THE
RANDALL HOUSE
BIBLE
COMMENTARY

THE
RANDALL HOUSE
BIBLE
COMMENTARY

1, 2, 3 JOHN
and
REVELATION

by
Thomas Marberry
Gwyn Pugh
Craig Shaw

FIRST EDITION

randall house

RANDALL HOUSE
NASHVILLE, TENNESSEE 37217

RANDALL HOUSE BIBLE COMMENTARY, 1, 2, 3 JOHN and REVELATION
© Copyright 2010
RANDALL HOUSE
NASHVILLE, TN 37217
ISBN: 9780892655373

General Editor:
ROBERT E. PICIRILLI
Professor Emeritus, Free Will Baptist Bible College
Nashville, Tennessee

Associate Editor:
Harrold D. Harrison
Nashville, Tennessee

PREFACE

This is the ninth volume in the series of Randall House Bible Commentaries on the New Testament. It deals with the Epistles of 1, 2, 3 John and the Book of Revelation. The combined talent, skill, and effort put forth by Drs. Craig Shaw and Thomas Marberry on the Epistles of John, and by Rev. Gwyn Pugh on Revelation, coalesce to create a spiritual tool of great value.

Scholars differ in their overall analysis of the content of 1 John. Wescott says: "It is extremely difficult to determine with certainty the structure of the Epistle. No single arrangement is able to take account of the complex development of thought which it offers, and of the many connexions which exist between its different parts."

On the other hand, A. T. Robertson says: "There is movement, progress, climax. All the threads are gathered together by the close. But meanwhile truth is presented, now from this angle, now from that, with a new focus, a fresh facet that like the diamond flashes light at every turn. The thought is not rambling, not disjointed, not disconcerting, but the author's quick intuitions of parallel lines of thought call for keen attention on the reader's part. The reward, however, is worth the trouble."

Alexander Ross, in his commentary on James and the Epistles of John, takes issue with the statement by Moffat that "we would not have suffered much loss if these two tiny notes [2 and 3 John] had been excluded from the N.T. Canon." "There is good reason," Ross insists, "for saying that we would have been spiritually poorer if we did not have the subtle rebuke of 'advanced' thinkers in 2 Jn. 9

and the mordant pen-portrait of Diotrephes in 3 Jn. 9."

Many people tend to shy away from a study of the Book of Revelation because of its strong, intricate, apocalyptic language. This was not so with the people of John's day. They were well acquainted with this type and style of writing.

The Book itself singly holds title to the fact that it is the only New Testament book that gives primary attention to prophetic events. Author Pugh has gently and carefully sieved out extraneous material that makes the text easily understood— whatever millennial point of view one holds. The treatment of various millennial views and approaches to interpreting Revelation, in the Introduction, is thorough and easy to grasp.

The author himself, who takes a premillennial, futurist approach to the book (but does so with grace and without extremism) has taught and preached these concepts to his own congregation for many years. His full and careful interpretation, analysis, and application give credibility to his adequate research, citations, and bibliography. He takes pains to make clear how those who take different approaches will interpret the various passages.

In these post-modern days. when the authority, inspiration, and truth of Holy Scripture are not only challenged but also denied, we can be confident that these truths are firmly upheld, defended, and applied in this commentary.

Harrold D. Harrison
Nashville, Tennessee
2010

CONTENTS

Commentary on the Books of 1, 2, 3 John
by
Thomas L. Marberry
and
Craig Shaw

COMMENTARY ON THE EPISTLES OF JOHN

INTRODUCTION

The letters of John are important. They give modern believers a snapshot of what life was like within the Christian community of Asia Minor in the first century. They point out that life was not always easy for Christians of the first and second generations. They had to battle enemies from without and within; their daily lives were filled with struggles and difficulties. Modern Christians readily admit that first-century churches struggled against persecution and opposition from an unbelieving world. It is more difficult to admit that they also struggled with internal problems of heresy, jealousy, envy, and conflict (Burge 17). These three brief letters bring modern readers face to face with the external opposition as well as with the doctrinal errors and internal conflicts that the early churches confronted on a regular basis.

These letters also give modern believers a picture of the vibrant life and faith of the early Christians. They remind us how seriously these believers took their faith commitment and how willing they were to contend for "the faith which was once delivered unto the saints" (Jude 3). The author of these letters challenged them to respond with faith and love to a situation that had shaken the very foundations of their newfound faith. They never lost hope, but they were realistic in their appraisal of the current situation. They demonstrated great courage,

faith, and commitment. These brief and often neglected letters contain a message that the church of the twenty-first century needs to hear and heed (Burge 18).

The Johannine Epistles are normally numbered among the Catholic or General Epistles. The word "catholic" in this context means "universal." They are called "Catholic Epistles" or "General Epistles" because they were not written to one specific church but to a group of churches.

Even so, 1 John does not reflect several of the characteristics that were commonly found in first-century letters. It identifies neither its author nor its recipients. It also lacks the farewell that is customarily found at the end, and the organization is different. First John is difficult to outline because themes are repeated and often overlap. (For more analysis of the organization and structure of 1 John see Burge 42; Jackman 17, 18; Kruse 1-15; and McDowell 188, 189.) McDowell (188) suggests that the book is a tract or a homily. Many scholars believe that 1 John is a circular letter designed to meet the needs of a community of churches in Asia Minor. Burge (42) suggests that it may be a pamphlet, a brochure, or an encyclical.

Second and Third John also differ from the other General Epistles. While they follow the customary way of writing

1

letters in the first century, they are very brief and more personal than the other General Epistles. They are addressed to individuals and respond to very specific situations in a local church. The other General Epistles are longer, more well-developed, and written to groups of churches.

Second and Third John have never enjoyed widespread popularity. They are the shortest books in the New Testament. They seem to have circulated only in certain areas and are not widely quoted by early Christian writers (Akin 21-27). Since they deal with very specific situations in a local church, many writers find it difficult to isolate teachings that can be applied in a variety of different contexts. They have always lived in the shadow of 1 John (Marshall 2), and the fact that they are so closely related to it has led many in the history of the church to see little value in studying them (Burge 13). Even so, these brief letters make a significant contribution to the thought of the New Testament. As Akin (22) writes concerning them, "Here we discover nuggets of gold that, when carefully mined, yield a small but valuable treasure that will better adorn the Lord's church with truth."

First John is more widely known and used. Many new believers find assurance of eternal life in John's faithful words. They also find encouragement to continue in the face of earthly challenges and spiritual unfaithfulness. Marshall (1) suggests that 1 John is an excellent starting point for one who wishes to study the theology of the New Testament. He notes that 1 John is concerned with "the very fundamentals of Christian belief and life."

Authorship

These epistles, like the Gospels, do not name their authors. First John launches directly into the subject matter of the letter. Second and Third John identify their author only by the title "Elder." Apparently, the identity of the author of these letters was so well known to his spiritual children that he knew they would recognize him by what he wrote (Barker 299).

Three views of the authorship of these letters are found in the field of New Testament studies. The first is the traditional view, that the author of all three was John, the son of Zebedee and brother of James. Early church tradition is virtually unanimous in attributing the first epistle to the Apostle John. Kruse (11-14), after analyzing early statements about the authorship of 1 John, concludes: "What is clear from these citations is that early Christian tradition is unanimous in ascribing 1 John to John, the disciple and apostle of the Lord." Lenski (363) reflects this traditional viewpoint when he writes, "The fact that the First Epistle of John was written by the apostle John and by no one else is beyond serious question."

The authorship of 2 and 3 John was apparently more difficult for the early church, but a clear majority considered John the Apostle to be their author as well (Plummer, *Introduction* ii-iii). A minority of the early Christian writers distinguished between John the Apostle and John the Elder and attributed these letters to John the Elder. The majority, however, viewed the term "elder" as a title describing John the Apostle, the author of all three letters (Kruse 42; Marshall 46). The traditional view that John the Apostle is the author of all three epistles is still widely held today (McDowell 189-191).

A second view which finds considerable support in contemporary scholarship is that the author was not the Apostle John himself, but one of his disciples commonly known as John the Elder. Hunter (174, 175) and Brooke (lxvii) defend this position. Brooke (lxvii) extensively analyzes both the similarities and the differences between the Gospel of John and the Johannine Epistles and devotes considerable attention to statements made by early Christian writers. He concludes that the most likely interpretation is that the Epistles were written by John the Elder, not John the Apostle: "His relation to John the son of Zebedee is a mystery which, at present at least, we have not enough evidence to enable us to solve." He asserts that the view that John the Elder was a pupil of John the Apostle, and in some sense a disciple of Christ, is "perhaps the hypothesis which leaves the fewest difficulties unsolved."

The third view that is found in N.T. scholarship today is that these epistles were written by early leaders in or near the city of Ephesus who were not directly connected with the Apostle John. The best known defender of this position is C. H. Dodd (lxix) who argues that these epistles were written by one of the "Presbyters" who lived in Asia Minor between A.D. 96 and 110. He suggests that we do not have sufficient evidence to identify the author. He writes that it is "highly unlikely" that the author should be identified with the Apostle John.

Dodd analyzes the possibility that the author was "John the Presbyter," a rather shadowy figure mentioned by the early Christian writer Papias. John the Presbyter was, supposedly, a follower of Jesus, not the Apostle John, an early Christian leader who lived and died in Ephesus. Dodd concludes that John the Presbyter, if he ever lived, is not a good candidate to be the author of these Epistles. He would have been a very old man at the time they were written. Dodd's (lxxi) final conclusion is that we simply do not know who the author was, but "we know what manner of man he was, what he taught about faith and duty, and what part he played at a critical moment in the history of the Church."

Similarly, Grayston argues that 2 and 3 John share a common author who was an anonymous Christian leader, but who did not write 1 John (153). In his view, 1 John had more than one author. He argues that 1 John includes an "initial agreed statement" which was drafted by some anonymous Christians. Then the main author of the book, also anonymous, made use of this material to produce the final document (9).

Moffatt (594, 595) also argues that 1 John was written by an anonymous author. He suggests that the author of 1 John may have been one of those who brought the Gospel of John into its final form, but there is insufficient evidence to come to any firm conclusions.

Some scholars prefer to leave the authorship of these Epistles an open question. Marshall (46), for example, writes that the author may be John the Apostle who came to be known as the "elder." The author also may be a follower of the Apostle who came to be known as "the elder." Burge (39) suggests that we do not have "unambiguous objective evidence of apostolic authorship" either for the Gospel of John or for the Epistles. He goes on to argue, however, that the absence of such evidence does not make apostolic author-ship "implausible." His position, then, is that the Apostle John is the most likely candidate for the authorship of these letters, but there is not sufficient evi-dence to arrive at complete certainty.

Law (43) arrives at similar conclu-sions, thinking it clear that the author of these three Epistles serves as a "spiritual guide and guardian" for the churches of Asia Minor. He writes that this agrees with the traditional interpretation of the relationship that existed between the Apostle John and these churches during the closing decades of the first century, but he adds this qualification: "Nothing has been, so far, adduced that points conclusively to an apostolic author-ship."

Since the Johannine Epistles do not name any author, we should investigate both the internal evidence and the exter-nal evidence before arriving at any con-clusion. We should not simply accept the opinions of other writers who have dealt with this important issue.

As for the *internal evidence*, 1 John seems to have been written by one who was an eyewitness to the life and minis-try of Jesus Christ, most probably an apostle (Stott 30-39). The opening vers-es give an account of one who saw Christ with his own eyes, both before and after His resurrection. "That which was from the beginning, which we have heard, which we have seen with our eyes, which we have looked upon, and our hands have handled, of the Word of life" (1 Jn. 1:1). Here the author force-fully makes his case for an intimate relationship with the Lord. He uses the three greatest of the five senses to bol-ster the case for his eyewitness account: hearing, sight, and touch. He further develops the account by saying in v. 2

that "we bear witness" (Greek *marture* , testify) and "show" (Greek *apangell* , declare) what we have known and "what was manifested" (Greek *phanero* , make apparent) to us. Verse 3 repeats the refrain, "that which we have seen and heard we declare unto you."

Many scholars have recognized that these letters come from the hand of an eyewitness. Stott (30) writes, "His decla-ration is a testimony, and his testimony depends on the personal experience granted to his ears, eyes, and hands." These bold assertions mark the fact that the author is able to speak authorita-tively. They also declare to the reader that the author is speaking from a posi-tion of leadership because of his close association with the Lord Jesus Christ, a position held only by one recognized as an apostle.

Kruse (9) proposes three facts con-cerning the author which we can learn from the text of 1 John. They are:

(i) he writes as an individual, some-thing which his repeated self-refer-ences in the first person singular indicate (2:1, 7, 8, 12, 13, 14, 26; 5:13); (ii) his language and thought bear very striking resem-blance to that of the Fourth Gospel, suggesting that he either wrote the Gospel as well or was deeply influ-enced by its language and con-cepts; (iii) he writes as an eyewit-ness of Jesus Christ, introducing himself, along with others, as one who has heard, seen with his eyes, looked at, and touched with his hands the incarnate Word of life (1:1-5).

At the time of the writing of the Epistles, there was only one living apostle, John, who was known by the church to have had an authentic personal experience with Jesus and who could make such a bold declaration. Without the widely recognized personal witness of the author, it is doubtful that the early church would have recognized these Epistles as authoritative. Kruse (9) explains that all three of these letters came to be accepted into the Canon because the church assumed them to be the work of the apostle.

The use of the term "elder" is important to this discussion because both 2 and 3 John identify their author as "the elder." The word (Greek *presbuteros*) originally meant an old man. In the first century, the word came to mean "one who exercises oversight and leadership" (Marshall 42). The term was used in this capacity to describe the leaders of the Jewish Sanhedrin; the early church also began using this designation for groups of leaders (Acts 14:23). Although the term "elder" is only used in 2 and 3 John, 1 John gives hint of the same understanding when he uses the words "little children" (Greek *teknia*) to emphasize the relationship of an elder to his followers.

With this understanding of the word "elder," it is possible to associate the elder of 2 and 3 John with the Apostle John. That is exactly what many in the early church did. Writers such as Polycarp, Papias, Irenaeus, Origen, Cyprian, Clement of Alexandria, Tertullian, Eusebius, and others all made this association. Plummer (*Second Epistle* 1) describes *elder* as "a not unlikely appellation to have been given to the last surviving apostle."

Some scholars have argued that John the Elder is not John the Apostle but a disciple of the great apostle. Hunter (62), for example, suggests that both the Gospel of John and the Epistles of John were not written by John the Apostle but by his disciple, John the Elder. He notes that the Gospel of John makes use of material from Matthew and Luke and argues that it would be unlikely for a disciple of Jesus to make use of a Gospel written by another disciple. Such conduct would be expected from the disciple of an apostle. Hunter finds many similarities in vocabulary and writing style between the Gospel of John and 1 John, as well as "the same distinctive idioms and phrases" (174, 175). After examining the evidence, he concludes: "First John is, therefore, in all probability, the work of John the Elder, the disciple of the Apostle John." The following quotation from Papias (as preserved in the writings of Eusebius) is most often used to support this hypothesis.

If anywhere one came my way who had been a follower of the elders, I would inquire about the words of the elders, what Andrew and Peter had said, or what Thomas or James or John or Matthew or any other of the Lord's disciples had said; and I would inquire about the things which Aristion and the elder John, the Lord's disciples, say (Akin 3).

In this quotation Papias mentions the name "John" twice. The first occurs in a very ambiguous context. Andrew, Peter, Thomas, James, John, and Matthew are described as "elders" and later as the "Lord's disciples." The second reference is to "Aristion and the elder John." We know nothing about the individual named Aristion. "The Elder John" is not clearly identified as the Apostle John or as some other person named John. This quotation from Papias is difficult to interpret, and it is not surprising that various interpretations have been suggested (Stott 38-41). Regardless, the quotation is ambiguous, and it is difficult to determine precisely the meaning that Papias intended. It certainly does not provide conclusive evidence that John the Disciple and John the Elder are two separate individuals.

Carson, Moo, and Morris (449) argue that it would have been natural for the Apostle John to refer to himself as "the" elder not just as "an" elder. He was not just an ordinary elder; he occupied a position of special authority. Stott (44) has a similar position. He suggests that the author's description of himself as an "elder," the authoritative tone with which he speaks, and his claims to be an eyewitness are "fully consistent with the early tradition of the church that these three letters were in fact written by the apostle John."

An understanding of the circumstances of the recipients of the letters may also help to identify the author of these letters. The readers of the three epistles may be identified as a group of believers, most probably in a church or churches, who were familiar with and accepting of the leadership and authority of the author. First John addresses its readers "little children" (1 Jn. 2:1, 12, 28; 3:7, 18; 4:4; 5:21) indicating that the relationship between the church and the author is an intimate one, that of a father to his children. (This diminutive term of affection appears only eight times in the New Testament, seven in 1 John and one in the Gospel). "The elect lady and her children" of 2 John is most certainly a designation for a church and

her members. Third John is addressed to Gaius and it appears that he is a leader among the members of a local congregation, perhaps the same congregation as that found in 2 John. The author is not a member of the churches addressed; they do, however, share a common fellowship with the Father and the Son (1 Jn. 1:3).

The group of churches for whom these letters and the Gospel were written has come to be known as the "Johannine community." Kruse (4, 5) summarizes the basic characteristics both of this community, and of those who had withdrawn from it, thus:

1. A number of churches in and around Ephesus in the Roman province of Asia.
2. Churches with a loose fellowship with the elder of 2 and 3 John.
3. A group of secessionists from the Johannine community whose beliefs involved a denial that Jesus was the Christ, the Son of God, come in the flesh (1 Jn. 4:2-3).
4. Belief by the community of believers that the death of Christ was necessary for the forgiveness of sins (1 Jn. 5:6-7).
5. The secessionists and the church both sent out itinerant preachers.

This evidence indicates that the author of these epistles was held in esteem by the congregations where he ministered. He was clearly an older man who exercised a high degree of influence. He spoke with authority and claimed to be an eyewitness to the events of Jesus' life.

Many scholars have recognized that there is a close connection between the authorship of the Johannine epistles and the authorship of the fourth Gospel. Kistemaker (197), for example, notes that there are many similarities in vocabulary and writing style; there also exist many similarities in content and expression. If it can be demonstrated that the letters were written by the same person who wrote the Gospel of John, then it would be appropriate to apply the arguments for the authorship of the Apostle John to the letters. To this end it is best to consider first the evidence of common authorship, first between the Gospel of John and the first epistle, then between the second and third epistles, and finally between the second and third epistles and the first.

A casual reading of both the Gospel and the first epistle lead the reader to conclude that both were written by the same person. Carson, Moo, and Morris (446) suggest that when reading the fourth Gospel and 1 John one finds many similarities in "theme, vocabulary, and syntax." Gromacki (368) gives a short list of these similarities:

> The similarities of vocabulary, thought phrases, and style of writing between the first epistle and the Gospel of John argue for the same author. For example, these distinctive words are common to both books: Father, Son, Spirit, beginning, Word, believe, life, keep, light, commandment, love, abide, and paraclete. In addition, these phrases are found in both: to do truth (1:6; Jn. 3:21); to be born of God (3:9; Jn. 1:13); children of the devil (3:10; Jn. 8:44); to pass from death to life (3:14; Jn. 5:24);

the Spirit of truth (4:6; Jn. 14:17; 15:26; 16:13); the only begotten Son (4:9; Jn. 3:16, 18); no man has ever seen God (4:12; Jn. 1:18); the savior of the world (4:14; Jn. 4:42); and the water and the blood (5:6; Jn. 19:34).

Brooke (ii-xix) gives an extensive analysis of the similarities in phraseology, writing style, and content between 1 John and the Gospel of John.

Numerous scholars have suggested that the similarities between the Gospel and 1 John are closer than the similarities between other New Testament writings that are unquestionably from the same pen. Examples include: Luke and Acts written by Luke; the Pastoral Epistles of Timothy and Titus written by Paul near the end of his ministry; the Prison Epistles of Ephesians and Colossians written by Paul; and the two letters to the church at Thessalonica written by Paul during his second missionary journey (Stott 28).

This evidence suggests that the Gospel of John and 1 John were written by the same person and that the Apostle John is most likely the author of both. For an analysis of the authorship of the Gospel see the comments of Stallings (1-6) who concludes, based on a review of both the internal and the external evidence, that John is the probable author of the book.

Since there is evidence indicating that both the Gospel of John and 1 John were written by the same author, one may then argue for the same authorship for 2 and 3 John based on their similarity to 1 John. Eight of the thirteen verses found in 2 John 4-11 are a paraphrase if not a direct quote from concepts introduced in 1 John. Kruse (36) suggests four reasons for unity of authorship between 1 and 2 John. (1) John addresses the same "historical situation" as that in 1 John. (2) He identifies the false teachers as antichrists, as in 1 John. (3) He emphasizes the love command, just as the author of 1 John does. (4) In both he finds joy in seeing his children walking in the truth.

Kruse (42) also points out that there are many similarities in content and writing style between 2 and 3 John. He cites four specific similarities that argue for common authorship. They are: (1) In John's greeting he addresses both recipients with the phrase "whom I love in the truth" (2 Jn. 1; 3 Jn. 1). (2) He rejoices greatly that his children are "walking in the truth" (2 John 4; 3 Jn. 3, 4). (3) He affirms the idea that if one does right he is of or abides with God (2 Jn. 9; 3 Jn. 11). (4) In both he concludes with nearly identical statements (2 Jn. 12; 3 Jn. 13, 14).

There is also considerable *external evidence* that points toward the Johannine authorship of these epistles. Possible allusions to 1 and 2 John begin as early as the end of the first century. Papias of Hierapolis, in the middle of the second century, is the first early Christian writer to specifically recognize the Apostle John as the author. By the time of Irenaeus in the late second century, 1 John is clearly regarded as the work of the Apostle John. After the time of Irenaeus, the early church consistently cited the Apostle John as the author of the Gospel and 1 John. Examples of this early attestation include such major figures and works as the *Didache,* Clement of Rome, the Epistle of Barnabas, and Polycarp (Carson, Moo, and Morris 446, 447).

The first person to specifically ascribe the Johannine epistles to the Apostle was Papias of Hierapolis in the middle of the second century. Eusebius quoted Papias as saying that John "used testimonies drawn from the former Epistle of John" (Carson 446).

Irenaeus attributed both 1 and 2 John to John, whom he identified as the disciple of the Lord and author of the Fourth Gospel. In his *Adversus Haereses,* he quoted from 1 Jn. 2:18-22; 4:1-3; 5:1; and 2 Jn. 7, 8. Clement of Alexandria knew of more than one Johannine letter, because he used the expression "the greater epistle" and ascribed it to the Apostle John. Clement quoted from each of the five chapters of 1 John.

In the first half of the fourth century, Eusebius included the first letter in the acknowledged books (*homologoumena*), while he placed the second and third letter in the disputed books (*antilegomena*). The reason cited for the inclusion of 2 and 3 John in the disputed list was the fact that some regarded the identity of the author of the second and third epistle as uncertain. However, Eusebius himself affirmed the Apostle John as the author of all three epistles (Stott 19, 20).

The many similarities between the Gospel of John and the three Johannine Epistles argue for a common authorship. The early Christian writers are virtually unanimous in attributing these letters to the Apostle John, and there are no competing theories that received serious attention. Although they do not identify any author by name, the available evidence, both internal and external, points toward the Apostle John as their author.

Date and Place of Writing

There is a remarkable degree of unanimity within New Testament scholarship on the date of John's Epistles. Many modern writers, based largely on the opinion of Irenaeus, date them during the closing decade of the first century (Moody 14; Hunter 175). Kistemaker (218) is typical of many who reflect a conservative viewpoint; he dates all three letters between A.D. 90 and 95. These epistles probably were written in or near the city of Ephesus, where, according to early Christian tradition, the Apostle John spent his final years (Moody 11; Hunter 175). Lenski (363) summarizes the traditional view of the final years of the life of the Apostle John. He posits that John was forced to leave Palestine before the year A.D. 66 when a major revolt against Roman rule began. He then moved to Ephesus and worked from there until his death about the year A.D. 100. Stallings (6) in his analysis of the place of writing of the Gospel supports this traditional view that John spent his final years in Ephesus. If that is the case, then it is likely to suppose that these three epistles were written in Asia Minor.

According to this traditional interpretation, John wrote these letters to churches in Asia Minor with which he had worked for a number of years. It cannot be determined with certainty whether or not he had founded these churches, but he had worked with them for many years and knew them well.

Marshall (48) agrees that Asia Minor is the most probable destination for these epistles, but he prefers to leave the date of the epistles an open question. He argues that there is not sufficient evidence to date them with precision.

He suggests a date between the sixties and the nineties of the first century. Burge (40) takes a similar approach; he notes, correctly, that the heresy refuted in these letters would have taken some time to develop. He suggests a date between A.D. 70 and 90. McDowell's (191) analysis of both the internal and external evidence causes him to date these letters during the last quarter of the first century.

These epistles were probably written about the same time as the Book of Revelation, but there is no solid evidence to indicate whether they were written before or after it. The epistles make no reference to John's time on the island of Patmos or to other historical events which would make a comparison of the relative dates possible.

Purpose

These letters are complex, and it is sometimes difficult to determine precisely why they were written. It is clear that they are designed to refute false teachings which were being widely circulated. The best course is to examine each epistle individually and analyze its content in an effort to determine the author's specific purpose or purposes.

According to McDowell (191), 1 John mentions three specific purposes: (1) to make his joy complete (1:4); (2) to warn his spiritual children not to fall into sin (2:1); and (3) to assure his readers that they possess eternal life (5:13).

In 1 Jn. 1:4 the author writes as a pastor who has a deep and abiding love for his spiritual children. He writes as the elder statesman of the Christian faith who wants to see his followers resist false teachings and continue in the truths that he has taught them. If they resist the false teachers, his joy as an apostle will be complete (Akin 58-61).

It should be noted that some early Greek manuscripts of this verse read "our joy" while others read "your joy." The manuscript evidence is about equally divided, and it is difficult to determine which reading is more likely original (Stott 70). Major English translations are divided on this issue, but the words "our joy" fit the context better.

John's second purpose is to exhort his children not to fall into sin (1 Jn. 2:1). Burge (84-86) suggests two possible interpretations of this verse. First, it may imply that the false teachers are denying the reality of God's truth about sin. Second, it may mean that some are misinterpreting John's teachings about sin. The fact that John emphasizes that forgiveness is available through Jesus Christ should not be taken as a license to sin. While there may be some doubt about the details, John's overall teaching is clear: his goal is to prevent sin and not to condone or encourage it (Stott 84).

The third specific purpose that John mentions is to assure his readers that they have eternal life (1 Jn. 5:13). The false teachers were spreading doubt among the believers of Asia Minor. They were teaching that the faith of these early Christians was incomplete and defective. Marshall (243) captures the author's purpose well when he writes, "John was ... writing not to persuade unbelievers of the truth of the Christian faith but rather to strengthen Christian believers who might be tempted to doubt the reality of their Christian experience and to give up their faith in Jesus."

It is clear that John is responding to the attacks of false teachers who are spreading false doctrines and causing believers to doubt their relationship with God. John is deeply concerned with the welfare of these believers in Asia Minor. He is their spiritual father. As Stott (45) notes, the situation is urgent and demands immediate attention. The term "secessionists" is often applied to these false teachers because it is clear that their teachings had not only produced division and strife, they had produced actual division within the churches. Although Jackman (13) does not use the term "secessionist" he calls attention to the fact that the false teachers "have separated themselves and their followers from the main body of believers." Barker (297) makes a similar point when he notes that the division had grown so sharp that some members of the church "had separated themselves from the others and were in the process of setting up their own community."

First John 2:19 explains the separation that these secessionists had brought about: "They went out from us, but they were not of us; for if they had been of us, they would no doubt have continued with us: but they went out, that they might be made manifest that they were not all of us." It is not clear just how many of the Christians had already left the churches of Asia Minor when this letter was written, but it is clear that John considered this to be a serious threat. If the internal strife and division could not be stopped, they would lead in the future to open division.

First John is a pastoral document. The author's goal is to promote the truth as well as to heal the division and conflict. John demonstrates a tender care and concern for his flock. He speaks of the members of these churches as "little children" or "dear children" in 1 Jn.

2:18, 3:7 and 3:18. In 3:2 he calls them his "beloved." He does not want them to fall victim to errors in doctrine or practice.

In another sense the letter is a polemical document (Stott 44). The apostle and his followers are in a battle for truth. The false teachers are trying to pervert the Christian faith. John writes, "These things have I written unto you concerning them that seduce you" (1 Jn. 2:26). A short time later he writes, "Little children, let no man deceive you" (1 Jn. 3:7). John's primary goal is to protect his readers from the heresies that threaten to destroy them and to establish them more firmly in the Christian faith (Stott 44).

Moffatt (583) writes that "this encyclical or pastoral manifesto was written neither at the request of its readers nor in reply to any communication on their part. What moved the author to compose it was anxiety about the effects produced on the church by certain contemporary phases of semi-gnostic teaching."

We have no firsthand description of the false teachings that were being circulated. Only John's response to them has survived (Burge 27). We can, however, reconstruct the false teachings by making a careful analysis of John's argument. It is clear that these false teachers were presenting a form of "Christianity" that is very different from what John and the other apostles of Christ taught.

John's opponents were clearly a sophisticated group of false teachers who were enjoying considerable success in spreading their heretical teachings (Jackman 13). Although we are not sure where they came from, these false teachers had entered into the churches where they were producing strife and

division. Some of the false teachers and their followers had separated themselves from the church (1 Jn. 2:19, 26; 3:7), but apparently they still had considerable influence and were capable of doing great harm (Marshall 14).

Some of the errors being propagated by these false teachers were doctrinal in nature, others were more practical. An erroneous view of Jesus Christ was at the heart of the heresy. First John 2:22 asks, "Who is a liar but he that denieth that Jesus is the Christ?" The word "Christ" (Greek *Christos*) in the New Testament refers to the *Messiah*. It appears that the false teachers refused to identify the man Jesus with the Jewish Messiah. They might have taught that Christ entered into the man Jesus at His baptism and then left Him before His passion (Moffatt 586). It is also possible that the false teachers denied the reality of the incarnation (Stott 46). First John 4:2b says, "Every spirit that confesseth that Jesus Christ is come in the flesh is of God." First John 4:15 says, "Whosoever shall confess that Jesus is the Son of God, God dwelleth in him and he in God."

While it is difficult to be sure about all the details, it is clear that the false teachers taught a heretical view of Christ. The most likely possibility is that they denied the real humanity of Jesus Christ. They would not accept the traditional Christian teaching that the man Jesus was, at the same time, both the Messiah and the incarnate Son of God (Kruse 16, 17). Akin (54, 55) describes the essence of the heresy this way, "The issue this epistle addresses is not that the heretics believed Jesus to be someone other than the Christ ... but rather that they believed Christ to be someone other than Jesus." According to Akin, the false teachers

11

were teaching that the man Jesus was not, in fact, the Jewish Messiah.

It is clear that the false teachers were presenting a perverted doctrine of Christ. They refused to affirm that the man Jesus was the fulfillment of the messianic prophecies of the Old Testament. Marshall (14-22) presents a thoughtful analysis of the false teachers and how they perverted the doctrine of Christ. Akin (29) presents a somewhat different but worthwhile perspective.

These false teachers were also propagating certain ethical errors. Burge (28) correctly notes that the false teachers "had embraced an aberrant form of Christology that led them to make wrong judgments about Christian living." They advocated, for example, a perverted view of sin. They claimed that one could know God and at the same time continue to live in sin (Stott 79). While it is difficult to reconstruct their false teaching with absolute certainty, it is quite possible that the false teachers taught that the sins of the body were of no consequence. In their view, one's spirit would still be blameless even though the body was living in sin (Kistemaker 245). Another possible interpretation is that the heretics were teaching that they had arrived at a state of sinless perfection (Kistemaker 245).

Such passages as 1 Jn. 1:6-10 and 2:1-6 serve to refute all such heretical teachings. The sins of the body do matter, and sin destroys the believer's relationship with God. John always connects true religion and morality. As Marshall (54) explains, "John claims that faith expresses itself in righteousness and sinlessness. The believer keeps the commandments of God and does not fall into sin." It is John's view that

the child of God must recognize the reality of sin and confront it.

It is difficult to identify the origin of the false teachings that were causing such havoc in the churches. The most commonly accepted view is that these Christians were battling an early form of the Gnostic heresy (Marshall 52). Gnosticism was the most dangerous heresy that the early church faced. Its most developed form was during the second and third centuries. For good summaries of this early heresy see the works of McDowell, Wilson, and Yamauchi.

Gnosticism taught that anything material or physical was automatically evil. That made it difficult for them to accept the reality of the incarnation. Many of them taught that Christ had no real human body; He only had the appearance of a man. Many Gnostics taught that the sins of the body had no effect on one's spiritual destiny. Only the sins of the spirit would affect one's relationship with God. These Gnostic teachings contributed to the development of heresies such as Docetism and the Monophysite heresy which several church councils would later condemn. For a good summary of how Gnosticism contributed to the development of other heresies see the works by R. McL. Wilson.

Plummer (*Introduction* iv-v) gives an excellent summary of the main differences between traditional Christianity and Gnosticism. The Gnostics taught that Christianity was a most worth-while teaching, but that it was incomplete. In order to be right with God, one needed to receive a "higher knowledge" that came through special revelations given only to them. They stressed the importance of the human intellect. Many

12

Gnostics denied traditional moral teachings and argued that what one did with the body was immaterial and unimportant to God.

The evidence is clear that 1 John was written to confront a complex and dangerous heresy that produced much strife and division. This heresy rejected the traditional view of Christ and replaced it with a view highly influenced by the pagan teachings of that era. It also rejected the traditional understanding of the Christian life. Early Christians always recognized the importance of moral purity and consistently struggled against the desires of the flesh. These false teachers saw no reason to struggle against the desires of the flesh. In summary, they were teaching doctrines that the Apostle John could not accept.

Second John is similar to 1 John in some ways, but different in others. It is much briefer than 1 John and is not written to a group of churches but to a single family (or to a local church). The major themes, however, are very similar. An unnamed Christian lady and her children are encouraged to walk in love and to avoid those who do not continue in the truths they have been taught. The main enemy seems to be the same early form of the Gnostic heresy that we meet in 1 John (Plummer, *Introduction* iv). John warns this Christian family not to provide hospitality to those who deny that Jesus had come in the flesh. Those who welcome the wandering teachers who spread such heresies become part with them (McDowell 193).

Third John is slightly shorter than 2 John (Akin 235) but is sharply different in content and purpose. There is no warning against false teachers who go around spreading false views of Christ.

There are three principal characters in 3 John. Gaius, the recipient of the letter, is urged to provide help and hospitality to those wandering teachers who propagate the truth. Diotrephes is singled out for condemnation because of his persistent refusal to provide hospitality to traveling evangelists who teach the truth. His refusal to provide hospitality does not seem to result from doctrinal error. He seems to be motivated more by his hostility toward the Apostle John than by any desire to impede the spread of the gospel. The third character is Demetrius, who is perhaps the bearer of the letter (Akin 237). In the final section of the letter, John encourages good works and specifically commends the work of Demetrius (McDowell 193; Kistemaker 209).

In all three letters John recognizes that right doctrines and right practices go together. Christians need to understand and accept the basic truths of the faith. They need to understand who Christ is, why He came, and how He came. Christianity and paganism cannot be combined. Believers also need to put their faith into practice in their everyday lives. They must recognize both the reality of sin and the danger of sin in their personal lives and in the larger community of faith. They need to commit themselves to lives of purity and service to Christ.

Teaching and Preaching from John's Epistles

Although we have not yet entered into the interpretation of the Johannine Epistles, there are several points in the introduction that should be kept in mind when preaching and teaching from these books. First, these epistles give much practical guidance to a pastor who is dealing with a problem within his church. In these epistles John confronts serious problems that are both doctrinal and practical in nature. He confronts these issues with kindness and respect, but he does confront them. He is not willing to stand idly by and allow the churches with which he has long labored to be torn apart by false teachings. He writes to the members of his churches with kindness and genuine love, expressing his affection for them. At the same time he writes to them as adults. He deals with the issues fairly and frankly. He never pretends that the issues are not important, and he never addresses his converts as people lacking maturity and judgment. He respects them and trusts them. Pastors and teachers today should do no less. Truth is important; the church is important; doctrinal integrity is important.

Second, these letters can help a pastor or a teacher distinguish between what is really important and what is secondary. All issues within a church are not equally important, and some battles do not have to be fought. A Christian leader needs to learn to pick his fights. John chose to fight over these particular issues because he understood that the truth of the gospel and the future of God's work in Asia Minor were at stake. The controversy was serious, with both doctrinal and practical dimensions. The fellowship was being disrupted. The love that binds Christians together was being destroyed, and the doctrine of Christ was being compromised. Issues of such importance must always be addressed.

Third, these letters provide good examples of how to deal with church members who manifest pneumatic or ecstatic tendencies (Burge 33). It is not unusual to encounter church members who claim to have had spiritual experiences or special "anointings" that other members of the church have not had. This can lead to unhealthy rivalry and contention within the fellowship. When this situation arose in Asia Minor, John responded by emphasizing that the Holy Spirit works in the lives of all believers and that no one has a monopoly on the leadership of God. Instead of being led astray by false teachers and their mystical experiences, the believers needed to remain faithful to the true gospel which they had received. Modern pastors and church leaders must not allow themselves to be intimidated by those who claim to have received such extraordinary experiences.

Fourth, these brief letters emphasize the commonality and necessity of interdependence between doctrine and practice. Our doctrines influence our practices, and our practices influence our doctrines. The false teachers claimed to be spiritually superior to other believers. This belief led them to deny the mutual love that had characterized these congregations before their arrival. John emphasizes that "walking in the light" involves both a correct understanding of doctrine (1 Jn. 4:15) and a genuine commitment of love (1 Jn. 4:16). Christian leaders need to understand that faith and practice go together. Both are necessary to have a healthy Christian fellowship.

EPISTLES OF JOHN

THE OUTLINE OF FIRST JOHN

Prologue, 1:1-4
- I. Walking in the Light, 1:5—2:29
  - A. Sin Breaks Fellowship with God, 1:5—2:2
    1. If we say we have fellowship, 1:5-7
    2. If we say we have no sin, 1:8, 9
    3. If we say we have not sinned, 1:10
    4. The advocate for the believer, 2:1, 2
  - B. Conditions for Fellowship, 2:3-29
    1. Obedience, 2:3-6
    2. Love for one another, 2:7-11
    3. Victory for the members of the body of Christ, 2:12-14
    4. Love for the Father not the world, 2:15-17
    5. Beware of the Antichrists, 2:18-23
    6. Abide in Christ, 2:24-29
- II. Walk in Love, 3:1—5:12
  - A. The Children of God, 3:1-3
  - B. Freedom from Sin, 3:4-10
  - C. Love and Obedience, 3:11-18
  - D. Evidence of Walking in the Truth, 3:19-24
  - E. Try the Spirits, 4:1-6
  - F. The Love of God, 4:7-16
    1. Know God, 4:7, 8
    2. The manifestation of the love of God, 4:9, 10
    3. Dwell in love, 4:11-16
  - G. Perfect Love Brings Assurance, 4:17-21
  - H. Obedience and Love, 5:1-5
  - I. Jesus, the Bearer of Eternal Life, 5:6-12
- III. Conclusion, 5:13-21
  - A. Assurance of Eternal Life, 5:13
  - B. God Hears Those Who Follow Him, 5:14-17
  - C. Do Not Continue in Sin, 5:18-20
  - D. Keep Yourselves from Idols, 5:21

Prologue (1:1-4)

**1 That which was from the begin-
ning, which we have heard, which
we have seen with our eyes, which
we have looked upon, and our
hands have handled, of the Word
of life;
2 (For the life was manifested, and
we have seen *it*, and bear witness,
and shew unto you that eternal
life, which was with the Father, and
was manifested unto us;)
3 That which we have seen and
heard declare we unto you, that ye
also may have fellowship with us:
and truly our fellowship *is* with the
Father, and with his Son Jesus
Christ.
4 And these things write we unto
you, that your joy may be full.**

These verses comprise the prologue
of the Epistle, similar to the prologue to
the Gospel of John and serving to introduce the main theme of the book, Jesus
Christ. See Stallings (15-18) for a summary of the main ideas found in the
prologue of the Gospel. See Brodie
(133-47) for an analysis of current
scholarly debate concerning the prologue to the Gospel.

The first three verses form one long
sentence. They present a challenge to
the interpreter because the grammar
and syntax are complicated and somewhat difficult to interpret. The letter
opens with four relative clauses, in
apposition to each another, followed by
the prepositional phrase "of the word of
life." The second verse is a parenthetical
statement clarifying the meaning of the
prepositional phrase "of the word of
life."

The main verb of the sentence,
"declare" (*apangellomen*), is not introduced until v. 3. All this complexity does
not, however, obscure the basic message. John declares to his readers the
reality of the incarnation of Christ and a
message of fellowship and joy that leads
to eternal life (1 Jn. 5:13). The author
stresses that he and other early Christian
witnesses have seen and touched the
physical body of Christ while He was
here on earth. He was not a phantom;
He was the Son of God who had come
in the flesh.

In the prologue John establishes his
credibility by pointing out that he is an
eyewitness to Christ's earthly life and
ministry. He also establishes that Christ
is the foundation of the Christian faith.
Verse 2 declares that God the Father
has a Son and that the Son is eternal.
The Son, Jesus Christ, lived in the world
as a man, and those who believe in Him
have fellowship with Him and, through
that fellowship, joy.

This unique opening is found where
one would typically expect to find a first
century letter-opening. There are three
elements which are normally found in
the opening of most letters from this
period: first, the name of the writer;
second, the name of the recipient; and
third, a greeting. According to Fee and
Stuart (57), a fourth element usually follows, in the letters of the N.T., namely,
"a prayer wish or thanksgiving."

Akin (50) suggests that the absence
of a formal salutation raises questions
over the type of literary genre that 1
John represents. Is it an epistle, a narrative, or a prophecy? This is an important question because the literary genre
of a given document will affect how it
should be interpreted. Should 1 John be
interpreted as an epistle with its own

specific rules or as another type of literature with different rules and expectations?

The letter unfolds to the reader much
like a sermon in which John applies his
theology to their specific problems. The
content of the text is directed to a particular congregation faced with a specific
heresy which appears to be an incipient
form of Gnosticism. The interpretive
tradition of the church is that 1 John
should be interpreted as an epistle.
Perhaps the best option for the modern
interpreter is to view this book as an
epistle written from a pastoral perspective (Akin 50).

John begins his polemic against the
heretical teachings of the antichrists by
reminding his readers that the message
he is writing to them has existed from
the beginning. It is not some newly
revealed knowledge of salvation as the
false teachers claimed to have received.
As was noted in the introduction, the
heretical teachings which John confronted in Asia Minor appear to deny
the reality of the incarnate life of Christ.
John, in sharp contrast to these heretical teachings, proclaims that the gospel
message is based on a historical reality,
the incarnation of Christ.

The phrase "Word of life" is the key
phrase of the first verse. Although it
occurs at the end of the verse, it is
clearly the most important idea. Many
interpreters, following Westcott, see this
phrase as a description of the Gospel
message rather than as a description of
Jesus Christ Himself. Westcott (7) writes,
"The obvious reference is to the whole
Gospel, of which Christ is the centre
and the sum, and not to Himself personally." Most commentators, following
Law, see this phrase as a reference to
Jesus Christ personally. Law (44)

explains, "With the great majority of
commentators, I conclude that the 'Word
of Life' here signifies the Personal
Logos." The term "Logos" is a transliteration of the Greek term (*logos*, meaning *word*) which is used here and in the
prologue to the Gospel of John to
describe Jesus Christ.

Although it is possible that the phrase
may refer to the gospel message, it is
more likely that it refers to Jesus Christ
personally. Several terms are used to
describe Jesus Christ in the Johannine
literature. He is, for example, called the
"Word" in Jn. 1:1 and the "Life" in Jn.
11:25 and 14:6.

The earlier phrases of v. 1 serve to
describe and introduce the Word of Life.
The first of these is "that which was
from the beginning," which reminds the
reader of both Gen. 1:1 and Jn. 1:1.
Both books begin with the concept of
beginning. Genesis describes how God
in the beginning created; John speaks of
how the Son and the Father existed
together from the beginning. Two interpretations of the word "beginning" in
this text are commonly found. First, it
could refer to the time before the creation of the universe when we first find
God existing as Father, Son, and Holy
Spirit. This is the interpretation preferred by Akin (52). The second option
is that it could refer to the beginning of
the gospel proclamation or to the traditional set of beliefs which the church has
proclaimed from its earliest days. For a
discussion of these two possibilities see
Grayston (37, 38). Dodd (5) suggests
that either interpretation is possible and
that it is not necessary to decide between
them.

John uses the word *beginning* (Greek
arche) ten times in his epistles (1 Jn.
1:1; 2:7, 13, 14, 24 twice; 3:8, 11; 2

Jn. 5, 6). First Jn. 1:1 is in reference to the word of life. In 1 Jn. 2:7; 3:11; and 2 Jn. 5, 6 it refers to the command to love one another. In 1 Jn. 2:13, 14 it refers to Christ, while in 1 Jn. 2:24 it refers to the gospel message and Christ. First Jn. 3:8 is a reference to the fact that the devil has sinned from the beginning. Given the various ways in which John uses this term, it could refer either to the time before the beginning of the creation or to the beginning of the proclamation of the gospel. Either interpretation would fit the context.

The fact that John uses "that which" (Greek *ho*, the neuter relative pronoun) may indicate that the 'beginning' refers to a thing, possibly the gospel message. Yet it is difficult to speak of a message in such a personal manner as something seen, heard, and (especially) handled. The eyewitness testimony better supports an interpretation centered on the person of the Son, Jesus Christ. In either case the "beginning" must refer, if only indirectly, to the Son; for the gospel message is nothing apart from the incarnation, crucifixion, and resurrection of Jesus Christ. The best understanding is that John's use of beginning is a reference to the incarnate Son of God.

John uses the three greatest senses— sight, hearing, and touch—to confirm the reality of the incarnate Christ and the gospel message. Citing these senses makes the testimony much more personal and draws the reader quickly into the author's perspective of the current situation. Both the first century and modern readers can identify with the use of the senses to verify information. Through the senses people come to know things.

The second verse is a parenthetical statement that gives further explanation of the 'Word of Life.' In this verse John chooses to use only the last word of the previous verse, *life*, rather than the complete phrase, "Word of life." In this parenthetical statement we learn at least five things concerning the life: it was manifested, it was witnessed, it was proclaimed, it is eternal, and it was present with the Father.

That the life was manifested is a reference to the incarnate life of Jesus as the second Adam. John uses this term (Greek *phaneroo*) often (20 times in his writings, 9 times in 1 John). He states unequivocally that the life (the Son) was not hidden, it did not have to be found, and it was openly revealed.

Much as in Hebrew poetry, John often repeats concepts for emphasis. In verse three, he restates the fact that his letter is based on the testimony of eyewitnesses. They have seen the life and are placing their own personal reputations on the line by publicly bearing witness to the reality of what they have seen. In contrast to the teachings of the secessionists, they proclaim a risen, living, and personal Savior. The Savior was not simply a man inhabited by a divine essence, but was divine—as noted in the reference to the divine attribute of eternality. The life is eternal and with the Father. John uses the term *Father* as a designation for God twelve times in this Epistle. It should be noted that the language is very similar to that found in the opening verse of John's Gospel, the only difference being that in the Epistle John uses Father rather than God; still, both words refer to the same divine being, God the Father.

In vv. 3, 4, John presents his objective in writing this Epistle. His goal is that his readers may have fellowship with the eyewitnesses and with those who share in the truth that the eyewitnesses have taught. Fellowship (Greek *koinonia*) means "to possess something in common, to participate in, or to share." It is an association involving close mutual relations and involvement. Jackman (23, 24) notes that the term found here is often used in classical Greek to describe marriage. It implies a loving and intimate relationship.

Christian fellowship, then, means to share or to participate in the common life in Christ through the Holy Spirit. It binds believers to one another and to God. Westcott (11) explains that John speaks of fellowship in two directions. First, there is the human fellowship that is found within the church. Second, there is the higher fellowship that the believer has with God.

Fellowship is an ongoing process that demands continued attention on the part of those within the community. Kruse (59-61) explains several of the most common uses of this term in the N.T. He suggests that in this verse it "appears to denote a personal relationship with the author or with God." It may also in this context "include the idea of commitment to a common task, that of the proclamation of the Word of Life."

In v. 4 John presents the central theme of the letter, "that your joy may be full." From this proposition John develops a case for the working out of a personal relationship involving God the Father, Jesus the Son, and the believer. It is important to remember that these things were written by one who had full authority to write, John an apostle of Jesus Christ (Westcott 13). The best commentary on this verse is 3 Jn. 4

which reads, "I have no greater joy than to hear that my children walk in the truth." John is writing about the spiritual joy that these believers can experience if they reject the false teachings and continue to walk in the truth of the gospel.

There is a minor manuscript variant found in v. 4. Some manuscripts read 'your' joy, while others read 'our' joy. The variant does not change the meaning of the text, because both ideas are obviously present. It is only as John brings his readers into true Christian fellowship that both his own joy and their joy may be made full. In the same way that seeing one's children do right brings joy to a father's heart, so does true fellowship bring joy to the heart of the aged apostle (2 Jn. 4; 3 Jn. 3, 4). At the same time the children find their joy in doing right. "Your joy" and "our joy" go together. Either way, true joy comes only from fellowship with God. (For discussions of this phrase see Kistemaker 238, 239; and Beyer 55, 56.)

Summary
(1:1-4)

The first four verses comprise the prologue to John's epistle. In these verses he sets forth a case for the incarnate Christ based upon his and others' eyewitness testimony. He vividly portrays the word of life using the most important of the five senses; sight, hearing, and touch (v. 1). He uses repetition as a device to emphasize the reality of the message he declares to his readers (vv. 2, 3). The primary reasons for declaring the message that "was from the beginning" were: (1) to show them the "eternal life, which was with the Father," thus expressing the eternal coexistence of Jesus with the Father, and (2) to draw the readers into fellowship with those who have seen Christ which in turn would bring them into fellowship with the "Father and with His Son Jesus Christ." The fellowship that results would then give to all involved complete joy.

Application: Teaching and Preaching the Passage

This prologue deals with important themes which should be preached and taught. First, these verses establish the historical nature of the Christian faith. Christianity is not just based on someone's opinion or subjective judgment. It is built on the solid foundation of eyewitness testimony. As Clemance (6) wrote many years ago, "The writer was one who had been brought into close contact with the Person of the Lord Jesus, who had himself intimately known him, and who had associates in knowledge of and fellowship with him." John was an eyewitness to the life and ministry of Christ. He also lived and worked among others who were also eyewitnesses. He is proclaiming what he and others had seen and heard.

Second, these verses establish a firm connection between doctrine and fellowship. In order to participate in the Christian fellowship one must understand and accept the doctrine of Christ. In other words, those who do not accept the doctrine of the incarnation cannot be accepted as a part of the Christian church. John is not saying that believers must agree on every detail to participate in the fellowship. He is saying that beliefs do matter and that those who do not adhere to the basic doctrines of the Christian faith, such as the incarnation,

cannot and should not be accepted into the church.

This is an exclusive message that is difficult for many moderns to accept, living as we do in an age which emphasizes religious toleration and acceptance. Many people teach that any belief should be accepted as long as it is sincerely held. Burge (56) writes, "Within the pews of America's churches, two-thirds of the people do not believe in the *exclusive* character of the Christian message, and almost half of all evangelicals say the same." John emphasizes that Christianity is a historical, doctrinal, and exclusive faith. It has historical roots and is built on a proper understanding of the life and ministry of Jesus Christ.

I. WALKING IN THE LIGHT (1:5—2:29)

A. Sin Breaks Fellowship with God (1:5—2:2)

1. If we say we have fellowship (1:5-7)

5 This then is the message which we have heard of him, and declare unto you, that God is light, and in him is no darkness at all.
6 If we say that we have fellowship with him, and walk in darkness, we lie, and do not the truth:
7 But if we walk in the light, as he is in the light, we have fellowship one with another, and the blood of Jesus Christ his Son cleanseth us from all sin.

John's use of *message* and *declare* connect this paragraph with what he has written in the previous paragraph. "Declare" translates two slightly different words from the same family (Greek *apangellomen*, vv. 2, 3; *anangellomen*, v. 5). The word translated "message" (Greek a*ngelia*), referring to what is announced or proclaimed, has the same root and is found in both paragraphs. For analysis of the meaning and usage of this family of words see Becker and Müller (44-48).

In these verses John further explains and applies the point he has made in vv. 2, 3. The message declared does not originate with the author or with any other apostles; it finds its origin in the risen Lord. The words "God is light, and in him is no darkness at all" are not a direct quotation from the Gospels but rather a declaration of the truth taught by Jesus, heard by His disciples, and understood by John. Westcott argues that the phrase "God is light" is a summary of the gospel message. He writes (14), "Thus the fundamental ideas of Christianity lie in this announcement: 'God is light'; and man turns to the Light as being himself created in the image of God and recreated in Christ."

It is significant that God's message is conveyed through the process of proclamation and hearing. The mystery religions of John's day placed major emphasis on seeing God rather than simply hearing God. The Jewish emphasis was just the opposite. Deuteronomy 6:4-9 begins, "*Hear*, O Israel" a passage now known as the "Shema" (from the Hebrew word meaning *to hear*). The pages of the O.T. are filled with statements about hearing God's message. Repeatedly we find statements like: God said (Gen. 1:3, others), come near to hear (Is. 34:1), and thus saith the Lord (Ex. 4:22, others). In the rabbinic tradition, hearing is related to the Word of God given in the O.T. Because it is read aloud, its study involves hearing.

Kittel (219) points out that hearing is just as important in the N.T. as it is in the Old. The N.T. message is both a word to be heard and a word to be proclaimed. He writes, "The mission of Jesus and the disciples was first regarded and treated as something to be received by way of hearing" (Kittel 219). The message proclaimed in the N.T. includes both the offering of salvation and ethical demands. In other words, hearing always includes both the message of God's grace and a call to repentance (Kittel 220).

The message that John declares is "God is light." Most commentators agree that this is a statement concerning the character of God (see Akin 62, 63). John uses the metaphor of light (Greek *phos*) often (37 times: 24 in John, 6 in 1 John, and 7 in Revelation). In all of John's writings, only here do we find "light" used to identify God. Stott (75) points out that the statement is absolute and that *light* has no article. "The Logos is '*the* light'; but God is light, just as he is 'love' and 'spirit' and 'consuming fire.'" Light reveals something about the essential being of God. Like light, He is good, pure, true, and holy. Jackman (28) notes that light is commonly used as a "symbol of God's presence in the Old Testament." It serves as "a picture of his perfect moral righteousness, his flawless holiness."

Marshall's (109) paraphrase of this verse illustrates the ethical sense of light: "God is good, and evil can have no place beside him." Akin (70, 71) suggests that the metaphor 'God is light' refers more specifically to the idea of life as eternal life, the life that comes from God.

John insists that God is completely light and there is absolutely no darkness in him (the Greek construction contains a double negative which is used for added emphasis). Where there is light there cannot be even a minute amount of darkness; darkness and light cannot coexist in the same place at the same time. Speaking metaphorically, light is the opposite of darkness, and darkness is the absence of light. God is wholly other than darkness and all that the metaphor of darkness represents. According to Westcott (17), light suggests truth, goodness, joy, safety, and life, while darkness suggests falsehood, evil, sorrow, peril, and death.

The message that God is light is the foundation for the ethical application found in the following verses. In vv. 6-10 we find three conditional statements that begin with the words "if we say." These statements describe claims that someone might make, but they are false statements. John is probably referring to the false teachings that were being circulated in Asia Minor. After each of the false claims John provides a parallel conditional statement that serves to correct the falsehood. In this way John accomplishes two important things: he reveals what is meant by the message he has just introduced, that God is light; and he introduces and corrects the errors of his opponents who have withdrawn from the genuine believers in the Johannine community. The three false claims probably represent variations on a single theme that the heretics emphasized: namely, that sin did not affect them (Smalley 21). The nature of their claims will become clearer as the thought of the Epistle develops.

The first of the conditional statements centers on the requirements for fellowship. Fellowship between God and man depends on a basic understanding of human nature and the nature of God as revealed in the person of Jesus. Here John confronts the claims of the false teachers that they could have fellowship with God and still walk in sin. John insists that fellowship with God involves more than the mere mental assent of the individual. It involves participation in something that is common to the parties involved. Since it is not possible for darkness to participate in and share the essence of light, there can be no fellowship with God for those who walk in darkness. Those who claim to have fellowship with God must live and walk in the light because God's very nature is light.

In John's view, the one who claims fellowship with God but who continues to walk in darkness is nothing more than a liar: "If we make such a claim we lie, deliberately, knowingly, self-evidently, and we do not the truth" (Stott 79). Kruse (63) suggests that these individuals are guilty of two offenses: "First, they are guilty of lying about their relationship with God." Darkness and light cannot have fellowship. "Second, they are guilty of not doing the truth." Not doing the truth is not a lie in word only but also a denial rooted in action. Doing the truth is the opposite of doing evil. It is not sufficient to say that one knows God and is in fellowship with Him. One must also live and walk in the light of truth and avoid sinful behavior.

The conditional clause in v. 7 provides the corrective and positive complement to the false claim in v. 6. Having outlined the consequences of walking in darkness, John now gives the benefits of walking in the light. Since God's nature is incompatible with darkness, only when we walk in the light may we walk with him. God is in the light because He is light. We must walk in the light without sinful conduct.

Walking in the light is to make no attempt to conceal anything, but to allow the light to illuminate one's entire life (Stott 80). It is not a singular act of perfection but a process of continually being shaped in the image of Christ. It does not mean that those who walk in the light never sin but that they do not try to hide their sin from God. Instead, their lives are cleansed of sin by the shed blood of Christ (Kruse 64, 65).

One important benefit of walking in the light is that we have fellowship with one another. John has already stated that we must walk in the light to have fellowship with God. In v. 7 he adds the natural corollary: we must also walk in the light to have fellowship with other believers. The fellowship of believers is, first and foremost, based upon a right relationship with the Father through the Son. Without this primary relationship with God, who is light, the only possible fellowship is with darkness. "There is no fellowship with God which is not expressed in fellowship with other believers" (Kruse 64). Jackman (31) writes that "to walk in the light means to become increasingly conscious of sin that would hinder our fellowship with God and our fellow Christians."

Another benefit of walking in the light is that the blood of Jesus Christ His Son cleanses us from all sin. To cleanse (Greek *katharizo*) carries the connotation of purification, an idea similar to forgiveness but that goes further by including the very removal of sin (see Lenski 389). The word may be under-

stood, then, as the removal or the cure for the stain of sin. It is important to note that the Greek verb occurs in the present tense which normally implies continuing or on-going action. The idea is that the blood of Jesus always cleanses or that it continues to cleanse (Barker 310, 311).

Cleansing comes only by the blood of Christ, which is a reference both to His life and to His death on the cross. The early Gnostic belief did not allow for the literal incarnation or the physical death of Christ (Lenski 389; Law 31-34; Brooke xliii-xlix). Here John clearly separates himself from the teachings of these early Gnostics by speaking of a literal death and shedding of blood for the cleansing of man's sin.

2. If we say we have no sin (1:8,9)

8 If we say that we have no sin, we deceive ourselves, and the truth is not in us.
9 If we confess our sins, he is faithful and just to forgive us *our* sins, and to cleanse us from all unrighteousness.

The second conditional statement, with its false claim, is a continuation of the first. John further exposes the false teaching of the separatists, namely that they claim not to have sin. The verb *have* is presented as an ongoing action (Greek present indicative). Thus, the false teachers claim that they do not continue to have sin.

Among leading interpreters there are three commonly held interpretations of the phrase "if we say that we have no sin." See Brooke (17, 18) for a good analysis of the various ways in which these words have been interpreted. The first possible interpretation is that the false teachers were saying that the believer no longer possesses the sin principle or the sinful nature. Such an interpretation would be quite consistent with what we know of early Gnostic teaching. According to the Gnostics, believers have been given a new nature which makes them superior to other men. This interpretation is defended by Dodd (21) who writes, "They have no need for moral striving; they are already perfect."

The second is that no guilt for sin is applied to the believer. Such an interpretation would also be consistent with what we know of early Gnostic teaching. This interpretation is defended by Lenski (390) who argues that these false teachers considered themselves to be immune to the guilt of sin. They believed that salvation came by knowledge, and that the sins of the flesh did nothing to contaminate them.

The third possible interpretation is that John's opponents are claiming to be innocent of personal sin. This view is defended by Akin (74) and Kruse (66). According to Kruse, these words should probably be interpreted to mean that the false teachers had committed no sins after they had come to know God and experienced his anointing. Marshall (113) presents a somewhat similar interpretation. He suggests that the false teachers refused to consider as sinful certain actions which John considered to be sinful.

According to most interpreters, these heretical views had developed out of the early Gnostic teaching that matter was evil and spirit was good. This belief led many Gnostics to conclude that what was done in the flesh was of no conse-

quence. We find this belief practiced in two forms: (1) total denial and subjugation of the flesh, thus not giving the flesh (the embodiment of evil) an opportunity to defile the spirit (the embodiment of good); (2) complete indulgence of the flesh because the flesh is always evil and the spirit is always good and cannot be tainted by the evil flesh.

The clause "we have no sin" is only found here in 1 John, but it is also found four times in the Gospel of John (9:41; 15:22, 24; 19:11). How these words are used in the Gospel sheds light on the meaning in 1 John. In all four instances in the Gospel the emphasis is on the guilt for actual sin rather than, as some commentators suggest, the sinful nature. Kruse (66) maintains that the secessionists were not claiming to be free of the sinful nature, but they were not guilty of committing sins. No matter what form the argument takes, whether free from the nature of sin or the guilt of sin, it is true that whenever the principle of sin is denied as an ongoing reality, there follows a denial of responsibility for one's individual actions. The result is the destruction of fellowship between man and God, and between man and the church.

According to John the denial of the reality of sin produces two dire consequences. The first is that "we deceive ourselves." According to John the deception begins with lying to others and then to one's self. The fact that the deception is self-inflicted demonstrates the responsibility of the individual. With responsibility comes a personal accountability for sin that leads to divine judgment.

The second is that "the truth is not in us." The Johannine idea of truth is personified in Christ, who communicates

25

both His message and Himself to humanity. Even Jesus equates truth with Himself (Jn. 14:6). Therefore, the one who claims that he does not have sin does, in fact, have sin imbedded within his very nature. What he does not have is the indwelling and redeeming presence of Jesus. A person in this condition has no part in the fellowship of God. See the excellent comments of Kruse (68). Barker (312) concludes, "When the principle of sin is denied, truth as an inner principle of life cannot exist. The futility and irony of our predicament then becomes evident: In God's name, we make God's presence and power an impossibility."

Verse 9 is one of the most well-known in John's Epistles. It explains that the believer should not respond to the sin in his life by denial but by confession. Many believers have found the amazing grace of God in practicing this important truth. Renewed commitment and zeal have been realized by many as a result of confession, forgiveness, and cleansing. Keeping with his pattern, John presents a positive complement to the admonition of v. 8. The believer is given directions for properly dealing with sin.

The verse begins with "If we confess our sins." Lenski (392) suggests that the tense of the verb *confess* (Greek present) implies a continuous or ongoing action. He translates the phrase "if we keep confessing our sins." In this verse John teaches that followers of Christ are to acknowledge their sins, which is the antithesis to saying that "we have no sin" in v. 8.

Confession and sin are both prominent concepts in the N.T. As Kruse (68) notes, we find the two concepts together only in four places in the N.T.: Mt. 3:6, Mk. 1:5, Jas. 5:16, and Acts 19:18. The first two occurrences refer to those who came to John the Baptist to be baptized while confessing their sins. The third instance concerns confessing faults to one another. The fourth describes how the people of Ephesus burned their books and confessed their evil deeds during Paul's visit. All three of these references appear to indicate a public confession (Kruse 68).

Some commentators also see a public confession in 1 Jn. 2:9. Westcott (23), for example, understands this verse to teach not only that men should acknowledge their sins, but that they should "acknowledge them openly in the face of men." Interpreters such as Westcott base their conclusions on the use of the verb *confess* in John's writings. The first use is by John the Baptist, confessing that he is not the Christ. In each of the other uses the confession is an acknowledgment of Christ as the Son of God or of some similar sentiment.

There is, however, one important difference between the confession made here and the confessions made in the passages cited above. The confession found in 1 Jn. 1:9 is not a confession of Christ but of one's sins. Most modern interpreters conclude that this verse says only that sins must be confessed; they do not believe that the passage specifies either a public or a private confession. Lenski's (392) comments are typical: he writes, "John does not say how, when, [or] where we do the confessing." In this verse we find what appears to be private confession before God resulting in forgiveness and cleansing. The confession is a private confession first because all sin is against God. David confessed, "Against thee, thee only have I sinned" (Ps. 51:4). To confess (Greek *homolo-*

geo) means to agree with someone on something; it embraces both the fact and event and also the act and action by which one bears witness to the agreement. Confession of sin is then the act of agreeing with God that sin is sin and embracing the sinfulness of personal sin. See the comments of Lenski (392).

According to John, God responds to this confession with forgiveness of sin and cleansing from unrighteousness. Forgiveness (Greek *aphiemi*) carries the understanding of a release from debt; no longer are persons' sins held against them. To *cleanse* bears the meaning of purification. One could substitute the word *purify*. For a most helpful analysis of usage of words from this family see Vorländer (697-703).

The text says that in forgiving and cleansing God is both faithful and just. *Faithful* signifies that God is trustworthy and is willing and able to carry through on His commitment to forgive and purify those who confess their sin (Kruse 69). *Just* indicates that God is acting righteously, or in a manner consistent with who He is. As Marshall (114) points out, "The justice lies in the inherent rightness of the act; if the conditions are fulfilled, God would be wrong to withhold forgiveness."

A most natural question then arises in the mind of the reader. How can God be just and, at the same time, forgive the guilty? Paul deals with this issue in a different context and comes to the conclusion that God can be both just and justifier through the sacrifice of Jesus (Rom. 3:26). Stott (83) brings the faithfulness and the justice of God together in a simple but powerful statement, "God is faithful to forgive because he has promised to do so, and just because his Son died for our sins." See also the insightful comments of Lenski (393).

3. If we say we have not sinned (1:10)

10 If we say that we have not sinned, we make him a liar, and his word is not in us.

The third false claim expressed as a conditional statement is a restatement of the second. Verse 8 says "If we say that we have no sin"; v. 10 says "If we say that we have not sinned." The only difference between the two is found in the choice of verbs and the tenses used. The first uses the present tense verb "to have" with "sin" as its object; the second uses the perfect tense verb translated "have sinned." The difference seems to be simply one of style. John does not seem to be introducing a new concept or idea.

The phrase "if we say," found in vv. 6, 8, and 10, is significant. The Greek is in the mood (Greek subjunctive) which is used to express several kinds of potential statements. In this context, it could be translated "if we should say." John is making a hypothetical statement; he knows that no true believer would ever say "I have no sin." Sincere followers of Christ will recognize their sins and deal with them. The statement describes the beliefs of the false teachers and their allies. The author's goal is to show where such false teachings will inevitably lead. See the comments of Lenski (386).

The author continues to develop his thought by using the word "liar." First Jn. 1:8 states that a man lies and deceives himself when he says that he has no sin. Here we find the additional

27

assertion that if such a claim is true, then God is also made to be a liar. God has often stated that man is a sinner (see Rom. 3:23). If the claims of the false teachers are true, God has lied about this most important matter. John's point is that the teachings of the heretics are not true to Scripture and must be rejected. If God is a liar, then He is less than perfect and holy and therefore cannot be God. Such teachings make a mockery of the gospel (Barker 313). John has carried the teachings of his opponents to their logical conclusion and has shown how dangerous they are.

The resulting condition for man would be that God's "word is not in us." There are two possible understandings for "word": first, that it refers to the message of the gospel, the proclamation about the "word" (Christ) in vv. 2, 3, and 5; second, that it refers directly to Christ. Just as the *truth* in v.8 may be identified with Christ so also the *word*. Either way, that "His word is not in us" is a very strong statement indicating John's rejection of the heretical teachings. One who says he lives above sin in himself does not have the source of life in him. Consequently, he is unable to walk in the light but must walk in the darkness. There is no fellowship with God or the body of Christ. As Barker (313) writes, "The possibility of receiving the forgiveness offered by God is lost."

4. The advocate for the believer (2:1, 2)

1 My little children, these things write I unto you, that ye sin not. And if any man sin, we have an advocate with the Father, Jesus Christ the righteous:

2 And he is the propitiation for our sins: and not for ours only, but also for *the sins of* the whole world.

In these verses John continues his discussion of sin and forgiveness, but with a different emphasis. His focus is no longer on the false teachers and their heretical views. He now speaks to his converts with the warmth, tenderness, and compassion of a father for his children. It is easy to envision an elderly John earnestly making his case to a church which he views as his family. John is the only author in the N.T. to use the exact phrase "my little children." The phrase translates a single word (Greek *teknia*) which is a term of endearment (Barker 313).

John's goal in these verses is not only to contradict false teachings but also to make a positive presentation of Christian truth. Rather than denying the guilt or presence of sin, John's spiritual children should confront the reality of sin in their lives and deal with it in the right way. They cannot serve God and at the same time continue to live in sin. John's goal is, first and foremost, that his children should not sin.

The statement "that ye sin not" has provoked controversy. There are those who interpret this statement to mean it is possible for a believer to attain a state of sinless perfection. In light of the correction given to the false teachings in the previous verses (1 Jn. 1:6-10) and the insistence upon sin as continued reality in the experience of the believer, this is a misinterpretation of the text. See the comments of Lenski (397).

A more likely interpretation of these words is that John does not want his previous statements to be taken as a license to sin. Sin should never be accepted as a normal part of the Christian life (Westcott 41). As Lenski (397) explains, "All that John writes has as its purpose that we may *not* sin."

John is an experienced pastor. He knows from his own experience, and from the lives of those to whom he has ministered, that believers always have to struggle against sin. Sometimes they may fall victim to sin's temptations. When believers do fall into sin, they do not need to deny the reality of sin. They need a remedy, and that remedy is Jesus Christ.

If a man does sin he has an "advocate with the Father." That advocate is, of course, "Jesus Christ, the righteous [one]." An advocate (Greek *parakletos*) is one who pleads another's cause or who helps another by defending or comforting him. Jesus uses it as a name for the Holy Spirit three times (Jn. 14:16; 15:26; 16:7, where it is translated "comforter"). In this text, it is applied to Jesus Christ, who comes before the Father to plead the cause of the believer who has fallen into sin. It is important to remember that He is not pleading the believer's cause based on the believer's righteousness. That would be futile because his sin has already condemned him. Jesus pleads the believer's cause based on *His* righteousness, which has been applied to the believer. Westcott (43) points out that the term *righteous* is much more than a simple adjective describing Jesus Christ. The idea is that Christ has fully satisfied the Father's demand for righteousness, and it is that righteousness which makes it possible for Him to serve as the believer's advocate.

There is another interesting aspect of the term *advocate*. Westcott (43) correctly points out that in order to receive the benefits of an advocate's intercession, one must first accept the services of the person serving as advocate. In other words, in order to receive forgiveness the believer must freely and voluntarily take advantage of Christ's work as mediator.

On what ground may the believer be assured that he has access to God's mercy and grace after he has sinned? It is because Jesus has paid the price for the sins of the whole world; He is the *propitiation* (Greek *hilasmos*), a most interesting word. It is sometimes translated *expiation* or *atoning sacrifice*. The term is used in classical Greek to describe an offering given by a guilty person to the one he has offended in order to placate or appease him (Barker 314). It is found six times in the Septuagint (Lev. 25:9; Num. 5:8; Ps. 130:4; Ezek. 44:27; Am. 8:14) and twice in the N.T. (1 Jn. 2:2 and 4:10).

There is some disagreement among leading commentators concerning the meaning and use of this term in the Septuagint and in the N.T. It seems clear that it is used to describe a sacrifice offered to appease the wrath of an offended deity. Man's sins have offended God, and Christ offers Himself as the propitiation for man's sins. He becomes the way to appease the wrath of God whose standard has been violated.

Propitiation alludes to the sacrifices offered for atonement in the O.T. In Judaism, the sacrifice on the Day of Atonement was for Israel alone; but Jesus offered Himself in sacrifice not only for Christians but for the whole world, leaving them without excuse (Keener 738). Romans 1:20 also states that all men are without excuse.

The word has another use, to describe an act which removes guilt or defilement (see Dodd 25, 26). The proper English term to describe this aspect is *expiation*. As McDowell (199) points out, this Greek term is used in the Septuagint to translate the Hebrew word (*kipurim*) that means "a covering." It is this covering for sin which makes it possible for the sinner to be reconciled to God. The most likely interpretation is that something of both ideas is involved here. The sacrifice of Christ serves both to appease the righteous anger of God and to provide the needed covering (or atonement) for man's sin. Akin (84) summarizes in these words, "Fellowship with God is possible because the sins that caused the offense to God have been removed through Jesus' atoning sacrifice, so that God's wrath no longer abides on those who have fled for refuge in the Lamb of God who takes away the sin of the world."

The last words of v. 2 are important. They state that Jesus is the atoning sacrifice not only for our sins but also for those of the whole world. What does John mean by this statement? Does this phrase mean that all will ultimately be saved (a belief commonly known as *universalism*)? The answer is clearly no. In this epistle John clearly distinguishes between those who are right with God and those who are not. There is nothing in the letter to suggest that all will be saved (see 1 Jn. 2:15-17; 3:7, 8; 4:2, 3).

John uses the term *world* several different ways in his writings. Westcott (45) explains thus: "The world, all outside the Church, is sinful. But for all alike Christ's propitiation is valid." As Jackman (47) explains, John uses the term "world" in several different ways in his writings.

The most common use is to describe those who are outside of Christ; those who are in rebellion against God; those who have no personal relationship with Him. The idea here is that Christ's atonement is sufficient for all who will accept His offer of pardon. His death has provided all the sacrifice necessary for those outside of Christ to be saved. They must, however, accept Christ's sacrifice and receive the forgiveness of their sins. There is no indication that they will be saved automatically.

Summary
(1:5—2:2)

This passage in 1 John connects several important themes. It speaks of the character of God. He is light, which means that He is totally pure and holy. He does not tolerate the presence of sin. Yet He is also forgiving and caring. He has provided a remedy for the tragic consequences of sin, the blood of His Son, Jesus Christ.

This passage points out the sharp contrast between walking in the light of Jesus Christ and walking in the darkness of sin. The false teachers were trying to obscure that distinction. Walking in the light does not mean a life of sinless perfection; it does mean a life of dedication to Christ, a life of repentance and faith. John does not say that the Christians of Asia Minor have actually left the light and begun to walk in the darkness; but they are clearly in danger of doing so. The false teachers have clearly made serious inroads into the Christian fellowship, and their negative influence must be stopped.

Another important theme in this passage is the danger of false teaching. John is no doubt amazed that his spiritual children have allowed themselves to fall under the influence of false teaching. It is difficult to reconstruct completely the content of the false teaching. It is possible that false teachers claimed to be sinless themselves and implied that the Christians could also become sinless by following their teachings. It is more likely that the false teachers were saying that the sins of the flesh were of no consequence. They would not cause one's relationship to God to be broken. Such distinctions between the spiritual and the material were common in the ancient world. Either way, the tragic consequences of false teaching are obvious.

These verses confront the reality of sin in the life of a believer. The child of God must always struggle against the forces of sin and Satan. Conversion does not mean the end of one's battle with sin; it is often the beginning of that struggle. The Christian is not, however, left to battle against sin on his own. Jesus Christ serves as his advocate, the one who speaks for him, the one who serves as his aid and counselor (Burge 85).

How can Christ serve as the believer's advocate in his hour of need? According to this passage, He can fulfill that role because He is the atoning sacrifice. He has fully satisfied the Father's demand for righteousness and provides the only adequate remedy for sin.

Application: Teaching and Preaching the Passage

Although it was written centuries ago, this passage deals with several of the most important issues of life with which Christians must deal every day. This passage points out that there is a clear distinction between appearance and reality. There is no doubt that the false teachers were persuasive, and their teachings were attractive. They had the appearance of something good, but the reality was quite different. Modern Christians must always be careful. We must not allow ourselves to be led astray by false teachings that appear to be good but are not. There is simply no substitute for wisdom and spiritual maturity.

This passage also helps us to understand the being and character of God. He is just; He does not take human sin lightly. He is, at the same time, merciful. He is willing to forgive, pardon, and cleanse. There is nothing in the passage which teaches that God's forgiveness comes automatically. The promise of God's forgiveness is ours only when we "walk in the light" of Jesus Christ. We should always present a balanced picture of God in our preaching and teaching. We must point out what God will do and what He expects us to do. We must emphasize that both justice and mercy are essential elements of God's character.

Another important theme in these verses is the reality of sin in the life of the believer. The fact is that Christians struggle with sin. We should never pretend that we are sinless or that our sins are not important to God. As Jackman (31) emphasizes, "Sin does matter." We need to walk in the light every day. That means that we must repent of our sins and accept God's pardon and restorative grace.

Fellowship is another important theme found in this passage. The term *fellowship* implies a growing and developing relationship. These verses speak of the importance of maintaining a proper relationship both with God and with other believers. The false teachers stressed the importance of maintaining fellowship with God and ignored the importance of fellowship between believers. Both are important; both should be stressed in our preaching and teaching.

B. Conditions for Fellowship (2:3-29)

1. Obedience (2:3-6)

3 And hereby we do know that we know him, if we keep his commandments.
4 He that saith, I know him, and keepeth not his commandments, is a liar, and the truth is not in him.
5 But whoso keepeth his word, in him verily is the love of God perfected: hereby know we that we are in him.
6 He that saith he abideth in him ought himself also so to walk, even as he walked.

In these verses John expands and further defines the relationship between man and God. In the previous section, that relationship was defined using the concept of "fellowship" (1 Jn. 1:3). Here the author moves on to the related concept of "knowing Him." This passage also deals with the related subject of assurance. How can one be sure that he in fact knows God? John's opponents were arguing that they came to know God through special revelations. These special revelations were evidence that they really knew God.

The aged apostle presents a totally different approach. He argues that a life of obedience to the teachings of God is a much better way to determine who knows God and who does not. Those who abide in Christ and walk according to His teachings are the ones who truly know God. Brooke (29) explains, "The writer can conceive of no real knowledge of God which does not issue in obedience."

The words "and hereby we do know that we know him" (v. 3) can also be translated "and in this we do know that we know him." The words "in this" refer to the phrase "if we keep his commandments" which come at the end of the verse. The main idea of the verse is that keeping God's commandments is the proof that one really knows Him. The point is that no one who truly knows God will live in direct opposition to His teachings.

John uses the verb *know* twice in the opening clause of v. 3. To know (Greek *ginosko*), in this sense, means to have knowledge grounded in personal experience (Schmitz 397-406). In John, knowing God is always more than mere intellectual assent. To know God includes both "obedience to the moral law" and "the presence of God's love in the believer" (Barker 315). To know God is to live in daily fellowship with Him. Anyone who makes the claim to "know God" but is disobedient to the Word "is a liar."

It should be noted that John uses two different tenses of this verb in v. 3. The first (Greek present) conveys the idea that we know, or are knowing, or continue to know. The second (Greek perfect tense) implies that we have come to know and continue to know. See the explanation of Robertson (210).

Knowing is a concept which is found often in 1 John. In this Epistle the author uses two different words to express this concept; together they occur a total of 42 times. The first

(Greek *ginóskó*, as in v. 3) occurs 25 times; the second (Greek *oida*) occurs 17 times. Schütz (391) examines the usage of these two terms, and he does not find a significant difference in meaning. He writes, "Both contain the implication of certainty based on experience" (403, 404). He also analyzes how these terms are used in the writings of John. He notes that on several occasions John uses Gnostic terminology to combat Gnostic ideas. He writes, "He faces the Gnostic on his own ground and combats him with his own weapons."

The believer who wishes to know if he is truly in a relationship with God in which he "knows" Him, regardless of any personal shortcomings, is given a simple test founded on obedience. The keeping of His commandments becomes the means by which the believer can be sure that he really knows God.

Logically following the assertion that one knows that he knows God by keeping His commandments is the negative opposite. If one does *not* keep His commandments but claims to know God, he is a liar. John uses direct and strong language to condemn the false teachers. They cannot claim to teach the truth when there is no evidence in their daily walk that they really know God.

In the last words of v. 4, John describes the false teacher by saying that "the truth is not in him." This statement has two implications. First, a lie is the opposite of truth, which like 'light and darkness' cannot exist at the same time in the same place. The truth was exchanged for a lie (Rom. 1:25). Second, they do not have the abiding truth of Christ dwelling in them.

There is a shift in vocabulary usage in the fifth verse. John substitutes "word" for "commandment." The word repre-sents the whole of revelation, which includes all commandments. The two vocabulary words are still easily connected because we are instructed to keep both the word and the commandments.

The phrase "the love of God" (v. 5) has provoked considerable discussion and can be interpreted in at least three different ways. The phrase may refer to: (1) God's love for man (Greek subjective genitive), (2) man's love for God (Greek objective genitive), (3) the type or kind of love God exhibits (Greek qualitative genitive). Westcott (49) says, "The love of God is God's love towards man welcomed and appropriated by man." Robertson (211), along with many modern scholars, proposes that it is "probably ... our love for God, which is realized in absolute obedience." Marshall (126) says that it is God's *kind* of love which He showed in giving His Son.

It does not appear that John adheres strictly to any one meaning. There are shades of each meaning found throughout the epistle (God's love for man, 4:9; man's love for God, 5:3; God's kind of love, 3:17; 4:7). Therefore it seems best to leave it without a specific identification. Whichever interpretation one adopts we must realize that each possibility has as its foundation God's love. Man's love for God is a reflection of His love for us. What is clearly communicated is that love is perfected in the person who obeys God's Word.

Some equate obedience with legalism, seeing obedience as keeping a list of rules and laws. Christian obedience is not a form of legalism. Christian obedience is concerned more with motives than with a list of rules. Obedience means that we are to abandon all selfishness and to take up our cross and follow

Him (Mt. 16:24; Mk. 8:34; 10:21; Lk. 9:23).

Assurance of salvation is an important theme for John. The experience of perfect love, whether it is the love of the Father for His creation or the love of the believer for his God, assures and helps the believer to accept and understand that he is in God. The believer who knows that he is in God is then enabled to continue to live in fellowship with the Father. If we are in Him we have fellowship with Him, we know Him, and we walk in the light.

The term "perfected" has also provoked considerable discussion. The meaning (Greek *teteleiotai*, perfect tense, passive voice) is *has been made perfect* or *has been made complete*. The tense indicates an action that was initiated and completed in the past with results that continue into the present. The voice indicates that something or someone else is performing the action on the subject. Who is acting from the outside to bring the love of God to perfection or completion? The obvious answer is that God is the active force in the perfecting.

The word does not necessarily imply that one has come to a state of absolute perfection. It often means "accomplished," "completed," or "brought to its appropriate result." The love of God accomplishes its work when we obey (Kruse 80). Perfected love is expressed in obedience.

Many times throughout his letter John uses words like *hereby* (Greek *en touto*) to connect and further develop his content—much as a preacher might do in a sermon. The phrase "hereby know we that we are in him" links what has been previously stated with what follows. Previously John has stated that we

know that we know Him because we obey Him. We abide in Him by walking as He walked. By using this transition device the reader is able to sense the forward motion of the text as one concept is defined and developed, and then a new concept is introduced, defined, and developed. The text unfolds like an upward moving spiral, "the line of thought simply spirals in rising, widening circles until all is complete" (Lenski 366). John develops his line of thought something like this: If one says "I know him," he must then demonstrate that knowledge in obedience. Knowing God leads to existence in Him which is then demonstrated by walking as Jesus walked. Smalley (50) explains, "John moves on from discussing the Christian's knowledge of God in Christ to consider one expression (and test) of that knowledge: 'abiding' in him."

"To abide" is a direct reference to the relationship between the individual and God. It also implies fellowship, friendship, dependence, harmony, and communion (Wuest 3:64, 65). Lieu (41) concludes, "Abiding is a claim the believer can justifiably make, but only when that claim is matched by a life of obedience and love; such obedience both is a precondition and at times seems almost a definition of abiding in and by God."

Verse 6 says that the one who says he abides in Him ought to walk as He walked. The current English connotation for "ought" allows the individual a choice to do or not to do; many understand this word to describe something that one should do but is not required to do. The word used here does not allow for this understanding. It denotes a duty or obligation based upon an indebtedness to another. If one is to abide in God it is his individual responsibility, duty, obligation, and debt "to walk, even as he walked."

Summary
(2:3-6)

The believer can know that he knows God; this knowledge is not simply a philosophical knowledge but a real knowledge. The one who knows God is recognizable to himself and others by his obedience to God's Word. The one who does not keep God's Word, but who claims to know God, is a liar. He does not have the indwelling presence of the truth to guide, build, and encourage him. He who keeps God's Word also has his love for God perfected, completed, and fulfilled. Man's love for God is a reflection of and flows from God's love for man. Love is another identifying mark that the believer knows God and is in Him. As a result of what God did for man, providing the opportunity to abide in Him, it is man's obligation or debt to follow the example of Jesus and walk as He walked.

Application: Teaching and Preaching the Passage

This brief passage contains a message about loving God, knowing God, and obeying God that the modern world needs to hear. There is a relationship between these three concepts. Too many people adhere to the false belief that it is possible to love God without obeying His teachings. John specifically denies the possibility of such a dichotomy. To love God means to know Him, and to know God means to obey His commandments.

The type of obedience that this passage calls for is radical in nature. John asks his followers to commit themselves totally to living out, every day, the teachings of Christ. At this time the Christian faith was new, and the church was an underground movement (see Burge 103). The pagan world did not understand or appreciate this new religion. If it was to have any chance of success, Christianity had to have the total commitment of its members.

This passage, and others like it, can be easily abused. John is writing to his followers about their obedience to God's commandments. He is not encouraging them to use this passage as a club to beat up on other believers. Unfortunately, too many Christians are quick to demand that others obey the teachings of God while they themselves fail to do so. We should never demand more of others than we demand of ourselves.

There is also the danger of selective obedience. All of us are tempted to select those aspects of the teachings of God that are the most acceptable to us and emphasize them. We also tend to downplay those aspects that are not so agreeable. We cannot, however, pick and choose the commandments that we wish to obey. We must do our best to observe all that the gospel teaches.

We must always remember, when teaching and preaching from this passage, that it deals with obeying God's commandments and not with obeying human traditions. Sometimes it is difficult to determine exactly where God's commandments stop and the implications we draw from those commandments begin. Preachers and teachers should be careful to distinguish between what God specifically teaches and their own personal beliefs and practices.

This passage does not justify a harsh, critical, or condemnatory spirit. It ties love and obedience together; it does not separate them. Our goal must always be to manifest a Christ-like spirit as we obey His commandments. We need to be honest, sincere, and loving followers of God.

2. Love for one another (2:7-11)

7 Brethren, I write no new commandment unto you, but an old commandment which ye had from the beginning. The old commandment is the word which ye have heard from the beginning.
8 Again, a new commandment I write unto you, which thing is true in him and in you: because the darkness is past, and the true light now shineth.

John opens this subsection with the term "brethren" (Greek *adelphos*). Some Greek manuscripts have the word "beloved" (Greek *agapetos*) instead. Both terms indicate John's intimate relationship with his readers and the affection with which he holds them. Such a personal address indicates that the brethren are part of the Christian community. Following his personal address, John continues expounding the conditions for Christian fellowship by citing the greatest of the commandments, that which sums up all the rest (Mt. 22:37; Mk.12:30; Lk. 10:27). Note the change to the singular "commandment" from the plural in vv. 3, 4.

This entire subsection deals with the commandment to love one another (as John will later point out in v. 10). The commandment to love is not new but old. In the N.T. there are two words translated *new*. One (Greek *neos*) describes something which is new in

time; the other (Greek *kainos*) means something which is new in kind. The word used here is the latter. The idea is that John is not giving some new kind of commandment to his followers. He is emphasizing the same commandment that God has always given.

Love is the fulfillment of God's Law (Rom. 13:8-10). The readers have known it from the beginning. In context, "beginning" probably refers to the beginning of the gospel message; that which the individual believer and the community had known from the beginning of their Christian experience. For the Jewish-Christian it could easily mean from the beginning of the law (Dt. 6:5; Lev. 19:18), for even at that beginning there is love.

In v. 8 the author presents something of a paradox. In antiquity, paradox was a graphic way of forcing an audience to think through the meaning of one's words (Keener 738). In v. 7 John had stated that he was writing a commandment that was not new but had been a part of God's plan from the beginning. Then in v. 8 he writes, "Again a new commandment I write unto you." "Again" (Greek *palin*) can also mean "on the other hand." In this verse the translation "on the other hand" more clearly communicates the intent of the author. John is not simply repeating himself; he is adding additional information to what he has already written. Although the command to love is old, it may also be identified as new. The commandment "to love one another" has been given a new depth of meaning by the life and ministry of Jesus. Akin (96) explains, "The law of love is new in the sense that it is seen in Jesus and established by Him through His death and resurrection."

A reader from within the Johannine community would have recognized this new command as a command from Jesus Himself: "A new commandment I give unto you, That ye love one another; as I have loved you, that ye also love one another" (Jn. 13:34). Jesus repeats the same sentiment in Jn. 15:12. The purpose of the paradox appears to be to cause the reader to grapple with the enduring meaning as well as to recognize and affirm the central place of the commandment.

Interestingly, John will not formally identify the commandment as the commandment to love until v. 10. The content must have been so familiar to the readers that he did not find it necessary to make a definitive statement of the commandment until then. John simply says that it is true both "in him and in you." The repetition of "in" with both pronouns indicates that the commandment is true for both but not in the same manner at the same time. The commandment to love is first realized in Christ. Because of Him, it can also be realized in man.

Love shows itself in that "the darkness is past and the true light now shines." "Past" is actually a verb (Greek present tense *paragetai*) and communicates the idea of continuous action: the darkness is passing away. Marshall (130) says it is as if the world is in the darkness of the predawn hours and the first rays of light are just breaking through. The incarnation of Jesus was the first light of dawn; the beginning of a new day for humanity (Mt. 4:16). The world remains in darkness, but that darkness is passing away because the believer is walking in the light as seen in the love that they have for one another. Just as the moon reflects the light of the sun in the night sky so the Christian reflects the light of God into the darkness of the world.

Just as the darkness is passing away so the light is continuing to shine (also Greek present tense). As the light penetrates deeper and deeper into the darkness of the world, more and more men are being set free. People everywhere have the choice to come into the light and walk in the light as He is in the light.

9 He that saith he is in the light, and hateth his brother, is in darkness even until now.
10 He that loveth his brother abideth in the light, and there is none occasion of stumbling in him.
11 But he that hateth his brother is in darkness, and walketh in darkness, and knoweth not whither he goeth, because that darkness hath blinded his eyes.

Those with whom John is dealing fall into two classes. On one hand are those who are in fellowship with God and walk in light and love. On the other hand are those who are not in fellowship with God and walk in darkness and hatred. Those who claim to have fellowship with God, to know Him, and to abide in Him must verify their claim by right conduct if it is to be recognized as true. The test of love provides appropriate verification.

The word *brother* (Greek *adelphos*) originally meant "one born of the same womb." As time passed, however, it came to be applied to family members other than brothers and sisters. Later it also came to be used to describe neighbors, comrades, companions, and friends (Günther 254). In the N.T. it is used to describe the close and loving relationship that exists within the members of the family of God (Günter 256, 257). Today, it must be understood to include both male and female members of a Christian church.

This passage draws a sharp contrast between the concepts of "light" and "darkness"—a common theme in this epistle, introduced in 1:6, 7. Hahn (494) gives a careful explanation of how these terms are used in the writings of John. He notes that believers must walk in the light because "he who is the light and the way does not want mere admirers, but believing followers."

Verse 9 adds the phrase, "and hateth his brother." If someone has hatred directed towards his brother; if he is displaying animosity toward his brother; or if he is not working with others, then that person is walking in darkness although he may claim to be in the light. The confession is meaningless apart from right conduct. His hatred for his brother reveals that darkness dominates his life; it is what controls him. He is not living in the grace and love that have been shown to him by God. This verse is probably directed against the Gnostic teachers who saw little relationship between one's earthly conduct and one's relationship to God.

Verse 10 presents the same truth in a positive manner. The one who truly loves his brother continues to walk in the light of Jesus Christ. In the second half of the verse John points out that the one who walks in the light has no cause for stumbling in him. The phrase "occasion of stumbling" is used in the N.T. in two different ways. It is most often used to describe causing another person to stumble (Akin 99; Robertson 212). It is occasionally used to describe placing an obstacle in one's own path (Robertson

212). The context must determine how the phrase is used in a particular verse.

Either interpretation of the phrase "there is none occasion of stumbling in him" is possible in v. 10. Following the first usage, it may mean that as long as one is walking in the light he will not cause another to stumble. If the second interpretation is correct, the idea is that the believer himself will not stumble. He is walking in the light and is able to see what is before him and where he is going. The path is clear before him (Ps. 119:105). Any obstacle or trap in his path is clearly illuminated and can thus be avoided.

Verse 11 helps to establish the context of v. 10. In v. 11 John writes that the one who hates his brother is walking in darkness and cannot see where he is going. Based upon the context, the meaning of v. 10 seems to be that the person walking in the light will not stumble (Akin 99).

The one who hates his brother is walking in darkness. The linkage is clearly and emphatically delineated. He not only is in darkness but walks in darkness. His spiritual progress is random and without clear direction and purpose, effectively resulting in being lost. His hatred for his brother blinds him so that he is unable to follow the path to eternal life.

Summary
(2:7-11)

In this passage John writes that the commandment to love is both old and new. It is old because it is found in the O.T. and because these believers have had it since the beginning of their Christian experience. It is new because the love of Jesus Christ has added a new

38

dimension to it. The love described in this passage is not what the world considers to be love. It is a love that is selfless and demonstrated by acts of the will toward the brethren, choosing their well-being. Love becomes the fruit that is visible to all. John presents the command to love as a true test of the spiritual position of his followers. Are they walking in the light or in darkness? If one hates his brother, he is in darkness and walks blindly in that darkness. If one loves his brother he is in the light and sees clearly the path before him, therefore having no occasion to stumble.

These verses should be understood in the light of the false teachings that John is battling. The Gnostic teachers claim that they have received special revelations. In their eyes, the special revelations confirm their relationship to God. In these verses John argues that true love is a much better indicator of one's relationship to God than special visions and revelations.

Application: Teaching and Preaching the Passage

There are many lessons that these verses teach us. The primary lesson is that there is simply no substitute for genuine Christian love. The command to love is not a new commandment; it has been a part of God's plan for His children from the very beginning. The life and ministry of Jesus Christ have, however, added a new dimension. The type of love that Christ taught is much more profound and much broader than any type of love that had existed previously. Jesus taught that we are not only to love our neighbors (those who are like us), we are also to love our enemies.

Genuine love leads to action. As followers of Christ we must always be looking for appropriate ways to demonstrate God's love in an unloving world. Love may simply be an expression of care and concern for a friend or loved one. It may be nothing more than a simple kindness shown to a stranger. If it is to be truly meaningful, our love needs to be demonstrated with integrity and without seeking reward. It must always be appropriate to the situation and without looking for glory or recognition. It must always seek the best interest of the person loved.

Genuine love is not, however, naïve. Christian love should never be used as an excuse to tolerate sinful conduct or heresy. Sometimes love has to be tough. In this passage, John is well aware of the danger presented by the false teachers, and he is committed to do everything he can to prevent the spread of their error. Love and truth go together. As believers, we have a responsibility both to defend the truth of the Gospel and to share the love of Christ in a fallen world.

3. Victory for the members of the body of Christ (2:12-14)

**12 I write unto you, little children, because your sins are forgiven you for his name's sake.
13 I write unto you, fathers, because ye have known him *that is* from the beginning. I write unto you, young men, because ye have overcome the wicked one. I write unto you, little children, because ye have known the Father.
14 I have written unto you, fathers, because ye have known him *that is* from the beginning. I have written**

unto you, young men, because ye are strong, and the word of God abideth in you, and ye have overcome the wicked one.

John moves from his discussion of what it means to walk in the light to a brief word of encouragement for his spiritual children. These verses seem to be almost parenthetical to the flow of the letter. His purpose in these verses is to "remind his readers of their victories in the Christian faith and to assure them of his approval of their steadfastness" (McDowell 201). The author introduces six statements concerning the believer, each beginning with a form of "I write unto you." The section can be divided into two stanzas; the second repeats the major ideas presented in the first and in some ways further develops them.

When investigating these verses, five basic exegetical questions arise. First, why does John repeat his thought nearly verbatim? Second, what do the different categories represent? Third, why does he change vocabulary using a different word for children (in Greek) in v. 13? Fourth, why does he change the verb tense of "write" in the second stanza? Fifth, what is the correct understanding of "because"?

The first exegetical question (Why the repetition of thought?) is the easiest to answer. In the first century, much like today, repetition is often used to place emphasis on a thought or idea. The repetition in this instance has a poetic flow that would have been appreciated by those in the Johannine community. The proposition that these verses are poetry is supported by the fact that they are set out as lines of poetry in modern printed Greek New Testaments and in some English translations.

The second question concerns the identification of the terms "children," "fathers," and "young men." These terms may be understood in several ways. First, they may be taken literally, with each term representing a specific age group in the church: children, young adults (young men), and older adults (fathers). In keeping with the accepted practice of the day the categories are listed in the masculine (men, and fathers) but incorporate both genders.

A second possible understanding of these terms is that they are metaphors for levels of spiritual maturity. The children represent those who are new believers. The young men represent those who are maturing in the faith. The third category, fathers, represents the mature, wise believers. See the insightful comments of Stott (96).

A third possible interpretation sees the "little children" of v. 12 and the "little children" of v. 13 as referring to the whole of the church. John has already addressed the body of believers to whom he is writing as his "little children" (2:1), and will do so at the end (5:21) so it would be logical to read this occurrence in the same way.

The order in which the groups are listed (little children, fathers, and young men) strikes some interpreters as illogical. One would expect the order to be fathers, young men, and children, or children, young men, and fathers). If, however, the words "little children" refer to the body as a whole, then the terms "fathers" and "young men" refer to specific groups within the fellowship. This view typically understands these terms to refer to chronological and spiritual age (or possibly to offices such as elder and deacon). Akin (103), Kruse (88),

Lenski (418), and Smalley (72) each support this approach.

A fourth possible interpretation views the little children, fathers, and young men from a totally different perspective. According to this view, these terms do not describe three different groups within the fellowship. Rather, they describe the three stages of growth that most Christians go through. They pass from the innocence of childhood through the strength of youth and finally into the maturity that comes with age and experience. Marshall (138) agrees with this interpretation and says that John uses the different categories to express general spiritual truths. Dodd (37-39) also accepts this interpretation. Although this interpretation is quite attractive, it is difficult to see how this line of thinking contributes to John's argument.

The third possible interpretation provides the best explanation of the text for the following reasons: (1) John refers to the church as a whole by using the term "little children" in 2:1; 5:21; (2) the statement "your sins are forgiven you" of 2:12 is applicable to all believers; (3) only two categories provides for a better logical order, fathers and young men; (4) to describe both children and fathers with the nearly identical statement of knowledge (vv. 12, 13) indicates that one is of or from the other.

The third exegetical problem in this passage centers on John's uses of two different words, both of which are translated "little children" in the KJV. The first "little children" (Greek *teknia*) was discussed earlier in the comments on 2:1. It is a term of affection. The second "little children" (Greek *paidion*) stresses the ideas of subordination and discipline more than the idea of kinship. Wuest (4:567) suggests the translation "little children under instruction."

Although there are slightly different meanings for the two words, to make a major exegetical statement based on this difference is to go beyond the evidence. One need not make a sharp differentiation between them; both words are diminutive and can be used as terms of affection. First century writers would often use a variety of vocabulary to keep their reader's attention. As Brooke (42) correctly notes, repetition of words, phrases, and ideas with slight changes is a common feature of John's writing style.

The fourth exegetical question involves a change in verb tense. In a quick reading of the passage one could easily miss the change in verb tense in v. 14. The first three uses of "write" (Greek *grapho*, present tense) are usually translated "I write" or "I am writing." The last three uses of "write" (Greek *egrapsa*, aorist tense) are more likely to be translated "I wrote" or (as in the KJV) "I have written." Some have suggested that this change in tense refers to another letter that we do not presently possess. A more plausible explanation is that John put himself in the place of his readers and described as past that which was to himself present, but which would be past to his readers. This kind of usage (Greek *epistolary aorist*) generally enables the writer to identify better with the reader and to emphasize his thought or idea.

Some translations end v. 13 after the description of the young men and begin v. 14 with the second description of the fathers. This is a versification problem that has no impact on the translation or interpretation of the text.

The fifth exegetical problem centers on the best understanding of the word "because" in the formula "I write to you . . . because" which occurs several times in the passage. The word (Greek *hoti*) is used in different ways in the N.T. It may establish a causal relationship between John and his disciples. If that is the correct interpretation, John is writing this message to his spiritual children because they are part of his spiritual family. An acceptable translation would be, "I write to you fathers because you have known him who is from the beginning." The implication is that if they were not his spiritual children, there would be no reason to write this message to them. He is challenging them to respond in an appropriate way to what he is writing.

This word can also be used declaratively, to introduce a statement or an assertion. When used in this way, it may be translated "that." If John is using the word with a declarative idea in this passage, an acceptable translation would be "I write to you fathers that you have known him who is from the beginning."

Marshall (136, 137) suggests that the grammarian may place too much emphasis on the subtleties of the translation of the term "because." Both the causal and declarative senses are probably intended by John. John is writing because they are saved and so that they may respond to the truth of his teaching. Smalley (71) supports this assertion by suggesting that John may have intentionally intended the double meaning.

As noted previously, vv. 12-14 are difficult and filled with ideas that are closely interwoven. For this reason, they present the interpreter with several interesting questions. The basic meaning of the paragraph, however, is clear.

John's goal is to remind his followers of the spiritual victory that they have already attained. In these three verses he makes such statements as "your sins are forgiven," "ye have known him that is from the beginning," and "ye are strong, and the word of God abideth in you." These are words of assurance. These believers have no reason to doubt the genuineness of their relationship with God; they should not allow themselves to be carried away by any false teaching.

4. Love for the Father not the world (2:15-17)

**15 Love not the world, neither the things *that are* in the world. If any man love the world, the love of the Father is not in him.
16 For all that *is* in the world, the lust of the flesh, and the lust of the eyes, and the pride of life, is not of the Father, but is of the world.
17 And the world passeth away, and the lust thereof: but he that doeth the will of God abideth for ever.**

The apostle begins this section with a command in the negative, much like the familiar formulation found in the Ten Commandments. He instructs his spiritual children not to love the world or the things in the world. This love of the world and the things in it is a selfish love that seeks to gratify one's own passions and desires and indulge in worldly pleasures. It is totally different from the kind of love that believers have for the Father and for others within the Christian fellowship. Love for the Father and love for the world are mutually exclusive.

42

Any discussion of these verses must begin with a proper understanding of the term "world" (Greek *kosmos*), a *world* with a wide range of meanings in the N.T. A basic lexical definition would define *world* as the sum total of all created beings in heaven and earth, or the universe (Arndt and Gingrich 446-48). Joachim Guhrt (521-26) gives an excellent summary of the various ways in which this word is used both in the Septuagint and in the N.T.

Bruce (61) suggests that *world* is used in the Biblical text in two primary ways. First, the world is the object of God's love and redemptive work. Second, the world is that which falls under the dominion of the "evil one" and stands in opposition to the love and work of God. The second is the meaning in these verses. The command is not to be in love with anything that stands in opposition to the will of God, whether a worldly philosophy, possession, or prince. Law (145, 146) suggests that in this passage the term refers to "the mass of unbelieving men, hostile to Christ and resisting salvation." The meaning is "Do not court the intimacy and favour of the unchristian world around you" (Law 148).

John uses a conditional statement to clarify the condition of the one who loves the world. If anyone loves the world, the love of the Father is not in him. In v. 15, the context makes clear that "love of the Father" refers to the individual's love for God (an objective genitive in Greek). Because of the exclusive nature of this kind of love, one cannot love two things that are in opposition to each other. The one who loves the world, regardless of what he says or believes, cannot love the Father. John is refuting the claims of the secessionists who say that they can be both in the world and in fellowship with God at the same time.

The next verse provides a threefold definition of all that is in the world. Bruce (62) writes that these three designations comprise what is commonly identified as materialism. He further explains that worldliness does not reside in things, but in our concentration and affection on things. The "lust of the flesh" refers to a self-centered orientation which pursues its own ends independent of God (Thiselton 680). According to Schönweiss (458), the lust of the eyes, the lust of the flesh, and the pride of life are "external allurements appealing to the senses, material in their nature," that Satan uses to try to obtain our love.

The "lust of the eyes" refers to anything that entices one by seeing it. Greed, envy, and sexual lust all illustrate this form of worldliness. Eve's lust for the fruit, Achan's lust for the spoils of war, and David's lust for Bathsheba are Biblical examples of the "lust of the eyes." Law (151) asserts that the lust of the eyes is "the love of beauty divorced from goodness."

The "pride of life" is understood to refer to the boastings of an individual centered on things real or contrived. The man who continually brags concerning his wealth, possessions, or status in order to enhance his reputation, thus bringing glory to himself rather than to God, is one who has fallen to this form of worldliness (see Plummer, *First Epistle* 24). These sinful actions and attitudes do not come from the Father. They provide evidence of one's attachment to the world.

John concludes this portion of his argument at v. 17. Those whose love is devoted to the world have placed their confidence in something that cannot last. Interestingly, the "passing away" is communicated as an ongoing action (Greek present tense). The world is already passing away as a result of its own wretchedness and sin. The phrase "he that doeth" and the verb "abideth" have the idea of continuing to do and abide (Greek present tense). The idea is that the one who continues to do the will of God will continue to abide forever. The final destiny of those whose love is devoted to the Father is to abide with Him forever, which is the very definition of eternal life.

Summary
(2:12-17)

In these verses we find two threefold progressions, one negative, stated explicitly and one positive, stated more implicitly. As a negative, one finds that to love the world has its source in the world and results in death. The love of the world appeals to our fleshly desires and may provide temporary satisfaction. The long-term results, however, are tragic. The world is already passing away, and the one who loves it will also pass away.

As a positive, one finds that to love the Father has its source in the Father and abides forever (Smalley 80). The opposite of loving the world is doing the will of the Father. The one who does the will of God is not tied to the world. He will not share the world's fate. He has before him the promise of eternal life with the Father.

Application: Teaching and Preaching the Passage

Those who preach and teach need to note both what John is saying in this passage and what he is not saying. He is not saying that everything in the world is evil or that the Christian must totally avoid all aspects of life in the world. In reality, such an approach is simply not possible. Christians have been placed in the world to bear witness to Christ. In Jn. 17:15 Jesus prayed this prayer for his disciples, "I pray not that thou shouldest take them out of the world, but that thou shouldest keep them from the evil." Plummer (*First Epistle* 24) correctly points out that John is not forbidding the love of "those material advantages which are God's gifts, nor of nature which is God's work." In summary, God has placed us in this world to minister, and He expects us to use the things of this world wisely and for His glory.

In this passage John is dealing with priorities. For the child of God, serving his heavenly Father must always be his first priority. Earthly desires can easily become the most important things in a believer's life. We live in a world that places great value on material prosperity, luxury, power, influence, etc. The desire to accumulate these things must never take the place of our commitment to serve God and follow Him.

5. Beware of the Antichrists (2:18-23)

18 Little children, it is the last time: and as ye have heard that antichrist shall come, even now are there many antichrists; whereby we know that it is the last time.

19 They went out from us, but they were not of us; for if they had been of us, they would *no doubt* have continued with us: but *they went out*, that they might be made manifest that they were not all of us.
20 But ye have an unction from the Holy One, and ye know all things.
21 I have not written unto you because ye know not the truth, but because ye know it, and that no lie is of the truth.
22 Who is a liar but he that denieth that Jesus is the Christ? He is antichrist, that denieth the Father and the Son.
23 Whosoever denieth the Son, the same hath not the Father: [but] he that acknowledgeth the Son hath the Father also.

In these verses, John gives his spiritual children important personal instruction. His goal is to help them understand what is going on around them. The entrance of heresy into the churches of Asia Minor should not take them by surprise. They need to understand that their conflict is part of a larger struggle between God and the forces of this evil world.

The author identifies his readers as *little children* (or *dear children*), indicating his devotion to them and his relationship with them as both teacher and mentor. John often uses this designation for his followers. It is possible that he is using this phrase as a transition device. Its use here may indicate the beginning of a new unit of thought.

Verse 18 introduces two new and important concepts: *the last time* and *the antichrist*. The phrase *last time* (Greek *eschate hora*) occurs only here

in the N.T. It is similar to the term *last days* found in other N.T. writings (Acts 2:17; Heb. 1:2; Jas. 5:3). The word translated "time" (Greek *hora*) in this verse is often translated by the English word *hour*. The phrase could correctly be translated "it is the last time" or "it is the last hour."

The phrase has O.T. roots and is not easy to define; two interpretations are common. First, it could mean the period associated with the new age initiated with the Christ event, the incarnation, death, resurrection, and ascension of Jesus. This view stresses that the revelation that has come in Jesus Christ is God's final revelation that the world will receive. It is the "last time" in the sense that it is mankind's final opportunity to accept Christ. It does not necessarily imply that Christ will return within a short period of time. Kistemaker (274, 275) suggests that it is the time period beginning with the ascension of Christ and ending either with His return or shortly before His return. This is often referred to as the chronological or theological interpretation of this important phrase. (See the comments of Barker 323, 324; and Bruce 64-66.)

Lieu (98) finds the historical background for this phrase in the words "latter days" or "the following days" which are rather common in the O.T. She suggests that these phrases do not specifically speak of the end times. They speak rather "of the time when God's purposes will become manifest."

The second possible interpretation is that this phrase should be understood eschatologically, as a reference to the time immediately preceding the Second Coming of Christ (Kistemaker 275). It was a common Jewish belief that evil would multiply shortly before the end time (Dodd 48). The multiplication of evil in John's day could easily be understood as an indication that the end of time was drawing near. (See Yarbrough 142; and Smith 179.)

There is no general agreement among scholars concerning these two possible interpretations. Stott gives an excellent summary of those scholars which supports each position (108, 109). Each interpretation presents both advantages and disadvantages.

On the whole, the first interpretation seems to fit this context better. John was not writing in order to give his readers a detailed prediction of future events. His goal was to help them understand what was going on in Asia Minor then, and to help them respond to it in an appropriate manner. In particular, he wanted to assure them that the events which had transpired were part of God's plan. They were no surprise to God, and should not be a surprise to His children.

For the Christians of Asia Minor, it was the last hour (or the last time) in the sense that God's final revelation had come in the person of Jesus Christ. No new revelations were to be anticipated. Jesus had warned His followers that they would face opposition and false teachings, and the recipients of John's letter were certainly facing them. In this passage, the phrase "the last time" is being used in a theological sense and not in an eschatological sense. As Cox (335) writes, "Since Christ came the first time, the end of time is present. The conflict with antichrist has started, and will continue until the second coming."

The grammar of the passage also indicates that the theological understanding is better: literally, the words are "It is last hour" (no definite article in

Greek). This leads Westcott (69) to comment that it is a reference to the "general character of the period and not its specific relation to the end." He continues by saying that "It was a period of critical change, a last hour, but not definitely the last hour." Bruce (65) echoes the position by poignantly writing that "in the Christian era it is always five minutes to midnight. But as the course of things runs along the edge of the final consummation, that edge at times becomes a knife-edge, and at such times the sense of its being 'the last hour' is especially acute."

Stott presents an interesting approach which is somewhat different from the two common interpretations cited above. He (108) argues that John meant that the "last hour of the last days" had arrived. The old era has ended and the new era has arrived. John did not mean to say, however, that the Second Coming of Christ was imminent. John would never have tried to predict the time of Christ's return; there are too many warnings against doing so. It is more likely that John would have connected these events with the period of trials and apostasy that precede Christ's return.

The second important term introduced in v. 18 is "antichrist" (Greek *antichristos*) which occurs in this verse both in singular and plural forms. This significant and somewhat controversial term is a compound of two parts. The first, *anti*, originally meant "in place of" and later came to mean "against"— which is the idea here (Kauder 124). The second, *Christ*, is the Greek equivalent of the Hebrew term "Messiah" or "Anointed One." The term "Antichrist," then, describes someone who is opposed to Jesus Christ in some way.

This term occurs five times in the N.T. (four times in 1 John and once in 2 John). John is the only N.T. writer to use it and could have coined the term (Kruse 98). It is a general term which could include anyone who denies that the man Jesus has come to earth as God's Anointed One or Messiah.

Most interpreters see the term as a reference to the false teachers who were causing such division and strife within the churches of Asia Minor. Bruce (65) interprets the passage to mean that the end-time antichrist is now active in the world and that the spirit of the antichrist is working in the false teachers. Kauder (126) writes, "In the Johannine Epistles teachers of false doctrines are called antichrists." See Kruse (99-102) who presents an excellent summary of the O.T. background.

Yarbrough (144) takes a somewhat different approach. He first notes that early Christian writers explained the term in different ways. He then distinguishes between the singular "antichrist" and the plural "many antichrists." The antichrist will come at the end of time. He is "likely a human representative or incarnation of the evil one whom Christ explicitly acknowledged in his teaching." In his view, the antichrists are "forerunners of this end-time figure." They are the false teachers who are causing such problems for John and his spiritual children.

Verse 19 clearly identifies the antichrists of the previous verse as human teachers who were at one time part of the community but who had voluntarily withdrawn from it. Since they had departed from the church and were encouraging others to do so, many commentators refer to them as *secessionists*. John can easily identify those who

left the church as antichrists because they stand against what the church has taught concerning the incarnation.

In the first part of the verse John writes, "They went out from us, but they were not of us." In the last part he writes, "that they might be made manifest that they were not all of us." Both expressions present the same idea. Those who left the fellowship may have been members of the church, but the fact that they left raises serious doubts about the genuineness of their faith. As Bruce (69) notes, "Had they been securely built on the foundation of eternal life, they would not have been so easily shifted from it."

Verse 22 identifies the antichrists as liars who deny that Jesus is the Christ. Barker (325) points out that in the context of 1 John the liars are not Jewish teachers who argue that Jesus is not the Messiah, but the Gnostic teachers who denied that Jesus had come in the flesh. The next verse explains that one who does not have the Son does not have the Father either. The idea is that one who denies the incarnation of the Son cannot have a living relationship with the Father. He is by his own action outside the family of the faithful. Only those who recognize Jesus Christ as the Son of God and the only way of salvation enjoy a legitimate personal relationship with the Father.

In vv. 20, 21 John expresses his confidence that his followers in Asia Minor will not be carried away by all the false teachings. He also explains why he believes that they will continue to adhere to the true teachings they have received: because they have received "an unction from the Holy One."

The word "unction" (Greek *chrisma*) means an anointing. The basic idea is that the believers have been anointed by God and that this anointing will help them to stand firm and not be deceived by the heretical teachings. See the comments of Müller (122, 123). Moody (51, 52) gives a helpful analysis of the O.T. background of the concept. As Müller (122) explains, "Anointing is a metaphor for the bestowal of the Holy Spirit, special power, or a divine commission."

Believers who continue in the body are given an assurance that they may stand against the secessionists because they have an unction or anointing from the Holy One. The "Holy One" can be identified as either the Father or the Son, but in this context it is most probably the Son. (See Westcott 73; and Marshall 155.) The anointing by the Holy One is probably a reference to the outpouring of the Holy Spirit on the believer just as the Spirit was poured out upon Christ at His baptism. The anointing—the abiding presence of the Holy Spirit in the life of the believer—provides the source of power and authority with which the believer can overcome the antichrist.

The two expressions "unction" and "know" assure the believers that they possess what the antichrists claim to possess. These false teachers claimed a special anointing and knowledge that goes beyond what the average believer possesses. It was through this special knowledge that they claimed salvation. John contradicts their claims; he argues that true unction and knowledge come from God through His Son.

John reminds his readers that they know all things. This does not mean that they are omniscient but that they know the truth that Jesus is the Christ. As a result of their anointing they have all the knowledge necessary to stand firm in a difficult situation. Marshall (156) points out that the false teachers can claim no monopoly on truth. All believers have access to the truth. The basic idea of the passage is that God has bestowed the Holy Spirit upon the Christians of Asia Minor. He has given them the necessary understanding to withstand the false teachers.

John continues by encouraging the believers to rely on their knowledge of the truth and reject all that is not of the truth. His basic assertion is that they know the truth in Christ. It is not his purpose to inform them of new truth but to affirm the truth that they already know.

The spiritual condition of those described in v. 19 has provoked considerable debate. The verse describes those who have left the fellowship; it probably includes both the false teachers and those who have fallen under their influence. They are often called secessionists (Kruse 102). Kruse (105) outlines several possible interpretations of their spiritual condition. The two most likely interpretations are: (1) they were once believers but are no longer believers, or (2) they never really were believers. Kruse himself accepts the second interpretation. He (102) writes, "Their secession, as far as the author is concerned, only showed that they had never been true members of his own Christian community."

Marshall (152, 153) comes to some significant conclusions concerning those who left the fellowship. He writes, "They had been only apparent members." Marshall then explains that this passage illustrates clearly the distinction between the visible church (composed of those who belong to it) and the invisible church (which includes only those who have been redeemed).

According to Cox (336), it is difficult to determine whether or not they at one time had been true believers. He concludes that it is possible that some of them had been true followers of Christ in the past. For the Apostle John, the most important issue is not what they were in the past but what they are now. It is clear that when John wrote this letter they were no longer part of the Christian fellowship, and by their acceptance of false teachings they were undermining the proclamation of the gospel in that region.

It is clear that they had left the churches voluntarily. They were not commanded to leave; they went out by their own choice. Their voluntary departure coupled with John's statement that they were "not of us" suggests there was a long-standing theological difference. Later we will find out that the theological difference centers on the nature of Christ in the incarnation.

Membership in a local church does not guarantee that one has been truly redeemed, but remaining in the local fellowship is, at least, some evidence that a person is truly a Christian. These false teachers were once part of the church in Asia Minor, but they have since departed. For John, their departure is sufficient evidence that they are not truly part of the family of God. If they had truly been part of the church universal, they would have continued in fellowship with the Christians of Asia Minor. As Burge (127) explains, "Their departure is evidence … that they were never part of the church in the first place."

The clear message that the Apostle communicates is that although the secessionists were once part of the church they no longer are—because they did not continue in the true doctrine of Christ. The implications for the Christians of Asia Minor are obvious. If they wish to have a right relationship with God, they must continue in the true faith they have received and resist the efforts of the false teachers to lead them astray.

He who denies the truth that Jesus is the Christ is both a liar and the antichrist. The verb "denieth" (v. 22, Greek *arneomai*) denotes a continuous or habitual action (Greek present participle). It describes one who continues to deny the essential truth of the incarnation. The truth is that Jesus came in the flesh and died for man's sin. Denial of this core doctrine separates true Christianity from all other faiths. One who claims to be a Christian cannot say he believes in the Father but not in the incarnate Christ. John asserts that the one who denies the Son also denies the Father.

The converse is also true; the one who acknowledges (Greek *homologeo*, confess) the Son has the Father also. Acknowledgment or confession of the Son is more than mere intellectual assent. The devils do that (Mk. 1:24; Jas. 2:19). It involves recognition and personal acceptance that Jesus is both Savior and Lord. It is to agree with the truth of the cross event. He who does this is assured of a right relationship with God. See the excellent summary of Plummer (*First Epistle* 27, 28).

Summary
(2:18-23)

An element of conflict dominates these verses. John is convinced that the current situation can be tolerated no longer. The secessionists claim to be saved by the special revelations they have received. They reject the traditional

49

Christian teaching that Jesus Christ has come to earth in human form. While it is difficult to reconstruct their teachings with certainty, they are most likely teaching that Jesus had the appearance of a human being but not the reality. John views this teaching as the most serious of heresies. If it is not defeated, serious harm will be done to the church.

John's followers are facing the last hour—in a theological rather than an eschatological sense. The antichrists are those who were once part of the body of believers but left of their own volition, preferring to believe a lie rather than the truth. The believers are encouraged to hold to the truth as confirmed in them through the anointing of the "Holy One." By holding to the truth they are empowered by the Holy Spirit to stand against the false teachings of the antichrists, namely the denial of the incarnation. When one acknowledges the Son as Savior and Lord he also confesses the Father, for the Son and the Father are one. By this confession one can know he is in right relationship with God.

Application: Teaching and Preaching the Passage

This important passage contains many ideas that should be part of our preaching and teaching. The first lesson is that doctrine does matter. There is a difference between truth and error. In the modern world, much emphasis is placed on sincerity. It is not unusual to hear people say with both their words and their actions, "It doesn't matter what you believe as long as you are sincere." This passage forever stands as a testimony against such thinking. The Christian faith is built on truth, not on error. Heretical doctrines must always be rejected.

The second lesson is that conflict is sometimes necessary. No one likes discord, and the Bible itself encourages people to live in peace with one another. This does not mean, however, that the church should maintain peace by tolerating heresy. Doctrinal errors must be exposed and corrected.

Doctrinal error must be confronted in the right way. John did not deal with the situation through rumor and innuendo. He went directly to the source and confronted the heresy openly. We should do the same. The church must always operate in an atmosphere of openness and integrity.

The third important lesson is that John does not provoke a controversy over something that is really insignificant. The issue at hand in these verses is the incarnation of Jesus Christ, the Son of God. This is one of the cardinal doctrines of the Christian faith. It is not the kind of issue about which sincere Christians may disagree. The Christian faith has always held to a core of essential doctrines without demanding conformity on lesser issues. Some issues are worth fighting about, others are not. Christians need the wisdom and maturity to know the difference.

6. Abide in Christ (2:24-29)

24 Let that therefore abide in you, which ye have heard from the beginning. If that which ye have heard from the beginning shall remain in you, ye also shall continue in the Son, and in the Father.

25 And this is the promise that he hath promised us, *even* eternal life.
26 These *things* have I written unto you concerning them that seduce you.
27 But the anointing which ye have received of him abideth in you, and ye need not that any man teach you: but as the same anointing teacheth you of all things, and is truth, and is no lie, and even as it hath taught you, ye shall abide in him.
28 And now, little children, abide in him; that, when he shall appear, we may have confidence, and not be ashamed before him at his coming.
29 If ye know that he is righteous, ye know that every one that doeth righteousness is born of him.

John begins this section with an emphatic construction. He places the personal pronoun "you" first (in the Greek sentence), a maneuver often used to show emphasis on that word. The emphasis is further strengthened with an imperative main verb. A literal translation of this passage would be "You, therefore, let that which you heard from the beginning abide in you." The emphatic construction draws attention to the role of the believer in this sad situation. They are to keep the truth that was communicated to them from the beginning. The responsibility is on their shoulders.

There is some difference of opinion on the meaning of the words "from the beginning." According to Kruse (107), this looks back to the gospel message as they first heard it and by which they were saved. Akin (123) writes that this

phrase most probably refers to the original apostolic message that they had received. He also notes that this phrase possibly refers to the teachings of Christ Himself. Cox (337) summarizes well the meaning in these words, "The original teachings given by Jesus and confirmed by the apostles are to be held fast in the believer's hearts."

Verse 24 continues with a conditional statement. The idea is, "If you keep the truth then you shall continue in the Son and the Father." If the believer remains in the truth of Christ, then he or she is assured of a continuing relationship with God in Christ Jesus. If they wish to remain in a proper relationship with the Father and with the Son, the Christians of Asia Minor must maintain their commitment to the gospel message they had received.

If these believers continue in the Son and Father, God has a promise for them. The word *promise* (Greek *epangelia*) describes a declaration given by one who has the ability, desire, and resources to secure its fulfillment. The promise given by God is sure because He is the guarantor. The believer must, however, accept it by faith. The content of the promise given by God to the believer is eternal life. Eternal life is characterized by either timelessness or immortality. It is the kind of life attributed to God and distributed to believers (Elwell and Comfort 448). John's concept of eternal life is not only an anticipation of a future life but also a present experience of that life. Eternal life then is available in the present in Christ to the believer.

John declares to his readers his purpose for writing this section of the letter. His goal is to make the believer aware of the actions and character of the secessionists. They are seeking to deceive the believers, to lead them away from the faith which they possess. The text uses the word "seduce" which is a vivid and appropriate description of the behavior of the deceivers. The false teaching, like the dress of the seductress, is appealing. Christians must always be conscious of the attempts of the false teacher to lead them astray. One cannot help but see the connection of the deceiver in v. 26 with the deceiver of the world, the father of lies (Jn. 8:44).

In v. 27 we find the same emphatic construction as in v. 24. The "you" is placed at the beginning of the clause. John continues his instruction to the believer with a reminder that he has received the anointing of God. In this context, the anointing should probably be identified with the indwelling presence of the Holy Spirit (Westcott 73). The Holy Spirit serves to teach the believer; he is therefore not in need of other confirmation of the truth. Each Christian may rest in the fact that there is no lie in the truth.

The words "and ye need not that any man teach you" (v. 27) indicate that these Christians have already received the true apostolic teaching. They already have the truth and do not need the additional instruction that the false teachers wanted to provide. According to Plummer (First Epistle 28), the anointing of Christ remains with them as a permanent gift, and they need nothing more. Rather than seeking some new teaching, they need to concentrate their efforts on abiding in Christ.

Verse 28 forms something of a summary of this section of the epistle. The verb "abide" is a command (Greek imperative). The believer is given specific instruction to abide in Christ; to continue in that which they have heard from the beginning and in that which the anointing of the Holy Spirit continues to teach them. It is a matter of obedience. The purpose of continuing to abide in Him directs the readers' focus to the future coming (Greek paruousia) of Christ. When one abides he will feel no shame nor will he be put to shame because of his relationship to Christ, and he can be confident at Christ's coming (Kistemaker 288).

The noun "confidence" (Greek parresia) is used 31 times in the N.T., 13 of which are found in the Johannine corpus. It was originally used in classical Greek to describe the right of a free citizen to speak in public meetings. It later came to express the idea of courage, confidence, or boldness especially before important people (Arndt and Gingrich 635, 636). In this context, the idea is that the believer may come into the presence of God freely and without fear based on a right relationship with Him. According to John the right relationship is achieved by confessing Jesus as the Christ and abiding in Him. Smalley (130) makes the case that this is not an improper confidence because God Himself made it possible through Jesus.

There is some difficulty in determining the antecedent of "he" in v. 29. It could refer to either the Father or the Son. The preceding verse unquestionably refers to Christ, so it could easily be understood to refer to Christ. Westcott (83) takes this view saying, "It is most natural to suppose that He [Christ] is the subject in this verse also." The opposing argument is that nowhere in scripture is it said that the Christian is "born of Christ." However, John uses the phrase "born of God" six times (Jn. 1:13; 1 Jn. 3:9; 4:7; 5:1, 4, 18). This verse identifies those who practice righteousness as being "born of him." It is then most appropriate to identify God as the righteous one. It naturally follows that God's children will reproduce His righteous character. If anyone claims to belong to the family of God and does not practice righteousness (like the secessionists), his claim is false. Yet one who practices righteousness is identified as a child of God by his very actions and deeds.

John uses two different Greek words translated as "know" in v. 29. It is not necessary to draw far-reaching conclusions based on the subtle nuance of each word (see the discussion of v. 3 above). Still, the differences may enrich one's understanding of the passage. The first "know" (Greek *oida*) carries the idea of an awareness of fact. The second "know" (Greek *ginosko*) describes a knowledge gained by experience, or that which one learns (Akin 131; Westcott 82). One might translate the verse in this manner: "If you are aware of the fact that He is righteous, you have learned from experience that every one that does righteousness is born of Him." There is a relationship between the factual truth statement and one's experiential knowledge. It is a fact that must be accepted by faith that God is righteous. Knowledge learned through experience allows an individual to be identified with the family of God because of the reflection of God's righteous character in his own life.

John's goal in this verse is to give assurance to his spiritual children. They are living according to the teachings of Christ. The fact that they are living righteously is evidence that they have received Christ's righteousness (Burge 145). The false teachers have nothing

that they need; they should continue serving Christ as they are.

<h2 style="text-align:center">Summary
(2:24-29)</h2>

John wrote these words to a group of his spiritual children who were actively engaged in battle. Satan was trying to destroy them through the false teachers who were subverting the faith of many in Asia Minor. These false teachers were raising doubts of one sort or another about their relationship with Christ. What they needed was assurance, and that is what John gave them.

The false teachers tried to create doubt about their prior experience with Christ. John assures them that they have received the true gospel and encourages them to continue in it. They have received the anointing of the Holy Spirit and are truly born again. The false teachers can offer them only the teachings of men, which they do not need.

At this point, we should clarify what John is saying. He is not saying that all human teaching is bad or unnecessary. When human teachers can help believers to understand the gospel better, that is a good thing. That is not, however, what was happening in Asia Minor. The false teachers were not helping the believers to understand the gospel better, they were offering an alternative gospel which was, in reality, no gospel. John has already rejected them and their false teachings. His spiritual children need to do likewise.

The key word in this passage is "abide." These Christians need to abide in Christ and in the true teachings they have already received. They should not be led astray by these false teachers no

53

matter how attractive their teachings may be.

Application: Teaching and Preaching the Passage

Christians sometimes have doubts, and leaders such as pastors need to be able to respond to those doubts in appropriate ways. In this passage, John provides a good example of how the church should deal with those who are having doubts about their faith and their prior experience with Christ. It should first be noted that John responds with love and acceptance, not with rejection. He does not attack them or accuse them of being weak in faith. Instead, he takes their doubts seriously. He understands that even the strongest of believers may at times be overcome with doubt and fear. He responds to their doubts with assurance and seeks to restore their faith and confidence.

John begins this discussion by reminding them of what they have accomplished. They have heard and received the truth. Their experience with Christ is not defective. Rather than seeking some new experience with Christ, they need to affirm what has already happened to them.

He continues by reminding them of where they are spiritually. They have received the anointing of the Holy Spirit. They continue to live according to the gospel message they have received. The false teachers have nothing that will contribute positively to their Christian faith.

Then John turns his attention to the future. Because of their present relationship with Him, they can look forward to Christ's return with hope and assurance.

They have nothing to fear. They simply need to continue abiding in Christ.

Burge (153) makes some insightful comments about this passage. He reminds us that we should never make our feelings the main focus of our spiritual lives. Feelings will always go up and down. Conversion is a profound spiritual experience, but our emotional response to that experience will vary depending on the circumstances about us. In the final analysis, we are not saved by our feelings but by our relationship with Christ.

II. Walk in Love (3:1—5:12)

A. The Children of God (3:1-3)

**1 Behold, what manner of love the Father hath bestowed upon us, that we should be called the sons of God: therefore the world knoweth us not, because it knew him not.
2 Beloved, now are we the sons of God, and it doth not yet appear what we shall be: but we know that, when he shall appear, we shall be like him; for we shall see him as he is.
3 And every man that hath this hope in him purifieth himself, even as he is pure.**

The opening verses of chapter 3 continue the development of several important themes from the previous chapter. John continues to encourage his spiritual children to trust in Christ and to live as they have been taught to live. Regardless what the false teachers may have said to them and about them, they are in fact the children of God. They should allow no one to shake their confidence in Christ and in their commitment to Him. What these believers need is encouragement, and that is exactly what the aged Apostle gives them in this important passage.

First John 2:28—3:3 forms a natural division of the letter, with the final verse serving as a summary and conclusion to this section. A new division begins with v. 4 (Beyer 163).

In 1 Jn. 3:1-3 the author writes with a voice of authority instructing his spiritual children to behold the manner of love the Father had given to them. The command to *behold* comes in response to the awesome message of salvation they had received in the previous chapter. It challenges the Christians to reflect upon who they are and what Christ has done for them (Akin 132). It is a reminder to his followers of the sacrificial nature and perfect quality of the love that the Father has given to them. According to Jackman (81), the main idea is that Christians need to take time to contemplate the implications of the sacrificial love that God has bestowed on them.

The word translated "what manner" (Greek *potapos*) means "of what sort or kind" and can be literally translated "of what country." It occurs only seven times in the N.T. and always conveys a sense of astonishment. Many times it also implies a sense of admiration (Akin 132). Stott (122) suggests that this term refers to the unearthly or foreign nature of the kind of love that would cause the Father to redeem His creation. In other words, it is not the kind of love that human beings can generate. It is a special kind of love that has its origin in heaven.

In this context the phrase "to be called" means to be recognized as the children of God (Grayston 100). Marshall (171) suggests that the phrase "to be called" in many instances means "to be." That seems to be the idea in this verse. John's goal is to assure these believers in Asia Minor that they are in fact the children of God and heirs of His promises.

Being *sons of God* or *children of God* means that Christians are partakers of the very nature of God in the new birth. This phrase is more than a title. It declares the fact that believers are members of the family. As Beyer (165) explains, "The love of God is not given for no reason, but because He wishes to gain the lost so that they can become members of the family of God."

In the last part of v. 1, John reminds his readers that the special relationship they have with the Father puts them at odds with the world. Those who belong to the world do not have, and cannot have, the same personal, intimate relationship with the Father that the Christians have. The world does not know Him or His children. The term *world* (Greek *kosmos)* is used with several different meanings in the N.T. In this context it describes "the evil humanistic system that dominates the society around us, a hostile order that stands in opposition to God" (Akin 134).

There is a minor textual variant in this verse which does not affect the interpretation of the passage. Most manuscripts include the words "and we are" (Greek *kai esmen)* in the middle of v. 1, but some omit them. English translations are divided; some include these words and some do not. The KJV does not include them. See the discussion of Kruse (115).

The words "and we are" complete the thought begun earlier in the verse by the words "that we should be called the sons of God." John wishes to leave no doubt that his followers are the children of God even though his enemies may teach otherwise.

In v. 2 John addresses his readers as *beloved*. He then affirms "now are we the sons of God." These terms leave no doubt about their salvation and their present relationship both with the Father and with the Son. The word *now* also serves to connect their present relationship with God and the bright future that He has in store for them (Kruse 116). The precise nature of their future existence cannot be determined with certainty, but one thing is certain: when Christ returns they will be like Him and they will see Him as He is.

According to Kruse (116), the phrase "see him as he is" does not convey the idea that we will see Christ as He was during the days of His earthly ministry. Neither will believers see Him with the eyes of faith as the church sees Him now. Instead they will see Him in all His glory in heaven. The author's point seems to be that believers will, in the end time, have a much more complete understanding of Christ than we have now. (See the comments of Marshall 171, 172.)

Christians will be "like him." The phrase "like him" may mean "like Christ" or "like God." The meaning "like Christ" best fits the context (Akin 136; Beyer 169). The word "like" (Greek *homoios*) does not mean that believers become identical to Christ in being. The idea is that they will share certain aspects of His character. The believer carries the likeness of Christ in the new nature. The believer is like Christ because he walks in the light as He is in the light, because it is the righteousness of Christ that

dwells within him. This likeness does not lead to equality with Christ. Equality with Christ is impossible because Christ is divine, and man is His creation.

The last words of v. 2, "for we shall see him as he is," have provoked considerable discussion. Perhaps the best interpretation is that believers will come face to face with Christ on the day of His Second Coming. When that event occurs, the believer's transformation into the likeness of Christ will be complete. (See the comments of Akin 137; Beyer 169, 170; and Marshall 173.)

The first phrase of v. 3, "And every man that hath this hope in him," continues the thought introduced in the previous verse. The idea is that all who have this hope—the hope of seeing Him face to face; the hope of being transformed into His image; the hope of being eternally part of the family of God—will respond in gratitude and seek to mirror Christ's image in the present. The believer's hope is more than a wish; it carries the expectation of fulfillment in reality. The believer's hope in Christ is much more than wishful thinking or optimism about the future. It is a hope made sure by the work of Christ. (See the comments of Beyer 171.)

The phrase *purifies himself* does not mean that the Christian can purify himself through good works or personal effort. It is, rather, the believer's response to the grace bestowed upon him as a child of God. It is the moral and ethical responsibility of the individual to live according to the precepts of God. *To purify* means to cleanse oneself from the corruption of sin in a moral sense (Thayer 6). This term was first used to describe ceremonial purification; it later came to describe the personal cleansing of an individual (Robertson 221).

This kind of cleansing can only be accomplished in Christ. It is a continuing process of renewal that begins at the new birth and ends when we see Him. Because Christ is pure we must practice purity. Beyer (171) notes that in the N.T. the idea of purity implies much more than washing with water. It includes the moral purifying that the Christian receives as a result of Christ's blood. He summarizes in these words, "to purify ones' self means to live constantly in the forgiveness that Christ has obtained for us, and, at the same time, to renounce sin and live according to the will of God." This can be accomplished only through the power of the Holy Spirit.

The "great manner of love that the Father has bestowed upon us" explains the reason God includes the believer in His family. As a member of the family the child of God identifies with the Father and not with the world. Conversely the world does not have personal knowledge of the family and stands in opposition to God and His children. The exact nature of the familial relationship is unknown in the present, but at the Second Coming believers are promised that they will be like Him. Their likeness to Christ is not a statement of equality of being but likeness in nature. When they see Him in His glory at His appearing, He will affect our change to His likeness.

The love of God, inclusion in the family, re-creation into His image—all unite to elicit a response of hope in the believer. From a position of gratitude the follower of Christ seeks a moral purification that is made possible because of his position in Christ. This process of purification is ongoing from the time of the new birth. When the believer remembers the purity of the Son his desire is to be as much like Him as possible.

Summary
(3:1-3)

This passage should be interpreted in light of the false teachings that the Apostle John was refuting. Christians are not saved by some type of special revelation that God gives them. They are saved by the love of God as demonstrated through the person and work of Christ. The deeds of the flesh are not unimportant, as the various Gnostic schools argued. They are very important, and the true believer must commit himself to a life of purity which can only become reality through the continuing work of the Holy Spirit.

It is by His love that the believer becomes a child of God. The precise nature of this sonship is impossible to determine today. In these verses, John's emphasis is not on the present but on the future. The believer is now a son of God, but the full significance of being a child of God will only become apparent at the Second Coming of Christ.

The process of transformation that began at salvation will continue in the future. At Christ's second coming, the believer will be like Christ. The promise of becoming like Christ gives to the believer a desire to purify himself and be like Him in every respect. There is a measure of responsibility for moral purity that is placed squarely upon the shoulders of each member of the family. The Christian is able to begin his lifelong pursuit for moral purity because of his position in Christ.

Application: Teaching and Preaching the Passage

There are several important themes in these verses that contemporary Christians need to hear. These verses speak of the special relationship that Christians have with their Heavenly Father. While it is certainly true that God loves everyone and desires that all be saved, the Bible clearly teaches that those who have accepted Jesus Christ as their personal Savior occupy a special place in God's family. The promise of salvation is extended only to those who have been saved through the blood of Christ. The fact that God loves all does not mean that all will be saved.

These verses also point out that our knowledge of the future is incomplete. As John wrote, "It doth not yet appear what we shall be." God has revealed to us the information about the end times that we need to know now. The rest we will find out when Jesus returns for His own. Christians should not allow themselves to be caught up in unhealthy attempts to determine the precise order of future events.

There is a great need for purity in the lives of believers today. Unfortunately, too many Christians emphasize the fact that they are saved by faith to such an extent that they neglect a personal commitment to purity of life. The grace of God never leads into sin; it always leads away from it. The grace of God both saves and transforms. Part of that transformation is a sincere commitment to purity of life. Sin in the life of a believer must never be taken lightly.

B. Freedom from Sin (3:4-10)

**4 Whosoever committeth sin transgresseth also the law: for sin is the transgression of the law.
5 And ye know that he was manifested to take away our sins; and in him is no sin.
6 Whosoever abideth in him sinneth not: whosoever sinneth hath not seen him, neither known him.
7 Little children, let no man deceive you: he that doeth righteousness is righteous, even as he is righteous.
8 He that committeth sin is of the devil; for the devil sinneth from the beginning. For this purpose the Son of God was manifested, that he might destroy the works of the devil.
9 Whosoever is born of God doth not commit sin; for his seed remaineth in him: and he cannot sin, because he is born of God.
10 In this the children of God are manifest, and the children of the devil: whosoever doeth not righteousness is not of God, neither he that loveth not his brother.**

In these verses, John continues to confront the false teachings of the Gnostics. He considers them to be heretics because they do not take the sins of the flesh seriously. In their view, only the sins of the spirit can separate a believer from God; sins of the flesh do not. Marshall (176) points out that the Christians were likely being taught to regard sin "as a matter of indifference." (See the discussions of Beyer 177, 183; and Akin 140, 141.)

In the previous verses the author's attention was focused on the Second Coming of Christ, but in these verses the emphasis shifts to His first coming. John gives two reasons for the coming of Christ to earth: first, to take away the sins of humanity (3:4-6); second, to destroy the works of the devil (3:7-10). The very object of Christ's manifestation in the flesh was to take away sin, thus redeeming children of this world into sonship. Being God's offspring, our new nature is incompatible with sin.

"Whosoever committeth" is the same phrase used in 1 Jn. 2:29 where it is translated "every one that doeth," indicating action that is ongoing or continuous (Greek present participle). There is an obvious connection between the two passages; both describe the actions and attitudes that characterize the child of God. In 2:29 he is described positively as one who continues to do righteousness. In this verse the same truth is stated in the negative. The child of God does not continue in sin (Akin 139; Marshall 175, 176).

A person demonstrates who he is by what he does. If he does righteousness and does not do sin then his conduct confirms his profession as a child of God. Sin is incompatible with the new birth from God. As discussed earlier in chapters one and two, the false teachers whom John is confronting believed that sin was not problematic for one of two reasons: either the false teachers taught that they were incapable of committing sin because of their nature, or they believed that actual sin done in the flesh was of no concern to God and was not charged to their account.

John uses the construction (Greek *pas* with present participle) "every one" (2:29), "every man" (3:3), and "whosoever" (3:4, 6, 9, 10, 15) a total of eight times in this portion of the epistle (including twice in v. 6). His use of this

formula indicates the universal scope by which he provides a moral and ethical description of the child of God. The first two are positive descriptions of what the child of God does. The next six are negative, describing what the child of God does not do. This positive and negative description gives boundaries by which believers can evaluate themselves as to their position in the family of God. The same standards can be used to evaluate the teachings of those outside the community. Any teaching that offers a different picture of the follower of God must be heretical and should be rejected. John will return to this important point in 4:1.

Several terms are used in the N.T. to describe sin; two figure prominently in this passage. The first (Greek *hamartia*) is translated "sin." The second (Greek *anomia*) is translated "transgression of the law" in the KJV. In other English translations it is often translated "lawlessness." The latter part of 3:4 uses these two terms for sin interchangeably; sin is lawlessness and lawlessness is sin.

The first of the two words (*sin*) literally means "to miss the mark." It is used in classical Greek to describe a warrior who missed his target or a traveler who missed the right path (Akin 140). In the N.T. it implies a willful and deliberate departure from the way of the Lord. Akin (140) describes it as "an intentional breaking of God's moral standard." Beyer (176) defines it as "rebellion against God's norms."

The second word (*lawlessness*) is used in several different ways. It may refer to the violation or breaking of God's moral law (Marshall 176). Beyer (176) argues that it does not refer to one who ignores the law or who does not have the law. It describes one who is directly opposed to the law of God.

Kruse (117, 118) suggests that this word is often used in contexts referring to Satan, false prophets, or others who are actively opposed to God. He connects the term with the antichrists mentioned in chapter two. If this interpretation is correct, to live a life of lawlessness is to ally oneself with Satan and to be openly and actively opposed to the work of God in the world.

Lawlessness, then, may be defined as rebellion against God's law and is the very essence of sin. It is a general description of the nature of sin rather than of specific sins committed by the individual. Further, we find that rebellion against God's law is the definition of the Antichrist, who is against God and against Christ; we might even say that the person described here is "an antichrist." This is in keeping with John's earlier statement (1 Jn. 2:18).

In v. 5, John gives his spiritual children another reason why they should strive to avoid sin in their lives (Akin 141). He turns his attention to the purpose of the incarnation. Jesus came to take away sins, not to encourage Christians to continue living in them. He is uniquely qualified for this task because He is wholly sinless. The purity and holiness manifested by Jesus stands as the foundation for the claims of purity for the believer and continues to give definition to what it means to be a child of God. The words "in him is no sin" are included for a very practical reason. John is contrasting the sinlessness of Christ with the sinful lifestyles of the false teachers (Kruse 120). The Christians of Asia Minor need to see that only Christ is worthy of their allegiance.

Verse 6 begins with the familiar term *whosoever*. The idea is that anyone who abides in the sinless Christ cannot continue living a sinful lifestyle. He has received a new nature in Christ, and his life must manifest that new nature. The verbs used in v. 6 (Greek present tense) ordinarily denote linear or ongoing action (Cox 341). It is doubtful that John's message is that if a Christian commits a single act of sin, that single act of sin is evidence that he has never truly been born again. Such an interpretation simply does not fit the context. In fact, it is contrary to 1 Jn. 1:6-10 where the author confronts the problem of sin in the life of the believer. More likely, John's message is that no person who is abiding in Christ will choose to live a sinful lifestyle.

Leon Morris (1404) explains the meaning in these words, "John is not writing about individual acts of sin, but about habitual attitudes." As Beyer (180) correctly notes, the only way the believer can avoid sin is by remaining in Christ. While that is possible through the power of God, it is difficult to do. Sometimes believers sin in spite of their best efforts not to do so. When a believer does sin, he responds with repentance and rededication (2:1, 2). He seeks to reestablish communion with Christ and be restored as soon as possible (Beyer 180).

Kistemaker (299) sees in this passage a sharp contrast between the life of a believer and the life of an unbeliever. He suggests that the believer "occasionally stumbles into sin, and that if he confesses his sin, Christ forgives, and cleanses him from all unrighteousness." The unbeliever, on the other hand, "continues to sin and demonstrates that he has no fellowship with Christ."

This passage should not be used to teach that Christians may live a life of sinless perfection. There are too many passages in the N.T. that deal with the problem of sin in the lives of believers (1 Jn. 1:8–2:2, for example). Neither should the passage be used to minimize the demand for holiness in the lives of believers (Morris 1404). God will never be satisfied with believers who live in sin. To live in sin means to practice sin on a regular basis and to minimize its importance; it also means not to repent and not to seek for, or accept, God's pardon (see Beyer 182).

John's purpose in this passage is to contrast the commitment to righteous living that is found in the lives of his followers in Asia Minor with the unholy lifestyles advocated by the false teachers. This passage should be interpreted in light of the author's goal and the historical situation that existed in Asia Minor at that time. John's point here is not to teach that a child of God can live in sin and still be part of the family. His point is that sin is totally and completely incompatible both with the nature of Christ and with the nature of those who abide in Him.

In v. 7 John responds in a most direct and forceful manner to the false teachers by admonishing his followers not to be deceived by the false teachings they have heard. His use of the address *little children* is significant. This shows his care and concern for those in the family of God. The admonition not to be deceived is communicated in the strongest sense possible (Greek third person imperative). "Deceive" (Greek *planao*) is to lead astray or to cause to wander off the path. This is exactly what the false teachers were attempting to do. They sought to lead the believers away from the truth which they had heard from the beginning (1 Jn. 1:1). The false teachers placed their own defective version of the truth before the Christians of Asia Minor and attempted to use knowledge and persuasion to convince them to accept it.

The teaching of vv. 7, 8 is clear: if one is a child of God, he practices righteousness—not just any righteousness, but righteousness as defined by the standard of the perfect righteousness of Christ. The one who practices sin is of the devil. There is no truth to be found in the devil; he is the deceiver and the father of lies. Satan speaks lies, and when he does so, he reflects what kind of being he is (Jn. 8:44). It was Satan who first lied to Eve in the garden (Gen. 3:4) and deceived her.

According to v. 8 Christ also came "that he might destroy the works of the devil." Jesus' coming exposed the devil for what he is, a liar and deceiver. The light of truth destroys Satan's schemes and plans by stripping them of the power to confuse, manipulate, and deceive. By the power of Christ, the one who was once deceived by the devil is no longer a victim but is presently the victor over him and his works (Rom. 8:37). The victory of Christ over the devil and his works is the fulfillment of Gen. 3:15: "It [the woman's seed] shall bruise thy [the serpent's] head, and thou shalt bruise his heel."

It is important to remember that the believer is not able to do things that only Christ can do. The believer is not charged with destroying the works of the devil; Christ came to do that. Kistemaker (302) correctly notes, "The Son of God came to deliver his people from the bondage of sin and to restore them as children of God." The responsibility of the believer is to practice righteousness by being obedient to the will of the Father.

Verse 9 begins with the "whosoever" formula which draws attention to the universal application of the teaching that John is presenting. The theme of v. 9 is closely associated with v. 6. Both verses emphasize that sin is incompatible with abiding in Christ. Once again, the verbs suggest ongoing action (Greek present tense), and the passage could be translated "all the ones begotten from God do not continue doing sin." As Robertson (222) explains, "The child of God does not have the habit of sin." The propensity to sin is present in the believer but no longer reigns because he is born of God and the image of His nature remains in him. Cox (341) explains, "One must never assume from v. 9 that a person truly born of God is infallible and can never sin again. John is explicit that a child of God is liable to sin and thus needs an Advocate."

The words "his seed" (Greek *sperma)* in the second phrase in v. 9 are difficult and somewhat controversial. Some of the most common interpretations are that it refers to: (1) Christ, (2) the Holy Spirit (Kruse 125), (3) the Word (Lenski 463), (4) God's nature (Akin 149; Barker 332; Bruce 92; Morris 1265; Westcott 107), (5) the life-principle, and (6) the gospel message. Each of these possible interpretations has certain strengths and weaknesses, but the solution that fits the context of the passage best is that the seed is God's seed. It is God's divine agency that brings new birth, and that divine agency continues to operate in the life of the believer after conversion.

This affirms to the believer that God's abiding work in him continues to overcome the work of the devil. The false teachers and their followers do not have the abiding work of the Spirit of God within them. Kruse (124-26) analyzes carefully the various possible interpretations. He concludes that the most likely interpretation is that the seed is God's seed, and that God's seed dwelling in believers is a reference to the Holy Spirit.

First John 3:10 serves as a transition between two descriptions of the child of God. While 1 Jn. 3:1-9 emphasizes that the child of God does righteousness and does not continue to live a life of sin and rebellion against God, 1 Jn. 3:11-24 introduces the love of the believer. The believer not only lives righteously, he also demonstrates a genuine love for his fellow believers. The two themes are not new to 1 John, but in this chapter they are brought together to distinguish the true sons of God from the false teachers and their followers.

Summary
(3:4-10)

In these verses John is writing as a concerned pastor to a group of his spiritual children who are facing serious challenges to their faith. He is not dealing with hypothetical situations; he is confronting reality. The fact is that there is a sharp difference between the lifestyle of sincere believers and the lifestyle of those who have fallen into the trap of Gnostic heretics. John's point in this passage is not to teach that true believers never sin; he knows better than that. In several passages in this Epistle, he confronts the problem of sin in the life of the believer (1 Jn. 1:5—2:6, for example). His point in this passage is that the genuine followers of Christ have a very different view of sin and righteousness than do the heretics. The child of the devil ignores God's demand for righteousness and continues to live a life of sin. He seeks to justify his sin in some way. The child of God, on the other hand, is convicted when he sins and responds with repentance and rededication. He does not deny the reality of his sin or minimize its importance, he confronts it.

Application: Teaching and Preaching the Passage

There are two important themes in this passage that should be stressed in preaching and teaching. One is that the believer enjoys a relationship of love with his heavenly Father. The world may not recognize that Christians are sons of God, but they are. Christians may not always feel like children of God, but they are whether they feel it or not. Salvation is not based on emotions and feelings but on faith in Christ.

There is little doubt that the false teachers of Asia Minor used various strategies to cause these Christians to doubt the legitimacy of their salvation and commitment to Christ. Satan still uses every device at his disposal to undermine the faith of believers, and some of these strategies are very sophisticated and appealing. One of the most effective is that he tries to convince Christians that they are not good enough or that they can never live up to God's expectations. Those who preach and teach God's Word have a responsibility to strengthen the faith of believers and help them resist the subtle temptations that Satan sends their way.

The other important theme in these verses is the reality of sin. The false teachers had a defective view of sin.

They taught one of two things: (1) that sin did not matter at all, or (2) that only the sins of the spirit would hinder one's relationship to God. Such teaching was attractive because it downplayed the sins of the flesh and allowed people to live as they pleased. This false teaching gave those who were seeking some way to avoid the moral claims of the gospel an easy way to excuse their sin. John argues that all sin is important, that all sin affects one's relationship with God, and that all sin must be confronted. The consequences of ignoring sin are tragic.

Care must be taken to preach and teach this passage correctly. John is not saying that Christians never sin or that if a believer sins he or she was never truly saved. His message is that sin is serious and must be confronted. There is a remedy for the problem of sin, and that remedy is Christ. The one who continues to live in sin is not of God, he is of the devil.

C. Love and Obedience (3:11-18)

**11 For this is the message that ye heard from the beginning, that we should love one another.
12 Not as Cain, *who* was of that wicked one, and slew his brother. And wherefore slew he him? Because his own works were evil, and his brother's righteous.
13 Marvel not, my brethren, if the world hate you.
14 We know that we have passed from death unto life, because we love the brethren. He that loveth not *his* brother abideth in death.
15 Whosoever hateth his brother is a murderer: and ye know that no murderer hath eternal life abiding in him.**

16 Hereby perceive we the love *of God*, because he laid down his life for us: and we ought to lay down *our* lives for the brethren.
17 But whoso hath this world's good, and seeth his brother have need, and shutteth up his bowels *of compassion* from him, how dwelleth the love of God in him?
18 My little children, let us not love in word, neither in tongue; but in deed and in truth.

These verses are closely connected with the previous section. In the previous verses John has described the Christian life in largely negative terms. He emphasized that believers do not live in sin. In this section, the author turns the discussion in a more positive direction. Believers must not only avoid sin, they must also show genuine love for one another. Both sections should be seen as a direct response to the false teachers of Asia Minor who minimized both the consequences of sin and the importance of Christian love.

In this passage John introduces two Biblical illustrations of the importance of genuine love in a Christian life. The first is the negative example of Cain, from Gen. 4:1-15. Interestingly, this is the only illustration from the O.T. found in this epistle (Burge 160). The obvious conclusion is that Cain's lack of love contributed to his murder of Abel. Jackman (98) writes, "Instead of loving his brother, Abel, Cain's attitude was dominated by a hatred which eventually drove him to kill his brother."

The second illustration is the positive example of Jesus Himself. His great love led Him to lay down His life for us. The love of Jesus should serve as the example for believers. The phrase "from the beginning" (v. 11) draws the reader's attention back to the opening words of chapter one. The command to love is one of God's first commandments, and it is still in force (Plummer *First Epistle,* 73; Westcott 51). John's emphasis, both here and in chapter one, is that the message he shares with the believers of Asia Minor is nothing new. It has been God's message to His children from the beginning time. It is also what these believers have been taught from the time of their conversion.

The love that exists between believers is a common theme in the writings of John. He first introduces the commandment to love one another in Jn. 13:34. In that passage Jesus is in the upper room following the Passover meal; He washes the apostles' feet and foretells His approaching betrayal. Then He tells His disciples, "A new commandment I give unto you, That ye love one another; as I have loved you, that you should also love one another." First John 3:11 is a continuation of the discussion of love found in 1 Jn. 2:7-11.

There can be no doubt of Cain's evil nature, for John identifies him as being of the "wicked one." The "wicked one" is clearly Satan (Kistemaker 306). The proof that Cain is a child not of God but of Satan is found in what he did; he murdered his brother, Abel. John asks the question, "Why did Cain kill him?" In seeing an answer, one could attempt to analyze the apparent personality conflict between the two, investigate the parenting techniques of Adam and Eve, or even hypothesize concerning the validity of the individual sacrifices. John's answer is clear and precise: it was because Cain's works were evil and Abel's righteous.

This illustration clearly teaches that the distinguishing mark of the believer is not hate but love for fellow believers. Love is here specifically directed by the believer to those in the fellowship of the family of God. Does the specificity in the passage limit love only to other believers? Most assuredly not; in the account of the Good Samaritan (Lk. 10:25-37) Jesus extended the definition of the neighbor to include all people. In this passage John emphasizes the love that believers have for each other because of the particular context within which he is writing. He is responding to the false teachers who downplay the importance of brotherly love.

Those who hate are murderers and are therefore bound by death and are unable to partake in eternal life. In the Sermon on the Mount (Mt. 5:21-22) Jesus speaks of the relationship between the motive of one's heart and the resulting action. If one is angry with his brother for no cause, he is under the penalty of judgment. Cain had no reason to be angry with his brother Abel; his evil motive found fulfillment in the act of murder and he was judged to be a murderer.

In v. 16 the illustration changes from the negative example of Cain to the positive example of Christ. Cain was imperfect, full of hate, and operating in the nature of his father the wicked one. Christ, the perfect one, is full of love and one with his Father in nature. The illustration of Christ defines the source for the kind of love intended in the previous verses. Here is how one can perceive (Greek *ginosko*, "to know") this kind of love, the love of God. He laid down His life for us (Rom. 5:8). With the same sacrificial attitude we are to love the brethren. Jesus is the truest and most perfect example of the kind of love in which we are to operate. This kind of love is the mark of the true believer (Barker 336).

It is interesting to note the similarities between this verse and Jn. 3:16. In both verses the subject is the love of God. In both the divine demonstration of love is the giving of His Son for humanity. First John assumes that the believer has eternal life (v. 15) and gives moral instruction to the believer as to how to practice love, while the gospel account tells one how to escape death and acquire eternal life.

In vv. 17, 18 we find love in action, a simple but important application of the sacrificial love that John has just advocated. Verse 17 states a very simple truth. If one has the ability to meet a brother's need, he should meet it. In this way, one demonstrates the abiding love of God in his life. The verse actually presents this truth in a negative fashion by saying that "if you see a brother in need and you have the ability to meet that need but do not do so, how is it that the love of God is abiding in you?" The answer can only be that love is not abiding in such a one.

John then gives specific instructions in v. 18. He again addresses the believers as his "little children" and then firmly commands them not to love in word only but to love in deed and truth. "Let us not love" (a Greek hortatory subjunctive) is a form of exhortation. The KJV renders the idea very well in these words, "let us not love in word, neither in tongue; but in deed and in truth." True love demands action. Lenski (474) explains, "Let us not pretend love with sham, empty evidence, but let us furnish genuine evidence." Smith (186) insightfully adds: "Martyrdom is heroic and exhilarating; the difficulty lies in doing the little things, facing day by day the petty sacrifices and self-denials which no one notices and no one applauds."

It is not John's intention to downplay the importance of words in the Christian faith. His goal is to emphasize that words must be accompanied by actions. Akin (160) writes, "John is not condemning kind or comforting words. The expression of such utterances without the outward manifestation of them, however, is mere noise and therefore worthless."

Summary (3:11-18)

First John 3:11-18 places the relationship between love and action in a Christian perspective. This passage should be viewed as John's response to the false teachings that were then being circulated in Asia Minor. It is clear that the false teachers did not stress the relationship between loving God and loving one's fellow believers. The Apostle reminds his spiritual children that the command to love one another is nothing new; it has been an important aspect of God's work from the very beginning. Those who truly love God will also love their fellow believers.

This passage deals with the loving relationship that exists between believers; it says nothing about how a believer should relate to those outside the fellowship. We should not, however, conclude from this passage that Christians may treat those outside the faith with disdain. That is simply not the author's intent.

Application: Teaching and Preaching the Passage

All believers would agree that this passage teaches the importance of sacrificial love. All Christians would also agree that they should love one another. The difficulty comes in putting these beautiful teachings into practice in our daily lives. Living a life of love is never easy; it requires wisdom, maturity, and commitment. Christian leaders have a responsibility to show true love in their own lives; they cannot expect others to demonstrate love if they do not. They also have a responsibility to preach and teach in such a way that helps the members of their congregations to demonstrate in their own lives the kind of love that God wants to see. Here are some ideas and suggestions that the Christian leader should keep in mind in preaching and teaching on this subject:

1. Both the leader and the people must understand the situation. What is an acceptable expression of love in one culture or in one situation may not be in another. Both pastor and people need to pray for God's help in understanding a given situation. They also need to find out all the information necessary to make a wise decision within a specific context. Ignorance often produces tragic consequences.

2. We must look for ways to express love that preserve the dignity, worth, and self-respect of all parties. Some people find it very difficult to accept help from others. The goal is always to be of benefit; it is not to embarrass or humiliate. In many situations privacy is very important.

3. Helping others should never be used as an excuse to meddle in their

affairs and make decisions for others that they alone have the right to make.

4. A true expression of love is done unselfishly. It is never designed to make the giver feel good or to obtain something in return.

5. Love should be shown in appropriate ways to fellow believers who fall into sin. The goal should always be restoration rather than condemnation. Christians should not, however, condone sinful conduct.

6. Sometimes love has to be tough. Decisions must often be made based on what is in the other person's long-term best interest. Simply gratifying the desires of the moment may not be a genuine expression of love.

D. Evidence of Walking in the Truth (3:19-24)

19 And hereby we know that we are of the truth, and shall assure our hearts before him.
20 For if our heart condemn us, God is greater than our heart, and knoweth all things.
21 Beloved, if our heart condemn us not, *then* have we confidence toward God.
22 And whatsoever we ask, we receive of him, because we keep his commandments, and do those things that are pleasing in his sight.
23 And this is his commandment, That we should believe on the name of his Son Jesus Christ, and love one another, as he gave us commandment.
24 And he that keepeth his commandments dwelleth in him, and he in him. And hereby we know

that he abideth in us, by the Spirit which he hath given us.

The opening phrase of v. 19, "And hereby we know that we are of the truth," is the controlling idea for the concluding section of chapter three. This passage should be understood as an important part of John's response to the activities of the false teachers in Asia Minor. One of their strategies was to create unnecessary doubts in the minds of the believers. If the secessionists could convince the Christians that their relationship with God was defective, they could seriously weaken the Christian testimony in Asia Minor and bring about much division and strife.

John is an experienced Christian leader; he understands that Christians struggle with doubts and fears. He makes no effort to explain the origin of those doubts; he simply recognizes that they exist (Barker 337). The term "heart" is often used in the Bible as the center of the conscience or of self-knowledge (Lieu 154). Lieu notes that the believers' self-knowledge may lead to "self-criticism and self-doubt, undermining the security of being God's children."

Verses 19-24 are difficult to translate and hard to interpret. Barker (337) writes concerning vv. 19, 20, "The passage itself is complex in the Greek and allows several translations and interpretations." See Akin (163, 164) and Lieu (154-156) for good summaries of the difficulties we face in translating these verses. Kruse (139) summarizes the two most common interpretations of the passage. In this passage John answers two questions. The first is, "How do we as believers know that we belong to the truth?" The second is, "How do we as believers deal with our condemning hearts?"

In answer to the first question, John offers to his children some tests that they may use to confirm that they do indeed belong to the truth. The first of these tests concerns answered prayer. In v. 22a John writes, "And whatsoever we ask, we receive of him." The fact that God has answered the believers' prayers is an evidence of the soundness of their relationship with Him. Jackman (105) writes that our assurance as believers is based on the fact that "God treats us as dearly loved children, day after day, by answering our prayers." Moody (76) points out that confidence in prayer was a cardinal teaching of Jesus that is also found in other places in the N.T. The fact that these believers were able to pray with such openness and confidence testifies to their membership in the family of God.

Another way that these believers may know that they belong to God is by their obedience to His commands. In v. 22b John writes, "because we keep his commandments, and do those things that are pleasing in his sight." Believers must remember what the Apostle Paul wrote in Rom. 8:1, "*There is* therefore now no condemnation to them which are in Christ Jesus, who walk not after the flesh, but after the Spirit." John's disciples in Asia Minor had, in fact, ceased to walk after the flesh and had begun to walk after the Spirit.

John does not mean to imply that his spiritual children have always obeyed God's commandments perfectly. The idea is that they have taken God's instructions seriously and have made them the guiding force in their lives. Bruce (100) correctly notes that their obedience to God's commands is not the cause of their relationship with God but a result of it.

In v. 23 John points out the specific commandment that he wishes to emphasize. It is a two-fold commandment that involves believing in Jesus Christ and loving one another. Jesus, when asked what is the greatest of the commandments (Mt. 22:35-40), responded in a similar way: love God and love your neighbor. Believing in or placing one's faith in Jesus Christ implies a personal trust and commitment to Him. This personal trust and commitment is the foundation stone upon which any relationship with God must be built.

This commandment also teaches that the believer is to show love to other believers. Bruce (100) develops both aspects of John's thought in these words, "Faith in Christ, then, is the first step of life in the family of God, and this life is a life of love as well as a life of faith." The love that exists between fellow believers is an important theme in this epistle. John says nothing which indicates that his disciples were failing in this important area. They were demonstrating genuine love for other members of the family of God.

The last part of v. 24 adds one final proof of the genuineness of the faith of the Christians in Asia Minor: the ministry of the Holy Spirit. The fact that the Holy Spirit continues to work within them is a powerful testimony to the vitality of their faith. It is interesting to note that John here introduces for the first time in his Epistle the Holy Spirit and the Spirit's role in affirming the indwelling of God. At this point John begins an investigation of the role of the Holy Spirit in the heart of the believer and of the importance of the witness of the Spirit in the life of the Christian community; this investigation will continue in future chapters. See the comments of Moody (78, 79) for a discussion of the role of the Holy Spirit both in this Epistle and in the Gospel of John.

John's second question deals with how Christians should deal with a condemning heart. This question is difficult, and John's answer to it is subject to more than one interpretation. Verse 20 is the most difficult to interpret; it reads, "For if our heart condemn us, God is greater than our heart, and knoweth all things." Most modern interpreters take this verse to mean that Christians should focus their attention on God's promises rather than on their doubts, fears, and failures. In other words, these believers should have more faith in what God has said and done than they have in their own personal doubts and fears. Marshall (198) explains this important truth in these words, "For God understands us better than our own hearts know us, and in his omniscience he knows that our often weak attempts to obey His command springs from a true allegiance to him."

Jackman (105) points out that our hearts condemn us, and many times this condemnation is just. This just condemnation does not mean, however, that we are outside the family of God. We are conscious of our failures, and God understands them even better than we do. The fact that we are conscious of our failures and sins testifies to our membership in the family. See the comments of Bruce 98, 99.

There is another, more rigorous interpretation, which was found in the early church and is still held in some circles today. Moody (75) summarizes this interpretation in these words, "The argu-ment is advanced that if the heart knows things against the believer, then the great God knows even more, and if the heart condemns one, then God condemns even more." See also the explanation of Kruse (139, 140). This interpretation was used in the early church to produce conviction of sin and encourage Christians to take their sins seriously. The N.T. clearly teaches that Christians should take their sins seriously, but this interpretation simply does not fit the context. John's purpose is to assure his spiritual children that they are part of God's family. This interpretation contributes nothing to the accomplishment of that purpose.

Verse 21 sounds a note of joy and hope. After the believer has examined his own heart, he is not condemned but is able to stand confidently in God's truth. This confidence, established in God's promise and power, allows the believer to ask and receive whatever he may need to serve in God's family. John identifies the source of the privilege: it is God Himself.

John concludes this section in v. 24 by repeating the truth that the believer who keeps these commands dwells in God and God in him. The verbs (Greek present tense), once again, suggest that the one who *continues* to observe Christ's teachings *continues* as a part of God's family.

Summary (3:19-24)

In these verses John continues his refutation of the false teachings that the Christians of Asia Minor have had to confront. There is no doubt that the false teachers had sown the seeds of discord among the believers; they had tried to create a spirit of doubt and discouragement. They had also endeavored to cause the Christians to doubt their conversion and their relationship with Christ.

John assures the Christians that their relationship with Christ is legitimate and that they should not be carried away by the false, but attractive, teachings they had received. John proposes some simple tests that his disciples can use to confirm their relationship with Christ. They need to trust in God's promises more than they trust in their feelings or emotions. Ultimately God is the one who determines who belongs to His family. These Christians should also look at their relationship with one another. The fact that these believers manifest a loving and caring relationship with each other is a testimony to the legitimacy of their faith. Lastly, the believers should examine their own lives in the light of what Jesus has taught them. They are sincere; they are making a good-faith effort to live according to God's commandments. This commitment is a testimony to the genuineness of their faith. The Holy Spirit is actively working among them. They should not allow themselves to be carried away by the claims of the false teachers.

Application: Teaching and Preaching the Passage

There is much in these verses that contemporary believers need to hear and heed. Our faith is often challenged from without and within. False teachers are always saying that our experience with Christ is not complete. They will say that in order to be a true follower of Christ, we need to do this, that, or the other. Such claims should always be viewed with suspicion. Emotions and feelings are generally a very inadequate and incorrect measurement of our relationship with God.

Our acceptance before God is built on a personal relationship with Jesus Christ. Before we accept any teachings that create doubts, we should ask ourselves some important questions such as these: Have we accepted Christ as our personal Savior? Are we committed to Him and to His teachings? Is the Holy Spirit at work in our lives? Do we love our fellow believers? The love we have for our fellow believers is an indication of the genuineness of our relationship with Christ. If we love Christ, then we will love those who belong to Him. This love does not include, however, the acceptance of false teachings. Error must be confronted.

Obedience to Christ's teachings is another indication of the genuineness of our faith. Are we committed to living as Christ taught us to live? We may not always have the strength to do as we ought to do, but we can make a sincere effort to live as He taught us to live. If we have placed our faith in Christ and in Him alone, we should not allow others to create doubts and fears where none should be. Creating doubt is one of the best weapons that Satan uses to defeat believers.

E. Try the Spirits (4:1-6)

1 Beloved, believe not every spirit, but try the spirits whether they are of God: because many false prophets are gone out into the world. 2 Hereby know ye the Spirit of God: Every spirit that confesseth that Jesus Christ is come in the flesh is of God:

70

3 And every spirit that confesseth not that Jesus Christ is come in the flesh is not of God: and this is that *spirit* **of antichrist, whereof ye have heard that it should come; and even now already is it in the world.**
4 Ye are of God, little children, and have overcome them: because greater is he that is in you, than he that is in the world.
5 They are of the world: therefore speak they of the world, and the world heareth them.
6 We are of God: he that knoweth God heareth us; he that is not of God heareth not us. Hereby know we the spirit of truth, and the spirit of error.

In the previous chapter John has noted the essential nature of love in the Christian life. He challenged his followers in Asia Minor to commit to a life of love as Christ taught. In this passage John points out that love is "not indiscriminate affirmation but discerning devotion" (Yarbrough 219). To love does not mean that believers are to accept everything they hear; they must exercise spiritual discernment in order to determine what is true and what is not.

This passage is similar to 1 Jn. 2:18-29, where the author insisted that believers understand the doctrine of Christ and have correct beliefs concerning the person and work of Christ. There John warned that many false teachings were circulating and that the Christians must not be led astray by them. A similar emphasis is found here: many spiritual forces are at work in the world, and not all of them are good. John's followers must carefully test the spirits to see

which are genuine. Evil spirits may try to imitate the Holy Spirit and lead the Christians into error.

The Scriptures often warn about false prophets, as in: Dt. 13:1-5; 18:20-22; Mt. 7:15-20; 24:11, 23-26; Mk. 13:22; 2 Pet. 2:1-3; Jude 4. Three themes are prevalent in such passages. First, false prophets will be known by their actions. If what they do is not proven true, then the prophets are not from God: "Ye shall know them by their fruits" (Mt. 7:16). Second, false prophets seek to lead disciples astray by imitating the works of God: "False prophets shall rise, and shall shew signs and wonders, to seduce, if *it were* possible, even the elect" (Mk. 13:22). Third, false prophets must be rejected and cast out from among the body of believers: "So shalt thou put the evil away from the midst of thee" (Dt. 13:5).

The aged Apostle, communicating his fatherly instruction in a tone of love, continues to use contrasts to give clear parameters to his argument. In this letter, John uses six different contrasting concepts to communicate his message: between (1) light and darkness, 1:5-7; (2) obedience and disobedience, 2:2-6; (3) love and hate, 2:7-11; 3:11-24; 4:7-21; (4) truth and falsehood, 2:18-28; (5) sons of God and sons of the devil, 2:29—3:10; and (6) the Spirit of God and the spirit of the world, 3:24b–4:6.

In this passage John contrasts the Spirit of God with the spirit of the world. He assumes that there are various spiritual forces at work in the world. As Westcott (139) writes, "There are many spiritual powers active among men, and our first impulse is to believe and to obey them." He warns his followers that they must resist this temptation. The teacher or leader who comes proclaiming a message that is clothed in spirituality and uses a familiar, orthodox vocabulary is not necessarily delivering a message from God. The believer is to "try" or "test" the spirits in order to determine whether they are genuine.

There is a connection between the terms "spirits" and "false prophets" in v. 1. The word translated "spirits" is used in several different ways in the N.T. Beyer (226) points out that in many cases it is used to describe demons. He argues that in this verse the evil spirits are manifesting themselves in the false prophets. According to Barker (340), the false prophets are presenting the teachings of the evil spirits.

John is aware that there are many "false prophets" in the world. Because of the existence of these false prophets, John gives his readers two commands. First, they are told not to believe every spirit. Second, they are commanded to *test* all spirits to see if they are from God or from the world. The verbs used are second person plural imperatives (Greek *dokimazete*) because all the members of the church are expected to participate (Akin 170). The struggle against error is too important to be left to a few. The testing should be an ongoing process (Greek present tense); it should become a part of the church's daily life.

The test is simple, yet definitive: every spirit that confesses that Jesus Christ is come in the flesh is of God, and those that do not affirm this confession are of the world. False teaching is not new. The first-century church was plagued by it as is the church of the twenty-first century. According to vv. 2, 3, the church is responsible to discriminate between the message delivered by the true Spirit of God and that delivered by the false spirit of the evil one. The test by which the church may know without reservation which message is from God is a Christological test. Akin (172) suggests that John's test is both comprehensive and confessional. Those who teach the truth will readily confess that Jesus Christ has come in the flesh.

This test is comprehensive in that every spirit and its message must submit to this test before it can be regarded as true by the Christian community. It is confessional in that the test itself is a confession of the incarnation; "Every spirit that confesseth that Jesus Christ is come in the flesh is of God." To confess (Greek *homologeo*) means "to say the same thing, to agree with, to assent" (Thayer 446).

It is important to note the wording of the confessional test. To be counted true one must "confess, agree to, and assent," that Jesus Christ is come in the flesh. The confession has a two-fold significance. First, it is a confession of the legitimacy and accuracy of the incarnation of Jesus as the Christ. It does not mean that Christ simply appeared in human form as many heretics taught (see Yarbrough 223). He really became a human being. Second, it is also much more than the recognition of the historical fact of Jesus' coming into the world. It is a faith commitment to Christ and to His work. Genuine faith involves more than intellectual assent to a body of truth.

In v. 3, John describes the false teaching of the separatists as "the spirit of antichrist." Akin (267-70) has done an extensive analysis of the various ways in which *antichrist* is used in these epistles. It is used to describe "an eschatological figure of evil." John's goal is not to identify this figure but to warn the Christians of Asia Minor concerning his teachings. The word itself is composed of two parts: *Christos* means "Christ, the Anointed One," and *anti* means "against" or "place of." The idea here is that the false teachers have abandoned the true teaching about the incarnation for a heretical view. Apparently, they were teaching that Christ had the appearance but not the reality of a human being.

As Akin (269, 270) notes, there have been attempts down through Christian history to identify the Antichrist with a specific person, but no identification has won widespread support. In these Epistles the idea seems to be that these false teachers are dominated by a spirit of opposition to Christ and His work. That kind of error is still common today. As Jackman (113) writes, "The spirit of antichrist is still abroad in the spirit of our age, with its mind set against allowing even for a moment that Christ's claims could be true."

In vv. 4-6 of this chapter the discussion turns in a somewhat different direction. Now that John has identified the opponents, he turns his attention to the sharp contrast that exists between them and the true followers of Christ. He begins with the statement, "You are of God, little children." "Little children" is the diminutive form of "child." It could be translated, "dear children." In this context it is clearly a term of endearment and affection. The phrase "you are of God" indicates the special relationship which exists between God and His spiritual children. They have chosen to follow God and adhere to the truths they have received. For this reason, they stand in a special relationship with God.

The phrase "and have overcome them" is theologically significant (Greek

perfect tense), referring to a past action with continuing results (Akin 174). The idea is that the Christians of Asia Minor, by their decision to adhere to the truth, have already won a great victory and the results of that victory have not been lost. John does not deny the reality of the situation; he recognizes that many spiritual battles lie ahead. What he wishes to do is to assure his followers that Christ is with them and in Him they have already won the victory. (See Kruse 148.)

The latter part of v. 4 gives the reason these Christians can go forward with confidence: because the One who is in them (God or Christ) is much more powerful than the one who is in the world (Satan). The secessionists have left the true family of God; they have returned to the world (Kruse 148). For this reason, they can no longer count on God's strength and provision. As Lieu (171) explains, these words do not mean that no more battles remain to be fought. The idea is that the outcome of the struggle is already determined; God and those who are with Him will ultimately gain the victory.

Verses 5, 6 outline additional elements of the contrast between the secessionists and John's disciples. They are "of the world" in the sense that they are dominated by the world. They speak "of the world," meaning that they reflect in their teachings a worldly and heretical view of Christ. It is only natural that "the world" (those outside the faith) will listen to their false teachings and accept them. Kistemaker (328) notes that the term "world" occurs three times in v. 5 and that it is used differently in this verse than elsewhere. Here it denotes "a world of people who are opposed to God."

73

In v. 6 John changes from the second person "you" to the first person "we." John is preparing to make an important statement and he wants to insure that he and all of his disciples are included. He does not wish to limit his statement to the specific group of believers now facing the challenge of heresy. The important statement is, "We are of God." John and his followers have heard, accepted, and maintained the truth. They have not been carried away by the false teachings. Barker (341) suggests that the "we" includes all of the faithful followers of Jesus but has special reference to teachers who teach the truth.

The next two clauses, "he that knoweth God heareth us" and "he that is not of God heareth not us," go together. The entrance of heresy had produced division and strife within the Christian community. It is likely that many of these believers had seen friends and relatives carried away with the false teaching. They had tried to win them back, but were not always successful. The only possible conclusion is that those who refuse to hear and heed the truth do not truly belong to God. If they were truly part of God's family, they would respond to the truth. (See Jackman 114-16.)

In v. 6, John gives another test which these believers can use to determine which individuals are controlled by the "spirit of truth" and which are controlled by the "spirit of error." The word "hereby" refers to the test that John has established in the previous verses. Those who confess that Jesus has come in the flesh are the true children of God. Those who know God are willing to heed the truth that they have been taught. Those who do not know God are not willing to hear the truth; they are willingly carried away by the false teachings of the secessionists.

Summary
(4:1-6)

These verses contribute much to the progress of thought in this epistle. Lieu (162) points out that for many interpreters 6:1-6 and 2:18-22 hold the keys to correctly interpreting 1 John. The most important single theme of these verses is the need for spiritual discernment. The entrance of false teachings into the Christian community of Asia Minor calls for vigilance, common sense, and spiritual maturity. If they are to protect the infant Christian churches from destruction, they must develop both the capacity to distinguish between truth and error and the necessary resolve to confront the error wherever it may appear.

John emphasizes the fact that these Christians have received sound teaching. They have heard and obeyed the teachings of the apostles, and now they need to continue in them and not be carried away by teachings that are attractive but heretical.

The presence of the Spirit of God among them is another important theme of these verses. These believers wanted to have the presence of the Holy Spirit in their lives, but they were faced with an important question. How does a group of believers determine if the Holy Spirit is among them? John responds by saying that correct doctrinal beliefs are an important part of the answer. If He is really among them, the Holy Spirit will lead them to a correct understanding of the life of Jesus Christ. They will understand and proclaim that Jesus really did come in the flesh.

These verses also point out the sharp distinction between those who are "of God" and those who are "of the world." Those who are "of God" are controlled by Him and seek to please Him in all things. Those who are "of the world" are governed by their fleshly desires and seek to gain the recognition of men.

Application: Teaching and Preaching the Passage

For the child of God spiritual discernment is not an option. There are many who claim to speak for God and who claim to offer a better way of life to the believer. All such claims must be carefully examined in light of the teachings of Scripture because false teaching can be packaged and presented in a very attractive manner. This would be a good text for sermons dealing with spiritual maturity and the need to distinguish between truth and error. In vv. 5, 6 John reminds his spiritual children that he has given them the truth, and that they need to continue in the truth they have received. When John writes "we are of God" in v. 6, he does not mean that he has a perfect understanding of all things. He means that what he has preached and taught is the truth; it is in accord with what God Himself has revealed. The Christians should not abandon what he has taught them.

We live in an age when much emphasis is given to emotions and feelings; comparatively little interest is devoted to sound doctrinal teaching. This passage warns against such an approach to the Christian life. Doctrine does matter. The false teachers were presenting a view of Christ that was contrary both to the teachings of Scripture and to the traditional teachings of the Christian faith.

Emotions are certainly important; we are emotional beings. But the Christian life must never be based on emotions and feelings. It must always be built on a sound understanding of the basic teachings of the Christian faith. These verses would serve well as a text for a sermon or lesson on the importance of sound doctrine in today's church.

These verses also provide a good basis for a lesson on the power of God. Verse 4 says, "Greater is he that is in you, than he that is in the world." As Christians we sometimes feel alone and isolated. Such feelings are normal; most believers experience spiritual loneliness at some point in their lives. We need to understand that we are never really alone. God is always with us and His power is always available to us. We must be careful to note that God always uses His power for our good. His goal is to bring us to an understanding of the truth.

There is one final theme in these verses that must always be preached and taught: the child of God enjoys a special relationship with God that others do not enjoy. Verse 4 says, "Ye are of God, little children." The false teachers were doing all they could to raise doubts in the minds of John's followers in Asia Minor. John encourages his spiritual children to resist all such efforts. They had truly experienced the grace of God, and they did not need to allow others to destroy their confidence in Him.

F. The Love of God (4:7-16)

1. Know God (4:7, 8)

7 Beloved, let us love one another: for love is of God; and every one

that loveth is born of God, and knoweth God.
8 He that loveth not knoweth not God; for God is love.

John now turns his attention from discerning between good spirits and evil spirits to the relationship between knowing God and loving one's neighbor. He has dealt with this theme previously (2:10, 11; 3:11, 14), and it will become one of the dominant themes in 4:7—5:4 (see Lieu 175). As Beyer (241) correctly notes, the aged Apostle is addressing the theme of Christian love for the third time in this Epistle (see 2:7-11; 3:11-18); he writes concerning this passage, "There is no other passage in the Bible as clear, simple, and profound dealing with divine love and brotherly love and the mutual relationship between them." John stresses that a right relationship with God produces important changes in character, and one of those changes is a genuine love for other believers. John is probably responding to the attacks of the secessionists who have downplayed the importance of love within the Christian community (see Kruse 17).

He begins by addressing his readers as *beloved* (see 2:7). When he uses this term, John is not imparting new information to them; he is preparing them to receive the instruction on Christian love that he is about to give them. He is also reminding them of the deep personal love that he has for them. When John exhorts his followers to love one another, he is simply asking them to do for one another what he has already done for them.

"Let us love one another" (Greek hortatory subjunctive) has the form of exhortation. The idea is not that they should begin loving one another, but that they should continue doing so. As an experienced Christian leader, John understood well how times of conflict and difficulty can cause Christians' love for one another to grow cold.

In the latter part of v. 7, John gives two reasons Christians should continue loving one another. First, because "love is of God." Love is more than a commandment of God; it has its source or origin in Him (Lieu 177). If they have truly experienced God in their lives, they have also experienced His love. Love is a part of God's character which He communicates to those He redeems.

Second, they should love because "everyone that loveth is born of God and knoweth God." This important phrase must be interpreted in light of its context. John is not saying that everyone who shows any degree of love is automatically born again. As he has previously emphasized in 1 Jn. 3:23, loving one another and believing in Jesus go together (see Marshall 211). The point here is that those who have truly come to know God will manifest the love of God in their everyday lives (see Kruse 157).

The same truth that was presented in a positive fashion in v. 7 is presented negatively in v. 8. The one who does not have the love of God in his life has never really come to know God (see Kruse 157). The last words of v. 8, "for God is love," call for special comment. These words are not a definition of God's character or being. They are, rather, a description of how God acts in the world. Dodd (110) notes, "But to say 'God is love' implies that *all* of his activity is loving activity."

The concept of love is one of several analogies used in the Bible to help us understand better who God is and how He reveals Himself to the world. First John 1:5 speaks of God as light; Jn. 4:24 speaks of God as spirit (see Marshall 212, 213). No human words can adequately define God; love and the other human analogies help us to understand more about Him and how He relates to us.

2. The manifestation of the love of God (4:9, 10)

9 In this was manifested the love of God toward us, because that God sent his only begotten Son into the world, that we might live through him.
10 Herein is love, not that we loved God, but that he loved us, and sent his Son *to be* the propitiation for our sins.

First John 4:9 repeats the great truth found in Jn. 3:16, "For God so loved the world, that he gave his only begotten Son, that whosoever believeth in him should not perish, but have everlasting life." God has not left humanity to die in spiritual darkness; He has taken the initiative and demonstrated His love for us by sending His Son (Dodd 110).

The words "in this" sometimes point back to something that John has previously written; sometimes they point forward to what he is about to say. Here they point forward. The idea is that sending His Son to earth so that we might live through Him is the way that God has chosen to manifest His love for us. God's love is active. He has demonstrated His love for mankind in many different ways; the deliverance from slavery in Egypt is the great example of God's love in the O.T. In the N.T., the supreme example of God's love is in the life and ministry of Jesus Christ.

The word translated "sent" (Greek *apostello*) is not the one normally used (Greek *pempo*) to describe the act of sending. This word expresses the idea of sending someone on a special mission or with a special commission (Kistemaker 333). The idea is that God sent His Son to earth to accomplish a specific mission, and that mission is the salvation of mankind. Here the verb describes a past action with a result that continues (Greek perfect tense). The coming of Christ to earth was a one-time event with results that will continue to be felt until the end of time.

Jesus is described as God's "only begotten Son." The words "only begotten" translate one word (Greek *monogenes*) which occurs nine times in the N.T. in several different contexts. Kruse (158, 159) analyzes how this word is used and translated in different versions of the Bible. It generally expresses the idea of "one and only." In Lk. 7:12 the word is used to describe a widow's only son. In this passage the idea is that God loved us so much that He was willing to send His one and only Son to purchase our redemption. God has other "sons," but not in the sense that Jesus is His Son. Giving Him is the greatest possible demonstration of God's love for fallen humanity. Yarbrough (238) correctly points out that this term emphasizes "both the exclusivity and the uniqueness of the Father's revelation in the Son."

The last phrase of v. 9, "that we might live through him," states clearly and unequivocally the reason Jesus came to earth, suffered, and died: to bring eternal life to fallen humanity. As Westcott (149) correctly notes, the natural state of mankind is death. The coming of Christ made it possible for mankind to experience spiritual life, a life lived in relationship to God as never before possible. Human beings could never have earned or merited eternal life; it came as God's free gift to His creation. There is nothing in this verse that implies that God will force eternal life on anyone. The idea is that by sending His Son to earth He has made it available to all who are willing to receive it.

In v. 10 John defines in greater detail the kind of love that God has demonstrated for His children. He is not talking about the kind of love that human beings can and should have for God. He is talking about that special kind of love that God demonstrated when He took the initiative to send His Son, Jesus Christ, to earth. The word for "love" used in this and other passages in the N.T. (Greek *agape*) is not widely found in secular Greek literature. Plato, Aristotle, and other writers normally used another word (Greek *eros*) which expresses the idea of sexual desire (Dodd 111). The precise meaning of this "agape love" must be determined from its use in the N.T. Here and elsewhere it describes the kind of unselfish love that led God to send His only Son into the world to give His life in payment for the sins of fallen mankind.

The last words of v. 10 repeat an important idea that was first introduced in 2:2. Christ did not come simply to manifest God's love in a general sense; He came with a specific mission. That mission was to offer Himself as the atoning sacrifice for our sins. As was pointed out in comments on 2:2, the word *propitiation* (Greek *hilsamos*) is also sometimes translated as "expiation" or "atoning sacrifice."

This term is generally used to express the idea of placating or pacifying an offended person or an offended deity (Dodd 24). It is also used, but less commonly, to express the idea of performing an act that removes or expiates a moral or ritual defilement (Dodd 25). In this passage something of both ideas is probably involved. Man's sinful conduct has certainly offended God, and God has accepted the sacrifice of Christ as satisfying His righteous demand for justice. The sacrifice of Christ has also defeated the power of sin that has held people captive since the fall of Adam and Eve in the garden. (For more detailed discussions of the word see the comments of Barker 314; Kruse 73-76; Westcott 44; and Yarbrough 77-81.)

3. Dwell in love (4:11-16)

11 Beloved, if God so loved us, we ought also to love one another.
12 No man hath seen God at any time. If we love one another, God dwelleth in us, and his love is perfected in us.
13 Hereby know we that we dwell in him, and he in us, because he hath given us of his Spirit.

In these verses John outlines some of the results that the transforming love of God will produce in the lives of His followers. The first and most obvious result is that they should demonstrate the love that they have received in their relationships with others, especially in their relationships with fellow believers. Because they are finite human beings, they cannot demonstrate "agape love" as perfectly as God does, but they can demonstrate their love for God by their care and concern for their fellow believers.

The phrase "no man hath seen God at any time" refers to God the Father. Obviously, people who were living at that time could and did see the Lord Jesus during the time of His incarnation. John's emphasis is that God is Spirit and therefore cannot be seen with physical eyes. Since human beings cannot see God, neither can they see the love that Christians have for their God. They can, however, see the love that believers have for one another. Beyer (253) suggests that the idea of the passage is that through love we can have communion with God. Although we cannot see God with our physical eyes, when Christians love one another the world can see the nature of God revealed. As Jackman (123) explains, "Christ's physical presence is no longer with us in this world, but if people want to see Jesus, they should be able to meet him in the churches. They should encounter his love in the love that we Christians have for one another."

Beyer (253) argues that this statement also contributes to the anti-Gnostic message of this Epistle. The Gnostics taught that one could rise to such a level of mystical experience with God that he could obtain a "vision" of God and eventually be in "union" with Him. The statement "no man hath seen God at any time" serves to refute all such false teachings. Barker (343) comes to similar conclusions.

When Christians love one another with the true "agape love" described in this passage, two important things happen. First, this love demonstrates that God is, in fact, dwelling within this group of believers. Only God can create this special kind of love between human beings. Second, this love demonstrates that His love "is perfected in us." The word "perfect" in the N.T. often implies completeness or maturity. As Beyer (254) points out, "Mutual love is the sign that the love of God has accomplished its goal within us." John's point is that the love that these believers have for one another is proof of the genuineness of their relationship with God. They lack nothing that the false teachers can supply.

Verse 13 gives another proof of the genuineness of the faith of the Christians of Asia Minor. John points out that God has given "of his Spirit" to these believers, which means that they have the Holy Spirit dwelling within them. This verse should be interpreted in light of what John has written in the previous verses. The love that they have for one another is the proof that the Holy Spirit dwells within them. If they have the Spirit of God dwelling within them, they are true believers.

John's goal, here, is to give his spiritual children the assurance that they need in order to continue the struggle with the false teachers who were seeking to undermine their faith. Marshall (219) gives the following insightful explanation of John's argument:

> It is important to recognize that the grounds of Christian assurance and the tests of the reality of the Christian experience are multiple: one cannot say that simply because a person professes true belief, or loves his fellow men, or claims to have had charismatic experiences, he is a true Christian: it is the combination of these features in a harmonious unity that makes up true Christianity.

John's followers have had a genuine experience of the grace of God, and they should not allow anyone to convince them otherwise.

14 And we have seen and do testify that the Father sent the Son *to be* **the Saviour of the world.**
15 Whosoever shall confess that Jesus is the Son of God, God dwelleth in him, and he in God.
16 And we have known and believed the love that God hath to us. God is love; and he that dwelleth in love dwelleth in God, and God in him.

These verses form something of a summary of John's argument to this point. He has consistently taught that God sent His Son, Jesus Christ, to bring salvation to the world. This testimony is not something that John and his followers have created; it is based on what God has done as verified by the eyewitness testimony of the apostles.

Those who confess that Jesus Christ is the Son of God enjoy a special relationship with God that those outside the faith do not enjoy. That special relationship brings two important results. First, it means that God through His Spirit remains in the one who confesses Christ. Second, it means that the one who confesses Christ remains in the family of God. He does not have to seek additional signs or special revelations to continue as a part of the family of God. A personal relationship with Christ is all he needs.

The verbs "have known" and "have believed" in the first part of v. 16 are in the tense (Greek perfect) which implies a past action with results that continue. The idea is that John's spiritual children have come to know and come to believe

the love that God has demonstrated for them in the life and ministry of Christ. That experience has remained with them and continues to motivate them to follow the Lord. Westcott (155) notes that "The love of God becomes a power in the Christian Body. Believers are the sphere in which it operates and makes itself felt in the world."

On the words "God is love" (v. 16), see the comments above on v. 8; the statement does not define God's essence but describe the loving way in which God does many good things for his children (Kruse 157).

The verbs in this passage (Greek present tense) imply action that continues. The one who lives according to the kind of love that God has demonstrated remains in God, and God remains in him. A proper relationship with God does not demand some special revelation or unique experience; it is based on the demonstration of God's love in one's daily life.

Summary
(4:7-16)

This is one of the most important sections in 1 John. It draws together several important themes that are developed in the Epistle. As Dodd (115) notes, the major theme of these verses is assurance. The believer is not left to wander in doubt about his or her relationship to God. Two grounds of assurance are developed. The first is the gift of the Holy Spirit. Verse 13 reminds us that we know that we dwell in Him and He in us "because he hath given us of his spirit." John does not describe specifically how the Holy Spirit works in the lives of believers, but he emphasizes the Spirit's indwelling presence. The implication is that the believers of Asia Minor have the Holy Spirit living within them. The Spirit's presence assures them of their relationship with God and enables them to stand firm against the false teachers.

The second ground of assurance is the external testimony of Jesus Christ (Dodd 115). As v. 14 states, "And we have seen and do testify that the Father sent the Son to be the Saviour of the world." Salvation is based on the work of Christ; no special revelations are necessary. The false teachers are wrong when they insist that simple faith in Christ is not sufficient for salvation.

These verses give one of the most comprehensive treatments of Christian love to be found in the N.T. The theme of love is first approached from the standpoint of the love that God has shown for His children by sending His Son, Jesus Christ, to provide atonement for our sins. According to John, any definition of love must begin with a correct understanding of who God is and what He has done for us. God did not just tell us to love; He set the example for love when He sent His Son into the world.

After discussing the love that God has for His children, the passage moves to an analysis of believers' love for each other. Kruse (161) correctly notes, "In this context, the author is not interested in love for its own sake, but because it is the sign that God lives within us." The assumption is that John's disciples have received the love of God and are manifesting that love in their everyday lives. The fact that they love as God has taught them to love is a powerful evidence of the genuineness of their faith. It is important to note that John does not demand any particular manifestation

of Christian love. He understands that true Christian love can be demonstrated in a variety of different ways. The important thing is that it is demonstrated in the daily lives of believers.

There is a relationship between faith and actions in these verses. Verses 14, 15 point out that the love of these believers does not stand alone; it is accompanied by deeds. By their love they testify to the fact that God sent His Son into the world "to be the propitiation for our sins." They are not silent; they are confessing publicly that "Jesus is the Son of God." The fact that they bear faithful testimony to the person and work of Christ is another evidence of the genuineness of their relationship with God.

Application: Teaching and Preaching the Passage

This passage begins with an exhortation to love, and its hortatory nature is never lost. Christian love does not come quickly, easily, or automatically. It must be developed and put into practice every day. Love may be demonstrated in many ways, but it is always an essential element in the Christian life. The one who loves "is born of God and knoweth God." The implication is that one who does not love has not yet come to know God. These verses would provide an excellent basis for a series of lessons on the importance of love in the Christian experience.

In this important passage, love is more than a shallow emotion or a sweet sentiment. It has real content. Christian love is first defined, not in terms of what believers do, but in terms of what God has already done. Verse 9 explains, "In this was manifested the love of God toward us, because that God sent his only begotten Son into the world, that we might live through him." God has actively demonstrated His love for His children in meaningful ways. The children of God must do likewise. They must demonstrate both their love for God and their love for one another. The implication of the passage is that John's disciples in Asia Minor have experienced the love of God and are demonstrating the love they have received. Their love is a powerful testimony to the genuineness of their faith and a strong refutation of the arguments of the false teachers.

Many Christians have little understanding of what Christian love is. They view it from a primarily emotional perspective; they do not understand that it is an exercise of the will. Love is something that the believer makes a deliberate decision to do. This passage can be of great value in helping people to understand what Christian love is and how to apply it.

G. Perfect Love Brings Assurance (4:17-21)

17 Herein is our love made perfect, that we may have boldness in the day of judgment: because as he is, so are we in this world.
18 There is no fear in love; but perfect love casteth out fear: because fear hath torment. He that feareth is not made perfect in love.
19 We love him, because he first loved us.
20 If a man say, I love God, and hateth his brother, he is a liar: for he that loveth not his brother whom he hath seen, how can he love God whom he hath not seen?

21 And this commandment have we from him, That he who loveth God love his brother also.

Christian love has been one of the major themes that John has developed. Here he notes that it produces important results in the lives of believers both individually and collectively. Verses 17, 18 mention two of them. First, love gives us "boldness in the day of judgment." The word "boldness" (Greek *parresia*) is also found in 2:28; 3:21; and 5:14, where it is translated "confidence." It does not mean "arrogance" or "self-confidence." The idea is that the believer, because of his loving relationship with God, does not have to approach the Day of Judgment with an attitude of fear. The "day of judgment" is understood by most commentators to refer to the end time when God will judge the world through His Son. (See the comments of Yarbrough 260, 261.) The Christian can serve God without being paralyzed by an unhealthy fear of the future. His sins have been forgiven; he is in a right relationship with God.

The second result is closely related to the first. It is that "perfect love casteth out fear." One of Satan's best devices is to destroy the Christian's effectiveness through fear. Fear can render the strongest army totally ineffective. Love makes it possible for the believer to defeat the fear that seeks to destroy him.

The phrase "made perfect" does not imply perfection in an absolute sense. It means "to bring to completion," or "to bring to maturity." Beyer (263) correctly notes that the phrase means "that the love of God in and for us has accomplished its goal and is fulfilling its purpose in our lives." The word "herein" is a transition word. In this context, it probably refers not to what has gone before but to what is coming after. The idea is that when Christian love has come to maturity the believer loses his fear of God's judgment.

Verse 18 stresses that the love which exists between God and His spiritual children defeats the power of fear. First and foremost, it defeats the fear of God's judgment, as the previous verse has made clear. The last phrase, "because fear hath torment," can be translated "fear brings its own punishment" (Barker 346). Fear robs the believer of the joy and hope that he needs to serve the Lord effectively. John may well be responding to the false teachers who tried to create a climate of doubt and uncertainty within the churches of Asia Minor.

The words "he that feareth" at the end of the verse (Greek present tense) indicate continuing or ongoing action. The idea is that a believer whose life is controlled by love will not be dominated by his fear of God's judgment. His fears will not destroy his usefulness in the Kingdom of God.

Barker (346) notes that "the fear spoken of here is not to be confused with reverence for God." Believers should always have reverence and respect for God because He is King of kings and Lord of lords. This passage speaks of an unhealthy fear of God which grows out of a lack of understanding of God's love, care, and concern for His children.

Verse 19 probably reflects a common saying used in early Christian preaching and teaching. There is little doubt that this was a phrase that John himself had used many times as he taught these churches in Asia Minor. The early manuscripts of this passage do not all read exactly the same. Some say simply "We

love." Others say "We love God." Some say "We love him." A few say "We love one another." (See Kruse 169 for a helpful discussion.) The main idea is clear: that Christian love does not have its origin in the human heart but in the heart of God. We love because God has taught us how to love and has given us the power to love. Christian love does not depend on the believer's power to generate it within his own heart and soul. It is something that God works to produce in the life of the believer. (See Kistemaker 342.)

Verse 20 is a direct refutation of the Gnostic teachers who claimed to love God while they demonstrated contempt for the people of God (Kistemaker 342). A genuine love for God will always produce earthly consequences. Those who truly love God will also love those whom God has called to be members of His family. John states very frankly that one who says that he loves God while hating his brother is a liar.

The second half of v. 20 reinforces the idea of love presented in the first half by asking a very important rhetorical question. If a believer cannot love his Christian brother with whom he serves in the local church every day, how can he be expected to love God who cannot be seen with physical eyes? The answer is, emphatically, that he cannot. In order to love God as he should, a Christian must learn to love his fellow believer. John does not intend to say that the believer must first love his brother before he can learn to love God. The idea is that love for God and love for fellow believers cannot be separated. The sincere follower of Christ will love both.

Lieu (198) points out that this verse states explicitly, for the first time in the Epistle, that believers need to love God.

It has been implied in other verses (2:5, 15; 3:17), but this is the first specific instruction that the believer is to love God. As she correctly notes, the contrast here is not between love and some other human emotion. The contrast is between loving God and loving the world or loving some other deity. To love God means to serve Him and to obey His commandments.

Verse 21 is a summary of the truth that John has presented in the previous verses. The instruction to love both God and one's fellow believer is not a new commandment coming from John or from any other apostle. It is an old commandment that has come directly from God Himself; it is one of the basic teachings of the Christian faith. The "we" is inclusive; the commandment to love is designed for all believers and not just for the most dedicated. For the Apostle John, one of the axioms of the Christian faith is that the one who loves God will love his brother also. Love both for God and for one's fellow believer serves to distinguish between the true believers and those who had separated themselves from the faith.

Summary
(4:17-21)

As shown here and elsewhere in this letter, the false teachers were raising doubts about the genuineness of the faith of John's disciples in Asia Minor. The most likely explanation is that John's opponents were questioning the Christian experience of these believers. It is doubtful that they were attacking John's teaching openly. Probably they were saying that John's teaching was elementary and that his followers needed new revelations which only the false

teachers could provide. John had no choice but to respond.

John responds by saying that the Christian love that existed within the Christian community of Asia Minor was a strong evidence of the genuineness of their faith. John certainly does not assert that his followers are perfect and lack nothing; he asserts that they do not need what the false teachers are offering. The love that they have for God and for one another is an evidence of the genuineness of their faith.

John's followers were serious about their Christian faith. They wanted to live righteously and serve God faithfully. They were not interested in some type of Christian life that would leave them but little different from the pagan world around them. The important issue was how to attain this Christian maturity. John offered one answer; his opponents offered another. For the aged Apostle, genuine Christian love was the way to attain maturity. Only love could bring them into a right relationship with God and with their fellow believers; only love could free them from an unhealthy fear of future judgment.

John correctly recognized that Christian love does not come automatically; it is a deliberate decision. Christians must learn to love God and their fellow believers both in good times and in bad. Genuine Christian love is more than a shallow emotion that is here today and gone tomorrow.

Application: Teaching and Preaching the Passage

This passage was written to a group of Christians who were relatively mature in their faith and who were seeking to serve God faithfully and understand His teachings correctly. It was not written to shallow believers who were looking for a way to justify their unholy conduct. In these verses there is an important contrast, but not between love and obedience. It is between the true Christian faith, which is built on love, and the cheap imitation which the world offers. True Christian love leads us to obey the teachings of God, not to violate them.

These verses provide a good text for a sermon or lesson on the believer's relationship with God. That relationship is one of trust. The Christian should always have a healthy respect for God and His teachings, but this respect should never degenerate into an unhealthy fear. God is for us; He is not against us. We are His children, not His enemies. God has manifested His love toward us in many ways, and His love makes it possible for us to love others.

In these verses there is a clear relationship between the believer's love for God and his love for other believers. The two cannot be separated. Love for God will produce a love for the children of God. We should recognize that love is more than a shallow emotion or a sweet sentiment. It involves depth and commitment. Our love for God must lead us to seek Him in all areas of our lives and to follow His teachings diligently. Our love for other Christians must lead us to seek their best interest even when that may be painful or difficult. The most important goal of our love is always to glorify God and advance His kingdom.

H. Obedience and Love (5:1-5)

The first five verses of chapter five are closely connected with the final verses of chapter four. John continues to develop the theme of the importance of Christian love, emphasizing the content of Christian love and some of the results that Christian love produces in one's life. His main goal is to show that love is not just an emotional response; it is a decision with real theological content, one that makes a difference in how one lives and thinks.

**1 Whosoever believeth that Jesus is the Christ is born of God: and every one that loveth him that begat loveth him also that is begotten of him.
2 By this we know that we love the children of God, when we love God, and keep his commandments.
3 For this is the love of God, that we keep his commandments: and his commandments are not grievous.
4 For whatsoever is born of God overcometh the world: and this is the victory that overcometh the world, even our faith.
5 Who is he that overcometh the world, but he that believeth that Jesus is the Son of God?**

Verse 1 establishes the solid connection between Christian faith and love. The first clause establishes the basic Christian truth that a relationship with God is based on personal faith in Jesus Christ. Jesus Christ is the Son of God, and the one absolute requirement to be a child of God is personal faith in Him. The second half of the verse ties together the theme of faith in Christ with the love that believers demonstrate. Christian faith produces results, and one of those results is genuine love.

The phrase "him that begat" refers to God the Father. One of John's basic assumptions is that a Christian will love God in the same way that a child loves his father (Kruse 171). That is the normal response of one who has been redeemed by the grace of God. That is what John expected to see and had observed in the lives of his spiritual children.

In this context, the words "him…that is begotten of him" refer to a regenerate person, one's fellow believer (Kruse 171). In 1 Jn. 4:21, the author had written that one who loves God must love his brother also. The love that believers have for one another is the natural outgrowth of their relationship with the Father. Kistemaker (348) writes, "In essence faith and love are inseparable. In God's family, faith in God and love for him and his children are totally integrated." This exhortation is probably a response to the Gnostic teachers who tried to separate between love for God and love for one's neighbor. The Christian faith knows no such artificial distinction.

The point of v. 2 is that love for God and love for fellow believers go together. Dodd (125) explains, "No doubt the author holds that love to God and love to man are so inseparable that the presence of either is evidence of the other." It is interesting that the phrase "when we love God " is followed by the qualifying phrase "and keep his commandments." John's point is clear: the believer's love for God is a demanding one. It demands a commitment to live according to the instructions that God has given. Dodd (126) notes, "Love which does not include obedience is not worthy of the name."

Verse 3 should not be understood as a definition of love but as an explanation of the result that love produces in a Christian life. Love and obedience go together. A child who truly loves his father will obey his instructions. A believer who truly loves his Heavenly Father will live according to the Father's teachings. This verse repeats the teaching given by Jesus Himself in Jn. 14:15 and 15:10. Christians may fail to live up to this standard at times; they will not always obey perfectly. There must, however, be a serious personal commitment to live by the teachings of Jesus.

The last part of v. 3 explains that the commandments of Jesus are not *grievous*. This word (Greek *barus)* appears six times in the N.T. with several different meanings. It sometimes means "important." In this verse, the idea is that the commandments are not impossible to keep (Marshall 228). A similar idea (but not the same word) appears in the words of Jesus: "For my yoke is easy, and my burden is light" (Mt. 11:30). The same term is found in Mt. 23:4 where it is used to describe the heavy burdens that the scribes and Pharisees laid upon their followers.

John is not saying that obeying Christ's commands will always be easy; the idea is that keeping them is not so demanding as to be impossible. Obedience is possible because the believer is not left to do so in his own strength. The Holy Spirit is always present to guide, direct, and empower. Akin (191) explains, "God's moral standards are high, but God gives the Christian grace to be able to live up to that standard." (See also Stott 173, 174.)

The last words of v. 3 are closely connected with vv. 4, 5. The Christian overcomes the world by obeying the commands of Christ. *World* is used in several different ways in the writings of John, referring here to "worldly attitudes or values that are opposed to God" (Kruse 172).

The word *overcometh* (Greek *nikao*) is the key word in vv. 4, 5; it means to conquer, overcome, or gain the victory (Beyer 284). In v. 5 (Greek present tense participle), the idea is a victory that continues and not an isolated event; those who follow Christ are not dominated or controlled by the world, they are controlled by Christ. As Kruse (174) correctly notes, "To overcome the world, the readers must persist in their faith in him despite the propaganda of the secessionists."

In v. 4 John uses the neuter gender ("whatsoever") rather than the masculine ("whosoever"). This type of construction is sometimes used not to describe a specific individual but to present a general truth (see Akin 192; Marshall 228; Stott 174; and Yarbrough 275). That seems to be the idea here. John's emphasis is that all of those who have been born of God are overcoming and can overcome the world. Brooke (130) asserts that the neuter is used to emphasize that it is not the person who is victorious but the divine power within him. He explains, "Everyone who is born of God has within himself a power strong enough to overcome the resistance of all the powers of the world, which hinder him from loving God."

The phrase "born of God" is the key to understanding this passage. The promise of overcoming the world is not made to everyone, nor to those who make a merely verbal profession of faith. It is made to those who have been truly transformed by the power of God. The idea is that believers are spiritually reborn; they have a new quality of spiritual life bestowed upon them by God. They alone have the capacity to defeat the forces of this world. Stott (174) writes, "The new birth is a supernatural event that takes us out of the sphere of the world, where Satan rules, into the family of God." (See Barker 349; Kruse 172; Yarbrough 275.)

The last part of v. 4 explains clearly and succinctly that the believer does not overcome the world through his or her own strength. It is "our faith" that makes this victory possible. There is a connection between the words "our faith" in the latter part of v. 4 and the words "whosoever is born of God" in the first part. Both terms describe the source of the believer's victory over the world. The new birth is given by God; it is not earned by man. It is not, however, given by God indiscriminately. It is given only to those who have saving faith in the Lord Jesus Christ. Saving faith implies more than a recognition that Christ exists; it demands a personal trust in Him for one's salvation. Kruse (173) notes that this is the only place in the Epistles of John when the term "faith" is used as a noun. For a good exposition of the word "faith" in this context, see Clemance (144, 145) and Kruse (173, 174). For a discussion of the term "faith" in the larger context of the Johannine literature see Michel (602, 603).

Verse 5 is a rhetorical question that continues the argument that John has been making in the preceding verses. The only one who can gain victory over the world is the one who has personal faith in Jesus Christ. The phrases "he that overcometh" and "he that believeth" both imply continuous or ongoing action (Greek present tense participles). The point is that the one who continues to believe in Jesus will continue to gain the victory. Kistemaker (352) notes that it is not undefined faith that overcomes the world, but faith in Jesus Christ. It is a faith built upon the confession of Jesus Christ as the Son of God, a faith that reflects solid doctrinal content.

Summary
(5:1-5)

These verses contribute to a correct understanding of the true nature of the Christian faith. They remind us that our treatment of other human beings is important, even though this is but one component of the Christian faith. To assert that we are right with God simply because we treat other people as we should is an oversimplification (see Yarbrough 273). As v. 5 explains, true Christian faith involves the confession that Jesus Christ is the Son of God. Authentic Christian faith produces both right actions and right beliefs. Our love for God and our love for our fellow believers go together as parts of one whole.

There is also a relationship between love and action. Those who truly love God take His commandments seriously. They see that God's commandments are not just a heavy burden that must be carried. They understand that obeying God's teachings is the way to obtain victory in the Christian life. Being a child of God means overcoming the world, not being overcome by the world.

This passage reminds us that love, obedience, and faith go together; all three are necessary in the development of a mature Christian life. Love leads to obedience of God's teachings, not to a sinful lifestyle. Personal faith in Jesus Christ is also central. Verse 5 says, "Who is he that overcometh the world, but he that believeth that Jesus is the

Son of God?" The only way to overcome the forces of evil is through faith in Christ.

Application: Teaching and Preaching the Passage

This passage is about goals, about issues that are of primary importance and have eternal consequences. They must be an important part of any program of Christian preaching and teaching. They should be dealt with in a comprehensive way in every local church.

The first of these fundamental issues is overcoming the world. Too many Christians today view compromise with the world as a necessity; they see no other way to get ahead or even to survive. This passage clearly points out the fallacy of such thinking. The basic fact is stated in v. 4, "For whatsoever is born of God overcometh the world." For the committed follower of Jesus Christ there is simply no other option. Preachers and teachers need to help their congregations understand both what it means to overcome the world and how they can accomplish that goal.

These verses explain the correct relationship between love and obedience. Too many Christians feel that they must choose one or the other. They can either love their fellow human beings or they can obey God's instructions. This is a false dichotomy; the Christian has to make no such choice. True love does not mean unconditional acceptance; sometimes love has to be tough. Obeying God's teachings will lead us to love others, but it will lead us to love them in the right way.

The believer must establish proper priorities in life. This passage can serve very effectively as a text for a lesson dealing with establishing the right priorities for a successful Christian life. In particular, this passage can help to establish the proper relationship between faith and love. They go together, and both contribute to a well-rounded Christian life.

I. Jesus, the Bearer of Eternal Life (5:6-12)

6 This is he that came by water and blood, even Jesus Christ; not by water only but by water and blood. And it is the Spirit that beareth witness because the Spirit is truth.
7 For there are three that bear record in heaven, the Father, the Word, and the Holy Ghost: and these three are one.
8 And there are three that bear witness in earth, the spirit, and the water, and the blood: and these three agree in one.
9 If we receive the witness of men, the witness of God is greater: for this is the witness of God which he hath testified of his Son.
10 He that believeth on the Son of God hath the witness in himself: he that believeth not God hath made him a liar; because he believeth not the record that God gave of his Son.
11 And this is the record, that God hath given to us eternal life, and this life is in his Son.
12 He that hath the Son hath life; and he that hath not the Son of God hath not life.

These verses accomplish two main purposes. First, they explain more fully the doctrine of Christ that John has been developing. It is important that his spiritual children in Asia Minor have a correct understanding of the Christ in whom they have placed their faith. Second, they distinguish between the teachings of the secessionists and the true gospel message that John and his followers have presented. The false teachers and their secessionist followers have corrupted the faith by presenting a false view of the person and work of Christ.

While we cannot reconstruct these false teachings with absolute certainty, we have a very good idea of what was being taught. (See the Introduction.) The false teachers denied that Jesus Christ, God's Son, had come in the flesh (Kruse 174). It is likely that they had adopted the view of the Gnostics who taught that Christ had the appearance but not the reality of a human being (see Barker 350; Dodd 130; Westcott 183). Dodd (130) explains that some Gnostic teachers taught that Jesus was born as a mere man. The divine Christ entered into the man Jesus at his baptism and then left him at his crucifixion because they believed that the divine could not suffer. It is quite likely that John is refuting this teaching or something similar to it. See the analysis of Beyer 289, 290.

Verses 6-8 are the most difficult verses to interpret in this Epistle, for two reasons. The first concerns the original text of vv. 7, 8. The problem is that the early manuscripts of them do not all read the same way. The great majority of manuscripts do not include the latter part of v. 7 and the first part of v. 8: namely, the words "in heaven, the Father, the Word, and the Holy Ghost: and these three are one" (v. 7) and the words, "And there are three that bear witness in heaven" (v. 8). Most commentators are of the opinion that these words were not included in the original text of the Epistle but were added later in order to explain more fully the nature of Jesus' incarnation (see the helpful comments of Marshall 236, 237; Westcott 202-209). (For a more in-depth analysis of the textual issues see Akin 198-200; Beyer 292; Kruse 180; Moody 106-108; Stott 180, 181.) The basic meaning of the passage is the same whether these words were or were not included in the original.

The second difficulty we face in interpreting these verses is the meaning of the phrase "not by water only, but by water and blood" found in v. 6. The meaning of these words has been long debated, and several different interpretations have been offered since the earliest days of the church. Stott (177, 178) discusses three common interpretations.

The first is found in the writings of Luther, Calvin, and others who view the water and blood as a reference to the sacraments: the water to baptism and the blood to the Lord's Supper. This view is not widely held today. The difficulty with this interpretation is that this text says that Christ came "by water and blood." Christ instituted the sacraments *during* His earthly ministry, and it is hard to see how we can speak of His incarnation as *through* the sacraments.

The second common interpretation is found in Augustine and other writers of the early church period. It connects the water and blood mentioned in this passage with the blood and water which flowed from Jesus' side when the spear was thrust into him (Jn. 19:34). This interpretation also presents difficulties and is not widely accepted today. The two passages seem to present two very different ideas: in the Gospel of John the blood and water came from the body of Jesus, but nothing is said about Jesus' coming by water and blood.

The third interpretation, found in the writings of Tertullian and others, is the most widely-accepted today. According to these writers, the water is a reference to Jesus' baptism in the sense that His baptism marked the beginning of his public ministry. By the act of baptism He was commissioned and empowered for the task ahead of Him. The blood is seen as a reference to Jesus' death. The idea is that with his death on the Cross, Jesus completed the work the Father had sent Him to earth to do. It marked the culmination of his public ministry. (See Yarbrough 281, 282; Akin 196, 197.)

Although we should avoid being dogmatic when faced with such a variety of interpretations, the third view seems to fit the context better than the first two. His baptism and crucifixion were important events which contributed greatly to His public ministry. It was "through" them that He revealed His love and saving power.

Several writers (Dodd 130; Kruse 178; Stott 178) add the understanding that these words also served to refute the false teaching that was being circulated in Asia Minor. John responds to the error by saying that both Jesus' baptism and His crucifixion are proofs that He was both God and man during his entire lifetime. He was never one without the other.

Dodd (130) suggests that the author's main purpose for these words was to defend the full humanity of Christ: "Jesus Christ was both baptized and crucified, and both these facts are essential to our faith in him." Stott (179) presents a similar interpretation: "So John emphasizes not just that He *came*, but especially that He came by water and blood, since it is His blood which cleanses from sin." Kruse (178) takes a little different approach, arguing that the false teachers saw baptism as the primary ministry of Jesus. John corrects this by saying that Jesus came both to baptize and to offer Himself as the atoning sacrifice for our sins.

The last half of v. 6 obviously refers to the Holy Spirit, who has born witness to the incarnation of Jesus. That "the Spirit is truth" emphasizes that what the Holy Spirit has confirmed about Christ is the truth. The Holy Spirit always teaches the truth. The text does not explain how the Holy Spirit bears witness to the full humanity of Christ. Stott (180) suggests that this passage refers to the inner witness of the Holy Spirit that opens the eyes of the believer to see the truth that is in Christ. Akin (197) notes that this is similar to Jn. 15:26: "But when the Comforter is come, whom I will send unto you from the Father, *even* the Spirit of truth, which proceedeth from the Father, he shall testify of me."

Verses 7, 8 provide further evidence and support for the full humanity of Christ. They call attention to three important proofs of the incarnation of Christ that are found in the latter part of v. 8. They are "the Spirit, and the water, and the blood." The "Spirit" refers to the Holy Spirit, as already introduced in v. 6. The water and blood have the same meaning as in v. 6 (Akin 197). Jesus experienced a human baptism with physical water; He also experienced a physical death on the cross. These are powerful historical arguments for the reality of Jesus' human body. He

did not just *seem* to be a man, as the Gnostics argued; He *was*, in fact, a man.

The last words of v. 8 point out that all three witnesses—the Spirit, the water, and the blood—agree. They all point to the full humanity of Jesus Christ. In the Jewish legal tradition the testimony of two or three witnesses was necessary to establish the truth (see Dt. 17:6, 19:15; and Beyer 293). These three witnesses certainly fulfill all the legal requirements to establish the truth about Jesus' humanity.

Verse 9 continues to develop the ideas presented in vv. 7, 8. John notes that the testimony of men is received in any court of law; without it no case could ever be decided. If men are willing to accept the testimony of other men, should they not also be willing to accept the testimony of God? Indeed, men should be willing to accept what God has said about His own Son. The phrase "witness of God" (taken as a Greek subjective genitive) means a witness given by God (Yarbrough 285, 286). John is probably referring to one of several incidents when God spoke in a personal and direct way about the ministry of His Son. At Jesus' baptism: "And lo a voice from heaven saying, This is my beloved Son, in whom I am well pleased" (Mt. 3:17). At the transfiguration of Christ: "While he yet spake, behold a bright cloud overshadowed them: and behold a voice out of the cloud, which said, This is my beloved Son, in whom I am well pleased; hear ye him" (Mt. 17:5). The point John wishes to make is obvious: the Christians of Asia Minor should accept what God says about His Son rather than what the false teachers are saying about Him.

Verse 10 calls attention to another evidence of the truth about Christ, the inner witness of the Holy Spirit that resides within the believer. As the Gospel of John explains, the Holy Spirit bears witness to Jesus Christ. According to Dodd (131) this passage should be understood against the background of Jn. 5:19-47 where John the Baptist bears witness to Jesus, but the Jewish leaders refuse to accept his testimony. Jesus then offers two further proofs of His deity. The first is that He does the works that the Father has given him to do: "But I have greater witness than that of John: for the works which the Father hath given me to finish, the same works that I do, bear witness of me, that the Father hath sent me" (Jn. 5:36).

The second proof that Jesus presents is the testimony of His heavenly Father: "And the Father himself, which hath sent me, hath borne witness of me" (Jn. 5:37). The Jewish leaders also refused to accept these additional testimonies.

Since the Jewish leaders refused to accept the testimonies that Jesus offered, it is obvious that they did not have the truth abiding within them. Jesus explained, "Ye have neither heard his voice at any time, nor seen his shape. And ye have not his word abiding in you: for whom he hath sent, he ye believe not" (Jn. 5:37, 38). The problem was not the lack of evidence; the real problem was their unwillingness to believe. Unwillingness to believe is also the root of the problem with the false teachers in Asia Minor.

The aged Apostle uses very similar language in 1 Jn. 5:10. When one receives the testimony about Jesus, that testimony becomes a part of his being. He "has that witness in himself." The one who refuses to believe makes God a liar in the sense that he treats the testimony that the Father has presented about His Son with contempt. He treats God as if He were a liar.

Dodd (133) stresses that the false teachers had at one time been within the church. They had heard the truth about the incarnation and the crucifixion of Christ but had deliberately chosen to deny it. As he explains, "Such denial is tantamount to making God a liar— accusing the Truth of falsehood." The one who refuses to accept the testimony that God has given about His Son cannot be a teacher of truth. According to Marshall (241) "It is inconsistent to profess belief in God, as John's opponents did, and yet to disbelieve what God has said. Belief in God and in his Son, Jesus Christ, are inseparably joined."

Verses 11, 12 provide a most appropriate summary and conclusion to this portion of 1 John. They emphasize that the decision to accept the testimony about Jesus is not merely an academic matter; it is a decision with eternal consequences. The simple truth is that the one who enjoys a right relationship with the Son of God has eternal life; the one who does not have the Son of God has no promise of eternal life. Marshall (242) writes, "Eternal life is not possible apart from true belief in Jesus as the Son of God." Yarbrough (290) correctly explains that to "have" the Son of God means "to trust in him continually." This involves much more than accepting intellectually the facts about Jesus; it involves personal faith in Him and a personal commitment to Him.

Beyer (299) argues that "to have" the Son is a synonym for believing in Jesus Christ. He explains, "To believe in him is more than to accept certain dogmas. Faith is a close relationship, an intimate communion, in some way so real that the believer can 'have' the one in whom he believes."

Summary
(5:6-12)

The textual and interpretive difficulties that we face in these verses may cause us to overlook their basic message. The basic theme is that Jesus Christ, the real God-man, is the only Savior. He came to earth and was born as a human being. He was baptized in the Jordan River and lived among the people of the land of Palestine. He knew the people, and they knew Him. His earthly life came to an end when He gave His life on the cross of Calvary in payment for the sins of the world.

These facts were well known to John's disciples in the churches of Asia Minor because they had heard John's preaching and teaching. They did not, however, accept them based on John's testimony alone. Verse 7 mentions three testimonies that they had heard and received: the Father, the Word, and the Holy Spirit. The truth of the gospel did not depend on the opinion of John or any other apostle. It was built upon the revelation which God had given and which He had communicated in different ways.

These verses warn against being led away from the truth of the gospel that these believers had received. John reminds his spiritual children once again that they have received the truth and that they must never allow themselves to be carried away by any false teaching. Eternal life is to be found only in Jesus Christ; there is no other avenue whereby they can be saved. Only the one who has the Son living within him has eternal life.

Application: Teaching and Preaching the Passage

All believers of every generation confront the same important question: "Are we willing to accept the testimony that God has given us concerning His Son?" The separatists in Asia Minor were seeking to substitute their testimony for the testimony of God. They were asking the Christians to leave the traditional teachings of the Christian faith and accept a new doctrine. That might be acceptable if the new doctrine were built on more solid testimony, but what the false teachers advocated was not. It was merely the words of men. As Lieu (216) correctly notes, "To set trust in human testimony over trust in God's own self-witness would be nonsense."

Contrary to much popular opinion, faith is not a leap in the dark. People make decisions based on the evidence that they have. John's disciples have made a decision to follow Christ based on the evidence that has been presented to them. Their decision has been based on good authority, God's own authority. The false teachers have entered the picture and are asking them to reject the evidence that God has given and accept their testimony in its place.

Countless believers around the world have to make similar decisions every day. The world challenges them in respect to what God has said about Jesus Christ. They are, for example, challenged to view Christ as one way of salvation among many. They are taught that the moral and ethical teachings of Jesus are simply one option among many that are available. Whose evidence will they heed? Believers should accept the testimony of God and reject that of the world.

Those who preach and teach the gospel have a responsibility to help believers examine the evidence and come to right conclusions. They do not have the right to simply impose their beliefs on them, but they have a responsibility to help them evaluate the evidence, make the right decisions, and build their lives on a solid foundation. The wise preacher or teacher can make effective use of these verses as part of a program of instruction in the faith.

III. Conclusion (5:13-21)

A. Assurance of Eternal Life (5:13)

The final section of this chapter forms something of an epilogue in which John accomplishes two objectives. First, he reminds his spiritual children one final time that they may be certain that they have eternal life if they believe in the Son of God. Second, he describes some of the practical consequences that believing in Jesus will produce in a human life. Being a follower of Christ makes an important difference in the believer's thoughts, actions, and relationships with others.

13 These things have I written unto you that believe on the name of the Son of God; that ye may know that ye have eternal life, and that ye may believe on the name of the Son of God.

Verse 13 serves a dual function. First, it functions as the conclusion of the preceding section. It is a brief summary of some of the important doctrinal truths that John has presented in this Epistle. The words "these things" probably refer to the entire content of this letter (Kistemaker 359), although some commentators take them to refer only to the preceding section. (See Akin 203, 204; Beyer 202, 203; and Marshall 243.)

Second, this verse serves as the introduction to the final section of the letter. It prepares the reader to receive John's summary of what he has taught and will help them put his teachings into practice in everyday life in sometimes difficult and trying circumstances.

The author mentions that he has written this Epistle to his spiritual children, to "you that believe on the name of the Son of God." The words imply continuous or ongoing action (Greek present tense). The message is that the recipients do not have just an historic faith; they have a living faith in Jesus Christ as the Son of God. His goal in this passage is not to bring unbelievers into the fold but to instruct and encourage his spiritual children. He wants to keep them from falling into the errors presented by the secessionists. Stott (184) notes that the goal is "not that they may believe and receive, but that having believed, they may know what they have received."

The last phrase of v. 13, "and that ye may believe on the name of the Son of God," is not found in some of the early manuscripts (Lieu 220; Stott 184), leading some interpreters to suggest that they were brought over at some later time from Jn. 20:31 (Beyer 302). Their inclusion does not, however, affect the basic meaning of the verse.

B. God Hears Those Who Follow Him (5:14-17)

14 And this is the confidence that we have in him, that, if we ask any thing according to his will, he heareth us:
15 And if we know that he hear us, whatsoever we ask, we know that we have the petitions that we desired of him.

Verses 14, 15 address the specific issue of prayer because prayer is such an important aspect of the believer's relationship with God. The false teachers had tried to raise doubts in the minds of John's disciples concerning their relationship to God. It is possible that they also raised questions about whether the prayers of believers were being heard. John here assures his spiritual children that God is attentive to their prayers: "Not only can a believer have assurance of salvation, but he also can have assurance that God will hear his prayers and answer them" (Akin 205).

In context, John is not saying that God is obligated to grant every prayer that a believer may pray, even though that prayer may be contrary to God's will: "Prayer is not a convenient device for imposing our will upon God, or bending His will to ours, but the prescribed way of subordinating our will to His" (Stott 185). The implication is that John's followers in Asia Minor will, when they pray, seek God's guidance and direction (see Lieu 223).

The word "confidence" (Greek *parresia*), in v. 14, may also be translated "boldness." It is the freedom of speech granted to a citizen in a public assembly; it also implies speaking in the presence of someone with power and authority (Lieu 223; Stott 185). In this context it denotes acceptance. The believer is a part of God's family; he has the right to speak, and his words will be heard. God will then answer the believer's prayer according to His infinite wisdom, understanding, and purpose.

16 If any man see his brother sin a sin which is not unto death, he shall ask, and he shall give him life for them that sin not unto death. There is a sin unto death: I do not say that he shall pray for it.
17 All unrighteousness is sin: and there is a sin not unto death.

Verses 16, 17 are difficult. The "sin unto death" and "sin not unto death" are not easy to define, and the passage gives little context to help explain them. Lieu (226) notes, correctly, that the author makes no attempt to define either term. Westcott (209) points out that John's original readers were apparently close enough to the situation that they understood the terms and no explanation was necessary. He also notes that these terms were used by the Rabbinic writers. The difficulty lies in the fact that modern believers are far removed from the situation; what was at one time very clear is no longer so clear. Contemporary believers have to examine the various possible interpretations in light of the available evidence and come to the best conclusions possible.

John's words are: "There is a sin unto death: I do not say that he shall pray for it." He does not insist that they not pray for one who has committed this sin, he simply says that it is not necessary to do so. The implication is that the sin cannot be forgiven or that the believer's intercessory prayer will make no difference.

Stott (186) connects 1 Jn. 5:16, 17 with vv. 14, 15, which deal with one's personal prayer life. In his view, the main purpose of these verses is to remind the believers of the need for intercessory prayer. They must not forget to pray for believers who are facing difficulties and need the prayers of their fellow believers.

What, then, is the "sin unto death"? Stott (187, 188) analyzes several possible interpretations of this much-debated phrase. He suggests that there are three common interpretations, as follows.

1. This phrase refers to a specific sin. In the O.T. there were certain sins called "presumptuous sins" or "sins of the high hand." These were sins of direct rebellion against God, and there was no forgiveness for them in the Jewish sacrificial system. This list of sins could include murder, adultery, and the worship of pagan gods.

2. The phrase means apostasy. According to this view, the "sin unto death" is not any specific sin but the denial of Christ and renunciation of the Christian faith. This view is advocated by a number of interpreters including Brooke, Law, and Dodd. Stott himself refuses to accept this interpretation because he sees it as a contradiction of John's teaching that no true Christian can persist in sin.

3. The interpretation that Stott himself accepts is that the "sin unto death" is the blasphemy against the Holy Spirit mentioned in Mt. 12:31 and elsewhere. Stott (188) defines this as "a deliberate, open-eyed rejection of known truth." He argues that it was committed by the Pharisees who ascribed the mighty

works done by Jesus to Beelzebub, the prince of the demons.

In Stott's view, neither the one who commits the "sin unto death" nor the one who commits the "sin not unto death" is a true believer. He writes (189), "Both are 'dead in trespasses and sins' (Eph. ii:1)." The difference is that "the one may receive life through a Christian's intercession, while the other will die the second death" (189, 190).

Brooke (146) suggests that there is a connection between the "sin unto death" in 1 John and the sins of deliberate rebellion against God described in Num. 15:30, 31 and other passages. He argues that John is not thinking of one particular sin, but of a pattern of sin. He writes, "In the author's view any sin which involved a deliberate rejection of the claims of Christ may be described as 'unto death.' If *persisted* in, it must lead to final separation from the Divine life."

Law (141) takes a similar approach. He recognizes that the "sin unto death" is difficult to define with precision, but suggests that it may be "the sin of those who by deliberate and avowed action severed themselves from Christ and from the Christian community." In other words, it is apostasy or something very close to it.

Brooke (147) also points out that John does not *forbid* intercession for one who has committed the "sin unto death" but simply does not command it: "Such cases lay outside the normal sphere of Christian intercession. They must be left to God alone."

Beyer (308-15) offers a comprehensive discussion of various views of the "sin unto death." He cites the most common interpretations found in ancient and modern times and analyzes the strengths and weaknesses of the most important views. He finally comes to a very ambiguous conclusion, arguing that we should guard against any interpretation that claims to be the only correct way to interpret the text.

Westcott (211, 212) summarizes the most common interpretations found in early Christian writers such as Clement of Alexandria, Tertullian, Origen, Ambrose, and Jerome. He also writes that the simplest interpretation is to define the "sin unto death" as a sin which results in natural death as in Num. 18:22.

Lieu (227, 228) calls attention to the difficulties in trying to distinguish sharply between a "sin unto death" and a "sin not unto death." She analyzes several ways of making this distinction and finds none of them to be entirely satisfactory. She does, however, make one important observation: "The emphasis here is not on the inevitable consequences of the choices made by a member of the community, the sinner, but on the exercise by the community as a whole of the privileges of having the ear of God." The purpose of the passage is not to define precisely the difference between a "sin unto death" and a "sin not unto death." In her opinion, the goal is to help the Christian community pray in the most effective way possible.

One important question often arises in any discussion of this passage. It is, "Can the sin unto death be committed by a believer?" There are basically two responses to this question, and a particular author's response is often influenced by his theological orientation. Calvinistic interpreters generally argue that no true Christian can sin in this way. Stott (188), for example, argues that John has taught that no true

Christian can continue in sin. He writes, "Surely John has taught clearly in the Epistle that the true Christian cannot sin, that is, persist in sin (iii.9), let alone fall away altogether." The implication of Stott's interpretation is that anyone who commits the "sin unto death" has not been truly born again.

Marshall, an Arminian scholar, differs sharply. He sees no convincing evidence that a believer cannot commit the "sin unto death." John has warned his followers about the possibility that they might sin and fail to continue in the truth in such passages as 1 Jn. 2:24 and 2 Jn. 7-11 (Marshall 250). There is no reason to believe that a believer may not commit the "sin unto death." The entire argument of the letter is designed to meet the needs of believers who are faced with serious theological errors. Why would an author of John's understanding and experience warn Christians about a sin they could not commit? Law (137) writes, "It is a sin which may be committed by Christians, and it is only as committed by Christians that it is here contemplated."

Given the small amount of information in this passage, we should not be dogmatic about the precise definitions of the "sin unto death" and the "sin not unto death." Of the possible interpretations of the former, apostasy seems to be the most likely. There seems to be a connection between deliberate rebellion in the O.T., the blasphemy of the Holy Spirit in the Synoptic Gospels, and apostasy in the book of Hebrews. The connection is that these sins lie outside the normal provision for forgiveness. They produce truly tragic consequences in the life of a believer. It is quite likely that the "sin unto death" is not a single sin that a person commits but a pattern of sin and rebellion against God that ultimately leads to a rejection of Christ as the Intercessor. Without Christ's intercession, there is no forgiveness.

Nothing in the passage indicates that the "sin unto death" may not be committed by a believer. John is not writing to unbelievers; he is writing to Christians who are in danger of falling away into serious doctrinal and practical error. What reason would he have to warn them about a sin they could not commit?

C. Do Not Continue in Sin (5:18-20)

18 We know that whosoever is born of God sinneth not; but he that is begotten of God keepeth himself, and that wicked one toucheth him not.
19 And we know that we are of God, and the whole world lieth in wickedness.
20 And we know that the Son of God is come, and hath given us an understanding, that we may know him that is true, and we are in him that is true, *even* in his Son Jesus Christ. This is the true God, and eternal life.

Verses 18-20 introduce no new information. They remind the believers of Asia Minor of some of the most important truths that John has taught in this letter. John uses the words "we know" three times in these verses; this three-fold repetition serves to remind the readers of the knowledge they have obtained and the commitments that they have made. The first is "We know that whosoever is born of God sinneth not." The idea is that the believer cannot con-

tinue to live a life of sin, as already indicated in 3:6-9. As there, "sinneth not" (Greek present tense) implies continuing action. The idea is that a believer cannot continue to live the same type of sinful lifestyle that he lived before his conversion. There has to be a difference. Beyer (317) points out that John is not saying that the believer is totally incapable of sinning. In several passages, including 1:8—2:2, John has dealt with the problem of sin in the life of the believer. John's message is that sin cannot be taken lightly.

There is some variation in how the next phrase reads in the early manuscripts. Some read, "The one who has been begotten of God keeps him." Others read, "The one who has been begotten of God keeps himself." If the first reading is followed, the idea is that Christ (the one who has been begotten of God) keeps the believer from falling back into the ways of the world. If the second reading is followed, the idea is that "the one who has been begotten of God"—the believer—keeps himself faithful to the God who has forgiven his sins. Both readings yield meanings that are theologically correct. The believer does not have to depend on his own resources; Christ is the one who remains with him as he lives the Christian life. At the same time, the Christian has a responsibility to continue in the faith. He is a free moral agent. Christ will not hold him in the faith against his will. (See Beyer 318; Kistemaker 366; Kruse 195; Marshall 252; and Stott 192.)

In the last phrase, "and that wicked one toucheth him not," the "wicked one" refers to Satan (Akin 212; Kistemaker 366). The verb "to touch" in this type of context means to injure or do harm to a person (Kistemaker 366).

This should not be interpreted to mean that the Christian will not face serious trials and temptations. In Jn. 16:1-4 Jesus warned His followers of the serious persecutions that they would face because of their commitment to Him. (See Yarbrough 317; and Beyer 319.)

The second "we know" is found in v. 19, where John reminds his spiritual children of two basic things that they have learned from their Christian experience. They know that they are "of God" in the sense that they belong to God. They have been born again and are a part of His family. The false teachers may try to cause them to doubt their relationship to God, but that relationship is real.

The other basic truth known is that the entire world lies in wickedness. The term "world" is used in several different ways in the N.T. In this context, Dodd (138) defines it as "the organized pagan society in which he and his readers had to live." Akin (213) defines it as "human society under the power of evil and at war with God and his people." These first-century believers had to live and serve Christ every day in a hostile pagan environment. If they were to survive in such an environment, they needed to have a good understanding of their relationship to God.

The final "we know" is found at the beginning of v. 20. It introduces a brief but profound summary of the Christian faith. These Christians need to be assured that the Son of God has come and given them a correct understanding of how they can relate to God. The truth is not to be found in the false teachers; it is to be found in the message of Jesus Christ which they have received and accepted. The phrase "him that is true" is most likely a reference to God the Father (Akin 214; Stott 194). The idea is that these believers have received through Jesus the Son an accurate picture of God the Father. Any teaching other than that which they have already received cannot be the truth.

They are "in" Jesus Christ in the sense that they have a saving relationship with Him. They have heard the truth of the gospel and accepted it, and they should allow no one to shake their confidence. The last phrase of v. 20, "This is the true God, and eternal life," could be translated either, "This one is the true God and eternal life" or, "He is the true God and eternal life." Some interpreters see this phrase as a description of Jesus Christ; others see it as a reference to God the Father (see Akin 214; Brooke 152, 153; Kruse 197, 198; Stott 195, 196). Since the previous phrases of the verse have dealt primarily with the Son rather than with the Father, it is probably better to take this phrase as referring to Jesus the Son. In this context, the idea is that these believers have been taught the truth about the Son of God and have received eternal life. The false teachers have offered them a new doctrine which is radically different from what they have been taught. They should see this false doctrine for what it is and reject it.

D. Keep Yourselves from Idols (5:21)

21 Little children, keep yourselves from idols. Amen.

This verse forms a fitting conclusion to the message of hope and love that John has presented. The first phrase could be translated "dear children." It expresses the sincerity of John's love for the Christians of Asia Minor. He has known them for years and has seen them grow in the faith. He has gone through severe trials with them, and now he addresses them as his spiritual children.

John's final petition is that they will "keep themselves from idols." This exhortation is interesting in that it takes the aged Apostle's message in a new direction. Most of this Epistle deals with the problem of heresy. The author has consistently refuted the false teachings of those who have sown the seeds of discord and strife. Much of the content of the letter has dealt with a correct understanding of the life and ministry of Jesus Christ.

Here in the final verse, John adds a new dimension to his thought. He reminds his spiritual children to stay away from idols. "Idols" in the N.T. normally refers to the pagan gods that were worshipped in the Roman Empire of the first century. Many passages in the N.T. warn against the danger of worshipping pagan gods (Marshall 255). However, various interpreters debate the use of the term here. They point out, correctly, that there is no evidence within 1 John which indicates that the Christians of Asia Minor were tempted to worship pagan gods. (See Akin 215, 216; Beyer 326, 327; Brooke 154; Kruse 200, 201; and Marshall 255, 256).

Beyer (326, 327) suggests three possible interpretations of "idol" as used in this verse: (1) anything contrary to a true conception of God; (2) mixing Christianity with the pagan religions of the world; (3) the false conceptions of God which the Gnostic teachers were promoting. Brooke (154) argues that the term refers to "all false conceptions of God." Westcott (197) suggests that an idol is

"anything that occupies the place due to God." Kruse (200, 201) gives a good summary of how various interpreters handle this term.

These believers lived in a pagan world. They faced the daily temptation to compromise their faith in some way with the pagan religions around them. There is no doubt that John had taught and preached on this theme during his years of association with these churches. In this context, it is not unusual that John would include a final exhortation encouraging his children to avoid the destructive influence of paganism.

"Amen" comes from a Hebrew root word meaning to be certain or true. It is the normal Hebrew closing for a letter and is often found in the N.T. (For a helpful analysis see Graber 97.) The problem here is that the word is not found in the earliest manuscripts, leading most textual scholars to assume that it was a later addition. Its presence certainly does not detract from the message that John has given to his spiritual children.

Summary
(5:13-21)

Verses 13-21 form a fitting conclusion to this Epistle, reminding John's spiritual children of some of the most important lessons they have learned. They also challenge the believers to put their faith into practice by presenting a positive testimony in the midst of false teaching. They seek to strengthen the resolve of Christians to stand firm in the conflicts that lie ahead (Burge 219).

There are several key ideas in this passage. The first is confidence. A living relationship with the living God introduces a high level of certainty into a life.

The believer does not have to live in doubt, wandering from one idea to another. He has confidence that God loves him, cares about him, and answers his prayers. He has certainty about who Christ is and what He has done. In a world filled with uncertainty, the Christian has confidence in the One whom he serves.

A second key idea is intercession. We should not allow the difficulty in defining the terms "sin unto death" and "sin not unto death" to obscure the basic meaning of the passage. John's assumption is that his children will and should make intercession for one another. His goal is to help them do it in the most effective manner. The Christian community is built on the mutual relationship between believers, and praying for one another is an important part of that relationship. Intercessory prayer is both important and effective.

The third key idea in this passage is sin. The false teachers downplayed the importance of sin. They argued that the sins of the body had little or no effect on one's relationship with God. They could not have been more wrong. As v. 17 explains, "All unrighteousness is sin." The Christian community must always take seriously the tragic consequences of sin both in the individual lives of believers and in the corporate life of the church.

Application: Teaching and Preaching the Passage

Burge (219-23) argues that this passage has special relevance for Christians who have been hurt and wounded in churches. He (219) writes, "This section is a practical paragraph, aimed at rebuilding the personal lives of exhausted peo-
ple." John's final words can be of great value both to Christians who carry scars and wounds and to leaders who minister to them. This paragraph offers certainty in the midst of doubt. Christians can be sure of their relationship to God and certain about the truths of the Gospel that they have heard and received. God will never turn His back on His people when they are in the midst of trials; they can trust Him and rely upon Him.

These verses envision a Christian community in which believers love one another, help one another, and pray for one another. The first words of v. 16 are important, "If any man see his brother sin a sin which is not unto death, he shall ask, and he shall give him life for them that sin not unto death." At the time these words were written, Christians constituted a small percentage of the population in a hostile pagan world. In such an atmosphere the believers had to stand together, pray for one another, help one another, and even correct one another when necessary. That is the nature of a true Christian fellowship. This passage is an excellent basis for teaching dealing with the church and how believers can and should serve God together.

This passage emphasizes prayer. Verse 15 says, "And if we know that he hears us, whatsoever we ask, we know that, if we ask any thing according to his will, he heareth us." A victorious church is a praying church. Only a church committed to prayer can withstand the assaults, from within and without, that it will face. We cannot overestimate the important role that prayer plays both in an individual Christian life and in the life and ministry of a local congregation.

Purity is another important theme in these verses. According to v. 18,

"Whosoever is born of God sinneth not." As noted, the verb suggests an action that continues. The idea is that one who has been born again will not choose to live in sin. He will do everything that he can to avoid being caught up in the sinful lifestyles he finds in the world around him. He will seek for purity and holiness. Every generation of Christians needs to hear regular teaching and preaching about what purity is, how it can be obtained, and how it can be maintained.

This passage also outlines the relationship between doctrine and practice. John reminds his followers one last time about the importance of doctrine. What they believe about Jesus Christ is important because what they believe will affect what they do. The modern world increasingly sees doctrine as irrelevant. This passage can help modern believers see the importance of a proper understanding of the doctrine of Christ.

Few people in the western world still worship pagan gods, but that does not mean that the command "keep yourselves from idols" has become obsolete. There is always the temptation that we will put something in the place of prominence in our lives that rightfully belongs to God alone. As Dodd (142) writes, "Christians believe that the God revealed in Christ and attested in the Scriptures is the one real God, and the worship of any God-substitute is idolatry." We must always be on guard lest we give the priority in our lives to any political idea, economic theory, job, favorite hobby, or other factor. God alone is God, and He alone deserves our worship.

THE OUTLINE OF SECOND JOHN

  I. Greetings, 1-3
 II. Walking in Truth and Love, 4-6
III. Confronting the Error, 7-11
IV. Closing Remarks, 12, 13

COMMENTARY ON SECOND JOHN

INTRODUCTION

Second John illustrates the kinds of doctrinal and practical problems that early Christians encountered on a regular basis. Travel, for example, was safer and more practical than in earlier centuries, but it was still slow and dangerous. It was difficult for Christian travelers to find acceptable lodging when they traveled. Modern hotels and motels were unknown. There were many inns, but they were generally filthy and often doubled as houses of ill repute. They were not the kind of places where Christians felt comfortable. Because of this difficulty, it became customary for local believers to provide hospitality for traveling Christians. While this was a good system, it was subject to abuse. Sincere Christians did not want to provide hospitality to those whose claim to be followers of Jesus was not matched by their lives and doctrine. Early Christians needed firmness and discernment to deal with situations that concerned hospitality. Ramsay (375-402), in an old but still useful work, explains what traveling conditions were like for Christians in the ancient world. Kruse (215) gives a brief but insightful analysis of customs concerning hospitality in the ancient world.

Burge (231) suggests that John had two specific purposes in mind when he wrote this letter. First, he wanted to strengthen his readers' commitment to the truth of the gospel which they had received. Second, he wanted to warn them of the severity of their opponents. His goal was to help prepare them for the spiritual battles that they were sure to face.

There is much emphasis on love in this brief epistle. For these early believers their faith was much more than an intellectual belief. It demanded a genuine love for the gospel and for other followers of Christ. To walk in love meant to obey the commandments of Christ.

The doctrinal issues faced in 2 John are similar to those faced in 1 John. The main problem concerns those who "confess not that Jesus Christ is come in the flesh" (2 Jn. 7). This false teaching seems to have its origin in an early form of the Gnostic heresy (see the comments on the Gnostic heresy found in the Introduction). The challenge to the Christians who received this letter is to continue in the true doctrine that they have been taught and not to be led astray by false teachings, no matter how attractively they may be presented.

Burge (229) argues that this letter is best understood against the background of serious conflict within the church in Ephesus. While this is a possible explanation of the situation, there is no firm evidence to prove that the conflict was centered in Ephesus. This type of conflict could have occurred in any of the churches in Asia Minor that looked to the Apostle John for leadership.

I. GREETINGS (vv. 1-3)

1 The elder unto the elect lady and her children, whom I love in the truth; and not I only, but also all they that have known the truth;
2 For the truth's sake, which dwelleth in us, and shall be with us for ever.
3 Grace be with you, mercy, *and* peace, from God the Father, and from the Lord Jesus Christ, the Son of the Father, in truth and love.

This letter follows the normal pattern for letters in the first century, beginning with the identification of the author (Dodd 143; Morris 1271). The author does not identify himself by name as Paul does in his letters; he identifies himself by title (Stott 203). As noted in the Introduction, the term "elder" implies more than age. It implies one who occupies a position of respect and leadership within the Christian community (Burge 231; Kruse 203, 204; Stott 203). As noted previously, the Apostle John was the person most likely to be known by this title in Asia Minor in the late first century.

The words "the elect lady and her children" have provoked much discussion since the earliest days of the Christian church. Various interpretations generally fall into one of two categories. Some (Morris 1270, 1271) see this phrase as a description of an individual Christian woman and her children. Others (Akin 219, 220; Dodd 145; Kruse 204; Lenski 555-57; Stott 204) see these words as a personification of a local church and its members. Since first-century churches often met in the homes of members, it may be diffi-

cult to sharply distinguish between the host family and the church that met with that host.

Burge (231) explains that many interpreters in the early church understood the phrase to refer to an individual and her children. Morris (1271) suggests that the most natural interpretation is to see these words as referring to a woman and her family. He doubts that the author would have written such a brief letter to a congregation. Dodd (143) points out that some of the Greek words used in this passage might have been used as proper names: "to the lady Electa," for example, or "to the elect Kyria." Dodd (145) notes that in this context *lady* (Greek *kyria*) might be a proper name.

Most modern interpreters see the phrase, instead, as describing a local church and its members. Kruse (204) gives several reasons for this view. In vv. 6, 8, 10, and 12, John addresses the readers in the second person plural in a way that seems applicable to all members of a church. In 1 Pet. 5:13 the church in Rome is described as "she who is in Babylon." In the final verse of 2 John the author writes, "The children of thy elect sister greet thee." In the opinion of most commentators today, the most natural interpretation of this phrase is that one church is sending greetings to another church.

Such examples of personification are not new. They are used to describe Israel in the O.T. and to describe the church elsewhere in the N.T. Dodd (144, 145) suggests that the letter might have been written in this way to protect both the writer and the readers. If the letter fell into the hands of those who wished to persecute the church it would appear to be nothing more than a friendly, personal letter.

There are two common interpretations of the phrase, "whom I love in the truth": to mean "whom I truly love"; or that John loves the "elect lady and her children" because they continue to walk in the truth of the gospel which they have heard and received. Most interpreters (Burge 232; Dodd 145; Kruse 205; Morris 1271; Stott 205) prefer the second interpretation, which fits the context better.

The word "truth" (Greek *alētheia*), in various forms, occurs four times in these three verses. It is one of the most important terms used in John's Epistles. It includes an intellectual element in that it refers to the truths of the gospel which these believers have accepted and which have become the guiding force in their lives. The term also implies a very personal commitment to Jesus Christ and His work. Jesus said, "I am the way, the truth, and the life: no man cometh to the Father, but by me" (Jn. 14:6). Dodd (145) expresses the idea well in these words, "In these epistles 'truth' is not merely, as in ordinary speech, that which corresponds with the facts, but also, specifically, the ultimate Reality as revealed in Christ."

In this specific context, the idea is that John is confident that the elect lady and her children will reject the heretical teachings and will remain faithful to the true gospel that they have received. (See Burge 232, 233; Dodd 146; Kruse 205; and Stott 205, 206.)

In the closing words of v. 1, John emphasizes that his care and concern are not limited to this specific church. He extends his love to all who have received the truth and continue to walk in it. That they "have known the truth"

(Greek perfect tense participle) implies a past action with a continuing result: the idea is that John loves all who have come to know the truth and continue to live by it (Stott 205). Lenski (558) explains the idea well in these words, "John describes all these fellow Christians as being those who have known the truth, known it for a long time with its blessed effect upon themselves."

Verse 2 further develops the ideas that John has introduced in v. 1. It is difficult to determine the connection of the phrase, "for the truth's sake." Stott (205) connects it with the idea of love that the author has introduced in v. 1. The idea is that Christians have a special bond of love for one another because the truth of the gospel is working in their hearts. Lenski (558) explains the meaning this way: "It is ... for the sake of this truth remaining in us that John and all those who know this truth love the members of this congregation and do not want a single one of them to forsake the truth and fall prey to the deceivers."

Dodd (146) points out that the false doctrines being circulated threaten to destroy the very foundation of the Christian faith. True Christian fellowship cannot exist apart from a sincere acceptance of the truth. The closing words of v. 2 stress the eternal nature of the gospel message. John's purpose is to assure the Christians of Asia Minor that God will not abandon them as they strive to preserve the truth of the gospel. The gospel message has come to live in their hearts, and it will continue to live there.

Verse 3 is the formal salutation of the letter. It conforms to the common letter-writing practice of the first century and is similar to the greetings found in the letters of Paul. The three key words are grace, mercy, and peace, which are found in the salutations of some other N.T. letters (see Yarbrough 336; Brooke 171). Paul often uses grace and peace to introduce his letters, although grace, mercy, and peace are in the openings of the Pastoral Epistles. Each term has special significance for the followers of Christ. Grace and mercy are similar concepts. They stress that God has bestowed His goodness and kindness on those who do not deserve them. The term "grace" is often used in salvation contexts (as in Eph. 2:8). The idea is that these believers have not been saved by their good works but by the goodness of God.

"Peace" in this context does not refer to the absence of earthly conflict but to the peace with God which they have received. As a result of the forgiveness of their sins, they are no longer separated from God. (See Akin 222; Kruse 206; Lenski 559; and Morris 1271.)

The verb translated "be" in the KJV (Greek *estai*) is future tense. The idea is that the grace, mercy, and peace that God gives will be with these believers during the difficult days that lie ahead. John is careful to point out that grace, mercy, and peace do not come from the Father alone; they come from both the Father and the Son.

The last two phrases of v. 3 are not normally found in N.T. salutations. John has added them here in response to the specific situation that has caused him to write this letter. He emphasizes that Jesus Christ is "the Son of the Father." He also emphasizes the importance of truth and love. The idea is that these believers will enjoy the grace, mercy, and peace that God gives them because they continue to walk in truth and love. John's goal is to refute the heretical

teachings that seek to make Jesus inferior to the Father and disrupt the Christian fellowship. (See Akin 223; and Burge 233.)

II. WALKING IN TRUTH AND LOVE (vv. 4-6)

4 I rejoiced greatly that I found of thy children walking in truth, as we have received a commandment from the Father.
5 And now I beseech thee, lady, not as though I wrote a new commandment unto thee, but that which we had from the beginning, that we love one another.
6 And this is love, that we walk after his commandments. This is the commandment, That, as ye have heard from the beginning, ye should walk in it.

These verses are the heart of this brief Epistle. They encourage these Christians to do two things: to walk in truth and to love one another. Neither of these commandments is new; both represent the traditional teachings that they have received ever since the gospel first came to Asia Minor. Both sharply contradict the false teachers who sought to undermine the traditional doctrine of Christ and who desired to divide the believers into competing congregations.

According to v. 4, the aged Apostle rejoiced when he learned that the members of this church were "walking in truth" in spite of the efforts of the false teachers to lead them astray. A number of early manuscripts, including those preferred by many textual scholars, read "walking in *the* truth." Regardless, the author does not intend to convey the idea that they are walking according to truth in a general sense only. They are walking according to the specific truth of the gospel that they have been taught. Dodd (147) defines walking in the truth as "leading a truly Christian life." According to Stott (208), walking in the truth includes "both believing it, especially the central truth of the incarnation, and obeying it, seeking to conform our lives to it."

This commandment to walk in the truth is not new; the last words of v. 4 are "as we have received a commandment from the Father." This commandment to follow the truth is, then, part of the traditional teaching of the church. These specific words are not found on the lips of Jesus in the Gospels. Perhaps John is referring to 1 Jn. 3:23 which says, "And this is his commandment, That we should believe on the name of his Son Jesus Christ." It is also possible that John is giving a summary of Jesus' teaching rather than quoting a specific saying.

Regarding the preposition "of" (v. 4), Burge (233) suggests that the word may indicate that some of the members of the church have already left the faith. Lenski (561) writes that the verse leaves the impression that some "were found who were not walking in line with the truth." Akin (225) does not accept this interpretation. In his view, the Apostle John has not met all of the members of the church, and he can only speak about those he has met. He writes, "Given the positive and encouraging thrust of v. 4, to read a negative judgment between the lines seems unnecessary and unwarranted."

Verses 5, 6 emphasize the importance of walking in love. For the Apostle John, truth and love go together; both are important. He rejoices to find the members of the church walking in love just as he rejoiced to find them walking in the truth. The commandment to walk in love is just as old as the commandment to walk according to the truth. It is likely that this verse refers to the specific teaching of Jesus found in Jn. 13:34, "A new commandment I give unto you, That ye love one another; as I have loved you, that ye also love one another."

The first phrase of v. 6 must be interpreted in light of the context. Akin (226) has correctly noted that "love is a multifaceted concept in John that receives different emphases depending upon the need of the audience." In this specific context, the false teachers have divided the fellowship; they have sown discord and strife. They have not lived according to Jesus' instructions to love. They have not demonstrated love for the Father, for the Son, for the truth of the gospel, or for their fellow believers. Therefore, their false teachings should be rejected.

The last half of v. 6 provides something of a summary of what John has taught to this point. Beyer (355) notes that there are two possible interpretations of the phrase "from the beginning." It may refer to the beginning of the proclamation of the gospel or to the beginning of their new lives as believers. See the comments on 1 Jn. 1:1; 2:7.

Verse 6 should be interpreted in light of what John has written in the previous verses. The main idea is that the commandment of God to walk both in the truth and in love is not a new commandment. It has been an important part of the gospel from the beginning. These believers should not be led astray by the false teachings that have recently come into Asia Minor. The fact that a teaching has been around for a long time does not automatically make it right, but, in this case, what they have been taught is both traditional and true. They should continue to walk down the pathway of truth and love.

III. CONFRONTING THE ERROR (vv. 7-11)

7 For many deceivers are entered into the world, who confess not that Jesus Christ is come in the flesh. This is a deceiver and an antichrist.
8 Look to yourselves, that we lose not those things which we have wrought, but that we receive a full reward.
9 Whosoever transgresseth, and abideth not in the doctrine of Christ, hath not God. He that abideth in the doctrine of Christ, he hath both the Father and the Son.
10 If there come any unto you, and bring not this doctrine, receive him not into your house, neither bid him God speed:
11 For he that biddeth him God speed is partaker of his evil deeds.

The conjunction "for" (Greek *hoti)* in v. 7 connects these verses with what John has written in the previous verses. The believers must be careful to walk in truth and love because they are surrounded by false teachers and false teachings. The word translated "deceiver" (Greek *planos)* literally means "seducer." The idea is that they lead others astray from the truth of the gospel (Plummer, *Second Epistle* 2). One important aspect of their heresy is given in the next phrase: they deny that Jesus Christ has come in the flesh. This is

probably the same false teaching that we met in 1 Jn. 2:22, 23 and 4:2, 3. It seems to be an early form of the Gnostic heresy that taught that Christ had no real human body. He only had the appearance of a human being (Plummer, *Second Epistle* 2). The verb "are entered" (Greek *exelthon)* into the world expresses the idea of "going forth" into the world. These false teachers are making no effort to hide their heresy. They are going out among the churches and openly proclaiming a Docetic Christology.

The last words of v. 7 could be translated, "For this one is the deceiver and the antichrist." The specific reference is to the false teacher who is spreading his heretical teaching; John warns the lady and her children not to be deceived by him. "Antichrist" literally means "against Christ." This false teacher is advocating a heretical view of the person of Christ. Akin (230) and Lenski (567) describe this false prophet as the forerunner of the great Antichrist who will come in the future. See the comments on 1 Jn. 2:18-23.

The words of v. 7 are emphatic. As Plummer (*Second Epistle* 3) correctly points out, "The strong words of the apostle are the expression of a glowing conviction." The Apostle John views the situation as a serious one that demands a strong and immediate response.

The imperative verb in "look to yourselves" (v. 8) is a command form that implies continuous action (Greek present tense). The meaning is that these Christians must always be vigilant; they must never let their guard down (Akin 231).

There is some variation in the way the remaining verbs in this verse are translated. These variations are due to slight differences in the early Greek manuscripts. Some manuscripts have the verbs in the first person plural "we"; others have them in the second person plural "you" ("ye"). The KJV follows those manuscripts that use the first person plural "we." Following this reading, the verse is translated, "Look to yourselves, that we lose not those things which we have wrought, but that we receive a full reward."

Lenski (567) and others follow those manuscripts that use the second person plural. He translates the verse, "Look to yourselves lest you destroy what you have wrought but that you may receive full reward." Since the first part of the verse uses the second person plural, it would make sense for John to continue with it in the latter part of the verse. Either way, however, the author is concerned that these believers will be led astray and will forfeit all that they have accomplished.

There are two possible interpretations of the warning about the possibility of losing that which has been wrought. One possibility is that John is warning these believers that if they succumb to the false teachings they will lose their heavenly reward. The other possibility is that if they fall into this trap they may lose their very salvation. The context of the passage argues for the second interpretation; the incarnation is the doctrine that is at stake here, and it is one of the cardinal doctrines of the Christian faith. If these Christians are carried away to such an extent that they abandon this basic belief, how can they maintain a proper relationship with God? Plummer (*Second Epistle* 3) explains that what this lady and her children are in danger of losing "is nothing less than God himself." (See Akin 231; Kruse 212; Lenski

568, 569; and Marshall 72, 73.) If these Christians lose their relationship with God, they will also lose their hope of eternal life.

Verses 9-11 present the same basic truths but from a more general perspective. They warn all believers everywhere that they must remain true to the teachings of Christ that they have received. The first part of v. 9 could be translated, "Everyone who transgresses and who does not remain in the teaching of Christ, does not have God." The phrases "everyone who transgresses" and "who does not remain" are describing the same individual. The verb "transgresses" (Greek *proago*) literally means "to run ahead" (Kistemaker 382). In this context it refers to one who leaves or runs ahead of the Christian faith in order to follow the false teachers. The phrase "does not remain" refers to one who rejects the true Christian teachings about the person of Christ. Kistemaker (382) explains, "If someone progresses and leaves the faith, he regresses and faces spiritual ruin. Genuine progress is always rooted in Christ's teaching."

John's message is that the one who transgresses the teachings about Christ that he has received no longer has God. He has forfeited his personal relationship with his heavenly Father.

The phrase "doctrine of Christ" can be interpreted in two ways. Most interpreters see it as describing the doctrine or teaching that Christ has given (Greek subjective genitive). The other possible interpretation is that these words describe the doctrine about Christ that these believers have been taught (Greek objective genitive). The second interpretation fits the context better. See the helpful comments of Marshall (72).

The last half of v. 9 presents the same truth from a positive perspective. The one who continues to live according to the teachings he has received has "both the Father and the Son." In other words, if he continues to live according to the correct teaching he will continue to enjoy a personal relationship with God the Father and with Jesus the Son. See the comments of McDowell (227).

Verses 10, 11 give a very practical example of how these early Christians can hinder the spread of false doctrine. They can stop providing hospitality to the false teachers who are going from church to church spreading their heretical teachings. In the first century it was customary for Christian families to provide food and lodging to traveling missionaries. That did much to facilitate the spread of the Gospel in the Roman world. John is concerned that the false teachers will use this hospitality to further their evil ends.

The first part of v. 10, "if there come" states a condition that has come true or is likely to come true (Greek first class condition); see the analysis of Lenski (569). In other words, John is not responding to a hypothetical situation; the work of these false teachers is already well under way. John warns this Christian lady and her children not to fall into the trap of helping those who want to do damage to the faith.

The readers are given specific instructions not to receive the false teachers or to bid them God speed. In other words, this Christian family must not provide them with a place that they can use as a base of operations (Lenski 570). The phrase "neither bid him God speed" could be literally translated, "neither say to him 'Greetings.'" The idea is that

they are not even to wish him well in his work (Lenski 570).

Verse 11 explains why they are not to receive the false teachers or wish them well. If they do so, they will be sharing in their evil work. In the ancient world, providing hospitality to a wandering teacher was a sign of one's approval of his teaching (McDowell 228). Kruse (212) points out that accepting a visitor into one's household gave to that visitor a certain legal standing. He would then "enjoy the protection afforded by the local laws."

John's instructions may seem harsh to modern ears, but they should be understood against the background of the serious danger that the churches of Asia Minor were confronting. As McDowell (228) correctly notes, "The apparent harshness or even un-Christian nature of the prohibition testifies to the seriousness of the heresy and its inroads into Christian ranks." Heresy must never be taken lightly.

IV. CLOSING REMARKS (vv. 12, 13)

12 Having many things to write unto you, I would not *write* with paper and ink: but I trust to come unto you, and speak face to face, that our joy may be full.
13 The children of thy elect sister greet thee. Amen.

These two verses form a rather abrupt conclusion to John's brief, personal letter. The letter may end so abruptly because the author is nearing the bottom of his sheet of papyrus (McDowell 228). He has more that he would like to write, but he does not have space to do so. Therefore, he will share the remainder of his message with his friends in oral form when he goes to visit them.

Another possible understanding is that the author ends the letter abruptly because he prefers to communicate the rest of his message to them orally. That would give him the opportunity to share with them and answer their questions in a more personal manner. It will also give to John and his disciples the joy of being together. (See Marshall 76.) Lenski (571) suggests that John may wish to discuss with the family the matter of Diotrephes (a person we will meet in 3 John). Since this is such an important matter, it should be handled face to face rather than by letter.

The "paper" (Greek *chartos*) is papyrus, a writing material made from certain plants that grew in the marshes of the rivers of the ancient Near East (especially the Nile). It was one of the cheapest and most readily available writing materials in the first century. Most modern scholars are of the opinion that every book in the N.T. was written originally on papyrus. (See Brooke 179.) The ink (Greek *melanos)* was mixed by the writer primarily from soot and water (Stott 215).

In the second half of v. 12 John expresses his desire to visit the family personally. This visit will bring great joy both to the aged Apostle and to this dedicated family. Most commentators understand the words "the children of thy elect sister" to be a reference to the members of the church from which John was writing (probably Ephesus), although if this letter is addressed to a particular "lady," her "sister" could just as easily be taken literally. (See Burge 237; Lenski 572; and McDowell 228.) These churches were standing together in love and fellowship. They also were

involved in the same struggle against a dangerous heresy. Verse 13 is an eloquent expression of the mutual love and concern that exists between the aged Apostle and his spiritual children.

Summary
(vv. 1-13)

Second John has much in common with First John and with the Gospel of John (Dodd lx). Verses 5-7 are largely a summary of the teaching given in 1 John (Dodd lxiv). Second John seems to grow out of the same set of historical circumstances as First John and is much concerned with the spread of heresy. There are two main themes that are intertwined throughout this brief Epistle: truth and love. As Dodd (146) correctly notes there is for this author "no real charity, no Christian fellowship in the proper sense of the term, which does not rest upon a sincere acceptance of the Christian faith in its totality." The heretical doctrines which are spreading rapidly threaten to destroy the Christian life as these believers have come to know it (Dodd 146). For the Apostle John there is no conflict between living a life of love and standing firm for the truths of the gospel. The Christians must do both. They must not allow their battle for truth to destroy their love. Neither should they allow their love to lead them into accepting false teachings. They must maintain a proper balance between truth and love.

Spiritual understanding is a major theme of this letter. In the difficult environment of Asia Minor in the first century, ignorance was a dangerous thing. These Christians had received the truth from reliable witnesses, but an early form of the Gnostic heresy had come to challenge what they had been taught. They needed a good understanding of what they believed and why they believed it. They had to understand the difference between truth and error.

This epistle emphasizes faithfulness and perseverance. Verse 8 points out that the Christian life is not always easy; believers must always examine themselves to be sure that they continue to live and believe as God wants them to. They must always be vigilant to avoid falling into error.

This letter reminds us of the trials and difficulties that early Christian communities faced every day. Opposition came both from without and from within. All believers did not remain faithful to the message they had received; many were carried away by false teachings that sounded very attractive. Without doubt many families and churches were divided. These church members needed sufficient spiritual discernment and fortitude to accept that which was good and reject that which was bad.

Application: Teaching and Preaching the Passage

This brief letter was written many centuries ago in a context vastly different from the western world of the twenty-first century, but many of its themes are just as relevant as when John first wrote them. There are many important lessons that should be stressed as we preach and teach from 2 John.

The first important lesson is that doctrine matters. We live in a world that often says in one way or another, "It doesn't matter what you believe as long as you are sincere." Second John warns us of the danger of such relativistic thinking. There is a difference between truth and error, and Christians need to learn the truth and live by it.

The doctrine of Christ is the special emphasis of this letter. Throughout history cults and sects have often twisted or distorted Biblical teaching about Christ. Modern believers need to understand this important doctrine and teach it correctly. We must never forget that our beliefs have eternal consequences. We must always defend the truth—though not with bitterness but with a loving spirit.

The second great lesson we can learn from 2 John concerns love. This epistle addresses the subject of Christian love from two distinct perspectives. It emphasizes both the necessity of Christian love and its content. Genuine love is a necessary element within the Christian fellowship. This epistle bears eloquent testimony to the loving relationship that existed between the aged Apostle and the Christians with whom he worked.

The term "love," however, cannot be deprived of its content. If separated from the teachings of Christ it has little real meaning. Marshall (68) correctly notes, "The relevance of the elder's point is obvious in the modern situation where we are sometimes told, 'All you need is love.' Such advice is meaningless if the nature of love is not defined and unfolded." Within the Christian faith, love must be more than an emotion. It must include a firm commitment to the true gospel and to those who live by it.

A word of warning to modern-day believers: we must remember that the Apostle John is responding to a serious doctrinal error involving a basic teaching of the faith. He is not dealing with the kind of ordinary disagreements that Christians often face. Marshall (71) comments, "It should be noted that the elder's attack is on those who strike at the heart of Christian belief, not at those who may have happened to differ from him on theological points of lesser importance." This epistle does not justify bitter attacks against others just because they may not share our viewpoint on a particular issue.

This brief letter has never received the attention it deserves in preaching and teaching. It makes an important contribution to the overall teaching of the N.T., and that contribution should be recognized.

COMMENTARY ON THIRD JOHN

INTRODUCTION

Third John is the shortest book in the N.T.; according to Akin (235), the Greek text contains only 219 words. It is also the only letter of John specifically addressed to an individual by name. Lenski (577) suggests that 2 and 3 John were probably written on the same day to the same destination: 2 John was written to the entire congregation while 3 John was addressed to an individual within the congregation. Each of these brief letters was probably written on a single sheet of papyrus. There are many similarities in grammar and writing style between the two; Akin (235, 236) charts the most important similarities.

In content, 3 John is different from 2 John. The author is not concerned with the serious doctrinal problems that he had to confront in 1 and 2 John. The problems are more practical in nature. They concern a certain church member who was attacking the Apostle John and refusing to provide hospitality to the emissaries that John sent to visit the churches. (See Burge 244, 245.)

This brief letter reminds modern believers that conditions were not always perfect in first-century churches; they faced problems that were often strikingly similar to those faced in local churches today. These early followers of Christ often faced enemies both from without and within. The Christian faith has always had to stand against both doctrinal error and those who try to hinder the work because of their own pride and ego.

There are three principal characters in the story, all mentioned by name: Gaius, Diotrephes, and Demetrius. The letter is addressed to Gaius who is a close friend and ally of the Apostle John. The same name, common in the first century, occurs in four other places in the N.T. (Acts 19:29; 20:4; Rom. 16:23; 1 Cor. 1:14), probably describing several different individuals. We know nothing more about this person than the information contained in the letter. There is a Christian tradition that John ordained Gaius as Bishop of Pergamum, but there is no hard evidence to substantiate the tradition, and most authorities discount it (Akin 239).

He must have been a man of some means because he customarily provided hospitality to traveling missionaries. This ministry was a great help to John and his representatives as they visited the churches, won people to Christ, and helped develop the work. Lenski (578) suggests that this Epistle was carried to Gaius by missionaries sent by John. It served as a letter of introduction for them. John speaks well of Gaius and has high regard for his history of Christian service. He is confident that Gaius will again show hospitality to his representatives, as in the past. See Dodd (156) for a summary of what is known about him.

The second character in the story is Diotrephes, who will be discussed in greater depth in the commentary. Here, it is sufficient to say that he is not willing to show the same hospitality to traveling missionaries that Gaius has shown. John does not accuse him of doctrinal error, but of arrogance, shown in refusing to accept missionaries sent by John and in casting out of the church those who would receive John's emissaries.

The third character in the story is Demetrius, who receives only brief mention. He is commonly thought to be the bearer of the letter and the leader of the team of missionaries that John had sent (Akin 250; Dodd 166l; Kruse 232; Lenski 590; Moffatt 477, 478; Plummer, Third Epistle 3). Nothing more is known about him than the information in this Epistle. Probably John mentions him by name because he was not personally known to Gaius.

THE OUTLINE OF THIRD JOHN

I.   Greetings, 1-4
II. Commendation of Gaius, 5-8
III. Condemnation of Diotrephes, 9, 10
IV. The Apostle's Admonition, 11, 12
V.   Conclusion, 13, 14

I. GREETINGS (vv. 1-4)

1 The elder unto the wellbeloved Gaius, whom I love in the truth.
2 Beloved, I wish above all things that thou mayest prosper and be in health, even as thy soul prospereth.
3 For I rejoiced greatly, when the brethren came and testified of the truth that is in thee, even as thou walkest in the truth.
4 I have no greater joy than to hear that my children walk in truth.

Third John follows the customary letter writing practices of the first century, first identifying the author. As in 2 John, he is simply called the "elder." (See the Introduction and comments on 2 Jn. 1.) The traditional interpretation is that this is a reference to the Apostle John. The letter next introduces the recipient, Gaius. This was a common name in the first century; others in the N.T. by that name were not necessarily the same persons.

John uses two significant phrases to describe Gaius, thus indicating something of the nature of their relationship. He first calls Gaius "wellbeloved" (Greek *agapetos*), usually rendered, simply, "beloved." John then follows with the phrase "whom I love in the truth." These phrases indicate something of the special relationship which existed between John and Gaius.

"Whom I love in the truth" can be interpreted in two different ways. Dodd (157) points out that this type of phrase was common in first-century letters and may mean nothing more than "whom I sincerely love." (See also Kruse 220.) The second, and more likely, interpreta-

tion is that John and Gaius have developed such a close and long-lasting relationship because they have stood together in defending the truth of the gospel in the face of opposition. Defending the truth of the gospel is a major theme of all John's Epistles. It occurs four times in the first four verses of this letter. (See Dodd 157; Kruse 220; and Lenski 577.)

The second verse continues the personal greeting that John is sending to his close friend. This verse is probably an expansion of "I pray that you may keep well," a phrase common in letter-openings of this period (Dodd 157). The verb "prosper" (Greek *euodoo*) expresses the idea "to have a good journey" (Dodd 157). Lenski (579) suggests that these words imply more than John's personal care and concern for his friend. They refer to Gaius' ability to provide for the needs of the traveling missionaries that John is sending to him. The word "soul" (Greek *psuche*) is used in several different ways in the N.T. In the writings of John it is often used in the sense of "one's natural life." Sometimes it is used to express the idea of one's inner life as opposed to his outer or physical life (Kruse 221). Here the idea seems to focus on the totality of Gaius' life. John's prayer is that all aspects of his life—physical, mental, and spiritual—may go well.

Verse 3 refers to events about which we know nothing more than what is written here. Apparently John had sent an earlier group of traveling missionaries to this area, and they returned with a good report of Gaius and his work. The verb "walkest" (Greek present tense) often expresses the idea of continuing action. The idea here is that John's emissaries had reported that Gaius continued to walk, or live, in the truth.

Verse 4 concludes this section with a general statement. The Apostle John is the most important Christian leader in the area and bears much of the responsibility for directing the missionary work going on in Asia Minor. He is filled with joy when his spiritual children remain faithful to their commitment to the truth of the gospel.

II. COMMENDATION OF GAIUS (vv. 5-8)

5 Beloved, thou doest faithfully whatsoever thou doest to the brethren, and to strangers.
6 Which have borne witness of thy charity before the church: whom if thou bring forward on their journey after a godly sort, thou shalt do well:
7 Because that for his name's sake they went forth, taking nothing of the Gentiles.
8 We therefore ought to receive such, that we might be fellowhelpers to the truth.

These verses give us a brief overview of Gaius' personal commitment to the missionary work in Asia Minor. He used his time, talents, and resources to further the spread of the gospel.

Wandering teachers and philosophers of all kinds were common in the first century (McDowell 229). Paul and other early Christian missionaries traveled from place to place as they preached the good news along the major trade routes of Asia Minor. Some forty years later the Apostle John used the same strategy as he sent missionaries and teachers to plant new churches and

develop existing churches. Gaius made a significant contribution to this effort by providing hospitality to those whom John sent.

The words "thou doest faithfully" indicate that Gaius' hospitality was an outgrowth of the genuine faith that was within him (see Brooke 183, 184). Plummer (*Third Epistle 2*) suggests that the meaning is "to act as a faithful man would." The "brethren" are probably Christian missionaries personally known to Gaius. The "strangers" probably describe Christian workers not personally known to him.

The main idea of v. 6 is that when these missionaries return to their home base (probably Ephesus), they always testify to the goodness and love of Gaius. Plummer (*Third Epistle 2*) translates the last part of v. 6, "Whom thou wilt do well to forward on their journey in a manner worthy of God." These words are a commendation. They recognize Gaius' commitment to helping these missionaries on their way.

Verse 7 focuses the readers' attention on the missionaries. They do not ask for money as pagan teachers often did. They travel "asking nothing of the Gentiles"; they are not asking for contributions from the unsaved Gentiles to whom they preach (Plummer, *Third Epistle 2*). Their only goal is to further the cause of Christ, and they will not compromise the integrity of their ministry.

In v. 8, "receive" (Greek *apolambano* or *hupolambano*, depending on the manuscript) means "to receive with hospitality" or "to support" (Brooke 187). The teaching is that all believers should imitate the example of Gaius. They should become fellow workers with him

118

in spreading the truth of the gospel wherever they can (Brooke 187).

III. CONDEMNATION OF DIOTREPHES (vv. 9, 10)

9 I wrote unto the church: but Diotrephes, who loveth to have the preeminence among them, receiveth us not.
10 Wherefore, if I come, I will remember his deeds which he doeth, prating against us with malicious words: and not content therewith, neither doth he himself receive the brethren, and forbiddeth them that would, and casteth *them* out of the church.

The opening words of v. 9 refer to a previous letter that John had sent to the church to which Diotrephes belonged. The contents of this letter are never explained. There is some possibility that this may refer to 2 John, but Moody (130), along with most interpreters, posits that it is probably a lost letter. These words are probably included to remind Gaius that problems with Diotrephes are not new. John has been dealing with him for some time. Dodd (161) points out that there is nothing in 3 John that connects it with the doctrinal controversy addressed in 2 John. Neither is there any reference in 2 John to the conflict with Diotrephes.

The most likely assumption is that the earlier letter mentioned here is not 2 John. Apparently Diotrephes did not like what John wrote in that letter, and it served only to harden his opposition to the Apostle's ministry. The last words of v. 9 express the idea that Diotrephes refused to recognize John's authority as an apostle of Christ (Brooke 189).

Brooke (187) assumes that Diotrephes and Gaius were members of the same local church, but evidence of that is not conclusive. All that can be said with certainty is that Gaius is aware of the conflict and may have been involved in it. Dodd (161) suggests that Gaius was a member of a neighboring congregation.

John makes three principal accusations against Diotrephes. First, he was always seeking "the preeminence": in other words, he was seeking to be the one in control and refused to recognize the authority of the Apostle John. Second, he is "prating against us with malicious words." "Prating" (Greek phluareo) occurs only here in the Greek N.T. and expresses the idea of idle or empty chatter. As Brooke (190) correctly notes, "It emphasizes the emptiness of the charges which Diotrephes brings against the Elder."

The third accusation is that he used his power and influence to control the actions of others in the church and prevent them from aiding in the missionary efforts of the Apostle John. See the comments of Moody (131, 132). There are two possible interpretations of the last words of v. 10. One is that Diotrephes was in fact excommunicating those who insisted on remaining loyal to John and his missionary program. The other is he was trying to excommunicate those who remained faithful to the Apostle. (See Dodd 162; and Lenski 588.)

John could not allow such a situation to proceed unchallenged. The actions of Diotrephes were not only doing harm to John's missionary efforts, they were also dominating and controlling the actions of the local congregation in an improper way. His plan is to visit this area and confront Diotrephes personally. John's hope is that a face-to-face meeting with him may help resolve the issues. The phrase "I will remember his deeds" means that John will appear publicly in a meeting of the church and recount what this man has done (Lenski 587).

The words "if I come" (Greek *ean eltho*) may also be translated "when I come." The type of grammatical construction used (Greek third class condition) implies that there is some level of doubt in the author's mind. There is no doubt that John wanted to make the trip to resolve the important issues at stake. There is some doubt, however, that he would be able to make the trip. (See Lenski 586, 587.)

IV. THE APOSTLE'S ADMONITION (vv. 11, 12)

11 Beloved, follow not that which is evil, but that which is good. He that doeth good is of God: but he that doeth evil hath not seen God. 12 Demetrius hath good report of all *men*, and of the truth itself: yea, and we *also* bear record; and ye know that our record is true.

At first glance, John's admonition in v. 11 seems unnecessary. The fact that the word "beloved" is singular in Greek indicates that the verse is directed specifically to Gaius, who had been a friend and supporter of the Apostle for some time. Why should it be necessary to remind such a faithful worker of the need to avoid evil? In its context, this exhortation should be understood as a gentle reminder to Gaius not to imitate the evil example of Diotrephes (Dodd 165). The words "follow not" (Greek *me mimou*, present tense imperative) could also be translated "do not imitate." They

mean "don't have the habit of imitating" (Akin 249).

The remaining words of v. 11 are a general exhortation to do that which is good and avoid that which is evil. The one who does good is "of God" in the sense that he is motivated by God and his actions are done to please God. Moody (132) suggests that "doing good" in this context means "keeping or following the new commandment to love." According to Moody (132, 133), doing evil is "to hate." In his view, the one who does evil "hath not seen God" in the person and work of Jesus Christ. Perhaps John is suggesting that Diotrephes has never truly known God.

Verse 12 serves to introduce Demetrius, who is probably the bearer of the letter and the leader of the missionary team that John has sent. Perhaps John mentions him by name in the letter because he is personally unknown to Gaius (Lenski 590). Then the Apostle turns attention to the reasons he has entrusted such an important mission to him. First, Demetrius has a "good report of all men." Probably this refers to those in and around the city of Ephesus with whom Demetrius had worked (Lenski 591). In other words, Demetrius was no neophyte; he had earned the trust and confidence of those among whom he had ministered.

Second, John points out that Demetrius has the testimony "of the truth itself." There are two possible interpretations of these words. One option is that the Apostle means "the facts speak for themselves"; Demetrius does not have to depend on the testimony of others; his own actions demonstrate the truth of his ministry (Moody 133). The other is that Demetrius has consistently stood for the truth of the

Gospel in the face of the incipient Gnosticism then sweeping Asia Minor (Moody 133). The precise meaning of the phrase is difficult to determine, but either interpretation makes good sense within the context of this Epistle.

The third testimony is that of John and his colleagues: "We also bear record." John and the other leaders of the church in Ephesus know Demetrius personally and have confidence in his leadership and in his commitment to the truth. Brooke (193, 194) correctly notes that "we" is used in several different ways in the Johannine writings and provides a helpful analysis of them.

The last phrase "and ye know that our record is true" is a reminder to Gaius and the other members of the church that John has been a faithful leader for a long time. They can have confidence in the ambassador that he has sent.

V. CONCLUSION (vv. 13, 14)

13 I had many things to write, but I will not with ink and pen write unto thee:
14 But I trust I shall shortly see thee, and we shall speak face to face. Peace be to thee. Our friends salute thee. Greet the friends by name.

Verse 13 is very similar to the first words of 2 Jn. 12. According to Lenski (592), this similarity makes it likely that these two brief letters were written at the same time. This verse also explains why John is terminating the letter at this point. He is probably near the bottom of a sheet of papyrus and does not wish to continue on a second sheet. For a discussion of *paper*, see the comments on

2 Jn. 12. The "pen" (Greek *kalamos*) commonly describes a writing instrument cut from a reed and dipped in the ink (Brooke 194).

Since John enjoys a personal relationship with Gaius, it is only natural that he prefers to continue the conversation in person. Brooke (194) notes that the difficult situation in the church may add a greater sense of urgency to John's desire to visit Gaius.

Verse 14 contains several expressions that are common Christian farewells of the first century. The word "peace" probably refers to the peace with God that Christians enjoy. John knows that they have a special need for God's peace in the midst of conflict. The second phrase (literally, *the friends salute thee*) may mean either "*our* friends" or "*your* friends" send their greetings to Gaius. The latter translation makes better sense in the context, but the difference is not great. John is writing from Ephesus where, no doubt, Gaius has many Christian friends who send their greetings as well.

"We shall speak face to face" expresses a desire to communicate directly rather than by letter. Such expressions are common in letters of this time period (Kruse 234). The last words, "greet the friends by name," are a literal translation of the Greek text and probably mean, "Greet our friends by name." Just as Gaius has friends in Ephesus, the Apostle John has Christian friends in the church to which Gaius belongs. He wishes to send his greetings to them.

Summary
(vv. 1-14)

This brief letter should be seen from within the larger context of First and

Second John. In these two Epistles the emphasis is on standing fast against the false teachers who were causing division and strife within the churches of Asia Minor in the late first century. The basic conflict is between the true gospel that John and his associates were proclaiming and the heretical doctrines taught by the false teachers.

Third John also reflects the theme of conflict, but a different type of conflict that is more organizational and personal. It was John's custom to send out traveling preachers from his base of operations (probably Ephesus). These preachers helped found new churches, disciple those who had already been won to the faith, and watch out for the spread of heresy within the churches. It is quite likely that they also served as John's eyes and ears; they kept him informed about what was going on.

A group of these wandering missionaries returned home and reported to John about the faithfulness of his friend Gaius and the problems that were being caused by Diotrephes (Kistemaker 216). The problems seem to be more personal than doctrinal in nature. Diotrephes wanted to be the undisputed ruler of the church. He refused to recognize the authority of the Apostle John and sought the excommunication of any church members who dared to challenge him. Perhaps he had even dismissed Gaius from the church (Lenski 549). It is also possible that Diotrephes had not expelled Gaius and that Gaius belonged to a neighboring congregation (Kistemaker 216).

Diotrephes had refused to heed a previous communication, and John's only option is to make a trip to confront Diotrephes and attempt to remedy the conflict. John sends this letter to Gaius to commend him for the hospitality he has extended to traveling missionaries and to advise him of his plans to make a personal visit. He also wants to prepare Gaius for the upcoming meeting with Diotrephes.

Two important ideas stand out in this letter. First, John expresses his great love for the gospel and for those believers who are working with him to share it in Asia Minor. They are his true brothers and sisters in the faith; he is committed to them and cares about them deeply. Both the verb and the noun for *love* appear many times in John's Epistles.

Second, this letter reflects John's determination to do everything he can to remedy this personal conflict that has the potential to do great harm to the work. John is more concerned with the effective spread of the gospel than with his personal position and authority. He has no desire for a confrontation with Diotrephes, but in this situation he has no other option. Diotrephes' attitude and conduct are doing great harm to the spread of the gospel, and something must be done.

John does not wish to take Gaius and the other faithful Christians by surprise. He writes this letter to them and sends it by the hand of Demetrius so that these faithful men and women can prepare for John's visit. Perhaps there is the unspoken prayer that this brief letter will cause Diotrephes to reconsider what he is doing and change his ways before it is too late.

Application: Teaching and Preaching the Passage

Because of its brevity and personal nature, this letter has never received the

3 JOHN

attention it deserves. Early Christian writers make few references to it (Lenski 551). Brooke (lxxi) gives a list of the early Greek and Latin commentaries on the Johannine Epistles; as a general rule, they pay little attention to 3 John. This lack of emphasis is understandable but unfortunate. Although it is the shortest book in the N.T., 3 John is very useful for preaching and teaching. It develops several themes that were important in the first century and are equally important today.

First, this letter is important from a historical perspective. Our knowledge of the Christian faith in the closing years of the first century is fragmentary. This letter helps us to understand something of the personal and organizational dynamics of churches at that time. We see that first-century churches were not perfect; they always had to struggle against opposition from without and within.

Early believers were not perfect either. They did not always get along with each other. There were those like Gaius who were willing to serve at great personal sacrifice. Then there were those like Diotrephes who were determined to control the church and use it to further their own selfish ends. The lesson for believers is that we must serve within churches that are imperfect and with people who are not always what they ought to be. In our preaching and teaching we must continually remind people that the work of God on earth is done by men and women, not by angels. God can and does use us in spite of our faults and failures.

Second, this letter is important because of what it tells about resolving conflicts within the Christian community. We should, however, proceed with caution in this area. We must remember

that this is a personal letter dealing with a specific situation. John is not saying that all conflicts can or should be resolved as he has worked to resolve this one. He is, however, laying out several general principles that Christian leaders can use when they confront situations of conflict.

It is important to note that John did not give up on Diotrephes or on the church that he was leading astray. John maintained contact with them; he wrote letters; he sent emissaries; he planned a personal visit. It would have been easy for the Apostle to withdraw from this painful situation, but he was willing to risk personal insult and injury in an effort to resolve the problems and salvage as many people as he could for the Christian faith. Modern Christians can learn important lessons about perseverance, patience, and tenacity from this letter.

John understood his limitations and sought the counsel of others. He sent representatives with whom he talked upon their return. It is very likely that John wrote this letter and sent representatives to the house of Gaius because he wanted to hear Gaius' understanding of the conflict. John respected Gaius' judgment. He also understood that Gaius was much closer to the situation than he was. Christian leaders today also need to seek out the counsel of those who are mature in the faith.

Third, this letters points out the need for firmness and strength of character. John dealt with his opponents with courtesy and tact, but he refused to allow a strong personality to run over him or to dominate the church in an unchristian manner. He was committed both to the truth of the gospel and to the church. He was determined to do what

123

was necessary to keep the gospel moving forward in Asia Minor. Christian leaders of any period face formidable obstacles. They also need the firmness and strength of character that John demonstrates in this Epistle.

BIBLIOGRAPHY: WORKS CITED IN THIS COMMENTARY
(cited by author's last name)

Akin, Daniel L., *1, 2, 3 John* (NAC, Broadman and Holman, 2001).

Arndt, William F., and Gingrich, F. Wilbur, *A Greek-English Lexicon of the New Testament and Other Early Christian Literature* (University of Chicago Press, 1957).

Barker, Glenn W., *1 John* (EBC, Zondervan, 1981).

Becker, Ulrich and Müller, Heinrich, "Proclamation, Preach, Kerygma" in *The New International Dictionary of New Testament Theology* (III:44-68), ed. Colin Brown (Zondervan, 1978).

Beyer, Hartmut, *Las Cartas De Juan* (Editorial CLIE, 1998).

Brodie, Thomas L., *The Gospel According to John* (Oxford University Press, 1993).

Brooke, A. E., *The Johannine Epistles* (ICC, Charles Scribner's Sons, 1912).

Bruce, F. F., *The Epistles of John* (Eerdmans, 1970).

Burge, Gary M., *The Letters of John* (NIV Application Commentary, Zondervan, 1996).

Carson, D. A., Moo, Douglas J., and Morris, Leon, *An Introduction to the New Testament* (Zondervan, 1992).

Clemance, C., "The First Epistle General of John" in *The Pulpit Commentary* (XXII:105-19), ed. H. D. M. Spence and Joseph S. Exell (Eerdmans, 1950).

Cox, Leo G., *First, Second, and Third John* (WBC vol. six, Eerdmans, 1966).

Dodd, C. H., *The Johannine Epistles* (Harper and Brothers, 1946).

Elwell, W. A., and Comfort, P. W., "Eternal Life" in *Tyndale Bible Dictionary* (Tyndale House, 2001).

Fee, Gordon D., and Douglas Stuart. *How to Read the Bible for All Its Worth,* third edition (Zondervan, 2003)

Graber, Friedrich, "Amen, Hallelujah, Hosanna" in *The New International Dictionary of New Testament Theology* (I:97-99), ed. Colin Brown (Zondervan, 1975).

Grayston, Kenneth, *The Johannine Epistles* (NCBC, Eerdmans, 1984).

Gromacki, Robert G., *New Testament Survey* (Baker, 1974).

Guhrt, Joachim, "World" in *The New International Dictionary of New Testament Theology* (I:521-26), ed. Colin Brown (Zondervan, 1975).

Günther, Walther, "Brother, Neighbour, Friend" in *The New International Dictionary of New Testament Theology* (I:254-58), ed. Colin Brown (Zondervan, 1975).

Hahn, Hans-Christoph, "Light, Shine, Lamp" in *The New International Dictionary of New Testament Theology* (II:484-94), ed. Colin Brown (Zondervan, 1976).

Hunter, Archibald M., *Introducing the New Testament* (2nd ed., Westminster, 1957).

Jackman, David. *The Message of John's Letters* (The Bible Speaks Today. Edited by J. A. Motyer and John R. W. Stott. (InterVarsity Press, 1988)

Kauder, Erwin, "Antichrist" in *The New International Dictionary of New Testament Theology* (I:124-26), ed. Colin Brown (Zondervan, 1975).

Keener, Craig S., *The IVP Bible Background Commentary: New Testament* (InterVarsity, 1993).

Kistemaker, Simon J., *James and I-III John* (NTC, Baker, 1986).

Kittel, Gerhard, Ἀκούω in *Theological Dictionary of the New Testament* (I:216-21), trans. and ed. Geoffrey W. Bromiley (Eerdmans, 1964).

Kruse, Colin G., *The Letters of John* (PNTC, Eerdmans, 2000).

Law, Robert, *The Tests of Life* (3rd ed., Baker, 1968).

Lenski, R. C. H., *The Interpretation of The Epistles of St. Peter, St. John, and St. Jude* (Augsburg, 1966).

Lieu, Judith M., *I, II, & III John: A Commentary* (NTL, John Knox, 2008).

Marshall, I. Howard, *The Epistles of John* (NICNT, Eerdmans, 1978).

McDowell, Edward A., *1-2-3 John* (BBC, Broadman, 1972).

Michel, Otto, "Faith" in *The New International Dictionary of New Testament Theology* (I:587-606), ed. Colin Brown (Zondervan, 1975).

Moffatt, James, *An Introduction to the Literature of the New Testament* (ITL, T. & T. Clark, 1911).

Moody, Dale, *The Letters of John* (Word, 1970).

Morris, Leon, "2 John, 3 John" in *New Bible Commentary*, ed. D. Guthrie and J. A. Motyer (Eerdmans, 1970).

Müller, Dietrich, "Anoint" in *The New International Dictionary of New Testament Theology* (I:119-24), ed. Colin Brown (Zondervan, 1975).

Plummer, A., "The Epistles of St. John, Introduction" in *The Pulpit Commentary* (XXII:i-xii), ed. H.D. M. Spence and Joseph S. Exell (Eerdmans, 1962).

_____, "The First Epistle General of John" in *The Pulpit Commentary* (XXII:1-174), ed. H. D. M. Spence and Joseph S. Exell (Eerdmans, 1962).

_____, "The Second Epistle of John" in *The Pulpit Commentary* (XXII:1-18), ed. H. D. M. Spence and Joseph S. Exell (Eerdmans, 1962).

_____, "The Third Epistle of John" in *The Pulpit Commentary* (XXII:1-18), ed. H. D. M. Spence and Joseph S. Exell (Eerdmans, 1962).

Ramsay, W. M., "Roads and Travel in the New Testament" in *A Dictionary of the Bible: Extra Volume*, ed. James Hastings (T. & T. Clark, 1904).

Robertson, Archibald Thomas, *Word Pictures in the New Testament*, vol. VI (Broadman, 1933)

Schönweiss, Hans, "Desire, Lust, Pleasure" in *The New International Dictionary of New Testament Theology* (I:456-58), ed. Colin Brown (Zondervan, 1976).

Schütz, Eduard, "Knowledge, Experience, Ignorance" in *The New International Dictionary of New Testament Theology* (II:390-409), ed. Colin Brown (Zondervan, 1976).

Smalley, S. S., *1, 2, 3 John* (WBC, Word, 1984).

Smith, David, "The Epistles of John" in *The Expositor's Greek Testament*, vol. V, (Eerdmans, 1967).

Stallings, Jack W., *The Gospel of John* (RHBC, Randall House, 1989).

Stott, John R. W., *The Letters of John*, 2nd ed. (TNTC, Eerdmans, 1988).

Thayer, Joseph Henry, *A Greek-English Lexicon of the New Testament* (Baker, 1977).

Thiselton, A. C., "Flesh" in *The New International Dictionary of New Testament Theology* (I:678-82), ed. Colin Brown (Zondervan, 1976).

Vorländer, Herward, "Forgiveness" in *The New International Dictionary of New Testament Theology* (I:697-703), ed. Colin Brown (Zondervan, 1975).

Westcott, Brooke Foss, *The Epistles of St. John: The Greek Text With Notes* (Eerdmans, 1966).

Wilson, R. McL., *Gnosis and The New Testament* (Basil Blackwell, 1968).

Wilson, R. McL., *The Gnostic Problem* (A. R. Mowbray & Co., 1958).

Wuest, Kenneth W., *Wuest's Word Studies from the Greek New Testament*, vols. 3, 4 (Eerdmans, 1966).

Yamauchi, Edwin M., *Pre-Christian Gnosticism* (Tyndale, 1973).

Yarbrough, Robert W., *1-3 John* (BECNT, Baker Academic, 2008).

Commentary on the Book
of Revelation
by
Gwyn Pugh

COMMENTARY ON THE BOOK OF REVELATION

INTRODUCTION

Preliminary Considerations

The Book of Revelation has been an interpretive enigma throughout church history, partly because we view it through the smog of mysterious apocalyptic images. Otherwise known as The Apocalypse (Greek *apokalupsis*, 1:1), it is the New Testament's prime example of "apocalyptic" literature. Apocalyptic means an unveiling, a revealing of something hidden and perhaps future. Apocalyptic literature is a class of writings, especially ancient Jewish ones, characterized by visions and symbols intended to reveal mysteries about the role of the heavenly realm in earthly affairs. Much of Daniel, in the O.T., is apocalyptic, as are many apocryphal and pseudepigraphical writings of the post-captivity Jews and early Christians. It is strikingly ironic, therefore, that a work intended to reveal has often been found to cloud the truth. Apocalyptic imagery is by its very nature subject to more than one interpretation. (For an introduction to apocalyptic literature, see Mounce 1-8.)

But the major themes of Revelation are clear enough. God's purpose, as the title to the book suggests, is to reveal or unveil; "revelation" in the N.T. is especially associated with the Second Coming of Christ. Introduced by John in 1:1, 7 (cf. 22:7, 12, 20), this future eschatological event resonates throughout the book. This is true even in the letters to the seven historical churches of first-century Roman "Asia" in chapters 2 and 3. Christ's own predictions of His coming added weight to His exhortations to the churches (2:25; 3:11; cf. 2 Pet. 3:10).

Other important themes are also discernible. One is that Jesus will personally defeat the forces of evil, judge all mankind by the gospel, banish Satan and unbelievers to Hell, and reward the saints with eternal life in a new Heaven and earth minus sin. Another gives us a vision of Heaven, where the primary activity is the worship of God: its incredible beauty, its songs, its diverse population by an almost infinite number of angels and representatives of various groups of redeemed mankind. The quality of eternal life is described, including not only new things but also the absence of negative or sinful things, unbelievers, death, tears, sorrow, the sun, the moon, and oceans. Spiritual warfare between God and Satan is also a prominent theme, moving toward eternal resolution in the final triumph of Christ.

In spite of the difficulties, there is significant consensus within the major schools of conservative interpretation. Everyone recognizes that Revelation teaches principles for Christian living, makes real historical references, uses symbolical language and speaks of the literal realities of Heaven, Hell, and

131

eternity—not to mention the Second Coming. (See Sanders 1 for common understandings.)

To think that God would deliberately obscure or confuse rather than reveal is absurd and contradicts God's stated purpose (1:1). Bible students often speak of the perspicuity of Scripture: that is, that its meaning is clear or understandable. Our confidence is that Revelation, though complex and debated, is as understandable as the rest of the Bible. Great blessing is promised to those who "read, hear and keep" the words of this book (1:3). To ignore its instruction at this critical juncture of world history, because it seems too difficult or controversial, potentially forfeits personal blessing and future readiness. Revelation clearly instructs as to what everyone ought to be doing about the future right now.

At least three other considerations warrant another commentary on Revelation. First, its message is relevant for our times, as it has been for every generation of believers and unbelievers alike—from the contemporaries of the Apostle John to the present, postmodern generation. We have entered a new millennium carrying the excess baggage of inordinate sensuality, social ills, apostasy, new age philosophy, random mass murders, global terrorism, and various fears about our national, economic, and personal futures. Humanistic solutions have proved powerless to retard the downward spiral into the abyss of moral, civic, judicial, and spiritual confusion. Most are ill-prepared for the future events described in Revelation—Christ's return, the judgment, the creation of a new Heaven and earth—or for personal, eternal consignment to Heaven or Hell. Revelation is a warning for some to repent of evil behavior and an encouragement for others to persevere for Christ in such a time as this. The church must review the sobering messages of Christ to the seven churches as a mirror and guide for present behavior.

Second, fresh exegetical exposition takes into account the added insight gleaned from the latest Biblical scholarship. There has been renewed interest in eschatology during the last decade of the twentieth century. The ability to discern truth from error and false prophets from faithful preachers is paramount and is facilitated by knowing the Bible well.

Third, Revelation equips believers with abiding principles applicable to any church or believer in any age of church history. Much of it is intended for practical living here and now (1:3).

Authorship and Canonicity

If there is not enough evidence that the Apostle John wrote the Book of Revelation, there is even less for others. The acids of higher criticism fail to dissolve the consensus of conservative scholarship as to its apostolic origin, unity, canonicity, and divine inspiration.

The danger of the so-called "higher" criticism of Scripture, which typically challenges traditional views of authorship, is that even the doctrines of inspiration and the miraculous may be doubted. Such scholarship often leaves the student of Scripture with the impression that the Bible is merely human, not providing a supernatural revelation from God through the Holy Spirit. Scripture is the very breath of God (Greek *theopneustos*) according to 2 Tim. 3:16. Peter adds that it was produced by the Holy Spirit and not by any man (2 Pet.

REVELATION

1:21). As Scripture, everything within Revelation comes from God. John does not slavishly mimic Jewish apocalyptic literature as a model to express his own hopes within a first-century worldview; instead, he writes what God has given him. There is evidence within the book itself that John's material sources were more Biblical than anything else, drawing especially from the O.T. and Jesus Himself. The unusual subject matter of Revelation accounts for differences of vocabulary, structure, and style between Revelation and John's other writings (the Gospel and three espistles).

Proposed alternatives to apostolic authorship are unimpressive. One early group (the "Alogoi") assigned all Johannine writings to a Gnostic heretic named Cerinthus, a contemporary of the Apostle John. Dionysius of Alexandria (ca. A.D. 247-264) attributed the book to an alternative "John the Elder" in Ephesus; but that this alternative John even existed is disputed because the evidence is based largely on the statement of one historian, Eusebius, quoting another, Papias. As Harris (258) notes, Dionysius' arguments against apostolicity were "from diction and style rather than from any positive evidence against the ancient tradition." Even if we grant the existence of John the Elder as a person distinct from the Apostle John, there is no evidence connecting him to Revelation.

Objections to apostolic authorship based on so-called incongruities between Revelation and the letters of John in matters of style, structure, grammatical solecisms, or common themes is a matter of subjective opinion. Indeed, there is a significant amount of obvious thematic and verbal similarity between Revelation and other Johannine writings, thus pointing to the one author as John the Apostle (see Thomas I:2-19).

Revelation passes all the tests of canonicity outlined by Harris (199-271). It is apostolic. It exhibits the marks of divine inspiration as opposed to the absurdities of non-canonical literature. It was accepted immediately by the earliest church fathers, thus passing the patristic test. It was included in the important lists of inspired writings recognized by the early church (e.g., the Muratorian canon, the third council of Carthage in A.D. 397), though not without a few dissenting voices along the way (cf. Mounce 23, 24; Harris 257-260). Athanasius is given credit for finalizing Revelation's position in the canon of Scripture.

Aune (I:xlviii) suggests, appropriately, that the question of authorship in the Bible is often affected more by one's presuppositions than by objectivity. Dionysius' theory that the writer was not John the Apostle was apparently influenced by his own anti-chiliast (i.e., non-millennial) viewpoint. Devoted to the allegorizing school, Dionysius vigorously opposed the idea of a literal, thousand-year reign of Christ on earth. We must not let theological bias of any kind, whether involving critical assumptions or eschatological views, color our conclusions about the authorship or dating (or *interpretation!*) of the Book or Revelation.

I accept the traditional view of authorship: that the Apostle John, son of Zebedee and beloved disciple of Jesus (Mt. 4:18-22), wrote Revelation. The author identifies himself as John in 1:1, 4, 9; 21:2; 22:8.

133

Date

This commentary relies on the majority of early church fathers closest to John's own time—as championed by Irenaeus (ca. A.D. 115-200)—and on many other recent conservative scholars (Beale 4-27; Guthrie 949-961; Mounce 15-21). John wrote Revelation while exiled on the island of Patmos (1:9) toward the end of Domitian's reign around A.D. 96. Exile was another method of Roman punishment, cruel in its own right, requiring varying degrees of hardship and deprivation according to the crime. Ramsay (60, 61) believes John's sentence was severe.

The traditional date is consistent with first-century history and fits the internal evidence equally well. The historical context of emperor worship and persecution might fit the reign of either Nero (ca. A.D. 54-68) or Domitian (ca. A.D. 81-96). But persecution was probably more widespread and intense by the time of the latter (Beale 5-27; Aune I:lvii-lxix). Nero's persecution was more localized and short-lived, and the churches in Asia Minor were far from Rome. The later date allows time for the churches to have come into existence and for the deterioration of faithfulness described in Christ's warnings.

Pergamum was *the* official center for emperor worship during Domitian's reign, having a temple of the imperial cult (DNTB 967, 968). This may reasonably be equated with "the throne of Satan" (2:13). At Smyrna brave and faithful Polycarp (ca. A.D. 69-156) was martyred for refusing to confess Caesar as Lord (ANF I:41). To recognize that the first-century church faced this kind of hostility in an extremely pagan and idolatrous environment, and that this probably was the historical background of Jesus' messages to the churches in chapters 1-3, should not conflict with any of the major approaches to interpreting Revelation.

John addressed his letter to the local pastors (the Greek *angelos*, as in 2:1, means "angel" or "messenger") and congregations of seven cities within the small, Roman province of Asia in western Asia Minor (1:4). Ramsay (132) suggests that the location of these churches, connected by a great circular road, may account for the order of their messages. This is the order in which they are addressed, beginning with Ephesus and proceeding clockwise around the circuit to Laodicea (3:14). John may well have meant for the book as a whole to be distributed, eventually, to additional churches in Asia Minor and throughout the world.

Schools of Interpretation

We should begin by insisting that exegetical compulsion should be the primary basis of interpretation. George Mueller once said to A. T. Pierson (in regard to arguments for the latter's millennial position): "My beloved brother... not one of them is based upon the word of God" (Clouse, *Manual* 95). We should strive to rise above theological or eschatological bias and to avoid errors of application associated with sensationalistic identifications of Antichrist or date-setting. A faithful examination of the text will yield principles for living which may be applied by any generation of believers to equip them for end-time events whenever they occur.

There are four major approaches to the interpretation of Revelation. Each aims to provide a framework for understanding the book as a whole. And within each school of thought there are varieties that modify existing parent views and even serve in a measure to harmonize tensions between competing viewpoints.

The four major approaches to interpreting the Book of Revelation are the Preterist, Idealist, Historicist, and Futurist. A brief summary of each follows.

1. Preterist (Past-time)

Preterists (from the Latin for "the past") locate the fulfillment of Revelation's visions somewhere in early church history: especially in the first century before the fall of Jerusalem in A.D. 70, but possibly extending to the fifth century with the fall of Rome in A.D. 476 (Beale 44-46). "The sustained attempt to root the fulfillment of the divine prophecies of Revelation in the first century A.D. constitutes the preterist's distinctive approach" (Pate 19).

Mounce (27) finds the reasoning behind this view in the demands for emperor worship in the late first century and the severe testing of the church that resulted. Thus the preterist view, rather than relegating the book to some future period of time, sees its encouragements and warnings as having immediate application for the plight of the first-century churches to which it was first sent.

Revelation might be categorized, according to the preterist view, as a handbook on persecution, written for believers in John's day to encourage perseverance in a pagan environment hostile to Christianity. In light of dangers present then (emperor worship, idolatry, sensuality, false doctrines, and the threat of martyrdom), assurance of final justice or victory in the end was a welcome message.

The preterist emphasizes such statements as "things which must shortly take place" (1:1), or the warning that "the time is near" (1:3). These seem to put the entire book in the near future when written. Then the references to Christ's "coming" (as in 1:7) do not mean the Second Coming at the end of time but a "coming in judgment" upon first-century Jews for crucifying Christ. The ultimate event of this judgment would be the destruction of Jerusalem (A.D. 70). God's program for Israel would then cease once for all, His attention from then on shifted to the church and all nations (see Gen. 12:3).

This way, the opening of the book with seven seals, at the heart of Revelation (5:1-11:19), amounts to a divorce decree between God and his O. T. wife for spiritual adultery (Gentry, *Four Views* 51, 52). This includes the trumpet judgments, seen as continuing descriptions of the horrors the Jews experienced in their war against Rome culminating in Jerusalem's destruction (cf. Josephus 698, 719, 720). The beast of chapter 13 was the Roman Empire under Nero. Jerusalem was the great harlot or prostitute, called "Babylon" (17:1, 5) as a result of her unfaithfulness to God.

In the preterist view the marriage of the Lamb and Battle of Armageddon (chapter 19) refer to the Gentile Church's replacement of Israel as the people of God and to the judgment on Judaism represented by the destruction of Jerusalem—both first-century events. The millennial reign of Christ, the binding of Satan through the preaching of the gospel, and the first resurrection (chapter 20)—all of these dramatize the effects of Christ's redemptive work in creating and building the New Testament church, a work begun with Christ Himself and continuing throughout the Church Age. The *first* resurrection (20:4, 5) is spiritual, the new birth. The *second* (v. 5) is physical, the general resurrection of all mankind before God's throne at the end of time. (One might legitimately ask why the Great White Throne Judgment is not also located in the first century.) The New Jerusalem (chapter 21) is the church, and chapter 22 provides a metaphorical description of the experience of personal salvation in the present age.

2. Idealist (Para-time)

The *idealist* or symbolic perspective does not identify any of Revelation with specific historical events, persons, or things but interprets these as symbolic of deeper spiritual realities throughout history. Mounce (28) quotes Milligan: "We are not to look in the Apocalypse for special events, but for an exhibition of the principles which govern the history both of the word and the Church." G. K. Beale (48), a "modified" idealist, characterizes Revelation as "a symbolic portrayal of the conflict between good and evil, between the forces of God and of Satan." This way, the book is timeless; none of its symbols are to be identified with any particular historical events. Beale (48) acknowledges the "problem" that Revelation, interpreted this way, does not depict any *final* consummation or victory such as might be represented by the Second Coming or the ushering in of an eternal state after a last judgment. For such reasons he modifies the classic idealist position to include a *literal* Second Coming, judgment, the

new creation, and specific local churches identified in chapters 2, 3.

A key feature of idealism is its conviction that the symbols of Revelation may be applied throughout the church age. To locate the book in the first century (preterist), or at various points along the way (historicist), or just before the end of time (futurist), conceivably hinders its designed benefit for believers of all generations. Every believer of every generation, whether in the first or the twenty-first century, needs help facing persecution, false doctrine, pagan culture, or immorality—evils depicted in Revelation. We all must discern right from wrong, serve Christ faithfully in the church, deal with the devil, face persecution, and be ready for Christ's return. The messages to the seven churches are applicable to every generation of believers throughout history. No advocate of any school of interpretation would deny this; we should not ignore grounds for synthesis of the major viewpoints.

One writer sees the vision of Christ walking among the golden candlesticks as a lesson that the true church is a "light-bearer" of the gospel to a dark world (Hamstra 102). This is an example of idealism's allegorical method, a method of symbolizing Scripture traced to Clement of Alexandria (ca. A.D. 150-215) and his student Origen (ca. A.D. 185-254).

Consider also the idealist's allegorization of 10:9, 10: the little book may remind the church, in a time of bitter trial, that God has not forgotten and that the church must face its sin. Or, more likely (Hamstra 110), the book symbolizes the gospel, which itself is sweet but brings bitter persecution when preached. As for the two beasts in chapter 13, Hamstra (113) regards the first as the "spirit of the world" which persecutes the church, and the second as "false religion and false philosophy."

This way, Revelation is "a theological poem setting forth the ageless struggle between the kingdom of light and the kingdom of darkness," a "philosophy of history wherein Christian forces are continuously meeting and conquering the demonic forces of evil" (Kepler, quoted in Mounce 28).

3. Historicist (Continuous-time)

The historicist sees Revelation as depicting church history from the first century up to the end-times. Historicists are prone to link the predictions of Revelation to literal, historical fulfillments within history (often in their own generation). Beale (46) summarizes this view that Revelation predicts the "major movements of Christian history, most of which have been fulfilled up to the time of the commentator." This means that the major symbols—seals, trumpets, bowls, etc.—refer to successive, historical events in chronological order. Thus (though in differing interpretations), things in Revelation might be seen as referring to the invasions of the Christianized Roman empire by the Goths and the Muslims, or to the medieval corruptions of the papacy, the reign of Charlemagne, or to the Protestant Reformation, for example—or even to the acts of such persons as Napoleon or Hitler!

Perhaps the best known feature of historicist interpretation is to identify Babylon and the Antichrist in Revelation with Roman Catholicism and the papacy. A. Johnson (13) urges that this became a "common" element of this approach, and that Luther, Calvin, and other Reformers came to this view. (See Walvoord 18-20 for a summary.)

Many historicists have also tended to identify the seven churches of Revelation 2, 3 as referring to seven successive stages of church history.

Historicism has an impressive list of interpreters on its side, among them John Wesley, Finney, Spurgeon, and Matthew Henry (Gregg 34). Albert Barnes (v-ix) was impressed with the approach but did not adopt it. However, it is not now popular, perhaps due in part to false predictions and identifications. Pate (17, 18) did not include it in his survey of major views. Gregg (34) describes it only because many of the classic commentaries that are still widely used represent the historicist view.

It may be that the historicist approach, identifying parts of Revelation with one's own generation, helped open the door to various kinds of sensationalistic interpretation that continue in our day and are practiced by some futurists. We must not fall in with those who set dates for Christ's return (Mt. 24:23-28, 36, 42) or identify heinous figures (Saddam Hussein?) with the Antichrist. Suggesting that the creatures of Rev. 9 are modern military helicopters is speculation that misses the mark. Even so, the events and persons of Revelation *will* locate somewhere in real history at some specific point in time. The Antichrist will be a real person. Jesus Christ is literally coming again. But the precise timing and identity of these and other things in Revelation must remain a mystery until then.

4. Futurist (Future-time)

Futurism, often synonymous with "dispensationalism" (though there are many varieties) places most of Revelation (chapters 4-19) in a relatively short period of time (seven years, often designated as Daniel's seventieth week or the Great Tribulation) at the *end* of church history. This future period, mostly of tribulation and catastrophe, affects the entire population of earth. The three series of judgments——seals, trumpets, and bowls—are usually interpreted either chronologically and increasing in intensity or as recapitulations of the same events.

A literal, human Antichrist, revealed during this period, galvanizes worldwide rebellion against God in an attack on Israel at Armageddon. At His Second Coming, Christ personally defeats the Antichrist's forces, dissolves the world's systems (religious, political, commercial) and institutes His own literal, millennial reign on earth (chapter 20). At the end of the one thousand years are the final insurrection of Gog and Magog (distinct from Armageddon in chapter 19) and the resurrection and judgment of unbelievers at the Great White Throne (vv. 11-15). Here personal eternal destinies are assigned to everyone, based on their works, as recorded in God's books, and on whether or not their names are written in the Lamb's book of life. Immediately following, the present cosmos gives way to a new and final universe crafted by God, described in the final two chapters of Revelation.

It is important to distinguish two basic varieties of futurism. One, the presently popular *dispensational* type, typically places the rapture of the church *before* (by some, within) the tribulation period. The other, called "modified futurism" (Beale 47), places the rapture of the church at the *end* of the tribulation period. Many who hold this second view

blur the distinction between Israel and the church and believe that O.T. promises made to Israel are fulfilled in the church—much as in classic amillennial or preterist tones. (See the discussion below of progressive dispensationalism and historic or covenant premillennialism.)

Many futurists are willing, if not exegetically compelled, to acknowledge a first-century setting behind the first several chapters of Revelation. This view was typically associated with preterist contentions that most of Revelation reflects a first-century environment. That futurists adopt this view of the opening chapters is an example of how differing viewpoints often share common elements. But deeply rooted differences remain and are considerable. Futurists are confident, for example, that the New Jerusalem of chapter 21 is a literal city in the future, not the church, and that chapter 22 is a description of conditions in Heaven itself and the quality of eternal life rather than the experience of personal salvation in the present age.

In fairness to futurists, who believe that most of Revelation finds its ultimate fulfillment toward the end of time, the practical lessons of Revelation for the present are not minimized. The power of God and Satan were at work in John's day. They are at work in ours. They will most certainly be at work to the end of time. But the futurist, while appreciating the idealist's desire to universalize Revelation for the benefit of every generation of believers, cannot reject what seems to be the obvious implications of the book for a specific future time at the end of this age.

Millennial Views

Millennium (Latin) means "a thousand years." In eschatology it refers to the millennial reign of Christ in Rev. 20:1-6. Knowing what one believes about this passage and the four major frameworks for interpreting the book as a whole (above) is integral to a study of the book. What one believes about the millennial question invariably colors the interpretation of everything else. There are three basic views, with varieties: Premillennialism, Amillennialism, and Postmillennialism.

1. Premillennialism

Premillennialism advocates a literal, one-thousand-year reign of Christ on the earth after the Second Coming. It was the dominant viewpoint in early church history until the fourth century. Men like Papias, Irenaeus, Justin Martyr, Tertullian, Hippolytus, Commodianus, and Lactantius were advocates of a literal millennium. The "chiliast" (Greek *chilia*, "thousand") or literal viewpoint prevailed until the time of Augustine, whose allegorical work *City of God* helped turn thought to a "spiritual millennium" for about 1,200 years of subsequent church history: that is, until after the Protestant Reformation.

This shift away from the premillennial viewpoint continued until relatively recent times, gradually reemerging in the writings of men like Johann Alsted (ca.1588-1638), a German scholar, and Joseph Mede, an Anglican who helped popularize premillennial ideas in the English-speaking world. Others included Henry Drummond in Great Britain and the Lord brothers in America. J. N. Darby (ca. 1800-1882) of the Plymouth Brethren is usually cited as the father of the modern dispensational form of premillennialism (Couch 82-85), though the roots of dispensationalism are discernible earlier (Ryrie, *Dispensationalism* 61-77).

The Niagara Bible Conference movement in America, during the last quarter of the nineteenth century, "popularized premillennial doctrine in North America" but shifted it from *historic* to *dispensational* premillennialism and emphasized a pretribulational rapture of the Church (Reiter 11). Before Darby and the Niagara movement, most premillennialists (often called "historic" or "covenant" premillennialists) believed in a *posttribulational* rapture at the Second Coming proper—which meant that the church would have to endure the tribulation.

There were also emerging Bible schools that taught this perspective and popular books like Blackstone's *Jesus Is Coming* (1898), and the *Scofield Reference Bible* (1909), deeply influenced by the Niagara movement. All these combined to revive widespread interest in studying Bible prophecy.

In our day, interest in dispensational premillennialism and eschatology in general has increased. One reason is the success of well-known television personalities like Jack Van Impe and popular works like Lindsey's *Late Great Planet Earth* and LaHaye's fictionalized eschatological novels about end-time events (the *Left Behind* series). The film industry has also found it impossible to resist "doomsday" and apocalyptic scenarios and saviors.

The modern form of premillennialism, largely synonymous with the term dispensationalism, is the most popular way of interpreting Revelation at present. Dispensationalism pictures world history divided into a sequence of dispensations (Greek *oikonomia* meaning "management, administration, stewardship"), each with its own way by which God related to those living within that particular period: innocence in the Garden of Eden, conscience in the patriarchal period, law and works in the O.T., grace and gospel in the N.T., and the millennium and eternal dispensations to follow. Classic dispensational premillennialism views these as very distinct from one another; covenant and progressive varieties of premillennialism view them as more unified or complementary.

The foundation of dispensational premillennialism is its more "literal" hermeneutic, interpreting Scripture according to the "normal" principles of grammar and word meaning without "spiritualizing" beyond exegetical warrant. Figurative language is recognized when it is obvious, as in "the trees of the field shall clap their hands" (Is. 55:12). But most Scripture must be interpreted literally, and such ideas as the rebuilding of the Temple, reinstitution of Levitical sacrifices, Messiah's rule over the nations of earth with a rod of iron, and the fulfillment of other O.T. promises arise from a consistent application of this approach and are to be fulfilled in the millennial reign of Christ. As Benware (101) summarizes, "A literal approach to the prophetic Scriptures leads one to believe that the promises made to Israel have not been fulfilled in the past and are not being fulfilled today. This mandates that they be fulfilled some time in the future to national Israel, which means that the nation of Israel and the church of Jesus Christ must be kept distinct." This distinction is one of the key ingredients of dispensational premillennialism.

Premillennialists also believe there will be a literal, seven-year period of tribulation on earth immediately preceding the Second Coming of Christ, though some would allow the first half to be less precise. The concept of the church's imminent or "any-moment" rapture is prominent, teaching that the church, made up of previously deceased and living saints, will be taken up to meet Christ in the air (1 Th. 4:13-18). But the question often debated is at what point within this seven-year period of tribulation the rapture will occur. There are three major views about this: namely that the rapture is pre-, mid-, or post-tribulational.

Pretribulationists, usually classical dispensationalists, believe the rapture will occur at the very beginning of the tribulation period. The church is thus spared the outpouring of God's wrath on a Christ-rejecting world. Midtribulationists (e.g. William B. Harrison, ca.1941) believe it will occur after the first three-and-one-half years, delivering the church from what is often designated as the period of "great tribulation" in the last half. Posttribulationists believe the rapture will occur at the very end of the tribulation period at the Second Coming. This last is typically the view of covenant or historic premillennialists.

Varieties of these include the view that only believers who are *ready* will be raptured first, at the beginning of the period, with others taken at some point during the tribulation after they get right with God ("partial or successive rapture"). There is also a "pre-wrath" view which places the rapture about three-fourths of the way through the tribulation, just prior to a shortened but extremely intense period designated the "Day of the Lord" (Benware 157-241).

For a pretribulational rapture see Ryrie, Lahaye or Walvoord. For a "pre-wrath" rapture see Van Kampen or Rosenthal. For a midtribulational rapture see Archer (115-145). For a posttribulational rapture see R. Gundry. For the partial or successive view, see Seiss. All these views keep the church protected from God's wrath during the tribulation, either by removing it entirely or protecting it within the period.

The energy of dispensationalism is belief in this "any-moment" or imminent rapture of the church, inspiring personal readiness and evangelism. According to this view, all Scriptural conditions are fulfilled and there is nothing preventing Christ from rapturing the church at any moment. For it to be otherwise would compromise the sanctifying effect of imminency. A pretribulational rapture is necessary to keep the church from the outpouring of God's wrath on unbelievers, since this characterizes the entire seven-year period. Belief in an "any-moment" (and therefore pretribulational) rapture, along with an eternal distinction between the nation of Israel and the church, and the literal interpretation of Scripture constitute the triad which distinguishes classical dispensationalism (Ryrie, *Dispensationalism* 38-41).

All these views (except posttribulationalism) mean that there are actually *two* stages in Christ's return, with the rapture preceding the public manifestation of Christ by a shorter or longer period of time. This also leads to belief in multiple resurrections, as does any form of premillennialism. In the pretribulational scheme, for example, the first resurrection is of deceased believers at the rapture. These join living believers to meet Christ in the air. After the tribulation, before the millennium begins, trib-

ulation martyrs (O.T. saints also, according to many interpreters) are raised (20:4). A third resurrection, at the end of the millennium, will be for the ungodly of all the preceding dispensations, perhaps also of new believers converted during the millennium (20:5).

In classic dispensationalism, God's program for the nation of Israel and the church are eternally distinct. Non-dispensationalists usually hold that God's original program for and promises to Israel were fulfilled during Christ's first advent and finished with the destruction of Jerusalem in A.D. 70; from then on, the N.T. church has permanently taken Israel's place as the covenant people of God, thus making an earthly millennial reign unnecessary. Dispensationalists, rejecting this "displacement theory," believe that an earthly reign is necessary to fulfill God's promises to Israel as a nation. Even so, some classic dispensationalists (Walvoord, for example) suggest that the two separate peoples will merge at the end of the earthly millennium, becoming one thereafter. This concession softens the historically rigid distinction.

At some contrast to dispensational premillennialism is the view called historic or covenant premillennialism held, for example, by George E. Ladd. This form of premillennialism blurs the distinction between Israel and the church much like amillennialism's displacement theory. As Ladd (*Four Views* 27) indicates, this viewpoint "forms its theology from the explicit teaching of the New Testament. It confesses that it cannot be sure how the O.T. prophecies of the end are to be fulfilled, for (a) the first coming of Christ was accomplished in terms not foreseen by a literal interpretation of the O.T., and (b) there are unavoidable indications that the O.T. promises to Israel are fulfilled in the Christian church."

Dispensational premillennialism itself has not remained static through the twentieth century; a more recent variety known as *progressive dispensationalism* (Blaising and Bock; Saucy) emphasizes the "kingdom of God" as God's primary concern within history. Progressive dispensatonalists hybridize preterist and amillennial elements with futurist and premillennial ones by emphasizing an "inaugurated" kingdom without abandoning premillennialism's emphasis on future, end-time fulfillments. They also see a more unified and complementary connection between the dispensations while retaining elements of the displacement concept.

There is much that is common among all premillennialists (historic or covenant, dispensational, progressive varieties). The millennium in Rev. 20:1-6 is a *literal*, one thousand-year reign of Christ on earth, yet future. The rapture of the church and the Second Coming of Christ *precede* this reign. Christ's public return, to conquer and institute His reign over the nations, will occur at the end of a future period of catastrophic, unprecedented worldwide tribulation. Satan is bound and cast into the abyss as a holding place (20:3) until the end of this millennial reign. Afterward, one last devilish hurrah is permitted by God before Satan and his rebels are finally defeated and cast into Hell forever. Blissful millennial conditions predicted in Isaiah, such as lifting the curse of nature and worldwide peace, are fulfilled literally in the millennial period on earth. The judgment of unbelievers immediately follows, at the Great White Throne Judgment. Final destinies in either Heaven or Hell are determined. The old

creation then gives way to a new, eternal Heaven and earth with the New Jerusalem as its focus. All of these images are interpreted literally.

2. Amillennialism

Adding the prefix "a" to a word is a negation; "amillennial" therefore literally means "no millennium." This viewpoint does not see a *literal*, future one-thousand-year reign of Christ on earth in chapter 20 of Revelation, but interprets the millennial portion of the chapter in a *symbolic* or spiritualized way. John's vision is a figurative picture of Christ's reign with believers already in Heaven and in the hearts of believers on earth *during the present church age*. This period began at Christ's first advent and continues throughout church history.

The *binding of Satan* (20:2, 3) is not *total* during this spiritual "millennium." He continues to exercise his power and influence throughout the world, but is "bound" when the gospel is preached and men are saved. Revelation's picture of tribulation is not confined to a final seven-year period but continues throughout the church age, worsening toward the end with the appearance of Antichrist. At the end of this period, Satan is loosed to recruit a final rebellion culminating in the Battle of Armageddon, also known as Gog and Magog. This means that chapter 20 does not necessarily follow chapter 19 chronologically.

After this battle there is one general resurrection and judgment of all saints and sinners, consummating this age. This transitions immediately to the eternal state, where there is but one family of God, including saved Jews and Gentiles. Classic dispensationalism's dualism (one purpose for Israel, one for the church) is rejected. God's distinctive purpose for the nation of Israel ended in the first century A.D. with the destruction of Jerusalem. Much of O.T. prophecy about blissful "millennial" conditions (Is. 11:6-9, for example) is either fulfilled (spiritually) in conditions within the people of God here and now or actually in eternity in the new Heaven and earth. The two resurrections of 20:4, 5 are usually interpreted as (1) symbolic of the believer's new birth in the Church Age, and (2) literally as a physical resurrection of everyone at the general judgment.

In sharp contrast to premillennialism, amillennialism views the tribulation and the "rapture" of the church in a different light, regarding Daniel's seventieth week as fulfilled with the destruction of Jerusalem in A.D. 70. Sanders (75, 76, 79) indicates that the "great tribulation period" has therefore already taken place. However, he acknowledges that this is regarded by many amillennialists as "only an initial fulfillment," with others expected to follow, and that some consider the tribulation as past, present, and future, allowing that tribulation may "intensify during an end-time tribulation period."

Hoekema (156-159), following Hendriksen's "progressive parallelism," provides an example of how some amillennial interpreters view the structure or sections of Revelation as recapitulations of the same events. This way, Revelation provides seven parallel sections with each depicting church history from Christ's first advent to His Second Coming.

One of the major themes of amillennialism is the ultimate triumph of Christ and His church in the struggle over Satan and the world. From this perspective Revelation was written to encourage believers to persevere in each generation in the ongoing spiritual conflict which continues throughout church history.

Common to amillennialists, postmillennialists, and even some covenant or historic premillennialists is the "displacement theory" mentioned above. In this view the church has replaced Israel and O.T. promises initially made to the nation of Israel are now applied to the church (Sanders 37, 38, 53, 56, 63, 75, 76, 79). God no longer has a separate program for both the church and Israel but merges them as one. An example is God's promise to David that one of his descendants would rule forever (2 Sam. 7:16); this is fulfilled in Jesus, now ruling in Heaven over the church. After Christ's first advent, Jews and Gentiles are saved and relate to God eternally in the same way (Eph. 2:14-18). Everyone enters God's kingdom or family or church by the gospel of Jesus Christ. "Judaism has been abrogated... and the church has taken its place. The new covenant is now the authoritative instrument for God's dealings with his people. This...renders impossible both the historic premillennial and the dispensational premillennial position. It is compatible with either the amillennial or the post-millennial position" (Boettner 101, 102). Ladd's covenant premillennialism acknowledges this displacement but still advocates a literal, earthly millennium.

The amillennial concept, that O.T. prophecies to Israel are fulfilled in the church spiritually, is traced to Tyconius (ca. A.D. 390) in his *Book of Rules*. Augustine (ca. A.D. 354-430), partly in reaction to the abuses of chiliasm (the premillennialism of the early church), popularized the Alexandrian allegorical method in his book *The City of God* (NPNF II:1), which "spiritualizes" Bible truths. Christians relate to the "city of God." Satan and unbelievers relate to "the earthly city." Tyconius and Augustine interpreted the "millennium" of Rev. 20 as the present age.

The amillennial view has continued through the centuries to the present day as the viewpoint of respected early church fathers, Protestant Reformers, scholars, preachers, and laymen. It transcends denominational boundaries.

3. Postmillennialism

"Post" means *after*; postmillennialism holds that Christ's coming will be after "the millennium." Daniel Whitby (ca. 1700) is often credited as a leading representative of postmillennialism. Daniel Whitby's idea of the church's eventual triumph in the present age, leading to a "golden age" of Christian influence on the earth, was very popular in the last several centuries. The hallmark of postmillennialism is its *optimism*. This is in contrast to both premillennialism and amillennialism which have what postmillennialists term a "pessimistic" view of the end of world history.

In postmillennial thought, the world is gradually being changed for the better by the preaching of the gospel and by Christian influence. The Second Coming of Christ will not be combative or catastrophic but "icing on the cake" for what has already happened before He comes. He does not come to conquer the world by force because the world has already been conquered by the gospel. He comes to be willfully coronated as rightful King by a majority of the world population. "Postmillennialism expects the proclaiming of the Spirit-blessed gospel of Jesus Christ to win the vast majority of human beings to salvation in the present age...[This will] produce a time in history prior to Christ's return in which faith, righteousness, peace, and prosperity will prevail in the affairs of people and of nations" (Gentry, *Three Views* 13). Only after a long period of such conditions will the Lord return "visibly, bodily, and in great glory, ending history with the general resurrection and the great judgment of all humankind" (Gentry, *Three Views* 13, 14).

After tracing evidence of the postmillennial concept in early church history up through the Protestant Reformation, Gentry (*Three Views* 14-19) provides an impressive list of advocates from the time of the Reformation until relatively recent times. He credits Thomas Brightman (ca. 1562-1607), instead of British Unitarian Daniel Whitby (ca. 1638-1725), as the first "systematizer" of modern postmillennialism. However, it was Whitby's idea of the millennium as a "golden age" which popularized the view. And it is understandable that such a positive, triumphalist viewpoint appealed to theologians of the late eighteenth and early twentieth centuries and to human nature in general.

After a significant period of popularity, the postmillennial view declined in a twentieth-century environment of world wars, amorality, and the rising tide of dispensational premillennialism.

Reconstructionism today, as a revival of postmillennial sentiments, promotes the concept of theonomy, an effort to reintroduce God's laws into ethics and government. (See Bahnsen's *Theonomy In Christian Ethics*.)

For postmillennialism the one-thousand years represents an indeterminate amount of time: "The 'millennial' era has already lasted almost two thousand years; it may continue another thousand or ten thousand more, for all we know" (Gentry, *Three Views* 55). Following the golden age and the battle of Gog and Magog, a general resurrection and judgment will take place before giving way to eternity.

Postmillennial understanding of the tribulation is preterist, with such prophecies fulfilled in the first century. Tribulation will diminish as history unfolds. The world will not get worse but better toward the end of the age. The strength of this view is its encouragement of continual involvement in social concerns because it truly believes the gospel will transform society. Advocates of the "social gospel" were typically associated with this view.

Conclusion

On balance there is much common ground for students of Revelation to stand on. Indeed, even within some of the differing schools of interpretation there is awareness of important emphases in other approaches. O. Cullman's "already/not yet" principle becomes the umbrella concept, for example, of progressive dispensationalists (Pate; Blaising and Bock; Saucy) and provides a kind of bridge connecting otherwise opposing views. Historic or covenant premillennialism's advocacy of the "displacement theory" is in some ways more like preterism or amillennialism than like the dispensational premillennialism of Walvoord or Ryrie.

Progressive dispensationalists also stress how present kingdom realities and Biblical prophecies will ultimately be fulfilled in the tribulation period just before Christ's Second Coming, followed by a literal millennium; these realities are therefore not limited to a first-century or heavenly fulfillment. This realigns them with classic dispensational, futuristic interpretation. Covenant premillennialism sees the fulfillment of much O.T. prophecy in Christ and the church in a way that is similar to amillennialism.

At one end of the interpretive spectrum is "realized eschatology," which in its more radical (liberal) form spiritualizes the Kingdom of God within the present age to such an extent that it denies all eschatological significance. A more "consistent eschatology" responds by pointing out that there is a massive amount of Biblical data confirming a future aspect to the Kingdom of God, including in the mind of Jesus Himself. We must recognize both aspects of the Kingdom of God, the present and the future realities. It is possible to become so "heavenly minded as to be of no earthly good," but it is also possible to become so "earthly minded" as to be totally unprepared for eschatological events.

There is no denying an "already" aspect to prophetic or Kingdom Scriptures. There was a kingdom ethic and power already present in Jesus' earthly ministry. But equally undeniable is that the authors of Scripture, and Jesus in particular, truly believed that certain predictions are "not yet" fulfilled, awaiting specific events in the end-times. (See Erickson 17-34 and Ladd's *The Presence of the Future*.)

A study of Revelation should not lead to confusion. Every generation of believers must continue the quest to interpret, understand, and preach it. God promises to bless in the present those who do (1:3), and this increases in importance as we "see the day approaching." Let us continue practicing the abiding principles: to "hear what the Spirit says to the churches" of our day.

My own viewpoint is futurist and premillennial. I remain committed, though open to correction of my understanding, to the literal interpretation of the Scriptures. I dare not add to or take away from the text (22:18, 19).

John's Use of the O.T. in Revelation

On the use of O.T. images in the Book of Revelation, McComiskey (307) observes, "One of the striking features of the book of Revelation is its adaptation of O.T. imagery to its Christocentric proclamation....We frequently find in its pages imagery hauntingly familiar to us from the OT but different in form or application from its O.T. setting."

Still, as Bible scholars have recognized, it is odd that John never quotes the O.T. if in fact he uses it as a primary source. This may indicate that the Revelation is less dependent on the O.T.

than many recent interpreters have supposed. Certainly God gave John fresh revelatory content that often intersected with O.T. images or vocabulary. But these may only be similar descriptions of realities and types shared in common. One should remember that *the same Spirit* authored all Scripture. John is not so much looking at the O.T. type as he is to the heavenly reality. According to this principle, the descriptions, and at times the very words, of Bible authors may be similar or identical, to be noted more as agreement of sources than dependence.

John did not necessarily seek O.T. language or precedents to express what he heard and saw. The visions, and often interpretations of them, were given directly to him, so that Revelation is, by and large, a record of what he heard and saw—not interpretation governed by what he already understood. Although conservative views of Biblical inspiration generally recognize a degree of freedom of expression for the human authors, John's description was largely determined for him by the nature of the material—perhaps more so than for any other Biblical writing.

REVELATION

OUTLINE OF REVELATION

PROLOGUE TO THE REVELATION (1:1-20)
    A. Nature of the Revelation (vv. 1-3)
    B. Salutation to Recipients (vv. 4-8)
    C. Commission to John (vv. 9-11)
    D. Confirmation by the Glorified Christ (vv. 12-20)
I. REVELATIONS TO THE CHURCHES (2:1—3:22)
    A. Message to the Ephesian Church (2:1-7)
    B. Message to the Smyrnean Church (2:8-11)
    C. Message to the Pergamean Church (2:12-17)
    D. Message to the Thyatiran Church (2:18-29)
    E. Message to the Sardian Church (3:1-6)
    F. Message to the Philadelphian Church (3:7-13)
    G. Message to the Laodicean Church (3:14-22)
II. JOHN'S VISION INTO HEAVEN AND THE FUTURE (4:1—5:14)
    A. General Description (4:1-11)
    B. Successful Heavenly Search (5:1-14)
III. THE SEVEN SEALS (6:1—8:1)
    A. Four Horsemen of the Apocalypse (6:1-8)
       1. First Seal—the white horse and its rider (vv. 1,2)
       2. Second Seal—the red horse and its rider (vv. 3,4)
       3. Third Seal—the black horse and its rider (vv. 5,6)
       4. Fourth Seal—the pale horse and its rider (vv. 7,8)
    B. Final Three Seals (6:9—8:5)
       1. Fifth Seal—martyrs for Christ (6:9-11)
       2. Sixth Seal—catastrophes (6:12-17)
       3. First Parenthesis—two great multitudes (7:1-17)
       4. Seventh Seal (8:1-5)
IV. THE SEVEN TRUMPETS (8:2—14:20)
    A. First Trumpet (8:6, 7)
    B. Second Trumpet (8:8, 9)
    C. Third Trumpet (8:10, 11)
    D. Fourth Trumpet (8:12, 13)
    E. Fifth Trumpet (9:1-12)
    F. Sixth Trumpet (9:13-21)
    G. Second Parenthesis (10:1—11:14)
       1. A mighty angel (10:1-7)
       2. A little book (10:8-11)
       3. Two witnesses (11:1-14)
    H. Seventh Trumpet (11:15-19)
    I. Third Parenthesis (12:1—14:20)
       1. A celestial woman (12:1, 2)
       2. A great red dragon (12:3, 4)
       3. A child king (12:5, 6)

4. War in Heaven (12:7-17)
5. War on earth (12:13-17)
6. Two beasts (13:1-18)
7. The character of Christ's servants (14:1-20)
V. THE SEVEN BOWLS (15:1—16:21)
A. Preparation (15:1-8)
B. First Bowl (16:1,2)
C. Second Bowl (16:3)
D. Third Bowl (16:4-7)
E. Fourth Bowl (16:8, 9)
F. Fifth Bowl (16:10, 11)
G. Sixth Bowl (16:12-16)
H. Seventh Bowl (16:17-21)
VI. THE CONQUEST BY CHRIST (17:1—20:15)
A. The Great Prostitute (17:1-18)
B. Babylon the Great (18:1-24)
C. Celebration in Heaven (19:1-10)
D. Battle of Armageddon (19:11-21)
E. The Millennial Reign (20:1-10)
    1. The binding of Satan (vv. 1-3)
    2. The millennial reign of Christ (vv. 4-6)
    3. The final rebellion (vv. 7-10)
F. The Great White Throne (20:11-15)
VII. THE ETERNAL AGE (21:1—22:5)
A. The New Heaven and Earth (21:1-8)
B. The New Jerusalem (21:9—22:5)
    1. As the Lamb's wife (21:9-27)
    2. As Eden restored (22:1-5)
EPILOGUE (22:6-21)
A. Assurances (22:6-17)
B. Warnings (22:18, 19)
C. Conclusion (22:20, 21)

PROLOGUE TO THE REVELATION (1:1-20)

A. Nature of the Revelation (1:1-3)

1 The Revelation of Jesus Christ, which God gave unto him, to shew unto his servants things which must shortly come to pass; and he sent and signified *it* by his angel unto his servant John:
2 Who bare record of the word of God, and of the testimony of Jesus Christ, and of all things that he saw.
3 Blessed *is* he that readeth, and they that hear the words of this prophecy, and keep those things which are written therein: for the time *is* at hand.

"Revelation" (Greek *apokalupsis*), meaning an *unveiling*, identifies the contents of the book (v. 1). Many interpreters take "*of* Jesus Christ" to mean that Jesus was the *giver* of the revelation (Greek subjective genitive); others take it to mean that the revelation is *about* Jesus (Greek objective genitive). Both are true. He is the artist who unveils His work, but when the veil is removed He is the One revealed; and He pulls back the curtain of time to reveal present realities and future events.

This revelation comes about through a chain of communication: (1) God the Father, (2) Jesus Christ, (3) an angel, (4) John, and (5) God's servants. The *source* is God, establishing its absolute authority. Jesus Christ is both *agent* and *object*; He gives it to John by an angel. John *records* it and delivers it to the pastors of the seven churches.

The transmission is complete when delivered to Christians in those churches, here identified (along with John himself) as God's "servants" (Greek *doulos*), one who "belonged by nature not to himself, but to someone else" and thus subordinated his own will to another's (DNTT 592, 593). This role in John's day was not always as *harsh* as may seem to us: slavery was common and could be respectable in ancient society. These are *spiritual* slaves or "bondservants" (Vincent II:407); it is an honor to be *God's* bondservant. This initial transmission has continued throughout church history for God's "servants" of every generation. Revelation is therefore primarily for the saved rather than the lost; but unbelievers also need to be informed about the realities described.

God's stated purpose for Revelation is "to shew unto His servants things which must shortly come to pass." "Shew" (Greek *deiknumi*) means to make known (Vine 569). "Servants" (as above) refers to believers in general (Robertson 283), appearing fourteen times in the book. The events to be revealed are portrayed as near, indicated by "shortly" and "at hand" (v. 3).

But if these meant "near" in John's day, how are we to explain the apparent delay of Christ's coming for over two thousand years since then? (1) Some like Schweitzer (Erickson 21-29) suggest that Jesus and John believed He would return soon but were mistaken: His predicted return never happened. (2) Some preterists (like S. Russell) speak of a "judgment-coming" of Christ at the fall of Jerusalem in A.D. 70. Jesus was therefore correct about coming "shortly." (3) Others invoke God's perspective of time, with whom one day is as a thousand years and vice versa (2 Pet. 3:8).

149

Two thousand years is a short amount of time to God. (4) Some take "shortly" to mean "quickly": once things finally begin to happen, they will all transpire in a short period of time (Walvoord 35). (5) Yet others think that the soon *beginning* of the last age as a whole is in view in Revelation. Some of it has already been fulfilled, while much remains in the future (1 Cor. 10:11).

This last view accommodates the "already, not yet" characteristic of the Kingdom of God. Jesus saw the presence of the Kingdom in Himself and in His disciples (Mt. 12:28; Lk. 17:21). In this sense it has already arrived. But He also taught that its ultimate, literal fulfillment is at the end of time (Mt. 25). In this way the sense of imminence about the return of Christ is preserved without ignoring the suggested immediacy here and elsewhere in the N.T.

Angels figure prominently in Revelation, their importance implied by statements of Christ Himself (cf. 22:6, 16) indicating that the revelation was given through them. Angels are special beings created to serve God; some assist John in various ways as the revelation is passed on to him, including offering commentary. They assist in the process but are not the source of the revelation and refuse worship (19:10). The angel in v. 1 is distinct from God and Jesus Christ, but not otherwise identified. This angel is, however, described somewhat intimately as "his angel"; compare 22:16, "mine angel."

The revelations were "sent" by God through Christ and His angel to John on the island of Patmos, with "sent" indicating completed action (Greek aorist). "Signified" (Greek *semaino*) means "to give a sign or token" (Vincent 408), with the signs becoming part of the written Word; Revelation is filled with these. By the term John may imply "the difficulty in understanding the revelation narrated in the text that follows," thus indicating the need for "informed interpretation" (Aune I:15). Had Christ not interpreted the vision of 1:12-20, for example, John would not have understood it (cf. Dan. 2:19-23; 4:18). Even so, though in "sign" form, Revelation is not given to remain as a "mystery" (v. 20) but to reveal. "The revelation...includes not merely the thing shown and seen, but the interpretation or unveiling of the same" (Trench 354).

John's role is that of a humble servant who "bore record to" the revelation he received (v. 2; cf. v. 19). The word (Greek *martureo*) means to be or bear witness, to testify (Thayer 390). The entire revelation was faithfully witnessed and written down by John. His physical senses were fully engaged (cf. 1 Jn. 1:1, 2). He *heard* much of it spoken—by God the Father, the glorified Christ, or various angels—and such *audible* sounds as thunder, earthquakes, or heavenly music. And he *saw* much of it in the form of signs or images: "I saw" recurs repeatedly throughout the book.

John categorizes the revelation as: "the word of God," "the testimony of Jesus Christ," and "all things that he saw." As the Word of God—here specifically Revelation—it merits the respect given to all Scripture. As in v. 1, "the testimony of Jesus Christ" may be about Him or by Him; both apply. "Testimony," meaning "witness," has the same root as "bore record to." When the revelation reaches John, its transmission has been "traced from its origin in the Mind of God to the moment when it reached its human interpreter" (Swete 2).

The last part of John's opening (v. 3) is the first of seven "beatitudes" (blessings) in Revelation (1:3; 14:13; 16:15; 19:9; 20:6; 22:7; 22:14). This one is promised to believers who practice three activities: reading, hearing, and keeping.

"Reading" (Greek *anaginosko*) is singular—*one* person reading—where "hearing" and "obeying" are plural (all Greek participles). This probably reflects first-century worship services, referring to the *public reading* of Scripture to the assembled congregation (cf. Lk. 4:16-20). Public reading of Scripture was necessary, since copies of Scripture (all handwritten) were not plentiful; many could not read and relied solely on "hearing" the word. All three activities (Greek present tense) indicate continuing action and depict the nature and purpose of a worship service. God expects His church to manifest its nature with signs of life. "Keeping" (Greek *tereo*) means "to guard, keep, observe, reserve" (Thayer 622). The blessing is for those who practice these things. The messages to the churches (chapters 2, 3) show that failure to remain active leads to forfeiture of blessing.

"The things that are written" and "the words of this prophecy" indicate two additional qualities of Revelation: it is a *written* (verbal) revelation, and it is *prophetic*. "Prophecy" (Greek *propheteias*), though often "fore-telling" the future, includes all forms of speaking "for" God, whether of the past, present, or future (Vine 492). Some "prophecy" is divinely-given *wisdom* or guidance for present living, no less miraculous than prediction. Revelation does both, offering counsel about present realities (chapters 2, 3) as well as predicting future events (chapters 4-19). But the blessing promised here is for the *present*: one prepares for the future in the present.

Summary
(1:1-3)

Revelation, written by the Apostle John, is primarily a book which "unveils" Jesus Christ and the future. He is both *source and object* of the revelations. Though apocalyptic in nature, it is unique and dissimilar to other Jewish apocalyptic literature.

The message is urgent: everyone should know that the time of these predicted events is at hand. God transmitted this through a chain of communication consisting of God, Jesus Christ, an angel, John, and His servants. John himself carefully recorded everything.

A unique blessing is attached: reading, hearing, and obeying the words will bring special good. Perhaps as no other Scripture, Revelation alerts and helps prepare humanity for a truly catastrophic future. That future will culminate with the end of the world and time as we know them. The entire human race, from Adam until then, will meet Jesus Christ and God face to face.

Application: Teaching and Preaching the Passage

The prologue of Revelation is foundational. Upon it John confidently constructs the rest of the book. Our preaching and teaching are founded likewise. Knowing the quality and source of one's product makes for a much bolder presentation. This foundation, yea authority, is God Himself and the power of His Word given through Jesus Christ.

The message is also extremely urgent because "the time is at hand." Most people will be unprepared for the catastrophic events described. Urgency is demanded because Revelation speaks of the end of the world: there is no recourse beyond these pages. Present freedom of the will must be exercised to make it through a window of opportunity rapidly narrowing. Once closed, opportunities of repentance and service become eternal regret. Heaven and Hell beckon their future residents.

Suggested Outline. Revelation 1:1-13: (1) Authority [God], v. 1; (2) Account [John], v. 2; (3) Application [Word of God], v. 3.

B. Salutation to Recipients (1:4-8)

4 John to the seven churches which are in Asia: Grace *be* unto you, and peace, from him which is, and which was, and which is to come; and from the seven Spirits which are before his throne;
5 And from Jesus Christ, *who is* the faithful witness, *and* the first begotten of the dead, and the prince of the kings of the earth. Unto him that loved us, and washed us from our sins in his own blood,
6 And hath made us kings and priests unto God and his Father; to him *be* glory and dominion for ever and ever. Amen.
7 Behold, he cometh with clouds; and every eye shall see him, and they *also* which pierced him: and all kindreds of the earth shall wail because of him. Even so, Amen.
8 I am Alpha and Omega, the beginning and the ending, saith the Lord, which is, and which was, and which is to come, the Almighty.

After the brief prologue John includes an *epistolary* salutation for his readers (vv. 4-8), addressing it as a letter like many N.T. epistles. As typical, he first identifies himself (v. 4).

N.T. salutations typically include the intended recipients and pronunciation of a blessing of "grace and peace," perhaps a combination of the standard greetings in Hebrew (*shalom*, "peace") and Greek (*charis*, "grace"). Praise for one or more of God's attributes is usually included in the form of a brief doxology; John includes all three Persons of the Trinity.

The first reference to destination is general: "the seven churches, which are in Asia," identified later as Ephesus, Smyrna, Pergamos, Thyatira, Sardis, Philadelphia, and Laodicea (v. 11). As noted in the Introduction, Ramsay (132), crediting Hort, reports that these lay (in this order) on a great circular road in the Roman province of Asia. Mounce (57) adds that each served as postal headquarters for its respective district.

Seeing the seven "churches" as a prophetic sketch of future periods within church history is unlikely, a theory never suggested by the text itself which tends to confine the problems and the applications to a solitary time period. Surely the churches represent churches both in John's day and in every generation. To the degree that any church or believer experiences similar conditions, all seven messages apply to believers at all times.

Seven is the Biblical number of perfection or completeness, occurring 49 times in Revelation. There were certainly more than seven churches in Asia Minor at the time; these were enough for the Lord's greater purpose of giving Revelation to all believers.

God alone is eternal, unlimited by time. John highlights this attribute, which goes back to Ex. 3:14 in God's preferred and most sacred name, "I Am That I Am" (Hebrew *Yahweh, Jehovah,* or *the LORD*), from a verb meaning "to be or exist" (TWOT II:210-212). God's eternal existence and unchanging nature guarantee the fulfillment of John's message. A three-fold phrase expresses His eternal nature: "him which is" (literally, "the one being or existing") and "which was" and "which is to come" (literally, "the one coming"). He is the source of the revelations.

John's greeting also includes the Holy Spirit, named second rather than (as usual) third. Probably "seven" (symbolizing fullness or completion) represents the full retinue of the *one* Spirit's person and ministry (Is. 11:2), not seven different entities. But some commentators regard the "seven Spirits" as ministering angels before the throne, or as seven "archangels," or as the seven which minister to the seven local churches (3:1, etc.). This view seems, inappropriately, to place angels on a par with God the Father and Jesus the Son. Zechariah's description of the Holy Spirit as "the eyes of the *LORD*, which run to and fro through the whole earth" (Zech. 4:6, 10) supports the view that the "seven spirits" are a reference to the one Holy Spirit with something to say to each church (2:7, 11, 17, 29; 3:6, 13, 22).

Jesus is listed last in this greeting for a special reason. "The Revelation of Jesus Christ" (v. 1) is both subjective (the one who does the revealing) *and* objective (the one being revealed). The book is not primarily about the Father or the Holy Spirit but about Jesus the Son. John's introduction of Him includes impressive facts. The first three are personal attributes (v. 5). The next three describe His blessed activity on behalf of believers (vv. 5, 6). The seventh introduces us to the theme of the Revelation as a whole—His Second Coming (v. 7).

"The faithful witness" (v. 5) summarizes Jesus' entire earthly ministry: He was faithful to God in every way. "Witness" (Greek *marturos*) sometimes means "one who bears witness by his death" and always "one who can or does aver what he has seen or heard or knows" (Vine 680). Jesus was a faithful witness in both senses. He faithfully gave the message God had given Him (Jn. 17:6-8), but the greatest demonstration of His faithful witness was the crucifixion brought about by His positive confession of truth and refusal to deny it under the threat of death.

The "first begotten of the dead" also has two nuances. One is the recognition of pre-eminence or honor that comes from being first (Ps. 89:27; Col. 1:18). The second is the implication that others will follow: Jesus is the "firstborn" of a new family to come (1 Cor. 15:20). His resurrection will be experienced by all who believe in and remain faithful to Him.

"The prince of the kings of the earth" alludes to O.T. predictions about the ruling character of Messiah (Ps. 2:6-9; 72:8; Is. 9:6, 7; 11:4). This reign is pictured as worldwide in scope ("the nations" or "the earth"), militaristic in nature, and ultimately triumphant (19:15). Jesus' earthly ministry was primarily within Israel and focused on "spiritual" aspects of His kingdom. When questioned by Pilate, He replied that His kingdom was "not of this world" (Jn. 18:36, 37). Indeed, some interpreters (including amillennialists) view this reign as always *spiritual* in nature, equating it with His present rule over the church. But as Revelation will make clear, His kingdom will have a literal fulfillment in the millennial reign of Christ (20:4-6).

Following these attributes, John launches into a doxology of lofty accolades (vv. 5, 6) about what the exalted Christ does for believers: He cherishes, cleanses, crowns, and commissions believers as subjects in His triumphant kingdom.

First is His love for all believers—"the characteristic word of Christianity" (Vine 381)—expressed as ongoing action (Greek present participle): the risen and eternal Christ still loves and will love us forever. Such love has substance, is active and sacrificial, ultimately demonstrated in the cross of Christ where God gave Jesus for all mankind (1 Jn. 4:10; Rom. 5:8). The "blood of Jesus," shed in His death, effectively "washed" (Greek *louo*) or "released" (Greek *luo* in many manuscripts) us from our sins. Whether as the washing away of that which defiles or as freeing from that which binds, Jesus has delivered us from the stain, slavery, and penalty of our sins. Indeed, our Lord could not *free* us from our sins without *washing* or cleansing us from them. Both happened to every believer at the moment of the new birth by virtue of the blood of Christ.

That believers are "kings and priests" (v. 6; cf. Ex. 19:6) needs interpreting. One view is that these are two distinct offices; the other is that this should be understood as "a kingdom of priests" (as in many manuscripts). This way, Jesus is the one King and we make up His kingdom as priests before Him. Aune (I:47, 48) argues that comparing 1:6 with 5:10 settles the question in favor of the view that believers are both kings and priests, consistent with the earliest Jewish understanding of Ex. 19:6.

To be sure, by virtue of our union with Christ the King, believers will share together in His future and literal reign over the earth (2:26, 27; 20:4). Though in one sense we are not kings but subjects in God's kingdom, in this sense we will reign with Christ (2:26; 3:21; 20:4, 6; see 1 Pet. 2:5, 9). We also function as priests in the world, which implies at least two things. One, believers offer spiritual sacrifices to God in the form of worship, prayer, and Christian service (Rom. 12:1, 2; 1 Pet. 2:5). Two, every believer is a mediator of the Gospel for Christ to an unbelieving world (1 Pet. 2:9; 2 Cor. 5:20). We help bring them to Christ, the ultimate Mediator between God and men (1 Tim. 2:5).

Such a litany of benefits causes John to insert a benediction of praise, apparently to Jesus the Son, who has done these wonderful things for us, rather than to the Father—though such praise is appropriate for both: (literally) "to whom [be] the glory and the dominion (or might: Greek *kratos*) into the ages of the ages." John must have known the Lord's Prayer well. "Amen" (both Greek and Hebrew) means "faithful or true" (Vine 25). The word indicates agreement with or affirmation of truth.

John adds an even more arresting truth: resurrected and reigning King of Kings, Jesus is coming to this earth again! Important things about that event are made clear. For one thing, the Second Coming will not be secret but public: the mention of clouds means that it will be *visible* in the sky (v. 7), though perhaps they are attached to Him as a specially-created, billowy entourage that enhances His glorious appearance.

The Second Coming will be *universally recognized* the moment it happens: "Every eye shall see him"—including unbelieving Jews and Gentiles. "They also which pierced him," looking back to the crucifixion, singles out the Jewish nation in particular, but the entire planet will be affected. "Kindred" (Greek *phule*) refers to a "group of people related to one another in some way" (Vine 643). All such communities will "wail" (Greek *kopto*), literally "beat the breast" (Vine 418). Many will attempt to hide (6:15). Sadly, this is mostly regret rather than repentance, even in the face of horrible catastrophes (9:20, 21). Nonetheless, Jesus Christ will literally return in a sovereign manifestation of world rule (cf. Zech. 12:10).

John concludes with a direct quote of Christ about His deity: "I am Alpha and Omega"—the first and last letters of the Greek alphabet. This kind of literary device (sometimes called a "merism") "states polar opposites in order to highlight everything between the opposites" (Beale 199), thus including *everything* between the beginning and the end. When Jesus claimed to be Creator ("the Alpha") and Consummator ("the Omega") of all things, they understood this to mean sovereign control of everything between the beginning and end of time. One pillar of Christ's claim to full deity is His eternal existence: He is, was, and is to come (vv. 4, 8).

Jesus also possesses the attribute of sovereignty as "the Almighty" (Greek *pantokrator*). That Jesus is sovereignly and providentially present at the beginning, middle, and end of time guarantees the future. On the basis of His eternal presence and power, the church may expect to fulfill the Great Commission (Mt. 28:18-20). Because of

His enabling presence, believers may also anticipate personal triumph in overcoming the world.

Summary
(1:4-8)

At least two features distinguish Revelation within the genre of apocalyptic literature. One, a genuine apostle identifies himself personally as the author (vv. 1, 4). Two, it is epistolary: written as a letter, established by the salutation (vv. 4-8).

The greeting is Trinitarian, mentioning God the Father, the Holy Spirit, and Jesus the Son. But since the book is primarily about Jesus, more attention is given to Him and His activity. John expands his salutation into an impressive litany of Christ's personal attributes and blessings bestowed upon believers.

John addresses his letter to seven churches located in Asia Minor on a circular postal route in consecutive order. They also serve to represent believers in every generation until Christ's return.

The Second Coming is *the* central truth, coloring the contents of the entire book. Jesus' return is both triumphant and catastrophic for the earth and mankind. Opportunities to repent are replaced by mourning on the part of those who have rejected Christ.

There is also an unambiguous statement by Christ Himself about His own deity. He is not only our Savior, He is the Creator, Controller, and Consummator of the universe.

Application: Teaching and
Preaching the Passage

Surely a goal of discipleship is to know Christ and make Him known.

Revelation helps by providing understanding about Jesus and the future, about which we must inform the world. The imminent finality of this age calls for urgent proclamation in a generation increasingly ignorant of God and the Bible.

In postmodern America most are not Christians. Personal ignorance of what was basic Bible fact just a generation or two ago is appalling. Consumer-driven philosophy in church growth theory has abandoned the need for old-time, Holy Spirit power from on high. Our neighbors *have* "no clue" and must be reintroduced to the realities of Heaven and Hell, sin, the need for forgiveness, judgment, and—most important of all—Jesus Christ as Savior and Lord.

There is rampant failure, in a new age of post-Christian pluralism, to recognize the exclusive claims Jesus makes about being the *only* way to Heaven. Time-honored institutions like the church, family, and marriage are under assault. The pursuit of personal holiness is almost forgotten, even by many professing to know Christ. Belief is divorced from behavior. This breeds a twenty-first century style of Christianity similar to some of the groups Jesus condemned in Revelation.

Even when denied or ignored, the truth about Jesus Christ remains. Pilate's dilemma is everyone's: each must come to terms with Jesus Christ. Every church must see itself as Jesus sees it. Those who refuse are in significant jeopardy.

Suggested Outline. 1. Jesus Christ is: (a) Faithful Witness, v. 5; (b) First-begotten, v. 5; (c) Future Ruler, v. 5. 2. Jesus Christ: (a) Loves us, v. 5; (b) Liberates us, v. 5; (c) Lifts us up, v. 6.

C. Commission to John (1:9-11)

9 I John, who also am your brother, and companion in tribulation, and in the kingdom and patience of Jesus Christ, was in the isle that is called Patmos, for the word of God, and for the testimony of Jesus Christ.
10 I was in the Spirit on the Lord's day, and heard behind me a great voice, as of a trumpet,
11 Saying, I am Alpha and Omega, the first and the last: and, What thou seest, write in a book, and send *it* unto the seven churches which are in Asia; unto Ephesus, and unto Smyrna, and unto Pergamos, and unto Thyatira, and unto Sardis, and unto Philadelphia, and unto Laodicea.

Jesus personally commissions John (v. 9). Patmos is a mountainous island in the Aegean Sea off the coast of modern Turkey, approximately 60 miles southwest of Ephesus. Most agree that Patmos was used in John's time as a place of banishment or as a Roman penal colony (Aune I:78). Those banished there may have been forced to work under harsh conditions (Ramsay 59), but circumstances varied in severity. The severe form meant loss of certain privileges like Roman citizenship and loss of property. The less severe might be like "house arrest," temporary, with a measure of physical freedom on the island. Some think that Nerva ended John's banishment after the death of Domitian (ca. A.D. 96), allowing him to return to Ephesus.

John was sent to Patmos "for the Word of God and for the testimony of Jesus." Disregarding the unlikely view that he was there to evangelize the island (Bullinger 151), we are left with two possibilities. One is that "tribulation" means persecution, that he was banished there as a result of preaching the Word in Ephesus. "The Word of God," then refers to proclamation and "the testimony of Jesus" to John's personal faith or personal witness for Christ. The other interpretation identifies "the word of God" (as in v. 2) with Revelation: John was on Patmos, from God's perspective, to receive the revelations.

No doubt both of these are true, one from God's perspective and the other from man's. The Roman authorities exiled John to Patmos because of his faith in Jesus and preaching of the Word of God. God providentially allowed this in arranging for John to receive and record Revelation.

John identifies himself as a "brother, and companion in tribulation," defined as "in the kingdom and patience of Jesus." He thus identifies himself with his readers, automatically making his work more meaningful to them. Some recent scholars have questioned, though unconvincingly, the existence of serious persecution of Christians by the Romans during the lifetime of John. The weight of traditional sources (Pliny, Eusebius, Victorinus) is great; those living close to John's time, with many conservative scholars, must be heard.

"Kingdom" (Greek *basileia*) is the general term for the kingdom of God in the N.T.; the Kingdom of God and the Kingdom of Jesus are synonymous. "Patience" (Greek *hupomone*) means perseverance or endurance: "to abide under" (Vine 462, 463). The discipline or virtue of patience is characteristic of subjects within Christ's kingdom, integral to their survival. The three words—

tribulation, kingdom, and patience—are linked closely together: John is speaking about *kingdom tribulation* and *patience in tribulation*.

In John's world, Christians automatically encountered tribulation from the pagan world culture. Christ expected them to overcome the world and remain faithful even to death. Patience in tribulation is rewarded with more patience until a believer is perfected in character and ultimately rewarded with eternal life (Rom. 5:3; 8:25; Heb. 6:12; 12:1; Jas. 1:3, 4). He requires "overcoming," and patience is necessary for that. John's banishment testified to his personal triumph and would engender sympathetic understanding from his readers: "St. John wrote to the churches in those words of 1:9 because he was suffering in the same degree as themselves" (Ramsay 62).

The commissioning takes place on "the Lord's day" (Greek *kuriakos*), which some take to refer to the eschatological "Day of the Lord" (Walvoord 42), and others to Easter Sunday in particular (A. Johnson 29). But it seems clear that it means Sunday. The term became common in the early church because the resurrection of Christ was on the first day of the week (Mt. 28:1), and most interpreters agree.

John describes his condition as being "in the Spirit." This might mean "a state or spirit of worship," but more likely refers to the Holy Spirit, who communicated supernaturally from within John's own spirit while he remained physically on Patmos. He did not receive the revelations in a dream (Lenski 58) but was wide awake: in a "state in which the ordinary faculties of the flesh are suspended, and the inward senses opened" (Hort, quoted by Thomas I:90). The emphasis should be on *Jesus* as author, not on John.

The incomparable voice of Christ, like a trumpet behind him, must have startled John (v. 10). Jesus identifies Himself as the "Alpha and Omega," eternally in control of all things (v. 11; cf. 2:8; 22:13; see v. 8). *Trumpets* frequently herald special events or signal troops in war and have eschatological significance (1 Th. 4:16). But John's emphasis is on the volume and clarity of Christ's voice.

Jesus commands John to write, to record in a book the revelation he is about to receive—both in sight and hearing, as noted above. John's "book" (Greek *biblion*) would be in the form of a scroll of parchment or papyrus (Metzger 3-5). He would then send the entire book to the seven churches of Asia Minor, via trustworthy messengers. The messages would ultimately be delivered to the pastors of the churches to be read to their congregations.

The significance of the messages, though originally for real churches of the first century, should not be limited to them but speaks to God's church throughout history. Ramsay (134, 136) notes that there were other important cities with churches along the same road, including Hierapolis, Tralles, and Magnesia. Though not mentioned, they too might have received the Apocalypse. Regardless, the messages are still needed by the churches.

Summary
(1:9-11)

John identifies himself as a faithful brother in Christ to his readers, banished by the authorities to Patmos for preaching the Word of God and because

of his witness for Christ. He understands the need for courage and patient endurance. This is a mark of true discipleship, though providentially permitted for a higher purpose.

On Sunday, the "Lord's Day," God's revelation begins. Like the holy authors of Scripture before him, John is enabled to receive and write by the power of the Holy Spirit. He hears the mighty, trumpet-like voice of Jesus calling and commanding him. As "Alpha and Omega" He commands John with the authority of God the Son, as the one who creates, controls, and consummates the universe.

The recipients are seven local churches located in western Asia Minor, addressed in order as they were situated along a great circular road from Ephesus. These believers need the counsel of Christ; they have the same kind of problems encountered by all believers and churches, including those in our own generation.

Application: Teaching and
Preaching the Passage

The demands of discipleship are sometimes costly. Jesus, Peter, Paul, and John prepare us for persecution and suffering for the cause of Christ. They also connect suffering with growth in grace and achievement of God's design. But the believer remains triumphant: the principle of Rom. 8:28 in action.

God often uses tribulation and persecution to fulfill His purpose for us. Joseph's brothers sold him into slavery and he suffered for many years. But what they intended for evil, God meant for good. Jewish authorities crucified Jesus; but while Satan was doing his worst, God was doing His best for the world. God uses the wrath of man to praise Him.

The same may be said for John. His persecution and banishment to Patmos were not desirable, entirely apart from frailties typical of John's old age. But in God's providence that provided the circumstances for him to receive and write this marvelous work. Tribulation makes possible what cannot be achieved in any other way (Ps. 119:71). Today's church includes believers under equally great pressures. With them, as in the early church, we await the rapture of the church and the return of Christ. While we wait we must hear what the Spirit is saying to us through what He said to the ancient churches of Asia.

Suggested Outline. Tribulation, 1:9-11: (1) Companionship, v. 9; (2) Combination [kingdom and patience], v. 9; (3) Cause, v. 9; (4) Commission, vv. 10, 11.

D. Confirmation by the Glorified Christ (1:12-20)

12 And I turned to see the voice that spake with me. And being turned, I saw seven golden candlesticks;
13 And in the midst of the seven candlesticks *one* like unto the Son of man, clothed with a garment down to the foot, and girt about the paps with a golden girdle.
14 His head and *his* hairs *were* white like wool, as white as snow; and his eyes *were* as a flame of fire;
15 And his feet like unto fine brass, as if they burned in a furnace; and his voice as the sound of many waters.

16 And he had in his right hand seven stars: and out of his mouth went a sharp twoedged sword: and his countenance *was* as the sun shineth in his strength.
17 And when I saw him, I fell at his feet as dead. And he laid his right hand upon me, saying unto me, Fear not; I am the first and the last:
18 *I am* he that liveth, and was dead; and, behold, I am alive for evermore, Amen; and have the keys of hell and of death.
19 Write the things which thou hast seen, and the things which are, and the things which shall be hereafter;
20 The mystery of the seven stars which thou sawest in my right hand, and the seven golden candlesticks. The seven stars are the angels of the seven churches: and the seven candlesticks which thou sawest are the seven churches.

This last section of chapter one describes the first great revelation: a spectacular, visual portrait of the risen and glorified Christ that is not only impressive but instructive, emphasizing "the aspects of His nature that are most relevant to the needs and circumstances of the seven churches" (Thomas I:97). The obvious, intentional connection between this picture and the "Ancient of days" (Dan. 7:9, 10, 13; 10:6) reinforces the N.T. doctrine that Jesus is God.

John turns instinctively to see the person speaking to him (v. 12). What he sees traumatizes him, causing him to faint (v. 17). To identify the person as someone other than Christ—Charlesworth speaks of a "hypostatic heavenly being"—ignores the context, which clearly indicates that the voice (a metonymy representing the whole person: Beale 208) is Christ Himself. Fainting is not uncommon in the presence of deity (Dan. 10:5-11; Lk. 1:12; 2:9). Jesus intervenes and with the touch of His right hand revives the understandably fear-stricken apostle (v. 17).

There are three major parts in the vision, two of them *entirely* symbolic according to Christ's own interpretation (v. 20). There are "seven golden candlesticks" (lampstands: Greek *luknios*) and "seven stars" (v. 16), not yet interpreted but noted as parts of the vision. The third is a magnificent view of the glorified Christ, with considerable attention given to the details of His appearance: "a literary palette from which he creates in artistic language the image of the one who commissioned him" (Gregg 49). Even the position of Christ is instructive: in the center, surrounded by the seven lampstands (each a single pedestal with a simple oil lamp on top). Aune (I:88) believes they are modeled after menorahs like the one in the O.T. Temple.

"Son of man" (v. 13) is Jesus Christ, our Lord's own favorite self-designation in the Gospels. "One like" (Greek *homoios*) is equivalent to "similar to." Some contemporary translations render, "like *a* son of man" (cf. Dan. 3:25; 7:13, 14) since there is no article before "Son." This can be understood to mean "like a *human being*." But "the Son of man" in Rev. 14:14 and Jn. 5:2 unequivocally refer to Jesus and are also lacking the article. Mounce (57) argues convincingly that the construction means, precisely, "the Son of Man," an official title that in the context refers to Jesus Himself.

Jesus not only represented God to men as God in the flesh (Jn. 1:14; Col. 2:9), He represented men to God as fully human. He identified with humanity as the second Adam and perfectly fulfilled God's design for man (2 Cor. 5:21; 1 Tim. 2:5; Heb. 4:15). The title "emphasizes how he 'represents' God's people as he establishes for them God's kingdom" (Brighton 55) and leaves no question about His deity or identity here.

Every part of Jesus' appearance has an *otherworldly* but instructive quality. He is clothed in a full-length robe down to His feet and "girded" with a golden girdle or sash around His chest. "Paps" (Greek *mastos*) are "breasts." The '"girdle" (Greek *zone*) is probably sash-like, about the chest rather than the waist. The clothing is reminiscent of priestly attire but could suggest royalty as well. Both priestly and royal clothing fit Christ perfectly. Figuratively speaking, these were the holy and regal garments Christ willingly put aside to become flesh and become Savior of all (Phil. 2:6-8).

His head and hair are brilliant white, like snow or wool (v. 14), which often represents "radiance of light...transcendent glory and redemption" (DBI 944). The comparison to snow and wool more aptly applies to His "hair" than His face (Aune I:95; cf. Is. 1:18; Dan. 7:9). In Revelation white is applied to horses, stones, the clothing of righteous saints and angels, and the great judgment throne. Here, as referring to Christ's head and hair (v. 14), it is distinct from the "radiance of light" characterizing His appearance as a whole. Modifying the "hoary" head of Christ, it represents His infinite wisdom and experience, dignity, and eternal existence.

His eyes "like flaming fire" may imply a look that is "fierce," "penetrating," manifesting "supernatural intelligence," or "all-seeing" (Thomas I:101). Jesus is able to see into the past, present, and future and to probe the innermost recesses of a human soul (Heb. 4:12). Such keen vision validates Revelation's message: Jesus knows the future. His "eyes of flaming fire" contribute to a countenance connoting soberness, determination, and intensity.

His bare feet gleam like "fine brass" (v. 15). The rare word used here may be a metal alloy of gold and brass (Mounce 59) or a similar alloy. Polished bronze ("brass") was used for mirrors (DBI 124). The feet of Jesus glow as if just withdrawn from a purifying fire. This may relate to Christ's person, representing His absolute holiness, or to His activity as the future judge of the world and all mankind. In this latter sense, Christ purges the world of those things and persons that cannot enter into the holy presence of God in Heaven or into the new Heaven and earth (21:27).

His awesome voice sounds like a mighty waterfall cascading into a gorge, or ocean breakers pounding the coast of Patmos ("the sound of many waters," v. 15). Jesus speaks the Word of God with unique power, authority, and wisdom (Mt. 7:28, 29).

Christ holds seven "stars" in His right hand (v. 16). God's "right" hand generally signifies sovereign power or authority in action, whether providing for the needs of His people or raised in judgment against the wicked. Here the emphasis is *relationship*: Jesus "has" or holds these "stars" ("angels": messengers or pastors) in His right hand, with the "holding" (Greek present participle) representing an ongoing relationship.

There is no hidden astrological meaning. Jesus, not the stars, is in control of every aspect of the future. Everyone's future is revealed in Revelation. We look not to astrology but to Jesus Christ; He alone is a trustworthy guide and counselor.

A sharp double-edged sword is in His mouth, a N.T. metaphor for the all-powerful Word of God. In written form it is Scripture (Eph. 6:17; Heb. 4:12), but the "sword" is also the *spoken* Word (19:15). Ancient swords were long and heavy, requiring two hands to wield in combat, devastating on impact—though the Word may also be used like a surgeon's scalpel, probing a single individual (Heb. 4:12). The connotation is militaristic; the same metaphor is used when Christ conquers His enemies in literal battle at Armageddon (19:15), slaying thousands with the spoken Word.

His brilliant "countenance" (Greek *opsis*, "face"), compared to a powerful, noonday sun, makes it almost impossible to gaze upon Him. As with the sun at its zenith, this is the "high-point" of the vision (Mounce 60). Perhaps no other symbol in the Bible illustrates as much about the nature of God as the sun or light, in frequent contrast to the darkness, an integral component of the glory of God. No other light is needed in Heaven or eternity (21:23, 24).

As noted, John is overwhelmed by the spectacle (v. 17). He falls before Jesus in a dead faint, remaining so until the Lord touches him (cf. Dan. 8:17, 18, 27; 10:7-10) with the *right hand* of power or authority (as above) to revive and comfort His beloved apostle. Jesus also speaks, exhorting him to "fear not." Fear usually means the kind that "causes a person to run away" (Vine 229, 230):

a natural fear or terror (not to be confused with "the fear of the Lord"). Such fear may be replaced by faith on the basis of three absolutes spoken by Christ about Himself (vv. 17, 18), each relating to His sovereign control over all things. One, He is "the first and the last," an expression of preeminence, absolute control, and eternal existence (cf. "Alpha and Omega," vv. 8, 11). Two, "to live, die and live again" summarizes the essence of the Gospel message: Christ came to live in the flesh, died in the flesh, and was resurrected and lives forever. Three, He possesses "the keys of hell and of death," guaranteeing His ultimate control over every aspect of life and eternity. Death and Hell are the most dreaded fears of man; Jesus has mastery over sin, Satan, death and Hell, and He shares His triumph with us.

There are two kinds of "death" in Scripture. One is physical death, when the soul is (temporarily) separated from the body. The other is spiritual death, separation from God because of sin. Every human being since Adam is born spiritually dead because Adam represented the entire race (Rom. 3:23; 5:12-21; Eph. 2:2). We are sinners by nature. This spiritual death is eternal unless a new birth occurs (Jn. 3:3). In Revelation, eternal death is equated with Hell as the "second death" (see 20:14; 21:8).

Space allows only brief comments about Hell. Two words are thus translated in the A.V.: *hades* (v. 18) and *gehenna* (not in Revelation). *Gehenna* was originally a Hebrew word (literally "valley of Hinnom"), an area outside ancient Jerusalem where the city's refuse was burned that became associated with pagan ritual and the sacrifice of children (2 Kg. 16:3; 17:17, 31; 21:6; 23:10; 2

Chr. 28:3; 33:6). *Hades*, a Greek word, apparently indicates the unseen realm (Thayer 11), "the realm of the dead." In the Greek O.T. it represents the Hebrew *sheol*, apparently meaning the realm of *all* the dead. But by the time of Jesus, it was often used to refer to the place of the *wicked* dead. In one way or another, then, both of these apparently came to be metaphors equivalent to what we mean by "Hell," even if there were some subtle differences, at times, between the two. (For additional information, see J. Jeremias, TDNT I:146-149; Picirilli, "Hell in the New Testament.")

The main question for us, then, is what is meant by "Hell" (Greek *hades*) as it is used here. Clearly, it is the only destination possible—this side of the "lake of fire" at least—for the ungodly dead. The vivid picture in Lk. 16:19-31 provides the classic understanding of Hell as a place of fiery, eternal punishment. The rich man aptly summarizes the nature of Hell as "a place of torment": that is what Hell is in a word: *torment*. John is observing the very Person who created and controls Hell; He has the "keys"!

After reviving His faithful servant John, Christ commissions him and interprets the meaning of the vision in vv. 19, 20. Primarily, John is to *write* (v. 19), a command given contemporaneously with the first vision and before the rest of the revelations. Afterward, John would be less frightened and better prepared to comprehend and record what he would see and hear.

There are three views about *when* John actually recorded Revelation: (1) *immediately*, between revelations; (2) shortly *after* all the revelations were finished; (3) *after* he was released from

Patmos (note the past tense in v. 9). Locating the writing on Patmos seems preferable, making for better recall. There was no reason to wait, providing he had access to writing materials and opportunity. At the same time, it seems practical to think that he would have waited until all the visions were complete before setting them down. Assuredly, the Holy Spirit assisted John in writing, whenever he put pen to paper.

Many interpreters think v. 19 suggests a two- or threefold division of the book. If three, then the vision of Christ (vv. 12-20) stands for "the things which thou hast seen": the past. If two (Mounce 62), then the present ("the things which are") refers to the historical conditions of the seven churches at the end of the first century (chapters 2, 3). And the future ("the things which shall be hereafter") looks to chapters 4-22 (4:1: "after these things") and to the end-times, at least for futurist interpreters. But the distinction between these two views is somewhat artificial. The more important point is that the revelation began with the Apostle John on Patmos when Christ began speaking to him. The conditions of the churches described in chapters 2 and 3 were contemporaneous with him. Then, beginning in 4:1, we are rocketed forward from the first century to the end of time.

Interpretation is ideal when *Scripture interprets Scripture*. Here we have an excellent example: Jesus Himself interprets the two most significant things in the vision, the seven stars and the seven golden candlesticks (v. 20). The stars represent the "angels" of the churches. "Angels" (Greek *angelos*) basically means "messengers" and may less frequently refer to *human* messengers

(TDNT 1:74-83). The "candlesticks" ("lampstands") are the seven local churches in Asia Minor (vv. 4, 11). The "angels," therefore, are in all probability the *pastors* of these churches (Barnes 58). The pastor is God's messenger to a congregation, the most appropriate person to receive and deliver the message directed to a church.

Summary
(1:12-20)

Upon hearing the voice, John turns to see the person speaking to him and beholds the most spectacular visual representation of Christ in Scripture. Jesus' deity is undeniable. So is the authority behind the messages; the reason for listening and obeying could not be stronger.

The spectacle is overwhelming, causing the frightened apostle to faint, only to be strengthened by the touch of Jesus' right hand. John sees Jesus standing in the midst of seven lamps on stands, whether simple oil lamps or modeled after the O.T. Temple menorah (seven branches from a single pedestal). The awesome figure looks like the Son of Man, as John knew Him well. He had spent enough time with Jesus during His earthly ministry to recognize the one who called Himself "Son of Man."

The supernatural appearance of Christ communicated His nature and character. He was dressed in a robe down to His feet with a gold sash around His chest, indicating a priestly or royal function. He was both King and Priest (see Melchisedec, Heb. 7).

His white hair and flaming eyes were striking. Hair white like snow and the whitest of wool symbolizes absolute wisdom, dignity, holiness, and eternity. The eyes of flaming fire may very well represent His omniscience, including things hidden and future, or a resolute attitude for the stern mission and catastrophic future ahead.

The robe did not cover His feet, which were like polished brass, glowing as if just withdrawn from a furnace. The feet may symbolize His holy character, perfected in the fire of His sufferings on earth. The idea of Christ's future role as judge may also be implied.

His voice had a supernatural quality to it, compared to many waters—perhaps like waves pounding the coast of Patmos. He was holding seven stars in His right hand. A sharp, double-edged sword protruded from His mouth, representing the power of the Word of God. His countenance radiated like the sun at noon, impossible to gaze on.

Jesus personally strengthened the frightened apostle, reassuring and reminding him again of divine authorization for the messages. John was encouraged not to fear in light of several great claims of Christ, and to pursue his mission in confidence because Jesus is the Creator, Controller, and Consummator of all things, including death and Hell. This is so because He has been resurrected to live forever, thus proving His mastery over life, death, and Hell.

Jesus gave John an outline for writing—past, present, future (v. 19)—aiding our understanding of the contents of the book. This was followed by interpretation of the "stars" and "lampstands" in the vision. The stars probably represented the pastors of the churches and the lampstands the seven churches.

Application: Teaching and Preaching the Passage

The day is coming when "every knee shall bow and every tongue confess that Jesus Christ is Lord." For some this will be with great regret. Realization after the fact, that the Bible really is true and Jesus really is who He claims to be, will not avail. Our present generation is confused about who Jesus really is and about spiritual things in general, a confusion sustained by the politics of religious and philosophical pluralism and the prince of darkness. His devices have been all too successful. Jesus nonetheless remains as the way, the truth, and the life, the one and only Son of God and Son of Man.

An examination of Christ's attributes in this vision helps us know more about Him to make Him better known. John described the picture in detail, focusing on the glorified Jesus but including two other important symbols in the background. Those who teach and preach from this passage, and other texts throughout Revelation, should resist the tendency to find or read more into the text or symbol than even God Himself intended. Christ interprets only those two elements of the vision (v. 20), the stars and the lampstands. (Other aspects of the portrait will become important in the letters to the churches in chapters 2, 3.)

It is *this* Jesus before whom everyone must stand and give account. The secrets of men will be judged by the gospel of Jesus Christ. Life's most basic issue is reduced to what we do with Him. His voice speaks to us today as surely as it did to John on Patmos. Revelation is the source to consult about the future, informing us about everyone's future. It also informs us about the real Jesus that some intellectuals are unable to find.

Most people are unprepared for the days ahead, promised by Christ through John. They are like people in the path of a tornado, exposed to the the coming wrath and judgment of God against a Christ-rejecting world. We must be careful not to become so like the world that we pass away with it.

Even more, we must join with John in a continuing mission to broadcast this information to an unbelieving generation—a task made possible only by the Holy Spirit who enabled him to receive and record the information for us. The chain of communication in 1:1 has continued through teaching and preaching Revelation for two thousand years of church history. The eternal destinies of multitudes in our day depend in part on our faithfulness in getting the message to them.

Suggested Outline. Facing the Future in Faith versus Fear, 1:17-18. Jesus gives John three reasons: (1) He is the Sovereign of all time including past, present, and the future, v. 17. (2) He will be there in our future—having been resurrected to live forever, v. 18. (3) He has the keys governing the most dread ed aspects of the future—Hell and death, v. 18.

I. REVELATIONS TO THE CHURCHES (2:1—3:22)

Before examining the individual messages to the seven churches, it is helpful to view all of them together. They will be most appreciated when seen as both historical *and* illustrative rather than merely prophetic of the future or limited to any one generation of believers.

First, it would be difficult *not* to notice that Jesus uses the same basic, seven-fold pattern in each letter: (1) Commission, (2) Characteristics of Christ, (3) Commendation, (4) Concern, (5) Correction, (6) Challenge, (7) Compensation.

The *commission* given by Jesus includes the identity of the recipients and destination: namely, all believers residing there.

Second, Jesus identifies Himself with *characteristics* from the original vision of Christ (1:12-20). Some interpreters suggest that the attributes chosen relate specifically to that church; others see a connection with the city's historical background. The implications would be obvious to the readers.

The *commendation* is third, acknowledging each church's good qualities— except for the Laodiceans (3:14-22).

Fourth are one or more *concerns* or condemnations—except for Smyrna and Philadelphia. These warnings alert each church to serious problems, with weighty consequences if the problems are not addressed immediately with genuine repentance.

Specific steps of *correction* come sixth, required to restore God's blessing. Neither doctrinal error nor moral impurity can be tolerated. The threat of removing a church from its place is real, and repentance is not optional.

The *challenge* in each letter is identical: "He that hath an ear, let him hear what the Spirit saith to the churches." The Holy Spirit is speaking, as well as Jesus, implying the inspiration of the seven messages and of Revelation as a whole.

Each message concludes with the promise of future and eternal *compensation* for the "overcomers" within the churches. Overcoming means remaining faithful to the Lord in the face of moral and doctrinal compromise, even at the cost of martyrdom.

Second, it is helpful to consider the historical backgrounds of the seven cities, which Jesus apparently alludes to at times. Among the more important background elements, many of them affecting more than one church, are the following seven.

(1) The relationship to Roman authority, especially the *imperial cult* (emperor worship). Cities sought the honor of "temple warden," awarded to those with a temple devoted to this cult. Believers were often compelled to confess Caesar rather than Christ, under threat of execution, banishment, or loss of possessions.

(2) *Idolatry*, involving the worship of pagan deities. Each city had its favorite(s), perhaps native to the region or imported from other cultures. Roman, Greek, or Persian gods were often fused into those of native origin to accommodate and unify without bruising ethnic sentiment.

(3) *Jewish presence.* The hostile activities of this group—including informing Roman or local authorities against believers—often dramatically impacted the Christian population in the early church.

(4) *Geography.* Geographical situation often had important implications for a city's character and potential, whether involving roads, harbors, terrain, water supply, or other things.

(6) *Economics.* The kind of trade or natural resources available contributed to a city's prosperity. Some were known for a unique product and these are alluded to in the letters.

(7) *Special history.* Key persons, events, and cultural features affect the consciousness and character of a city, and the letters sometimes reflect such things.

We must be careful about reading the letters in the light of historical background; interpretation must always be grounded in what the text itself explicitly states. But historical information that potentially illustrates Scripture should not be ignored, and such factors help us understand the things that dramatically affected these believers.

A. Message to the Ephesian Church (2:1-7)

Background. Ephesus was perhaps the leading city of the Roman province named Asia. Pergamos to the north was the official capital and seat of emperor worship; Smyrna claimed to be "first in beauty and loyalty to Rome." But Ephesus was capital *de facto*, and addressing this church first is appropriate in that light and because of its Christian history. It had been in existence for around 40 years since Paul's lengthy, successful ministry there. Luke suggests that the entire province was evangelized while Paul was there (Acts 19:10). Other well-known Bible personalities ministered there, not least among them the Apostle John.

Roman officials traveling to Asia Minor first passed through it. Indeed, its wealth was in part because it served to connect eastern and western parts of the Roman Empire. It was also extremely idolatrous, with various temples to pagan gods and especially the great temple of Artemis (Diana), considered one of the seven wonders of the ancient world (Acts 19:24-28).

A natural harbor, the city was on the western seacoast of Asia Minor at the mouth of the Cayster River. Unfortunately, over time the harbor would silt up; this forced several relocations. It had been literally "moved from its place."

1 Unto the angel of the church of Ephesus write; These things saith he that holdeth the seven stars in his right hand, who walketh in the midst of the seven golden candlesticks;
2 I know thy works, and thy labour, and thy patience, and how thou canst not bear them which are evil: and thou hast tried them which say they are apostles, and are not, and hast found them liars:
3 And hast borne, and hast patience, and for my name's sake hast laboured, and hast not fainted.
4 Nevertheless I have somewhat against thee, because thou hast left thy first love.
5 Remember therefore from whence thou art fallen, and repent, and do the first works; or else I will come unto thee quickly, and will remove thy candlestick out of his place, except thou repent.
6 But this thou hast, that thou hatest the deeds of the Nicolaitanes, which I also hate.
7 He that hath an ear, let him hear what the Spirit saith unto the churches; To him that overcometh will I give to eat of the tree of life, which is in the midst of the paradise of God.

1. *Commission* (v. 1). Jesus directs John to address the pastor of the church. As already noted, "angel" (Greek *angelos*) may also be translated as "messenger"—in this case, the pastor

(Barnes 57-60). This is both consistent with the normal N.T. chain of authority in a local church and practical. There is no one more qualified than the pastor who teaches and preaches the Word to the congregation.

2. *Characteristics of Christ* (v. 1). The two characteristics Christ uses to introduce himself to the Ephesian church are from the vision in 1:20, where John saw Jesus holding seven stars in His hand and walking in the midst of seven candlesticks or lampstands. As Jesus Himself had explained (1:20), the "stars" represented the angels or pastors, the "lampstands" the churches.

Pastors of local churches have a special relationship to Jesus: He holds them in His right hand of power and authority. Knowing this is encouraging and challenging. Preaching and pastoring must be done with the power and authority of Christ, promoting confidence, boldness, and effectiveness in ministry. Furthermore, listening to or rejecting a messenger ordained by God is the equivalent of listening to or rejecting God.

Jesus walks among the lampstands, perhaps circling from church to church. Both "holding" and "walking" indicate continuing activities of Jesus (Greek present participles). This sovereign oversight will continue as long as the churches exist. The Lord relates to every church this way.

The all-penetrating "eyes of flaming fire" (1:14;2:18) enable Jesus to see or know everything about the church, and as He walks about He makes accurate inspection and administers personal care. After such an examination He is ready to tell them what the inspection reveals.

3. *Commendation* (vv. 2, 3). This section begins in each letter as "I know thy works," followed by one or more matters of commendation (for five of the seven).

"Works" broadly indicates an individual's or church's activity or characteristics. In the N.T. , works never serve as a means of justification but are an integral aspect of Christian behavior and service. They are crucial, though for different reasons, in the judgment of believers at the judgment seat of Christ (2 Cor. 5:10) and for unbelievers at the Great White Throne (Rev. 20:11-13).

The list of works commended in Ephesus is impressive: as many as ten, though some can be grouped in the same category. These are: (1) works, (2) labor, (3) patience, (4) inability to tolerate evil, (5) ability to discern false apostles, (6) exposure of liars, (7) burden bearing, (8) patience, (9) labor for Christ's name, (10) not having fainted. The first group of three relate to works in general. Items four, five, and six relate to zeal for doctrinal purity. Items seven through ten are related to, if not identical with, the first group.

"Labor" (Greek *kopos*), though similar to "work" (Greek *ergon*), characterizes work as "intense, troublesome, to the point of fatigue" (Thayer 355). "Patience" (Greek *hupomone*) is the ability to bear up under a heavy load or to remain constant in intense labor. The Ephesians are commended by Christ for their patient endurance of a heavy load over an extended period of time.

The church is also commended for its attitude toward holiness and zeal for doctrinal purity (v. 2), significant in light of two internal threats: "them which are evil," and "them which say they are apostles, and are not." Moral compro-

mise (sexual immorality) and doctrinal error (false apostles) were successfully resisted.

In appreciating the Ephesians' purity, we remember that at that stage they did not have the entire N.T. Further, there were pseudo-apostles usurping authority and pseudepigraphical documents impersonating real Scripture. Some traveling evangelists were sincere but many were not. A monumental challenge for the first-century church was to discern between the genuine and the counterfeit—without the benefit of the later councils and standard guides familiar today.

Those broadly described as "evil" (v. 2) might have been guilty of sowing false doctrine and corrupting others within the church—like the Nicolaitanes (v. 6); compare "Jezebel" in Thyatira (2:20). Or they might have been seduced by false teaching to compromise with the pagan environment around them. Lenski (84, 85) represents them as "disgraceful church members." But to use the word "evil" to describe fellow believers may be too strong, unless one differentiates between the persons and their rightly despised evil behavior.

"Bear" (Greek *bastazo*), used twice (vv. 2, 3), means to carry, including "bear what is burdensome" (Thayer 98). First the Ephesians are commended for their *inability* to bear or tolerate evil men; they hated destructive teaching as much as Jesus did. Then Jesus relates their bearing to His own name: "for my name's sake" (v. 3). The Ephesians carried their burdens, with steadfast endurance, for an appropriate reason: for Christ. Jesus looks at their effort as a successful whole (Greek constative aorist).

The final item in this lengthy commendation section adds a word about the Ephesian condition at the time of John's writing. Through their prolonged efforts, and against the natural tendency to grow weary or become satisfied with past success, they have "not fainted" (v. 3). The Ephesian church was still faithful.

4. *Concern*. In many ways the Ephesian church was exemplary. But one serious factor jeopardized their standing with Christ. For all its zeal in doctrine and holiness, the church had lost its original enthusiasm, its "first love" (v. 4). This could mean loss of love for Christ Himself, leading to a corresponding loss of love among believers (Thomas I:139-142), or loss of fervor for evangelizing unbelievers (Beale 230). At any rate, Christ's concern is not about the Ephesian church's response to its *external* enemies, but about what had become, by now, an *internal* attitude afflicting genuine believers.

We have contextual help to understand the meaning of *first love,* referred to in v. 5 as "the things you did at first." The preceding commendation rules out that the Ephesians had apostatized. Still, the concern is serious; it colors everything about them. The absence of the most necessary thing jeopardizes the whole. Achievement or success means nothing unless there is love (1 Cor. 13). The absence of this premier element even called into question the Ephesian church's future usefulness and existence.

To understand better this church's "first love" and "first works," we can glance back into its past. They immediately accepted Paul's gospel over their own limited experience (Acts 19:10). His lengthy ministry there (Acts 20:31)

indicates their eagerness to study. Their evangelistic fervor was obvious: the province was evangelized (Acts 19:10). The elders had apparently heeded Paul's farewell appeal, faithfully shepherding their flocks and guarding against false doctrine (Acts 20:28-31). Subsequently, Paul had commended their faithfulness (Eph. 1:1) and love for other believers (Eph. 1:15). He had prayed for them to be "rooted and grounded in love" and "know the love of Christ" (Eph. 3:17, 18). Their great love for Paul himself is also beyond question (Acts 21:37, 38). The Ephesian church had manifested love, but that has waned.

5. *Correction*. The threat is real: Jesus raises the possibility of "removing their lampstand from its place" (v. 5). Many scholars see a connection between this warning and Ephesus' literal relocations; see the background above. The Ephesians would immediately understand this threat.

Acts and Ephesians depict the Ephesian church, in Paul's day, as vibrant, full of life, a beehive of activity. That success was due in part to their great love for Christ, for Paul, for one another and for others. But their future place was in jeopardy, and the first step on the way back to first love is taken on the bridge of memory. Jesus commands, in effect: "Be remembering how it used to be."

"Thou art fallen" (Greek perfect tense) indicates that the departure from their first love has already happened. Consequently, Jesus warns them of a serious negative consequence. They desperately need to repent in order to survive the judgment of Christ (v. 5). The threat of removal is conditional and may be avoided. The forfeiture of a believer's salvation, although possible, is not in view here (as perhaps at Laodicea). The threatened removal more likely refers to the church's future usefulness, perhaps even to the continuing existence of a church in Ephesus. The mostly positive analysis, above, argues for the more lenient consequence: the church's effective functioning is in jeopardy.

"Repent" (Greek *metanoeo*) means "to change one's mind." Jesus commands the Ephesians to repent, requiring first a decision to do so. But this is only the first half of repentance. They must also do something about their situation. As Paul appealed in Acts 26:20—"that they should repent and turn to God, and do works meet for repentance"—so after commanding the Ephesians to repent Jesus commands them to "do" their first works.

Verse 6 inserts an additional commendation: namely, the Ephesians' rejection of the Nicolaitanes. The precise identification of this group is difficult. The name combines two roots (*nikao* and *laos*) meaning "to conquer the people." A popular suggestion is that they were followers of someone named Nicolas, perhaps even the early deacon in Jerusalem (Acts 6:5). They might have become a class of authoritarians or have been influenced by elements of incipient Gnosticism; see further the comments on 2:12-17.

6. *Challenge.* "Hear what the Holy Spirit is saying to the churches" (v. 7) is a strong command. The challenge is vital because the Holy Spirit gives it and because *hearing* is prerequisite for a positive response to Jesus' concerns. Obedience is implicit in the command to hear.

Anyone reading or hearing the invitation is included by "he that hath an ear

to hear." This encompasses every church, every believer, and every particular in the messages, negative or positive. However, obedience to the voice of the Holy Spirit is voluntary; God's grace may be resisted. The Holy Spirit may be ignored or grieved; a positive response is therefore invited.

7. *Compensation.* "Overcomer" (Greek *nikao*, v. 7) is a term originating with Jesus (Jn. 16:33) and borrowed by John (1 Jn. 5:4, 5). It means "to conquer, to be victorious" over "foes, temptations, persecutions" (Thayer 425, 426). Jesus was victorious over the world, the flesh, the devil, and ultimately death itself. Jesus empowers those who follow Him to do the same. This includes overcoming external enemies like Jewish or Roman persecutors and internal ones like false doctrine and worldliness.

The "tree of life" harks back to the Garden of Eden and points forward to its reappearance in Heaven (22:2). Amazingly, Jesus locates the tree of life, still alive, in the paradise of God—not an intermediate holding place but synonymous with Heaven itself (Lk. 23:43). The eternal existence of the tree of life in Heaven symbolizes God's gift of eternal life, the "reward" of salvation in Christ. Eating from the fruit of this tree symbolizes the fulfillment of salvation (Rom. 6:22, 23).

Summary
(2:1-7)

The deified Christ addresses the pastor of the Ephesian church, identifying Himself as holding the pastors in His right hand and walking in the midst of the churches.

He commends them for ten things (vv. 2, 3, 6), demonstrating the church's maturity or completeness. It is a model church, the most important of the seven.

However, the church is in danger of losing its "place" (v. 5), referring to the loss of mission or existence. The reason: they no longer love as they did at first (v. 4). Their first love was multidimensional, including love for Christ, for the Word, for one another, and for unbelievers. The threat is serious, reflecting loss of their original zeal and effectiveness in evangelism.

Furthermore, the church had successfully resisted Nicolaitane influence (v. 6). There was no equivocation on their part about this evil influence: they hated this group as much as Jesus did.

After being admonished to repent and resume the activities demonstrating their first love, the Ephesians are challenged to respond because this message is also from the Holy Spirit. Those who overcome will be rewarded to eat from the tree of life forever.

Application: Teaching and Preaching the Passage

Even model churches sometimes need revival and require a strong shock. We must not remove the "teeth" from Biblical threats because they serve this purpose and are real. Churches do not always remain faithful. Believers may be overcome rather than being overcomers. Churches go out of existence, sometimes after much success. Churches lose their original enthusiasm or first love, discontinuing the things they did at first.

This is one reason Revelation contains all seven messages: they provide needed exhortations for contemporary believers. Pastors should not neglect them; they often mirror problems within our own congregations.

Christ's influence transforms culture rather than conforming to it. Christians in these churches were called by Christ to make choices that ran against culture, and the price was often high. Nevertheless, He encouraged oppressed believers with guarantees of eternal rewards as compensation.

God offered eternal life from the beginning: Adam and Eve could choose between the tree of life and the tree of the knowledge of good and evil. He requires the same choice today. *Overcoming* is a choice. Overcoming the loss of first love for Christ insures continued effectiveness for Christ.

A major feature of our new nature in Christ is the restoration of freedom of the will. The spirit of the world that works in unbelievers no longer dominates the believer. Where the unbeliever is said to be "unable to not sin," the believer is "able not to sin" by virtue of the indwelling Holy Spirit. Only then is a person really free. If a believer sins, he *chooses* to do so; he is free to do otherwise.

Eating from the tree of life symbolizes participation in eternal life with God. It is the long awaited fulfillment of God's original design. The invitation from God is extended. Our response is a matter of choice.

Suggested Outline. First Love, 2:5: (1) Remember, v. 5; (2) Repent, v. 5; (3) Resume, v.5.

B. Message to the Smyrnean Church (2:8-11)

Background. Smryna was 35-40 miles north of Ephesus, along the post road. It too claimed the title "first-city of

Asia"; the physical layout, with streets and buildings on a gently sloping hillside leading to the acropolis with its stately buildings, was impressive. At each end of its main street ("the golden street") was a pagan temple, one to Zeus and the other to Cybele, mother goddess of Smyrna. Smyrna was also loyal to Rome, the first to erect a temple to "Roma" in 195 B.C. She was rewarded in A.D. 26 with the honor of constructing a temple to emperor Tiberius.

The city contained a significant number of Jews, who may have played an adversarial role against Christians. Some have estimated the Jewish population of Asia Minor to be as many as one million by the end of the first century. This would mean that there were a number of synagogues in the larger cities. The one unearthed in Sardis could seat a thousand.

The strength of the "imperial cult"—official worship of the Roman emperor—and the worship of local deities created a hostile environment for true Christians. Loyalty to Caesar and local gods was the norm of citizenship. Those who failed to confess Caesar as Lord or to participate in local pagan activities suffered. For the Christian this could mean death or at least poverty because of economic discrimination. In the mindset of the time, "loyalty" required participation in Caesar worship, the trade confederacy, and a given city's pagan temple activities. In their view, one could not be loyal to a city without worshiping Caesar and the patron deity. This was the dilemma for Christians in Smyrna and elsewhere. True Christians would not confess Caesar and did not receive their yearly certificate indicating allegiance. Failure to participate might also mean being reported to the Roman proconsul. Some scholars suggest that the Jews participated in informing the authorities against Christians.

As possibly background for "was dead and is alive," Smyrna was destroyed in about 600 B.C. and later rebuilt in 195 B.C. It is the only one of the seven cities which continues to exist at present, known as Izmir (renamed following its conquest by Muslims) in Turkey.

8 And unto the angel of the church in Smyrna write; These things saith the first and the last, which was dead, and is alive;
9 I know thy works, and tribulation, and poverty, (but thou art rich) and *I know* the blasphemy of them which say they are Jews, and are not, but *are* the synagogue of Satan.
10 Fear none of those things which thou shalt suffer: behold, the devil shall cast *some* of you into prison, that ye may be tried; and ye shall have tribulation ten days: be thou faithful unto death, and I will give thee a crown of life.
11 He that hath an ear, let him hear what the Spirit saith unto the churches; He that overcometh shall not be hurt of the second death.

1. *Commission.* Jesus gives John a letter for the pastor (Greek *angelos*) of the church in Smyrna (v. 8). Though Smyrna was known for its wealth and beauty, Christ notes the material poverty of the church there (v. 9). His message offers comfort and counsel.

2. *Characteristics of Christ.* Harking back to John's vision of Christ, Jesus identifies Himself as "the first and the last" who "was dead, but is now alive" (v. 8); see comments on 1:8, 11, 17.

Both phrases support His claim of deity and highlight specific aspects of His character. As "first and last," Jesus is eternal and preeminent. The second phrase emphasizes His resurrection. Perhaps these two characteristics had special significance for Smyrnean believers, relating directly to their material poverty and martyrdom (vv. 9, 10).

3. *Commendation*. Jesus, as God, is all knowing, His knowledge of each church absolute. The analysis of the Smyrnean church is wholly positive and includes their "works, tribulation, and poverty" (v. 9). Their faithfulness is exemplary, having remained so in an environment hostile to Christianity.

Though "works" is not in all manuscripts, most include it. This could mean their works as a whole, or specific works associated with tribulation and poverty (which closely follow in the clause). The word applies equally well either way.

The Smyrnean church was faithful in "tribulation" (Greek *thlipsis*), which at root means "pressure" (Thayer 291). Some (like Polycarp later) were perhaps martyred. Others most certainly were impoverished. "Poverty" (Greek *ptocheia*) suggests that one is reduced to begging (Thayer 557). The temptation to compromise with the culture and avoid such poverty would be great. The Smyrnean believers did not yield.

All of them had to endure mental tribulation as targets of the "blasphemy of the Jews." "Blasphemy" (Greek *blasphemia*) apparently refers to speech that is "injurious" to God or Christ (Vine 69). This type of tribulation can be as difficult to endure as any.

Against the reality of their material poverty, Jesus inserts an important contrast: though materially poor, they are spiritually "rich" in Christ, in two senses.

First, as believers they already possess present spiritual riches in Christ. Second, there are future rewards. In the great Sermon on the Mount (Mt. 5:1-12), Jesus predicts that the "poor in spirit" will inherit the kingdom of heaven, that the "meek" will inherit the earth, that those "persecuted for righteousness' sake" will be greatly rewarded. These compensations are of far greater worth than the temporary gain acquired by compromise or renunciation of Christ.

Two specific commendations follow. The first (v. 9) most likely reflects Jewish antagonism. Unbelieving Jews might participate in economic pressures against Christian Jews, forcing uncompromising believers into poverty. Even worse, hostile Jews could inform the authorities against Christians, forcing a crisis in regard to Caesar worship. Roman "don't ask, don't tell" policy, often dormant in the cities until aroused, would obviously be set aside when the loyalty of given individuals was challenged. This varied from place to place and emperor to emperor. Those more infatuated with the idea of being worshiped, like Domitian (ca. A.D. 96), were more inclined to enforce the practice. Smyrna was indeed very loyal to Rome. This clever technique of persecution may have been what evoked the Lord's stern words describing them (apparently the non-Christian Jews) as a "synagogue of Satan."

The second commendation reflects what Jesus, whose perfect knowledge also includes the future, sees as coming. There will be intense persecution from Satan himself, leading to literal imprisonment and, in some instances, death (v. 10).

4. *Concern*. Smyrna is one of two churches (with Philadelphia) not rebuked

in any way. The concerns are about issues or persons external to the church. The first of these is the "blasphemy of the Jews," as just discussed. The form of this is not stated but refers to Jews who had rejected Christ as Messiah. Some Jewish believers in Smyrna might have been expelled from the synagogue because of their faith in Christ. Among Jews, the synagogue was much more than a place of worship. It sponsored Jewish worship, culture, government, education, and other daily activities. A strong relationship with the synagogue was considered to be an integral aspect of Jewish life. Exclusion from the synagogue was a serious blow for any Jew.

The object of Jesus' ire ("synagogue of Satan") was not the Jewish race as a whole but the activities of a specific, antagonistic element within Asia Minor. Christ loves every race and invites all to become a part of the church. However, *unbelieving* Jews created much havoc for Christians in the first century, stirring up conflict and confusing new converts. No wonder both Jesus and Paul (Phil. 3:2) strongly denounced their activity against Christ (cf. Jn. 8:39-44).

5. *Correction.* Because no negative concerns are expressed, the section outlining steps of correction is also absent. No doubt the church there was less than perfect, but any problems must have been minor compared to those in the other churches. There was no immediate threat to the church's mission or existence.

The counsel Jesus offers relates to preparing for increasing persecution. He expects them to do this in several ways.

First, they should "fear none of those things" (v. 10), meaning things in the Smyrneans' near future and including imprisonment and severe persecution. The prediction that this "tribulation" will last "ten days" is probably symbolic of completeness. Believers in Smyrna (and elsewhere) would be called to endure such conditions for quite some time.

Next, they should "be faithful unto death," resisting the temptation to give in under difficult circumstances. There would be great temptation to participate in pagan activities or burning incense to Caesar in order to avoid impoverishment or to save their lives. But Christ does not waver in His expectations; they must remain faithful even in the face of death.

6. *Compensation.* Jesus promises the faithful of Smyrna a "crown of life" (v. 10). Such a "crown" (Greek *stephanos*)—wreaths made from plants or flowers—was bestowed as a reward for victorious athletes (1 Cor. 9:25) or generals, or for other occasions of celebration. (They are not "royal" crowns, indicated by the Greek *diadema*, as in Rev. 19:12.) Even if their lives end in martyrdom, Jesus will give them the crown of eternal life.

These eternal rewards are *conditional* because they are based on faithfulness, also expressed as "overcoming" (v. 11). Being faithful until death is tantamount to overcoming every obstacle along the way. Opposition often translated into material poverty, social persecution, or physical death. The risen and coming Christ expected His followers to overcome all of them.

7. *Challenge.* The Smyrnean church is also exhorted to heed Christ's message because it is what the Holy Spirit is saying (Greek present tense) to them— suggesting the ongoing relevance of the message. The Holy Spirit has no doubt continued speaking about these princi-

ples until now; He will continue to do so until He is taken out of the world when Jesus comes again.

A victorious Christian, one who "overcomes," will not experience the "second death" (v. 11). Fortunately, this term is defined for us as "the lake which burneth with fire and brimstone: which is the second death" (21:8)—another term for Hell itself. All men are appointed to die physically (Heb. 9:27), but the "second death" is *eternal*, spiritual death, an irrevocable state of physical and mental torment in a literal place. Thankfully, new birth in Christ cancels the second death for believers.

Summary
(2:8-11)

The link between the vision of the glorified and deified Christ in 1:12-20 is preserved: the Christ identified there speaks to Smyrna by virtue of His attributes of preeminence and eternity.

This risen and exalted Christ knows all about them: their works, tribulations, and poverty. He knows that their difficult circumstances are compounded by persecutions in two forms. One is from the Jewish presence in Smyrna. The other is a spirit of persecution from Satan himself, resulting in imprisonment for some and martyrdom for others. The symbolic use of "ten days," rather than suggesting brevity, more likely indicates a lengthy period that will test their faithfulness. Hence, Christ speaks to encourage them to endure: sure and severe persecution is coming.

Jesus promises that their faithfulness in such trying times will be rewarded in two ways. They will receive the crown of eternal life. And they will escape the second death, another name for Hell

itself, where unbelievers and apostates are consigned eternally by God.

Application: Teaching and Preaching the Passage

Christians should be able to avoid surface judgments based on what is visible to the eye. Scripture warns about the danger of being judgmental and of making comparisons. Things or persons are not always what they seem. The Smyrnean church was not as outwardly impressive as the Ephesian church. Yet the silence of Jesus about negatives implies that Smyrna was considered by Him to be a successful church also.

In the eyes of the world, the believers were materially poor. But Jesus saw beyond this and said they were rich. He commended them for faithfulness under extremely difficult circumstances. Success, then, is being what God has called us to be. A health, wealth, and superficial happiness model, often promoted today, is not the N.T. description of spiritual success. Faithfulness may lead one to forfeit his life. It often means giving up material things rather than stockpiling them. For some it is simply being faithful or unnoticed by others in difficult circumstances. It means remaining where God has called us to serve rather than setting forth on a quest for greener grass. It is a call to anonymity.

Suggested Outline. True Riches, 2:9-11: (1) Invisible, v. 9; (2) Invincible, v. 10; (3) Insulated, v. 11.

C. Message to the Pergamean Church (2:12-17)

Background. Pergamos was 35-40 miles north and east of Smyrna, its acropolis and fortress on a plateau

1,000 feet from the valley floor. Major temples were erected for Zeus, Athena (Greek goddess of victory), Dionysus (Anatolian bull god), and Asclepius (serpent god of healing). Many traveled to Pergamos to be healed. It was also home to the world's second largest library, boasting some 200,000 volumes.

This center of pagan religion was also *the* official seat of emperor worship in provincial Asia. The status of "temple warden" was conferred on Pergamos by Rome in 29 B.C., with the temple to Augustus officially establishing the cult of emperor worship in Pergamos before Ephesus or Smyrna (Charles I:60).

Pergamos was also the official capital of the province, and so the residence of the Roman proconsul. Proconsuls enforced their rule with the "right of the sword"—the authority to execute whomever they pleased.

Like the other cites, Pergamos had all the components antagonistic to public confession of Christ. Mandatory emperor worship, the presence of unbelieving Jews, and the essential interconnection between idolatry, economics, and citizenship made it truly difficult to practice Christianity.

12 And to the angel of the church in Pergamos write; These things saith he which hath the sharp sword with two edges;
13 I know thy works, and where thou dwellest, *even* where Satan's seat *is*: and thou holdest fast my name, and hast not denied my faith, even in those days wherein Antipas *was* my faithful martyr, who was slain among you, where Satan dwelleth.

14 But I have a few things against thee, because thou hast there them that hold the doctrine of Balaam, who taught Balac to cast a stumblingblock before the children of Israel, to eat things sacrificed to idols, and to commit fornication.
15 So hast thou also them that hold the doctrine of the Nicolaitanes, which thing I hate.
16 Repent; or else I will come unto thee quickly, and will fight against them with the sword of my mouth.
17 He that hath an ear, let him hear what the Spirit saith unto the churches; To him that overcometh will I give to eat of the hidden manna, and will give him a white stone, and in the stone a new name written, which no man knoweth saving he that receiveth *it*.

1. *Commission*. Again, Jesus directs John to write a message, this time to Pergamos (Latin *Pergamum*), another city where believers faced pagan idolatry, emperor worship, and (we may assume) hostile Jews. This church was not as successful as those in Ephesus or Smyrna in withstanding this three-fold enemy.

2. *Characteristics of Christ*. Jesus identifies Himself as one "that hath the sharp sword with two edges" (v. 12), reflecting 1:16 (see comments there and at 19:15). The sword metaphor is often used for the Word of God (Eph. 6:17; Heb. 4:12; Rev. 19:15), and Jesus is the Incarnate Word.

3. *Commendation*. The commendation centers on the faithfulness of Pergamean believers in spite of the triad of external threats noted above. The identification of "Satan's seat" (v. 13) is debated: some propose the famous altar

to Zeus atop the city's acropolis; others point to the city's healing cult (Asclepius) with its school of medicine. But the fact that Pergamos was the seat of emperor worship is the most likely candidate. The demand of this "imperial cult" to confess Caesar as Lord caused many to be martyred for their faith.

Jesus commends their faithfulness. They are "holding fast" to the name of Christ and have refused to deny their personal faith in Christ before either local or Roman authorities, knowing fully what this might cost them. Antipas' martyrdom might have been the result of refusing to deny Christ or confess Caesar as Lord.

Jesus leaves no doubt about the origin of all persecutions by using Satan's name twice. He labels *all* the enemies of the church as satanic ("seat" and "dwelling place" of Satan, v. 13; see Mt. 12:25; Jn. 8:44; Eph. 2:2), thus accounting for their evil behavior in general and for their hostility to believers in particular.

Every member of the human race falls into one of two spiritual categories: for Christ or against Him. Paul sees all the unsaved as under the influence of the satanic spirit "that now worketh in the children of disobedience" (Eph. 2:2; 6:12). Each of the three groups identified—imperial cult, pagan authorities, unbelieving Jews—manifests the same hellish hate for believers.

4. *Concern.* Two groups who purvey false doctrine are at Pergamos, blights against its otherwise commendable features: the "doctrines" (teachings) of "Balaam" (v. 14) and of the "Nicolaitanes" (v. 15). Toleration of these errors endangers the church's holiness, mission, and future existence.

The "doctrine of Balaam" is connected with its O.T. precedent (Num. 22:5; 25:1-3; 31:16). Balaam was hired by Balak to curse the Israelites but was unable to do so, finally blessing them instead. However, under his influence the Israelites sinned by committing whoredom with Moabite women, bringing severe judgment from God (Num. 25:9). The end result was the one Balak originally sought. The "stumblingblock" (v. 14) is two-sided: eating meat offered to idols coupled with sexual immorality. Balaamism as a term apparently evolved to symbolize those who advocated similar behaviors.

Those who advocated this doctrine in the church at Pergamos saw nothing wrong with eating food that had been offered to idols; they probably also advocated participating in pagan temple feasts, and these often included immorality. Whatever their justifications, Jesus rejected the practice entirely. Balaamism violated the decree in Acts 15. This earliest of church councils clearly forbade Gentile converts from participating in idolatry and from sexual immorality.

Nicolaitane influence, also present, might have been similar (v. 15). Membership in trade guilds required sacrifice to pagan deities and often involved immorality. DeSilva (273-302) notes, "Some commentators regard the practice of fornication as part of the entertainment of these feasts, but one must hold the spiritual dimension clearly in mind as well, namely, forsaking a faithful relationship to Jesus." He thinks that they might have picked up on the Corinthians' idea that "an idol is nothing" and that "their participation in an idol feast would be without spiritual significance." Whatever the Nicolaitanes' precise error, Jesus denounced it strongly. They appear again in the messages to Ephesus (2:6, above) and may be connected with the fallacies of both "Jezebel" in Thyatira (2:20, 24) and "Balaam" here.

There is no information about the Nicolaitanes except for what we find in this chapter. It is possible that John uses the term symbolically and pejoratively, describing those in general who practice or tolerate idolatrous and immoral behavior in the church (cf. ISBE 534). Jesus "hates" the Nicolaitane doctrine; though this is not in some manuscripts in v. 15, it is in 2:6. Their deeds include the eating of food offered to idols and sexual immorality. Jesus rejects Nicolaitane doctrine, those who teach it, and its practice by those who profess Christ.

5. *Correction*. Remedy requires immediate and decisive response: "repent" (v. 16), a mandatory command in light of the accompanying warning. If they do not, the omnipotent Christ, prepared for battle with His "sword," will deal with the problem personally. There is every reason to fear the sword wielded by Christ, even more than the sword of Rome.

"Quickly" reinforces the seriousness of the errors, and the warning is directed specifically to those who are guilty. Christ's judgment has precise accuracy, affecting only the advocates of these false doctrines.

6. *Challenge*. The standard challenge to "hear what the Spirit saith to the churches" (v.17) leads quickly into promised compensation to overcomers; see comments on 2:7, 11.

7. *Compensation*. The condition of overcoming is the same as in the other messages. One must overcome the doctrine of the Nicolaitanes and the idola-

trous and immoral behavior promoted thereby. "Hidden manna" and "a white stone" will be given in eternity to overcomers (v. 17). The first of these is likely an allusion to the pot of manna hidden in the ark of God behind the veil in the Holy of Holies (Ex. 16:14, 31-36; Heb. 9:4). This manna was a memorial to God's ability to provide for His people throughout their wilderness years. God will continue to provide for His children throughout eternity.

The significance of the white stone is not as obvious. In the culture of the times, white stones were sometimes used like modern tickets for admission into theaters, games, or temple activities (ISBE 769), or in court (in contrast to black stones) as votes for acquittal. Stones were carried as lucky amulets inscribed with the name of one's favorite god.

Those who were faithful to Christ often lost certain worldly privileges and possessions. But they could count on "hidden manna" provided by the Lord Jesus throughout eternity. Those who were not given admission to the world's activities would have eternal access to Heaven.

The "new name" may refer to the name of Christ or the name of the believer. It could be a new name literally, commemorating the new birth or being enrolled in the Lamb's book of life (20:12, 15). Any historical link for "no man knoweth except the one receiving it" is at best speculative.

Summary
(2:12-17)

Pergamos also claimed the title "first city of Asia," the official capital of Roman government in the province and the seat of emperor worship. Jesus' references to "Satan's seat" and "where Satan dwelleth" were probably metaphors for the imperial cult.

The Pergamean church is commended for remaining true to Christ's name. One of the believers there, Antipas, has been martyred: probably for refusing to confess Caesar as Lord. There may have been a yearly requirement to demonstrate allegiance to Caesar by offering a pinch of incense and verbally confessing Caesar as Lord. Ties with Domitian would have been strong in Pergamos.

Jesus gives the church mixed reviews. There is a faithful element in the church. But there are also those teaching false doctrine. Two doctrinal errors are that of Balaam and that of the Nicolaitanes. These two, if not identical, were at least complementary.

Eating meat offered to idols at pagan feasts violated Scriptural principles. Allowance was made when idol meat was eaten ignorantly, but the norm was abstinence (1 Cor. 10:14-28). Participation in pagan feasts and eating meat offered to idols hindered the church's mission as salt and light.

They are confronted by a Christ who, like the Romans, wields a powerful sword. Unlike the Romans, who have power over physical life, Jesus possesses power over *eternal* life. He should be feared more than Caesar. Jesus promises to deal with those guilty of promoting false doctrines; they must be confronted and purged from their church.

Those who overcome these doctrines will be compensated with eternal rewards beyond comparison: far greater than temporary Pergamean honors acquired by the high price of unholy cultural compromises.

Application: Teaching and Preaching the Passage

The gospel had successfully invaded the Mediterranean world through the journeys of Paul and others; as a result there was a church in Pergamos. As the years had passed, there may have been a waning of enthusiasm for truth, holiness, and evangelistic fervor. But Jesus requires that zeal for Him be maintained. Like most of the other churches, the one in Pergamos needed defenses against paganism from without and error from within.

The Lord intends that His church function as salt and light, but Christians can lose their identity or saltiness by becoming like the pagans. Some in the church advocated compliance and compromise. But Jesus expected triumph over culture and separation from certain aspects of the first-century world instead.

Some taught that participation in local festivals (involving eating meat offered to idols), indulging in sexual immorality with temple prostitutes, or confessing Caesar as Lord were acceptable, perhaps "necessary evils." There was no other choice, they said, in order to survive economically or otherwise. Others might have advocated indulging the flesh, based on an erroneous view of Christian liberty.

The ghosts of this old pagan triumvirate against the early church, and of advocates of compromise from within, still haunt us today. They include idolatry, covetousness, immorality, false doctrine, advocates of worldly compromise, and government censure of Christianity.

Whenever the church is not different from the world around it, it has ceased being a light in the darkness. Recent research points out that, although the number of professing Christians in America has increased, there has not been a corresponding change in behavior. Christians are not really different from their unbelieving neighbors.

Let us hear what the Spirit is saying to the church of the twenty-first century. He may very well be saying that we reflect the image of the seven churches of Roman Asia. If so, we too must repent.

Suggested Outline. Sword of the Lord, 2:12-17: (1) Weapon, The Word of God, vv. 12, 16; (2) Warfare, vv. 13-15; (3) Warning, v. 16; (4) Winning, v. 17.

D. Message to the Thyatiran Church (2:18-29)

Background. Forty miles east of Pergamos was Thyatira, which began as a military garrison. It changed hands often before Roman rule brought stability to the region. Nevertheless, Thyatira was in a valley between important commercial centers, a strategic stop along the imperial post road. Roman protection contributed to its thriving economy; it was famous for its trade guilds for "wool workers, linen workers, makers of outer garments, dryers, leather workers, tanners, potters, bakers, slave dealers and bronzesmiths" (Ramsay 238).

Paul's convert, Lydia in Philipi, was a "seller of purple" from Thyatira (Acts 16:4, 15). Thyatira was famous for its "turkey red" dye from the plentiful madder root in the valley (Mounce 85). "Purple" may have been considered a class of red.

Tyrimnos the sun god was the city deity. Each guild also had its own patron god, and feasts to such gods included sexual revelry. Good standing in the guilds meant participating in such activities (Acts 15:28, 29; 1 Cor. 10:20, 21). Christians, therefore, faced serious economic pressures to *compromise* with the world in the form of participation in idolatrous guild feasts and the immorality associated with them. This was necessary to maintain standing with their respective guilds, with economic hardship being the alternative. Apparently, in dealing with this problem, a faction arose within the church; some suggested that it was not harmful to "tip the hat" to pagan expectations while maintaining belief in Christ—the mistaken belief that one may have it both ways.

Some view this as "the longest and most difficult of the seven letters" (Hemer, quoted by Mounce 84). But the Thyatirans had about the same number of problems as the others. There is doubt that the Thyatiran church existed beyond the end of the second century (Swete 41).

**18 And unto the angel of the church in Thyatira write; These things saith the Son of God, who hath his eyes like unto a flame of fire, and his feet *are* like fine brass;
19 I know thy works, and charity, and service, and faith, and thy patience, and thy works; and the last *to be* more than the first.
20 Notwithstanding I have a few things against thee, because thou sufferest that woman Jezebel, which calleth herself a prophetess, to teach and to seduce my servants to commit fornication, and to eat things sacrificed unto idols.**

21 And I gave her space to repent of her fornication; and she repented not.

22 Behold, I will cast her into a bed, and them that commit adultery with her into great tribulation, except they repent of their deeds.

23 And I will kill her children with death; and all the churches shall know that I am he which searcheth the reins and hearts: and I will give unto every one of you according to your works.

24 But unto you I say, and unto the rest in Thyatira, as many as have not this doctrine, and which have not known the depths of Satan, as they speak; I will put upon you none other burden.

25 But that which ye have *already* hold fast till I come.

26 And he that overcometh, and keepeth my works unto the end, to him will I give power over the nations:

27 And he shall rule them with a rod of iron; as the vessels of a potter shall they be broken to shivers: even as I received of my Father.

28 And I will give him the morning star.

29 He that hath an ear, let him hear what the Spirit saith unto the churches.

1. *Commission.* Christ's fourth letter is to the church in Thyatira (v. 18). Though it was not famous for any particular reason, no church, individual, or sin is insignificant to the Lord.

2. *Characteristics of Christ.* Jesus identifies Himself as "the Son of God" (v. 18; cf. 1:2, 5), a direct reference to His deity and authority. The other characteristics relate specifically to the vision of Christ (see 1:14, 15) with "eyes of flaming fire" and "feet of brass" (bronze) glowing as if recently removed from a furnace.

The portrait of Jesus in the gospels is mostly benevolent: the suffering servant who humbly displays His power to heal sickness, control the elements, and deal with the devil, who eventually dies on the cross. By comparison, the picture of Christ presented in Revelation focuses on more sobering aspects of His character, helping us balance our understanding of Him. The eyes of Jesus (His countenance) can be compassionate or frightening, at times communicating forgiveness but at others holy concern directed at those who persist in sin.

His vision is always clear or accurate, able to penetrate into human hearts or telescope into the future. The molten feet probably symbolize His holiness and judgment. Fire purifies or makes holy. Feet transport us where we want to go. The implication is a warning of impending action taken by Christ Himself in regard to His concerns about problems in the Thyatiran church (see 2:16). The tone is serious.

3. *Commendation.* The standard evaluation, "I know thy works," introduces several positive qualities (v. 19): "charity" (or love), "service," "faith," "patience," and "works." Their presence must not be minimized: the Christians had not succumbed wholly to the advocates of false doctrine within the church. They loved the Lord sincerely. The penetrating gaze of Christ revealed works prompted by genuine love for the Lord and for one another.

"Service" is an expression of love, a distinguishing characteristic of discipleship. Servanthood is the pathway to greatness according to Christ (Mt.

20:26, 27). His own mission was so characterized.

"Faith" is essential for several reasons, first because we are saved by grace through faith. But Christ highly valued displays of faith, as mentioned often in the gospels: Mt. 8:5-10; 9:20-22; 15:27, 28; Mk. 2:1-5. Jesus sees faith in Thyatira.

"Patience" (Greek *hupomone*) is the ability to endure a heavy burden over an extended period of time. The church has endured the things threatening its existence. Indeed, their "last" works are more than the first ones, suggesting continuing progress (cf. the opposite in 2:4).

4. *Concern*. The "few things" (v. 20) that greatly concern Christ originate with a woman named "Jezebel." Whether she is so named symbolically or literally makes no difference, she is a real person in the church who has usurped the title of "prophetess" and is teaching false doctrine.

That some godly women exercised the gift of prophecy, to some degree, in the N.T. is clear, including Anna (Lk. 2:36) and the four unmarried daughters of Philip (Acts 21:9). Paul gives instruction about the head-covering for women who prophesy (1 Cor. 11:5). The "Jezebel" at Thyatira claimed this gift but her teaching gave the lie to her claim. Her erroneous teaching is identified by the same two markers (fornication and idolatry) as the doctrine of Balaam in the message to Pergamos (2:14).

The situation is serious because the church *permits* Jezebel to teach her falsehood, leading some believers into sinful behaviors. "Seduce" (Greek *planao*) means "to cause to stray or lead astray" (Thayer 514), "fundamental

departure from the truth" (Vincent 455). Like the original Jezebel (1 Kg. 18:18, 19; 21:25, 26), this N.T. counterpart led Thyatiran believers astray into sexual immorality and idolatry. As Elijah promised God's judgment against the original, Jesus promises to judge this "Jezebel" and her associates.

The fact that several verses describe this judgment underscores the Lord's unwavering demand for holiness in doctrine and lifestyle. Final judgment will come only after ample opportunity to repent has been extended. But "she repented not," her recalcitrance setting in motion judgments administered by Christ Himself against her and her unrepentant confederates (vv. 22, 23).

"I will cast" is, literally, "I am casting" (Greek progressive present, used futuristically), hinting at immediacy and certainty. The problem is so flagrant that it cannot be tolerated. Only those who repent of the two evils will escape (v. 22).

Some may have straddled the fence, and the warning might rescue many of them from Christ's judgments. Apparently, not many were influenced by Jezebel. They "have not this doctrine" and they "have not known the depths of Satan" (v. 24). The "depths of Satan" is enigmatic but may have reference to a Gnostic-like idea of *indulging the flesh* by exploring sinful behaviors, done under the wicked pretense of trying to understand those behaviors better.

There is no need to argue whether the "fornication" was literal or spiritual in nature; both were involved. Idolatry is "spiritual adultery" and participation in sexual immorality was associated with idolatry. Jezebel and her followers were guilty of advocating eating food sacrificed to idols and of the sexual immorality typically involved.

Jesus promises to throw all of the offenders into a common bed of great tribulation (Greek *thlipsis*), meaning affliction or pressure (v. 22), though this may be avoided by repentance (v. 22). Christ's promise to "kill her children with death" raises the question of whether the children in question were physically her own or those converted to her doctrine. The latter is probable, logically extending the "bed" metaphor immediately preceding (v. 22). It is not characteristic of the N.T. to punish children for a mother's sins.

Christ's swift and severe judgment will have a sanctifying effect on the believing community elsewhere ("all the churches," v. 23). The Son of God sees everywhere and into the hearts of everyone with His eyes of flaming fire. "Reins and hearts" identify the inner source of human behavior in the soul of man. "Reins" (Greek *nephros*, literally the kidneys) and "hearts" were both used by the ancients to represent the innermost being, perhaps respectively the seat of emotions and thoughts. External behavior originates as feelings, emotions, thoughts, motives, and attitudes. These eventually find expression in visible behavior, good or bad. Jesus, as presented in awesome and frightening detail (1:12-20), guarantees to come and examine their spiritual condition. This special visitation of judgment is for one purpose: He will judge Jezebel and her followers.

This judgment will not affect the faithful of Thyatira. Christ has no other "burden" (Greek *baros*; literally "a weight") to place on them other than continuing faithfulness (v. 24), manifesting itself in two ways: to continue rejecting false doctrine and to endure. Thyatiran believers must remain faithful until Christ returns.

5. *Correction.* The issue in the church may be resolved only by the repentance of the guilty. The church's leadership had not effectively dealt with this problem or had not tried, and Jesus calls for action: this unrepentant woman, with her unrepentant victims and false doctrine, must be expelled. Guilty individuals could regain a right relationship with Christ by immediate repentance of the sins of idolatry and fornication (v. 22).

Meanwhile, the faithful must "hold fast" to their commended features (v. 25; cf. v. 19). This verb (Greek effective aorist imperative) helps us picture a strong grasp that does not lose its grip. Jesus counsels them to hold on to the good until He comes.

6. *Compensation.* "Overcoming" is, in every letter, the condition for receiving various rewards (v. 26). Christ expects every believer to overcome the leaven of "Jezebel."

A second condition is "keep my works unto the end." To Christ, the end is as important as the beginning, especially in regard to the Christian life and the Second Coming. Believers should live in continual readiness for the Lord's return. They must be prepared and watching, because Christ's return is unpredictable and sudden. Eternity will greet us as that moment finds us. This emphasis is found particularly in the Olivet Discourse (Mt. 24, 25), Christ's most comprehensive statement about the end-times.

The basic thrust of Jesus' promise to overcomers is sharing in Christ's future world conquest (vv. 26, 27). This rule is universal, encompassing all the nations of earth. It is both sovereign and militaristic, authorized by God Himself. This portrayal is clearly messianic, closely matching David's prophecy in Ps. 2.

The militaristic aspect of this rule ("with a rod of iron") makes it difficult to reconcile or identify it with a "spiritual rule" through the church in the present age. The phrase simply does not fit the present situation. Furthermore, the end-time scenario painted by the N.T., worsening for the church in the last days (2 Tim. 3:1), makes the likelihood of such a time in the church age even more remote. Equally unlikely is that the church will somehow manage to "shatter the nations" like broken pottery (literally or symbolically), a metaphor that does not fit well with the presentation of the gospel. The time frame for all this was certainly future (future tense verbs) to readers of the first century.

The rule is also shared: as the Father has given this rule to Jesus (v. 27), He will give it to His faithful followers. The "morning star," which He promises to overcomers, becomes a symbol of this rule (v. 28); this star rules the morning sky alone. The image of ruling most aptly applies to Christ Himself, but ruling the nations becomes our privilege by virtue of our union with Him.

7. *Challenge.* The message ends with the standard invitation from the Holy Spirit to all seven churches, to be heeded by those with "ears to hear" (v. 29). Discerning the voice of the Holy Spirit is not only for the spiritually mature, it is the mark of discipleship. The Holy Spirit dwells within every believer (Rom. 8:9, 14) from the moment of conversion. Thus every believer can hear what the Spirit is saying. Those who hear and obey are blessed.

Summary
(2:18-29)

Jesus addresses the Thyatiran church as the Son of God having eyes flaming like fire and feet glowing like molten bronze. These characteristics (from 1:12-20) anticipate dealing with the problem of false doctrine in the Thyatiran church.

The picture is not entirely negative. They are commended for a number of qualities: their love, service, faith, patience, and a growing enthusiasm (v. 19). Many remained faithful in spite of Jezebel's corrupting influence (v. 24). They had not experienced the "depths of Satan" as some had.

Christ's concern is directed against the church for allowing a false prophetess, identified as "Jezebel," to teach false doctrine (v. 20). This apparently charismatic woman seduced some into idolatry and immorality. Although it is possible to conceive of idolatry as "spiritual" adultery, the naming of both makes it more likely that both sins were really involved. Participation in sexual immorality was often associated with idol worship.

Both eating food offered to idols and fornication are wicked. Jesus confronts the guilty, urging repentance in order to avoid promised judgment. The all-seeing and all-powerful Christ will execute the judgments personally.

After exhorting the faithful in the church to hold fast to their commended works, Jesus promises that overcomers will share in a future, earthly, militaristic rule over the nations. He promises to give them "the morning star," perhaps a symbol of millennial rule.

The message concludes with the invitation to hear what the Holy Spirit is saying to all the churches.

Application: Teaching and Preaching the Passage

The question of how to respond to the presence of evil in a church concerns us all. God allows this: Satan and sin often find their way into congregations and something must be done when they do. Jesus wants His church to be holy in doctrine and practice; such problems must be confronted and resolved without procrastination.

Exercising church discipline is a Scriptural mandate. Failure in this regard has a negative effect on others within the body. False doctrine or evil behavior must not be tolerated; wickedness breeds and multiplies.

There is a Scriptural model for discipline on an individual level in Mt. 18:15-20, where Jesus also vests great binding authority in the decisions of a local church. Paul gives us a model in 1 Cor. 5:1-12. Pastors have authority and responsibility as well (Heb. 13:7, 17). Contemporary society has discarded this high view of the local church and its officers, to its detriment. A church that consistently and fairly confronts various evils within is not unloving.

The positive impact of this message is clear: it really is possible for believers to remain faithful to the Lord even when others do not. While some dabbled in "the depths of Satan," many remained undistracted and were growing in grace and good works in the same church.

Welcoming one and all to visit and hear the Word in our churches, without respect of persons, is the "whosoever will may come" characteristic of the gospel itself. But we differentiate between those who simply attend our services and those who occupy the offices or teaching positions sanctioned by the church. Inviting everyone to attend does not carry with it the corollary of inviting everyone to teach. The way of salvation and doctrine is "narrow" because it is Biblically based. All of it is defined and controlled by Scripture. These standards must be preserved for the church to continue being the salt and light Jesus intended it to be in the world.

When there is no basic difference between the behavior of professing believers and the behavior of unbelievers in the world, the church has lost its savor. Its light is put under a bushel. It no longer fulfills the commission of the Lord. Christians should not be negatively influenced by the culture around them. Christ transforms and conquers culture. He shares with us the power to do the same. The truth is that after the new birth we are different at the most fundamental level. We have a different way of thinking and a different way of doing—God's way.

Suggested Outline. Faithful Soldiers, 2:18, 29: (1) Inspection, vv. 18, 19; (2) Infiltration by enemies, vv. 20-23; (3) Interim responsibility, v. 25; (4) Invincible reign, vv. 26-29.

E. Message to the Sardian Church, (3:1-6)

Background. Sardis, about 30 miles southeast of Thyatira, was for a time the most powerful city of Asia, a trade center at the end of a great trade route from the East. It was the capital of the Lydian kingdom, known for its textile industry, and claimed invention of the wool-dyeing process.

On a plateau atop 1,500 feet of sheer rock walls, Sardis was nearly impregnable. But invaders (Cyrus in 549 B.C. and Antiochus in 195 B.C.) had discovered paths to the unwatching city. By the time of Revelation, the city had relocated to a lower elevation, abandoning the old location as an acropolis. Much of Sardis' glory had faded.

Like the others, Sardis had pagan temples and cults, its patron goddess being Cybele, equated with Artemis. Near Sardis there were famous hot springs, claimed able (via Cybele) to restore life to the dead (Mounce 92).

Sardis was also famous for its decadence, its goddess worship debasing and including "orgies like those of Dionysus" (Walvoord 79). Though all six cities were known for immorality, pagan temples, and emperor worship, the reputation of Sardis for immorality and sexual obsession rivaled that of the Corinthians.

There was a significant Jewish population in Sardis, as evidenced by an archaeological discovery of the ruins of the largest Jewish synagogue building in the world (Aune I:218). However, Jesus does not mention Jewish opposition in this message. Christianity was at first recognized by the Romans as a Jewish sect, and this tolerance might have lingered in Sardis. Regardless, *external* pressure on the Sardian church was not the primary concern.

1 And unto the angel of the church in Sardis write; These things saith he that hath the seven Spirits of God, and the seven stars; I know thy works, that thou hast a name that thou livest, and art dead.

2 Be watchful, and strengthen the things which remain, that are ready to die: for I have not found thy works perfect before God.
3 Remember therefore how thou hast received and heard, and hold fast, and repent, If therefore thou shalt not watch, I will come on thee as a thief, and thou shalt not know what hour I will come upon thee.
4 Thou hast a few names even in Sardis which have not defiled their garments; and they shall walk with me in white: for they are worthy.
5 He that overcometh, the same shall be clothed in white raiment; and I will not blot out his name out of the book of life, but I will confess his name before my Father, and before his angels.
6 He that hath an ear, let him hear what the Spirit saith unto the churches.

1. Commission (v. 1). Christ commands John to write the pastor at Sardis (v. 1), following the pattern of the other letters with one exception: this message contains no *commendation* (compare Laodicea), except for reference (v. 4) to a faithful few who had not "soiled their garments." Caird (48) characterizes this church as "the perfect model of inoffensive Christianity, unable to distinguish between the peace of well-being and the peace of death."

2. Characteristics of Christ (v. 1). Christ introduces Himself as having "the seven Spirits of God, and the seven stars," again reflecting John's initial vision of Christ (1:4, 16, 20). The "seven stars" are the pastors of the churches. Whatever the reason for selecting these two characteristics, they support the divine authority and origin of the message. Possessing the "seven Spirits of God" (4:5; 5:6) may well imply: (1) Jesus' infinite knowledge, enabling Him to see beneath the veneer of Sardis' good reputation into its real condition; or (2) His ability to restore life to the dead church through the life-giving Spirit (Rom. 8:11)—thus countering the goddess Cybele's supposed ability to restore life. That Christ holds the pastors ("stars") in His hand may well intimate that He stands behind the messengers and their messages.

3. *Commendation.* Recognition of a faithful element within the church, whose garments were unsoiled, does not change Christ's negative opinion of the church as a whole (v. 4). The omission of commendation adds to the already sober tone of the message.

4. *Concern* (vv. 1, 2). "Know" (Greek *oida*) indicates knowing in a state of completion with continuing significance (Greek perfect). It reflects Christ's examination of each church's "works" through the omnipresent Holy Spirit ("seven Spirits of God," Rev. 5:6; 2 Chr. 9:16; Ps. 139:7-12; Zech. 4:10) and by His own eyes of flaming fire (1:14; 2:18). The examination motivates Christ to advise the church; the need is urgent because the *diagnosis* of their condition vitally affects the church's *prognosis.*

Many churches, like this one, degenerate into inactivity; members do not busy themselves with good works and do not seem bothered by the lack. Perhaps they are unintentionally convinced, by teachers stressing justification by faith alone, that they do not have to work in order to be saved. But though we must uphold the doctrine of justification by faith, the Bible's interest in the believer's works must be seen for what it is. Christianity is properly balanced

when grace and works complement one another, as in Eph. 2:8-10 (cf. Jas. 2:14-26).

The Sardian church had quit working, creating an imbalance unacceptable to Christ. This potentially fatal spiritual condition required immediate attention. The *inspired* character of the message argues for its urgency; failure to comply is not a sensible option because spiritual rigor mortis is already taking hold.

Christ's concern about the Sardian church is sobering (v. 3). It has "a name" as a good church, but the reality is that it is alive no longer, referring to spiritual life (Jn. 1:4; 3:16; 14:6; Rom. 6:23; 8:1). This life is the "antithesis of death" (Trench 91) and should characterize the church as a living organism.

Sardis was once alive and active with good works, perhaps having survived since Paul's original ministry in Ephesus 40 years previously (Acts 19:1-22; 20:17-38). But like the city itself, the church relied on its good reputation; now—in sharp contrast to public perception—it lives no longer. This does not seem to be hyperbole; the church is spiritually dead (v. 1). Providentially, the eternal Christ speaking to them holds the keys of life and death (1:18; 2:8; 3:7). He possesses the life-giving Spirit (v. 1). As desperate as their condition, Christ offers hope as the one who truly restores life to the dead.

Second, their works are "not perfect before God" (v. 2). "Found" refers to what Christ's examination has revealed about the church's true condition. "Perfect" (Greek *pleroo*)—not the usual word for maturity—means "to make full, to fill, to fill up" (Thayer 517): the works of the church had not been fulfilled. Forward motion in progressive sanctification had stopped.

"Before God" means in the presence of God Himself (some manuscripts read "before my God"). All our works will one day be examined in the presence of God (Ec. 11:9; 12:13, 14; Rom. 2:16; Rev. 20:11-15; Rom. 14:10-12), yielding results for all eternity. Meanwhile, the grading of our present works may be changed for the better. Christ's examination is not for *condemnation* but *correction*, revealing strengths and weaknesses. Sardis' "score" is not final and can still be improved.

"Things which remain" and are "ready to die" qualify Christ's remark only minimally. Like a tree already dead inside but with green leaves in its extreme branches, the Sardian church's works were no longer giving evidence of spiritual growth and vitality. "Apparently, untroubled by heresy and free from outside opposition, it had so completely come to terms with its pagan environment that although it retained the outward appearance of life it was spiritually dead" (Mounce 92).

5. *Correction* (vv. 2, 3). Though their condition is serious, Jesus' help is available for five steps of correction: (1) watch, (2) strengthen, (3) remember, (4) hold fast, (5) repent. The first, "be watchful," calls hearers to awaken from *spiritual* slumber—*a matter of life and death*. Like the old city falling to invaders, the church was guilty of not watching. Her security was overestimated and therefore false. Christ Himself has an eternally watchful Spirit ("the seven Spirits of God," v. 1). The "seven Spirits of God" are the "eyes of Christ" whereby He knows all things.

In the N.T. in general and in Revelation, watchfulness is essential for Christians in light of the unpredictable and imminent Second Coming of Christ (1:7; 3:2; 16:15). A believer must watch for the Lord's return in order to be ready. The Sardians' failure to watch had led twice to the city's destruction. Jesus may well have been using this history as an object lesson to emphasize the importance of *continual*, spiritual watchfulness.

The second step of correction is to "strengthen" (Greek *sterizo*) the church, which means "to fix, to make fast, to set" (Vine 206). The desired resuscitation must occur within a rapidly narrowing window of opportunity; the process of death was already in motion. The "things that remain" may imply that there is little to be salvaged. Even so, something of their former good reputation is still alive and worth saving. Or one can view the church (as a whole) as having just expired and subject to resuscitation if action is prompt; this preserves the force of Jesus' pronouncement (v. 1) that they are *already dead*. A risen Christ certainly has the power to raise the dead.

The third step of correction is to "remember" (v. 3; cf. 2:5). When a person backslides, memory can serve as a bridge to reconnect with the past—like the prodigal (Lk. 15:17), who "*remembered*" how it used to be in his father's house. Indeed, the Sardians' past contains the model for restoring spiritual health. "What [or, how] they had previously heard and received" summarizes their new birth and instruction in Christ. When someone carried the gospel to Sardis, some heard and put faith in Christ and a church came into existence, flourished, and became known as a living church. Reflecting on this will show the way to renewal.

Jesus' fourth step for their recovery is "hold fast," referring back to "what they had heard and received." The verb (Greek *tereo*) means "watch over, watch, preserve, guard, keep, reserve" (Vine 307), thus closely complementing "watch."

The fifth corrective step, "repentance," goes beyond merely "remembering" their former obedience. Biblical repentance embraces a change of heart and mind and external behavior. One "holds fast" after truly repenting, posting a fresh guard in the soul and continually watching in order to protect spiritual ground reclaimed. This renewed grip readies the church (or believer) against future attack and protects against the sure judgment of Christ. Failure to watch spiritually will be repeated unless action is taken, and they will be caught by surprise, as by a "thief."

Some interpret this threatened "coming" (v. 3) as a type of *judgment-coming* rather than the Second Coming of Christ. The threatened judgment in this symbolic sense would be a unique (and imminent) one, directed only against the unfaithful in the Sardian church. But it is much more likely that this "coming" refers to the Second Coming of Christ at the end of time. The "thief" metaphor argues strongly for this because it is the same language used elsewhere by Christ to refer to the Second Coming (Mt. 24:43; 1 Th. 5:2, 4; 2 Pet. 3:10; Rev. 16:15). His return is unpredictable, sudden, catastrophic, and imminent. Here, the reference to Christ's Second Coming is perhaps *proleptic* (speaking of the future as if it were present). Although the Second Coming is in the future, the consequences of Sardis' condition will be reserved for judgment then, and changes of behavior inspired by Christ's coming must be made within one's own lifetime.

6. *Compensation* (vv. 4, 5). Jesus makes three promises to those who overcome. First, a faithful few have "not defiled their garments" with the death of Sardis; these will be compensated in eternity with "white" garments, symbolizing undefiled clothing and eternal life with Christ. White clothing was preferred by pagan worshippers or by the Romans when celebrating victory. Accordingly, for faithful believers, white clothing not only represents holiness but also victory in overcoming the enemies of Christ.

Furthermore, they will "walk" forever with Christ in white because they are "worthy." Throughout Scripture, "walking" with God is one of the most endearing symbols of Christian life, whether for Adam before the fall (Gen. 3:8, 9), Enoch who *walked with God* (Gen. 5:22-24), David (Ps. 1:1; 15:2; 39:6; 101:6; 128:1), or Christ with two disciples (Lk. 24:13-17). The N. T. apostles pervasively use "walking" as a metaphor for the Christian life. Walking with Christ forever will be each believer's reward.

"Worthy" (Greek *axios*) implies "having weight" or value or meriting good or bad (Thayer 52). A believer has weight or merit with God because the merits of Christ's righteousness are imputed to him or her at the moment of conversion in the forensic act of justification. This "worthiness" comes by faith (Rom. 3:10, 23; 4:13, 22, 25). Later in Revelation, "white robes" symbolize "the righteousness of the saints" (6:11; 19:8, 11). A believer's righteousness *is* the righteousness of Jesus Christ.

Second, Jesus promises that He will *not* "blot out his name out of the book of life" (v. 5). The concept of a "book of life" has parallels in O.T. and secular history. Citizens of ancient society were often listed in a town's registry, with names of the dead or criminals removed. Moses spoke of being blotted out of God's book (Ex. 32:32, 33). David spoke of a "book of God" (Ps. 56:8; 139:16; cf. Mal. 3:16). A book of life is also prominent in the N.T. (Lk. 10:20; Phil. 4:3; Rev. 3:5; 13:8; 17:8; 20:12, 15; 22:19). It is the same as "the Lamb's book of life" (21:27).

The possibility of "blotting out" raises the question whether it is possible for a genuine believer to forfeit salvation and become apostate. A vast amount of O.T. and N.T. data confirms this possibility (2 Chr. 15:2b; 1 Cor. 10:1-13; Heb. 6:4-6; 10:26-31; 2 Pet. 2:20-22; Jude 5, 6). Jesus would not waste time warning against a danger that was merely hypothetical; some names will be blotted out after having been written there. Otherwise, the promise is meaningless; it "suggests that fidelity to God rather than any type of predestinarian system is the reason for having one's name inscribed in the Book of Life in the first place (see Rev 17:8)" (Aune I:223; cf. Thomas I:261-263; Caird 49ff).

A third promise for overcomers, with two additions, is that Jesus will "confess" their names. If believers have not been afraid to confess Him in life, He will not fail to confess their names in Heaven (cf. Mt. 10:32, 33). The most likely time for such a confession will be in conjunction with the Great White Throne Judgment, during "roll call" from the Lamb's Book of Life (20:11-15).

Public confession was not easy for believers in that culture. In the context of the imperial cult, many were asked to confess Caesar as Lord and deny Christ, on pain of death. And there was public pressure to be a loyal citizen and participate in local pagan festivals. Thompson (27) describes the processions that took place during such festivals: "As the procession passed by, householders would sacrifice on small altars outside their homes." *Uncompromising believers would not take part.* Whatever the cost on earth, Christ promised to reward those who faithfully confessed Him before the world.

Compensation is not earned, it is reciprocated! It is not merited but "given" (2:7, 10, 17, 26, 28). Christ reciprocates faithful behavior; He confesses those who confess Him.

7. *Concluding Challenge* (v. 6). All the churches must "hear what the Spirit saith unto the *churches.*" The challenge is fourfold. (1) Every *individual* is personally challenged to "hear." God's Spirit speaks to anyone who listens. (2) *Each church* should hear what Christ says to it specifically; the admonitions require attention. (3) Each church should listen to *the other messages.* (4) The open-ended invitation ("the churches") invites *churches of every generation* until the Second Coming to hear what the Spirit is saying. The messages are for every church, every believer, and every unbeliever in the world—whose future is predicted therein.

Summary
(3:1-6)

The church in Sardis had a reputation for being alive but was in reality dead (v. 1). The diagnosis is reliable, given by an all-knowing Christ. The pastors, who will convey Jesus' messages, are held in Christ's right hand.

There is no commendation, putting this church in the same category as Laodicea. There were, however, vestiges of life worthy of being salvaged.

A deeply concerned Christ outlines five steps to correct the situation: watch, strengthen, remember, hold fast, and repent (vv. 2, 3). Jesus calls the church back to its former high standard, warning them about judgment linked to His coming. Constant watchfulness is necessary to be ready.

Those who overcome will be rewarded to walk with Christ for eternity (vv. 4, 5) in white clothing, symbolizing righteousness and victory. Their names remain written in the Lamb's Book of Life and will be confessed before God and the angels of Heaven.

The message ends with the common challenge to heed it, important not only because the situation mandates an immediate response, but also because it is a message given by the Holy Spirit (v. 6).

Application: Teaching and Preaching the Passage

The message to Sardis is relevant to our times: many formerly successful churches are declining. Often, neither flagrant sins nor external pressures are the cause, but contentment with past achievements. The good news is replaced by talk about the old days. A false security develops, resting on reputation rather than watchful reliance on the Lord.

The history of ancient Sardis illustrates vividly the importance of the spiritual principle of watchfulness. We must be watchful, not only for the Second Coming of Christ but also in maintaining personal holiness. Believers must guard their hearts and minds.

Some sheep invariably stray from the shepherd and the safety of the fold. Just so, genuine believers sometimes lose their way. Remembrance (v. 3; 2:5) of former experiences in one's Christian life may serve as a bridge that helps take us back where we should be. There is a way for dying churches, churches that live on their past reputations: start over again. The place of departure may be the point of return; pick up where you left off. As long as you have breath and desire, you are not dead. *Resume* the things that brought spiritual success.

Repentance is making up our minds to return, the bridge that enables us to go back to past achievement. The Chief Shepherd encourages His wandering sheep to do this. There are not many feelings comparable to the one a lost person feels when he finds his way home again.

Suggested Outline. Revival Recipe, 3:1-5: (1) Reconnoiter the ruins, vv. 1, 2; (2) Reinforce the ramparts, v. 2; (3) Remember the reasons, v. 3; (4) Regrip the rules, v. 3; (5) Repent to revive, v. 3; (6) Ready for the return, v. 3; (7) Rejoice in the rewards, vv. 4, 5 (also Lk. 15:1-32).

F. Message to the Philadelphian Church (3:7-13)

Background. On the imperial post road, Philadelphia was 25-30 miles southeast of Sardis. It was founded in the second century B.C. by Attalus II, who named it Philadelphos ("brother-love") because of his love for a brother named Eumenes (Ramsay 286). It was destroyed by the great earthquake in A.D. 17, rebuilt with assistance from Tiberius, and became a prosperous and enduring city.

Its most important natural feature was the volcanically enriched soil around the valley, making it ideal for vineyards (Mounce 98). Predictably, its major cult was to Dionysus, Anatolian bull god. The cult following this god justified immorality when done in connection with worship (Worth 195, 196).

Though Jesus did not admonish them, as the other churches, about external dangers, they were just as real in Philadelphia (Aune I:234, 235). A subsequent letter of Ignatius to Philadelphia (ca. A.D. 110) refers to a Judaizing presence there (Worth 197). Philadelphia also subsequently earned the nickname "Little Athens" because of its pagan temples and cults (Brighton 89).

These threats against faithfulness, similar to those present in all seven cities, made the Philadelphian character even more remarkable. As about Smyrna, Jesus had nothing negative to say about the church: they were overcomers.

7 And to the angel of the church in Philadelphia write; These things saith he that is holy, he that is true, he that hath the key of David, he that openeth, and no man shutteth; and shutteth, and no man openeth;
8 I know thy works: behold, I have set before thee an open door, and no man can shut it: for thou hast a little strength, and hast kept my word, and hast not denied my name.
9 Behold, I will make them of the synagogue of Satan, which say they are Jews, and are not, but do lie; behold, I will make them to come and worship before thy feet,
and to know that I have loved thee.
10 Because thou hast kept the word of my patience, I also will keep thee from the hour of temptation, which shall come upon all the world, to try them that dwell upon the earth.
11 Behold, I come quickly: hold that fast which thou hast, that no man take thy crown.
12 Him that overcometh will I make a pillar in the temple of my God, and he shall go no more out: and I will write upon him the name of my God, and the name of the city of my God, *which is* new Jerusalem, which cometh down out of heaven from my God: and *I will write upon him* my new name.
13 He that hath an ear, let him hear what the Spirit saith unto the churches.

1. *Commission* (v. 7). The commission to write is identical to the others, emphasizing that the risen Christ is the source.

2. *Characteristics of Christ* (v. 7). Jesus identifies Himself as "the holy one, the true one," strengthening His claim to deity and equality with the Father. Though these are *not* taken from the magnificent vision of the glorified Christ in chapter 1, they are consistent with it as fundamentally a picture of holiness. The holiness and truthfulness of Christ undergird the authority, accuracy, and potential acceptance of the message. The nature of Christ is absolute holiness.

Christ also "hath the key of David," indirectly reflecting "the keys of death and hell" in the original vision in 1:18. Many interpreters see an O.T. connection with the stewardship of Eliakim over Jerusalem in Is. 22:22; he was to have absolute power over the Davidic throne as king (Beale 284,285). Just so, the stewardship of Christ includes the nation of Israel, the Kingdom of God, Gentiles, the church, eternal life in Heaven, and even Hell. A key, of course, opens or locks a door: Christ claims nothing less than absolute control over all things.

The fourth characteristic is (literally) "the one opening and no one shuts, and shutting and no one opens," expanding further on possessing the key of David. The Jewish synagogues might claim the power to admit or exclude from the synagogue rolls, but only the risen and glorified Christ has the authority to admit to or exclude from the Kingdom of God. Faith in Christ brings membership in the church. After Calvary and Pentecost, the church became *God's true synagogue.*

3. *Commendation* (vv.8, 9). As in all the letters, "I know thy works" introduces the diagnosis. Jesus prefaces His positive review of the Philadelphian church in a unique way, obviously eager to share good news with them: "Behold" has the form of "a demonstrative particle to prompt attention" (ALGNT 202).

There are at least two possible meanings for "an open door." (1) Philadelphia had been founded for the purpose of exporting Greek culture into Phrygia and beyond. By this analogy the "open door" would be a *door of evangelism* or "missionary activity" (Mounce 101). This way, Christ wants the church to seize the opportunity to spread the gospel throughout their region (cf. Acts 14:27; 1 Cor. 16:9; 2 Cor. 2:12). (2) Others suggest *Christ Himself* as the door into God's kingdom or to eternal life (Beale

285; Mounce 101). Jesus did apply the metaphor of "the door" to Himself in Jn. 10:9. These two views are not incompatible: both are true.

"Have set" (Greek *didomi*, literally "have given") implies that the door has been opened and now stands open to them (Greek perfect tense). That no one is able to shut what Christ opens also suggests sovereign causation and future consistency. The fact that Jesus is the major cause of the open door fits well with interpreting the open door as evangelistic opportunity. Even so, the context also supports the view that Christ is the door. The "synagogue of Satan" has expelled believers and claimed to be the true people of God. But Jesus alone governs membership in God's household. He is the door and possesses all the keys (v. 7; 1:18).

Christ commends several characteristics about the Philadelphian church (vv. 8, 10). One, they have "little strength," which—in view of the positive context—need not be viewed as a negative assessment. Perhaps this reflects their material poverty or low social class, or they may have been small in number. Christ brings attention to an existing good characteristic of the church, however slight it may have been. Or He cites their smallness in contrast to the magnitude of the revelations about to be made to them. Either way, He has sovereignly opened a door of evangelistic opportunity for them, irrespective of their limited resources. Indeed, even in that "little strength" they have managed to remain *faithful* to Christ despite the pressures of pagan environment and Jewish antagonism.

Two, they have "kept" Christ's word, amplified as "the word of my patience" (v. 10): they have "kept my command to endure patiently" (NIV). This is a positive review of past behavior or activity and stands in contrast to the compromising of some other churches. That the glorified Christ held such an opinion of their church would bring tremendous encouragement.

Three, they have "not denied Christ's name," stressing successful resistance against pagan practices and the imperial cult. Upon discovery to the Roman authorities and on pain of death, a believer could be asked to confess Caesar as Lord and thus deny Christ (Heb. 11:35). And apart from physical martyrdom, there was the specter of economic boycott and material poverty: Christians were often perceived as unpatriotic, disloyal, unsociable, or simply "strange" for not participating in pagan activities (1 Pet. 4:3, 4).

4. *Concern.* As in the letter to Smyrna, Christ does not cite any negative concerns. Philadelphia's "little strength" is a positive citation that potentially showcases God's glory through meager human resources. Many feel that the churches at Smyrna and Philadelphia were poorer and perhaps smaller than the other five. If so, the reason might have been their bold, public confession of Christ. Such open witness could lead to expulsion from the local synagogue, or martyrdom for resisting the imperial cult, or economic pressures for civic disloyalty.

The congregations at Pergamos, Thyatira, Sardis, and Laodicea may have been larger or wealthier, but Jesus rated them less faithful. They either tolerated false doctrine internally or compromised externally. Had they been faithful in doctrine and public witness, they might have been more like Smyrna and Philadelphia.

Jesus' only concern for Philadelphia is about the church's *enemy:* unbelieving Jews identified again as a "synagogue of Satan" (v. 9; 2:9; cf. Jn. 8:44; Phil. 3:2.; Rev. 22:15).

He exposes the unbelieving Jewish assemblies as a counterfeit household of God, to which they naturally evolved after the resurrection of Christ. The gospel of Jesus Christ and the birth of the church changed the nature of God's family dramatically, requiring more than Jewish lineage, tradition, or synagogue membership.

Jesus denies the unbelieving Jewish claims at three levels. First is a direct denial: "they are not." Second, they are "lying"—a form (Greek middle *peseudomai*) that exposes their direct responsibility for the lie and for persecuting those who professed Christ (Mare 5). Third, Jesus gives promise and prediction of vindication against their lie, thus comforting believers who have been expelled from the synagogue by unbelieving Jews.

Some interpreters suggest that the expectation of Is. 45:15; 60:14, 15—that the Gentile nations of the world will bow before the glory of Israel—is reversed here. Unbelieving Jews will eventually acknowledge their doctrinal errors, bow and worship before the very group they persecuted, and realize Christ's special love for His true church. Furthermore, some interpreters see implications of an eschatological conversion of the nation of Israel here. But Jesus' promise to Philadelphia has Jews bowing before Gentiles and not vice versa (as in Is. 60:14). More likely, Christ is referring only to the situation in Philadelphia in the near future.

5. *Correction.* With no complaints to offer correction for, Jesus introduces,

instead, a significant and unprecedented announcement about *the hour of temptation*. This telescopes the readers into the distant future (cf. 2:10) and expands in scope to include the whole world (3:10)! It includes a promise to keep them from that trial.

The promise is given because the believers have "kept the word of my patience" (v. 10) and so is on the basis of reciprocity. "Patience" (Greek *hupomone*) means "steadfastness, constancy, endurance" (Thayer 644). The phrase may mean "the word of My perseverance" (NASB) or "my command to endure patiently" (NIV). The first refers to Christ's own patient endurance culminating in the cross, the second to His word or command to endure patiently. Either the faithful in Philadelphia followed Christ's own example of perseverance or their endurance was in obedience to Christ. Either way, the meaning is similar. Christ often rewards obedience in reciprocal fashion. The promise "to keep thee from the hour of temptation" is for those who have been faithful to Christ in their temptation.

More than one factor is involved in saying that "the hour of temptation," as described in v. 10, refers to the eschatological future. First is the meaning of "from" (Greek *ek*). Some interpreters think it means deliverance from trial by being sustained in it; Gundry (54ff.) cites Jn. 17:15 for this meaning. More likely, however, it means to be kept entirely from; Townsend (255) cites examples of this meaning. Pretribulationists believe this "hour of temptation" is the Great Tribulation at the end of the age and that the church will be kept "from" it by means of the rapture (1 Th. 5:9). Posttribulationists believe the church remains on earth during the Great

Tribulation but is preserved by God all the while and thus in that way escapes His wrath (Jn. 17:15). In the end, one's view of the rapture is involved, though all of us recognize that any reference to the rapture, here, is inferred and not explicit. (See definitions of eschatological views in the Introduction to this commentary.)

The second factor is in the expressions "all the world" (Vine 191: "inhabited earth") and "them that dwell upon the earth." Both seem clearly to indicate that Jesus has looked far beyond the situation at Philadelphia. As the rest of this commentary will show, Revelation shows that creation itself will undergo catastrophic changes during and after the Great Tribulation (cf. 2 Pet. 3:10-13; cf. Rom. 8:19-22).

"Temptation" (Greek *peirasmos*) indicates trial, testing, or proving (Thayer 498). In the N.T. a trial or test has one of two possible outcomes: it may refine genuine character or it may reveal flaws in character. The effect of the predicted "hour" or "time" of trial will be to test or prove the character of those then dwelling on the earth. The faithful (converted during the Tribulation) will have their character perfected (7:14). For those who remain unrepentant, the Tribulation confirms God's justice in pouring out His wrath (9:20, 21). Those who "overcome" through faith in Christ will be rewarded with eternal life in Heaven, and those found faithless and unrepentant will be cast into Hell forever.

"Shall come" is, literally, "is about to come," preserving an emphasis on the "nearness" of the hour and fitting what Christ says in the very next verse: "I come quickly" (v. 11); see comments on 1:1. The special focus of the testing will be against "them that dwell upon the earth." This expression typically describes the world's unbelieving population in Revelation (6:10; 8:13; 11:10; 13:8, 12, 14; 17:2, 8). Unbelievers receive the brunt of God's wrath during the period.

6. *Compensation* (vv. 11, 12). Biblical "patience" leads to "overcoming": it is the ability to persevere, to endure a heavy load for an extended period of time, applicable in three ways. First, persevering believers have remained faithful to Christ in an environment of hostile paganism and Jewish persecution. Jesus likes what He sees and exhorts them to "hold fast." Second, they are positioned before an "open door" of evangelistic opportunity to the regions beyond. Third, a firm grip is needed to hold to a promised "crown." This is a victor's crown (Greek *stephanos*, wreath; Vine 139), to be distinguished from a king's crown, one of several mentioned in the N.T. that will be given to overcomers in Heaven (Phil. 4:1; 1 Th. 2:19; 2 Tim. 4:8; Jas. 1:12; 1 Pet. 5:4; Rev. 2:11; 3:11; see 14:14).

This crown may be taken away (v. 11). Jesus alerts believers to spiritual enemies that are aggressive, militant, and opportunistic. Believers must be on guard against any temptation, whether imperial pressure to deny Christ, social pressure to compromise with the pagan and idolatrous environment around them, or persecution from unbelieving Jews—not to mention false doctrine, indifference, and spiritual inertia within the churches. Any of these might overcome the believer and have the effect of taking one's crown.

Permanence and *presence* are major aspects of the compensation Christ offers (v. 12) to "overcomers." In con-

trast to the temporary glory of athletic or military victories, Jesus promises to make overcoming believers into "pillars in the temple of His God," a perfect choice to visualize the permanence of eternity and proximity to God's presence. Envisioning oneself as a permanent fixture in God's eternal temple is an effective object lesson of encouragement against the background of earthquakes, edicts by emperors, and excommunication.

"He shall go out no more" apparently refers to *access or fellowship* with God, given the proximity of a pillar to the sanctuary of a temple. This is especially meaningful in Heaven because there is no literal temple there; God Himself is the temple (21:22-27; cf. 11:1, 2, 19). The promised status as "a pillar in God's temple" is *permanent*. Once in Heaven, "he shall go no more out." To be a pillar in God's temple is tantamount to being eternally in the presence of God.

"Temple" (Greek *naos*) refers to the building, room, or place where deity dwells (ALGNT 269; TDNT IV:880, 888). The O.T. Temple and Levitical system were grand but temporary, visual object lessons representing greater spiritual realities. In Heaven the symbol gives way to the reality: unbroken fellowship with God. (Though the Temple is visible in Heaven during the Tribulation, it apparently disappears in the transition to a new Heaven and earth: 7:15; 11:19; 14:15, 17; 15:5, 6, 8; 16:1; 21:22.)

Christ also promises to write new names. The background of this may have been memorializing, similar to modern practices. The name of a former emperor, city patron, or dignitary was often inscribed on a plaque, statue, or pillar at a pagan temple. "In the building of some temples, wealthy contributors had *their name* inscribed on a column to indicate that this particular column had been placed there because of their support" (Gonzalez 34, 35). In v. 12 the inscription on every believer (pillar) in Heaven is threefold: the name of God, the name of the New Jerusalem, and the new name of Jesus.

The name of God probably suggests *ownership*. The name of the New Jerusalem suggests heavenly *citizenship* (Phil. 3:20). Jesus' "new name" suggests *identification* with Christ or commemoration of the transformation into a glorified body. All three names, and the realities indicated, are eternal. How and where these will be written on each believer's glorified body or clothing is not indicated; what is paramount is the truth thus represented.

7. *Challenge.* (v. 13) The challenge for all seven churches—"He that hath an ear, let him hear what the Spirit saith unto the churches"—is repeated here. (See commentary above.)

Summary
(3:7-13)

There was a great door of evangelistic opportunity opened to the church in Philadelphia. The risen Christ wanted the believers to walk through that door to spread the gospel in the regions beyond. He encouraged them to remain faithful in the midst of the difficult circumstances they shared in common with most of the churches. But He also offered special counsel for the somewhat unique situation in Philadelphia.

Christ introduces Himself as the one who is "holy," "true," and "possesses the key of David" controlling access into the Kingdom of God (v. 7). This authority is exercised specifically in setting an "open door" before the church at Philadelphia and by allowing believers excommunicated from local synagogues into the true and eternal kingdom of God.

The all-knowing Christ commends their works in a wholly positive way. Their faithfulness was demonstrated by "a measure of strength," "keeping God's Word," and "confessing Christ's name" (v. 8). They were positioned and qualified to take advantage of a sovereignly created and sustained opportunity. Unbelieving Jews in the synagogue persecuted believers in a number of ways, evoking a strong denunciation from Christ who describes them as "the synagogue of Satan" (v. 9). Christ offers comfort to His true household. He promises to reverse the privilege of stewardship over God's household, claimed by their Jewish antagonists, by humbling the unbelieving Jews before the Christians they had persecuted. He also promises to convince the believers' foes of Christ's great love for His church.

The promised compensation includes a reciprocal "keeping" (v. 10). The faithful in Philadelphia had been careful to keep Christ's Word and example. Christ would therefore keep them from a future time of worldwide tribulation. The focus jumps well beyond the local situation in time, scope, and degree, placing the Second Coming in proximity with the predicted testing (v. 11). Christ advises them to "hold strongly" to what they have in light of the great opportunity before them, in light of the imminence of Christ's return, and in light of attempts to take their crowns away.

Much of the eternal compensation is illustrated with the image of a temple pillar (v. 12), representing the privileged nature of a believer's status in Heaven: permanent proximity to the presence of God and the associated blessings and activities of worship. Three new names will be written on believers as pillars, comparable to ancient and modern memorialization: "the name of God," "the name of the new Jerusalem," and "the new name of Jesus."

An invitation to "hear what the Spirit saith to the churches" concludes the message (v. 13).

Application: Teaching and Preaching the Passage

Most feel that Christ's description of Philadelphia as a church with "little strength" is positive rather than critical, meaning that it was probably a small church with limited resources, a "poor" church. It did not have the wealth of Ephesus or Laodicea. Yet Christ speaks more favorably about it.

Two major points can be made. One, being small or poor is not unspiritual. Christian merchants who refused to sell or buy meat offered to idols, or any other product associated with idolatry (such as amulets or carvings), sacrificed profit for principle. Those who refused to join a trade-guild because it meant participating in pagan festivals would suffer economically. And if the imperial cult was aroused in a given area, with it the threat of martyrdom, that would tend to dampen enthusiasm for church membership.

The second point is much more pleasant: the message to Philadelphia should encourage smaller churches. Not only may a small church be considered a faithful or successful church in the eyes of Christ, but it also provides God with a wonderful opportunity to bring glory to Himself. He delights to use weak and small things in order to confound the mighty (1 Cor. 1:18-31). When He uses a church or individual in this way, He gets the glory and that is where the credit rightfully belongs.

Furthermore, little is much when God is in it. God often does great and mighty things through small groups. We should learn to be thankful for the numbers God has given and not frustrated by what He has not given. Someone wisely said, "God does not have as many people in Heaven as He would like to have." We must not be satisfied by smallness, but neither should we be unthankful and feel powerless.

Third is a tremendous thought about the sovereignty of God in this message. The "open doors" of the new birth, evangelism of others, and opportunity are created, sustained, and offered to us by God in spite of men. And we ought to walk through the doors that God has clearly placed before us. Furthermore, the doors opened to the Philadelphian church remain open to us in our generation. The promised compensations also still apply, as does the urgency. The coming of Christ and the period of tribulation are nearer than ever before. We must be ready for these awesome events!

Suggested Outlines. Sovereign Keys (doors opened by Christ), 3:7-13: (1) Door of Davidic Kingdom, v. 7 (see Is. 22:22); (2) Door of Evangelism and Service, v. 8; (3) Door of Synagogue, v. 9; (4) Door of Earth's Future, vv. 10, 11; (5) Door of Heaven, vv. 12, 13.

Pillars in Paradise, 3:12a: (1) Permanence in God's presence; (2)

Proximity to God's presence; (3) Privilege of being in God's presence.

What's In A Name? 3:12b: (1) Ownership; (2) Citizenship; (3) Fellowship.

G. Message to the Laodicean Church (3:14-22)

Background. Laodicea was in the Lycus river valley some 40 miles southeast of Philadephia, 90 miles due east from Ephesus, in the province of Phrygia, intersected by two major roads: the great trade route from Ephesus into Syria and one from Pergamum to Perga on the southern coast.

Laodicea was a banking center, so wealthy that when the city was destroyed in A.D. 60 by an earthquake, it refused Roman aid. Mounce (107) calls it the wealthiest city of Phrygia, attributing its prosperity to the textile industry: the city was famous for the production of a unique, glossy-black, soft wool for clothing and carpets and for a certain highly desirable tunic (Ramsay 307). There was also a famous Phrygian powder used as an eye salve (Ramsay 309), manufactured in tablet-like form, suitable for export, probably produced in connection with Laodicea's medical school (Hemer 179).

Emperor worship was active in Laodicea, subsequently awarded the honor of temple-warden. There was also a large Jewish presence characterized by its heterodoxy and worldliness (Mounce 107, 108).

Laodicea's great weakness was the lack of an adequate water supply to support its burgeoning population. Sufficient substitutes for its own undrinkable water were miles away: Hierapolis, six miles to the north, had hot water and Colossae to the south had cold water (Hemer 188), either of which would be tepid after being transported. From Denizli, five miles to the south, the city brought water by an aqueduct of three stone pipes (Mounce 107), conduits extremely vulnerable to enemies. Excavations have revealed heavy lime deposits in the pipes, which must have made the water nauseating.

14 And unto the angel of the church of the Laodiceans write; These things saith the Amen, the faithful and true witness, the beginning of the creation of God;
15 I know thy works, that thou art neither cold nor hot: I would thou wert cold or hot.
16 So then because thou art lukewarm, and neither cold or hot, I will spue thee out of my mouth.
17 Because thou sayest, I am rich, and increased with goods, and have need of nothing; and knowest not that thou art wretched, and miserable, and poor, and blind, and naked:
18 I counsel thee to buy of me gold tried in the fire, that thou mayest be rich; and white raiment, that thou mayest be clothed, and *that* the shame of thy nakedness do not appear; and anoint thine eyes with eyesalve, that thou mayest see.
19 As many as I love, I rebuke and chasten: be zealous therefore, and repent.
20 Behold, I stand at the door, and knock: if any man hear my voice, and open the door, I will come in to him, and will sup with him and he with me.
21 To him that overcometh will I grant to sit with me in my throne, even as I also overcame, and am

set down with my Father in his throne.
22 He that hath an ear, let him hear what the Spirit saith unto the churches.

1. *Commission* (v. 14). Christ commands John to "write" the "angel" (pastor) of the church at Laodicea. Mounce (108) speculates that the church might have been founded by Epaphras, Paul's coworker (Col. 1:7; 4:12). Paul's letter to them (Col. 4:16) has either been lost or is the same as Ephesians.

Laodicean distinctives are perhaps the best known in our generation. Because of the *prophetic-historic* view of the seven churches, the present period of church history is often identified as the Laodicean. But all seven messages are relevant to every generation of church history.

2. *Characteristics of Christ* (v. 14). Christ establishes divine authority for the message by claiming three characteristics: "the Amen," "the faithful and true witness," and "the beginning of the creation of God."

"Amen" transliterates Hebrew or Greek words meaning to confirm: "the acknowledgment of that which is valid and binding" (Mounce 108). One function is to express verbal assent or approval after something is said or written—in the N.T., doxologies and prayers, for example (DNTT I:99). Thayer (32) says the custom of saying "amen" originated in the synagogue and carried over into Christian assemblies, uttered after a sermon or prayer by a worshiper as a way of affirming personal belief in the truth of what had been said. Here it is another affirmation of Christ's deity, consistent with (though

not taken from) the vision of the glorified Christ in chapter 1.

The second characteristic is in apposition: "the faithful and true witness" (v. 14); compare "the faithful witness" (1:5), "Faithful and True" (19:11; 22:6). Jesus was absolutely faithful as a witness for God in the world to the point of crucifixion (Jn. 8:12-18; 17:4-8, 14, 26) and sets the norm for discipleship in the messages to the churches. He commends and compensates those who are faithful. He chastises and warns those who are not.

"True" (Greek *alethinos*) distinguishes the "genuine" from the "counterfeit" (Thayer 27). A "witness" "faithfully avows what he sees, hears and knows," often sealed by death (Vine 680, 681). The exalted Christ may be trusted to tell the whole truth. His testimony perfectly corresponds to reality, whether in Heaven, Hell, or earth. His description of the Laodicean condition is accurate, as are His revelations of the future.

Third, Christ is "the beginning of the creation of God." "Beginning" (Greek *arche*) might mean "ruler" (NIV) or "origin or source" (NASB margin). The expression has been used as a cultic proof-text (by ancient Gnostics or modern Mormons) undermining the deity of Christ. And it has special significance for the Laodicean situation because every good thing they possessed came from Christ, whether material or spiritual wealth.

In Col. 1:15—written earlier to a sister church of Laodicea—Paul describes Christ as "the image of the invisible God" (cf. Heb. 1:3) and "the firstborn of every creature." This latter is an expression of *preeminence* or rank over the created universe (cf. v. 18), not an indication that Christ is a created being, made clear from the very next words, "For by him were all things created" (v. 16). That He is "before all things" (v. 17) indicates His eternal existence as God the Son. In the same way, here in Rev. 3:14, "the beginning of the creation of God" does not mean the first created thing but the one who stands over all creation as both source and initiator.

3. *Commendation.* This is omitted: Christ's examination of the Laodicean church reveals nothing positive. The deafening silence is a severe condemnation. Even so, their condition is not hopeless if they heed Christ's counsel in the end.

4. *Concern* (vv. 15-17). Christ's "I know" is impartial, accurate, exhaustive, and urgent; His concern is singular and sobering. The "faithful and true witness" must bear honest witness about them.

The church is "neither cold nor hot," but "lukewarm" (tepid). There is difference of opinion as to the implications of cold (freezing) and hot (boiling) on either side of "lukewarm." Some view "cold and hot" as both *positive* (Brighton 101). Cold and hot water are useful. Lukewarm would then mean *a loss of effectiveness or usefulness*. Others interpret "cold" negatively, referring to an unregenerate person in whom the work of salvation has not even started (Lenski 154), who may even be antagonistic toward the gospel.

"Lukewarm" can likewise be interpreted differently. Walvoord (92, 93) and A. Johnson (62) think this refers to someone familiar with the gospel, who professes but is never genuinely saved. But this seems to skirt the N.T. principle of *increasing accountability* based on one's knowledge or previous experience; see Lk. 9:62; Heb. 6:4-6; 10:26-31; 2 Pet. 2:19-21. In the classical structure "hot" is indicative of spiritual life and zeal for God; cold is the opposite: spiritually cold or inactive. The one who is unsaved or makes insincere profession would fit better in the "cold" category. Lukewarm is obviously somewhere in between the two extremes, implying a genuine new birth that weakens over time and tribulation from hot to lukewarm, leaving them apathetic, neither angry with nor enthusiastic toward God (Brighton 101).

Laodicea lay between the hot springs of Hierapolis and the cold waters of Colossae. Christ may have been comparing the church to this: the water from either would become tepid by the time it was transported to Laodicea. Regardless, Christ is concerned about the tepid spiritual temperature of Laodicea. This condition puts them in danger of being spit out of God's mouth—something the readers understood well since the local water was foul and tended to make one sick. "I *will* spue" means "I *am about to* (Greek *mello*) or *on the verge* of spewing"—a present threat but not yet a final decision. This fits well with the gracious invitation in 3:20.

Some interpreters suggest that Laodicean "effectiveness" is the focus instead of diminished spiritual interest. But the charge seems more serious than that, and interpretations suggesting that the "lukewarm" individuals were never saved bend the text severely. Halfhearted, lukewarm effort is inconsistent with the norm of N.T. discipleship. The Christian life should be characterized by growth in grace and knowledge (1 Pet. 2:2; 2 Pet. 1:5-9; 3:18), fruitfulness (Jn. 15:2-16), and maturity (Phil. 3:12-16). Lukewarmness indicates that this process had slowed or stopped, with further degeneration into apostasy a definite possibility. Being vomited out of God's mouth is tantamount to being rejected by God. Laodicean believers were cooling to a temperature unable to sustain Christian life.

Christ indicates the symptoms of the "lukewarmness" (v. 17), thus exposing their true condition from God's point of view. "Because thou sayest" shows how they saw themselves. "Knowest not" indicates gross ignorance about how Jesus saw them. In stark contrast to the hubris of "rich," "increased with goods," "have need of nothing," Jesus counters with the truth that they are "wretched," "miserable," "poor," "blind," and "naked."

Material wealth does not translate into spiritual wealth. Materially speaking, the Laodiceans did not need anything or anyone. Scripture warns us about the sense of self-sufficiency and independence from God that may be generated by material wealth (Mt. 6:19-21; 19:23, 24; Lk. 12:18-21; 1 Tim. 6:4-11). The church's material wealth probably contributed to its self-sufficiency and spiritual conceit (Barnes 100).

The Master Accountant lists five adjectives illustrating their spiritual poverty, the first two and the last three being grouped together. They are "wretched" and "miserable" ("pitiable," Vine 412). A wretched (afflicted) condition produces misery.

The Laodiceans are spiritually "poor" in the eyes of Christ. True riches are spiritual and eternal, stored up by believers in Heaven (Mt. 6:19-21; 2 Cor. 4:18; Phil. 3:19, 20; Col. 3:2), but the Laodiceans put far too much confidence in earthly treasures. Material wealth tends to choke the Word (Mt. 13:3, 7, 22) and in time passes away (1 Jn.

2:17). Spiritual wealth increases in value throughout eternity. The Laodicean Christians failed to take eternity into account.

Furthermore, they are "blind" to their own spiritual condition. Peter warns that being blinded comes from lack of growth in grace and fruitfulness (2 Pet. 1:5-9). They are also "naked," damning because clothing is a symbol of spiritual status. Righteous saints are clothed in white linen, symbolizing their "righteous acts," at the marriage supper of the Lamb (19:8,9,14). There was nothing positive to say about the Laodiceans' works or behavior.

5. *Correction* (vv. 18, 19). After exposing their true condition underneath the veneer of spiritual conceit, the Great Counselor advises His readers what to do, outlining four steps to rehabilitate their condition: "buy," "anoint," "be zealous," and "repent."

"Gold tried in the fire" (v. 18) is pure, with the dross smelted away in hot furnaces, here representing true spiritual wealth (Mt. 5:3-12): virtues added to faith (2 Pet. 1:5-8), godliness with contentment (1 Tim. 6:6-12), fruits of the Spirit (Gal. 5:22, 23), and spiritual achievements in general. Jesus counsels them to "buy" (seek, acquire) spiritual wealth or character in order to become rich from God's point of view.

He also counsels them to buy "white raiment" (v. 18) to cover their spiritual nakedness. The manufacture of clothing was a significant point of pride in Laodicea. But the church was not wearing any *spiritual clothing*. Their righteousness by faith and faithful service had been stripped away. The proper clothing—truly righteous values—would cover the shame of their pitiful spiritual condition in the eyes of Christ. The contrast between a material wealth generated in part by Laodicean "*black*" wool and the absence of true spiritual wealth ("white raiment") is pointed.

Christ urges the Laodiceans to "anoint" their eyes "with eye salve." There was a school of ophthalmology at Laodicea (Beale 306), and the region was famous for its production of "eye-salve" (Greek *kollurion*), identified as "Phrygian powder" (Worth 217) and used for various eye ailments: "a coarse bread, cylindrical in shape," which was "impregnated with medicines and used as a bandage for sore or weak eyes" (Thomas I:315). Ironically, the Laodicean believers were blind to their "spiritual malaise" (Beale 306). Jesus counsels them to "anoint" their eyes with "medicine" in order to help them "see" how spiritually poor, blind, and naked they are.

Christ's motivation is "love" (Greek *phileo*, v. 19), which reflects more the emotional side than the volitional: something felt in the heart (ALGNT 399). This love governs Christ's "rebuke" and "chastening" (cf. Heb. 12:5, 6), which may not seem "loving" at the time but are prompted by His love for the backslidden church. "Rebuke" (Greek *elencho*) means convict or reprove and produces shame and conviction (Vine 510; Thayer 202). "Chastening" (Greek *paideuo*) is for the training or discipline of children and thus implies genuine sonship.

Christ summarizes His own corrective counsel by commanding the lukewarm believers to "be zealous and repent." "Repent" is "a definite change once for all" (Moffat 372), a condition of discipleship (Lk. 13:3, 5; Acts 26:20) that is incomplete without a corresponding change in behavior.

6. *Compensation* (vv. 20, 21). Compensation is promised to overcomers, possible by following the four steps of correction already outlined. "God resists the proud but gives grace to the humble" (Jas. 4:6).

The first compensation is highlighted with "Behold," a glorious invitation arising from the major point of the message: Christ the Judge still loves them! The compensation for immediate and sincere repentance is *restored fellowship*. Though v. 20 has often been applied evangelistically (and it is consistent to do so), the original application is to a backslidden condition like that in Laodicea. Christ stands outside the church as a whole or an individual's heart in particular, taking initiative to mend the broken relationship by presenting Himself as "standing," "knocking," and "calling" at the door (Mounce 106).

The conditions are "hearing" His voice and "opening the door," a wholly voluntary response. In response, Christ will enter into intimate "fellowship"— typified by the warm image of relaxing at home with family or friends during the evening meal (Greek *deipnon*, "main evening meal"; cf. S. of S. 5:2).

The second compensation will be at the end of the present age (20:4, 6) and in the eternal future as *a share in the reign of Christ* (v. 21). Christ obtained His royal position at God's right hand because He overcame the world; those "in Christ" who overcome the world will share in His reign (1:6; 5:10; 20:4, 6; 22:5). There is no reason to view vv. 20, 21 as a departure from the standard pattern or as a special conclusion for all the churches in chapters 2 and 3 (Ramsay 318, 319). Such an interruption in the pattern would leave Laodicea without the typical compensatory and challenge sections, without any reason for such omissions. Universal applicability is already established in the common challenge section of all seven messages. (See "unto the churches" v. 22.)

7. *Challenge* (v. 22). The challenge at the end of each message is consistent, repeated verbatim. See comments on 2:7.

Summary
(3:14-22)

After commanding John to write the church, Jesus introduces Himself with three titles: "the Amen," "the faithful and true witness," and "the beginning of the creation of God." These establish the message's divine source and authority. As "the Amen," Christ is God's ultimate confirmation of the truth of His Word and gospel. As "faithful and true witness" He obeys God and gives His Word to mankind as reliable testimony about the realities of the kingdom of God, discipleship, sin, Heaven, Hell, and eternal life. As "the beginning of the creation of God" He is preeminent over creation, its Source and Creator.

Christ's concern was that the affluent Laodicean church was "lukewarm" spiritually (vv. 15, 16). The material prosperity and conceited attitude of the city bled over into the church, affecting a similar spiritual attitude of self-sufficiency and independence. This put the church in grave jeopardy. Christ rebuked them sharply, warning them that God was "about" to spit them out of His mouth. The Laodicean church was as disgusting and useless to God as the city's emetic water to its citizens.

The self-sufficient attitude boasts that the church is "rich, increased with goods,

in need of nothing" (v. 17). Christ counters, charging them with ignorance of their true condition in the eyes of God. In reality they are "wretched, miserable, poor, blind, and naked."

Christ counseled them about how to correct the problem, in terms they would understand (v. 18): buy spiritual gold (character purified by fire) to be truly rich; buy spiritual clothing (white, symbolizing the righteousness of Christ) to cover their nakedness; use spiritual medicine (eye salve of eternal values) to heal their eyes. They would then be eternally wealthy, clothed, and sighted. These are the true riches.

Christ rebukes and chastens these genuine children because He truly loves them (v. 19). The proper response to discipline is a change in behavior. Christ counsels them to make the necessary changes immediately: "Be zealous therefore, and repent."

The great invitation in v. 20 was to a genuine church that had become lukewarm. Christ patiently presented Himself at the door of the Laodicean church, wanting to reestablish a right relationship with them. The principle may be expanded to anyone, including the unsaved, to any situation where Christ is on the outside desiring entrance and fellowship.

Christ promises to compensate eternally those who overcome, rewarding them with the privilege of reigning with Him forever (v. 21). The promises are not for Laodicean believers only, but are universal, for anyone who will listen (v. 22).

REVELATION

Application: Teaching and Preaching the Passage

The characteristics of Christ revealed to Laodicea reinforce the N.T. teaching about the deity of Jesus Christ. Tendencies that subsequently led to Gnosticism developed in the Lycus River valley during Paul's generation. His letter to Colossae dialogued against the error that Jesus was a created being less than God (Col. 1:15-19; 2:3-10). John's generation needed this reminder (v. 14).

The prophetic-historicist school (seeing church history as seven stages) often identifies the present generation of church history as the Laodicean age. While this may fit many churches today, it is not true for every church or believer. Many are "boiling" hot with activity and blessing. Some are zealous but have lost their "first love" like Ephesus. Some are suffering the fires of persecution and poverty like faithful Smyrna. Some have been infiltrated with false doctrine and sensuality like Pergamos and Thyatira. Some, like the church at Sardis, are *not* watching or living for the Second Coming of Christ but living on past reputation. Some are like Philadelphia, with doors of evangelistic opportunity open and unreached people groups at hand: God is bringing the nations to the United States to hear and receive the gospel.

Another mission field remains largely unharvested in our day: believers who have backslidden into spiritual lukewarmness. We must reach them before they are spewed from God's mouth. They no longer bother attending church or practicing spiritual disciplines. The picture of Christ standing and knocking at someone's door (v. 20) is relevant: He desperately wants to come back into the hearts, homes, and marriages of those who have known Him but are spiritually lukewarm.

Suggested Outlines. The Lukewarm, 3:15-19: (1) Classified by Christ, vv. 15, 16; (2) Conceit that must be corrected, v. 17; (3) Counseled to take steps, v. 18; (4) Commanded with urgency, v. 19.

Fellowship With Christ, 3:20: (1) The Christ of fellowship (standing, knocking, calling—patiently and graciously); (2) Calling every man fairly for fellowship; (3) Conditions of fellowship (hearing and opening); (4) Communion experienced within the soul (voluntarily, certainly).

Sins of Self (Laodicea), 3:14-22: (1) Self-righteousness; (2) Self-sufficiency; (3) Self-interests.

II. JOHN'S VISION INTO HEAVEN AND THE FUTURE (4:1—5:14)

Chapters 4 and 5 are foundational to the rest of Revelation. The trustworthiness of the revelations in the remainder of the book is reinforced by what we learn from this second great vision.

The door of Heaven is opened, allowing John and his readers an extended look inside the residence of God Himself, the source of the created universe. What he sees is not simply a sentimental picture of Heaven. The throne room of God was, and continues to be, the basic source of truth and metaphysical reality. The look also reveals Heaven to be a place of activity inhabited by other persons, objects, and constant worship. Knowledge that there is such a place of peace and providence, where God's will is done enthusiastically and unanimously, is an anchor in times of trouble or unbelief.

A. General Description (4:1-11)

1. An open door into Heaven (4:1)

1 After this I looked, and, behold, a door *was* opened in heaven: and the first voice which I heard *was* as it were of a trumpet talking with me; which said, Come up hither, and I will shew thee things which must be hereafter.

As compared to chapters 2 and 3, chapter 4 introduces three shifts in perspective. "After this" and "hereafter" are the same (Greek *meta tauta*, literally "after these things"), both indicating major transitions. The first links up with 3:22, signaling a major transition into a new revelation. There is no mention of how much time has passed—whether moments, minutes, hours, or days—before the revelations continued in 4:1.

The second ("hereafter") does not indicate a sequence of progression in receiving the revelations; instead it both introduces new subject matter and establishes a "time" separate from—*future* to—the first-century conditions described in chapters 2, 3. Though the length of time or position on the timeline of history is not stated specifically, *every* school of interpretation must allow for this temporal divide between 3:22 and 4:1.

The third major shift in perspective is the leap upward from earth to Heaven. John was "in the Spirit" while on Patmos when he saw the first great vision and received the revelations about the seven churches. He remained physically on earth while being transported spiritually into Heaven (1:10; 4:2; 17:3; 21:10).

A number of significant changes begin in 4:1. Place and time have already been mentioned. The differences are as great as the differences between the Roman province of Asia and Heaven itself, the locale of chapters 4 and 5. John saw: God sitting on His throne, spectacular colors, a bow above the throne, lightning, fire, a glassy sea, an infinite number of angels, living beings, elders sitting on other thrones, types of clothing, golden crowns, a seven-sealed book, a dramatic search, the Lamb of God, musical instruments, and bowls of prayers. He *heard* the sounds of Heaven: trumpet-like voices, thunder, singing, and antiphonal hymns of worship from various groups.

John's tour begins when he is commanded by a trumpet-like voice to "come up hither." "Open" indicates a settled state of being (Greek perfect tense). Whether opened by an angel or the One seated on the throne, the door stands open for John to peer into the throne room of Heaven. This special visual access into the presence of God was granted to John because of how intertwined the throne room of God is with the revelations about the future history of mankind. From here God created, governs, and guides the course of history to its consummation.

As an introduction to the future, John saw a timeless portrait of God in Heaven, a revelation that is the eternal, metaphysical foundation underlying all spiritual and material reality. The focal point of the vision is *the throne of God* and consequently God Himself, and the primary activity of those in Heaven is *the worship of God*.

In the structure of Revelation, the truths of chapters 4 and 5 legitimize the predicted future as God's sovereign acts of judgment and redemption. These revelations of what is to come (chapters 6-22) are from the *Creator* (v. 11) of the universe, who is presently governing, sustaining, and guiding it toward consummation in spite of mankind's sinfulness and the opposition of God's enemies. For these reasons the throne of God (referenced 38 times in Revelation) is the ultimate reference point within our universe, whether for the past (creation), present (providence), or future (judgments to come). All mankind will appear before this throne, either for condemnation or confirmation in eternal life (20:11, 12; cf. 2 Cor. 5:10).

2. A throne in Heaven (4:2-8)

a. The One sitting on the throne (vv. 2, 3)

2 And immediately I was in the spirit: and, behold, a throne was set in heaven, and *one* sat on the throne.
3 And he that sat was to look upon like a jasper and a sardine stone: and *there was* a rainbow round about the throne, in sight like unto an emerald.

John would not have been able to see, understand, or record the visions in Revelation were it not for the Holy Spirit: "in the spirit" (cf. 1:10) refers to John's being enabled by God's Spirit within his own spirit. The mind, will, and emotions of John were engaged but the ecstatic process was dominated by the Holy Spirit.

The throne room of God is the "control tower" (Poythress 97-99) in the field of future events from which God sovereignly governs world history. Our God is

in control because He is omniscient and omnipotent. Symbolized by His right hand, God's omnipotence is *the* fundamental *power source* of the universe. Neither wisdom (knowing what to do) nor power (ability to do) would be effective without the other. God, from His throne in Heaven, exercises His own infinite knowledge, wisdom, and power to create, sustain, and finally consummate the original universe. He will eventually replace the original one with a re-created one (6:12-14; 2 Pet. 3:10-13).

In a way somewhat analogous to the flow of electricity from the world's powerful generators, God distributes *all* power, wisdom, and benefits from His throne in Heaven. The power to create, sustain, and consummate the material and spiritual universe is generated from God's throne room, largely hidden to humanity but revealed now in chapters 4 and 5.

The One who sits on the throne (v. 2) is God Himself. The colors of three jewels—jasper, sardius, and emerald—are associated with God in this vision; (see Ezek. 1:26-28; Dan. 7:9; 10:5, 6; Rev. 1:12-20; Ex. 24:10). Not that God is multicolored: the brilliant colors should be viewed as distinct from God Himself. Jasper comes in a variety of colors, even white, normally associated with God's head or hair (Dan. 7:9: Rev. 1:14). The sardius or carnelian (the sixth foundation stone in 21:20) is typically red and is also used in descriptions of God's glory in Ezek. 1:26, 27 and Dan. 7:9; 10:6.

John's revelations were not only verbal but visual, stirring the senses. The glory of God in Heaven is *visible* (Ex. 24:9-18; Ezek. 10:1-4), often expressed with vivid colors. In addition to the colors of jasper and sardius, there was a "rainbow" around the throne. In Jewish theology, the rainbow—an emerald green "circle of light" (ALGNT 205)—is a symbol of God's glory (Brighton 115). The colors impress us that God is infinitely *beautiful*.

The bow and colors probably have significance. Red reminds us of Christ's blood in redemption, or it may symbolize the fire of God's holiness and judgment (Vine 547). Shades of red suggest judgment in 1:15. Green may represent God's mercy or eternal life. The original rainbow was created as a "sign" of the Noahic covenant (Gen. 9:9-17) following the flood, the greatest demonstration of God's wrath in the O.T. But God is equally merciful; He promised never to destroy the world in the same way again (Gen. 8:21, 22; 9:15). Instead, He has provided the sacrificial Lamb of God to meet the demands of His holiness, and the resurrection of that Lamb became the "sign" of the new covenant. The colors memorialize these aspects of God's nature.

Some suggest that only the rainbow is symbolic, that the individual colors have no special significance and serve only to enhance the overall effect of the vision. Because the colors were selected by God, they more likely symbolize some aspect of His nature.

b. The entourage around the throne (vv. 4-8a)

**4 And round about the throne *were* four and twenty seats: and upon the seats I saw four and twenty elders sitting, clothed in white raiment; and they had on their heads crowns of gold.
5 And out of the throne proceeded lightnings and thunderings and voices: and *there were* seven lamps of fire burning before the throne, which are the seven Spirits of God.
6 And before the throne *there was* a sea of glass like unto crystal: and in the midst of the throne, and round about the throne, *were* four beasts full of eyes before and behind.
7 And the first beast *was* like a lion, and the second beast like a calf, and the third beast had a face as a man, and the fourth beast *was* like a flying eagle.
8a And the four beasts had each of them six wings about *him*; and *they were* full of eyes within:**

Surrounding God's throne are 24 "elders" seated on smaller "thrones," the same word used for God's throne in v. 2. This may give a clue about the function and identity of the elders. Some hypothesize that the throne room and heavenly entourage proceed from the throne in concentric circles outward in the order given in chapter 4 (Hendriksen 83). It seems preferable (and logical) to picture the 24 lesser thrones as *flanking* God's throne, 12 on each side. They wear white raiment and gold crowns—a situation of royalty and honor in close proximity to God's own throne.

There is a wide range of suggestions about their identity: whether men or angels, why 24, and their function. A wider number of views can be reduced to two main ones: they are human beings or angels. Some interpreters are convinced they are angels (A. Johnson 66) who represent redeemed people and whose function is not different from that of O.T. or N.T. dignitaries or glorified saints. That these are angels would seem plausible only if they function as agents of worship or service in their own right, rather than as representing saints. But since their function seems to be representative, it seems more appropriate to have saints representing saints. Furthermore, "elders" is *never* used in Scripture to designate angels (Vine 195). Nor are angels ever seen sitting on thrones or wearing crowns (Brighton 118). All O.T. and N.T. precedents are *human* (see Aune I:287).

The spectrum of ideas ranges all the way from the absurd (equating them to Babylonian astral deities of the Zodiac!) to plausible Old or New Testament backgrounds; see Beale (323-326) for a helpful survey. Some suggest that this reflects the 24 courses of the O.T. priesthood established by King David (1 Ch. 24:1-4); while this would explain the *priestly* role of saints, it does not account so well for the *royal* nature implied. Some think of the 24 as a *heavenly council*; but there does not appear to be any interchange of counsel between the elders and God.

The more classic view sees the elders as signifying the twelve patriarchs of Israel and the twelve apostles of Christ (Brighton 116-120). The two dispensations of God's people are also prominent in chapter 7: 144,000 sealed representatives of Israel's 12 tribes (7:1-8) and a great numberless multitude of Gentile tribulation saints (7:9). Further, the names of both are inscribed in the gates and foundations of the New Jerusalem (21:12, 14). Similarly, some see the 24 elders as unnamed, glorified saints representing the entire community of the redeemed in both O.T. and N.T. Either way, the elders apparently represent the family of God throughout history, though Barnes (110, 111) thinks they represent the victorious *church* only.

There are also different ideas about their *function*. Though neither the names of the elders nor whom they represent is identified, their activity in worship is clear, as the liturgy indicates (vv. 10, 11). Furthermore, their regal attire suggests *rule* with God to some degree. The fact that they are seated on thrones of their own does not suggest they are objects of worship themselves. They eventually cast their crowns and fall prostrate before God who alone is worthy to be worshiped.

It seems best, then, to see these elders as divinely appointed representatives of redeemed humanity of all time (including Tribulation saints!) who participate in the eternal worship of God. Specifically, they may represent the 12 tribes of Israel (not necessarily all of Jacob's original sons) and the 12 apostles (cf. 21:12, 14).

John's description of the throne continues with both visual and auditory manifestations: "lightning," "thunder," "voices," and "seven lamps burning with fire" (see Ex. 19:16-19; 24:9, 17). Lightning and thunder manifest God's power, requiring respect. Those who come into the presence of a holy and omnipotent God must do so in awe and reverence (2 Kg. 1:9-14).

"Voices" (possibly "sounds": NIV, NASB) are probably the utterances of God, angels, living creatures, elders, and the redeemed. The voices John heard could have been from any or all of these, from ceaseless worship around God's throne (vv. 8, 10, 11).

The "seven lamps of fire" are "the seven Spirits of God" (v. 5; see 1:4; 3:1; 5:6; Is. 11:2)—a reference to the Holy

Spirit, not to seven angels (cf. 8:2), and a way of seeing the activity and nature of Him who is otherwise invisible.

The "sea of glass" before the throne (v. 6; 15:2) has stimulated much speculation whether it represents God's triumph over evil, separateness from or above His creation, the splendor or beauty of God's throne, or His sovereign control over the universe in peace (Beale 328; Thomas I:353). Interpretations include: it is the "reservoir of evil" from which the beast of 13:1 arises (Caird 65); it "has no special significance" except to heighten "the sense of God's separateness from his creatures" (Mounce 123); it recalls the great bronze "sea" in the courtyard of Solomon's temple (Aune I:296; see Ex. 24:10; Ezek. 1:22; 10:1); it represents the "divine providence of God" (Lenski 178) or "the cleansing blood of Christ" (Hendriksen 86).

While one may read too much into the text, one may also fail to see divinely intended symbolism. There may be elements of truth in some of the views just cited. The "sea of glass" and many other images in Revelation are perhaps purposely *dynamic* (not limited to one aspect), capable of suggesting many Scriptural ideas, doctrines, or backgrounds. However, the primary emphasis should never be obscured by speculation about indefinite particulars.

Also surrounding the throne are "four beasts" (v. 6). "Beast" (Greek *zoon*) is not derogatory and simply means a "living creature" or "living being"; it is used 20 times in Revelation referring to good angels. (A different word for "beast" refers to the Antichrist in 13:1, etc.) These uniquely-designed, angelic, living creatures are assigned to God's throne—though Lenski (180, 181) identifies

them as agents of God's providence and *not* angels. Mounce (124) sees them as "an exalted order of angelic beings who, as the immediate guardians of the throne, lead the heavenly hosts in worship and adoration." They are similar but not entirely identical to those described in Ezekiel or Isaiah.

The function of the four is threefold. (1) Their form is apparently symbolic and may be twofold, representing both the attributes of God and the entire animate creation (Hughes 74, 75). (2) They function as leaders in worship, their major responsibility being the unceasing worship of God's holy, eternal, and creating nature. (3) They illustrate select attributes of God, with a view to how these are used in His government over the universe.

The worship of God is clearly *the primary activity* around God's throne. All in the entourage serve in this way: the 24 elders, the four creatures, an infinite number of angels, and the redeemed (7:9-15). While there may be mystery about the identity or symbolism of the living creatures, there is no doubt that they function in this way (vv. 8-11; 5:6; 6:1, 6; 7:11; 14:3; 15:7; 19:4; see Ezek. 1:5-28; 10:1-22; Is. 6:1).

As to the identity of the four, there are various views. Some, like Irenaeus, Victorinus, and Augustine, identified them with the four gospels—though not all agree as to which is represented by the man, the eagle, the ox, and the lion (Charles I:124). Irenaeus also saw in them "four aspects of Christ's work" (Brighton 126). These connections are somewhat arbitrary, not founded in the text itself.

Others, in varying ways, think the four living beings represent the entire animate order. "The four forms suggest whatever is noblest, strongest, wisest, and swiftest in animate Nature…, including man" (Swete 71, 72). Mounce (124), while emphasizing that they lead Heaven in the worship of God, allows that they may "represent the entire animate creation." If this is the case, the lion may represent the wild animal kingdom; the ox, domesticated animals; the eagle, creatures in the skies; and man, the human race.

Another idea worthy of consideration is that the four represent the attributes of God (Barnes 113-117) as the basis for His government over the universe. This way, a lion might symbolize God's sovereignty; a calf or ox the strength or patient endurance of God; the eagle His swiftness, grace, or power; and intelligent man God's omniscience.

"In the midst" (v. 6), "middle," and "around" are adverbs describing the position of the living beings in relation to the throne, most likely "in the immediate vicinity" (Brighton 123) and apparently closer to the throne than the 24 elders.

Many interpreters see a link between John's living beings and the cherubim of Ez. 1 and/or the seraphim of Is. 6. But there are many differences in detail, so that these four would have to be a composite borrowing from both O.T. images. If they are identical with Ezekiel's cherubim, for example, they may even be positioned as pillars underneath the throne in each corner (Ezek. 1:22, 23, 26; 10:1). But this is more than we can say for sure. Regardless, the four here are "full of eyes within" (v. 8; see v. 6), indicating full knowledge ("omniscience," Barnes 114) or "alertness" (Thomas I:360). Vigilance and great knowledge are therefore attributed to the living beings.

The most logical explanation of the differences between these four and those in other Biblical passages is that there are many classes of angelic creatures, with different characteristics, surrounding God's throne. This would include cherubim, seraphim, and specially designed living beings. God's penchant for great variety in creation makes this plausible.

3. The manner of worshiping God in Heaven (4:8b-11)

8b And they rest not day and night, saying, Holy, holy, holy, Lord God Almighty, which was, and is, and is to come.

9 And when those beasts give glory and honour and thanks to him that sat on the throne, who liveth for ever and ever,

10 The four and twenty elders fall down before him that sat on the throne, and worship him that liveth for ever and ever, and cast their crowns before the throne, saying,

11 Thou art worthy, O Lord, to receive glory and honour and power: for thou hast created all things, and for thy pleasure they are and were created.

The worship of God in Heaven never ceases. The four beings "rest not day and night" (v. 8). It is right for the creature to worship and serve its Creator (Rom. 1:25), and they represent the whole animate creation, while the 24 elders represent specifically the redeemed, in this activity forever. Not all saints on earth worship God as often and sincerely as they ought, but their representatives in Heaven do. Jesus instructed us to pray that God's will be done "in earth, *as it is in heaven*" (Mt. 6:10).

The first characteristic of worship around God's throne is its regularity: "day and night." One may wonder how many times a day the "holy, holy, holy" (sometimes called the "Trisagion") is actually recited (Metzger 204), especially since the 24 elders respond each time by prostrating themselves and casting their crowns before the throne.

The "holy, holy, holy" is matched with three names of God: Lord, God, and the Almighty. "Lord" (Greek *kurios*) is God's most common name in the Greek O.T. (LXX), translating "Yahweh" ("Jehovah")—the personal or covenantal name of God (Vine 140). "God" (Greek *theos*) is usually the LXX's choice for translating either "*Elohim*" or "*Jehovah/ Yahweh*" (Vine 271). "Almighty" (Greek *pantokrator*), meaning "all-strength or all-ruling," is used nine times in the N.T., only once outside of Revelation (2 Cor. 6:18). The threefold repetition of "holy" rightly addresses each member of the Trinity and magnifies God's character as absolute holiness. At least five attributes of God are implied in the recitation: holiness, lordship, monotheism, omnipotence, and eternality.

God's eternal existence is in view with "which was, and is, and is to come" (cf. 1:4, 8; 11:17; Ex. 3:14; Jn. 8:58). Although the title may be rightfully applied to any member of the Godhead, in the context of chapter 4 it relates to the worship of *God the Father*, seated on His throne. An "echo" of the Second Coming, or other future events, is not wholly lacking (Thomas I:363).

The worship of the living beings continues when they give "glory, honour and thanks" to the Eternal God (v. 9). This triad suggests the substance of true worship, recognizing and confessing who God is and what He has done in creation and in all His works, past, present, and future.

The glory of God was visible in the O.T. tabernacle and temple (Ex. 40:34) as well as in the created universe (Ps. 19:1) and the written Word (Ps. 19:7). The throne-room vision (vv. 2, 3) is a visual picture of God's glory, but the greatest expression of God's glory is Jesus Christ (Heb. 1:1-3): "One sees the fullness of God's glory only when one sees also the enthroned Lamb who was slain" (Brighton 107). Thus chapters 4 and 5 offer a unified picture: God's glory inheres both in His Greatness as Creator of the universe (chapter 4) and in the redemptive work of the risen Christ as Redeemer of creation (chapter 5).

The throne of God remains the focal point: John refers to Him as "him that sat on the throne...who liveth for ever and ever" (v. 9), leaving no doubt about His identity. Some interpreters see this as an intentional rebuttal of the emperor worship involved in the imperial cult. While the truth may be applied in this way, the limitation truncates the scope too severely. God is worthy of such worship in all times and places; whether Roman emperors deify themselves or others usurp the role of God, Satan is the ultimate imposter (Ezek. 28:12-19). The praise and worship of God indicated here are never rightfully directed to anyone but God alone.

"Honour" (Greek *time*) is the reverence or respect God deserves as a result of His glory. "Thanks" or gratefulness is also an appropriate response since mankind directly benefits from the glory of God. God pledges His attributes of holiness, wisdom, power, love, and eternity for the benefit of those who worship Him in faith.

The 24 elders respond to the worship of the four living beings in an antiphonal way (v. 10), offering worship in response, substituting "power" for "thanks"—suggesting the individuality of the elders' own experience if nothing else. Their relationship to God is independent of that of the living beings. The elders prostrate themselves before the throne in worshiping God and cast their crowns before Him in submission to recite God's worthiness. All the elders share the same conclusion about God's worthiness to receive worship. The ceaseless worship of both the living beings and the elders guarantees that God forever receives the worship He deserves.

Chapter 4 concludes with two reasons God is worthy of our worship (v. 11). The first is that the universe (material and spiritual) and mankind exist because God created them (Gen. 1:1; Jn. 1:1-3), speaking them into existence from nothing (ex nihilo). The second is that all creation, especially mankind and animals, has been created for God's "pleasure" (Greek thelema)—more accurately, "will" (Eph. 1:5, 11; 2:10). One should also recognize two important boundaries within creation in light of how these distinctions are blurred within the theory of evolution and new age pantheism. One, God is wholly and eternally distinct from His creation. Two, man is created with an eternal soul, physically similar to, but spiritually distinct from, other animals or forms of life.

Worship is a recurring theme in Revelation, including at least seven worship services (4:8-11; 5:8-14; 7:9-12; 11:15-19; 14:1-3; 15:1-8; 19:1-10). These underscore the eternal relevance

of worship, offered to God in hymns (songs) or recitations extolling His great attributes, His triumphant judgments against the world, and His redemptive work.

Summary
(4:1-11)

Revelation 4:1 introduces a major transition, indicated by "after this" and by an invitation to John to "come up hither." John is transported in his spirit by the Holy Spirit into the throne room of God, especially to see *future* events: "things which must be hereafter." (Although many place the rapture of the church between 3:22 and 4:1, even advocates recognize there is no contextual mandate for doing so. However, it is logical to do so in the pretribulational view.)

What John sees in this vision is perhaps the most exhaustive Scriptural picture of the throne of God; cf. Ex. 24:9-11; Is. 6:1-6; Ezek. 1:22-28; Dan. 7:9, 10. The control room of the universe is exposed and remains in focus throughout chapters 4 and 5. Chapter 4 is an incredible visual and audible spectacle of the glory of God.

This first glimpse of God's throne reveals an entourage of four living beings and 24 elders in royal attire. The four living beings—somewhat distinct from other angels like the cherubim in Ezekiel or seraphim in Isaiah—are apparently specially crafted to represent the entire animate creation. They may also represent God's attributes and government. The 24 elders are most likely glorified human representatives of both O.T. and N.T. saints. This fits better with the term "elder," their royal attire, and the song of redemption to come (5:9, 10).

The vision also reveals the liturgy of a heavenly worship service (vv. 8-11). Worship is constant or daily. It acknowledges God's great attributes such as His holy, omnipotent, and eternal nature (v. 8). The living beings praise God with "glory, honour and thanks." The 24 elders respond by casting their golden crowns before the throne (v. 10) and acknowledging God's "glory, honour and power" (v. 11).

God is worthy of our worship, which acknowledges that the One seated on the throne is our Sovereign Creator. The universe should therefore worship Him, and the activity displayed fulfills this ideal perfectly.

Application: Teaching and Preaching the Passage

Famous Olympic gold medal winner Eric Liddell, hero of "Chariots of Fire," once said, "God created me to run fast and I must run for His pleasure." The fourth chapter of Revelation essentially says the same thing in a more elaborate way. Because God has made us, we should worship Him. Because He has made each of us for a purpose, we must seek to discover and fulfill it.

Chapter 4 also reassures its original readers and us that the future will be exactly as predicted by God because His sovereign power as Creator guarantees it.

The transitional language of 4:1 says nothing about a rapture of the church, nor will any careful exegete suggest that it does. The rapture of the church is not the subject. Advocates of a pretribulational rapture like John Walvoord acknowledge this. Even so, to place the rapture here is logical in the pretribulational view. This view, which puts the rapture of the church before the seven-year Tribulation, locates the rapture before the opening of the first seal (6:1). Though some interpreters (idealists, perhaps some historicists) see the seals as having been inaugurated at the ascension of Christ, futurists relegate the opening of the seals to the end-times. Explicit distinctions of time within the flow of the narrative of Revelation, and the absence of interpretation of the symbolism as present inauguration, strengthen the futurist viewpoint.

Cross-referencing other throne-room visions in Scripture (Exodus, Isaiah, Ezekiel, Daniel) can be helpful in interpreting the one given in chapters 4 and 5. Such a comparison reveals both similarities (sometimes equivalents) and differences. The different features of the "living beings" in Revelation, as compared to the angels in Isaiah and Ezekiel, may lead one to conclude that they are distinct from "cherubim" and "seraphim" around the throne.

Great care should be exercised when evaluating the symbolism of particulars in the vision. Often, interpreters offer sanctified speculation about things that are not explicitly stated. When we do that, we should qualify our teaching or preaching as such; most of the time there is enough that is clearly stated. John describes the rainbow around God's throne, for example, but does not interpret or assign meaning to the details; it is part of a general description of the glory of God. Nor does he inform us that the elders and living beings have a representative function, although this seems apparent. The text is silent about their precise identities.

Still, there are plausible interpretations informed by other Scriptural data— the rainbow of the Noahic covenant, for example, or the use of the colors red and green elsewhere. Consequently, while some things are not clear or explicitly stated, we should not reject enigmas outright because they are difficult to resolve. Some details are not left mysterious; the "seven lamps of fire," for example, are interpreted as the "seven spirits of God" (v. 5).

In this passage, the most important thing is clear: the personalities about the throne of God *worship* Him, an activity that is literal and described in great detail.

Suggested Outline. The Control Room of the Universe, 4:1-11: (1) The Creator, vv. 1-3; (2) The Crowned, v. 4; (3) The Creatures, vv. 6-8; (4) The Confession, vv. 9-11.

B. Successful Heavenly Search (5:1-14)

Chapters 4 and 5, as one unit, provide transition to the revelations about the future in chapters 6—22. The description begun in chapter 4 continues in chapter 5: now we see that "the One sitting on the throne" is not only our *creator*, He is also *redeemer* of His creation and of mankind in particular. The fifth chapter is a dramatic visual picture of the agent and activity of redemption, Jesus Christ, the Lamb of God.

1. John sees the seven-sealed book (5: 1-5)

**1 And I saw in the right hand of him that sat on the throne a book written within and on the backside, sealed with seven seals.
2 And I saw a strong angel proclaiming with a loud voice, Who is worthy to open the book, and to loose the seals thereof?
3 And no man in heaven, nor in earth, neither under the earth, was able to open the book, neither to look thereon.
4 And I wept much, because no man was found worthy to open and to read the book, neither to look thereon.
5 And one of the elders saith unto me, Weep not: behold, the Lion of the tribe of Juda, the Root of David, hath prevailed to open the book, and to loose the seven seals thereof.**

"And I saw" (or similar words) appears 33 times in Revelation and functions either as "a major break in the narrative," as in 4:1, or as "a change in focus of the unit," as here in 5:1 (Aune I:329). John's gaze is still focused upon God sitting upon His throne in Heaven, but it is now time to look beyond the overwhelming splendor.

The One on the throne has a seven-sealed "book" in His right hand (v. 1). The "right hand" of God is a common Scriptural symbol of His sovereign power, position, or authority. Thomas (I:375) says that this position of the scroll "indicates its divine source, the supreme authority of the revelation contained in it, and the assurance of adequate power to translate its contents into action." It is beyond the ability of anyone or anything to take the book from Him, reveal its contents, execute its contents, or thwart the fulfillment of God's design for future history. As the seals are broken, God will reveal His plan for the future, with emphasis on the end-time Tribulation culminating in the Second Coming of Christ.

"Book" (Greek *biblion*) may be either a "scroll" or "book" (ALGNT 91), and there are differences of opinion as to which is meant here (Metzger 5, 6). The "codex" or book form was known by the late first century (Zahn III:395, 396), but scrolls were more common, usually papyrus or parchment rolls. The "scroll" form seems more likely here, given the use of seals, which would be awkward for a "book." But the *content* of the sealed document is more important than its form.

The form and significance of the seven "seals" are also debatable. Ford (84) defines these as impressions made in material like clay or wax, observing that they "were used as a stamping device instead of signatures to make a document valid." Some suggest that the document is analogous to the ancient *Roman will,* which was customarily sealed by seven witnesses (Beale 344). Others think of ancient practices in Persia and the Near East, when official documents were sealed with impressions in wax or clay, signifying the authority of the source (Thompson 93, 94). Still others think the writing outside, by the seals, provides a summary of what is within, reflecting a common practice used for a contract or title-deed (Beale 344-346). In a similar way, J. A. Seiss thought of the scroll as the "title deed to creation" (A. Johnson 70); compare H. A. Ironside (Thomas I:376-379).

More likely, a scroll with writing "within and on the backside" implies complete or abundant revelation (v. 2; cf. Ezek. 2:9, 10; Dan. 12:4). The number of the seals is also important: seven is the "sacred number," especially to the Jews because of the Sabbath and the numerous sevens connected to the temple ritual (Ford 84). The "seven seals"

suggest not only completeness but *security* as well, indicating "the impossibility of any unauthorized person gaining access to what has been sealed...by God" (Aune I:346). They imply inaccessibility, authorization or certification, and ownership or protection. Accordingly, the sealed document is an authoritative, truthful, and protected disclosure about the future, given by God Himself.

The most important discussion concerns the *content* of the scroll. A. Johnson (71) says that it "ultimately includes the unfolding of the consummation of the mystery of all things, the goal or the end of all history....how God's judgment and kingdom will come." By analogy with the ancient "will," the scroll contains the revelation of God's will to be executed in the end-times. Others, in a similar vein, suggest that the scroll represents: "God's plan and destiny for the world" (Poythress 108); "God's purpose with respect to the entire universe throughout history.... The closed scroll indicates the plan of God unrevealed and unexecuted" (Hendriksen 89); the "future history of the world to the end" (Charles I:138).

Beale's survey (339-341) cites four major approaches to identification of the scroll: (1) the Lamb's Book of Life, (2) "a covenantal promise of inheritance," (3) the entire O.T. with Christ as the hermeneutical key of interpretation, and (4) the futurist view of an eschatological "Great Tribulation" period before the Second Coming.

Some idealists or preterists tend to hold that the scroll represents all of church history, in one way or another. This way, the opening of the seals of the scroll began with the ascension of Christ after His resurrection: a revelation of history "from the ascension of Christ to the Second Coming" (Brighton 139); then the taking of the scroll (5:7) symbolizes "the coronation or enthronement of Christ's reign at His ascension" (Brighton 145).

However, this view is problematic; nothing in the text links the exaltation of Christ after His resurrection to the opening of the seals. Furthermore, "after this" and "things which must be hereafter" (4:1) does *not* allow for the opening of the seals before, during, or immediately after the first-century conditions described in the letters to the churches in chapters 2 and 3. We simply cannot ignore the chronological sequence in the text itself. After chapter 3 there is a clear demarcation between the time of the seven churches (whether idealism's church age or historicism's Laodicean age) and the visions beginning in chapter 4. Neither John nor the interpreting angel attempts to indicate that the opening of the seals applies to the seven churches or throughout church history.

Exposition of the "seals" passages (6:1—8:1) also fails to support this view. By nature, the seals indicate catastrophic judgment. These conditions are nowhere referenced or implied in chapters 2 and 3, nor have any of those things occurred during 2,000 years of church history. The view that points to an unprecedented end-time fulfillment is preferred on both a *textual* and *historical* basis.

Neither is there anything to support identifying the scroll with "the Lamb's Book of Life." "When the Lamb does break its seals to open it, the writing discloses the objects of divine wrath rather than the recipients of divine redemption" (Wall 100, 101).

From every perspective, then, the view that the scroll's content deals with the end-times (eschatological view) is the most consistent. "The book in Revelation 5 concerns a predestined plan that is eschatological in nature, since its contents are revealed in chs. 6–22 and are summarized in 4:1 as 'what must take place after these things': a Danielic allusion indicating the end-time" (Beale 341, 342).

John's vision changes focus when he sees a "strong angel" (v. 2)—whether Gabriel (Dan. 8:16; 9:21; Lk. 1:19, 26) or Michael (Dan. 12:1-3; Jude 9) or some other angel. Regardless, a voice loud enough to be heard throughout the universe issues a universe-wide challenge (cf. 10:1; 18:21; 20:1), published throughout "Heaven, earth and under the earth" (v. 3), apparently corresponding to angels, living humans, and the dead. The dramatic "search," being universal and exhaustive, extends even into Hell. The challenge itself is rhetorical: God knew that no one would be found but used the challenge as an object lesson to demonstrate the uniqueness of Christ.

The challenge of the search is to find someone "worthy" to open the scroll: to "loose" or break its seven seals (v. 2). "Worthy" (Greek *axios*) means "having the weight of another thing, of like value, worth as much" (Thayer 52). The text separates its own prerequisites of worthiness into two parts: *moral* worthiness, without which no one could even approach God, and *ability* to open (break) or look on (read) the seals—and thus to execute or put them into motion. The catastrophes involved—miraculous plagues and eventual world destruction—suggest that infinite power is necessary.

217

The requirements for "worthiness" are high. First, retrieving anything from the right hand of God demands absolute holiness of character, sinlessness, or *moral excellence*, since God Himself is absolutely holy. Many interpreters therefore equate Christ's worthiness with "moral competence" (Hughes 78) or "moral fitness" (Swete 76).

Second is the Lamb's unique *identity* as the fulfillment of O.T. predictions of the Messiah. Some of these are cited by one of the elders in v. 5 (Gen. 49:8-12; 2 Sam. 7:12, 13, 16; Is. 11:1; 53:2). Eternal promises were made about the lineage of the tribe of Judah and the house of David in regard to the Messiah. Jesus was both "Lion of the tribe of Judah" and "root of David" (see Mt. 1:1-16).

A third requirement is implied: *divine attributes* are necessary to execute the catastrophic judgments of the seals and thus to guarantee that the things revealed will take place. Such a person must be *omnipotent*, *omnipresent*, and *omniscient*, truthful, wise, loving, and eternally unchanging. All these merge in the Person of Jesus Christ. (Additional requirements, cited in the song of redemption [vv. 9, 10], will be discussed below.)

The *initial* result of the "search" is stated next (vv. 3, 4): no one is found able to open, read, or look into the seven-sealed book, no one fulfills the prerequisites of worthiness. At this news, John is overcome with tears: (literally) "I was weeping" (Greek imperfect tense), continuing for a time before being interrupted by an angel. It first appears that the mysterious scroll must remain unopened and its contents unknown. Caird (73) suggests that faith cannot survive unless right finally triumphs over wrong, and that therefore "John weeps with disappointment because the hope of God's action appears to be indefinitely postponed."

The dramatic search has accomplished two things: it has illustrated the uniqueness of Christ and underscored mankind's need for total dependence upon Jesus Christ as the sole redeemer of mankind and sovereign Lord of future history. Jesus is the only champion able to rescue us from enemies pledged to our destruction. He is the only redeemer able to restore us to God's fellowship and favor and guide future history to its Biblical conclusion.

The grieving apostle is suddenly interrupted by the voice of one of the 24 elders (see comments on 4:4) commanding him to stop weeping (v. 5). This unidentified elder has wonderful news to report: someone equal to the task (worthy) has come forward. This one's resumé is impressive. He is the "Lion of the tribe of Juda" (Gen. 49:8-12) and "Root of David" (Is. 11:1, 10; Rom. 15:12).

The lion, symbolizing strength, fierceness, or royalty, is appropriate for the concept of the Jewish warrior-Messiah (Ford 85). Messianic hope was that this great deliverer would vanquish Israel's oppressors forever and secure her future glory on earth. As the Lion of Judah, he is a "David-like warrior Messiah who fights God's battles and wreaks vengeance on God's enemies" (Boring 108).

"Root" (Greek *hriza*) can be translated "shoot" or "sprout" (Lenski 196), marking Jesus as the fulfillment of prophecies that a descendant of King David would govern Israel forever. Both titles connect "the one found worthy" with Israel's Messiah predicted in the O.T.

But Jesus' worthiness derives from more than linkage with O.T. predictions of Messiah. In addition to His identity as Messiah, these titles highlight the sovereign strength, triumph, and royalty of Christ. The ability to open or loose the seals upon the earth requires authority from God and the raw power to execute what they reveal, both because of the catastrophic judgment involved and because of the strength of the opposition.

That Christ "has prevailed" adds further to the basis of His worthiness, actively demonstrated by His triumph over the world through His righteous life, death, burial, and resurrection (1 Cor. 15:1-4). "Prevail" (Greek *nikao*) is the same as "overcome" in the messages to the seven churches (2:7, etc.): the "key christological verb" in Revelation (Boring 111). The existence of either enemies or obstacles is implied, over which Christ has triumphed. He has conquered the world, the flesh, the devil, and death by His own life, death, and resurrection.

His triumph is personally and presently shared with all who are born again (Jn. 3:3-7), though full realization of that triumph—when soul and body are reunited in glorified condition—is not experienced until the rapture and resurrection of believers. Presently, on the individual and behavioral level, Christ's victory must be personally appropriated by faith through the power of the Holy Spirit. This is the *progressive* element in sanctification: believers should already be experiencing this victory, made clear in the challenge to be *overcomers* in the messages to all seven churches.

Furthermore, the victory is *eternal*. Thomas (I:386) says that "prevailed" (Greek aorist tense) suggests that Christ's triumph was a "once for all act within history." It stands in contrast to earthly championships that must be won again every season or from contest to contest (cf. 1 Cor. 9:25). "To open" indicates that Christ's ability to open the scroll is one of the assured *results* (and not the sole purpose) of this once-for-all triumph (Thomas I:388).

The act of breaking the seals sets the events in motion (6:1, 3, 5, 7, 9, 12; 8:1) and they are depicted in *proleptic* form: future events are described *as if they were presently happening*. This begins in 6:1: Christ opens them *sequentially*, revealing their contents, one at a time.

2. John sees the Lamb that has been slain (5: 6, 7)

6 And I beheld, and, lo, in the midst of the throne and of the four beasts, and in the midst of the elders, stood a Lamb as it had been slain, having seven horns and seven eyes, which are the seven Spirits of God sent forth into all the earth.

7 And he came and took the book out of the right hand of him that sat upon the throne.

The central image in chapter 5 is Christ as a "slain Lamb" (v. 6). "And I saw" shifts to this focus, alerting us to the most important aspect of Christ's worthiness. John sees the champion of Judah and David standing, "in the midst" of the throne and its heavenly entourage, like "a slain Lamb." No angel or elder needs to explain this to the apostle

219

who recorded the Baptist's words, "Behold, the Lamb of God" (Jn. 1:29, 36).

The point of "in the midst" is that Christ is "the Centerpiece of the whole *tableau*" (Swete 78). Jesus may well have been in human but glorified form, still bearing the marks of His crucifixion (Jn. 1:29, 36).

The image of a slaughtered Lamb with seven horns and eyes is not that of a "normal" lamb. The unusual features represent Christ's character and mission. He is *slaughtered* (dead) and yet *standing* (alive). "Slain" refers to "the violent slaughtering of a paschal lamb (Ex. 12:6; 1 Cor. 5:7; 1 Pet. 1:18, 19)" (Wall 103). The form of this verb (Greek perfect tense) suggests that "the efficacy of his death is still present in all its power" (L. Morris 95), thus emphasizing "the lasting benefits of his sacrificial death and resurrection" (Mounce 134). "Standing" may also imply "readiness for action" (Lenski 199).

Horns were an ancient and Scriptural symbol of power. Seven horns, the number of perfection, represent infinite power or omnipotence (Ford 86, 87). The death of Christ demonstrated not only God's love for the human race (Rom. 5:8) but also Christ's power in overcoming the world, the flesh, and the devil (Col. 2:14, 15)—not to mention His amazing self-control and the moral strength seen in His prompt forgiveness of those who had offended Him the most.

The picture of Christ as the slain Lamb of God does not suggest weakness or defeat but infinite power under self-control, absolute holiness of character, worthiness to redeem, vicarious sacrifice, pure love, and eternal victory. It "redefines omnipotence," not as the

power of unlimited coercion, but as the power of infinite persuasion, the invincible power of self-negating, self-sacrificing love" (Caird 75).

Eyes are a Scriptural symbol of knowledge (2 Chr. 16:9). Seven eyes symbolize infinite knowledge (omniscience). The eyes of the slain Lamb are interpreted as "the seven spirits of God sent forth into all the earth," a reference to the Holy Spirit (1:4; 3:1; 4:5). The Holy Spirit is Christ's agent in the world, manifesting Christ's own presence and power.

The focus has purposely shifted to Jesus *the Lamb*, an image that evokes the ideas of substitution and sacrifice. "Lamb" is one of John's favorite expressions of Christ, used 29 times in Revelation. Boring (108) notes that this is the first time Jesus has been represented as a Lamb: "John has reserved it for its dramatic entree precisely here." For the remainder of Revelation, the Lamb and "the One on the throne" remain in close association (6:16; 7:9, 10; 14:4; 21:22, 23; 22:1, 3).

The images of Jesus as *both* Lion and Lamb are paradoxical: lions eat lambs! Furthermore, this Lamb has been slain—a picture of weakness in comparison to the roaring king of beasts. But both images illustrate certain aspects of His character and mission. "This is perhaps the most mind-wrenching 'rebirth of images' in literature....The slot in the system reserved for the Lion has been filled by the Lamb of God" (Boring 108).

This apparent contradiction of images bears on the Jewish failure to recognize Christ as the Messiah. The sacrificial or *atoning* work of the Messiah—in spite of significant O.T. Scriptures like Ps. 22 and Is. 53—was not anticipated in the Judaism of Jesus' day. As Schurer's great survey of the Jewish Messianic hope (II:126-187) concludes, "In not one of the numerous works discussed by us have we found even the slightest allusion to an atoning suffering of Messiah" (186).

While the Lamb of this passage exhibits omnipotence and omniscience by its seven horns and seven eyes, the emphasis of the context is obviously upon the *sacrificial* character of the Lamb and His blood (vv. 9, 12). "It is blood even more than death that connotes sacrifice; for one may die without being slain and may be slain without being made a sacrifice" (Lenski 206). "The purpose of the term 'lamb' seems to be to identify the glorified Christ of Revelation with Christ the Lamb of sacrifice in His first coming" (Walvoord 115).

The uniquely worthy Lamb of God approached the throne of God and took the scroll from God's right hand (v. 7); He offered no resistance. Some interpreters think this corresponds to what "occurred at the ascension of Christ when Christ sat down at the right hand of God" (Lenski 202). (See Heb. 1:3; 10:12; Ps. 110:1.) By contrast, Mounce (134) expresses the futurist viewpoint, that it looks to "an event yet to take place at the end of time." The basic intention of the dramatic act is certainly a nonverbal, symbolic *confirmation* of Christ's worthiness. Specifically, the act is a dramatization that the control and denouement of future history is now in the hands of Christ.

Though God the Father, as Creator of the universe, administers sovereign control of history in the created order with His "right hand," He freely allows the Son to take the scroll. This effec-tively symbolizes a transfer of authority and control of the end of world history to Christ. Specifically, end-time events ("the things which shall be hereafter," 1:19), described when the scroll's seals are broken (including trumpet and bowl judgments in chapters 6–22), are in the hands of Christ. Present conditions in the church have already been described in chapters 2 and 3 as "the things which are" (1:19). Aune (I:374) is correct in labeling chapters 6–22 as an "eschatological scenario," "a transcription and revelatory preview of eschatological events."

In the hymns of chapter 5, Christ's worthiness is based on His successful redemptive mission, that is, by the shedding of His *blood* on the cross, the only soteriological currency that God accepts as sufficient to remove the debt of sin and purchase man's salvation (v. 9). In releasing the scroll from His all-powerful right hand, God could confidently give control of the future to the Lamb of God because He knew Jesus was fully endowed with the attributes necessary.

3. John hears the new song of the redeemed (5: 8-10)

8 And when he had taken the book, the four beasts and four *and* twenty elders fell down before the Lamb, having every one of them harps, and golden vials full of odours, which are the prayers of saints.

9 And they sung a new song saying, Thou are worthy to take the book, and to open the seals thereof: for thou wast slain, and hast redeemed us to God by thy blood out of every kindred, and tongue, and people, and nation;

221

10 And hast made us unto our God kings and priests: and we shall reign on the earth.

Heaven breaks out in *spontaneous* worship of the Lamb when He takes the book from the right hand of God (v. 8). The holy entourage around the throne falls prostrate, this time before Christ. The same language describing the worship of God in 4:10 is transferred unhesitatingly to Jesus the Lamb. This worship is offered *unanimously* and *antiphonally* and soon engulfs the entire population of Heaven.

Both the living beings *and* the elders prostrate themselves before the Lamb, but the acts and words in vv. 8-10 are apparently those of the 24 elders. Though the four living beings join in worship, the emphasis shifts to the elders as representatives of the redeemed; they are described in more detail than when first introduced (4:4) and their linkage with the saints is clearer. Each has a "harp," apparently to accompany the song of the redeemed in v. 9. This word (Greek *kithara*) may refer to a ten-stringed harp (Vine 291) or a "lyre" (similar to a guitar). Stringed instruments—relatively easy to make and sing with—were often used to accompany singing in Bible times, as in ours, and are prominent throughout the Psalms (33:2; 92:3; 144:9; 150:4). The four living beings and angels offer their own worshipful recitations, but not as song (vv. 11, 13); nor can they sing the song of redemption, having never experienced it.

Each of the elders also has a golden vial or "bowl" (Barnes 126) filled with incense, representing the prayers of saints (cf. 8:3-5). Old Testament worshipers in the Temple courtyards pros-

trated themselves in silent prayer as incense was burned in the Holy Place in conjunction with the morning and evening sacrifices. King David pictured his prayers ascending before God in this way (Ps. 141:2). The symbolism pictures every believer's prayers stored up in Heaven, with their pleasing aroma rising like fragrant, burning incense from the bowls held by the elders to be remembered by God. A. Johnson (72) sees these prayers as specifically related to martyrdom; Ladd (*Commentary* 89) limits them to "prayers for the coming of the kingdom." But such limitations seem unlikely; the bowls may as easily represent all the prayers of all saints throughout history.

The 24 elders sing "the song of the redeemed" in vv. 9, 10; but are they singing this for themselves or about others (the church)? This question arises because a number of manuscripts, in vv. 9, 10, read "them" rather than "us." Interpreters who think the 24 elders are angels will naturally prefer that reading. Ladd, for example, thinks they are angels and are singing *about* the redeemed (*Commentary* 92) rather than for themselves. But there is good manuscript evidence for "us," and this reading more accurately reflects the identity of the elders as glorified saints who participate fully in singing the song of the redeemed.

The song itself extols the worthiness of Christ, as the slain Lamb of God, to "take the scroll and open its seals" (v. 9). It is "new" (Greek *kainos*), "not simply new in point of time" but "new and distinctive in quality" (TDNT III:447).

Three reasons for Christ's worthiness are cited in this song about Christ the Redeemer. First, He was slain, apparently emphasizing the past, once-for-all sacrifice of Christ (Greek aorist tense). The writer of Hebrews argues this repeatedly and effectively (Heb. 7:27; 9:26, 28; 10:10; cf. 1 Pet. 3:18). Christ offered Himself once in history, a sacrifice never to be repeated.

Second, Christ freely offered His blood as a sufficient *purchase* (redemption) price: it "denotes a commercial transaction, typified by the purchase of people as slaves" (Wall 103). "To God" means "purchased back to Him" (Wall 104). Jesus' death, then, is the price that was paid; it is of infinite worth and as a result the believer is His bond-slave (cf. 1 Pet. 1:18, 19; 1 Cor. 6:9). In N.T. times, a slave could purchase his freedom by depositing money in the name of a god at the local pagan temple. The slave owner eventually received the money and the slave his freedom; the false god received the credit (see Ladd, *Commentary* 91). Freedom from sin and Satan are wonderful results of redemption taught in the N.T., but this is only half of what redemption intends: not just freedom from an old master but *transfer of ownership* to a new one. The emphasis here is more on Christ's ownership, secured by the price He paid for us, seen in the expression "redeemed us *to God*."

The life of Christ, represented by His blood, was the purchase price of our redemption. Again, "redeemed" or "purchased" (Greek aorist) indicates once-for-all action. The verb is active (not passive, as in "slain"): Christ offered His own blood voluntarily (Jn. 10:17, 18). The blood of Christ provided propitiation or covering for the sins of all, expiated God's wrath, and restored believers to God's favor. The provision was universal and application (though not universal) is without favoritism; the

redeemed represent "every kindred, tongue, people and nation" (v. 9; cf. 1 Jn. 2:2; 2 Pet. 3:9). This fourfold division of humanity makes the point of universal provision more emphatic (cf. 1:7; 5:9; 7:9; 10:11; 11:9; 13:7; 14:6; 17:15). Simply put, redemption provisionally includes everyone on earth.

"Kindred" (Greek *phule*) means "a company of people united by kinship or habitation, a clan, tribe" (Vine 643). It is a way of subdividing a larger association of people related to one another; compare the twelve "tribes" within O.T. Israel. "Tongue" (Greek *glossa*) in the N.T. is used (by metonymy) for "language" and so identifies people-groups by the languages they speak. "People" (Greek *laos*) denotes "an assembly" of those with common characteristics or of people in general (Vine 465; Thayer 372). "Nation" (Greek *ethnos*) has a number of senses (Thayer 168) but here probably focuses on the larger divisions of humanity associated by lineage, language, race, or basic citizenship. The purpose of these categories is no doubt for effect, to illustrate the universal scope of Christ's redemption.

Third, Christ is worthy of the redeemed community's worship because He "has made" them into "kings and priests" (v. 10; cf. 1:6; 20:6). The redeemed do not usurp this honor and mission for themselves; Christ grants it to them, commissioning and equipping them (Mt. 28:19, 20; Acts 1:8; Eph. 4:7,12; 2 Tim. 3:17; 1 Pet. 2:5, 9; Ex. 19:6). Some manuscripts read "kingdom of priests"; the meaning is not very different. "Kings" makes good sense, in that Christ has promised that the redeemed will "reign" with Him (v. 10; 20:4; 22:5).

The sure promise is that members of this redeemed body will participate in a definite *earthly* and *heavenly* reign (v. 10; cf. 20:4-6; 22:5). (Some manuscripts have "they" instead of "we.") The idea of believers sharing in the reign of Christ is included: "And we shall reign on the earth." "Shall reign" makes the predicted reign *eschatological* and not simply "spiritual" in nature.

This does not deny that kingdom rule and priestly function are important parts of the church's *present* experience. "To make [Christ's] act of amnesty and reconciliation known to the world is the royal and priestly task of the church" (Caird 77). Our priestly privilege includes "immediate and full access to God's presence for praise and worship" and "priestly service to God" (Thomas I:402). But the ultimate reference in v. 10 is to the end-times. On one hand, realized aspects of Christ's present kingdom continue to transform us spiritually and societally—to a *limited* degree. But evil will be present until the end (2 Th. 2:3-8; 2 Tim. 3:1; 1 Pet. 5:8). Because most people will resist Christ for the remainder of world history, an eschatological, militaristic triumph will be necessary to establish Christ's rule on earth in its O.T. millennial dimensions (Wall 105-107). This will happen at the Second Coming of Christ.

4. John sees, hears, and counts a great angelic host (5:11, 12)

11 And I beheld, and I heard the voice of many angels round about the throne and the beasts and the elders: and the number of them was ten thousand times ten thousand, and thousands of thousands;

12 Saying with a loud voice, Worthy is the Lamb that was slain to receive power, and riches, and wisdom, and strength, and honour, and glory, and blessing.

A countless number of angels offer a recitation of worship in recognition of the Lamb's worthiness (vv. 11, 12). These are positioned as an outer circle around God's throne and the living beings and elders, who are not involved in the recitation. The number of angels is "ten thousand times ten thousand" and "thousands of thousands," expressing their *seemingly infinite number*.

Their sevenfold tribute to the Lamb is antiphonal to the elder's song but more *recitation* than song (Mounce 137). John does not compose these "hymns" as such but records what he hears in Heaven. They are not traditional Jewish or Christian hymns but "new hymns... making use of some traditional Jewish and Christian liturgical traditions and forms" (Aune I:315). Any similarities to imperial cult hymns in honor of various emperors would imply a veiled rebuke of the imperial cult (Aune I:316). If Domitian or others required such terms of honor they usurped them; they rightfully belong only to God and the Lamb.

"With a loud voice" this numberless throng of angels offers tribute to the Lamb, affirming His worthiness to receive power, riches, wisdom, strength, honor, glory, and blessing. One cannot imagine the impressive volume of the voices of thousands or millions of angels. A. Johnson (74) suggests that the sevenfold doxology is methodological: "a Qumran liturgical method for creating the feeling of God's majesty and glory (7:12; 4QSL)." Thomas (I:405) thinks of this as *polysyndeton* which "enhances rhetorical emphasis by producing the impression of extensiveness and abundance."

Power (Greek *dunamis*) indicates "ability" or "capacity" (TDNT II:284), especially "the ability to carry out an action" (ISBE III:927). Jesus, the all-capable one, is worthy of the ascription of utmost power. He is also worthy to receive "riches," material or spiritual. Christ's sacrificial work merits all the wealth of God, Heaven, and earth, including all the redeemed as His inheritance, purchased by His blood.

To recognize that the Lamb *possesses* infinite "wisdom" (Col. 2:3; 1 Cor. 1:24, 30) is only part of the truth: He is the very *personification* of wisdom. Thomas (I:405) defines this as the attribute of God demonstrated "in the conscious and purposeful creation and government of the world" which "establishes the rule of righteousness on earth and is the moral power pervading and effecting the progress of world history."

The triad "honor," "glory," and "blessing" completes the angel's doxological tribute. "Honor" is the value, respect, or recognition someone deserves, "the public acknowledgment of a person's worth" (DNTB 518). Christ's exaltation at the right hand of God is symbolic of the high honor accorded Him by God.

The "glory" of Christ is comprehended in His redemptive character, work, and eternal exaltation at the Father's side. Because all glory rightfully belongs to God alone (Mt. 6:13), this tribute is additional confirmation of Jesus' deity. Jesus shared God's glory eternally (Jn. 17:5) and spoke of His future glory (Jn. 17:22, 24), which encompasses the sights, sounds, and service of everything

that Heaven is and of all that will be experienced there in eternity.

"Blessing" is "good speaking, praise, the giving of thanks" (Vine 70). The worthiness of Christ virtually commands such a response. Jesus' unique identity as the Lamb of God who was slain and who takes the seven-sealed scroll from God's right hand, is the paramount reason to "bless" Him in worship eternally.

5. John witnesses Heaven's doxology to God and the Lamb (5:13, 14)

13 And every creature which is in heaven, and on the earth, and under the earth, and such as are in the sea, and all that are in them, heard I saying, Blessing, and honour, and glory, and power, *be* unto him that sitteth upon the throne, and unto the Lamb for ever and ever.
14 And the four beasts said, Amen. And the four *and* twenty elders fell down and worshipped him that liveth for ever and ever.

An abbreviated version of the angels' sevenfold tribute is repeated by all of animate creation, offering the Lamb a fourfold doxology of "blessing, honor, glory, and power," corresponding in number to the four living beings. The last four of the seven in v. 12 are offered again (see comments above), except that a different word for "power" is used (Greek *kratos*), which "denotes the superior power of God to which the final victory will belong," that belongs to God exclusively (TDNT III:907, 908). (Where the seven, above, were united under one article in Greek, focusing on them as a composite whole, each of these four has a separate article, emphasizing the absoluteness of each.)

All creatures in Heaven and earth participate in this doxology through their representatives around the throne, the four living beings, corresponding also to the number of realms cited: "in heaven," "on the earth," "under the earth," and "in the sea" (cf. Phil. 2:10). The fourfold tribute to God and the Lamb also matches the number. All creation's tribute is appropriate because it too will experience and celebrate the effects of the Lamb's redemption (Is. 55:12, 13; Rom. 8:19-23).

After the living beings provide the final "amen" to the worship of the Lamb (v. 14), the worship scene concludes when the 24 elders, cued again by the four living beings, prostrate themselves before the throne in worship of the One who lives forever. Barnes (128) suggests that the three doxologies in chapter 5 demonstrate *universal agreement* in Heaven. "These last two verses, 5:13, 14, relate to the conjoined glory and adoration of God and Lamb. All the universe praises God and the Lamb because of their work in creation and redemption" (Hendriksen 92).

Summary
(5:1-14)

Chapters 4 and 5 are a thematic unit in Revelation. This description of the throne room of God in Heaven is John's *second* great vision, shifting dramatically from Patmos and the seven churches in chapters 1-3 to Heaven and the distant future in chapters 4, 5.

Chapter 5 looks beyond John's view of the splendor of God seated on His throne (ch. 4) to focus first on a seven-sealed scroll in the right hand of God (v. 1) and then on the slain Lamb of God (v. 6). This is done in high drama that is didactic in purpose.

First, a strong angel issues a challenge to find someone worthy to open the seven-sealed scroll (v. 2), which contains an exposition of end-time events. A universal search ensues, encompassing Heaven, earth, and under the earth. No one is found worthy, and therefore able, to open the scroll (v. 3).

John is overcome with weeping (v. 4), raising the possibility that the contents of the scroll will remain unknown, leaving the human race to face an unknown future, unprepared. The stakes are high and John's emotion is understandable.

The grieving apostle is interrupted by one of the elders with good news (v. 5). Someone has come forward with the necessary qualifications. He is described as "the Lion of the tribe of Juda" and as "the Root of David." These O.T. metaphors identify Him as the royal, warrior-Messiah of Israel and seed of David—the fulfillment of O.T. prophecy (Gen. 49:8-10; Is. 11:1). Thus John is further instructed about qualities that describe the identity and character of Christ in Revelation (cf. 1:12-20).

When John looks toward the throne he sees this Messiah as "a slain Lamb" (v. 6), a picture implying two great truths. One is the suffering and sacrificial aspect of Messiah's mission, seen in the marks of slaughter (Is. 53:7). The second is paradoxical: He is also *standing* and therefore alive, a clear reference to His triumphant resurrection.

The slain Lamb has seven horns and seven eyes, symbolic of Christ's omnipotence and omniscience. The slain Lamb manifests His power and presence in the world through the Holy Spirit (Jn. 14:26; 15:26; 16:7-11; Acts 1:8; see 1:4).

Jesus Christ, as the slain Lamb of God, is uniquely qualified and able to take the scroll from God's right hand and open its seals (v. 7). He is the fulfillment of O.T. prophecy. He is absolutely holy. He has been slain, thereby purchasing the redeemed from sin to God. He is able to execute the seals in future history because He is sovereign, omnipotent, omnipresent, and all wise. The opening of the seals will happen in the end-time Tribulation, culminating in the Second Coming.

The Lamb's ability to take and open the scroll is celebrated by all the host of Heaven (vv. 8-14). The living beings and 24 elders begin their worshipful response by falling prostrate before the Lamb. The 24 elders sing the "song of redemption" (vv. 9, 10), extolling the twofold *purchase* aspect of redemption. Redemption is both "from" an old owner (Satan and sin) and "to" a new one (God). The blood of Christ is the purchase price. The goal of redemption is the entire human race, summarized as "every tribe, tongue, people and nation." The ultimate result is that believers are made into "kings" and "priests" who will share in Christ's reign on earth.

An infinite number of angels recite an antiphonal, sevenfold response to the elders' song (vv. 11, 12). Not only is the Lamb worthy of this tribute because He has been slain, He is worthy because He already possesses these attributes. It is therefore a recitation of affirmation and praise. All animate creation joins in with a fourfold tribute (v. 13), most likely through the four living beings surrounding God's throne who are themselves the representatives of creation (4:6-8).

The four living beings conclude the antiphonal worship scene with an affirming and concluding "Amen" (v. 14). We are left with a picture of the 24 elders prostrating themselves in worship before God and the Lamb. The scene ends somewhat abruptly, providing a helpful pause within the narrative before the opening of the first seal in 6:1.

Application: Teaching and Preaching the Passage

The Greek verb tenses in chapter 5 are especially instructive in regard to the work of Christ. The aorist is used to indicate *a completed action* in past time (Mare 30), and some of these in context convey the *once-for-all-time* quality of Christ's work on the cross (as stated explicitly in Heb. 7:27; 9:12,27, 28). "Has prevailed" (or "triumphed"), in v. 5, is an example: the triumph has occurred in past history, never to be repeated. That took place on the cross of Christ (Col. 2:14, 15), an objective reality that was finished the day Christ died, confirmed in His resurrection and exaltation in Heaven. We cannot and do not have anything to add to the finished redemptive work of Christ. God is forever pleased with us on this basis. We are challenged to believe the gospel and to enter into His victory.

The Greek perfect tense is also significant in this regard, typically used to indicate "a state of completion" (Mare 26). An action may be completed and have *continuing results*. The perfect-tense verbs that describe the Lamb's activity in v. 6—"standing" and "slain"— draw our attention to the *continuing and settled effects* of the work of Christ. Jesus was slain on the cross but the effects continue forward throughout eternity.

The fifth chapter expands our knowledge of Christ. This began in 1:12-20 with the first great vision of Christ and continues with His identification as the Messianic Lion of Judah and Root of David in O.T. prophecy. The imagery of a slaughtered but living Lamb is also instructive.

The nature of redemption in Christ is seen in the term "redeemed," which may also be translated as "purchased." There is power in the blood of Christ in its ability to serve as the purchase price of our redemption. Believers are redeemed *from* the old masters—the world, the flesh, and the devil. The other side of this is *new ownership* by God. The vast scope of universal redemption is also clearly in view ("every tribe, tongue, people, and nation")—a powerful complement to the "whosoever will" emphasis. The result of redemption is the transformation of believers into "kings" and "priests." This involves present mission and future hope.

Continuing glimpses about the nature of worship in Heaven should be observed. Various distinctions within the host of Heaven are apparent. Musicians sing and play instruments. Praise and thanksgiving are recited or sung. The living beings, elders, saints, and angels are united in this activity. Worship is forever focused on God and the Lamb. There is an eternity of sincere wonder about their persons and attributes that will never be exhausted. Worship should never be considered boring; it certainly is not in Heaven.

A particularly encouraging image about the prayers of saints is in v. 8. Believers' prayers are stored before God in Heaven in "golden bowls" and rise

before Him like fragrant incense. Prayers, once prayed, are stored and continue to work for us, they are not lost. Each time we pray, we add to those already prayed. God never forgets legitimate prayers. Knowing this brings great comfort about past efforts in prayer and is an incentive to pray even more.

Suggested Outlines. The Scroll of Eschatology, 5:1-14: (1) The Seals, v. 1; (2) The Search, vv. 2, 3; (3) The Sadness, v. 4; (4) The Solution, vv. 5-7; (5) The Song, vv. 8-10; (6) The Sayings, vv. 11-14.

The Worthiness of the Lamb—worthy to be worshiped because of who He is and what He has done, 5:5-10: (1) The Sovereign Lamb, v. 5 (cf. Gen. 49:8-10; 2 Sam. 7:12-16; Is. 11:1; 53:6, 7); (2) The Slain but Standing Lamb, v. 6; (3) The Spirit of the Lamb, v. 6; (4) The Seeking and Saving Lamb, v. 9; (5) The Sanctifying Lamb, v. 10.

III. THE SEVEN SEALS (6:1—8:5)

A. Four Horsemen of the Apocalypse (6:1-8)

There has been much discussion about the symbolism, identity, and mission of the "four horsemen," especially the first. One perspective is that all four horsemen are *divine agents*, executing God's will in the earth (Michaels 103, 104); this way, the first horseman represents Christ or something equally positive.

A second perspective, at the opposite end of the spectrum, identifies all four as *satanic*; this requires that the first horseman represent an evil person or force—Antichrist himself, in the view of many.

A third view sees both God and Satan at work in the four horsemen: the agents are evil, but God uses or permits their destructive work in order to achieve His grand purpose for the redemptive and judicial consummation of world history. "The direct perpetrators of the eschatological woes [are]...demonic anti-God forces permitted and used by God as agents of divine judgment" (Boring 124).

Idealism, as a fourth variety, does not limit fulfillment to one particular example. Although the horsemen may be related to God and Satan, the focus is less sinister and broader. The white horse and its rider, for example, represent *the spirit of militarism or conquest* in general within world history. All four horsemen (conquest, war, famine, and pestilence) represent "*chief components* of society" throughout *all* of world history (Ellul 50).

As this indicates, one's viewpoint of the first horseman seems to be determinative for identifying whether the basic agency of all four is divine or satanic. Respective advocates of each view cite an impressive array of Scriptural evidence and logic; ironically, those holding opposing viewpoints often use the same O.T. and N.T. Scriptures for support and seek to bolster their argument with parallels from antiquity.

1. First Seal–the white horse and its rider (6: 1, 2)

1 And I saw when the Lamb opened one of the seals, and I heard, as it were the noise of thunder, one of the four beasts saying, Come and see.
2 And I saw, and behold a white horse: and he that sat on him had a bow; and a crown was given unto him: and he went forth conquering, and to conquer.

"And I saw" (v. 1) does not introduce a new vision but a new feature within the vision that began in chapters 4, 5. John still focuses on the Lamb of God. After taking the book from God's right hand (5:7), and after a crescendo of worship and praise throughout Heaven (5:9-14), the Lamb began opening the seven-sealed scroll.

"One of the seals" is the first; the rest will be numbered accordingly. Each of the first four is opened dramatically, following a call from one of the four living beings, whose loud voices reminded John of the sound of thunder (cf. 14:2). Since the four living beings are not identified, there is no implied correlation between their specific identities and the four horsemen.

In each case, the call is "Come and see" (A.V.) or, simply, "Come" (in a number of manuscripts). "Come and see" implies that the call was for John's attention to what he was about to witness (Walvoord 125). If the simple "Come" is original, the call was probably addressed to the horseman to ride forth: "Go" is equally correct as a translation (Aune I:380). One may compare Zech. 1:8-10 and 6:1-8 where colored horses and chariots are sent out by God to patrol the earth. Swete (85), citing how "come" is used exclusively in Revelation by God or in relation to Christ, sees it as a request of "nature" (represented by the living beings) for Christ to come. The symbolism of the horsemen is not affected by this difference: the seals are opened and the riders are sent out.

The color of each horse (white, red, black, and pale), together with other features, indicates the symbolism. But, unlike the other three, the meaning of the first horse is not stated. This results in a number of different interpretations about the identity and mission of the first rider. Is this Christ, or Antichrist, or some other good or evil force? Thomas (I:419-424) lists as many as eight different identifications: military victory, a Roman emperor, the Word of God, the victorious course of the gospel, the Parthian invasion, warfare in general, the Jewish Messiah, and a counterfeit Christ. Most frequently, interpreters regard the first horseman as representing either Christ or the Antichrist.

That the rider on the white horse represents Christ, directly or indirectly, may be called the "classical" view, going as far back as Irenaeus in the third century and held by more contemporary scholars like Alford, Hodge, Hendriksen, and Ladd. Oecumenius regarded Christ as the rider and the white horse as the gospel (Aune I:394). Similarly, some have interpreted this as the triumphant gospel (Charles I:164) or the Word of God (Lenski 222).

This view is based largely on: (1) the symbolism of the color white in Revelation; (2) the incongruity of this color with the nature of Satan; (3) the use of *the divine passive* "to whom it was given"; (4) the throne-room context beginning in 4:1; and (5) similarities to Christ in 19:11-16.

We should look at the symbols in v. 2 for help: one adjective ("white"), three nouns ("horse," "bow," and "crown"), and four verbs ("sitting," "was given," "went forth," "conquering and to conquer").

"White" appears consistently in Revelation as a symbol of righteousness, reward, victory, and heavenly regalia (1:14; 2:17; 3:4, 5,18; 4:4; 6:2, 11;

7:9,13, 14; 14:14; 15:6; 19:8, 11, 14; 20:11). This makes it difficult to justify using it, here, to denote the Antichrist or evil forces. Even outside the Scriptures, in the ancient world, white was often the color of victory (Swete 86) or "symbolic of purity and joy" (Ford 97).

The "horse" itself was often symbolic of war, in contrast to animals used as beasts of burden (Ford 97), reflecting their strength, speed, and versatility in warfare (Prov. 21:31). Kings rode on horses (Est. 6:8; 1 Kg. 20:20). White horses, in particular, were used in Roman triumphal processions in celebration of military conquests (DNTB 1004.). The additional use of the "bow" and "crown" and the verb "conquer" support this identification with militaristic or conquering activity—though some resist this by observing that generals rode in chariots pulled by horses rather than on the horses themselves, as here.

The rider has a "bow" (v. 2), with arrows implied, as prolific a symbol of warfare and strength as the horse. It often appears in Scripture, by metonymy, for the military might of a nation, or even of God (Ps. 7:12, 13; 45:5; 58:7; 64:7; Is. 66:19; Jer. 49:35; Lam. 2:4; Ezek. 39:3; Hos. 1:5; Zech. 9:10; Hab. 3:9,11-15). Hosea 1:7 lists bow, sword, battle, horses, and horsemen as instruments of warfare.

The rider on the white horse wears a "crown": the crown of a victorious athlete or general (Greek *stephanos*, as in 14:14) and not a royal crown (Greek *diadema*, as in 19:12). This victor's crown was typically a wreath made of plant material, awarded for celebration of victory (Trench 78, 79). Perhaps Christ is pictured this way to illustrate the *victorious* rather than *regal* aspect of His activity in the end-times.

Apparently the passive verb "was given" implies God as the giver, a construction called a "divine passive." Though Caird (81) insists that this construction, in Revelation, refers mostly to God's *permission* given to evil agents, Aune (I:394,395) has pointed out that it is also used for commissioning *divine* agents; a survey of the 20 uses of this divine passive in Revelation supports Aune. For that matter "was given" could well emphasize God's sovereign control of all end-time activities.

"He that sat" indicates the posture of the rider, mounted and ready to ride forth. "Conquering, and to conquer" ("a conqueror bent on conquest," NIV) indicates the mission of the first rider, using the same verb as "overcomes" in the letters to the seven churches. The basic activity portrayed by the double verb construction combines the idea of "continual effort in conquering" (Greek present participle) with total conquest or victory in "to conquer" (Greek aorist subjunctive)—the ultimate object in view. Since such a mission could fit Christ or Antichrist, it is not by itself determinative as to the identity of the first horseman; even so, it fits well with the view that the first horseman depicts Christ.

The strongest alternative to the classical position is that the first horseman represents, directly or indirectly, the Antichrist, masquerading as the true Messiah in order to deceive the world. This view is based largely on: (1) similarities between the seal judgments and the Olivet Discourse, which predicts the coming of false Christs first (Mt. 24:1-14; Mk. 13:1-10; Lk. 21:5-11); (2) parallels with 2 Th. 2:1-10; (3) dissimilarities with the picture of Christ in Rev. 19:11-16; (4) the frequent use of the "divine passive" for permission given to

evil forces (as observed by Caird, above); (5) the description of the beast in 13:1-18; (6) viewing the other three horsemen as satanic confederates who wreak havoc in the world; and (7) the appropriateness of conquest as a mission of the Antichrist. After presenting some of these arguments, Wong (227) summarizes: "The first horseman...represents the Antichrist or a trend or movement of which he would certainly be a chief example....The object of his overcoming probably includes inhabitants of the earth in general and tribulation saints specifically. [His] triumphs...will be characterized by violence, but Christ will return to earth and put an end to them." Wong links Ezek. 38, 39, where he interprets Gog, wielding a bow (Ezek. 39:3), as referring to Antichrist. However, a link between Antichrist and the first horseman is never supplied here in 6:2, and the use of a bow for conquering activity is equally appropriate for Christ, whose victory is eternal and a major theme in Revelation.

Beale (377) lists alternative identifications within the satanic category as "governments that persecute Christians," "the devil's servants in general," or "the forces of false prophecy and false messiahs." Some who hold such views would still identify these as agents of Antichrist.

Some have suggested that the first horseman represents the invasion of Parthian [Persian] cavalry, who rode white horses into battle (Charles I:163) and were a perennial threat to the peace of the eastern Roman empire. This view fits the preterist interpretation of Revelation, rooting the fulfillment of the first seal long ago in past history (ca. A.D. 62). This conflicts with the future-time reference indicated in 4:1: "things which must be hereafter." It is far more consistent to place the activity portrayed in this heavenly drama in the end-time Tribulation period. Preterists regard the judgment language of Revelation as a poetic way of describing God's judgment of Jerusalem and the nation of Israel in the first century (Gentry, *Four Views* 53-55).

Idealist interpreters suggest that the seals were inaugurated with the ascension of Christ: "The picture presented by this rider on the white horse is one of a tyranny that will dominate and be the rule, not the exception, throughout the time period from the ascension of Christ up to the end of history" (Brighton 165). Idealists see all four horsemen as symbolical representations of perennial scourges within history (military conquest, famine, disease, and death).

All things considered, the forces at work in all four seals are more properly credited to God, favoring the view that Christ is the Rider on the white horse. Neither Satan nor Antichrist has appeared in the throne-room vision leading up to the opening of the seals; Antichrist does not appear until 13:1. The worthiness and activity of Christ the Lamb in opening or inaugurating the seals also tends to support identifying the first rider as Christ or His agent.

Indeed, none of the four riders appears to be demonic as such but divine agents of judgment sent forth into the world. The fact that no interpretation is supplied for the first horseman, as for the others, seems to imply a *difference* in nature rather than absolute uniformity. Identifying the first rider as Christ preserves the unity of the four horsemen as agents of God's judgment.

Appeals to dissimilarities with Christ as the rider of 19:14 are unimpressive.

O.T. precedents, when God used the same phenomena—sword, famine, beast, and pestilence (Ezek. 14:21)—as agents of judgment on the righteous and unrighteous alike are weighty. Furthermore, that the "crown" here is the victor's crown, rather than a king's, is not a problem: in 14:14 (and Heb. 2:9) the victor's crown is worn by Christ (Hodge 334). Christ's conquest of the world will chastise a recalcitrant human race, vindicate His followers, abolish the world's religious and economic systems, save a vast multitude of Jewish and Gentile believers, defeat the Antichrist's regime, and establish His millennial glory on earth.

2. Second Seal—the red horse and its rider (6: 3,4)

3 And when he had opened the second seal, I heard the second beast say, Come and see.
4 And there went out another horse *that was* red: and *power* was given to him that sat thereon to take peace from the earth, and that they should kill one another: and there was given unto him a great sword.

Sequential opening of the seals affords opportunity to appreciate each and may indicate their sequential nature. The horsemen do not appear to be riding forth at once, and even if they did it would not affect the meaning. Common to each is the opening by the Lamb, whose God-given authority, moral worthiness, and sovereign ability for the task were established in the first part of the vision (5:5, 9).

We need not assume that the order of the living beings who introduce each seal corresponds to the order given in 4:7 (lion, ox, man, eagle). That the second living being is the "calf" or "ox"—domesticated and peaceful—has no obvious association with the war represented by the second horseman. On "Come and see" (versus simply "Come" or "Go"), see the comments above on v. 1.

The second horse is "red" (cf. Zech. 1:8; 6:2): "fiery red" (Aune I:381), in contrast with others in the red family (chestnut, bay, sorrel). The color of the second horse (and perhaps the others) may have had an exaggerated, supernatural quality: *bright* red for effect. Red can symbolize things such as the fire of God's judgment, redemption by blood, bloodshed (Ford 106), violence, etc. (see 1:14, 15; cf. 12:3; 17:3, 4).

As with the other three (implicit for the third), this horseman's authority is "given to him" by God (v. 4)—the "divine passive" construction referred to above. Though the mission of each has a negative effect on the inhabitants of earth, it is better to emphasize the *divine* rather than satanic agency. The Lamb opens each seal, effectively sending the riders on their missions. The second, third, and fourth horsemen are probably meant to be viewed as angelic beings, acting as divine agents.

In contrast to the first horseman, an interpretation is supplied with the second, third, and fourth seals: in this case, "to take peace from the earth" as represented by a "great sword" (v. 4). This particular "sword" (Greek *machaira*), "a knife for killing or cutting up" (ALGNT 255), was the *short* variety used in close fighting (Thomas I:429). (For the *larger* sword, see the fourth horseman in v. 8.) "Great" apparently indicates the large scope of the violence, perhaps the great

number of individuals killed. The sword was basically an offensive weapon, used frequently in Scripture as a symbol of authority, judgment, the Word of God, war, bloodshed, etc. (cf. 19:15; Mt. 10:34; 26:52; Rom. 13:4; Eph. 6:17; Heb. 4:12).

Ford (107) says that the second rider is "an angel of Yahweh who implements His (disciplinary) punishment by permitting civil strife (of which the sword is a symbol)." Charles (I:165) cites Is. 27:1; 34:5; 46:10; 47:6; Ezek. 21:3 as eschatological references where "the sword is wielded by Yahweh Himself." Limiting this reference to martyred believers is too restrictive; the sword of the second horseman potentially falls on the entire population of earth.

There are other identifications for the second horseman. Some see him as Roman domination or one of the emperors in the early centuries (preterist viewpoint). Some refer to the dissolution of the empire itself in the bloody period after the assassination of Commodus (Boring 122). Idealist Hendriksen (99) sees the rider as "religious persecution of God's children," the natural consequence of the first rider's spreading the gospel. But no such limitations are justified by the text. "The earth" implies that *the world's entire population is affected,* including believers and unbelievers. Futurist Thomas (I:426,427) views the second seal as "the beginning of a broader period called 'the tribulation' (2 Th. 1:6)," with the second horseman "representative of forces of war and bloodshed with their consequent horrors." Some have identified the second horseman with Russia and her Arab allies hostile to Israel in the Battle of Armageddon in the future (Gregg 109).

The combination of "to take peace from the earth" with "that they should kill one another" (cf. Is. 19:2) leaves no doubt about the activity involved. The first action leads naturally to the second as its consequence (cf. 2 Th. 2:6, 7). "Kill" (Greek *sphazo*) means "to slaughter or to murder by violence" (Mounce 143). The removal of external peace between nations and individuals leads invariably to *war*. Furthermore, it is worldwide, affecting the entire population of earth, including those converted during the Tribulation and unbelievers alike.

Although there have been worldwide and civil wars throughout history, the degree of chaos brought about by the second horseman (and his companions) reflects unprecedented conditions and seems clearly to be eschatological. (Note the "fourth part of the earth," below, in v. 8.)

Some interpreters tie the mission of the second horseman to the breaking of a covenant of peace by the Antichrist in the end-times. There is a "the" with "peace" (in the Greek), perhaps indicating a "previously existing peace." The desire for world peace may factor into the rise of the Antichrist to power, who makes a covenant with Israel at the beginning of Daniel's seventieth week—referenced in this commentary as the end-times Tribulation (Dan. 9:27). Those who identify the first rider as Antichrist (discussed above) see a covenant of false peace, brought about by the world leader, dissolving in the middle of the Tribulation period. Thomas (I:427) locates the second seal in the first half of the seven-year Tribulation.

But the second horseman *takes peace from the earth* rather than establishing a covenant of peace (even if a false one), as the Antichrist does at the beginning of Tribulation week. The spirit of military conquest in this sense does not originate with Antichrist but is what makes him attractive as one able to provide "peace" (cf. 1 Th. 5:3).

Those who locate the second seal in the first half of the Tribulation period do so because of the similarities between the first four seals and "the beginning of sorrows" section in the Olivet Discourse (Mt. 24:5-8). Jesus predicted that a significant amount and variety of bloodshed would occur during this period. These signs are present well before the midpoint of this period and do seem to correspond on a number of points with the horsemen's activities (Mt. 24:9-21).

3. Third Seal—the black horse and its rider (6: 5, 6)

5 And when he had opened the third seal, I heard the third beast say, Come and see. And I beheld, and lo a black horse; and he that sat on him had a pair of balances in his hand.
6 And I heard a voice in the midst of the four beasts say, A measure of wheat for a penny, and three measures of barley for a penny; and see thou hurt not the oil and the wine.

When the third seal is broken, the third horseman rides forth, introduced according to the same pattern as the two preceding; see comments on v. 1. This rider is on a black horse. "Black" often symbolizes "death or mourning" (Ford 107), but the symbol of death among the four horsemen is the pale horse and rider, interpreted for us as "death and hell" in v. 8. Here, then, black represents severe deprivation, as in famine, inflation, and perhaps poverty. Nonetheless, death is indirectly present since it may result from such conditions.

The rider holds "a pair of balances" or weighing scales in his hand: "a crossbeam suspended by a hook or cord with a pan suspended from each end of the crossbeam....Weights placed in one pan were used to determine the weight of commodities placed in the other" (Aune I:396). "In the ancient world food was distributed by rationed amounts (using scales) when it became scarce" (Beale 381). The empty scales, then, represent scarcity and famine, a frequent phenomenon in the ancient world and in first-century Asia Minor.

Additionally, John heard a voice coming from the vicinity of the four living beings (v. 6). Some suggest that this is one of the four living beings or an unidentified angel (cf. 9:13; 10:4, 8; etc.). Others suggest that it was the voice of the Lamb (Bousset, cited by Charles I:166) or God Himself (Thomas I:431, 432), or even "the protest of Nature against the horrors of famine" (Swete 87). Since this is the throne area, the primary point is that this command was of divine origin and authority.

Most feel that this depicts literal famine, and it is popular to link the famine with the conditions of war indicated by the second horseman (Walvoord 129). Some interpreters, instead, believe that the famine results from injustice, with food not scarce but inaccessible to the masses because of oppression and inflated prices (Lenski 228). A "measure of wheat" equals "the daily consumption of a man," and a "penny" (Greek *denarius*) "the ordinary daily wage" (Charles I:166). After buying a single day's worth

of food for one individual, there is nothing left over for anything or anyone else. If the worker has a family he may buy the cheaper barley, instead. Beale (381) says these inflated prices were eight to sixteen times higher than average.

The command to spare "the oil and the wine" (cf. 7:3) is addressed to the horseman rather than anyone in general (Barnes 151). "Oil and wine" may refer to the luxuries of the rich or may indicate that the scarcity did not affect the entire food supply. The roots of the olive tree and grape vine go deeper (Mounce 144) and could survive drought when other staple grain could not. Indeed, oil and wine were not luxuries but basic foodstuffs in the ancient world (Ladd, *Commentary* 101).

Hendriksen (102) sees the poor here as persecuted believers throughout the church age, suffering economic hardship because of their faith. Similar futurist interpretation might see them as Tribulation saints persecuted for religious reasons similar to those that prompted persecution of first-century believers in Asia Minor. Believers often suffered economically because they refused to give allegiance to "patron deities and trade guilds" (Beale 382), and Tribulation believers will experience similar persecution for refusing the "mark of the beast" (13:17). Even so, there is no reason to exclude the general population of earth, including all the unbelieving poor, during this time. The basic impact of the four horsemen is to portray the Lamb's preliminary judgments against the Christ-rejecting world and *not* Tribulation saints.

The third seal is likely inaugurated in the first half of Tribulation week (Mt. 24:7, 8), but the deprivation continues

235

for those refusing the mark of the beast in the second half (13:17).

4. Fourth Seal—the pale horse and its rider (6:7, 8)

7 And when he had opened the fourth seal, I heard the voice of the fourth beast say, Come and see.
8 And I looked, and behold a pale horse: and his name that sat on him was Death, and Hell followed with him. And power was given unto them over the fourth part of the earth, to kill with sword, and with hunger, and with death, and with the beasts of the earth.

The opening of the fourth seal revealed a pale horse and its rider, introduced in the same way as the preceding horsemen; see v. 1.

"Pale" (Greek *chloros*) is "the color of plants: *green, pale green, yellowish green*" (ALGNT 409); others suggest "pale yellow" (Charles I:169), "corpse-like" (Ford 108), "pale, greenish, gray... associated with sick and corpses" (Aune I:400). Here it symbolizes death, well represented by this lurid, ugly color, which might characterize "a corpse in an advanced state of corruption" (Ford 108). Some see the fourth seal as a summary of the effects of all four horsemen, since war (the second) and famine (the third) would also lead to death.

The name of the rider is "Death," with "Hell" following—riding on the same horse or another (Aune I:401), or walking behind (Thomas I:437): "death's inseparable comrade" (Swete 89). (For the combination "death and hell" see 1:18; 6:8; 20:13, 14; cf. 2 Sam. 22:6; Ps. 49:14; Is. 28:15.)

As with the first three, the power of the co-riders of the fourth seal is "given to them," a "divine passive" that sets this "in the context of the authority that belongs to God and to Christ" (Rowland 612). Though we are often reluctant to blame God for evil things, "John... intends it as encouragement, reminding us that no matter what happens, God and the Lamb are on the throne, setting limits to evil and bringing their own wise purposes to realization" (Michaels 103, 104). The keys to "death and hell" belong to the risen Christ (1:18) and not to Satan or the Antichrist.

Authority "to kill" is given to the fourth horseman and his hellish comrade, using four agents: the sword, hunger, death (pestilence), and wild beasts (cf. Lev. 26:21-26; Ezek. 14:21). Together these destroy *one quarter of the earth's human population* at this time. (For other massive destructions, see 9:15, 18; 19:17-21.)

"Sword" (Greek *hromphia*, v. 8) is different from that in v. 4; see there. This is the larger sword, typically associated with warfare (Hendriksen 104)—though the Romans were also known to use the shorter sword in close combat. (This larger sword also appears in 1:16; 2:12, 16; 19:15.)

"Death" (Greek *thanatos*) sometimes refers, specifically, to *pestilence* or *plague* (see comments on this word in 2:23), which explains why a number of versions render the word this way here; cf. Aune (I:382), who observes that the LXX uses this word for the Hebrew word "plague, pestilence" over 30 times. This understanding links the four agents of judgment to their O.T. precedents (Lev. 26:18-28; Dt. 32:24, 25; Jer. 15:1-4; 16:4, 5; Ezek. 5:16, 17; 14:13-23). The full-orbed effects of destruction, deprivation, and disease, associated with warfare, are thereby present during the Tribulation.

The "wild beasts" should probably be taken literally, matching the literal warfare and death resulting in the decimation of one-quarter of the earth's population. "A breakdown of those bonds that prevent murder and strife and ensure a proper food supply prompts the invasion of beasts of the earth into areas from which they are normally excluded" (Rowland 613). Following traditional Jewish interpretations, Beale (386, 387) favors identifying "beasts" with the satanic agents revealed in 12:3; 13:11 (or nations hostile to Israel and Tribulation saints) rather than literal animals. This view requires too much manipulation of the context.

How or why does God use these seals during the Tribulation period? As a group, they indicate the beginning of a breakdown of law and order, an order not to be reestablished until the New Jerusalem, when "no one will hunger or thirst anymore, and death will be destroyed." Do they affect Tribulation saints in the same way? Lenski (230, 231) suggests that they are "evidences" of God's love and not judgment or wrath. Idealist Hendriksen (105) says that they represent "*all* universal woes which believers suffer along with the rest of humanity throughout the entire dispensation [the church age]," used "for the sanctification of His Church and the extension of His kingdom." Michaels (102) states, "The trials here not only affect nations in general but have the dual purpose within the covenant community of purifying the faithful and punishing those disloyal to Christ."

Beale (382, 383) represents those who see satanic utility in all four horse-men, though "under the ultimate governance of the throne room." But there is no necessity to see Satan as actively involved: the O.T. precedents of these four are clearly instruments of judgment used directly by God Himself to chastise Israel or others.

The seals affect Tribulation saints and unbelievers differently, then, with a positive, *sanctifying* effect for true believers and a negative, *confirming* effect for the ungodly who remain recalcitrant in their sinful behavior and unbelief—as in 9:20: they "repented not." God's justice requires severe judgment on those who would, in the end, rather curse God than turn to Him in saving belief.

Does the fourth seal refer to physical, spiritual, or eternal death? The activity of any of the four horsemen could lead to physical death, and Hell is the ultimate destination of all unbelievers at any time. Thomas (I:437) notes that including Hell with Death implies "death for both the material and immaterial parts of man." The picture of "Hell" following after Death is therefore an accurate theological representation. The unbelieving rich man (Lk. 16:19-31) died and immediately awoke in Hell. This makes the appalling figure of "Death" even more somber, adding a note of final judgment. There is no recourse or resurrection; the spiritual condition of someone at death is final or eternal. Thankfully, these enemies of mankind—Death and Hell—are themselves put away at the end of Christ's millennial reign, when both are cast into the lake of fire forever (20:13, 14).

The destruction brought about by the first four seals is *unprecedented* in world history and points to an *eschatological* fulfillment (Boring 122). Even so, the catastrophe is *limited* and therefore merciful and not as severe as in the trumpet judgments to come (8:7-10, 12; 9:15, 18). While both series of judgments are universal, the effects intensify from "fourths" (the seals) to "thirds" (the trumpets), making it plausible to identify the less severe, seal judgments with "the beginning of sorrows" (Mt. 24:8). The first four seals are "harbingers of more terrible judgments to come" (Michaels 102). This argues against recapitulation as explanation for how the three series of sevens relate to one another, with the increase in intensity pointing to chronological separation and progression.

Preterists often identify the four horsemen with catastrophes in the early centuries, including the destruction of Jerusalem in A.D. 70, a Jewish revolt in A.D. 132-135 when 580,000 died, a period in A.D. 248 to 296 when pestilence took the lives of 5,000 people each day in Rome alone. As fulfillments these must be rejected, largely because more modern events typically surpass them in degree: Europe's bubonic plague, the Jewish holocaust of WW II, the purge of more than 100 million Russians by Lenin, etc. And even after these catastrophes, the end-time destruction described in Revelation remains *unprecedented*.

B. Final Three Seals (6:9—8:5)

The sequential opening of the seals continues. The last three are relatively independent of one another as compared to the "four horsemen" as a unit. The fifth seal provides a vision of yet another feature of the throne room in Heaven itself and of a unique group in Heaven (6:9-11). The sixth reveals a series of catastrophic natural disasters affecting the material world and describes

the effect of these on unbelievers (6:12-17). Between the sixth and seventh comes what is widely characterized as a "parenthesis" (ch. 7), when John saw two prominent groups: the 144,000 sealed from the twelve tribes of Israel (7:1-8) and the numberless multitude of Tribulation saints (7:9-17). The seventh seal is opened (8:1-5) and is followed by the seven trumpet judgments.

1. Fifth Seal—martyrs for Christ (6:9-11)

9 And when he had opened the fifth seal, I saw under the altar the souls of them that were slain for the word of God, and for the testimony which they held:
10 And they cried with a loud voice, saying, How long, O Lord, holy and true, dost thou not judge and avenge our blood on them that dwell on the earth?
11 And white robes were given unto every one of them; and it was said unto them, that they should rest yet for a little season, until their fellowservants also and their brethren, that should be killed as they *were*, should be fulfilled.

The fifth seal reveals persons "slain for the word of God," introducing us to the subject of *martyrdom* in the end-times (cf. Mt. 24:9; Mk. 13:9; Lk. 21:12). The scene shifts from the activity of the four horsemen on earth to "the altar" in Heaven (v. 9)—though the martyrdoms took place on the earth.

John sees *an altar* in the throne room, not noted previously. One assumes that it has been present all along, situated somewhere near God's throne. Some interpreters do not feel this is a permanent altar in Heaven but a temporary, symbolical vehicle to convey general truths. The weakness of this reasoning is that it also raises a question about the existence of *all* the components in the throne-room vision.

This heavenly altar apparently corresponds either to the golden altar of incense (L. Morris 105) or to the brazen altar (Barnes 158), where sacrifices were offered in the O.T. Tabernacle and Temple (Ex. 25:9, 40; 27:1, 2; 30:1, 2; cf. Heb. 8:5; 9:23). Both of these were anointed with sacrificial blood. The altar of incense was closest to God's presence, positioned before the veil leading into the Holy of Holies. It was also associated with prayer: incense was burned there twice a day to symbolize prayers offered up to God (Ps. 141:2; Rev. 5:8; 8:3, 4). This idea fits well with the scene portrayed by the fifth seal because the martyrs are seen and heard offering imprecatory prayers before God.

On the other hand, that they were "under the altar" might reflect the blood of sacrifices sprinkled at the base of the O.T. brazen altar (Lev. 1:5, 11, 15; 3:2, 8, 13; cf. 4:6, 7). This would mean that the martyred "souls under the altar" are viewed as lives sacrificed to God. Their faithfulness to the point of martyrdom has earned them a special place in God's sight. The image of sacrifice is significant and also works well here since the blood of martyred saints was literally and symbolically poured out for Christ.

It is possible that this heavenly altar was unique, representing *both* O.T. altars. Mounce (146) suggests that the altar image evokes equally well the ideas of both *prayer* and *sacrifice*. However, the clear identification of the altar as a "golden altar of incense" in 8:1-5 seems to be determinative in identifying the altar here as counterpart to the golden altar of incense in the holy place.

This occasions a somber prediction of future martyrdoms for Christ (v. 11). The verb "slain" (Greek *sphazo*) is typically used for slaughter, indicating *a violent* or *sacrificial death* (Vine 581). These "souls" belong to deceased believers who were martyred for their faith.

The martyrs at this altar represent the sacrificial death of all Christian martyrs and not of Tribulation saints only (Beale 392). The location of these "souls" ("lives" or "persons") in proximity to the throne is significant, consistent with N.T. doctrine about what happens to believers immediately after death (2 Cor. 5:6, 8; 12:2, 4; Lk. 16:22; 23:43; Rev. 2:7). "Under the altar" symbolizes "divine protection" (Beale 392) of these who are "especially precious in God's sight" (Thomas I:441). The Church has often asked what happens to those who are martyred for Christ. At death they are immediately taken into the presence of God.

Those in different schools of interpretation regard the scene differently. Preterists tend to associate these martyrdoms with first-century persecutions by Nero or Domitian (Summers 142), or more generally as martyrs "from the time of Stephen until the time of John's vision" (Lenski 235, 236). Idealists would spread the martyrdoms throughout the church age in general, from the ascension of Christ to His Second Coming (Brighton 172). Historicists would locate them somewhere specifically in church history, usually after the first century—during the reign of Diocletian (A.D. 284-304), for example (Barnes 160).

Futurists, on the other hand, typically refer the fifth seal to the end-times Tribulation, especially the latter half (Walvoord 133). But the designation "the souls of those that were slain" is a *general* one, and they are already in Heaven at the time the seal is opened, revealing what has already occurred without designating a specific time period. This group may therefore include the entire group of martyred saints throughout history as well as Tribulation saints. "Prophets" may just as well be included since "prophets and saints" are mentioned as martyrs in 18:24 (Michaels 105). And, since the elders in 4:4 already represent O.T. saints in Heaven, it would be consistent to include O.T. varieties with their N.T. counterparts here in 6:9-11. Nonetheless, the Tribulation period is particularly noted for a large number of martyrs. Walvoord (134) hypothesizes, "It may very well be that the majority of those who trust Christ as Savior in that day will be put to death." (See 13:7, 15; 20:4; cf. 7:9.)

These martyrs were killed because of "the Word of God" and "their testimony" for Christ (cf. 1:2, 9). Idealist Beale (390) takes these to mean "bearing witness in word and deed to Christ's redemptive work"; but for him the martyrdom is "metaphorical" of all believers' suffering in general, whether martyred or not—a view sustained with unconvincing arguments, given the specific context of 6:9-11. Literal martyrdom distinguishes this group from the universal family of God. Thomas (I:444) sees the "testimony" of the martyrs as their personal profession of Christ, which marked them as candidates for martyrdom during the highly anti-Christian Tribulation.

The imprecatory prayers of the martyrs were audible, and John heard them (v. 10). Aune (I:407) cites Ps. 7, 35, 55, 58, 59, 69, 79, 83, 109, 137, 139 as examples of this type of prayer, serving as a precedent for such imprecation on the part of God's people. All martyrs may have a nagging sense of injustice about their premature and violent death. This is not a prayer for "bitter, personal revenge" but refers to those "*ultimately* rebellious and reprobate" and is a "prayer that the reputation of God and his people be vindicated....God is being asked to bring wrongdoers to justice" (Beale 392). Ladd (*Commentary* 105, 106) suggests that it is not the martyrs' *voices* but their *blood*, poured out at the altar, crying out for vengeance (cf. Gen. 4:10; Lk. 18:7). The judgments that are ultimately poured out against the Christ-rejecting world serve to finally confirm the validity of every saint's faith.

Vengeance belongs to God, and He will unleash it at the proper time (2 Th. 1:8). The martyrs ask God "to judge" the unbelieving earth-dwellers who took their lives. In this context "judge" means "make the appropriate discrimination or distinction among people, to punish the inhabitants of the earth, and to vindicate and deliver the saints" (Thompson 104, 105). And "avenge" means the judicial righting of wrongs, not personal spite or vindictiveness. God's vengeance takes place in two ways: in the judgments described throughout Revelation, culminating at Armageddon (19:2); and when unbelievers and Satan are finally and permanently cast into Hell (20:10).

"Them that dwell on earth" or "earth-dwellers" is a general designation of all unbelievers in the world during the Tribulation (3:10; 6:10; 8:13; 11:10; 13:8, 14; 17:8): "the human race in its hostility to God" (Mounce 148). It obviously does not include believers. As with the martyrs (above), it is not necessary to limit these "earth-dwellers" to persecutors during the Tribulation. Christ's victory at the end of the age is not for Tribulation saints only, and the judgment or vindication of past generations is no doubt included in this cry. It is a response against the evil world system of all history.

"Lord" (Greek *despotes*, v. 10) means "Master" and "emphasizes the absolute power of God" (Mounce 147)—especially appropriate in a context where "servants" (Greek *doulos*) is also used (v. 11). Though the word was used for Roman emperors (Aune I:407), the titles "holy and true" distinguish God from such earthly rulers—perhaps best understood against the backdrop of injustice at the hands of the evil authorities that condemned believers to martyrdom. God is the ultimate Judge who judges individuals according to absolute fairness, purity of motive, and truth without error.

While they await final justice, compensation is given to martyrs in the form of "white robes" (cf. 7:9, 14): full-length robes (ALGNT 357) representing either *holiness* or *victory*. They also receive, in response to their cry, an explanation why they must wait. Beale (394) suggests that the robes also serve as "an annulment of the guilty verdict rendered against them by the world." This reward is therefore judicial, symbolic, and anticipatory of their final estate in eternity.

Some interpreters raise minor objections to the awarding of these robes before the final judgment or when the "souls" are still disembodied and unable to wear robes. Such objections reflect overpressing of details beyond the basic symbolism. We should not attempt to read into this a clear indication of the condition of believers between death and the final resurrection. Some suggest that they have "temporary" bodies that will eventually be replaced by permanent, resurrection bodies. But even that seems speculative. Regardless, in Revelation white robes stand as a multisided "metaphor for salvation, immortality, victory, and purity" (Aune I:410). This might simply be an early award given in anticipation of reunification with their glorified bodies, an immediate compensation marking the martyrs' ultimate sacrifice for Christ's sake. Somewhat similarly, others regard the robes as metaphorical for "justification" (L. Morris 107); "blessedness and rest" (Ladd, *Commentary* 106); or "a pledge of future and final glory" that proves "that no judgment awaited them" (Moffat 392). Charles (I:187, 188) even views the "robes" as "spiritual bodies" given to the martyred saints.

The martyrs are immediately instructed (by God, perhaps through an angel) that they must "rest yet for a little season" before they are avenged or vindicated (cf. 15:3; 16:5, 6); other believers will yet suffer the same fate as they. The answer to "how long?" is "a little season"; the actual fulfillment may be in chapters 18 and 19 with the destruction of the world systems and Battle of Armageddon (19:1, 2). Only then will the desired final justice come. God has a timetable that is certain but unyielding.

"Rest yet for a little season" represents encouragement: resting confidently in the meantime. Some take this as a mild rebuke, but this is out of character with the gentle tone of the verb "rest" and the positive award of white clothing just given. The prayerful martyrs are instructed to "rest a little longer" because some time remains even after the opening of the fifth seal. Martyrdoms will continue throughout the remaining Tribulation. This may correspond to a similar pattern in the Olivet Discourse where persecutions begin long before the end actually comes (Mt. 24:6-14).

We need not view the "fellow servants" as a specific number of martyrs that will push God's patience to the limit (though God obviously knows the exact number), but simply as indicating that there are more to come. As in 2 Pet. 3:9 others need more time to come to Christ, even in the Tribulation period—many from within the remnant of Israel. Judgment will take place when the number of martyrs and their missions are completed. "Their brethren" is another characterization of their "fellow servants."

2. Sixth Seal—catastrophes (6:12-17)

12 And I beheld when he had opened the sixth seal, and, lo, there was a great earthquake; and the sun became black as sackcloth of hair, and the moon became as blood;
13 And the stars of heaven fell unto the earth, even as a fig tree casteth her untimely figs, when she is shaken of a mighty wind.
14 And the heaven departed as a scroll when it is rolled together; and every mountain and island were moved out of their places.
15 And the kings of the earth, and the great men, and the rich men, and the chief captains, and the mighty men, and every bondman, and every free man, hid themselves
in the dens and in the rocks of the mountains;
16 And said to the mountains and rocks, Fall on us, and hide us from the face of him that sitteth on the throne, and from the wrath of the Lamb:
17 For the great day of his wrath is come; and who shall be able to stand?

If the language of the sixth seal is taken literally, as it should be, the catastrophic upheaval described here catapults us to the end of the Tribulation period—or, as some (Lenski 239, for example) think, to the end of the present world. Mounce (150, 151) also speaks of cosmic disturbances that herald the beginning of the last days, but he is reluctant to insist that all of the things described occur "in a completely literal sense." Others agree that they are symbolic of the destruction of political, social, or ecclesiastical traditions.

Ford (112) suggests that the pattern of destruction corresponds to the original order of creation in Genesis, with God systematically taking out of existence what He created. There are other similarities: as Adam and Eve attempted to hide after they sinned, so do unbelievers seek here to hide from God's wrath. When things within the material universe that are viewed as permanent—the sun, moon, stars, sky, mountains, and islands—begin to disintegrate, the world's inhabitants are stricken with great fear and panic. The truth regarding Jesus Christ becomes undeniable at His Second Coming. Some feel that the miraculous signs of the sixth seal are catastrophic phenomena associated exclusively with the O.T. "Day of the Lord."

The Creator never intended for human beings to worship His creation (Rom. 1:21-25). The destruction of this present world order, and eventually the material earth, effectively takes away the false idols of mankind. Charles (I:180,181) suggests, following Jewish apocalyptic thinking, that when the sun, moon, and stars forsake the stabilizing order God made them to have, the end of the world is at hand (Zech. 14:1-21). This may be the non-verbal message intended by the sixth seal.

Additionally, these upheavals point to a special visitation of God: "The Old Testament constantly pictures the divine visitations of God to His people in terms of a theophany, that is, in terms of majesty and power and glory so great that the physical world is shaken" (Newport 190). The Second Coming may certainly be viewed as *the ultimate theophany* of world history. Convulsions in the universe will accompany the O.T. *Day of the Lord* proper, culminating with the return of Christ to earth (Is. 13:10; 24:23; Jl. 2:2,10, 30, 31; Mt. 24:29, 30).

For idealist Beale (395-397), the events of 6:12-17 represent a "response to the plea in 6:9-11" and figuratively represent the "final judgment" rather than judgments of unbelievers prior to the parousia. He cites four "apocalyptic" O.T. images (Is. 2:19; 34:4; Hos. 10:8; Jl. 2:10, 31; Hab. 3:6-11; cf. Mt. 24:30; Lk. 23:30) from which John has drawn: "the shaking of the earth or mountains; the darkening or shaking of the moon, stars, sun and/or heaven; and the pouring out of blood." He regards the stars as symbolic of "heavenly powers of good or evil," the mountains as "forces of good or evil," islands as "Gentile nations or kings," and earthquake imagery as "God's judgment of nations" (402). For Caird (89), this symbolizes "the overthrow of human arrogance...[and] of a worldly political order organized in hostility to God"; the rolled-up scroll indicates "the punishment of principalities and powers" who control earthly authorities in Is. 34:2-4.

Favoring the literal view of the catastrophes are recent scholars like Ladd, Lenski, Walvoord, and Thomas. Initially, the natural disasters of v. 12 do not appear necessarily uncommon. Examples of great earthquakes are numerous. The sixth seal, however, refers to a single and unique earthquake "which is a precursor of the end of the world" (Charles I:179): "the climatic, eschatological earthquake that truly removes mountains" (Keener 220). Additional phenomena accompanying this catastrophe, also pointing to an eschatological time because of their magnitude or uniqueness, will be: (1) extinguished sunlight; (2) change of moon's normal color to red; (3) displacement of stars; (4) disappearance of the sky; and (5) displacement of earth's terrain (mountains and islands).

The catastrophe is universal in scope and affects the whole world's population, as suggested by the *seven* components (vv. 12-14) and *seven* groups of humanity (v. 15). "The double set of sevens shows that the destruction is total....Nothing remains in place and no one is high enough or low enough to escape" (Gonzalez 52).

Various analogies help us envision the nature of these events: (1) sackcloth, (2) blood, (3) figs, and (4) a scroll. "Black sackcloth" was a "garment of mourning... an emblem of sadness and distress" (Barnes 163) or perhaps of *death*. It was made of the hair of a black goat

(Robertson 345). Black obscures sunlight better than other colors and could suggest an eclipse of the sun. But this picture is worse than an ordinary eclipse, suggesting that the sun itself is significantly diminished.

"Blood" is red and may symbolize "death," "war," or "redemption"—here apparently an omen of great doom or calamity. Hughes (91) says that "blood" symbolizes "the horror of carnage." It is not difficult to envision tremendous loss of life resulting from the massive destruction.

"Figs" are late or summer figs, "that grow under leaves during winter and seldom ripen...that dry up and blow off in a wind" (Thomas I:454). Hughes (91) sees this as "a simile of the sterile futility of all that is unblessed by God and exposed to his judgment." Other interpreters regard the "falling stars" as symbolic: of "kings and rulers of the earth" (Barnes 163, 164); of "the angels of the churches" (Rowland 614); or of "the dislocation of all that has been regarded as stable" (Hughes 91). However, this is most likely a literal description of the disintegration of the universe with actual displacement of stars, meteor showers, and comets (cf. Is. 13:10; Mt. 24:29).

The "scroll" metaphor evokes an image of a scroll, with one end rolled forward and the other chasing behind. Returning to their original position would require rolling them backward to remove the slack, though Swete (93) and Brighton (173) see the scroll (and sky) as split apart with each side recoiling into its own roll (cf. Is. 34:4). The moving of mountains and islands out of their places could refer to a literal "shifting of the earth's crust" (Thomas I:455), so that they disappear (Lenski 241), or symbolically to "political and moral con-

vulsions" (Barnes 164). (Compare 16:20; Mt. 24:29; Mk. 13:24; Lk. 21:25.)

Aune (I:415) lists several metaphorical interpretations of "falling stars": (1) an omen needing interpretation; (2) an anticipation of the judgment of God; or (3) the fall of Satan and his angels. He adds, "In ancient dream interpretation, seeing stars falling down to the earth meant that many people would die." The phenomena of the sixth seal are "heavenly" and "terrestrial" prodigies: *heavenly* ones being thunder and lightning, comets falling to earth, and darkening of the sun, moon, and stars; and *terrestrial* ones being earthquakes, waters turning to blood, and famines (Aune I:418,419). He concludes that these are not meant to be "ends in themselves" but "stern messages of warning from God intended to produce repentance (9:20, 21; 16:9), although this is never the result" (I:419).

The type and scope of panic portrayed in vv. 15, 16 is inexplicable apart from some sort of universal catastrophe affecting all mankind. All seven classes of humanity, from kings to slaves, beg for the mountains and rocks to hide them from the face of God and the wrath of the Lamb (cf. Hos. 10:1-3, 8; 11:2; Jer. 4:23-30; 5:7; Gen. 3:9). (1) *Kings* include "heads of state" in the nations of the world, whatever their form of government (Thomas I:455). (2) *Great men* are "high-ranking officials... implementing the executive functions of government" (Thomas I:455). (3) *Rich men* are those of wealth, power, and influence. (4) *Chief captains* are commanders of large numbers of troops— in that time of a thousand (Vine 88). (5) *Mighty* (or strong) *men* could be persons of great influence over numbers of people (Thomas I:455); more generally, "the elite of the land" (Thompson 106); or "men of great prowess in battle" (Barnes 164). (6) *Bondman* and (7) *free man* may represent the two lowest classes. As a whole, the list is "a collective way of characterizing the enemies of God" and "a complex way of saying 'everyone'" (Aune I:419).

A significant number from each class will seek to hide in the dens and rocks of the mountains (v. 15). The catastrophic destruction will create mass hysteria that will engulf the entire unbelieving population. "What sinners dread most is not death, but the revealed Presence of God" (Swete 94). Many will beg mountains and rocks to fall on them in order to escape God's wrath (v. 16). The prospect of a suicidal, brutal death by natural catastrophe is more welcome than the only alternative—to come face-to-face with a Holy God and the slain Lamb (Summers 143).

With the inauguration of the sixth seal, the world will finally recognize with great regret the truth about Jesus Christ as the Lamb of God. With this goes a universal sense of irremediable doom (v. 17): "a graphic picture of terror and despair" (Thomas I:456). The point of no return has been passed (cf. Is. 2:19; Hos. 10:8; Lk. 23:30).

The depth of the wrath of the Lamb is clearly demonstrated in these judgments. Some manuscripts read "their" wrath, referring to the wrath of God and the Lamb. Either way, the Father and the Lamb are so united in nature and purpose that when either is referenced, the other is included.

Thomas (I:457) says that the wrath of God, in the N.T., is usually "a technical term for the eschatological visitation of God" to punish "rebellious mankind."

Newport (191) defines the wrath displayed in the sixth seal as "the response of God's holiness to persistent and impenitent wickedness." That the Lamb of God is also capable of wrath is ironic but neither surprising nor incompatible with His gracious nature.

The identification of the sixth seal as the wrath of God goes well with viewing the four horsemen as *divine* agents (above). The seals, as a unit, express God's judgment, and the sixth "originates in God as a divine punishment inflicted on a blasphemous world" (Walvoord 136).

"The great day" (v. 17) recalls the O.T. and N.T. concept of "the Day of the Lord" (Jl. 2:11,31; Zeph. 1:14; Mal. 4:5; Mt. 7:22; 1 Th. 5:2; 2 Th. 2:2; 2 Pet. 3:10). Those who advocate a "pre-wrath" rapture of the church limit this "Day" to one literal day, but pretribulationists tend to view it as *a series* of events throughout the Tribulation and millennial reign of Christ. Aune (I:421) defines the "Day of the Lord" as "a climactic eschatological event set in the indefinite future when God will judge the world" (see 16:14).

The sixth seal ends with a rhetorical question, "Who shall be able to stand?" (cf. Nah. 1:6; Mal. 3:2). The most obvious prompting for this lies in the catastrophes of the seal judgments, but it may also have reference to God's judgment of unbelievers at the Great White Throne. The final judgment and subsequent eternal consignments made there are the culmination of this ongoing process of wrath that started in motion with the first seal.

When, during the end-times, does the sixth seal occur? Thomas (I:451-453) concludes it does not refer to events immediately before the Second Coming, that the question who can stand serves as a harbinger of crisis events to be seen when the seventh seal is opened; he places the sixth seal just before the midpoint of a seven-year tribulation period. But this is problematic because of the degree of destruction portrayed in the sixth seal. More likely, the sixth seal is a proleptic view of what happens later, *after* the trumpet and bowl judgments. "The sixth seal brings us to the threshold of the end; and then John stands back, as it were, to tell the story of the end in greater detail" (Ladd, *Commentary* 109). In this case the seventh seal, the seven trumpets, and the seven bowl judgments, along with the rest of Revelation, provide that greater detail. All three series of judgments, once they begin, do not necessarily require a great deal of time.

The rolled-up scroll imagery apparently suggests the dissolution of the material universe itself; earthquakes and the darkening of heavenly luminaries may not be so serious, but the *disappearance* of the sky is quite another category. "The progression of eschatological woes has proceeded through 'normal' historical catastrophes (seals 1-4: war, famine, plague), through extraordinary historical pressures (seal 5: martyrdom), to the opening of the sixth seal in which the cosmos itself convulses" (Boring 126).

Summary
(6:1-17)

Chapter 6 reveals the first six of the seven seal judgments. The first four (four horsemen) reflect the beginning of Christ's mission of conquest (vv. 1-8), which begins when He (not Antichrist) rides forth upon the white horse, His character symbolized by the color of the horse. His bow and crown reflect His mission of conquest, and the action seems to indicate that this conquest is ultimate.

The next three seals personify God's instruments of judgment, the agents described in Ezek. 14:21 as "my four sore judgments": sword, famine, wild beasts, and pestilence. These strong precedents, as well as the throne-room context (chs. 4, 5), point to the four horsemen as agents of God rather than as satanic. These Scriptural precedents make identification of the first horseman less uncertain.

The second horseman rides a red horse, symbolizing bloodshed in the form of world war and perhaps rampant murder in society. This horseman is successful because peace is removed—a judicial act of God. The third horseman, on a black horse, represents significant worldwide famine and inflation. The fourth horseman, riding a pale horse, summarizes the effects of the first three. One-quarter of the earth's population perishes in these judgments, which include disease and wild animals. Death and Hell ultimately receive the unbelieving victims unfortunate enough to have perished with this initial wave of Christ's conquest.

The fifth seal (vv. 9-11) refocuses attention on Heaven's throne room, introducing another important component of the Tribulation: martyrdom. The souls of Christian martyrs huddled under an altar in the presence of God and heard God promise to answer their imprecatory prayer for vindication in due time. He would not avenge the premature, unjust deaths of the martyrs *until* the blood of the very last martyr was shed. Meanwhile, they are compensated for their great personal sacrifice with white robes.

The sixth seal (vv. 12-17) telescopes forward to the Day of the Lord at the end of the Tribulation, using the same language of eschatological destruction that a number of O.T. prophets used. The literal, material catastrophes described in the sixth seal cannot refer to any other event. The universe literally unravels—beginning with the earth, then extending to its luminaries in the solar system, and ultimately culminating when the sky itself disappears like a rolled-up scroll. Mountains and islands are dramatically displaced. Worldwide panic ensues; people from every class of society seek to hide from what is universally recognized as the wrath of God and the Lamb.

Application: Teaching and Preaching the Passage

Although it has been popular to identify the rider of the first horseman as a counterfeit Christ, no textual cue indicates this. There is more Scriptural evidence, in both testaments, that God uses these forces as instruments of *His* judgment against a Christ-rejecting world. Satanic activity through the Antichrist and his regime, prominent later in Revelation, are directed against believers rather than against unbelievers.

Christ's judgment of the unbelieving world begins with the first seal, and the end is pictured in the sixth. Tribulation saints (7:9, 14) will no doubt be affected by the natural disasters, by the spirit of violence, and by the collapse of the economy; indeed, many will be martyred. But this does not imply that they are being judged by the wrath of God in the same way as unbelievers.

The forces in the seal judgments—war, famine, disease, and death—will be present throughout the Tribulation, even when other judgments such as the trumpets and bowls are ongoing. There is war in the middle (13:7) and at the end (19:11-21; cf. 20:7-9). Even so, the first four seals focus on the first half of the Tribulation, while seals five and seven apply from the middle of the period, roughly, to the end. What the sixth seal reveals looks ahead to the end of the Tribulation or of the millennium.

Suggested Outlines. The Conquest of Christ, 6:1-17: (1) Commissioned by God to conquer, vv. 1, 2; (2) Cavalry confederate with Christ—horses and riders, vv. 3-11; (3) Catastrophic events, vv. 12-16; (4) Conclusion, "Who shall be able to stand?" v. 17.

Destiny of Doom, 6:1-8; The world is destined for: (1) Domination, vv. 1, 2; (2) Destruction, vv. 3,4; (3) Deprivation, vv. 5, 6; (4) Death, vv. 7, 8.

3. First Parenthesis—two great multitudes (7:1-17)

"After these things" (v. 1) introduces *a new vision* between the sixth and seventh seals, expanding the unfolding drama with new subject matter. It is still closely related to the contents of the preceding seal and may answer the rhetorical question of 6:17, "Who shall be able to stand?" This so-called "parenthesis," "interlude," or "intercalation" is inserted to focus on how the Tribulation period affects two particular groups of saints, clearly distinct from each other in a number of ways: the first numbers 144,000, the second is numberless; the first is from one nation, the second from every nation on earth; the first is located on the earth, the second is already in Heaven; the first is heading into the rigors of the Tribulation, the second has already come through it.

a. 144,000 sealed (7:1-8)

1 And after these things I saw four angels standing on the four corners of the earth, holding the four winds of the earth, that the wind should not blow on the earth, nor on the sea, nor on any tree.
2 And I saw another angel ascending from the east, having the seal of the living God: and he cried with a loud voice to the four angels, to whom it was given to hurt the earth and the sea,
3 Saying, Hurt not the earth, neither the sea, nor the trees, till we have sealed the servants of our God in their foreheads.
4 And I heard the number of them which were sealed: *and there were* sealed a hundred *and* forty *and* four thousand of all the tribes of the children of Israel.
5 Of the tribe of Juda *were* sealed twelve thousand. Of the tribe of Reuben *were* sealed twelve thousand. Of the tribe of Gad *were* sealed twelve thousand.
6 Of the tribe of Aser *were* sealed twelve thousand. Of the tribe of Nepthalim *were* sealed twelve thousand. Of the tribe of Manasses *were* sealed twelve thousand.
7 Of the tribe of Simeon *were* sealed twelve thousand. Of the tribe of Levi *were* sealed twelve thousand. Of the tribe of Issachar *were* sealed twelve thousand.
8 Of the tribe of Zabulon *were* sealed twelve thousand. Of the tribe of Joseph *were* sealed twelve thousand. Of the tribe of Benjamin *were* sealed twelve thousand.

"And after these things" marks the transition; the venue, unchanged since 4:1, 2, is still the throne room of God. "These things" refer back to the six seals of chapter 6.

John saw four angels standing on the four corners of the earth: divine agents given special authority. "Four corners of the earth" does not reflect the ancient view of a *flat* earth but is a way of referring to the entire planet. "The four winds of the earth" indicates the four points of the compass as directions from which the wind blows. A *mixture* of wind directions carried a negative connotation in Jewish thought (Charles I:204).

The four angels stand ready to execute their mission, having been placed (Greek perfect participle) there with authority over the winds, indicated by the "holding." They "withhold" or temporarily hold back the God-given, destructive winds of judgment. Thus they have power to hurt "the earth, sea, and trees" (vv. 2, 3) when they loose the winds: by implication, after the sealing of God's servants.

This pause is necessary for two reasons: (1) these winds of judgment are severely destructive and must be withheld until God's time for them; (2) a specific number of Israelites must first be sealed (v. 3). The winds may be literal (Ryrie, *Revelation* 60) or symbolic. Barnes (171) conjectures that they represent something like the seething forces of worldwide war and anarchy that are restrained until fully unleashed for destruction.

The expression "earth, sea, and trees" represents totality but also may be taken literally or representatively. Lenski (246, 247) interprets literally: the material earth or inanimate objects. The end of the world will include catastrophic disintegration of the material universe; the winds may be harbingers of, or instrumental to, that ultimate event (cf. 2 Pet. 3:10-13). If the three are symbolic, they may represent unbelieving humanity or evil world systems as objects of God's judgment (Ford 115, 116). Or the expression might convey the general idea of the universal nature of God's judgments during this period. Since no textual cue points otherwise, it seems best to view these as literal judgments, with violent winds directed against the earth, sea, and trees. Even so, the destruction serves indirectly as judgment against the inhabitants of earth, particularly (but not exclusively) unbelievers. However, the sealing that must occur first means that the winds will not harm the 144,000. Advocating literalism, by the way (as when interpreting wind, earth, sea, and trees literally), does not exclude the possibility of associated spiritual implications. The material universe *and* the evil, spiritual realm are *both* judged by God in the catastrophes. What affects one invariably affects the other.

"To whom it was given" (v. 2)—the "divine passive" discussed earlier—indicates divine agency in Revelation (6:2, 4, 8, 11; 7:2; 8:2, 3; 9:1, 3, 5; 11:1, 2; 12:14; 13:5, 7; 16:8; 20:4). The angels' destructive mission is under the sovereign control of God. There does not appear to be any direct correspondence between these four angels and

the four living beings (4:6-8) or the four horsemen (6:1-7). Neither should they be viewed as intrinsically "rebellious and wicked" or as "evil angelic agents of judgment" (Beale 406). The close, working relationship between these four angels, God, and the sealing angel argues the opposite: they are God's agents.

John saw "another angel" ascending "from the east" (literally, "from the rising of the sun")—another indication of divine origin and commission: eastern origin has been associated with deity throughout antiquity. This angel had "the seal of the living God," indicating that he was acting as God's proxy. (The reference is too general to identify him with an archangel; nor is Christ a good candidate for any of the unnamed angels in Revelation: He already occupies a central place as the risen Lamb in the visions.)

"Seal" (Greek *sphragis*) is the noun form of the verb "sealed" (5:1; 6:1): a mark of ownership, security, and authority. A document of any sort might be "sealed" in this way, often with the imprint of a signet ring (the "seal") in a blob of wax. In the ancient world, slaves and even devotees to false gods were often branded or tattooed with marks of ownership and devotion. This seal is apparently literal, used to mark the 144,000, equated with the name of God and the Lamb in 14:1 (cf. 3:12). Many see this seal as the Holy Spirit or Christian baptism, but the context points to a specific mark involving some form of the name of God and Christ (3:12; 14:1).

John was either told, knew intuitively, or read that the seal belonged to the one true God. "Living" sets God apart from the lifeless and therefore powerless gods of the nations or dead Roman emperors. That the owner of the seal is alive, God Himself, makes everything about this seal more consequential.

The four angelic judgments in the Tribulation wait "till we have sealed the servants of God in their foreheads" (v. 3; cf. 9:4). The homes of ancient Israelites were marked with the blood of a Passover lamb when the destroying angel passed through Egypt (Ex. 12:7). All sorts of things have been marked with seals or brands, throughout history, for various purposes. Seals could take various forms. As 14:1 indicates, the mark here in 7:3 is visible, in the form of a written name (Newcombe 195). There is no reason to equate it to the rite of circumcision, Christian baptism, or of Holy Spirit baptism (Hughes 94). The contrast with the mark of "the beast" (13:16) on the forehead or right hand of the world's inhabitants, for evil purposes, strengthens this literal understanding.

God's seal does not protect against martyrdom or suffering in general. But it does insulate the 144,000 from specific manifestations of the wrath of God and perhaps from apostasy (D. Johnson 134). The basic purpose of this group's marking is protection from the destructive effects of the "four winds." If these are literal winds, the protection is from physical harm—though some interpreters, like idealist Beale (404), view this as protection from apostasy or "spiritual harm" (Poythress 117). This visible seal of identification, in the form of the names of God the Father and the Lamb (14:1; 9:4), protects from the wrath of God, but not necessarily from every rigor of the Tribulation.

However, it is Scripturally consistent to speculate that some who profess faith in Christ initially in the Tribulation period (not the 144,000 elect of Israel) may subsequently deny Christ in the face of coercion or persecution. Christ admonished the churches in chapters 2 and 3 against being "overcome" by various threats. He expected those believers to be "overcomers"; He has the same expectation for all believers including those during the Tribulation. After outlining a variety of tribulations indicative of "the end," Jesus said, "But he that shall endure to the end, the same shall be saved" (Mt. 24:14). God's seal is secure but perseverance is required.

The specific number of Israelites sealed is 144,000 (vv. 4-8), suggesting completeness. Both this number and its Jewish identification are taken literally (Walvoord 143) and figuratively (Mounce 158; Barnes 173). If figuratively, the 144,000 may represent the entire church or Tribulation church comprised of both Jews and Gentiles: "*the church militant* viewed in its completeness" (Lenski 245). But 144,000 is much smaller than the numberless multiethnic multitude of Great Tribulation saints in 7:9; the latter group is more like the church. The sealing of the 144,000 may indicate either a unique need for preservation in order to fulfill their Tribulation mission or to prevent them from suffering God's wrath directly. The reason for the number 144,000 is perhaps twofold, being large enough to represent the size of the remnant of Israelite believers and a group adequate for their mission during the Tribulation. The elaborate attempts to explain the number by mathematical formulas appear to be largely arbitrary and inconsequential.

The 144,000 are identified in a number of ways: three major views are: (1)

the remnant of believing, ethnic Israelites (Thomas, Walvoord, Gonzalez); (2) all the redeemed, both Jew and Gentile, in the church (Mounce, Ladd, Poythress); (3) a select army of Christian witnesses (martyrs) during the Tribulation (Caird, Aune, Beale).

Since John provided such a specific list, specifying their patriarchal lineage and number, this group is best identified as believing Israelites during the Tribulation (cf. 14:1-5). This points to God's continuing commitment to the nation of Israel in the end-times (see Rom. 11:25, 26). The smaller group of 144,000 Jewish servants coexists with the much larger multiethnic group of believers in the Tribulation period. If the 144,000 are viewed as symbolic of the entire church, the distinction between these and those in 7:9, where the church *is* clearly in view, becomes pointless.

They are described as "the servants of our God" (v. 3), denoting their service and *ownership*. They belong to God and perform valuable service for Him during the end-times. They may simply be "witnesses" who preach the gospel and bear the testimony of Christ to their neighbors and others (cf. 11:3), or they may preach more broadly in a formidable and final evangelistic campaign. Their basic activity is more fully described in 14:1-5; in the present context *protection* from the wrath of God is emphasized. Walvoord (143) sees their sealing as an indication that they survive the Tribulation period without being martyred.

Of special interest about this particular list of Israel's patriarchs is the fact that Judah is listed first (v. 5), focusing attention once more on Christ, "the Lion of the tribe of Juda" (5:5). The absence of the tribe of Dan is noteworthy, as also Ephraim—though the latter is represented by his father Joseph. Both Dan and Ephraim are included in Ezek. 48:1, 6; their exclusion here may be because of their role as the seedbed of idolatry in Israel (Gen. 49:17; Jg. 18:27;1 Kg. 12:29). Levi, whose tribe was not counted in Israel's census because they were priests with no land allotment (Num. 1:47), is included in this listing.

b. Great Tribulation saints identified (vv. 9-17)

9 After this I beheld, and, lo, a great multitude, which no man could number, of all nations, and kindreds, and people, and tongues, stood before the throne, and before the Lamb, clothed with white robes, and palms in their hands;

10 And cried with a loud voice, saying, Salvation to our God which sitteth upon the throne, and unto the Lamb.

11 And all the angels stood round about the throne, and *about* the elders and the four beasts, and fell before the throne on their faces, and worshipped God,

12 Saying, Amen: Blessing, and glory, and wisdom, and thanksgiving and honour, and power, and might, *be* unto our God for ever and ever. Amen.

13 And one of the elders answered, saying unto me, What are these which are arrayed in white robes? and whence came they?

14 And I said unto him, Sir, thou knowest. And he said to me, These are they which came out of great tribulation, and have washed their

robes, and made them white in the blood of the Lamb.

15 Therefore are they before the throne of God, and serve him day and night in his temple: and he that sitteth on the throne shall dwell among them.

16 They shall hunger no more, neither thirst any more; neither shall the sun light on them, nor any heat.

17 For the Lamb which is in the midst of the throne shall feed them, and shall lead them unto living fountains of waters: and God shall wipe away all tears from their eyes.

"After this I beheld" (v. 9) turns attention to another distinct group; as indicated, a comparison reveals that the two groups are distinct in several ways. "Which no man could number" points to a *seemingly infinite number*: "an ancient hyperbole for a large number of people" (Aune I:445). The size and ethnic variety of this multitude point to the success and "broad appeal" of the gospel during this otherwise sobering period of world history (Wall 119), in contrast to the smaller group of 144,000 of the twelve tribes of Israel.

Further, the location is different: the 144,000 are on earth and this great multitude gathers in the throne room of God for another of Heaven's glorious worship services (v. 9). The 144,000 are still in the flesh on earth; the numberless multitude has already experienced death by natural causes or martyrdom and has no need of the protective sealing given to the 144,000. Indeed, this lack of sealing argues that the two groups are intentionally distinct (Thompson 108).

Another major difference is ethnic. Where the 144,000 are entirely Israelite, the numberless group includes (Gentile and Jewish) saints of "all nations, kindreds, and people, and tongues" (v. 9; cf. 5:9; 10:11; 13:7; 14:6; cf. 17:15). These subdivisions are social units within humanity like nationality, race, physical lineage, or language; see comments on 5:9; they represent the entire human race (Aune I:428).

Walvoord (149) suggests a "causal" connection between the two groups; A. Johnson (89) credits A. C. Gaebelein with the popular dispensational view that the 144,000 are Jewish evangelists who preach the gospel during the Tribulation period, with the numberless multitude their converts. But the text does not indicate any connection between the two groups. Such reading between the lines can never be determinative, especially for those who value grammatical-historical interpretation. Nonetheless, it seems likely that many Tribulation saints come to Christ as a result of the witness of others like the 144,000 (or the two witnesses of 11:3).

As with the 144,000, interpreters' identifications of this numberless multitude vary (for a survey see Thomas I:484, 485): a symbolic representation of those finally saved, Tribulation saints (corresponding to Daniel's seventieth week), martyrs who receive white robes at death, etc. Thomas (I:485) views them as "Gentile and Jewish believers who have died either natural or violent deaths during the period of the first six seals and come out from the Great Tribulation." Aune (I:445, 446) lists four major viewpoints: Christian martyrs, Christian Gentiles, all Christians, and Diaspora Jews. It seems clear that this gathering fulfills in some way the promise made to the martyrs in 6:9-11.

As to the time involved, the numberless multitude apparently offers the final snapshot of God's family when the Tribulation is over; the number of martyrs and additional conversions to Christ is by then complete. "Most interpreters view this scene as a proleptic vision of the future eschatological consummation" (Aune I:447). But some think these are Christians who die before the Parousia, when Heaven and earth are still separate. Still others divide the description into two time periods, the present through v. 15b and the final consummation in vv. 15c-17. Mounce represents those who place the scene "when those who are to pass through the final persecution will enter the blessedness of the eternal state" (161).

John's description of the numberless multitude of saints is detailed (vv. 9b-17). That they are "standing before the throne and before the Lamb" indicates that access has been granted into God's holy presence. This privilege has been granted primarily on the basis of the Lamb's own victory (ironically, through death on the cross) and secondarily as a reward for those who have "overcome."

They are "clothed with white robes," awarded to saints because of faithfulness to Christ (3:4, 5). "Robes" (Greek *stolas*) indicates long robes, "more appropriate to glorious garments than workaday clothing" (L. Morris 113). They may be symbolic both of the *imputed righteousness* of Christ (justification) and of the *righteous acts* of the saints (sanctification). Together, these constitute the totality of *spiritual victory* from God's perspective, encompassing belief (faith) and behavior (good works).

They hold "palms in their hands," a token of victorious celebration in Jewish history (1 Maccabees 13:51). Palm branches were used in the Jewish Feast of Tabernacles (Lev. 23:40), and it is possible that the gathering of the great multitude here is modeled after this (cf. Zech. 14:16-21). *Victory* or triumph, then, is by far the prevailing symbolism of the palm branch in antiquity (Aune I:468-470; Moffat 398). The scene symbolizes the saints' *victory* achieved by remaining faithful to Christ in the Tribulation.

Most idealists regard this group as composed of "tribulation" saints throughout all of church history (Poythress 119). Futurists often restrict the group and time to a future, literal, seven-year period of unprecedented tribulation (often equated with Daniel's seventieth week) that culminates with the Second Coming of Christ. But though martyrs are included in this great group (see 6:9-11), and a great number of saints will be martyred during the Tribulation, it is not likely that *every* saint on earth during the Tribulation will be martyred. Some may die of natural causes and some will survive; this group includes them.

They shout, "Salvation to our God which sitteth upon the throne, and unto the Lamb" (v. 10). Though "salvation" may refer to deliverance of many kinds, "the" before "salvation" (in Greek) emphasizes this salvation's uniqueness and primacy. In the end this is the only kind that matters, the one and only eternally enduring salvation. God and the Lamb alone are able to save. By including the Lamb, the great multitude is "claiming for the Lamb an honor and a worship that traditionally belong only to God" (Gonzalez 57).

This is not only personal salvation from spiritual death to eternal life. It is also salvation from destructive forces and spiritual enemies during the Tribulation. (Idealists would say, from the tribulations of Christian life in general.) In this context Aune (I:429) prefers "salvation in the sense of 'deliverance' or 'victory' over persecution" (cf. Caird 100). Their faith was neither denied nor destroyed by the catastrophes in the material universe, the dispossession of their earthly wealth, the deceit of false doctrine, or in the face of diabolical persecutions and pressures. And even this aspect of their salvation they owe to God and the Lamb. In the case of martyrs it is an ironic victory, in that it included their deaths. As with the slain Lamb of God, victory in Revelation is often portrayed as a victory through sacrifice or suffering (Mounce 162).

The praise generated by the numberless multitude prompted an antiphonal response from the permanent entourage of angels, elders, and living beings around God's throne (vv. 11, 12). Although angels do not personally experience redemption, they gladly join the celebration (1 Pet. 1:12; cf. Lk. 15:7, 10). The permanent throne-room entourage typically falls down before God from their standing position when offering worship to God (4:10; 5:8, 14).

The host of angels surrounding the inner circle around God's throne offered a sevenfold doxology of worship (v. 12) that "enhances rhetorical emphasis by producing the impression of extensiveness and abundance" (Thomas I:405; cf. 1 Ch. 29:11, 12). In the original, "the" appears before each term, emphasizing that "in the fullest, deepest sense these excellencies pertain to God and to Him alone" (Hendriksen 112). This doxology is similar to the one offered to the Lamb by the same angels in 5:11, 12. The order around the throne is listed in reverse, beginning with the angelic host in the outer perimeter, then the elders, and finally the four living beings (cf. 4:4, 6). Perhaps the angels initiate the worship with the others following their lead. Or they could very well be the only group involved in this particular doxology, as the A.V. and NASB translations seem to imply.

"Amen" (often spoken *after* other words) precedes the doxology (v. 12). "Blessing" (Greek *eulogia*) is "good speaking, praise, the giving of thanks" (Vine 70). The worthiness of God and Christ virtually commands such praise. Salvation comes from God ("the one sitting upon the throne"), and its administration has been delegated to Jesus, the Lamb of God. Jesus' unique identity as "the Lamb of God who was slain," the One who takes the seven-sealed scroll from God's right hand, who successfully shepherds His followers through the Great Tribulation period, is reason enough to bless Him in worship eternally. The "glory" of God shines brightest in the Person of Christ, demonstrated in His redemptive character, work, and eternal exaltation at the Father's right hand. Because all glory rightfully belongs to God alone (Mt. 6:13), this tribute to Christ, by the angels in v. 12 and living beings in v. 13, is additional confirmation of His deity.

Recognition that the Lamb possesses infinite "wisdom" (cf. Col. 2:3; 1 Cor. 1:24, 30) is significant. "Wisdom" (Greek *sophia*) is "insight into the true nature of things" (Vine 678). Ultimately Christ is the very *personification* of wisdom. Christ needed infinite wisdom to create and sustain the universe (Jn.

1:3, 10; Col. 1:16, 17). This attribute of God is specifically manifested in the creation and government of the world, in how He executes His will and shapes destiny, and in finally effecting the rule of righteousness on earth: "the moral power pervading and effecting the progress of world history" (Thomas I:405). It includes "the divine knowledge God exhibited in his plan of redemption (cf. Eph. 3:10)" (Mounce 163). Finally, Christ needed wisdom to redeem the remnant of Israel (144,000) and all Tribulation saints (7:9, 14) while also bringing the present world to its appointed consummation. The wisdom needed to create the universe is also needed to destroy it.

Thanksgiving is offered to God by the angels in recognition of the wonder of redemption (1 Pet. 1:12), even though angels have not experienced redemption. The salvation in view is redemption from sin but also from the Tribulation: the latter is specifically cited in v. 14, along with cleansing from sin by Christ's blood.

"Honor" (Greek *time*) may be defined as the "public acknowledgment" (Mounce 163) or respect someone deserves, the proper estimation of a person's worth, "granted on the basis of how fully that individual embodies qualities and behaviors valued by the group" (DNTB 518). The highest honor is the honor given by God to Christ, awarded especially in His exaltation to the Father's right hand. We may also honor Christ by acknowledging His lordship over us and by proclaiming or confessing Him to others.

"Power" (Greek *dunamis*) means, basically "ability" or "capacity" (TDNT II:284), "the ability to carry out an action" (ISBE III:927). "Might" (Greek *ischus*) is similar in basic meaning, per-

haps indicating raw strength (TDNT III:397). Mounce (163) says God's "strength" is His "redemptive presence in the events of history."

The angels' doxology concludes with the benediction "be unto our God for ever and ever" and "Amen" (v. 12). The praise and worship of God by angels and saints will continue throughout eternity since God is Himself eternal and immutable. This final "Amen," along with the opening "Amen" in the same verse, like bookends (sometimes called an *inclusio*) doubly affirm the truth of everything said between.

Verse 13 focuses attention on the specific identity of the multiethnic, numberless multitude wearing white robes. The rhetorical questions about their precise identity and source, asked by one of the 24 elders, anticipate some of the answers by mentioning "white robes" and by suggesting that they have "come from" somewhere (v. 13). The questions serve as a "didactic" device (Gonzalez 57). John's answer, "Sir, thou knowest," defers to the elder whose knowledge is more perfect; it may indicate uncertainty on John's part. The elder's prompt reply confirms that the question was asked rhetorically and is also an example of how Scripture sometimes supplies its own interpretation. "Sir" (Greek *kurios*), though often used for deity as "Lord," can also be applied to other dignitaries as a title of "respect," as here.

The answer to the "where" question is first, important because it adds significance to the worship and introduces the concept of *the Great Tribulation period*, only hinted at in the message to Philadelphia (3:10) and now introduced in its proper chronological context. Before both "great" and "tribulation" there is a "the" in the original: (literally) "the tribulation the great"—the Great Tribulation, in other words, to be distinguished from tribulation in general, in any period of church history (Mt. 24:21; Mk. 13:19; Dan. 12:1).

The group has come out: literally, "the ones coming out" (of this Tribulation, v. 14), which has the effect of making the action more vivid (Greek present tense participle). Nonetheless, for John and us, the whole scene is proleptic—portraying a future event as if presently happening for dramatic effect. It is plausible that the proleptic vision of victorious Tribulation saints was included at this point in Revelation to answer the question posed in 6:17; and the picture of these victorious Tribulation saints serves as an encouragement to believers of every generation who undergo tribulation to any degree. However, the Great Tribulation of 7:14 is eschatological and falls within the final seven-year period of history at the end of this age.

Jesus qualified the Tribulation in question with "such as was not since the beginning of the world to this time, no, nor ever shall be" (Mt. 24:21). Add to this prediction of unique severity the words of 3:10, indicating that the "hour of temptation" to come "shall come upon the whole world to try them that dwell on the earth." The troubles are *worldwide* in scope and were future in A.D. 96 when John wrote. The destruction of Jerusalem in A.D. 70 is therefore ruled out as the "Great Tribulation," which will be unprecedented in degree according to Christ's description (A. Johnson 89; Newcombe 200, 201). Furthermore, the reference to the Tribulation after a number of other events in the Olivet Discourse (cf. Mt. 24:1-14) lends credence to distinguishing the last half or so of the seven-year

period from the first half of the period as the Great Tribulation proper. Brighton (197, 198), typically an idealist, accepts the concept of a literal Great Tribulation period as "The evil days *immediately before Christ's Second Coming,* together with their sufferings and persecutions."

They have "washed their robes and made them white in the blood of the Lamb" (v. 14; cf. 22:14), both past actions (Greek aorist) implying the cleansing that occurs at conversion. The language indicates a N.T. salvation experience. Both expressions refer to a singular experience of personal redemption by the blood of Christ: "In other words, they have placed all their trust in the saving blood of Jesus Christ" (Hendriksen 114). As a result of this "washing," their "robes" (a metaphor for one's spiritual condition) became white or clean in the sight of God (cf. Is. 1:18; 64:6). The "blood of the Lamb" not only washes sins away, it also represents the righteous life of Christ, since the life is in the blood. Their sins are forgiven and the righteousness of Christ is imputed to them.

The merits of the righteousness and blood of Christ must be distinguished from the individual merits or rewards of personal faithfulness and martyrdom during the Great Tribulation: "Redemption, not martyrdom, is the essential basis of their deliverance" (Moffat 400). The forensic benefits of salvation, including the forgiveness of sins, are merited by the blood of Christ and are applied when a person places his or her faith in Christ. "Their act of washing the robes is not a meritorious work but a way of portraying faith" (Mounce 165). It is not necessary or possible to add to the finished work of

Christ in order to merit God's salvation—though each individual is responsible to be faithful after receiving salvation by faith (Rom. 10:9-13; Eph. 2:8, 9; Rev. 3:20; cf. Acts 26:20; Eph. 2:10).

The conditional requirement of *overcoming*, in the messages to the churches, is not contradictory to the doctrine of justification by faith. "God never bestows his gifts or wins his victories without the free consent and choice of his human agents; the martyrs must wash their robes and make them white by the means which God's grace has provided" (Caird 102). Even so, the only way a believer can "overcome" the enemies of faith (during the Tribulation or otherwise) is by the grace of God operating through the new-covenant dynamic of a personally indwelling Holy Spirit. But an individual's willful choice to do so is also necessary. The Tribulation environment will be toxic to casual faith. People will be called on to make a clear choice either for or against Christ in the context of tremendous pressures to compromise. For Tribulation saints *overcoming* means "identifying with the ways of Christ" and "abstaining from the ways of the beast" (Rowland 624). The ability to overcome confirms the existence of true saving faith.

Many Jews and Gentiles will be saved during the Tribulation, and the language used to describe their salvation is the same as used throughout the N.T. for the salvation of those who belong to the redeemed *church*. Nowhere does Scripture indicate that there is a new way of salvation in the Tribulation. If any are saved, they are saved in the same way as at any other time; the language of vv. 7-19 indicates as much. The work of the Holy Spirit in convicting, drawing, and regenerating, together with the preaching of the Word, will still be necessary. In my view, therefore, the Holy Spirit must remain on earth during the Tribulation, *whatever one's view of the rapture.* Ryrie's view (*Revelation* 64) that the Holy Spirit is withdrawn, albeit in a "special sense," is therefore soteriologically problematic.

This vast multitude standing before God's throne have done two things. First and foremost, they have been born again by the blood of Christ during the Tribulation. But they have also endured catastrophic and satanic tribulations to the end of the period, or until their own natural death (cf. Mt. 24:13). They have achieved victory by overcoming their tribulations and enemies of faith in the world (cf. 1 Jn. 5:4, 5).

The rewards of these saints' salvation are described (present and future tenses) in vv. 15-17. First, they are "before the throne of God" (cf. "standing," v. 9). While the main point of this is relational (spiritual), there is also a spatial (physical) element (Lenski 263; cf. 4:1-11). The blood of the Lamb opens the way for access to the throne of God (Heb. 10:19-22), a privilege granted to Tribulation saints and *all* saints throughout church history. This positioning implies both the holiness of those standing before God (and therefore unhindered fellowship) and God's perennial desire to dwell in the midst of His people.

Second, they are positioned there to "serve" the Lamb, indicating that "heaven is not only a place of rest from earthly toil but also a place of privileged service" (Walvoord 148). The verb indicates continuing service (Greek present tense), reinforced by the "day and night": "unceasingly or without pause" (Mounce

257

165). It conveys the idea of "carrying out religious duties in a spirit of worship" (ALGNT 244).

Many see "in his temple" (Greek *naos*, the inner sanctuary) as reminiscent of O.T. priestly service. This service is now performed in Heaven and will continue into eternity. It is not the service of the 144,000 on the earth. And there is no cue that this is service in a millennial rather than heavenly Temple. Walvoord (148) rightly rejects the view that restricts this to service in a rebuilt millennial Temple on earth. It speaks rather of service for God in eternity that will be worshipful and unceasing (cf. Ryrie, *Revelation* 63). The particular service of these Tribulation saints is doxological worship rather than other duties such as those reflected in the O.T. priesthood (cf. Charles I:214, 215). But the O.T. symbol gives way to the eternal reality: "Heaven itself is the sanctuary" (Mounce 165). Though some material forms remain—such as "the throne of God" (22:1) or perhaps "the golden altar" (6:9; 8:3)—the commentary of 21:22 is determinative: "And I saw no temple therein: for the Lord God Almighty and the Lamb are the temple of it."

Though this scene is placed, in Revelation, between the sixth and seventh seals, it is proleptic: it looks to the future and is not located between the sixth and seventh seals chronologically. Many events are yet to transpire, from 8:1 and forward. The latter elements of the scene in 7:9-17, though true at the end of the Tribulation, blend into eternity proper and need not be limited to the Tribulation. The least that may be said is that the Great Tribulation is either continuing or has ended in 7:9-17. Nevertheless, though the scene's *start-ing* point is *eschatological*, it contains blessed conditions that are typically associated with the new Heaven and earth in eternity (cf. Ladd, *Commentary* 118).

There is *direct* fellowship with God, the One that sits on the throne, and this is unprecedented. Historically, God's presence has been manifested among His people as the *Shekinah* glory filling the O.T. tabernacle and Temple (Ex. 40:34-38; 2 Chr. 7:1-3), or in the person of Christ (Jn. 1:14), or in the indwelling presence of the Spirit (1 Cor. 3:16; 6:19). The new and eternal relationship is expressed with the use of seven future tenses calculated to express the perfect or complete nature of every believer's eternal future in Heaven.

The first of these, "shall dwell among them," fulfills O.T. promises (Ex. 25:8; Num. 35:34; Ezek. 37:27; 43:7, 9; and Zech. 2:10, 11). God will become the direct, loving, and eternal Source (protection and provision) of all they will ever need. "Dwell" (Greek *skenoo*) means "to tabernacle or spread a tent" (Vine 188). A major component of Mosaic and O.T. eschatological hope was God's desire to dwell with His people forever (Lev. 26:11; Ezek. 37:27; 43:7, 9). God's presence with Israel during her wilderness wanderings meant His protection from her enemies, provision for their material and physical needs, and precepts for living in terms of worship and social interaction. God's tabernacling and shepherding presence with His people in eternity will mean the unprecedented, permanent, and inexhaustible supply of all that His people ever need. God's mediated presence in the wilderness years did not protect His people from the heat of the day or wipe away their tears. His *unmediated* presence in eternity will do both.

As a result of God's unmediated, eternal presence, Tribulation saints will never hunger, thirst, or experience the sun's negative effects since God protects and provides for them (v. 16; cf. 21:4; Is. 4:5, 6; 9:10; 25:4, 5; 49:10). Charles (I:216) calls thirst, "the pain of unsatisfied desire." Hunger can be thought of in the same way. Sunlight or "intense desert heat" (Barnes 187) brings physical pain. A significant part of the rich man's torment in Hell was unquenched thirst and the agony of unimaginable heat (Lk. 16:19-31). In contrast to those who are in Hell, eternally separated from God's presence and provisions, God and the Lamb will provide the food, water, light, and protection needed in the new heavens and earth.

Paradoxically, the Lamb, with God the Father at the throne, assumes the role of *shepherd* (v. 17). It comes as no surprise that the shepherd analogy carries over into eternity. More than 400 references to sheep in the Bible (DBI 782)—more than to any other animal—suggest that this is God's favorite analogy to describe His relationship with His people. He will continue to shepherd those who have faithfully followed Him through the Great Tribulation into and throughout eternity. Once in Heaven, the relationship continues. He will "feed them" and He will "lead them unto living fountains of water" (Jn. 4:14; 6:35; Rev. 21:6; 22:1, 17). "Living water" is "flowing water" (Aune I:478) such as in a spring or river, pure and nourishing, whereas still water, as in a pond or cistern, may stagnate and become unsuitable for consumption. He will "wipe away all their tears from their eyes" for-

ever (cf. Is. 25:8; Rev. 21:4). These may not necessarily be tears of regret for wasted lives but could just as well be tears because of tribulations or even tears of joy over long-awaited victory (Walvoord 148).

These conditions comprise a description of the quality of eternal life with God to be experienced by every believer in the new Heaven and earth. Though similar to every believer's present experience with Christ as the Good Shepherd, this relationship perfected in Heaven is infinitely better. There are no negatives. The goodness and mercy of Ps. 23:6 never end.

4. Seventh Seal (8:1-5)

1 And when he had opened the seventh seal, there was silence in heaven about the space of half an hour.

2 And I saw the seven angels which stood before God; and to them were given seven trumpets.

3 And another angel came and stood at the altar, having a golden censer; and there was given unto him much incense, that he should offer *it* with the prayers of all saints upon the golden altar which was before the throne.

4 And the smoke of the incense, *which came* with the prayers of the saints, ascended up before God out of the angel's hand.

5 And the angel took the censer, and filled it with fire of the altar, and cast *it* into the earth: and there were voices, and thunderings, and lightnings, and an earthquake.

The seventh seal provides seamless transition between the seals and the trumpet judgments. The "slain Lamb" of 5:6 opened the seals. When ("whenever" in some manuscripts) the seventh seal is broken, the main contents of the scroll (8:6—22:21) come into view. "Whenever" could suggest that the precise timing of the opening of the seventh seal is unknown (Swete 106); regardless, the *certainty* of its opening is not in doubt.

When Jesus opens this seal there is a brief period of "silence" in Heaven (v. 1). Some suggest that the content of this seal is nothing more than this silence; in that case, it has no content other than to introduce the following trumpet judgments (Ladd, *Commentary* 122). Another view is that the trumpet judgments *and* bowl judgments comprise the content of the seventh seal. Mounce (170) sees the silence as a "dramatic pause," during which "the angelic activity of vv. 2-5 takes place": "Silence underscores the gravity of the crisis" (Beale 446). It may also indicate reverence: worshipers in Temple liturgy bowed in silence as the incense was being offered inside (Edersheim 128). Given the significance of silence in the O.T. (Ex. 14:14; Hab. 2:20; 3:3-6; Zech. 2:13-3:2; Zeph. 1:7, 11), this silence apparently signifies much more than a mere transitional pause.

The silence may recall the silence in Goshen on Passover night, when the last plague fell upon Egypt (Ex. 11:7; 12:29, 30). This way, the "silence" in the seventh seal is *the calm before the storm* of additional judgments (the trumpets and bowls), a silence contemplating pending divine judgment. The immediate context is judgment, not creation.

The "interlocking" (Collins 1006) of both series of judgments (seals to trumpets; trumpets to bowls), in the seventh member of the seals and trumpets, fits well with the idea of a general momentum forward in the judgments. The other major view of the relationship holds that each series "recapitulates" the preceding ones, albeit from a different perspective. Since there is no textual cue indicating repetition or recapitulation, it is better to view each of the series (seals, trumpets, bowls) as going forward in time. The seventh seal and seventh trumpet serve to interlock their series with the one that follows, ending their group and beginning the next. The opening of the seventh seal or the sounding of the seventh trumpet introduces the next series of judgments.

Comparisons advocating that the trumpets are a recapitulation of the seals break down because of obvious differences. One such difference is the math: "one-fourth" in 6:8, but "thirds" in 8:7, 8, 9, 10, 11, 12. Another is the lack of uniformity in subject matter between the various sevens when they are compared. However, both the seventh seal and the seventh trumpet seem to depart from a strict sequential arrangement, telescoping us to the end of the Tribulation or perhaps the end of a literal millennium (6:12-17; 11:15-19; 16:17-21).

The pause of "one half-hour" is appropriate in light of the awesome seal judgments just revealed and the increased intensity of the trumpet judgments to follow. This may be a precise half-hour (Ryrie, *Revelation* 65) or "a figurative expression to emphasize the suddenness and unexpectedness of a decreed judgment" (Beale 453). It probably indicates a *brief* period; an indefinite period would probably be represented as an "hour."

Since the first trumpet is not sounded until v. 6, it is convenient to include the material of vv. 2-5 with the discussion of the seventh seal. "And I saw" introduces a new vision. However, before the seven trumpets sound, "the prayers of the saints" are portrayed as integral to the unfolding drama (cf. 5:8; 6:9). The initial focus changes from the "seven angels with seven trumpets" (v. 2), who are "standing before God" and whose trumpets "were given" to them, to the priestly action of "another angel."

The opening of the seventh seal, then, reveals *the* seven angels, perhaps "seven archangels who occupy a very particular role in the angelic hierarchy" (Aune I:509). "The" seems to set them apart as a distinct group, introduced for the first time, who have a special position to "stand before God"; cf. Gabriel (Lk. 1:19; Mt. 18:10). Though this may indicate "readiness for service" (Thomas II:7), the frame of reference is clearly throne-oriented and the expression equals being in God's presence.

Whether these are seven archangels, permanently positioned before the throne, we cannot say: neither that there is such a group or that they are the seven archangels of Jewish tradition (1 Enoch 2:2-8). There is no reference to seven archangels anywhere in Scripture. Michael is called an "archangel" in Jude 9; Gabriel, though thought of as an archangel, is never called this in Scripture. These are the only two angels named. Neither is it clear that the seven here have a permanent position around the throne; they are not mentioned in the earlier survey of the throne room (chapters 4 and 5). They may simply be a specially commissioned group ("ordi-

nary angels" Lenski 268) called into service for the sounding of the trumpet judgments, numbering seven for no reason other than that the judgments number seven. (This will hold for the seven angels of the bowl judgments as well.)

"To them were given" (the *divine passive* again) points to the divine source of the judgments. God's sovereign control of everything and everyone in the end-times—including Satan and the Antichrist—is fundamental throughout Revelation.

That there are *seven* trumpets emphasizes the complete nature of the associated judgments. Trumpets have a variety of purposes in Scripture, other than for music: heralding special religious events, military signals, celebrations, and warnings. Important in Scripture is the *eschatological* use of the trumpet; in the N.T. see Mt. 24:31, 1 Th. 4:16, and 1 Cor. 15:52. Some suggest that all three of these refer to the same event. If so, this has significance for the rapture question since the one in Mt. 24:31 is blown *after* the Great Tribulation depicted in Mt. 24:29-31. (Cf. also the seventh trumpet in Rev. 11:15.) The trumpet of 1 Cor. 15:52 is the *last* trumpet; Borland's (70, 71) pretribulational perspective seems correct, but his exegesis of "last" as "last of a series to be followed by more to come" is unlikely, being an attempt to explain why "last" does not really mean *last*.

We note the deliberate manner in which this interlude unfolds. First, "another angel" was positioned at the golden altar of incense (cf. 5:8; 6:9). Beale (455) cites two views about the identity of this angel. One, he may be similar to "the angel of the presence" (Is. 63:9), mediating God's presence in some way. A second view is that the angel is "Christ himself" (Seiss, Walvoord). Christ is presently in the form of a slain Lamb, occupied with opening the seals; identifying Christ as "another angel" seems highly unlikely. "Would the central figure of Revelation be introduced into the text with such an indefinite title?" (Mounce 173, 174).

The angel, then, "came and stood," probably in response to God's command. Incense was then "given to him." Directing this carefully scripted symbolism is God Himself, whether directly or indirectly. The altar is apparently the one identified in v. 3 as "the golden altar of incense" (Mounce 174), from which the "fire of the altar" (v. 5) is cast into the earth. Fire was as available from the altar of incense as from the brazen altar.

All this helps clarify the identity of the unidentified altar in 6:9. The golden altar of incense is more properly associated with prayer than the brazen altar of the Temple courtyard (Ex. 30:1-10; Heb. 9:4). The "golden censer" was probably a small, shovel-like instrument used to carry live coals on which incense was burned (ISBE I:628). Incense was burned on the golden altar twice a day, morning and evening, to symbolize the prayers of God's people (Edersheim 127, 128; cf. Ps. 141:2).

"Much" incense symbolizes "the prayers of all the saints," which have already been identified symbolically as "incense" in 5:8 (surely this explains "with the prayers" in 8:3, 4). The suggestion that the incense is offered with the prayers "to make them more acceptable to God" (Thomas II:10) is unwarranted; prayers are efficacious on their own and do not need enhancement. Further, the idea that the incense represents "the intercession of Christ for his church" (Hendriksen 117) reads too much into the text. Though the merits of Christ are always the basis of answered prayer, "the prayers of all saints" are in view here. The opening of the seventh seal reveals both God's decision that the time of His vindication had come and the close connection between prayer and divine response.

The aroma and smoke of the incense, ascending from the altar of incense in front of the Holy of Holies, is "a symbol of divine acceptance" (Mounce 175) and a visual image of what happens when saints pray. Prayers come into the immediate presence of God to be accepted and eventually answered by Him (cf. 5:8). While the prayers of Tribulation martyrs (6:9-11) may especially be in view here, there is surely a sense in which God's eschatological vengeance is a response to saints in every generation. Their prayers are stored in golden bowls in the hands of the 24 elders (who represent all believers).

All this makes an important contribution to *the theology of prayer*. The 24 elders, flanking the throne of God (4:4), have harps and *golden bowls of incense* that contain the "prayers of saints" (5:8). Christian martyrs are praying underneath the altar (6:9-11), their prayer offered in expectation of God's vindication (6:10). Now the trumpet judgments are introduced as an answer to the prayers of God's saints (8:1-5). The prayers of God's people play a significant role in the end-times and contribute to the ultimate victory of Christ and His church. God never forgets sincere prayer.

Application of fire to the incense, or vice versa, activated the incense's fragrant aroma (vv. 4, 5), symbolically offering the prayers of all saints to God. Afterward, the angel filled the censer with coals scooped from the golden altar and cast the fire "into the earth," and the trumpet judgments began (v. 5; cf. Ezek. 10:2). This fire from God's throne has a purifying, judging effect on the cosmos and the unbelieving inhabitants of earth and seems to reproduce itself in most of the trumpet judgments against the earth. Fire is manifested in some way with the first six (vv. 7, 8, 10, 12; 9:2, 17, 18).

The significance of this moment is dramatized by accompanying phenomena such as "voices, thunderings, lightnings, and an earthquake" (cf. 11:19; 16:19). Many view this expression as the effects of a "theophany": a miraculous manifestation of God's presence. Some of these may be typical throne-room phenomena, but they reaffirm a connection between God's presence and judgments against the earth. Beale concludes that the use of this fourfold formula at the end of each series of judgments (seals, trumpets, and bowls) indicates that the ending of each series points to the same event, the last judgment. But that is unwarranted simply on the basis of similar supernatural phenomena which can accompany the divine presence equally well on Mt. Sinai (Ex. 19:16-18) or in the throne room of Heaven (4:5)—neither of which is necessarily judgmental. As here, 11:19 and 16:18 reflect the end of a judgment series, and each seems to take us *near* the climax of the present world order (pictured in greater detail in chapter 19). But even the Battle of Armageddon is *not the last judgment*. The ultimate end of things occurs with the Great White Throne Judgment, and that does

not occur until after the millennial period and one final world rebellion.

Summary
(7:1—8:5)

Chapter 7 provides an interlude between the sixth and seventh seals. Two distinct, redeemed groups are described. Before the first (vv. 1-8) is introduced, John sees four special angels who control the earth's four winds (v. 1). Another appears and temporarily suspends their mission in order to seal or mark this first group with the seal of God in their foreheads (vv. 2, 3). This seal protects the marked group from the pending destruction represented by the first four angels.

The first group is composed of 144,000, an exclusively ethnic group of 12,000 from each of the 12 tribes of Israel named—omitting Dan and Ephraim and including Levi. They are "men" (14:4), described as "firstfruits unto God and the Lamb" during the Tribulation. These parameters keep them from being an adequate symbol for the entire church as some suggest.

The second group (vv. 9-17) is numberless and multiethnic, already in Heaven, their mission completed. They are pictured as victorious saints gathered before the throne in worship and celebration. They are on the other side of the Tribulation period, not in it (v. 14). Their condition and victory are final and not subject to change.

The brief snapshot of the second group's victorious gathering and heavenly worship extends into eternity proper (vv. 15-17). The existing relationship with Jesus as their Good Shepherd is made eternal: they will forever relate to Him in this way. In Heaven He will

guide, guard, and provide for them forever. This includes provisions for eternal
happiness, satisfying hunger and thirst,
giving light, comfort, and living water,
and the absence of all tears.

The seal judgments conclude with the
seventh seal in 8:1-5. When Christ
opens it there is silence in Heaven (v. 1),
remarkable for the vast number of angels
and saints who are busy worshiping,
singing, and reciting doxologies to God.
The silence contrasts with other supernatural phenomena associated with the
revelations, such as thunder, lightning,
earthquakes, and voices shouting loud
commands. It apparently indicates a
calm before the storm of the coming
trumpet judgments.

The seven trumpet angels stand
before God and receive their trumpets
from Him (v. 2), indicating the divine
origin and utility of the judgments.
Seven trumpets will be "sounded"
against the Christ-rejecting world during
the eschatological Tribulation (8:6—
11:19). The blowing of each symbolizes
the beginning of a specific judgment on
earth.

An unnamed angel performs a liturgy
reminiscent of O.T. Temple ritual (v. 3),
apparently designed to connect the
trumpet judgments to the prayers of all
God's saints. The angel burns a great
amount of incense, symbolically representing the prayers of all saints, on the
golden altar before God's throne. The
smoke and aroma of the burning incense
provide a visual representation of what
happens when saints pray (v. 4): their
prayers rise up into the presence of God
and are accepted by Him.

Fire is then taken from the golden
altar of prayer and cast into the earth (v.
5). Various theophanic phenomena
occur on the earth as a result. The inau-

guration of God's trumpet judgments is
thereby confirmed. The seven angels
prepared to sound their trumpets when
the prayer liturgy was completed.

Application: Teaching and Preaching the Passage

A good illustration of the sovereignty
of God is how He controls even evil
agents according to His will. The best
example of this was the crucifixion of
Christ. The powers of God and Satan
were both at work. Two agendas were
plainly in view. Both were successful.
Yet the triumph of Christ was achieved
in part *through* the agency of evil men.
Even those who favor identifying the
four horsemen as evil agents, rather
than instruments of God's judgment,
should allow for God's sovereign control
of them, using them to achieve His
greater purpose.

Revelation provides us with the ultimate answer to the question why God
allows evil or bad things to happen. One
reason is that much good comes to us
through affliction. We may be either
chastised for our own unacceptable
behavior, given grace to endure those
who offend us, or sanctified in character
in preparation for greater achievements.
The application of final justice against
our enemies and the enemies of Christ
is reserved for the end-times. The present generation of believers must exercise
confident patience in waiting until then
for some issues to be resolved. We know
our Sovereign God is in control of future
history.

Gonzalez (52) makes an interesting
point: some affluent believers, comfortable in the present world, may be reluctant to think about the end of this world:
"To us who have a significant invest-

ment in our society and whom the present order rewards with relative comfort and security, all of this may sound unbearably negative." This tension may explain in part the contemporary reluctance to embrace the Second Coming of Christ with enthusiasm. Still, the fact remains that all the bad *and* the good of this present world are coming to an end. Wisdom accepts this, is willing to turn loose the present when called upon, and makes preparation for the end by walking with Christ.

The present world is often toxic to faith in Christ. This was true for believers in the churches of first-century Asia Minor, is true now, and will be true during the Great Tribulation before the Second Coming. Threats to faith and security are real. Acts of individual apostasy by true believers are never the result of God's inability to keep believers eternally secure. He is more than able to do that. But God chooses to let men choose. And the possibility of apostasy remains on the table for the duration of the present church age and into the Tribulation because the enemies of faith are ever alive and well.

Theological presuppositions color one's interpretation of the "sealing" in 7:3. But the danger of apostasy, real throughout church history, will continue during the Tribulation when those things that are opposed to faith in Christ are most intense. We are reassured to know that tribulations, temptations, or satanic attacks cannot overcome the superior dynamic of the indwelling Holy Spirit; only a believer's free choice to deny Christ, as under threat of martyrdom, for example, can bring about apostasy (2 Pet. 2:20-22; Heb. 6:4-6; 10:26, 29). Nothing external to a believer can force him toward apostasy.

Suggested Sermon Outline. The Family of God, 7:9-17: (1) Around God's throne, v. 9; (2) Assisted and Admired by angels, vv. 11, 12; (3) Arrayed in white robes, v. 13; (4) Already triumphant, vv. 13, 14; (5) Active in worship and service, v. 15; (6) Absolute satisfaction, vv. 16, 17.

IV. THE SEVEN TRUMPETS (8:6—11:19)

The seven trumpets herald seven supernatural judgments against the Christ-rejecting world in the end-times Tribulation—judgments against the material world, unbelieving mankind, the Antichrist, and the evil world system. Even those judgments that are primarily directed against the material earth invariably affect mankind; the literal devastation of the fishing industry in the second and third judgments, for example, has a corresponding economic effect on the nations of the world. Thus all these judgments may be viewed as ultimately against the world's nations, governments, and economies. They are less severe than the bowl judgments to follow and therefore serve both to prompt repentance and as harbingers of the final judgment of this world.

Preterists view the trumpet judgments as symbolic of the destruction of Jerusalem in A.D. 70 (see Ezek. 5:12) while yet others try to connect them with the fall of the eastern Roman Empire late in the fifth century (Barnes 195f.). Idealists spread them out over the entire period of church history: "These trumpets of judgment...indicate *series* of happenings, that is, calamities that will occur again and again throughout the dispensation...woes that may be seen any day of the year in any part of the globe" (Hendriksen 116).

But it is clear that the trumpet judgments, more literally, hasten the demise of certain aspects of the material world, including trees, vegetation, water sources, sun, moon, and stars. "While the first four seals depicted judgments that are the inevitable consequences of human sinfulness, the trumpets reveal the active involvement of God in bringing punishment upon a wicked world" (Mounce 176). Though these judgments are not directed primarily against believers, they nevertheless sound notes of an ever-nearing final salvation for them.

Though some interpreters think so, the trumpet judgments do not reflect a recapitulation of the seal judgments. Earlier, I pointed out some differences that make this clear. The seals, trumpets, and bowls show progression from fourths to thirds to totality, demonstrating a difference in the intensity of the forces at work or in the scope of their application. Note 16:3, for example, when in the corresponding bowl judgment *every* living soul in the sea dies. The increase from series to series culminates in complete destruction by the end of the Tribulation.

There are structural similarities between the seal and trumpet judgments. Within each series, the first four display a unity distinct from the final three. In the trumpet judgments, for example, the difference is marked by an angel (or eagle) flying through Heaven (8:13). The first four bring literal judgments against nature whereas the last three ("woes") target the unbelieving human population. Furthermore, a "parenthesis" stands between the sixth and seventh members of the seals and trumpets. The sixth seal, seventh trum-

pet, and seventh bowl all telescope to the end of the Tribulation period.

There are also similarities between the first five trumpet judgments and the plagues in Egypt leading up to the Exodus (Ex. 7-12). The "hail and fire" (8:7) compare to the seventh plague (Ex. 9:23). The pollution of the Nile (Ex. 7:20, 21) compares to the devastation of the second and third trumpet judgments affecting salt- and freshwater sources of the earth (8:8-12). The demonic plague of locusts from the abyss (9:1-11) recalls the swarms of flies (Ex. 8:17), lice (Ex. 8:24), and locusts (Ex. 10:13, 14). The boils (Ex. 9:10) are similar to the stings inflicted on unbelievers by the demonic locusts (9:5). The darkening of sun, moon, and stars (8:12) compares to the plague of darkness in Egypt (Ex. 10:21).

Just as the Israelites in Goshen were not affected (Ex. 8:22, 23; 9:4, 6, 26; 10:23; 11:7), so with the seal, trumpet, and bowl judgments poured out on the world during the Tribulation. They are primarily judgments of God on unbelievers. Even the plague of demonic locusts (9:1-11) is an instrument He uses to chastise unbelievers, who largely remain recalcitrant even though the trumpet plagues are calls to repentance (9:20, 21). Though Satan is active during the Tribulation, his agenda is *a subplot* in Revelation.

A. First Trumpet (8:6, 7)

6 And the seven angels which had the seven trumpets prepared themselves to sound.

7 The first angel sounded, and there followed hail and fire mingled with blood, and they were cast upon the earth: and the third part

of trees was burnt up, and all green grass was burnt up.

Verse 6 brings our attention back to the seven trumpet angels introduced in v. 2; see the comments there. That they are first seen standing at God's throne indicates their "readiness for service" (Mounce 173), perhaps a permanent position for some angels.

These seven readied themselves to blow their trumpets, escalating further the sense of drama already enhanced by the dramatic silence (v. 1). As discussed above, the activity of vv. 3-5 may have intentionally represented the trumpet judgments as God's response to the prayers of saints, which play a role in God's decisions.

"Prepared themselves" suggests raising the trumpets to blow, to be "sounded" one at a time in order: probably one great blast of sound from each, since produced by angelic effort. The blowing of each is equivalent to the beginning or inauguration of each particular judgment, with the trumpet sound serving both to *warn* and to *herald* the judgments.

The sounding of the first trumpet produces "hail and fire mixed with blood," perhaps suggesting "a shower of blood" (Vincent 506). Brighton (225), comparing pagan prophecies (the Sibylline Oracles), suggests that this imagery "symbolizes the destruction of warfare on the land and people." Many interpreters cite the seventh plague of Ex. 9:24, which involved hail and fire; though "blood" is not mentioned there, the hail beating down on men and animals would have produced much blood. Likewise, the blood here may indicate the destructive effect that this divine concoction will have on human beings and animals when cast upon the earth.

There are other options. Perhaps the reddish tint of lightning (fire) associated with the hail storm is in view. Swete (110) mentions an instance when *red* sand particles from the Sahara reportedly produced "blood-red rain." Barnes (195) cites instances of "red snow" but interprets the blood here as "properly expressive of blood and carnage." "Mixed with blood" could refer to the color of the lightning or sky or could even mean literal blood supernaturally included by God. Thompson (114, 115) thinks this reflects the "sacrificial blood" mixed with incense offered on the Day of Atonement. Joel predicted that the Lord would "show wonders in the heavens and in the earth, blood, and fire, and pillars of smoke. The sun shall be turned into darkness, and the moon into blood, before the great and terrible day of the LORD come" (Jl. 2:30, 31; cf. Ezek. 38:18-21). Wall (126) even suggests that the "blood" symbolizes the death of Christ, but that connection is not apparent here. On balance, "mingled with blood" likely symbolizes what will clearly be the literally destructive effect of this first trumpet judgment on human, plant, and animal life (see Walvoord 153).

Hail and fire are also associated with the throne of God in Heaven, at times instruments of God's judgment (Jos. 10:11; Ps. 18:12; Is. 28:2; 30:30; Ezek. 13:11, 13; 38:22; Rev. 11:19; 16:21). The destructive potential of hail is well documented. Fire or "lightning" (Barnes 194) is also a terrible form of judgment (Gen. 19:24; Dt. 29:23; 2 Kg. 1:10,12,14; Lk. 16:23,24; 1 Cor. 3:13; 2 Th. 1:8; 2 Pet. 3:10, 12).

For the casting of this mixture of hail, fire, and blood upon the earth, Ford

(137,138) suggests the idea of an ancient "slingshot" in the hands of God as Warrior. She points out that ammunition was sometimes set afire before being hurled at an enemy. At any rate, the action is aimed at the enemies of God.

The first trumpet judgment catastrophically affects the entire material world in at least two major ways: a third of all the earth's trees and all green grass are burned up. In the majority of Greek manuscripts, there is a third effect, preceding these two: "a third of the earth was burned up." If this is original, it may simply be explained by the other two or may mean "the cultivated soil on earth's surface" (Thomas II:17). Regardless, the use of thirds in this judgment is also apparently meant to qualify "all the green grass" as well, though this might include grass and other kinds of small vegetation in contrast to trees.

At any rate, the description, combined with that of the other trumpet judgments, confirms the worldwide scope of all these judgments; compare the darkening of the sun, moon, and stars by thirds in the fourth trumpet judgment (8:12). This casts doubt on the preterist viewpoint that seeks to confine the trumpets to first-century Palestine and the destruction of Jerusalem, which "does flagrant injustice to the worldwide scope of the prophecy" (Thomas II:17). As already noted, the measuring of effects in thirds is different from the fourths of the seal judgments (cf. 6:8). Still, this means that the judgments are *limited* (merciful) rather than final.

A symbolic view interprets the "trees" and "grass" as representing the earth's unbelieving population. Scott (cited in Ryrie, *Revelation* 67), views *the third part of the earth* as representing the Western confederation of nations, the

trees as leaders and great people and *grass* as people in general. Alas, this view is contradicted by how the very same components appear in the fifth trumpet judgment (9:4), where the demonic locusts must not hurt "the earth, grass, or trees" but rather "those men which have not the seal of God." If "the earth, grass, and trees" symbolize people, then in 9:4 they must be *believers*, while here in 8:7 they must be *unbelievers*, an inconsistency that rules out this interpretation. There is no reason for interpreting these components other than as literal trees and grass and the judgments as supernaturally provoked catastrophes that affect the natural order directly and humanity indirectly. "Trees" would include fruit trees and "grass" would include cultivated grasses (like grain) and plants as well as pasturage for herds. Burning up a third of these in the earth would seriously affect the world's food supply.

B. Second Trumpet (8:8, 9)

8 And the second angel sounded, and as it were a great mountain burning with fire was cast into the sea: and the third part of the sea became blood;
9 And the third part of the creatures which were in the sea, and had life, died; and the third part of the ships were destroyed.

The second angel's trumpet affects the earth's oceans or salt-water sources by means of "a great mountain burning with fire" cast there. (Some manuscripts omit "with fire," but the "burning" directly implies this.) The qualification "as it were" (Greek *hos*) suggests that the burning object was *like* a burning mountain: "a large object falling from the heavens" (Walvoord 154). Naturally occurring phenomena might include a "giant meteor" (Alford, cited in Thomas II:19) or a volcano erupting with fire and hot lava (Ford 138). But a volcano would have to be incredibly huge to affect a third of the earth's seas as described here, not to mention that it is awkward to envision a volcano being uprooted and cast into the sea—though it is always possible that such an eschatological phenomenon is uniquely prepared by God.

Still, a meteor-like object seems more logical. Fiery meteors occasionally penetrate the earth's atmosphere; some have left great craters in the earth's surface. Scientists theorize that a meteor shower or one great meteor could wreak catastrophic devastation on the earth if not annihilate all life entirely. Some that presently exist within the solar system are sufficient in size to account for the destruction foreseen here. All that God would need to do would be to redirect the trajectory of one. It is easy, then, to take this judgment literally.

With the casting of this "mountain" into the sea, one-third of earth's oceans became blood. There are two possibilities here: perhaps the seawater is turned into *literal* blood, causing the death of sea life as a result (v. 9); or perhaps the blood of one-third of the marine life, killed by the impact, turned the water red as blood. The latter seems logical, but one should remember that in the first plague affecting the rivers in Ex. 7:17, 18 the water was first turned into blood—a precedent or model for eschatological judgments affecting nature. Since there is no indication of simile or symbolism here, it seems best to interpret this as literal blood; but the out-

come is the important thing, the same either way: a third of sea life dies.

A third of ships are also destroyed, apparently literal ships directly destroyed by the great burning mountain or the upheaval it causes: "the intense turbulence of the sea" (A. Johnson 96). This could, of course, be taken as a symbolic reference to the destruction of a third of the world's maritime economy, but that would inevitably follow from the natural disaster. With shipping fleets drastically reduced, the area for fishing and amount of fish similarly affected, there will be a third less maritime profits. Other aspects of the shipping trade would likewise be dramatically curtailed. The first two trumpet judgments invariably affect the world's economy; afterward, there is a third less of every commodity. The purpose of such graduated devastation thus far "is to warn and lead to repentance" (Mounce 180).

A number of interpretations take the "burning mountain" as symbolical; in them are obvious excesses of speculation: "a hopeless quagmire of contradictions" (Thomas II:16, 17; Mounce 179 has a list). Some think the mountain represents a fallen angel expelled from heaven, or the destruction of spiritual "Babylon" (Rome), like "a star falling into the sea" (Caird 114). Idealist Beale (476) cites Jer. 51:25 and connects the second trumpet with the fall of spiritual Babylon in Rev. 18:21. Historicist Barnes (199) takes this to represent "the second great event" that contributed to the destruction of the Roman Empire.

But such suggestions founder largely because the burning mountain is *not the object* but the *agent* of destruction. "The heavenly origin of this fiery judgment is implied" (D. Johnson 144); "In Revelation the mountain is no ordinary mountain, but a vehicle for fire sent down from God" (Michaels 122). In the analogy in 18:21, spiritual Babylon is not "a burning mountain" but a giant "millstone." On balance, it seems best to view the burning mountain as a literal instrument of God's judgment and not as a kingdom (Jerusalem, Babylon, or Rome) being judged.

C. Third Trumpet (8:10, 11)

10 And the third angel sounded, and there fell a great star from heaven, burning as it were a lamp, and it fell upon the third part of the rivers, and upon the fountains of waters;
11 And the name of the star is called Wormwood: and the third part of the waters became wormwood; and many men died of the waters, because they were made bitter.

With the third trumpet came a "great star" falling from heaven. All the trumpet judgments are sent by God upon the earth (8:5). The first four affect the material earth directly and the human population indirectly. Though literal, these judgments against nature may also foreshadow the destruction of the economical, political, social, and spiritual systems of the evil world.

The falling star is described as "burning as it were a lamp" (NIV: "blazing like a torch"). Apparently this "star" was still burning while it fell through space and as it impacted the earth's surface. Poison, either from the point of impact or from the atmosphere while passing through, spread to one-third of the earth's freshwater sources on land. Smaller objects like meteorites typically

disintegrate in earth's atmosphere, but some of the larger ones have impacted the earth, leaving huge craters. "Shooting stars or meteors were deemed bad omens in the ancient world and the darkening of the stars was thought to manifest the wrath of God" (Ford 139). This particular star might be specially crafted by God or an existing star, meteorite, or comet adapted for use at this time.

The star is named "Wormwood," from the effect it has on the waters (cf. Dt. 29:17,18; Jer. 9:15; 23:15; Am. 6:12). Wormwood is a flowering plant from the absinthe family, sometimes described as extremely bitter but not poisonous; but others say that it is "deadly" (Thompson 116). Even if it is not always life-threatening, "Biblical symbolism makes wormwood's bitter taste emblematic of lethal consequences" (D. Johnson 145). For that matter, the burning star's bitter, poisonous qualities were likely far more powerful than earthly wormwood.

The falling star fouls a third of the earth's fresh-water supplies, which perhaps tasted only mildly bitter since many apparently used the water and died—or they might not have had much choice. At any rate, this judgment is more serious than the first plague of Exodus that affected only aquatic life in the river (Ex. 7:21). It is catastrophic in scope: using or drinking this contaminated water caused human beings to die, affecting a third of earth's population.

There are various symbolical interpretations. That this represents judgment of pagan spirits connected with the waters (cited by Mounce 179, 180) seems unlikely, since real human beings die. Historicist Barnes (203) suggests that this "star" points to Attila the Hun, who contributed to the demise of the Roman Empire in the fifth century. Idealist Beale (479) says the bitterness is a "metaphor for the bitterness of suffering resulting from judgment." Lenski (281), resisting a literal or futuristic reading, says, "The third trumpet makes visible the advance of religious delusion in the world which scorns the gospel" (cf. Jer. 23:15). But the third trumpet makes no such claim for itself. God does not need to send additional delusion into an unbelieving world that is already deluded and recalcitrant.

Again, there is similarity between the effects of the third trumpet judgment and the first plague (Ex. 7:20; cf. Jer. 9:15). Both judgments pollute freshwater sources and spoil their use for drinking, and both kill the fish in the affected waters. The devastation of this food source dramatically affects mankind. In sharp contrast to the healing of the "bitter waters" at Marah (Ex. 15:25), God *spoils* a third of *the unbelieving* world's freshwater supply. The lessons from such comparisons are certainly obvious: God provides for those who believe in Him and judges those who do not.

D. Fourth Trumpet (8:12, 13)

**12 And the fourth angel sounded, and the third part of the sun was smitten, and the third part of the moon, and the third part of the stars; so as the third part of them was darkened, and the day shone not for a third part of it, and the night likewise.
13 And I beheld, and heard an angel flying through the midst of heaven, saying with a loud voice, Woe, woe, woe, to the inhabiters of the earth by reason of the other voices of the trumpet of the three angels, which are yet to sound!**

The fourth trumpet affects "the sun, moon, and stars" of our solar system. Aune (II:523) sees a connection with the *fourth* day of creation when the sun, moon, and stars were created (Gen. 1:14-19). This supports the ancillary idea that in addition to everything else He is doing, God is using the judgments of the Tribulation to dismantle, slowly but effectively, the material world He created (cf. 2 Pet. 3:10-13). Each of these light-bearers is "smitten" (Greek *plesso*), a word that suggests an aggressive action, striking a blow. This action "darkened" these light sources.

Who or what strikes them is not specifically identified but the action doubtless originates with their Creator and Sustainer. This is more likely a supernatural intervention than some natural phenomenon like volcanic ash in the atmosphere, smog from a polluted environment, or an eclipse. Ford (139) suggests that the darkening may have happened "because of the brightness of the theophany." But God's part is more active here. The God who spoke the lights into existence in Gen. 1 is able to turn their light down in the same way. Though this darkening occurs when the fourth trumpet sounds, it may well continue throughout the rest of the Tribulation, with normalcy resuming only at the beginning of the millennium.

Interestingly, darkness may be symbolic of deity (Ex. 20:21; Dt. 4:11; 1 Kg. 8:12; Ps. 18:11), judgment, or wickedness and lostness in general (Pr. 4:19; Is. 9:2; Jn. 3:19). Hell is a place of complete darkness (Mt. 8:12). Darkness in the fourth trumpet carries heavy tones of judgment. The plague of darkness (Ex. 10:21-23) is an O.T. precedent, and darkness is characteristic of the Day of the Lord (Is. 13:10; Jl. 2:2; Am. 5:18). Jesus predicted eschatological darkness (Mt. 24:29).

The direct effect of this darkening is an unprecedented shortening of the 24-hour solar day by a third. "And it shall come to pass in that day, saith the Lord God, that I will cause the sun to go down at noon, and I will darken the earth in the clear day" (Am. 8:9). All three light sources are equally "darkened" by a third. That "the day shone not for a third part of it," conclusively confirms "the total absence of light for a third part of both day and night" (Mounce 181). Whether the solar day is shortened or the amount of darkness in each 24-hour period is increased is not clear. Perhaps the luminaries remain intact but their light is prevented in some way from reaching earth. Regardless, this is a fearsome harbinger that world conditions will continue to disintegrate in increasingly threatening ways.

Many interpret the "darkening" non-literally: the taking away of the "light" of truth, or the spiritual darkness of Mohammedism, or the fall of long-established governments in the western empire. Beale (485) calls it "figurative," a judgmental reminding of unbelievers of their separation from God and final condemnation. Spiritual darkness undeniably plays a significant role in the Tribulation and in present world history, but by itself does not satisfy the phenomena described here.

"And I beheld" (v. 13) introduces a brief vision between the first four trumpets and the last three. An "angel" ("eagle" in the majority of manuscripts) is seen flying "in the midst of heaven"

(cf. 14:6; 19:17) with a message for unbelievers. The creature "speaks with a loud voice" and another angel executes the same maneuver when he flies through "the midst of heaven" in 14:6; this argues that an "angel" is more likely than a "bird" (cf. Thomas II:24). "Whether announced by an angel or an eagle, the effect of the trumpet is much the same....The earth is warned of judgment to come" (Walvoord 156).

Most scholars interpret "the inhabiters of the earth" in Revelation as an exclusive reference to unbelievers: "In Revelation 'those dwelling on earth' is regularly used as a designation for all those who reject the gospel and love the earth instead" (Lenski 283). Indeed, the trumpet judgments are directed primarily against them. "All four trumpets are concerned with sufferings imposed on the ungodly that indicate their separation from God and the beginning of their judgment" (Beale 485).

The angel's announcement identifies the last three trumpet judgments to come as three "woes." This word (Greek *ouai*) can also be rendered "alas!" and "is used especially in dirges" (Brighton 224). It is spoken by Jesus 30 of the 46 times it appears in the N.T. Perhaps the last three trumpets are especially woeful because they are directed against people instead of nature.

That "trumpet" in v. 13 is singular focuses on each individual trumpet. The objection of Charles (I:236) and others that the luminaries have already been affected in the sixth seal (6:12, 13) is significant only for an absolutely consecutive chronological sequencing. But sixth seal events have telescoped to the end of the Tribulation period. The language there clearly reflects the catastrophic upheaval of the material world and universe.

Summary
(8:6-13)

A brief period of silence in Heaven followed the Lamb's opening of the seventh seal (8:1). The content of the seventh seal was revealed to be the next series of judgments known as "the seven trumpets" (v. 2), with seven angels who stand before God preparing to blow them. But first this series is introduced in a dramatic way, by another angel, in order to demonstrate the close connection between the prayers of God's people (symbolized by the golden altar of incense) and the judgments themselves (vv. 3-5). The trumpet judgments are in part an answer to the prayers of all saints whereby God not only punishes the unbelieving world but also vindicates the faithful.

After the object lesson on prayer, the seven angels prepared to sound their trumpets (v. 6). John then proceeded to give an account of the first four trumpet judgments (vv. 7-13), which represent an increase in severity over the judgments that began with the seals, moving from "fourths" (6:8) to "thirds" (vv. 7-12). The first four trumpets are eschatological judgments directed primarily against the material earth during the end-time Tribulation. The last three affect unbelieving mankind directly.

The first trumpet judgment consisted of "hail and fire mingled with blood." This divine combination produced a devastating effect on a third of the earth's vegetation, destroying "trees" and "green grass" and other plants within the affected areas.

The second trumpet judgment (v. 8) was "a great burning mountain" cast into the sea. One-third of the sea turned into "blood" as a result. This had an equally catastrophic effect, killing "one-third of sea life" and destroying "one-third of the earth's ships."

The third trumpet judgment (vv. 9, 10) was "a great star from heaven" named "Wormwood," meaning "bitter." This flaming star fell and poisoned one-third of the earth's freshwater sources including "rivers" and "fountains of waters" or subterranean sources. "Many men" died as a result—and probably also from the previous trumpet judgments.

The fourth trumpet judgment (v. 12) was directed against the luminaries of the universe. These were "darkened" in a way that dramatically affected their ability to shine. This was likely a decrease in the intensity, eclipse, or alteration of the 24-hour solar day—either would cause devastating changes on the earth.

The trumpet revelations paused long enough for John to see an angel flying through the midst of Heaven in order to make an announcement. This heavenly messenger heralded a significant change in the application of the remaining three trumpets, introducing the last three trumpets as three "woes." These would cause increased distress since they would be of a more personal nature. Whereas the first four trumpets were directed primarily against the material earth, the last three are terrible judgments directed primarily against the unbelieving population.

Application: Teaching and Preaching the Passage

A study of judgment is more sobering than inspirational. To be honest, it can be depressing to contemplate the end of things in all its tragic ugliness. Millions of recalcitrant unbelievers, fellow human beings, will be doomed to an eternal Hell as a result. This should grieve us profoundly, knowing also that the beauty of the material world is slated for destruction.

And yet there is great comfort and assurance in knowing that the judgments of the Tribulation will be directed primarily against the unbelieving population of earth. Paul said, "For God hath not appointed us to wrath but to obtain salvation by our Lord Jesus Christ" (1 Th. 5:9). Tribulation judgments are the wrath of the Lamb against unbelievers, not believers. This is true whether the church is raptured before the seven-year period begins, in the middle, or at the end. Those who place the rapture of the church somewhere within the period invariably find a way to insulate believers from experiencing the wrath of God in any way. Unfortunately, many Tribulation saints will suffer the wrath of Satan and be martyred for their faith because they refuse his mark.

Those who interpret the apocalyptic images in Revelation should never make the mistake of getting lost in the particulars at the expense of the message itself. In the end it does not make any difference to the victims of exploding volcanoes, flaming meteorites, falling stars, or poisoned water. All are deadly. The question is whether the world is prepared for the kind of future predicted here. Are those we teach and exhort prepared to face this kind of future and meet Christ at the Second Coming?

Suggested Outline. The First Four Trumpets—God's Brass Quartet, 8:2-12: (1) Tune-up or Prelude, vv. 2-6; (2) First trumpet, v. 7; (3) Second Trumpet, v. 8; (4) Third Trumpet, vv. 9, 10; (5) Fourth Trumpet, v. 12.

E. Fifth Trumpet (9:1-12)

1 And the fifth angel sounded, and I saw a star fall from heaven unto the earth: and to him was given the key of the bottomless pit.
2 And he opened the bottomless pit; and there arose a smoke out of the pit, as the smoke of a great furnace; and the sun and the air were darkened by reason of the smoke of the pit.
3 And there came out of the smoke locusts upon the earth: and unto them was given power, as the scorpions of the earth have power.
4 And it was commanded them that they should not hurt the grass of the earth, neither any green thing, neither any tree; but only those men which have not the seal of God in their foreheads.
5 And to them it was given that they should not kill them, but that they should be tormented five months: and their torment *was* as the torment of a scorpion, when he striketh a man.
6 And in those days shall men seek death, and shall not find it; and shall desire to die, and death shall flee from them.
7 And the shapes of the locusts *were* like unto horses prepared unto battle; and on their heads *were* as it were crowns like gold,

274

and their faces *were* as the faces of men.

8 And they had hair as the hair of women, and their teeth were as *the teeth* of lions.

9 And they had breastplates, as it were breastplates of iron; and the sound of their wings *was* as the sound of chariots of many horses running to battle.

10 And they had tails like unto scorpions, and there were stings in their tails: and their power *was* to hurt men five months.

11 And they had a king over them, *which is* the angel of the bottomless pit, whose name in the Hebrew tongue *is* Abaddon, but in the Greek tongue hath *his* name Apollyon.

12 One woe is past; *and*, behold, there come two woes more together.

The fifth trumpet judgment is the first of the three "woes" (8:13): John sees a "star" that had fallen to earth. This obviously refers to an angel, given both the heavenly origin and the personal pronoun ("him," for example) and activities that follow. "The stars, personified as deities in ancient paganism, were sometimes identified with angels in the Old Testament and in Jewish tradition" (Boring 136). The *falling* is a poetic metaphor for this angel's *descent* from Heaven to earth, not a reference to an evil angel (Ladd, *Commentary* 126). The angel is distinct from the fifth trumpet angel and has an important role in the fifth trumpet judgment.

That the key to the abyss "was given" to him is another instance of the "divine passive," an important hermeneutical key in Revelation pointing to the divine

origin and sovereign control of Tribulation events and persons, good or evil (cf. vv. 4, 5, 10). But, for perhaps the first time, the more hellish aspects of the Tribulation emerge with the introduction of "the bottomless pit," especially since the locusts are likely demonic creatures confined in the abyss by God. A great *spatial* contrast is portrayed here: John's visions have enabled him and his readers to see three levels in the spectrum of eternal reality—the classical "three-tiered universe" of Heaven, earth, and Hell.

The angel proceeded to use "the key" to open the bottomless pit (v. 2), implying that the confinement there is involuntary. "Bottomless pit" is literally "the well (or, pit, or shaft) of the abyss." "Abyss" (Greek *abussos*) itself means "bottomless (place)," sometimes used for the abode of the dead (Rom. 10:7) and especially for the place where evil spirits are held (Lk. 8:31; Jude 1:6; Rev. 20:3). It appears in Revelation seven times (9:1, 2, 11; 11:7; 17:8; 20:1, 3), always as a kind of prison for evil powers, including "the beast" (Antichrist) of 11:7 and 17:8, something like the "death row" of the spiritual world. Some suggest that it "indicates hell before the final judgment" (Hendriksen 120) or "a preliminary place of incarceration" (Thomas II:28).

The key given to the angel fits the pit or well or shaft (Greek *phrear*) leading down into the abyss. "The two definite articles in the phrase 'the shaft of the abyss' indicate that the notion of a shaft to the abyss, as well as the concept of the abyss itself, was well known to the readers" (Aune II:525). Ladd (*Commentary* 130) offers: "He now refers to the underworld, which is conceived as a great hollow space in the depths of the earth...connected with the world by a shaft." But that may be more than we know.

Two things followed the opening of the abyss, both supernatural, hellish, and literal (vv. 2, 3). (1) An ominous smoke poured out into the earth's atmosphere, perhaps implying that fires were burning somewhere in this great subterranean abyss (Mounce 185). This smoke and the resulting darkening carries a negative, "judgmental tone" (Thomas II:29). (2) A great horde of supernatural locusts or "evil spirits/ evil angels/ demons" (Mounce 185) arose with the smoke from the abyss.

John compares the supernatural "smoke" to "the smoke of a great furnace," pictured perhaps as a column of smoke rising upward out of a chimney. (Compare the plume of smoke from a nuclear detonation or the eruption of a volcano.) The smoke is ominous, literally obscuring the sun and "darkening" the atmosphere. Some take this figuratively, as "spiritual darkness" (Brighton 236) or "the smoke of deception and delusion, of sin and sorrow, of moral darkness and degradation that is constantly belching up out of hell" (Hendrikson 120). Even Walvoord says, "It seems to portend the spiritual corruption which will be caused by these demons released from their confinement, and it identifies the character of the judgment involved in the fifth and sixth trumpet as that of demonic and satanic oppression" (159). But what John saw was literal smoke, irrespective of the symbolism one might wish to attach to it.

The smoke is not the greatest concern, however; the primary focus is on a plague of supernatural locusts unleashed on the earth—reminding us of the plague of locusts in Ex. 10:1-20 (cf. Jl. 1:7-12,

15; 2:1, 11). "Throughout the O.T. the locust is a symbol of destruction (Deut. 28:42; 1 Kg. 8:37; Ps. 78:46)....They invade cultivated areas in search of food...[and] may travel in a column a hundred feet deep and up to four miles in length, leaving the land stripped bare of all vegetation" (Mounce 186). A locust plague is "one of the severest evils (plagues) of mankind" (Brighton 232, quoting Palmoni).

But these eschatological creatures are not ordinary locusts. The lengthy and surreal description of them and their mission underscores their supernatural nature and points to the basic judgmental, terrifying nature of certain events during the Tribulation. The description of their uniqueness, the kind of torment they inflict ("scorpion-like"), and their selective, persecuting mission argue for an end-times scenario that far exceeds Exodus or any other historical precedent.

Their power is compared to the power of a scorpion (vv. 3, 5). Certain features of the scorpion—its hideous appearance and clandestine and destructive methods—make it especially appropriate to represent future Tribulation horrors. Its most prominent feature is its powerful *sting*, which inflicts significant pain and may paralyze or kill its victim— though not usually fatal to humans. These supernatural locusts with scorpion-like stings are not given the power to paralyze or kill their victims. Instead, they are "given" (the divine passive, again) power to inflict great pain by their sting (v. 5) and thus to "*terrorize*" (Aune II:527).

God places limits on their power and mission (vv. 4, 5). Unlike normal locusts they are *not* to hurt or damage grass, "green things" (plants, crops), or trees.

Instead, these hellish beings, perhaps demons, have been uniquely designed to torment "wicked people" (Mounce 187) for a limited period of time during the Tribulation. Keeping the analogy, they "devour" humans rather than vegetation. These are not literal locusts, then, but literal, hellish demonic creatures that are corporeal and tangible, that persecute real people in a physical way. It is a spiritually inspired plague to judge unbelievers.

A second limitation is that they "hurt only those men which have not the seal of God in their foreheads," and so *not* those who are "sealed" (2:17; 3:12; 7:1-8; 14:1; 22:4). The seal of God upon individual believers (Jews and Gentiles) in the Tribulation indicates belief in Christ and ownership by God and serves as a mark of protection from God's wrath. The sealing of 144,000 Jewish servants has just been recorded in 7:1-8. The last three trumpet judgments are directed exclusively toward unbelievers who have, instead, "the mark of the beast" (13:16-18; 14:9).

Like the Israelites in Goshen, marked with the blood of the Passover Lamb during the plague of the firstborn (Ex. 12:13), Tribulation believers are protected from this demonic plague. The "locusts" must skip over those "marked" with the seal of God (belief) and afflict only those who have not the seal of God in their foreheads. *Satanic persecutions* of Tribulation saints should be distinguished from those judgments that God sends against unbelievers such as the seal, trumpet, and bowl judgments. The latter are divine in origin and utility. The satanic beast practices a type of *reverse discrimination* against Tribulation saints because they refuse to carry his mark (13:16-18; 14:9).

"And to them it was given" (v. 5)—another instance of the *divine passive*, indicating divine origin and control—points to the locusts' God-given power over unbelievers. Again, God limits them: they are not to kill, but to torment those under this judgment with an intense, physical torment.

The final limitation imposed by God is the duration of "five months" (v. 5). This limitation also illustrates mercy even in judgment. "Five months" is a somewhat unusual designation. One explanation is that this reflects the natural life cycle of a locust (Charles II:243). Aune (II:530) thinks that "five" in the Bible suggests a "few," thus indicating the plague's *limited* time period. At any rate, the limitation is merciful; but it is short-lived in light of the additional "woes" of judgment yet to come.

"In those days" (v. 6) telescopes the reader to the distant future. Thomas (II:33) notes a subtle change in the narration: John's comments on the fifth trumpet use the future tense throughout v. 6, thus changing from mere description to prediction and making the entire verse *prophetic*. The very phrase "in those days" has the ring of prophecy, since "those" (Greek *ekeinos*) looks away from one's present situation (Aune II:486).

The pain from the "stings" of these demonic locusts is so severe that men seek death for relief. But they are unsuccessful because of God's strict design for the judgment. The last part of v. 6 is reminiscent of Hebrew parallelism, expressing the same basic truth as the first part (Lenski 292). The repetition adds emphasis: the certainty of judgment during the Tribulation period contrasts with worldly justice that is often aborted through imperfect lawyers, judges, juries, and laws. Judgments administered on unbelievers during the Tribulation cannot be avoided. The inability to find relief through death intensifies the torment.

All of this indicates real and unprecedented catastrophe, in sharp contrast to unsatisfactory attempts to make the fifth trumpet figurative for things like "spiritual warfare" or psychological turmoil, or even to identify it with events in past church history. These creatures, in appearance and ability, have an otherworldly quality. Besides, the picture is not of Christians seeking relief but of *unbelievers seeking relief*. It is also incongruous to think that this judgment is directly under Satan's control, even though the locusts arise from the abyss and have a leader or king named "Abaddon" or "Apollyon" (v. 11), meaning Destroyer. It is absurd to think that Satan, if given a choice, would afflict his own followers during the Tribulation or at any other time. Additionally, the abyss and Hell itself are places created by God for the purposes of judgment and confinement. The Sovereign God alone governs all entrances, exits, and confinements according to His purposes.

These extrordinary locusts "have to be reckoned among the more bizarre creatures in the Apocalypse" (Mounce 188). The physical characteristics of their bodies form a composite monstrosity that would make any modern creator of science fiction envious. Thomas (II:34) notes that "as" or "like" is used nine times in John's description, so that though it is literal it probably provides rough equivalents only, indicating "the inability of John to describe precisely what he has seen" (Beale 499, quoting Prigent).

That the "shapes" of the locusts were "like unto horses prepared unto battle" (v. 7) suggests the appearance of a war-horse (NASB). Moffat (407) says that Arabian poets often compared locusts to horses. But these are not actual horses nor are their "riders" human: the comparison is not strict identification.

Further, something similar to "golden crowns" was on their heads. These are crowns of victory or celebration (Greek *stephanos*), perhaps pointing to the success or irresistible execution of their mission (Aune II:532). Ford (151) suggests they may be the "bronze helmets of Roman legionnaires burnished with gold." (See Thomas II:35 or Keener 267, 268 for various views.)

Their faces are like "the faces of men," but they are not men, as their other inhuman features make clear. The similarity may represent their "intelligence" (D. Johnson 149). Still, the human-like faces serve to demonstrate that they are not ordinary locusts.

They have hair *like* "women's hair": that is, *long* (v. 8; cf. 1 Cor. 11:14, 15). Some think the hair was "disheveled" (Aune II:532), suggesting "the roughness of barbaric hordes" (Hughes 111). Swete (118) notes the suggestion that the long hair indicates immorality; but in fact the only thing indicated is that their hair is long.

Their "teeth" (v. 8) are *like* lions' teeth, perhaps "a proverbial expression for something irresistibly and fatally destructive" (Aune II:532). Ladd, (*Commentary* 133) thinks this may symbolize "the voracity with which the locusts devour the vegetation." Long hair and long teeth contribute greatly to their grotesque physical appearance and may have no symbolism beyond evoking terror. They use their "tails" and not their teeth to torment unbelievers. Historicist interpreters might point to the ancient Parthians who were "known for wearing long hair" (Ladd, *Commentary* 133).

Warhorses were often fitted with breastplates for protection. Likewise, these creatures wear something like "iron breastplates" that suggest a degree of invincibility (v. 9). Additionally, they have "wings" (v. 9) that together sound like a great number of horse-driven chariots "thundering" (NIV) into battle. The frightening sound contributes greatly to the dreadfulness of their activity (cf. Jl. 2:1-11; Jer. 51:27).

The "locusts" have tails, *like* a scorpion's tail (v. 10; see v. 3), with "stingers." They use this power to "hurt" earth's unbelieving population, referring to the excruciating physical pain thus inflicted—apparently far worse than that of a natural scorpion or other stinging creature: "As awesome to the eye and ear as these other elements are, they are only peripheral in comparison to the damage caused by their tails" (Thomas II:37).

Interestingly, more is recorded about the grotesque appearance of these creatures than about their mission: the picture may well be worth more than a thousand words! It is also interesting that some interpreters view these "locusts" as entirely symbolic, though with wide variety: "the self-defeating... tormenting nature of wickedness in the human soul" (Poythress 123); "the venom of inhumanity which is engendered by ungodliness" (Hughes 110); things like "alcohol and drug abuse, insatiable yearning for sexual promiscuity, sexually transmitted diseases, collective hysteria and subgroup tantrums, neurotic drives in diverse forms, driving

passions for power, prestige, and wealth at the expense of one's own humanity, torments of psychic disorders, debilitating inability to maintain personal relationships, and other 'locusts'" (Krodel, quoted in Mounce 190). D. Johnson (148) says, "The plague they represent is not agricultural but spiritual...demonic torment inflicted on the minds and souls of 'those who dwell on the earth,' who lack the seal of God's name on their thoughts and lives." Beale (497), a modified idealist, calls the torment "primarily spiritual and psychological." But even though mental torment may drive many to seek death for relief, there is no reason the element of physical torment or pain should be ruled out. No doubt both are components of fifth trumpet torment. But the basic purpose of these literal, hellish beings from the abyss, as portrayed in the text, is physical torment of the unbelieving population of earth during the Tribulation. The cause is a literal sting; the effect is literal pain. The hope that some will repent as a result is an ancillary purpose if at all.

An "angel king" from the abyss, known as "Abaddon" in Hebrew and translated as "Apollyon" in Greek (ALGNT 69), rules the demonic "locust" army (v. 11; cf. Pr. 30:27). The two names are equivalent, meaning "Destroyer," and reflect an O.T. background (Job 26:6; 28:22; Ps. 88:11; Pr. 15:11). In the O.T. the term is associated closely with hell, death, and the grave (Thompson 119). There is no justification for identifying the evil angel with the pagan god "Apollo," nor does this seem to be a veiled reference to an evil Roman emperor.

Predictably, some identify Satan as this demon king (Hughes 111). A core motivation of Satan is destruction (Jn.

10:10) and he is the ultimate ruler in Hell. "King" seems to imply authority over a demon hierarchy (Eph. 6:12), making this identification plausible. "The angel" may also suggest a specific and well-known person, Satan himself. But Aune, though acknowledging this, cautions: "It is not at all clear that the angel of the abyss is a designation for Satan, for he is carefully named elsewhere with a selection of aliases in two different contexts (12:9; 20:2), and neither Abaddon nor the angel of the abyss is mentioned again" (II:534). Perhaps Apollyon is not Satan himself but his proxy or field commander in the form of another evil angel (Beale 503). At any rate, the fact that he is *named* points to his existence as a real person rather than a symbol, and if this were an alias of someone else, that would likely have been indicated.

This angel has an evil nature, associated with the hordes of demon creatures as their leader. He is appropriately named "Destroyer" inasmuch as he commands destructive minions. It seems surprising that Apollyon's army of demonic creatures torture *unbelievers* rather than believers. However, it should be noted that whatever authority he has in this position, it coordinates in a subservient way with God's sovereign purpose through the fifth trumpet judgment.

Verse 12 serves as transition to the sixth trumpet judgment, the second "woe." One woe is considered past when, mercifully, at the end of five months, the infernal locusts have finished their mission. Two more—the sixth and seventh trumpet judgments—remain; the woes—the last three trumpets—follow one another chronologically. This is preferred to viewing them only as the order in which the visions, which reflect simultaneous events, were received (Beale 505). "Hereafter" is literally "after these things."

As noted, there are various suggested identifications of the star, the "locusts," and other particulars. Idealists generally avoid connecting any particulars with *one* historical fulfillment. Preterist interpreters typically focus on the destruction of Jerusalem in A.D. 70 or in the dissolution of the Roman Empire in the fifth century. Historicists look at specific individuals, institutions, or events within broader church history, sometimes overlapping with the preterist viewpoint, with Rome being the common denominator. Futurists put most things within a final, seven-year Tribulation. However, there are exceptions, as when an idealist interprets something literally or a futurist something symbolically. Idealist Brighton believes there will be a period of intense tribulation preceding the Second Coming. Futurist Walvoord interprets the locust army as symbolic of "demonic possession." Futurist Mounce often counsels against interpreting things too literally.

John's detailed description of locust-like creatures would seem to be a case of metaphorical overkill if these creatures were merely symbolic of demonic activity, false doctrine, or something else. It is obvious that they are not ordinary locusts, but they are literal creatures nonetheless. The portrait that John gives us is that they are corporeal, vicious, predatory, militaristic, and demonic in nature, and that they will arise from the abyss during the Tribulation.

F. Sixth Trumpet (9:13-21)

13 And the sixth angel sounded, and I heard a voice from the four horns of the golden altar which is before God,
14 Saying to the sixth angel which had the trumpet, Loose the four angels which are bound in the great river Euphrates.
15 And the four angels were loosed, which were prepared for an hour, and a day, and a month, and a year, for to slay the third part of men.
16 And the number of the army of the horsemen *were* two hundred thousand thousand: and I heard the number of them.
17 And thus I saw the horses in the vision, and them that sat on them, having breastplates of fire, and of jacinth, and brimstone: and the heads of the horses *were* as the heads of lions; and out of their mouths issued fire and smoke and brimstone.
18 By these three was the third part of men killed, by the fire, and by the smoke, and by the brimstone, which issued out of their mouths.
19 For their power is in their mouth, and in their tails: for their tails *were* like unto serpents, and had heads, and with them they do hurt.
20 And the rest of the men which were not killed by these plagues yet repented not of the works of their hands, that they should not worship devils, and idols of gold, and silver, and brass, and stone, and of wood: which neither can see, nor hear, nor walk:

21 Neither repented they of their murders, nor of their sorceries, nor of their fornication, nor of their thefts.

When the sixth angel sounded, John heard "a voice" coming from the vicinity of "the four horns of the golden altar" (v. 13; cf. 16:7; Ex. 30:1-10). This golden altar of incense in Heaven has already been in view with the fifth (6:9-11) and seventh seals (8:3-5). The voice could be from God, Jesus the Lamb, or an elder; but it is probably an angel's voice since they are employed so frequently and no other voice is designated here: perhaps "the angel of 8:3-5" (Mounce 193). Some suggest that "voice" is a metonymy for "all the prayers" of the saints that were offered at the golden altar in 8:3-5 (Swete 121), or that the altar itself is "endowed with speech" (Aune II:536). Regardless, the close connection between this altar and the prayers of saints should be noted (6:9-11; 8:3-5); the reference to it here may represent a continuing attempt to make the connection between the prayers of all the saints and the execution of the trumpet judgments. The sixth trumpet would then be viewed as a vindication of faith in Christ (especially for those who have been martyred) and as an answer to the prayers of all saints.

Placing the voice in the vicinity of "the golden altar which is before God" emphasizes again that God's authority lies behind these actions: "This curse comes by direct divine judgment" (Lenski 301). Otherwise, as for all the judgments revealed, the amazing spectacle portrayed in the sixth trumpet would likely be unbelievable to the readers of Revelation.

The sixth trumpet angel is commissioned to "Loose the four angels that are bound in the great river Euphrates" (v. 14), thus the only one of the seven trumpet angels actively involved in implementing the actual judgment (Mounce 193). There is no apparent connection between these four angels and the four horns of the golden altar or any other group of four mentioned in Revelation (4:6; 6:1f.; 7:1) The four angels of 7:1, for example, are at the four corners of the earth; these are "bound" in the Euphrates. Those controlled "the four winds of the earth" (7:1), whereas these control the "cavalry" of 9:16. It is likely that these four are evil since "bound" typically has a negative connotation: "Good angels are never bound" (Thomas II:43). Even so, that they are bound, and that the command to loose them comes from the vicinity of the golden altar before God, implies that they are under God's sovereign control.

The Euphrates is prominent as one of the greatest rivers mentioned in the Bible (Gen. 2:14; 15:18; Dt. 11:24; Jos. 1:4; Is. 8:7; Jer. 46:2, 6), the eastern extremity of God's original land grant to Israel (Jos. 1:4). "To the prophets the Euphrates was the symbol of all that was disastrous in the divine judgments" (Vincent II:511; cf. Is. 8:7). Many feel that, according to certain O.T. prophecies, an army from the north will one day invade Israel (Brighton 243), needing to cross the Euphrates to reach Jerusalem (Ezek. 38:1-23). The "kings of the east" lead a great army across the Euphrates in 16:12. These four angels could be instrumental in holding these great armies in check until the appointed time (v. 15). Or they might be involved in actually leading the

cavalry (L. Morris 131). When they are "loosed," perhaps their prohibiting ability is primarily in view.

The impact of these four angels is negative: "one-third" of the earth's population is killed as a result (vv. 15, 18); they participate in some confederate way with the deadly activity of "200 million cavalry." The seamless transition from the *angels* (v. 15) to the *"horsemen"* (v. 16) suggests that angels and horsemen are equal partners in the destruction, though if their mission has been simply to withhold the army, their participation is more indirect. The infernal "cavalry" is the actual agent of destruction (vv. 16-18). "Were prepared" (Greek perfect tense) implies that the angels have been bound in the Euphrates for this particular purpose.

"For an hour, and a day, and a month, and a year" points to a divine schedule or agenda within history, sovereignly managed by God (v. 15). The eschatological events predicted in Revelation are not by chance but by design of an intelligent Creator who does things on time every time for a reason (cf. Gal. 4:4), possible because He is omnipotent and omniscient, designing and controlling history from its creation to its consummation. The hellish cavalry, perhaps confederates of the Antichrist, are like a *pawn* moved into place on time by God in order to judge the world.

"To slay the third part of men" indicates the purpose for the releasing of the angels. Unlike the limited torment of the fifth trumpet judgment, the personal judgment of the sixth trumpet is total, the most sobering period of world history to date because of the unprecedented numbers affected. As already noted, the difference between one *third* of men, here, and a *fourth* part of the earth in the fourth seal judgment (6:8) indicates an unambiguous and chronological intensification of the judgments within the Tribulation.

There is even an increase in severity between the fifth and sixth trumpet judgments. The demonic locusts only *tormented* mankind for five months (9:5, 10), while the hellish cavalry *kills* one-third of unbelieving mankind. The clause "the rest of the men which were not killed by these plagues yet repented not of the works of their hands" (v. 20) clearly indicates that physical death, rather than some form of spiritual suffering (psychological torment, demonic oppression, etc.), is in view. Those *not* killed refuse to repent and are themselves spiritually dead; consequently those killed suffered more than "spiritual death." The death inflicted by this "cavalry" must therefore be "physical death, not spiritual or metaphorical death" (Thomas II:45), and this corresponds with viewing the action and torment literally.

Some degree of chronological sequencing between the seals, trumpets, and bowls must be recognized. The recapitulation theory, suggesting that each of these "sevens" retells basically the same events from a different perspective, cannot adequately account for these differences.

Since the sixth trumpet is a display of the wrath of God, the scope of destruction is apparently confined to unbelievers (7:3; 9:4, 20, 21). Believers are clearly distinguishable from unbelievers during the Tribulation, their respective marks being either the seal of God for Tribulation saints (7:3; 9:4) or the mark of the beast for unbelievers (13:16-18).

John "heard" rather than "saw" the number of the horsemen: since he would not have been able to count such a large army, the number must have been revealed to him. The way the number is stated in the various manuscripts varies, but all apparently mean either two hundred million (2 x 10,000 x 10,000), as in several versions, or less precisely an extremely large, uncountable number (10,000's of 10,000's; cf. 5:11). The fact that the vast number of this particular army has *no historical precedent* points to an eschatological fulfillment.

"And thus I saw" (v. 17) marks John's specific focus on the sixth trumpet judgment, viewing the "horses" and their "riders" in a vision—the only time John uses "vision." But the riders are barely noticed before John describes the horses in striking, apocalyptic detail. At first it is difficult to tell when John is describing the horse or its rider, but since horse comes first and is repeated midway in the verse, it seems clear that the breastplate belongs to the horse (Thomas II:47)—and the use of breastplates on warhorses is well documented. The rider becomes incidental and seems to have "morphed" with the horse into a solitary unit of destruction.

The multicolored "breastplates" are of "fire, jacinth, and brimstone"—red, blue, and yellow (NIV: "fiery red, dark blue, and yellow as sulphur"). "Red" (Greek *purros*) is "fire-colored or fiery red" (Vine 515). "Jacinth" (Greek *huakinthos*) is "a hyacinth or dark blue iris" or "sapphire stone" (Vine 332). "Brimstone" (Greek *theiodes*) is "connected with sulphur" (Vine 80) and thus yellowish. Each breastplate probably showed all three colors, corresponding to the "fire, smoke, and brimstone" issuing from the horses' mouths—listed in the same order, with blue meaning bluish smoke.

Their heads looked like "lion's heads" (cf. "lions' teeth," 9:8), thus evoking terror and symbolizing "cruelty and destruction" (Mounce 196). Destructive "fire, smoke, and brimstone" is belched from their mouths (cf "Leviathan" in Job 41:19, 20). These are hideous monstrosities reminiscent of some of the hybridized creatures of Greek mythology, *not* normal horses and riders and therefore not a normal cavalry. Perhaps the riders are demonic, evil angels (Thomas II:46), but if so their origin is not clearly identified (as was that of the demon locusts in 9:1-3). There is some similarity to the sixth bowl judgment to come (16:12-16) but the army there is an earthly one, does not attack fellow unbelieving earth-dwellers, and is itself the eventual object of destruction at Armageddon.

A. Johnson (98) favors a supernatural, demonic identity: "The actual raising and transporting of an army of the size spoken of in v. 16 completely transcends human ability....All the allied and Axis forces at their peak in WW II were only about 70 million." Charles (I:253) notes that "brimstone" is associated with demons and likely points to their demonic identity. Thomas (II:46) calls them "superhuman." Mounce characterizes them as "demonic horsemen who ride across the pagan world spreading terror and death" (194) rather than as symbols of implements of modern warfare (196).

Walvoord and others believe that the riders are men rather than demons. But, while God has used foreign armies (Assyrians and Babylonians, for example) to chastise His people, it is not

Israel but unbelieving peoples who are being judged here. On balance, the riders on the monstrous horses of the sixth trumpet may be either human or demonic. The horses they ride, however, are apparently specially created monstrosities utilized by God to bring judgment against one-third of the earth's unbelieving population during the Tribulation. Attempts by some to identify them with specific modern weapons or vehicles of war should be qualified as sanctified speculation at best (cf. Walvoord 167).

The destruction under the sixth trumpet judgment is catastrophic (v. 18): fully "one-third of men"—one-third of earth's unbelieving population—perishes as a result of the "fire, smoke, and brimstone" issuing from the horses' mouths and from their "serpent-like tails" (vv. 18, 19). Literally, the fire, smoke, and brimstone are "three plagues," plagues (Greek *plege*) being the same word used in the Septuagint for the "plagues" in Egypt (Ex. 11:1; 12:13). Mounce is correct to view each as "a separate plague" (197); the presence of "the" before each —"the fire," "the smoke," and "the brimstone"—points to their individual significance. Collectively, this trio of plagues calls to mind the judgment of God and Hell itself. God used these as instruments of judgment when He rained down "fire and brimstone" on the cities of Sodom and Gomorrah (Gen. 19:24,28). Hell is as a place of fire and brimstone. Summers (a modified preterist), following Gibbon, sees the "fire, smoke, and brimstone" as "three great things combined to overthrow the Roman Empire": namely, "natural calamity, internal rottenness, and external invasion" (159).

There is also power in their "serpent-like tails" (v. 19), distinguished from actual serpents by the word "like." The tails functioned *like* a poisonous snake striking at its victim, with some sort of "head" *on the end* of each tail. Their power to "hurt," though this is the same verb used for the locusts (9:4), is likely as lethal as the "plagues" from the horses' mouths (Aune II:549), giving the horses double power to kill: they are purposely designed to be lethal. The tails with serpent heads may also allude to their demonic nature (Mounce 197) since Satan is described as a "serpent" (12:9, 15; 20:2). Thomas (II:49) suggests that this image may have been especially meaningful to the church at Pergamum where the cult of Asklepios, god of healing symbolized by a serpent, was prominent.

As usual, Lenski interprets the "cavalry" nonliterally as *the world curse in its ultimate stage, delusions of hell overrunning what should be Christian nations*" (306). He thinks that these fatal delusions are presently operating in history and will continue to do so until the end of time. Idealist Beale suggests that this involves both physical and eternal, spiritual death, resulting from "all forms of death" such as "illness or tragedy" (512). But literal, physical death must be in view since unbelievers are already spiritually dead (Eph. 2:1, 5). Furthermore, the attempt to find a historical precedent for these unusual horses in ancient mythology or militant Mohammedism is unproductive in that it fails to address the eschatological and previously unknown nature of these creatures. We must remember that John was simply describing images provided for him in visionary form, not building images to fit things he was familiar with.

Especially incredible is the display of indifference by those who are mercifully spared from the infernal cavalry (vv. 20, 21). They ignore or misunderstand the awesome displays of God's power, much like Pharaoh disregarded those against ancient Egypt (Ex. 7:1-5). Unbelieving survivors are "the rest of the men which were not killed by these plagues." These kept their recalcitrant attitude and "repented not." "Repent" (Greek *metanoeo*) means either "a change of mind leading to change of behavior" or "a change of opinion in respect to one's acts" (ALGNT 260). The unbelieving survivors of the sixth trumpet judgment do not repent in any sense of the word but "continue to worship the very malignant forces that are bringing about their destruction" (Mounce 198). God's judgments during the Tribulation are not simply retributive but are designed to prompt sincere repentance and to turn unbelievers to Christ (2:5, 16, 21, 22; 3:3, 19; 9:21; 16:9, 11). But in the end, the effect is similar to the hardening effect the Exodus plagues had on Pharaoh; they refuse to repent of idol worship or of the immoral behavior associated with it. History has amply demonstrated that the sin of *idolatry* never goes away. It is still a problem during the end-times Tribulation and appears on the major list of sins in 21:8.

"The works of their hands" is idolatry: "All men must worship either the God who made them or gods of their own making" (Caird 123). Those who have survived the seal and trumpet judgments to date continue to make their idols or images, using various materials; John lists five: gold, silver, brass, stone, and wood. Though idolatry is typically associated with the *image* of some pagan god, Paul argued that it is also (1) the worship of demons (1 Cor. 10:14, 19, 20, 21, 28); (2) the worship of "the creature more than the creator" (Rom. 1:25); and (3) "covetousness" (Col. 3:5; cf. Gal. 5:20). "The works of their hands is an expression denoting the full range of human activities in life, particularly occupations and livelihoods. Therefore, any alternative to Christ and to faith in Him alone is idolatry (1 Jn. 5:21)" (Brighton 247). Idolatry was one of the major obstacles that Jesus exhorted the first-century Christians to overcome (2:14, 20). Most cities of the first century were rife with idolatry.

The unbelieving survivors of the sixth trumpet judgment are undeterred in their worship of "devils" (Greek *daimonion*), literally "demons. Aune (II:543) suggests that "and idols of gold, silver, and etc." may be "epexegetical": "that they should not worship demons, *that is,* idols." Worshiping an idol becomes the same thing as worshiping a demon since demons are behind them. Offering a sacrifice to an idol is the equivalent of offering a sacrifice to a demon—the very connection made by Paul in 1 Cor. 10:20, 21.

The unrepentant people of earth also persist in other sinful behaviors (v. 21; cf. 16:11,21): "Immorality of every description was the natural sequel of demonic worship and idolatry" (Charles I:255). These acts include "murders" and "sorceries" (Greek *pharmakeia*), which involve the use of magic potions, charms, or drugs; in the plural, as here, it equates to "*casting of magic spells, witchcraft, sorceries*" (ALGNT 397). "The practice of magic was widespread in the ancient world and was particularly prevalent in Asia Minor and Egypt" (Aune II:544).

Further, the unrepentant continue to practice "fornications" (Greek *porneia*), which may mean (1) "generally, every kind of extramarital, unlawful, or unnatural sexual intercourse"; (2) "distinguished from adultery (*moicheia*) in the same context"; (3) "as a synonym for unfaithfulness, adultery"; (4) "metaphorically, as apostasy from God through idolatry" (ALGNT 323). Here, it probably refers to sexual sins in general.

They also continue to steal. Together, the sins violate the sixth, seventh, and eighth commandments (Ex. 20:13, 14, 15). In the end, those who do not repent of idolatry and its associated sins cannot enter Heaven (21:8).

Summary
(9:1-21)

When the fifth trumpet sounded (first "woe"), John saw a "star" fall from Heaven to earth (v. 1)—actually an angel, since the key to the bottomless pit was given to him. His falling is a poetic way of describing the specially commissioned angel's descent to the abyss. The key represents God's sovereign control over this special holding place where evil angels are confined before being placed in Hell permanently. The angel is similar to the one in 20:1-3.

When the angel opened the shaft of the abyss, an ominous "smoke" poured out into the earth's atmosphere (v. 2), obscuring the sunlight and heralding the arrival of an unnatural "locust plague" originating from the abyss (v. 3). The demonic nature of the locusts becomes apparent from John's description: they had power like the scorpions of the earth to sting their victims—not to destroy earth's vegetation (like normal locusts) but to torment the unbelieving population of earth, "who did not have the seal of God in their foreheads." The torment is limited: the demonic locusts do not kill but inflict pain—for only a "five-month period." Even so, those affected will attempt suicide to gain relief (v. 6). They will not be successful: this is a judgment against unbelievers decreed by God.

These demonic "locusts" (v. 7) were shaped like horses dressed for battle, wearing what looked like "crowns of gold." Their faces seemed human, their hair long like a woman's (v. 8). Their teeth looked like a lion's teeth. They were wearing breastplates of iron. Their movements were noisy like the sound of many horse-drawn chariots on a battlefield (v. 9). Their tails looked and functioned like a scorpion's tail (v. 10). They were ruled by an evil angel named "Destroyer" (v. 11).

After the sixth angel sounded his trumpet (second woe), John heard a voice coming from the vicinity of the golden altar before God (v. 13), commanding to loose the four angels bound in the Euphrates (v. 14). These angels had been confined there until the divinely ordained hour and are now loosed "to slay one-third of the unbelieving population" on earth.

These angels assist an incredibly huge "cavalry" (200 million) (v. 16), God's agents of destruction. Their demonic nature is likewise apparent from John's description, which treats each horse and rider as a unit (v. 17). The horses wore brightly colored breastplates of red, blue, and yellow (fire, smoke, and brimstone). Their heads looked like lions' heads, capable of spitting fire, smoke, and brimstone from their mouths. Their victims are killed by one of these three weapons (v. 18) or by their equally lethal tails (v. 19).

Survivors refuse to repent in spite of the catastrophic loss of life (v. 20). They continue worshiping their lifeless idols and practicing sins associated with idolatry (v. 21).

Application: Teaching and Preaching the Passage

Interpreters of Revelation are tempted to read it in terms of their own time, a practice often associated with historicism. This unfortunately tends to tie the text down. Some contemporary Bible students equate the locust plague with modern military weapons, and the vast cavalry with the army of one of the world's belligerent nations. Some suggest that John is representing some type of nuclear phenomenon in first-century language. The Antichrist is often identified with a given period's most infamous personality. The kingdom of the beast, or spiritual Babylon, is likewise related to a hated nation or institution. Historicist Barnes thinks the sixth trumpet is the record of the fall of the eastern Roman Empire at Constantinople to the Turks in 1453.

Such interpretation is sanctified speculation at best, guesses that should be qualified as such. When we sensationalize beyond the text we often do serious damage. If the text does not say something outright, it is best to leave it there and major on the principle of what is being said. The bottom line in chapter 9 is that the world's inhabitants during the Tribulation will suffer physically and spiritually. Excruciating physical torment will eventually give way to catastrophic death tolls. Yet God's increasingly severe judgments do not bring people to repentance.

There is an element of comfort for believers here, assured and grateful that we are not destined for such wrath (1 Th. 5:9). But such knowledge also challenges us to witness even more actively because that Day fast approaches. The clocks of personal life and time are running down, and windows of opportunity are narrowing. We must inform our world of the awesome future predicted in Revelation and help as many as we can to come inside before it is too late.

Suggested Outline. Trial By Terror, 9:1-11: (1) Terrorists, vv. 1-4; (2) Time, tools, and tyranny of terror, vv. 5, 6; (3) Tracing or profiling the terrorists, vv. 7-10; (4) Tyrant of tormentors, v. 11.

G. Second Parenthesis (10:1—11:14)

1. A mighty angel (10:1-7)

1 And I saw another mighty angel come down from heaven, clothed with a cloud: and a rainbow *was* upon his head, and his face *was* as it were the sun, and his feet as pillars of fire:
2 And he had in his hand a little book open: and he set his right foot upon the sea, and *his* left *foot* on the earth,
3 And cried with a loud voice, as *when* a lion roareth: and when he had cried, seven thunders uttered their voices.
4 And when the seven thunders had uttered their voices, I was about to write: and I heard a voice from heaven saying unto me, Seal up those things which the seven thunders uttered, and write them not.
5 And the angel which I saw stand upon the sea and upon the earth lifted up his hand to heaven,
6 And sware by him that liveth for ever and ever, who created heaven, and the things that therein are, and the earth, and the things that therein are, and the sea, and the things which are therein, that there should be time no longer:
7 But in the days of the voice of the seventh angel, when he shall begin to sound, the mystery of God should be finished, as he hath declared to his servants the prophets.

"And I saw" (v. 1) introduces both a new vision and a change in subject matter—often called a "parenthesis" because it occurs between the sixth and seventh trumpets (like one between the sixth and seventh seals in chapter 7). It inserts additional revelatory material or a pause within the normal narrative. This parenthesis serves a dual purpose: preparing the reader for the sounding of the seventh trumpet (vv. 6, 7) and recommissioning John to record the revelations (vv. 8-11). "This section... validates John's calling as a prophet and indicates that his message...is from on high" (Gonzalez 69).

Idealist Beale, however, says, "The parenthesis does not intervene chronologically between the sixth and seventh trumpets but offers a further interpretation of the church age" (521). Brighton (252) sees the two witnesses of chapter 11 as "the church in mission," and the measuring of the temple as "God's protection of the church that enables them to carry out their mission." But taking chapter 10 as symbolic of *the church* unnecessarily complicates what is being portrayed and requires a significant leap beyond the text. Granted, the role of Tribulation saints in witnessing and preaching during the Tribulation is paramount. But the great angel's pronouncement that the end of time has come (10:6, 7) and the recommissioning of John (10:11) are straightforward enough. Besides, the angel's pronouncement about *the end of time* applies more to the end of the period, when witnessing and preaching are mostly over.

A significant portion of this new vision is devoted to a detailed description of "another angel" (cf. 8:3). As an *angel*, he is unique in appearance and chosen for a special task. "Another" may simply distinguish between this angel and the seven trumpet angels (Ladd, *Commentary* 141) or numerous other angels. Various identifications have been proposed: Gabriel or Michael; the angel of 5:2; or the angel of 1:1; 22:16 (see Brighton 274-278). Some interpreters favor identifying him as "the divine Angel of the Lord, as in the OT, who is to be identified with Christ himself" (Beale 522-525). But all angels by virtue of their presence in Heaven reflect God's glory; more likely, the angel's features are consistent with theophanic elements but not identical, designed not to indicate deity but to enhance the authority of the angel's proclamation about the end of time. The designation offered to us is, simply, "another strong angel." However, the argument that this cannot be Christ because the oath of v. 6 would be beneath His dignity is not by itself convincing; economic submission or subordination is not foreign to Him (Phil. 2:7, 8). As Ford (160) observes,

God even swears by His own Person (Dt. 32:39-41).

Charles (I:259) convincingly argues that Christ is never designated as an angel in Revelation. "In the Apocalypse angels are always angels" (Ladd, *Commentary* 141). All the angels in Heaven probably have supernatural strength (cf. Ryrie, *Revelation* 78). Michaels (133) is appropriately balanced: "Although he is not Christ in person, he can be viewed as a divine agent acting on behalf of God and the Lamb."

John calls the angel "mighty" or "strong" (cf. 5:2; 18:21), perhaps discerned from his size and the impressive volume of his speech, indicating "exalted rank" (Barnes 249). This draws special attention to the dramatic announcement that the end of time has come. The mighty angel's descent from Heaven *to earth* is appropriate because his announcement is from God and concerns what is going to happen to the earth and its unbelieving inhabitants in the end-times of its history.

John's basic vantage point has not changed since 4:1 and continues to be the throne room in Heaven, though some think that the angel's descent to earth (10:1) and John's approach to him (vv. 8, 9) mean that "John has moved from heaven" (Thomas II:60). But such a shift in venue is not indicated; John could see the angel's descent from his original position in Heaven and approach him from there, considering the angel's cosmic height.

The positioning of the angel is supernatural. "Clothed with a cloud," a continuing state (Greek perfect tense), refers as much to his great height as to his heavenly origin or "glory" (Ladd, *Commentary* 141). "Cloud" may also have eschatological significance (Mt. 24:30), since clouds are associated closely with the Second Coming (Mounce 201). Clouds are referred to seven times in Revelation (1:7; 10:1; 11:12; 14:14, 15, 16). Clouds were often thought of as a vehicle for heavenly beings (Acts 1:9), but here the clouds indicate, instead, the angel's colossal stature (Brighton 257), a carefully designed symbolism enabling him to put one foot on the sea and the other on land (v. 2).

Likewise, his head was fitted with a surrounding "rainbow," perhaps distinct in color from the one surrounding God's throne (4:3) and "due to the light from the angel's face on the cloud" (Charles I:259). Thomas (II:61) appropriately suggests that the rainbow "betokens mercy in the midst of judgment as it did in Noah's day." Historicist Barnes (250) calls the rainbow an "emblem of peace," but then boldly identifies it as the Protestant Reformation—making too much of symbolism.

That "his face was as it were the sun" indicates that his countenance was intrinsically bright, suggestive of heavenly glory or "Christ's glory" (Brighton 261; cf. 1:16). "The radiance of the angel's appearance marks him as one who bears the image of his Master" (D. Johnson 158). Moses experienced a similar transfer of divine radiance after being in the presence of God on Mt. Sinai without being confused as God (Ex. 34:29-35).

His feet (and legs, no doubt) look like "pillars of fire," a figure typically symbolic of judgment (cf. 1:15; 4:2, 3; Ezek. 1:26-28). Some suggest, instead, that it has an O.T. precedent as God's guidance or light or warmth over Israel (Ex. 13:21), but this link is not clear;

Beasley-Murray calls it "coincidental" (cited in Beale 529).

John eventually focuses on "a little book" or "scroll," held by the angel, in an already opened position (Greek perfect tense). This "book" (Greek *biblaridion*) is a diminutive form, perhaps in contrast to the full-size "book" or "scroll" (Greek *biblion*) in 5:1, 2; the differences between the two are obvious. That the latter word is used for this little book in v. 8 does not necessarily discount that contrast, since it refers back to the "little" book already introduced. "The scroll here is small enough for the seer to swallow" (Beale 526).

That it is "open" indicates that its contents are to be revealed rather than sealed. The key to its contents is perhaps given in v. 11 when the angel informs John that his commission from God will continue. It seems, then, to be symbolic of this recommissioning of John and may contain precisely the remaining contents of Revelation (cf. Aune II:555): "In this scene the Revelation of Jesus Christ is symbolically entrusted to John, completing his commissioning as a spokesman for the Risen Lord" (D. Johnson 157). There are other views: "the Word of God" (L. Morris 133); "the substance of the book of Revelation" (Keener 280); "the reign of Antichrist" (Charles I:260). Brighton (262, 263) has a helpful survey.

The angel positions himself with "his right foot on the sea" (earth's oceans) and "his left foot on the earth" (earth's continents). The combination indicates "the totality of God's creation" (Beale 529), with the angel's exaggerated size probably symbolizing the sovereign authority of God over all and the certainty of the announcement. "This asserts the divine right and determination to execute judgment against a world that exhibits its rebellion through idolatry and immorality" (Thomas II:63). No significance is attached to the distinction between his right and left feet.

Then the angel cried out in a "loud voice" (v. 3). "Cried" (Greek aorist) may suggest a short outburst similar to the roar of a lion. The loud volume would match his great size. Exactly what the angel said is not immediately revealed, and whether it was a specific word or sound is immaterial: he cried out to gain everyone's undivided attention. Or it is possible that the announcement of v. 6 was itself the loud cry. Regardless, immediately following the important announcement, the angel proceeded to recommission John for future service (vv. 8-11).

The loud cry of the great angel prompted an antiphonal response, from (literally) "the seven thunders" (v. 3). These seem to be more than echoes of the angel's great voice or a simple "literary device" (Spitta, cited in Charles I:261). The "thunders" are probably metaphorical for *angelic voices* (Beale 533), not further identified. The sound of loud thunder evokes a response similar to that of a lion's roar, and the Bible likewise connects the sound of thunder with the power of God (Ex. 20:18; Ps. 29:3-9; 77:18). Here it "forbodes the coming peril of divine retribution" (Mounce 203).

John was moved to write down what the seven thunders said (v. 4), indicating that the thunders spoke intelligibly (L. Morris 135). It was obviously his habit, immediately, to record all the revelations he received (Beale 533), as originally commissioned (1:11, 19). In this case, however, he was interrupted and prohibited from doing so by "a voice from

heaven." This might have been the voice of another angel or Christ Himself, since He commissioned John to record the revelations, or even the voice of God (Brighton 268).

The voice commanded John to "seal up" the revelations and "write them not." "Seal" (Greek *sphragizo*) is the verb form of the noun used for "the seven seals" (5:1, 2); see comments there. Perhaps the two actions, sealing and not writing, refer emphatically to the same act. "Write them not" may emphasize "do not begin to write" (Robertson 372, viewing the verb as ingressive aorist). Regardless, "To seal or shut up a vision is to keep it secret from mankind" (Moffat 412). This meant that what the seven thunders revealed was to remain unknown to everyone but John (cf. Dan. 8:26; 12:4, 9; cf. 22:10). Consequently, the revelations remain inaccessible or enigmatic; their content is never supplied.

Nevertheless, interpreters speculate about these unrecorded revelations. Some offer a reason God would reveal something to John and then forbid him to write it down: "This illustrates a divine principle that while God has revealed much, there are secrets which God has not seen fit to reveal to man at this time" (Walvoord 170). Or: "They likely were uttering holy things of God's heavenly glory that were too sacred and beautiful for anyone to hear while still on earth" (Brighton 268). Caird (126) suggests that the "cancellation" anticipates "the shortening of the Great Tribulation period" (cf. Mt. 14:22; Mk. 13:20).

But "thunder" evokes fear and judgment as easily as beauty and grace. In that light, they might have spoken of "another series of warning plagues"

(Mounce 206), no longer needed in light of the final, unrepentant posture of unbelievers after the sixth trumpet judgment (9:20, 21). "In all the other passages where thunder occurs, they form a premonition of coming judgments of divine wrath (8:5; 11:19; 6:18)" (Ladd, *Commentary* 143). On balance, we must remember that whatever is essential to us has been revealed. "We must be content to trust God in the midst of our partial knowledge, confident that He knows everything and governs everything for our benefit (Rom. 8:28-39)" (Poythress 125).

The colossal angel, still standing on the sea and earth (v. 2), "lifted up his hand to heaven" (v. 5)—his *right* hand in the majority of manuscripts. This posture is typically associated with taking an oath to tell the truth (Gen. 14:22, 23; Dt. 32:39, 40; Dan. 12:7). Here it is "a gesture that symbolically appeals to God, who dwells in heaven and therefore sees and knows everything, as a witness to the oath" (Aune II:564).

It is impossible to swear by any higher standard than by God in Heaven (Mt. 5:33-37; Heb. 6:13). No greater authority may be invoked to validate a proclamation that the end of the present world has come. The angel gives two major reasons (v. 6). First, God lives forever and ever (cf. 4:9, 10; 5:14; 15:7), a reference to His eternal existence. That God is eternal and immutable guarantees the fulfillment of His revealed plans for history. Second, God created Heaven, the earth, and the sea and everything in them (cf. Acts 14:15): the repetition of "and the things that therein are" with each tier of creation, is emphatic. Since God created these things to begin with, He also has the power to dismantle them when He

chooses. The decision that "there should be time no longer" (v. 6) did not originate with the angel but with God; the announcement should therefore be accepted as authoritative and certain.

At face value, the word that "time as we know it is about to come to an end" is astonishing, indicating that the condition of the present world is terminal (2 Pet. 3:10-13; 1 Jn. 2:17). The entire scene emphasizes God's sovereign control over creation in general, as its Creator, and over the clock of world history as well. The mighty angel, unchallenged, gives God's decree that "time" is ready to expire. This may also answer the question posed by the martyrs in 6:10, "How long?" (Mounce 205). The suggestion of Charles (I:263) that this means that the time has come for Antichrist's reign to begin, is too narrow, based on equating the seventh trumpet and the Antichrist's reign as the predicted "third woe."

A number of commentators interpret "time" (Greek *chronos*) in the sense of "delay" rather than as a literal end of time. Thomas (II:68) says, "The 'delay' is best seen as that before fulfillment of the mystery of God." This way, the announcement does not mean that there will be no more "time" but no more "delay" in fulfilling "the mystery of God" (v. 7). Certainly, *time* does not cease to exist at the end of the Tribulation— unless it is viewed as something like *time as we know it*; a millennial period is still to come. But the primary meaning of the word is not "delay," and to choose the secondary meaning seems selective (Ryrie, *Revelation* 79): "'Delay' is an inappropriate translation of *chronos* in v. 6, for it assumes that eschatological events have been postponed;

there is no hint that this is the case in Revelation" (Aune II:568).

On balance, it does not seem to make much difference whether we interpret this as "the end of time" or as "the end of delay"; either brings us to that point when the sovereign plan of God for present world history is finished. But "time" has a different nuance than "delay" and is to be preferred (cf. Lenski 318).

The angel's proclamation also connects the fulfillment of "the mystery of God" with "the days of the voice of the seventh angel" (v. 7), referring to the seventh trumpet judgment (11:15). "Days" surely refers to a period of time (cf. Mt. 24:37, 38): the *duration* of the seventh trumpet rather than one single act (Ladd, *Commentary* 145).

The use of "finished" (or, fulfilled) supports the position of this commentary that both the sixth seal and the seventh trumpet telescope to the end of the Tribulation period. Mounce (206) suggests that this is a reference to the entire period inaugurated by the sounding of the seventh trumpet, which means that with the last (seventh) trumpet even "time"—world history as we know it—is finished. The seventh trumpet judgment includes the seven bowl judgments. (This may be the reason some view the "seventh" trumpet as "the last trump of God" heralding the Day of the Lord and the Second Coming; see Is. 27:13; Jl. 2:1; Zech. 9:14; Mt. 24:31; 1 Cor. 15:52; 1 Th. 4:16.) Even though there is much revelatory material to be recorded by John after this point, all events, once inaugurated, snowball toward their consummation at the Second Coming. Idealists view this as the end of the vast church age (Beale 540), whereas futurists identify it with the end of the seven-

year Tribulation. In both views, the period culminates with the Second Coming of Christ.

"Mystery" (Greek *musterion*) appears four times in Revelation (1:20; 10:7; 17:5; 17:7): "In the N.T. it denotes, not the mysterious...but that which, being outside the range of unassisted natural apprehension, can be made known only by divine revelation, and is made known in a manner and at a time appointed by God" (Vine 424). Unregenerate men cannot understand the mysteries of God. Charles (I:265) identifies "mystery" here as "the whole purpose of God in regard to the world." Brighton (270) identifies it as "the coming about of the kingdom of the cosmos of Yahweh and of his Messiah at the end of the present world (11:15)." Michaels and Ladd appropriately suggest that the "mystery" is in fact not so secret since it has been "declared to the prophets." Indeed, Revelation as a whole is a grand exposition of the mysteries of the end-times.

Eschatological mysteries have in fact been previously made known to "his servants the prophets" (v. 7; cf. Am. 3:7). But is this a reference to O.T. or N.T. prophets? Old Testament prophets were certainly familiar with eschatological themes, especially in regard to the hope of a Messiah, and it is hard to exclude them here. They predicted He would rescue and restore the nation of Israel. It is also possible that this is a reference, specifically, to N.T. prophets since the "mystery" aspect of the gospel is a N.T. phenomenon according to Paul (Eph. 3:5; Col. 1:25-27). Still, "his servants the prophets" is a "repeated O.T. formula" (Beale 546). This weighs heavily for including O.T. prophets with the N.T. variety.

At any rate, the angel's proclamation that "there should be time no longer" answers the "mystery" regarding the end of present world history, indicating both when it will happen and that the full manifestation of the kingdom of God is ready to transition completely into history (see 11:15-17). For believers this is good news; for unbelievers it is a message of doom.

This connection between the sounding of the seventh trumpet and the fulfillment of the gospel and kingdom mystery may further indicate that the sixth seal, seventh trumpet, and seventh bowl *telescope* to the end of the Great Tribulation: "The drama has now moved to that moment immediately preceding the final scene" (Mounce 207). The mighty angel's proclamation prepares for the sounding of the seventh trumpet (11:15), which introduces another throne-room vision where the host of Heaven is seen giving tribute to God because the time of the world's judgment has finally come (11:15-19). The fulfillment of this "mystery," therefore, coincides with the sounding of the seventh trumpet and the following events that comprise it.

2. A little book (10:8-11)

8 And the voice which I heard from heaven spake unto me again, and said, Go *and* take the little book which is open in the hand of the angel which standeth upon the sea and upon the earth.
9 And I went unto the angel, and said unto him, Give me the little book. And he said unto me, Take *it,* and eat it up; and it shall make thy belly bitter, but it shall be in thy mouth sweet as honey.

10 And I took the little book out of the angel's hand, and ate it up; and it was in my mouth sweet as honey: and as soon as I had eaten it, my belly was bitter.
11 And he said unto me, Thou must prophesy again before many peoples, and nations, and tongues, and kings.

The "voice from heaven" (v. 4) spoke to John again and commanded him to take the "little book," still "open," from the hand of the mighty angel (v. 8). These repetitions preserve the unity of the chapter: John's vision of the great angel started the vision, and his recommissioning by the same angel brings the chapter to a close.

The authority signified by the heavenly origin of the voice in v. 4 applies equally here. The two halves of chapter 10 are closely linked. For one thing, the same angel continues to speak to John. Further, the focus on the "little book" continues. Yet more, the positioning of the angel on the sea and land is noted "three" times (vv. 2, 5, 8). The connection becomes fairly obvious. The word that "there should be time no longer" (v. 6) and that "the mystery of God should be finished" (v. 7) required a messenger to make these things known to a world unacquainted with the mysteries of God. Thus, the great angel not only reaffirmed John's commission, he also entrusted to him the message of the seventh trumpet, apparently including the remaining contents of Revelation.

John's emotions should not be overlooked; Thomas (II:72) suggests that he was "reluctant." The thought of approaching this colossal angel was daunting. However, one may also assume that the enabling power of the

Holy Spirit was operative here as it had been throughout the revelations (see 1:10; 4:2; 17:3; 21:10 "in the Spirit").

So John approached the angel and asked for the book (v. 9), thereby participating in the visions for the first time. Swete (130) thinks this was done to test John's "fitness." But he did not question that it was the right thing to do. "From heaven" (vv. 4, 8) indicates, each time, that the voice was divine in origin.

The great angel complied with John's request but added an unusual command: "eat it up." "Eat up" (Greek *katesthio*) is intensive: "consume, devour" (ALGNT 224). John must *thoroughly* ingest the contents of this little book. Many commentators point out parallels with Ezek. 2:8—3:3. In both accounts there is an open book of new revelations. Both Ezekiel and John are commanded to "eat" the book before going forth to deliver its message. Both obeyed the command and did in fact find that the Word tasted "sweet." But there are some differences as well: Ezekiel's experience did not include bitterness, and he was commissioned to speak to the nation of Israel; John was commissioned as a prophet to the entire world (v. 11; cf. Jer. 15:16).

The angel explained that though the tasting would be "sweet as honey," it would make his stomach "bitter." The "eating" takes place within the vision and is probably *symbolic* rather than literal. Thomas (II:73) says, "Eat is a Hebrew idiom for receiving knowledge" and he believes that John physically consumed a literal book. But this is one of those instances where advocating too strict a literalism seems to lead to absurdity. John clearly portrays himself as taking and eating the book (v. 10), but this is a *visionary* experience only—

"transparently metaphorical" (Aune II:572), representing "identification with and submission to the divine will" (Beale 551). Just as the angel's great size in the vision is not normative for angels, so it should be obvious that John's eating of the scroll is a symbolic demonstration of how important it is to internalize the Word of God.

The contrast between sweet and bitter is instructive. The Word of God is usually sweet to those who love God (Ps. 119:103; Prov. 24:13, 14; Jer. 15:16). "Sweet as honey" is "a metaphor for agreeable or pleasing speech" (Aune II:572): "life-sustaining" (Beale 550). Hendriksen (125) identifies the book as "the Word of God," the sweetness as "the gospel," and the bitterness as "persecution." A. Johnson (101) says, "Receiving the Word of God is great joy," and bitterness is "the unpleasant experience of proclaiming a message of wrath and woe." The sweetness may refer to delight in God's Word in general, the sweetness of proclamation, or the sweetness of anticipated vindication. The bitterness may reflect genuine sympathy with believers' tribulations during the Tribulation, as objects of persecution by the Antichrist. Or it may reflect the terrors of world judgment for unbelievers. The ultimate conquest by Christ portrayed in Revelation does not provide an optimistic picture for unbelievers. There is no joy in seeing anyone suffer, including unbelievers. Beale (552) identifies the bitterness as "John's anguish over the thought of inevitable judgment and that there will be many who do not respond to the Christian witness." "Every person who struggles to preach and teach the word of God knows this taste, this satisfaction, this sickness in the stomach" (Boring 142).

No doubt John was encouraged by the angel's charge, "Thou must prophesy again" (v. 11). To prophesy may be understood in two basic ways, either as the proclamation of the Word in general (forthtelling) or in the more limited sense of predicting (foretelling) future events. Perhaps the reference is to John's eventual departure from Patmos to continue his mainland ministry. Or it might be understood in the sense described by L. Morris (139): "He has spoken of his book as a prophecy (1:3), so he can be said in a measure to have prophesied already in what he has recorded." In this sense, the remaining revelations to be recorded by John would fulfill the promise.

Instead of "he said" (v. 11), most manuscripts read "*they* said." If this should be correct, then it may be either an example of "indefinite reference" (Thomas II:74), as in 12:6; 13:16; 16:15, or a combination of the heavenly voice (vv. 4, 8) and the great angel (vv. 9, 11).

John *must* continue to prophesy: after recording the revelations, it was important for him to give them to the world. The revelations were not over, only at the midway point. Roughly half of Revelation remained to be given. Once completed and codified in scroll or book form, it must be delivered to the churches and the world at large.

"Before" (Greek *epi*) can also mean *against* the unbelieving population of the world; indeed, a major thrust in the remaining revelations is God's continuing judgments against the Antichrist, Satan, the world systems, and those who follow them. But it sometimes has a more neutral sense, accurately represented by the translation "before" or "about or concerning" (Aune II:573,

574). The result of the prophesying affects unbelievers ultimately in the same way, whether the revelations are conceived as "about" or "against" them (Ladd, *Commentary* 148). Either way, the message of the revelations must be "proclaimed" to a world ignorant of the information regarding its future and powerless to avoid that divinely ordained future. The predicted catastrophic judgments that devastate the material and political world, the degree of individual suffering and torment, and the government of Antichrist will overwhelm the population of earth.

John's audience will include "peoples," "nations," "tongues," and "kings" (v. 11; cf. 5:9; 7:9; 11:9; 13:7; 14:6; 17:15): in other words, everyone. The terms indicate groups of humanity distinguished by ethnicity, nationality, language, and class. Including "kings" is noteworthy: "In Revelation 'kings' are almost universally arrayed with the dragon, the beasts, and the harlot against the Lord and his Messiah" (D. Johnson 164). Indeed, they have a prominent role in the Antichrist's confederacy before being eventually conquered by the *King of kings* and *Lord of lords*.

Summary (10:1-11)

The second parenthesis of Revelation yields additional revelations between the sixth and seventh trumpets, opening as John sees a mighty angel descending from Heaven to earth (v. 1). The angel is impressive. That he was clothed with a cloud apparently refers to his tremendous height, his head reaching into the clouds. A rainbow about his head may be due to the prismatic effect of his radiant countenance, bright like the sun. His feet and legs were like fiery pillars. Even though these features were similar to phenomena typically associated with deity, the angel was likely not Christ—he is not so designated—but, as John states, another of God's mighty angels. His great size and radiant appearance confirmed the angel's heavenly origin and authority.

The great angel was holding a little book, open in his hand (v. 2), and placed his right foot on the sea and his left foot on the earth. This posture represented God's position of sovereign control over all the earth.

Then the angel cried out loudly, compared by John to the fearsome roar of a lion and commanding the attention of those who heard (v. 3). Seven thunderous voices from Heaven responded antiphonally (v. 4). John was about to record what the seven thunders said but was stopped by another voice from Heaven, commanding him to seal them up instead.

The great angel raised his hand toward Heaven (v. 5) in order to take an oath before God. The oath itself extolled two of God's attributes as a basis for the authority and truth of what he was about to announce (v. 6): His eternal existence and His role as Creator of Heaven, earth, the seas, and everything in them. With the authority of God the angel gave his amazing, sobering proclamation that "time should be no longer."

The angel explained that this would happen in connection with the sounding of the seventh trumpet (v. 7). He equated this as the end of things, the fulfillment of the mystery of God that had been predicted through Old and New Testament prophets. This was another way of saying that the end of time or the

end of God's plan for the ages revealed in the Bible had finally arrived.

John then took part in his own recommissioning ceremony (vv. 8-11). A voice commanded him to take the little book from the great angel's hand. John promptly obeyed and was instructed to consume the book, that it would be both sweet and bitter. This was done to symbolize John's continuing role in receiving the Word of God and as preparation for future mission.

John consumed the book and experienced exactly what the angel had said. The sweetness is consistent with the more pleasant features of God's Word. The bitterness indicates the more negative features: coming judgment and perhaps the persecutions and tribulations of God's people. The little book probably included the parts of Revelation yet to be recorded.

The angel gave John a sure prediction that his ministry would continue beyond his banishment on Patmos. He must prophesy again before "peoples, nations, tongues, and kings."

Application: Teaching and Preaching the Passage

This chapter should provide encouragement to those who teach and preach the Word of God, even as it must have to the beleaguered Apostle. John was probably an old man at the time of his banishment to Patmos. He might have suffered harsh conditions of deprivation and hardship. Whatever our circumstances, they are probably not worse than John's.

In this light, the news of John's continuing ministry beyond Patmos takes on added significance. His usefulness was not over. There was still a job to do, and an important one at that. The revelations that John had faithfully recorded must be delivered to the mainland churches and to the unbelieving nations and kings of the world. Likewise, our mission is never finished: we too have been commissioned to deliver God's Word about the future, predicted in Revelation, to our world.

Neither the Word nor the Christian life is all sweetness. Persecution, physical ailments, death, and the spiritual perishing of many are not pleasant but must be treated in a balanced presentation of God's truth. Though the ninety and nine take comfort because they are safely within God's fold, their joy must be tempered by the sober realization that many are lost or astray. A teacher or preacher cannot take delight or deliver his message of judgment and hell with sweet relish that God is going to punish one's enemies.

Suggested Outline. Our Continuing Commission, 10:1-11: (1) The Awesome Authority (behind our commission), vv. 1-4; (2) The Announcement (the world is coming to an end), vv. 5-7; (3) The Action (renewal of commitment to "prophesy"—to teach and preach), vv. 8-10; (4) The Area (peoples, nations, tongues, kings), v. 11.

3. Two Witnesses (11:1-14)

The "parenthesis" that began in 10:1 continues with the presentation of the "two witnesses," providing an excellent example of the complexities involved in interpreting Revelation. Some scholars suggest that it is the most difficult material in the book.

The commentaries reveal wide differences. Mounce (212), though a futurist, advocates a *symbolic* view of the chap-ter, calling the first section "the fate of the witnessing church during its final period of opposition." For him the two courts of the Temple represent the church from "two different perspectives." Thomas (II:82), also a futurist, interprets the images *literally*: "a literal temple that will exist in actuality during the future period just before Christ returns."

A. Johnson (103) suggests that there are two ways of characterizing all the basic viewpoints. One casts the chapter as dealing with "the Jewish people and their place in the plan of God"; the other treats it symbolically as "a reference to the Christian church." (Ladd, *Commentary* 149, 150 surveys four basic viewpoints.)

**1 And there was given me a reed like unto a rod: and the angel stood, saying, Rise, and measure the temple of God, and the altar, and them that worship therein.
2 But the court which is without the temple leave out, and measure it not; for it is given unto the Gentiles: and the holy city shall they tread under foot forty *and* two months.
3 And I will give *power* unto my two witnesses, and they shall prophesy a thousand two hundred *and* threescore days, clothed in sackcloth.
4 These are the two olive trees, and the two candlesticks standing before the God of the earth.
5 And if any man will hurt them, fire proceedeth out of their mouth, and devoureth their enemies: and if any man will hurt them, he must in this manner be killed.**

6 These have power to shut heaven, that it rain not in the days of their prophecy: and have power over waters to turn them to blood, and to smite the earth with all plagues, as often as they will.
7 And when they shall have finished their testimony, the beast that ascendeth out of the bottomless pit shall make war against them, and shall overcome them, and kill them.
8 And their dead bodies *shall lie* in the street of the great city, which spiritually is called Sodom and Egypt, where also our Lord was crucified.
9 And they of the people and kindreds and tongues and nations shall see their dead bodies three days and a half, and shall not suffer their dead bodies to be put in graves.
10 And they that dwell upon the earth shall rejoice over them, and make merry, and shall send gifts one to another; because these two prophets tormented them that dwelt on the earth.
11 And after three days and a half the spirit of life from God entered into them, and they stood upon their feet; and great fear fell upon them which saw them.
12 And they heard a great voice from heaven saying unto them, Come up hither. And they ascended up to heaven in a cloud; and their enemies beheld them.
13 And the same hour was there a great earthquake, and the tenth part of the city fell, and in the earthquake were slain of men seven thousand: and the remnant were affrighted, and gave glory to the God of heaven.
14 The second woe is past; *and,* behold, the third woe cometh quickly.

John's personal participation continues: he is given, as a measuring device, a "reed-like rod" (v. 1). "The" angel is "the mighty angel from heaven" (10:4, 8); he delivered the measuring rod to John while still standing on the earth and sea (10:2). "Reeds" were bamboolike canes found in abundance in areas near the Jordan, used for measuring in three- or six-cubit lengths (ISBE IV:63; cf. Ezek. 42:16). After giving John the measuring reed, the angel commanded him to "Rise and measure the temple of God," following a pattern found in O.T. prophets; cf. Is. 20:2-5; Ezek. 12:1-7.

Taking the Temple's measurements is symbolic. The scene has apparently transitioned from Heaven to earth, made clear by the reference to earthly Jerusalem as "the holy city" (v. 2; cf. Is. 48:2; 52:1). The angel predicted that "Gentiles" would rule ("tread under foot") Jerusalem for a period of "forty-two months" (three-and-a-half years; cf. Dan. 8:13, 14; 9:26; Lk. 21:24). This clearly differentiates it from the heavenly city and makes problematic identifying "the holy city" symbolically as the new Israel or church, requiring an explanation how unbelieving Gentiles ever "rule" over the church. The New Jerusalem does not come into view until much later.

"Measuring" may be for destruction or preservation (Aune II:604); most take it here for the latter. Ford (176) lists four possible meanings: (1) "rebuilding or restoring"; (2) destruction; (3) preservation from physical harm; (4) preservation from spiritual harm. Walvoord (176) cites three Scriptural examples: Jerusalem was measured (in Zech. 2) to outline it as the object of God's judgment; the measurement of Ezekiel's Temple (Ezek. 40) suggested a restored Jerusalem; and the New Jerusalem is measured (Rev. 21:15-17) to amplify its amazing physical dimensions. While the first is negative, the latter two are positive. But the "city" here is designated as "where also our Lord was crucified," symbolized spiritually as "Sodom" and "Egypt" (v. 8), which were judged by God. The idea of judgment is therefore to be included.

John is to measure three things, the first being "the temple of God." "Temple" (Greek *naos*) is the Temple proper, the sanctuary that included "the holy place" and "the holy of holies," rather than the entire complex. The word can be used figuratively for the believer's body (1 Cor. 3:16, 17; 6:19; 2 Cor. 6:16) or for the church (Eph. 2:21, 22; 1 Pet. 2:5). Further, Paul predicted that the Antichrist would enthrone himself in an eschatological Temple (2 Th. 2:4). And the "heavenly" Temple or throne room has been prominent in Revelation since 4:1. Finally, God the Father and Jesus the Lamb are described as "the temple of God" in Heaven (21:22).

Many scholars view the "temple of God" here as the church, suggesting that "measuring" the Temple and its worshipers symbolizes "protection in the period of trial" (Beasley-Murray 1439). Beale (558-562) also interprets the "measuring" to be symbolical of the *spiritual* preservation of true Israel (the church). In summary, idealist interpretation potentially includes a twofold protection or preservation: the faith of individual believers and the success of

their mission as witnesses—not necessarily precluding martyrdom.

But does Revelation suggest that the faith of every believer is preserved during the Tribulation? A major motif in the messages to the seven churches (chapters 2, 3) suggests otherwise, pointing to the ever-present threat of external opposition (the imperial cult, for example) and internal dangers (false doctrines, for example) leading to compromise or apostasy. The measuring of the Temple may indicate a *refining* of those who profess to be in God's family: "John's prophetic ministry calls for a clear separation between those who are holy and those who have defiled themselves with the idolatry of the beast" (A. Johnson 104).

Walvoord (175) represents those who advocate a literal interpretation. He thinks the Temple will be rebuilt "for the worship of the Jews and the renewal of their ancient sacrifices," then "desecrated as the home of an idol of the world ruler" during the Tribulation. This implies that the "measuring" is for judgment, revealing that God's standards have been violated. Ryrie (*Revelation* 83) mostly concurs, defining the measuring as "an act of knowing, claiming, or staking out," but includes the idea that God also takes note of those who are faithful during the first part of the Tribulation and promises to uphold them.

John was also commanded to measure the Temple's altar and worshipers. The altar was probably the brazen altar situated in the courtyard, since worshipers were allowed closer to it. "These worshipers in John's vision represent a future godly remnant in Israel who will worship God in the rebuilt temple" (Thomas II:82). Ladd (*Commentary* 151), less directly, believes that "the prophecy in Revelation 11 is John's way of predicting the preservation of the Jewish people and their final salvation." "Measuring" the worshipers may be the equivalent of "counting" them (NIV) or simply a "zeugma" where one verb is used with three objects but does not fit all three in exactly the same way (Aune II:605).

D. Johnson (167, 168) cites several views of the identity of those "measured": "first-century Jews who believed in Jesus," "the whole church," and "the preservation of the spiritual significance of the temple—worship in the presence of God." On the identity of those represented by the "outer court of the Gentiles" he cites as potential candidates "those who rejected and killed the promised Messiah," "the Jesus-rejecting Jewish community or Jewish polity as a whole," or "the destruction of the physical Temple and city of Jerusalem in A.D. 70."

The angel commanded John not to measure the "court of the Gentiles" (v. 2: literally, "cast/put out the court of the sanctuary that is outside"), apparently the outermost court of the Temple complex (Mt. 21:12, 13). During the Second Temple era, Gentiles were forbidden to go any farther than this. The Jewish areas were measured here, probably not only because they are sanctioned in the O.T. and represent access into God's presence, but because special significance is being attached to the Jews during the Tribulation.

Ladd (*Commentary* 152, 153) explains the significance of distinguishing between preserving the Temple itself, representing a Jewish remnant who are true worshipers of God, and the city of Jerusalem, representing the Jewish people as a whole. The nation (Jerusalem, the outer court) as a whole is judged as apostate, made clear by the characterization in v. 8. But a believing remnant has accepted Jesus as the Messiah and is preserved. This correctly combines both elements of preservation and judgment happening during the Tribulation; the faithful will be spared from God's wrath, the wicked will be judged.

Another viewpoint equates the outer (Gentile) court with "worldly" or false Christianity not under God's protection or "measurement." Ryrie (*Revelation* 84) calls the symbolism of the outer court "utter rejection." According to this viewpoint, the command to "cast out" refers to worldly, compromising, false believers; they are "excommunicated" (Hendriksen 128). Only those who are "measured" (v. 1) are safe. Even if referring to the outer court itself, being left out symbolizes "removal or exclusion from God's favor" (Thomas II:83).

The distinction may suggest that the Temple and its Jewish areas (a believing Jewish remnant: 12:6) will be protected, whereas the Gentile area—whatever it symbolizes—will not be. "For it is given" (v. 2) is *the divine passive* again, used to indicate divine origin or control. Old Testament history is replete with examples how God has "given" or "allowed" judgment to fall on Israel, particularly the city of Jerusalem and the Temple. During the Tribulation Jerusalem will once again be given over to Gentile aggressors (Antichrist's regime) for the time period prescribed in v. 2.

"The holy city" (v. 2) refers to earthly Jerusalem during the Tribulation, an identification made clear in v. 8—though some interpret it figuratively as "the community of the faithful to Jesus Christ, composed of believing Jews and

301

Gentiles" (A. Johnson 106). Beale (568) echoes this idealist perspective, identifying "the holy city" as "the persecuted true people of God" and "the outer court" likewise as "the community of faith in which God dwells." But though the principle of divine protection of the church is valid, the idealistic viewpoint errs here by identifying "temple" as the church instead of the remnant of Israel and "Jerusalem" as something other than the literal, eschatological city of Jerusalem. Different advocates of a figurative interpretation differ radically, and that is the problem with this approach: there is no governing standard once a literal or historical approach is abandoned. When "the New Jerusalem" is intended elsewhere, it is identified by a phrase like "coming down from God out of heaven" (21:2); here the earthly city is carefully referenced in typical terms.

"Tread under foot" is an expression of *dominance* (Lk. 21:24), apparently indicating Gentile political control of a literal Jerusalem during the Tribulation. References to Antichrist's activities during this period gradually develop and become clearer subsequently, and we must resist reading what is ahead back into these initial hints. But we note that until relatively recently the city of Jerusalem was dominated by foreign nations, going as far back as the Babylonians.

Mounce, though a futurist, offers a symbolic interpretation: "The measuring of the church is a variant of its being sealed, and the trampling of the city is the great tribulation" (214). Idealist Beale (566) equates it with "an attack on the community of faith throughout the church age." Predictably, some futurists attribute this persecution or "trampling" to the Antichrist in the latter half of the Tribulation. Though many believers (Jews and Gentiles) are martyred (trampled), those "measured" (the believing remnant of Israel and other Tribulation saints) are preserved by God (cf. 12:6, 14).

"A time, and times, and half a time" or "42 months" (v. 2) is the prescribed *limitation* of the period in view: "a standard symbol for that limited period of time during which evil would be allowed free rein" (Mounce 215). Though the Scriptural expressions vary in the way they refer to the three-and-a-half-year period, the time is the same whether measuring in "times," weeks, days, or months. Idealist Brighton (285) sees the Temple that John measures as Ezekiel's Temple, and stretches the symbolism out over *the entire church age*. Even so, he foresees an intense period of eschatological tribulation culminating with the Second Coming. Some historicists ascribe to the theory that days equal years, making the time period approximately 1,260 years. But as with most such formulas, there is typically no agreement about when the purported period begins or ends. We are left largely unsatisfied because such speculations are arbitrary.

Jesus and Paul predicted Gentile political dominance over Jerusalem (Lk. 21:24; Rom. 11:25); history has confirmed. But the limitation imposed here suggests a relatively *brief* domination, unlike the general church age predicted by Jesus and Paul. Further, it appears to be primarily *political* rather than spiritual, though it is not always easy to separate the two. The specific number (as in Daniel) suggests a period more definite than the entire church age, fitting well with the second half of the seven-year Tribulation, since the

Antichrist's treaty with Israel is not broken until midweek (Dan. 9:27).

The Antichrist is a real person not easily symbolized for an entire age (cf. Thomas II:85). A. Johnson (107, 108) suggests that the preaching of the two witnesses takes place in the first half of the Tribulation, followed by the reign of Antichrist in the last half. But that seems too early in the period for the climactic conflict portrayed in chapter 11. More likely, their ministry takes place in the latter half: the sounding of the seventh trumpet is close at hand. The relatively brief time period of three-and-a-half years will culminate with the Second Coming; it is therefore a reference to *a literal and limited period of time*: "a symbolic apocalyptic number for a divinely restricted period of time (often a limited period of eschatological tribulation)" (Aune II:609).

The precise Temple meant here is also debated. Jerusalem and its Temple have been destroyed or profaned on several occasions: by the Babylonians (586 B.C), by Antiochus Epiphanes (ca. 167–164 B.C.). and by the Romans (A.D. 70). It has not existed since then; at present there is a mosque on the ancient site.

Interpreting "temple" in this context as a literal, "earthly temple" in Jerusalem is preferable to viewing it as the church. Some advocate a *rebuilding* of the Temple in the Tribulation period: "An assignment of the period to a future defilement and domination of Jerusalem and the rebuilt temple is more satisfactory" (Thomas II:860). No Jewish Temple existed when John wrote Revelation, so there was none for him to measure at the time. Then one implication of the command may be that one will exist during the Tribulation to be "measured."

The Temple John was to measure is certainly not the *heavenly* Temple, since Gentile dominance obviously cannot take place there. An earthly location is also consistent with the character and activity of the two witnesses: Heaven does not need their witness. Finally, the seamless connection between "the temple" and "the holy city" (Jerusalem) in vv. 2, 8 also points to an earthly context.

Interpreting this "temple" as symbolic of the church is problematic for several reasons. First, there is no textual cue to do so. Second, since Gentiles and Jews alike comprise the N.T. church, an appeal to *the exclusively Jewish areas* within the Temple is not an ideal analogy to reflect the new oneness in Christ (Thomas II:81). Third, the "temple" and "the holy city" are two separate entities here, as are also the altar, the worshipers, the courts, the Gentiles, and the 42 months. Taking them literally avoids the incongruities that result from seeing everything as a symbol of the church in some way.

Indeed, the "measuring" of the Temple may imply its reconstruction (Ford 176). This, in turn, implies a *regathered Jewish nation* in the land of Israel. One current dispensationalist interpretation is that this three-and-a-half-year period equals the latter half of the Great Tribulation. In this scenario, the regathered Jewish nation rebuilds the Temple with the approval of the world leader (Antichrist) during the first half of the period. The Antichrist breaks this treaty in the middle of the seven-year period (Dan. 9:27), throwing the land of Israel into the center of the increasing world chaos described in the seal judgments. God counters the resulting upsurge of evil by sending the two witnesses of chapter 11 to prophesy for most of the latter half of the period. After a great supernatural ministry, the witnesses are killed by the Antichrist. The unbelieving world's celebration over their deaths is dramatically cut short when the witnesses are resurrected and taken up into Heaven.

God's "two witnesses" are commissioned for a period of 1,260 days—three-and-a-half years (v. 3; cf. Dan. 9:27; 12:6; 13:5). The choice of two may reflect the law of evidence that every word must be established by at least two witnesses (Dt. 17:6; 19:15). The time appears to be the same as that given to the Gentiles' trampling of Jerusalem (v. 2). God's two witnesses are apparently raised up for this very period when anti-God sentiment is rampant.

"Witness" refers to both the character and activity of these two super-servants during the Tribulation. A witness (Greek *martus*, whence our "martyr") bears testimony to what he sees or knows (Vine 680), which may sometimes lead to martyrdom (6:9). These men exercise their "witness" by "prophesying" (preaching). "Prophesy" (Greek *propheteuo*) means to either "tell forth" or "foretell" (Vine 492, 493). Revelation obviously does both, and preaching its contents would also involve both. The message of the two witnesses probably included the basic gospel and the predicted events of the Tribulation and beyond as indicated in Revelation. Their personal testimony of Jesus (cf. "the testimony of Jesus" in 1:2, 9; 12:17; 19:10; 20:4), their character, and their miracle-working power will be part of their witness for God.

"I will give *power*" (v. 3) apparently refers to *an extra dimension* of miracle-working power. Since "power" is supplied, the text might simply mean that He gives *them* as witnesses to the world—or, as Barnes (273) suggests, that He gives them "the right" to bear witness. Nonetheless, He ordains and empowers them for their prophetic ministry. The central feature in Zech. 4:1-14, to which John alludes, is how the Spirit of God will empower Zerubbabel to rebuild the Temple. The two witnesses bear the light of God's Word and the testimony of Jesus to the world while the Holy Spirit keeps them supplied with fuel (olive oil) for burning (witnessing). Though all believers have, by the Holy Spirit, the power necessary for witness (Acts 1:8), these are special cases.

They will "prophesy" (preach the Word) wearing "sackcloth," "a dark-colored fabric made of goat hair or camel hair originally used for making grain sacks" (Aune II:611); cf. 6:12. It was the garment of mourning and repentance (Mounce 217), here apparently symbolizing their message "of impending judgment and a call to repentance" (D. Johnson 170; cf. Is. 37:1-2; Jon. 3:5; Mt. 11:21). The garments befit warnings about judgment, eternal Hell, and the end of the world, likewise appropriate for the urgent message of salvation proclaimed during this period. Many will no doubt respond to the preaching of these witnesses, the preaching of the 144,000 elect of Israel, and other Tribulation saints who share the gospel. But many will refuse their message and celebrate when the witnesses are martyred and silenced.

Views about the identity of the two witnesses fall into three categories (Aune II:599): (1) the *embodiment* of some ancient prophet; (2) the *reincarnation* of an ancient prophet or figure; (3) *symbolical*. If such a pair in history can be identified, then perhaps we can determine which of the three is meant.

Among the pairs proposed are Moses and Elijah, Elijah and Jeremiah, Zerubbabel and Joshua the priest, Enoch and Elijah, James and John, two otherwise unidentified Christian prophets martyred by Titus, Peter and Paul, and John the Baptist and Jesus. Enoch and Elijah have often been suggested, perhaps because neither experienced a natural death (Gen. 5:24; 2 Kg. 2:11). There has also been speculation that Moses was translated, and this, coupled with his and Elijah's appearance at the Transfiguration (Mt. 17:30), has made them popular candidates; see also the predictions of Dt. 18:15, 18 and Mal. 4:5 attributed to them.

The last pair compares very well in terms of the miracles the witnesses perform (Mounce 216), commanding fire and rain like Elijah (2 Kg. 1:10f.) and turning water into blood and calling forth plagues like Moses (Ex. 7:17-25). But it is probably better to say that the two witnesses are modeled after them, or others, than that they are literally resurrected. D. Hill (401) has argued that the two witnesses are raised up in the tradition of O.T. prophets who were called to prophesy to the nation of Israel. This is appropriate for those who see the conversion of a Jewish remnant in the last days.

An entirely symbolical view regards the vision of two witnesses as representing the witness of the church as a whole. "It is more likely, however, that they are not two individuals but a symbol of the witnessing church in the last tumultuous days before the end of the age" (futurist Mounce 217). "They represent the whole community of faith [of all time], whose primary function is to be a prophetic witness" (idealist Beale 573). Hendriksen (129) calls them "the church militant bearing witness through its ministers and missionaries...from the moment of Christ's ascension almost until the judgment day." Charles (I:284) equates them with "the Law and Prophecy." Others suggest that they represent the witness of the O.T. and N.T. or the Word of God and the testimony of Jesus Christ. Where Mounce takes the 1,260 days literally, the idealists view them as representing the "day by day" nature of witnessing during the church age.

John's portrayal of these two witnesses simply does not fit well with the idea that they are symbols. Although such rationalization is understandable, the text does not justify it. "Two" simply does not translate well into "an entire church age of saints" or "all the Tribulation saints" even though it is true that the church always has a kingly and priestly witnessing function. Furthermore, it is extremely awkward to envision "the witnessing church" in any generation as "breathing out fire" that scorches and kills their enemies, or as stopping rain, turning water to blood, or smiting the earth with plagues. This is not the picture of evangelism portrayed in the N.T. When a large group is intended, it is indicated, as in 7:1-8 (144,000) or 7:9-17 (numberless multitude).

Considering the entire context of Revelation, the likely period of activity for the two witnesses is the latter half of the Tribulation (cf. Ryrie, *Revelation* 84). But their personal identity remains an enigma. What we can say for sure is that they are ordained and equipped by

God for ministry during this period. At the least, they embody the spirit, principles, and power of all the Bible's great prophets.

"The two olive trees" and "the two candlesticks" are specific, probably going back to Zech. 4:1-14, where a Jewish candlestick (seven-branched menorah) illustrated the rebuilding of the Temple by governor Zerubbabel (Zech. 4:2) and Joshua, the other "olive tree" of the pair, who was high priest (Zech. 3:1). Zechariah prophesied that the enabling Holy Spirit would bring the task to completion (Zech. 4:6). He identified the "two olive trees" as "the two anointed ones that stand by the Lord of the whole earth" (Zech. 4:14), often interpreted as Zerubbabel and Joshua (Wall 144).

But the figure of two living olive trees supplying oil (the Holy Spirit) for light originally indicated the limitless divine resources *of the Spirit* for building God's house. Both in Zechariah and in Revelation, "They indicate a plentiful supply of oil" (L. Morris 144). The vision here obviously means to link the two witnesses to the precedent in Zechariah. They are also supernaturally empowered by the Spirit of God for their mission. That they stand before the Lord indicates their spiritual qualifications and readiness for service.

These witnesses prove indestructible until their prophetic mission is finished, toward the end of the Tribulation (vv. 5, 6). They are not only empowered for witness, they are protected and endowed with supernatural defensive and punitive abilities. The first of these is "fire from their mouths" (v. 5). Although "if any man will hurt them" is expressed conditionally (the manuscripts vary on the exact form), the point remains that

whenever men attempt to hurt these witnesses, they defend themselves with deadly force, as did Elijah (1 Kg. 18:24, 38; 2 Kg. 1:10, 12): though the fire did not come from his mouth directly, it might as well have. The repetition in v. 5 underscores how serious an offense "hurting them" is: even those who attempt (Greek *thelo*, "desire") to hurt them will be considered guilty of a capital offense. No doubt the witnesses will be attacked both because of the message they proclaim and in retaliation for the punitive miracles they perform (vv. 6, 10).

Though there is a sense in which fire might be a metaphor for the preaching of the Word or a message of judgment, the fire used by these witnesses is not portrayed as proclamation but as a deadly, *defensive* response to attacks. Idealist Beale (580) chooses to regard the "fire" as "the legal pronouncement of the ensuing judgment of the enemies." But this approach downplays the miraculous. A pious platitude has no power to preserve a witness from bodily harm, and mere words do not have power to "kill." Nor can this mean spiritual death, since as unbelievers they are already spiritually dead.

The works of the two include powers over nature. They can (and apparently do) prevent rain in the latter half of the Tribulation (v. 6; cf. 16:12). This too recalls the ministry of Elijah (1 Kg. 17:1), who stopped the rain for a three-and-a-half-year period and later successfully prayed for the rain to return (1 Kg. 18:41-45). They can also turn waters to blood and "smite the earth with all plagues, as often as they will" (v. 6), reminiscent of Moses and the plagues in Egypt. Such power can only come from

God and is a nonverbal affirmation of the witnesses' authority and message.

These prophetic powers serve as more than defense against personal threats; they are mini-judgments applied against specific manifestations of wickedness. Apparently some situations during the Tribulation will merit an immediate response similar to that against Sodom and Gomorrah. The powers are not exercised vindictively but necessarily in order to endure to the end of their designed ministry (Caird 135).

Divine protection lasts until their mission is complete (v. 7). Conflict between them and "the beast that ascendeth out of the bottomless pit" is inevitable since they represent kingdoms in conflict with one another. In v. 7, "beast" (Greek *therion*) "connotes a cunning of unreasoning violence that acts according to its own cruel nature" (Thomas II:92): a *wild animal*, in other words. This beast, introduced here for the first time (used 36 times), refers to the Antichrist of 13:1. Wall (145, 146) appropriately emphasizes that the lack of reference to the "beast" until now matches "the primary emphasis of the first section of John's composition on God's triumph over evil through the exalted Lamb," and that "the parameters for the exercise and effect of his evil power are set by the sovereign God." The beast eventually kills the two witnesses only when God allows.

The beast's ascent from "the abyss" is a figurative description indicating the hellish origin or inspiration of this real man who becomes a nefarious world ruler. Lenski (342) makes "the beast" symbolical of "the whole antichristian power in the world" (and mentions Kretzman's historicist view that the beast is "the Roman antichrist, personified in the pope of the Roman Church"). Idealist Poythress (129) calls him "demonized state power persecuting the church." Antiochus Epiphanes and various Roman emperors no doubt foreshadowed the beast, and the satanic power of the beast is at times institutionalized. But this particular "beast" is the epitome of all who have persecuted the people of God before him, a literal person who comes to power in the end-times.

Already present on earth since the beginning of Tribulation week, the beast demonstrates his ruthless nature when he begins stalking the saints of God as prey. He makes war against them, overcomes them, and kills them (v. 7). Antichrist will have been forced by then to endure the three-and-a-half-year ministry of the two witnesses, powerless to harm them before their ministry is finished. In the end—as was the case with Christ—the authority to kill is divinely granted, but the apparent defeat turns into an even greater display of God's glory: the two witnesses are miraculously resurrected to life after three days.

Those who interpret the "two witnesses" as symbolic (discussed above) suggest that the "death" of the two indicates the destruction of the church's witness as a result of the hostility of the anti-Christian world. But this is not theologically accurate; surely the power of the Word of God or of the Holy Spirit, in witness, can never be quenched (cf. Hughes 129). Nor does it seem likely that God would leave Himself without living witnesses, even to the very end. Jesus said, "I will build my church; and the gates of hell shall not prevail against it" (Mt. 16:18). These contradictions are avoided if one interprets the two witnesses as two literal, specially called prophets who preach and witness during the last half of the Tribulation.

Their bodies are denied burial and put on public display in "the street of the great city" (v. 8). The literal city of Jerusalem is clearly indicated, a logical place for the witnesses' ministry and often conceived in Jewish apocalyptic tradition as the focal point of God's eschatological activity. The witnesses likely begin their ministry there and, in the end, are martyred there. Beale (593) lists five interpretations on the identity of "the great city": (1) Rome, (2) Jerusalem in general, (3) unbelieving Jerusalem, (4) the antagonistic world, and (5) the apostate church. As an idealist, he regards it as representing "the ungodly world in general" (591). L. Morris (146) agrees: "The 'great city' is every city and no city." A. Johnson (110) suggests that, in Revelation, Sodom, Egypt, Jerusalem, Babylon, and Rome refer to the one symbolic "trans-historical city of Satan, the great mother of prostitutes" opposed to God.

It is difficult to understand futurist Mounce's identification of the city as "Rome" instead of Jerusalem (220, 221); perhaps it represents a desire to read "Rome" into Revelation as a polemic of John against the emperors (similar to historicist interpreters). Many interpreters will agree that Revelation often refers to Rome (as "Babylon," for example) but argue for Jerusalem here (Ford 180).

John describes "the great city" as *spiritual* —that is, figuratively—"Sodom and Egypt" (v. 8; cf. 14:8; 16:19; 17:18; 18:2-21). "The figurative likeness suggests utter moral degradation" and the phrase "where also our Lord was crucified" makes any identification other than Jerusalem impossible

(Thomas II:93). Identifying Jerusalem as "Sodom and Egypt" is sharp irony, as is the fact that God's beloved and chosen city was where His Son was crucified. "The author has transformed the historical Jerusalem into a symbol of the unbelieving world, which violently rejected the divine messengers sent to proclaim the word of God" (Aune II:619; cf. Mt. 23:37-39; Lk. 13:34, 35). Jerusalem continues to be focal in the end-times (Walvoord 181).

The residual hatred in the "beast" and his followers against the witnesses is so great that their deaths cause world-wide celebration (vv. 8-10). The "people, kindreds, tongues, and nations" of the world will view the lifeless bodies of the two witnesses for three-and-a-half days (v. 9). Though the entire world cannot be physically present, modern technology has made it possible for the entire world to view the scene, causing unbelievers to marvel even more at Antichrist's power. Refusing them a decent burial is the ultimate and deliberate indignity. (Some manuscripts have "body" instead of "bodies" in v. 8 or v. 9 or both; but this "collective" use has the same meaning.)

"They that dwell upon the earth" is the common designation for *the unbelieving population of earth* (v. 10; see 3:10; 6:10; 8:13; 11:10; 13:8, 14; 14:6; 17:8). At the death of the witnesses these earth-dwellers rejoice, make merry, and send gifts to one another (v. 10), indicating great celebration. The preaching and powers of the witnesses had "tormented" the unbelieving population, with both guilt and the plagues and fiery deaths.

The world's glee is terminated by the miraculous resurrection of the two witnesses (v. 11); celebration turns to dismay. After "three-and-a-half days" (most manuscripts have "the" before "three"), "the spirit of life from God entered" or *resurrected* the witnesses. Though some interpreters do not regard "spirit of life" (there is no "the" in the original) as a direct reference to the Holy Spirit (NIV: "a breath of life from God"), it is clear that God miraculously restored their lives by the agency of the Holy Spirit, as with Jesus Himself (Rom. 8:11). Many see an allusion to Ezek. 37:5, 9, 10 (Beale 597), and there are several similarities; but the witnesses' resurrection and ascension in a cloud is even more reminiscent of Christ (Acts 1:9), though the watchers—their enemies—are antagonistic and horror-stricken. That the earth-dwellers "saw" means that the resurrection was bodily, visible, and undeniable. Unlike Christ, the two witnesses rise in open view of those who saw their corpses.

"They" who "heard a great voice" are the two witnesses (v. 12), the voice probably that of an angel though possibly God's or Christ's. At the command to "Come up hither" the resurrected witnesses "ascend up to heaven in a cloud" in full view of everyone, including their enemies. Since idealist interpreters see the two witnesses as *the church*, it would follow that this is a picture of the rapture of the church (cf. Hendriksen 130). But if the symbolic interpretation of the two witnesses is wrong, so is that view. The "cloud" indicates *divine transport* (Aune II:625; cf. Dt. 33:26; Ps. 68:34). Clouds are often associated in Scripture with *ascents* into or *descents* from Heaven, such as the great angel in 10:1 or the rapture of the church in 1 Th. 4:17.

Within the "same hour" a great earthquake destroyed a tenth of the city of Jerusalem (v. 13; cf. 6:12; Ezek. 38:19, 20; Zech. 14:1-5; Mt. 27:51; 28:2). This is not symbolic of "social upheaval" (Swete 140) or "political revolution" (Barnes 282) but a literal earthquake that damages a portion of Jerusalem and kills a significant number of its inhabitants: "seven thousand men" apparently located in the affected part of the city. "Men" is, literally, "names of men," taken by most to mean 7,000 individuals. Brighton (302), on the other hand, suggests that "names" may refer to 7,000 "men of renown, famous, or notorious persons."

The survivors ("the remnant") were "frightened" by the deadly earthquake (v. 13), a natural response that does *not* suggest a mass conversion of some sort (as a few scholars have suggested). The timing, within "the same hour," may indicate that God sent the earthquake as a prejudgment of Jerusalem and its unbelieving inhabitants. His two witnesses and their message are thereby vindicated (cf. A. Johnson 111). Warning of continuing judgment is served (Beale 606).

The judgment affects a limited portion of the city and its inhabitants. This earthquake therefore appears to be distinct from the great eschatological earthquake predicted in the O.T. and in the sixth seal (6:12) in two ways: it is limited to Jerusalem instead of the entire world; and the result is giving glory to God rather than "cowering panic" (Caird 139). D. Johnson (173) calls this "the first tremor" of the ultimate great earthquake to come.

Some of the surviving citizens, grateful to be alive, rightly connect the miracles with God and give glory to "the God of heaven." This does not *necessarily* suggest conversion (Beale 607) but may indicate a grudging acknowledgment of God's power. Still, it is possible that some will turn to God as a result of these catastrophes, even this late in the Tribulation. But Aune (II:628, 629) thinks the words express conversion, and others (Thomas II:99, for example) suggest that it indicates the conversion of Israel associated with the Second Coming (cf. 14:7; 15:4; 16:9; 19:7; 21:24). If this is genuine conversion it indicates that conversions will occur throughout the entire Tribulation, to the very end. It would also confirm that the deaths of the two witnesses does not reflect the death of the church or of gospel witness at that point.

The statement "The second woe is past" (v. 14) includes the ministry of the two witnesses with the sixth trumpet contents that began in 9:13 and now concludes. The "third woe," to follow immediately, is the seventh trumpet judgment. Many suggest that "cometh quickly" is closely associated in Revelation with the Second Coming and that at this point Christ's coming is very near (Wall 149).

H. Seventh Trumpet (11:15-19)

The sounding of the seventh trumpet ushers in the "third woe." It need not be identified with one of the trumpets of Mt. 24:31; 1 Th. 4:16; or 1 Cor. 15:52. It *telescopes* us to the end of the Tribulation; cf. the sixth seal (6:12-17) and the seventh bowl (17:17-21).

This short section is a heavenly commentary on the *inauguration* of God's Kingdom in its *final and eternal* form, yet to come. With the events just preceding the Second Coming of Christ and following the establishment of His millennial kingdom on earth, that final

form of the kingdom, described in 21:1—22:21, draws nearer. Calling this "inauguration" is necessary: many things, which John will record, will follow the sounding of the seventh trumpet that factor into the transition into eternity proper. "The sounding of the seventh trumpet is not said itself to introduce the end, but to introduce the period of the end" (Ladd, *Commentary* 160). For example, the remaining "bowl" judgments are yet to be poured out on the earth; indeed, many see the bowls as the content of the seventh trumpet (Gonzalez 74). The Battle of Armageddon is yet to come, and the final judgment. But the doxologies of the seventh trumpet reflect that the final form of the Kingdom of God, toward the end of the Tribulation, is at the threshold.

15 And the seventh angel sounded; and there were great voices in heaven, saying, The kingdoms of this world are become *the kingdoms* of our Lord, and of his Christ; and he shall reign for ever and ever.

16 And the four and twenty elders, which sat before God on their seats, fell upon their faces, and worshiped God,

17 Saying, We give thee thanks, O Lord God Almighty, which art, and wast, and art to come; because thou hast taken to thee thy great power, and hast reigned.

18 And the nations were angry, and thy wrath is come, and the time of the dead, that they should be judged, and that thou shouldest give reward unto thy servants the prophets, and to the saints, and them that fear thy name, small and

great: and shouldest destroy them which destroy the earth.

19 And the temple of God was opened in heaven, and there was seen in his temple the ark of his testament: and there were lightnings, and voices, and thunderings, and an earthquake, and great hail.

When the seventh trumpet sounds, *recitations* come from within Heaven's throne room (11:15; 11:16-18; 12:10-12). There is a difference between recitations and songs (as in 5:9, 10): the redeemed sing songs of redemption but the angels recite doxologies—though the doxological content of the two is similar.

"Great voices in heaven" introduces another *throne-room vision* and points to the heavenly origin of the first recitation (v. 15). Since the 24 elders are involved in the doxology immediately following, these voices might belong to a number of angels otherwise unidentified. But since the "worship" of the four living creatures surrounding God's throne often prompts similar worship from the 24 elders (4:8-11; 5:14), that identification is appealing. Regardless, the doxology commemorates Christ's ultimate victory over the kingdoms of the world at the end of the present age (cf. Dan. 2:44; 7:14, 26, 27): "this great eschatological event that establishes once and for all the universal sovereignty of God" (Mounce 226).

"The kingdoms of this world" (v. 15) may be "the totality of creation" or "the human world that had been in opposition to God and in conflict with his purposes" (Aune II:638), a world that has been ruled temporarily by Satan (Mt. 4:8, 9). "Kingdoms" (singular in most manuscripts) refers to all the world's kingdoms as "a unit" (L. Morris 148). This domain, by conquest, will be wrenched from the control of those who are opposed to God and transferred permanently to God "our Lord" and to Jesus "his Christ" (cf. Ps. 2; Zech. 14:9). They are its rightful owners by creation in the beginning (Gen. 1:1; Jn. 1:1-3, 10), and by the Lamb's redemption by His own blood (5:9).

This future fact is stated emphatically as if it has already happened: "are become" (Greek aorist tense), either "to emphasize its certainty" (Aune II:638) or as "a proleptic preview" into the actual event. Either way, the reference must include both the establishment of Christ's earthly millennial kingdom (20:4-6) and "its blending into the eternal kingdom" (A. Johnson 113). Christ's millennial reign eventually transitions into an eternal reign over the new Heaven and earth. Some interpreters place this scene at the end of the millennial period; even so, the reign of Christ portrayed in v. 15 is eschatological in application. It should not be confused with a spiritual reign of Christ during the church age (Wall 152).

Christ will reign "for ever and ever," His kingdom encompassing not only the spiritual realm and the material universe but also the kingdoms or nations of the earth. The seventh trumpet heralds the final events that lead up to the Second Coming and the imposition of Christ's literal millennial rule on this earth. Once this threshold is crossed, Christ's reign will endure "for ever and ever," with no further successful challenges and with nothing sinful or antagonistic in its final form (21:27).

The literal reign of Christ over the material earth and its nations comes about militaristically or by force, representing a "visitation of God's wrath" (Ladd, *Commentary* 162). The last great event of the present age is the Second Coming of Christ at the end of the Tribulation. At this coming, Christ immediately destroys all the world's armies under the control of Antichrist (19:11-21) and proceeds to institute His reign on earth.

The 24 elders (representing saints of both testaments; see 4:4; 5:8, 9), prompted by the recitation, offer a doxology of their own about the change of world rule (v. 16). Their prostration ("fell on their faces") before God's throne is a nonverbal expression of worship. They begin with giving "thanks" to God (v. 17), momentous for all redeemed humanity formerly enslaved by the tyranny of sin and Satan.

God is addressed by three of His distinct names: "Lord, God, Almighty" (cf. 1:8; 4:8; 15:3; 16:7; 19:6; 21:22), "repeatedly used in the prophets to refer to God as the one who sovereignly directs his people's history" (Beale 613). The combination may purposely draw attention not only to God's ability to impose His rule over the earth but also to the inability of anyone to prevent Him (Thomas II:108).

The elders' thanksgiving continued with the recognition of His eternal nature: "which art, and wast, and art to come." (Most manuscripts lack "and art to come," but the sense of it is nonetheless justified.) Since God is sovereign, self-existing, and eternal, there is no beginning or end to God's existence; He is Creator, not created. And what is true of God the Father is also true of Jesus the Son and the Holy Spirit (cf. 1:4, 8; 4:8).

The way God is identified in v. 17 may call to mind His sovereign rule over time itself. Even the idealist Beale (613) affirms that this "is not merely a general reference to his sovereignty" but looks to "the end-time when God will break into world history and end it by overthrowing all opposition to his people and setting up his eternal kingdom." It is not therefore to be identified with an *inaugurated kingdom* at Christ's death and resurrection (idealism) or with the destruction of Jerusalem in A.D. 70 (preterism) but with the kingdom in its eschatological, final form. "Thou hast reigned" (Greek ingressive aorist) looks to the point at which Christ is finally and permanently enthroned.

The specific object of the elders' thanksgiving is that the time has come for God to exert His "great power" in fully establishing His eternal reign over the nations of the earth (v. 17). The "already" aspects of God's kingdom in the present church age and the "not yet" aspects waiting for the end-times will finally merge. God's eternal reign will be *fully* realized after the execution of the trumpet and bowl judgments, the victory of Christ at Armageddon, the millennial reign of Christ on earth, the final defeat and banishment of Satan to Hell, the Great White Throne Judgment, and the creation of a new Heaven and earth.

"The nations were angry" (v. 18) is a reference to unbelievers who refuse to repent and accept God's rule (9:20, 21; 16:9, 11, 21). This angry reaction to the imposition of Christ's earthly rule was predicted as early as Ps. 2 and is in part what necessitates the catastrophic means used by Christ to destroy the present world system before establishing His millennial reign. (This argues against hopes of a voluntary coronation of Christ by the world as suggested in post-millennialism.)

"The time of the dead, that they should be judged" (v. 18) refers to the judgment of the unbelieving dead at the Great White Throne (20:12, 13)—because their names are not found written in the Lamb's Book of Life and because their sinful works on record in God's books condemn them. As a result they are cast into an eternal Hell (20:15). But the doxology suggests that God's judgment is not completely negative: three classes of believing humanity, who have served God faithfully, will be *rewarded*, primarily on the basis of the righteousness of Christ but secondarily on the basis of their faithfulness and fruitfulness (Rom. 6:22). They are: "thy servants the prophets," "the saints," and "them that fear thy name."

There is obviously a sense in which all of God's people may be classed as "servants," "saints," or "God-fearers." But these are probably separate classes within God's family. The first could be either O.T. or N.T. prophets or, generally, God's people in the O.T. dispensation. "Saints" could also be either O.T. or N.T. saints or those of the N.T. dispensation only. The third group, the "small and great," suggests that individuals from all classes of society are conditionally rewarded on the basis of "fearing God's name," perhaps pointing specifically to Gentile believers (Aune II:645). (As an alternative, the third designation can be taken as additional description of the first two groups, the "prophets" and "saints.")

In sharp contrast, but also subject to God's final judgment, are those who "destroy" the earth who will themselves be "destroyed" or judged by God (19:20,

21; 20:10, 15). The judgment is deserved, and this group probably includes all those who have contributed in any way to the destruction of God's original design for the earth, whether Satan and his minions, the Antichrist, religious and political Babylon, or all unbelievers as members of a common, evil, spiritual confederacy (19:2). All of these are ultimately responsible in some way for the eventual destruction of God's material and spiritual designs.

After the two throne-room doxologies, John receives a brief, refocusing vision (v. 19), seeing "the temple of God" instead of His throne, where attention has been centered. This temple is "in heaven," open to reveal "the ark of his testament" (covenant). The O.T. Ark of the Covenant was a symbol of God's presence with the nation of Israel, normally housed in the Holy of Holies but also carried before the Israelites in their journeys and before their armies into battle. The mercy seat on top of the ark was the place of atonement.

The appearance of the Ark at this point in the narrative may be a literary way of introducing *the nation of Israel* into the revelations (cf. 12:1-6, 13-17), though this must be the original, heavenly Ark after which the O.T. one was patterned (Heb. 8:5). Charles (I:297) suggests that "the heavenly ark is a witness to the covenant between God and the Christian community, which is true Israel." But it more likely signifies that God fully intends to keep all His promises, particularly to Israel (Ladd, *Commentary* 164).

"Lightnings, voices, thunderings, earthquake, and great hail" are also phenomena associated with a manifestation of God's presence (theophany);

cf. 4:5; Ex. 19:16, 18; Ezek. 1:13-28. Here they confirm the reality of God's continuing and controlling presence in Heaven's throne room.

Summary
(11:1-19)

After recommissioning John, the great angel of chapter 10 commanded him to measure the Temple of God and its worshipers (v. 1), symbolically marking off the Jewish precincts of the Temple from the Gentile area—apparently indicating God's protection of a righteous remnant of Israel during the Tribulation and also the temporary but dominant role that unbelievers (Gentiles) would play during its latter half. End-times Jerusalem will come under Gentile control for a period of 42 months or three-and-a-half years (v. 2).

God raises up two men to witness or "prophesy" (preach) of coming judgment (probably the gospel as well) during this period (v. 3). Their clothing is made of sackcloth, befitting their woeful message. John connects them to an O.T. precedent in Zech. 4:1-14, thus indicating God's Holy Spirit as their empowerment. Success is thereby guaranteed.

The completion of their mission is further guaranteed because God endows them with supernatural ability to defend themselves (vv. 5, 6). Like Elijah of old, they use fire to destroy their enemies and perform miracles much like Moses did in turning water into blood and smiting the earth with plagues. Though their ministry is reminiscent of various Bible heroes of the past, they are not identified as any of them.

At the conclusion of their mission, God allows Antichrist ("the beast") to overcome and kill them (v. 7). They are refused burial and their dead bodies are put on display in end-times Jerusalem for the whole world to see (v. 8). A worldwide celebration follows, now that their message and miraculous powers have ceased (vv. 9, 10).

The world's glee is dramatically ended by an even greater display of God's power: in a way reminiscent of the resurrection and ascension of Christ the two witnesses are resurrected by the Holy Spirit (v. 11). In response to a voice from Heaven they ascend to Heaven in a cloud (v. 12). Unbelievers hear this voice and see the miraculous ascent.

Within the hour God sent an earthquake to authenticate the ministry of the witnesses (v. 13): a limited catastrophe affecting one-tenth of the city and producing 7,000 casualties. Remarkably, in contrast to the recalcitrant attitude reflected in 9:20, 21, some of those who survived the earthquake "gave glory to the God of heaven," perhaps indicating that conversions to Christ will occur during most of the Tribulation. The earthquake marks the end of the second woe or sixth trumpet (v. 14).

Verses 15-19 record the blowing of the seventh trumpet, refocusing attention on Heaven's throne room (v. 15). Two doxologies are offered. Those who offer the first are "great voices," probably some number of the heavenly host of angels and/or saints. They offer praise for the inauguration of God's Kingdom in its final form.

This is followed by a similar recitation from the 24 elders (vv. 16, 17). These representatives of all the redeemed of both testaments worship and thank God for His sovereign imposition of total theocratic rule over the earth (vv. 16,

17), a kind of reign that has not yet existed in the world's history.

Predictably, the nations of the earth do not submit to God's rule but respond in anger (v. 18). However, no one can hinder the process of Christ's conquest that was set in motion with the first seal in 6:2. He will ultimately destroy Satan, the Antichrist, and their evil minions before bringing recalcitrant humanity into final judgment before God at the Great White Throne.

A fleeting glimpse of the Ark of the Covenant is given along with typical throne-room manifestations of divine presence in the form of "lightnings, voices, thunderings, earthquakes, and hail" (v. 19). This glimpse of the Ark may signal the continuing role of Israel in the remaining Tribulation events beginning in chapter 12.

Application: Teaching and Preaching the Passage

The O.T. background of 11:4 is Zech. 4:1-14. God raises up these two witnesses to preach the gospel during the latter half of the Tribulation period. They are equipped with supernatural powers to defend themselves. Not until they have finished their mission do they become vulnerable and are martyred by the Antichrist. Of course, even this leads to yet another display of God's sovereignty when He miraculously resurrects them while the world watches. This reminds us of two familiar truths about Christian service: namely, "where God guides He provides"; and servants of God are truly "indestructible until God is finished with them."

The allusion to Zech. 4 is especially instructive. The method of divine enablement for ministry is the same at the end

of time as in Zerubbabel's day. As God's Spirit made possible the "impossible" task of rebuilding the Temple in the face of severe opposition (Zech. 4:6), so He provides power for ministry. This is reflected in the two living olive trees that connected directly into the menorah, providing it with a never ending supply of fresh oil to keep the light burning (Zech 4:3, 11-14). In the same way, God's two witnesses accomplish their mission by the inexhaustible power of the Holy Spirit.

So it is for those who are called into Christian service today. God's work must be done in God's way: it cannot be done successfully in any other way. The same applies to Christian living in general: every Christian must learn to live and serve in the energy and leadership of God's Spirit. The truth of Rom. 6-8 should be part of every new convert curriculum.

Suggested Outline. Equipped For World Witness, 11:1-12: (1) Sent to those outside God's house, vv. 1, 2; (2) Sent to preach the gospel, v. 3; (3) Sent in the power of the Spirit, vv. 3,4; (4) Sent to perform miracles, vv. 5, 6; (5) Sent to face persecution, vv. 7-10; (6) Sent to be faithful unto death, vv. 11, 12.

I. Third Parenthesis (12:1—14:20)

This third "parenthesis" begins with what John described as "a great wonder in heaven" (v. 1). "Wonder" in vv. 1, 3 (Greek *semeion*) is literally a *sign*, underscoring the symbolic nature of these visions. "It is a sign or symbol of important truth rather than merely a wonder" (Walvoord 187): a nonverbal revelation on par with the other forms of revelation given to John. The "signs" in chapter 12 are visual metaphors of God's truth that portray earthly realities *and* convey spiritual truth; defining them as representing "the struggle in the spiritual world which lies behind history" (Newport 232) does not go far enough. Spiritual reality invariably intersects the material world of time and history.

The drama transpires with "heaven" as a stage. The vision's characters, much like the great angel in 10:1, 2, are portrayed in supernatural dimensions. The vision in vv. 1-6 is obviously symbolic of real persons, objects, events, or realities and "embodies a surrealistic word-picture which describes the spiritual struggle standing behind historical events" (Ladd, *Commentary* 167). The universe is transformed into a gigantic obstetric delivery room where a great woman (Israel) gives birth to a child (Christ). A nemesis is presented in the form of a "great red dragon" (Satan), ready to devour the child as soon as it is born. The vision is a *reenactment* of past historical events: the birth of Christ and His ascension to Heaven.

A second vision (vv. 7-12) is inserted in the first vision, putting it on pause in order to describe a war in Heaven between Michael (with good angels) and the dragon (with evil angels). This results in the defeat and expulsion of the dragon (Satan) and his angels from Heaven and their subsequent descent to the earth. The visions of chapter 12 portray the intensely bitter conflict between these principal characters within history in general. It is therefore universal and spiritual in scope, historical in manifestation. It is the story in "sign" form of the conflict between God and Satan, between the seed of the woman and the serpent's seed (Gen. 3:15). Though

some of the elements of the visions are obviously caricatures larger than life, Satan's hatred of the woman's seed, the heavenly contest between Michael and Satan, God's protection of His chosen people, and Christian persecution are literal. Idealist Beale is right to say that the vision portrays "the deeper dimension of the spiritual conflict between the church and the world" (622) and that its purpose "is to encourage the readers to persevere in their witness despite persecution" (624). But he is not right to explain this simply as "the destiny of believers during the church age" (623). The visions of chapter 12 encompass specific historical events such as the birth and ascension of Christ of past church history and the war in Heaven that has an eschatological fulfillment.

It is popular among conservative interpreters to explore potential O.T. backgrounds for the apocalyptic material of Revelation. But John's descriptions reflect real visions he received and are not entirely controlled even by O.T. imagery.

1. A celestial woman (12:1, 2)

1 And there appeared a great wonder in heaven; a woman clothed with the sun, and the moon under her feet, and upon her head a crown of twelve stars:
2 And she being with child cried, travailing in birth, and pained to be delivered.

On "wonder," see above; John began by citing unusual features about the woman's appearance (vv. 1, 2), described in dramatic, cosmic dimensions. She is "clothed with the sun," perhaps a gigantic figure superimposed above the earth and enveloped in sunlight (cf. 10:1), perhaps like "a radiant bride" (Mounce 232).

The "moon" is "under her feet" as she stands above the earth, suggesting dominion (Mounce 232). She wears a "crown" (Greek *stephanos*; see 4:4) of twelve stars. She is pregnant and in labor (cf. Is. 66:7, 8), a realistic image of childbirth. She literally "cries out" in her labor. "Travailing" (Greek *odino*) means to "suffer birth pains" (ALGNT 415). "Pained" (Greek *basanizo*) is similar, meaning "to be tested, tormented, or in pain" (ALGNT 88), the only time this word refers to childbirth in the N.T. (Brighton 319). The combination suggests the painful labor of a woman about to give birth, striving to deliver (Greek middle voice).

Many suggest a direct allusion to Is. 66:7, but *that* woman gives birth *without* experiencing travail or labor pains (Ford 189), thus pointing to a blessing on "Jerusalem" in general (Michaels 148). The woman here has a specifically eschatological reference and more likely reflects Is. 26:17 (Ford 198), where the resurrection of a remnant (26:19), the preservation of Israel (v. 20), the judgment of the world (v. 21), and the conflict with Leviathan (27:1) are referenced.

The key issue is the "identity" of this "woman." Idealists tend to view her as representing the saints in general; Hendriksen (135), for example, speaks of "the church" as the one family of God of both dispensations. Even some futurists tend to agree that she represents "the messianic community, the ideal Israel" which combines the faithful of Israel and the church into one (Mounce 231).

However, considering the similar description of Jacob's family in Gen. 37:9, it seems more likely that the twelve patriarchs of Israel, and therefore the nation of Israel, are in view (Walvoord 188). If the church were included in this "crown," surely the number would be enlarged (as with the 24 elders) or this would be specifically designated (as with the foundations of the New Jerusalem in 21:14). Furthermore, she has not yet given birth to Christ and is therefore not the N.T. church. In the final analysis, the only identification that fits both giving birth to the Messiah and being the continuing object of Satan's ire, distinct from Tribulation saints in general (12:17), is *the nation of Israel* or *the faithful remnant of Israel* (Ryrie, *Revelation* 90). Jesus gave birth to the church, not vice versa. Dispensationalist Walvoord (188) says, appropriately: "Here is the godly remnant of Israel standing true to God in the time of the great tribulation." But he is wrong in viewing her travail not as for the birth of Christ but the pangs of persecution that the godly remnant will suffer during the Tribulation. Ford (198) is better: "Taken altogether these phrases depict the birth pangs, that is, the sufferings, which would precede the coming of the Messiah and the new era."

2. A great red dragon (12:3, 4)

3 And there appeared another wonder in heaven; and behold a great red dragon, having seven heads and ten horns, and seven crowns upon his heads.
4 And his tail drew the third part of the stars of heaven, and did cast them to the earth: and the dragon stood before the woman which was

ready to be delivered, for to devour her child as soon as it was born.

A second "wonder" (sign) appears (v. 3): "a great red dragon" as the "woman's" adversary (see v. 9). "Dragon" (Greek *drakon*) is used for "leviathan" or "serpent, sea-monster" in the Greek O.T. (LXX: Job 40:15; Psa. 74:13, 14; etc.), as well as metaphorically for Egypt (Ezek. 29:3) and Babylon (Jer. 51:34) as enemies of Israel, thus corresponding to the "beast" that arises out of the sea (13:1). Its negative connotation and association with Satan is clear: the same metaphor is used for both. Satan is the driving force behind the "beast."

"The red...symbolizes the murderous character of Satan" (Mounce 233); though reminiscent of monsters in pagan mythology, the one John sees is a caricature of Satan designed by God Himself. With the "seven heads and ten horns" (cf. 13:1; 17:9-12) one may compare the seven-headed hydra of Greek mythology. "Horns" symbolize power; that there are "ten" suggests complete or unchallenged power (cf. Dan. 7:7, 10, 24). Each of the seven heads wears a crown (Greek *diadema*), a *royal* crown that points to earthly rule. The number "seven" probably indicates "the universality of his power" (Mounce 233).

This multifaceted symbolism, therefore, points to an all-powerful, worldwide, religious, political, satanic, endtime confederacy. Non-futurists suggest a variety of identifications: "OT imagery of evil kingdoms who persecute God's people" (Beale 632); the Roman emperor Domitian and the imperial cult of Asia Minor (Summers 171); "the rise of the papacy," with the seven heads being "the seven hills of Rome" (Barnes 303).

Futurist Walvoord (189) is closer to the truth when he suggests that this represents a "revived Roman Empire" with Antichrist as its leader. But in fact the "dragon" is clearly identified as "Satan." He cannot be the Antichrist since this "dragon" has *all* seven heads and ten horns; Antichrist eventually comes from one of three of its horns (Dan. 7:24, 25). This dragon is also seen in Heaven in vv. 7, 8; his identity as Satan is undoubtedly made in v. 9 where four of his aliases are listed.

John's description includes the dragon's activity (v. 4). First, he gathered "the third part of the stars of heaven" with his tail and "cast them to the earth" (cf. Dan. 8:10)—in the manner of some animals with powerful tails. What happens to these "stars" seems more than mere dramatic effect. They are not *literal* stars but apparently indicate the dragon's successful, large-scale recruitment of other angels who fell with Satan from God's favor before the creation of the world. "The third part of the stars in heaven" (v. 4) points to the magnitude of the "initial rebellion of Satan" (Thomas II:115) (see 2 Pet. 2:4; Jude 6).

Other opinions about this drawing of the stars include: a picture of *persecution*, the stars being "Israelite saints who are the primary objects of the persecution" (Beale 635, 636) before the birth of Christ; "pagan nations under the devil's command" (Caird 149); a picture of Domitian and the cult of emperor worship in Asia Minor (Summers 171); "those who oppose [Antichrist] politically and spiritually" (Walvoord 189). But there is not enough exegetical weight to overturn the classical, conservative view that this depicts the original fall of Satan and evil angels.

The dragon positioned himself before the woman in labor (v. 4) in order to devour the newborn child (cf. 1 Pet. 5:8; Jn. 8:44), referring to the actual birth of the Messiah through the nation of Israel and indicating that the conflict takes place on earth (Aune II:686). The antagonism of Satan toward the woman's seed (Gen. 3:15) may be traced throughout Bible history. Cain murdered Abel. Pharaoh tried to destroy Israel at the Red Sea. King Saul attempted to kill David (1 Sam. 18:11; 19:10; 23:15). Athaliah attempted to destroy Judah's royal seed (2 Kg. 11:1, 2). Haman sought to destroy the exiled Jews in Esther's day (Est. 3:13). King Herod sought to destroy the Christ child (Mt. 2:16). This conflict continues into the end-time Tribulation, not to cease until Satan is put away forever. When Christ was born, Satan realized that his own illegitimate rule over the earth was at stake, and he sought to devour the rightful King.

3. A child king (12:5, 6)

**5 And she brought forth a man child, who was to rule all nations with a rod of iron: and her child was caught up unto God, and to his throne.
6 And the woman fled into the wilderness, where she hath a place prepared of God, that they should feed her there a thousand two hundred and threescore days.**

The woman delivered a baby boy: literally, "a son, a male" (apparently emphasizing the child's maleness), special because he would ultimately "rule all nations with a rod of iron" (v. 5). The ruling "speaks of absolute authority" (L.

Morris 154); the "rod"—apparently a typical shepherd's "crook" (Aune II:653)—continues the metaphor of *Jesus as Shepherd*, but an *iron* scepter "cannot be broken or resisted" (Thomas II:126).

This prediction of *ruling* over the nations identifies this "male child" as Israel's Messiah, Jesus Christ (cf. Ps. 2:1-12; Rev. 2:27; 19:15; cf. Ps. 110:1, 2). The stern nature of this rule does not easily harmonize with the idealist view that Christ's rule is now taking place in Heaven or in the hearts of believers on earth. Certainly, believers are under Christ's rule in the church age, but in no sense has Christ yet manifested universal rule over the nations. "Christ will strike the nations that oppress and persecute his church" (Mounce 234), a concept that accords best with a future, earthly, millennial reign. It alludes to Christ's triumph over the nations at Armageddon (19:15-20) and again at the end of the millennium (20:8-10).

That the child was "caught up unto God and *to* his throne" obviously refers to the ascension (Aune II:689) and exaltation of Christ, including His resurrection. "Caught up" (Greek *harpazo*) indicates that something is taken "forcefully" (Beale 639). Christ was indeed taken up to Heaven but not before the dragon made an attempt to destroy Him via the crucifixion. Ironically, the cross was the very thing that sealed Satan's eternal doom (Col. 2:15). Therefore, God's deliverance of the "child" from the "dragon" was not by preventing the child's birth but by *resurrection*, an "ironic victory" (Beale 639) indeed.

After giving birth, the woman fled to a safe place "in the wilderness" (v. 6): "The overtones of the Exodus are unmistakable" (Gonzalez 79). The wilderness is an apt place to hide, a metaphor for a place of safety. The primary factor here is that the place was "prepared for her by God" (cf. Jn. 14:1-3); He is the woman's defender and provider. God "feeds her" through unidentified agents ("they") for at least "1,260 days"— three-and-a-half years, again, the time of Antichrist's reign in the latter half of the Tribulation.

The means and nature of this provision are not indicated: perhaps by a great number of angels (cf. Is. 26:20). Material provisions will otherwise be in short supply because of rapidly increasing chaotic world conditions. The "nourishment" no doubt includes spiritual nourishment (Ford 202), equally vital in an environment that is doctrinally toxic and hostile to believers.

As noted, the woman represents a righteous remnant of *Israel* (in the end-times), not Christians who fled to Pella in A.D. 66 to escape the Roman siege of Jerusalem (Swete 152). Nor do the "1,260 days" cover all of church history (idealism), but the last half of the Tribulation during which Israel's then-believing remnant will be preserved. Satan is thus foiled on two counts: Christ has been caught up to Heaven beyond his reach; and the "mother" of Christ has fled to a safe hiding place in the wilderness. The verses to follow (vv. 7-12) indicate yet a third eschatological defeat.

4. War in heaven (12:7-12)

7 And there was war in heaven: Michael and his angels fought against the dragon; and the dragon fought and his angels.

8 And prevailed not; neither was their place found any more in heaven.

9 And the great dragon was cast out, that old serpent, called the Devil, and Satan, which deceiveth the whole world: he was cast out into the earth, and his angels were cast out with him.

10 And I heard a loud voice saying in heaven, Now is come salvation, and strength, and the kingdom of our God, and the power of his Christ: for the accuser of our brethren is cast down, which accused them before our God day and night.

11 And they overcame him by the blood of the Lamb, and by the word of their testimony; and they loved not their lives unto the death.

12 Therefore rejoice, ye heavens, and ye that dwell in them. Woe to the inhabitants of the earth and of the sea! for the devil is come down unto you, having great wrath, because he knoweth that he hath but a short time.

The "war in heaven" (v. 7) transpires where God dwells and not in the earth's sky, as in vv. 1, 3, 4 with the first two "signs." Heaven as the scene of a battle would be paradoxical except that Satan and his angels originated there (Is. 14:12-16; Ezek. 28:12-19). And even after his fall, Satan apparently has had some degree of access as the "accuser of the brethren" (v. 10; see Job 1:6-12; Zech 3:1, 2).

Good angels are led in this battle by the archangel "Michael" (Dan. 10:13,21; 12:1; Jude 9), prominent in the angelic hierarchy and the only angel named in

Revelation. He is generally considered to be the protector of Israel, evidenced by the high esteem accorded to him in Jewish tradition (Brighton 321, 322). "Early Jewish belief held the view that Michael would cast Satan from Heaven as the first of the last-time struggles to establish the kingdom of God on earth" (A. Johnson 120). He should not be confused with Christ even though he defeats the devil in battle; his strength and victory are from God.

Some suggest that Michael initiated this "war" for the specific purpose of eliminating Satan's accusatory presence permanently (Brighton 323). Though Satan might be reluctant to initiate such a conflict, he would certainly fight against his permanent expulsion. This war should not be confused with Christ's victory over Satan on the cross, symbolized in vv. 1-6. This is, instead, an *eschatological* event that builds on and goes beyond the significance of Calvary and takes place roughly midway through the Tribulation. It also appears to be more than a "legal battle in which the losing member is disbarred" (Caird 155) since many of the angels in Heaven from both sides are involved in what appears to be a titanic but short-lived struggle.

Evil angels are led by "the dragon," clearly identified as Satan by *four* different aliases (v. 9). One can only speculate about the form of such a battle between these two groups of angelic beings. Believers in the church age also war against such powers (Eph. 6:10-20), obviously stronger than unregenerate human nature (Eph. 2:2,3; Gal. 5:17). They can be overcome only by the power of the Spirit of God (Rom. 8:4,11; 2 Cor. 10:3-5; Gal. 5:16,18).

The war need not be explained as the direct result of Satan's attempt to devour God's Son (Aune II:691); that attempt (the crucifixion) is separated from the eschatological expulsion described here by a considerable amount of time. Nor does it appear to be an attempt on Satan's part to regain lost ground. Satan is not naive; having been controlled by God throughout the ages, he would not wait until the final period of earth's history to make such a move. On the other hand, he is prone to press hard for the last thing remaining to him at this point: his accusatory access to God. And the determination to terminate that precipitates this final conflict. This is in effect God's decision to listen to the advocacy of His Son Jesus Christ over the accusations of Satan *permanently*, a decision based on the merits of Christ as the slain and risen Lamb of God. Viable grounds for Satan's accusations against believers are forever removed because the righteousness of Christ and His atonement for their sins have been imputed to them.

The dragon and his angels "prevailed not" (v. 8), leaving Satan and his angels without place or reason for being in Heaven and cast out (v. 9). This does not refer back to Satan's original fall from Heaven before the creation of the world, or to the crucifixion and resurrection of Christ. The context of chapter 12 is not the beginning or middle but the *end* of time; this expulsion is eschatological and amounts to the curtailing of what had only been an accusatory access since the original fall (Beale 656). The devil's remaining "time" is "short" (v. 12).

As noted, four aliases make clear that this "dragon" is none other than Satan himself (v. 9). "That old serpent" connects with the serpent in Eden (Gen. 3:1-15), which emphasizes his *subtlety*.

"The Devil" (Greek *diabolos*) means "accuser" or "slanderer." The verb form means to "bring charges, bring complaint against, or accuse" (ALGNT 108). "Satan" means "adversary" (Vine 547). Finally, he is the one who "deceiveth the whole world" (cf. 1 Pet. 5:8). "That John piles up synonyms for Satan suggests that he is consciously attempting to expose the real role of this antagonist of God throughout cosmic and human history" (Aune II:697).

For the second and third time in v. 9, John reiterates that Satan and his angels "were cast out of Heaven to the earth." God is mightier than Satan and we have had significant demonstrations to prove it, ranging from Jesus' contest with Satan in the wilderness (Mt. 4:1-11) to this final, eschatological defeat of Satan in Heaven. The scene of the conflict therefore shifts from Heaven to "the whole inhabited earth," that is, the human population that *continues* to be the dragon's primary objective in his nefarious war.

The devil's chief weapon is "deception" (cf. Gen. 3:13), ongoing since the beginning of time and presently continuing (Greek present participle)—no doubt to continue until he is confined to the abyss for the duration of Christ's millennial reign (20:3). His nature and tactics have not changed since the Garden of Eden. His names indicate his nature and methods. He is a monstrous beast (dragon) that stalks the nation of Israel, Christ, and those children who have been begotten by Christ (believers). His work of accusation, previously permitted, is no longer possible after the war in 12:7-12. In the narrowing time remaining, he is driven by anger and remains recalcitrant to the bitter end.

Victory over the dragon prompts yet another doxology of praise from "a loud voice in heaven" (v. 10). "Our brethren" probably includes the speaker as one who has been accused by the devil, thus pointing to a fellow believer (not necessarily a martyr), perhaps one of the 24 elders representative of the redeemed (Brighton 337). The voice extols God's salvation, strength, and kingdom, and the power of his Christ—sovereign attributes employed to cast Satan down to earth.

The basic issue here (and often elsewhere) is that idealists see "Now is come salvation, and strength, and the kingdom of our God, and the power of his Christ" (v. 10) as the beginning of the church age (*inaugurated* kingdom; see D. Johnson 184). Futurists understand this to refer to the final form of the kingdom that will be established in the end-times as a millennial and then eternal kingdom (*consummated* kingdom). Both groups accept either characterization of the kingdom as legitimate but disagree over the time in view here, a difference not of principle but of perspective. It is true that Christ triumphed over the devil in the cross. But the devil keeps fighting (1 Pet. 5:8; Eph. 2:2). Likewise, it is true that by Christ's redemptive work there are no more grounds for the condemnation of believers (Rom. 5:1; 8:1), leading idealists like Beale (661) to view the "war" of 12:7 as a *legal* battle between opposing lawyers (Michael and Satan) that is lost by the devil. But even when legally defeated in God's sight, the devil continues to accuse the brethren until near the very end (cf. Caird 157). And Christ, not Michael, is our Advocate.

Several kingdom components—salvation, strength, and power—were all demonstrated by the war and its results. "Salvation" encompasses every aspect of redemption, specifically indicating the rescue of each believer from Satan's charges. "Strength" (Greek *dunamis*) is ability or power; Michael drew upon the great power of God to defeat the dragon in this battle. "Power" (Greek *exousia*) indicates authority: "supreme administrative power in both war and in the interpretation of law" (Aune II:700). Christ has indeed received "all authority in heaven and in earth" from the Father (Mt. 28:18). He has "the power" to make the laws and to enforce them, absolute power that leaves the devil with no ability to resist his expulsion.

As a result "the accuser of the brethren" was cast down from Heaven. "Accuser" (Greek *kategoros*) means "bring charges against" (Vine 10). The "brethren" are all believers, accused before God "day and night," meaning continually or incessantly. Job (1:9-11) and Joshua (Zech. 3:1, 2) provide examples.

The precise sense of this is debated. Some think of Satan as a "prosecuting attorney" who appears before a heavenly court to lodge or support charges. This appears to imply that God makes decisions based on arguments presented to Him. This is doubtful in light of Eph. 1:11, where Paul states that God does everything after "the counsel of His own will." Nor would it make sense for Satan to bring *false* charges before an Omniscient God. Slanderous accusations might be truthful ones, deviously used to damage someone's reputation. On the other hand, the basic accusation brought against Job turned out to be untrue; though Job was not sinless, Satan misjudged him. Satan is not beyond twisting the truth to suit his own purposes.

There is also a sense in which God's mercy and grace are magnified against the backdrop of forgiveness, a great part of God's glory. We may be sure that Satan's accusatory access was ultimately granted for a good purpose. If for no other reason it suggests that justification by faith in Christ, rather than human merit, is the eternal basis of salvation. God hears everything there is to know about believers and still grants them Heaven on the basis of faith in Christ.

The devil is powerful, but believers overcome him by appropriating the superior power of God (v. 11). "Overcome" (Greek *nikao*) means to gain the victory, a major theme in the messages to the seven churches. The report indicates that many believers were successful (Greek aorist tense). The devil and his accusations were overcome by those who trusted in "the blood of the Lamb." Whether his accusations are true is not finally determinative: every sin has been forgiven on the basis of the blood of the sinless One (2 Cor. 5:21).

Overcomers do so by "the word of their testimony," by confessing Christ to others as faithful witnesses. He confesses before the Father those who confess Him before men (Mt. 10:32, 33). Furthermore, they have maintained their confession to the point of martyrdom: they "loved not their own lives," they refused to deny Christ on pains of death (cf. Mt. 16:24-28). There were martyrdoms in first-century Asia Minor; there will be even more during the Tribulation.

The elimination of Satan and his cohort from Heaven is reason for great joy; the righteous host of Heaven are exhorted to show it (v. 12). The "heavens," here, represent all who dwell there (by metonymy). Conversely, the presence of the angry devil on earth is reason for great "woe" to "the inhabitants of the earth and sea." A warning is therefore in order. Satan's "great wrath" (Greek *thumos*) and confinement to earth during the Tribulation period will only increase chaos and suffering, dooming his followers to Hell with him.

One reason for the devil's great wrath is that he realizes his time before being cast into Hell forever is "short." This motivates him in a negative way, spurring him to even more evil. (Those same constraints can motivate believers positively to redeem the time.)

5. War on earth (12:13-17)

13 And when the dragon saw that he was cast unto the earth, he persecuted the woman which brought forth the man *child*.
14 And to the woman were given two wings of a great eagle, that she might fly into the wilderness, into her place, where she is nourished for a time, and times, and half a time, from the face of the serpent.
15 And the serpent cast out of his mouth water as a flood after the woman, that he might cause her to be carried away of the flood.
16 And the earth helped the woman, and the earth opened her mouth, and swallowed up the flood which the dragon cast out of his mouth.
17 And the dragon was wroth with the woman, and went to make war with the remnant of her seed, which keep the commandments of God, and have the testimony of Jesus Christ.

Having been "cast unto the earth," the dragon began persecuting the "woman which brought forth the man child" (v. 13). "Persecute" (Greek *dioko*) means "put to flight, drive away, pursue" (Vine 468). For emphasis, there are *seven* references to Satan's expulsion from Heaven: he is "cast out" (v. 9), "cast out into the earth" (v. 9), "cast down" (v. 10), "come down" (v. 12), "cast unto the earth" (v. 13).

It is not surprising that Satan persecutes Israel during the Tribulation. Conflict between the woman's seed and Satan is old news, beginning with the prediction in Gen. 3:15 and only finally to be resolved in the Tribulation. Satan hates Christ as the primary threat to his own rule; consequently he hates the nation that gave birth to Him. Furthermore, he hates the godly seed: both O.T. and N.T. saints and particularly those who turn to Christ during the Tribulation (see v. 17).

The previous reference to the woman's escape (v. 6) is now amplified. The method of escape is that she "was given two wings of a great eagle" (v. 14)—an analogy used before in the O.T. to describe God's special relationship to the nation of Israel and His role as Israel's deliverer (Ex. 19:4; cf. Is. 40:31). The reference to the eagle's two wings may be a metonymy (a part for the whole) implying that she was carried by a great eagle into the wilderness. We do not need to press such detail: the principle of divine protection is the main point and the wings represent "divine deliverance and enablement" (Mounce 241). God Himself bears the faithful remnant of His people to a place of safety.

Satan's efforts are unsuccessful because God protects and nourishes the "woman" during the latter half of the Tribulation; the dire conditions of this period necessitate her supernatural preservation. Famine, inflation, a food supply controlled by Antichrist's regime, and catastrophic changes in the material earth are involved (see 6:5, 6; 13:17).

"A time, and times, and half a time" (v. 14) is an alternative way of referring to this final three-and-a-half years before the Second Coming, and not to "the entire time of the church's existence" (Beale 669). It is clear by now that any of the various ways of referring to this period yield the same result (cf. 11:3; 12:6). The believing remnant of Israel (the woman) is effectively isolated in safety by God (vv. 6, 14; cf. 1 Kg. 19:4-8). God frustrates every effort made by "the serpent" to harm, or even to find, his prey. Thomas (II:139) suggests that this is "a literal flight from Jerusalem" (cf. Mt. 24:16).

Satan's failures infuriate him and fuel further desperate attempts to destroy Israel and her seed. That he "cast out of his mouth water as a flood after the woman" (v. 15) is an example. There are various interpretations of this "flood": an O.T. metaphor for "overwhelming evil" (Mounce 241); "a metaphor for destruction" (Aune II:707); "a tangible use of force by an authority figure" (Thomas II:140); "the nations which come to Jerusalem, or the soldiers who besiege it" (Ford 203, citing Giet); "Satan's attempt to destroy the church by deception and false teaching" or "a flood of words" (Beale 673); "all manner of delusions" (Lenski 384); "deceptive teaching" (D. Johnson 185). Regardless,

the floodwater from the dragon's mouth is symbolic of an attempt to locate and destroy the woman (literally, "to carry her away by a river"). Since the use of deception or false doctrine is one of Satan's devices, there is much to favor this interpretation; indeed, Jesus predicted that there will be rampant deception during the Great Tribulation in a context of flight (Mt. 24:5, 11, 24).

Satan's final attempt to destroy "the woman" failed when the water was miraculously absorbed into "the opened mouth of the earth" (v. 16)—an anthropomorphic expression pointing to God's supernatural protection. God has often performed miracles of deliverance for His people, even manipulating the laws of nature when necessary (Ex. 14; Jos. 10:10-14; Mt. 8:27). At the end of history, none of Satan's attempts to destroy Israel or the Messiah's lineage will have succeeded.

The previous "war in heaven" (v. 7) now transitions to war on earth (v. 17). "Make war" (Greek *polemeo*) refers here to a spiritual, literal conflict, reflecting God's judgment against both *religious* and *political* "Babylon" (God's enemies) in chapters 17 and 18. "Was wroth" (Greek *orgeo*) indicates the kind of anger that reaches deep and lingers long: "the strongest of all passions" (Vine 26). This wrath continues to energize the dragon's attempts to persecute God's seed.

"The seed of the woman" includes Jewish and Gentile saints of the Tribulation period: "actual Christians who constitute the empirical church on earth" (Ladd, *Commentary* 174). Limiting this to Jewish believers is too restrictive for the terminology used here. The use of "seed" "suggests that Gen. 3:15...is still in mind" (Michaels 153).

The objects of the dragon's wrath are, further, those "who keep the commandments of God, and have the testimony of Jesus Christ."

Jewish Christians come to Christ by faith in the same way as Gentiles during the church age or the Tribulation. They will relate to God in this way eternally, joining Gentiles as one people or family of God in Heaven—a view different from *classic* dispensationalism's eternal dualism. A contribution of the relatively recent progressive dispensationalist perspective is that maintaining a continuing role for Israel is not antithetical to the N.T. oneness of God's family.

Nor is "commandment keeping" antithetical to grace: N.T. believers also keep the commandments of God— which might refer to the Mosaic "commandments," or to the commands of God in general (both O.T. and N.T. varieties), or even to N.T. commands (cf. Mt. 5:19). The Apostle John argued in his first letter that keeping God's commandments indicates N.T. faith (1 Jn. 2:3, 4; 3:22, 24; 5:2, 3). "The traditional commands of God, understood from a Christian perspective, are seen as complementary rather than antithetical to the requirements of Christian faith" (Aune II:709).

Having "the testimony of Jesus Christ" suggests that a believer in the N.T. sense is in view (cf. 1:9; 14:12). This clause may be taken to mean either "the testimony that Jesus bore" (Greek subjective genitive) or "the witness that one bears (in faith) to Jesus" (Greek objective genitive). The two are so closely related within one's experience of Christ that it is difficult at times to discern the shade of meaning intended.

Summary
(12:1-17)

These visions help us understand the nature of spiritual conflict in general and during the Tribulation in particular. The first "sign" was cosmic in dimension: "a woman" clothed with sunlight, standing on the moon, wearing a crown with 12 stars (v. 1). Symbolic of the nation of Israel, she was about to give birth to a child (v. 2).

The second "sign" was "a great red dragon" (v. 3) with "seven heads and ten horns" and each head wearing a crown, symbolic of Satan. The dragon used his tail to cast one-third of the stars of heaven to earth (v. 4)—evil angels involved in Satan's original rebellion. The dragon positioned himself in front of the woman in order to devour her child as soon as it was delivered.

The woman gave birth to a male child (v. 5), identified as the One destined to "rule all nations with a rod of iron"—the promised Messiah, Jesus Christ. He was caught up to Heaven, harking back to His resurrection and ascension (Acts 1:9; 7:56). Afterward, the woman (Israel) fled into a special hiding place in the wilderness (v. 6)— a place of God's provision and protection. This occurs in the latter half of the Tribulation, designated as 1,260 days.

The theme is amplified by John's account of a war in Heaven (vv. 7-9), marking the end of Satan's accusatory access before God (Job 1:6-12). God employs the archangel Michael and the good angels to drive the dragon and the evil angels from Heaven permanently. Four of Satan's aliases are "the great dragon," "serpent," "Devil," and "Satan"; he is cast down from Heaven to the earth.

This momentous, end-time event prompts a doxology of praise in Heaven (vv. 10-12). God is praised because He exerted His great power to bring an end to Satan's accusatory presence. Satan had heretofore accused believers before God, accusations overcome on the basis of "the blood of the Lamb" that justifies them in God's sight. Believers also overcame Satan by maintaining their testimony even to the point of martyrdom.

Satan's expulsion creates havoc on earth; he is incensed and realizes that his time is short (v. 13). The drama that left off in v. 6 resumed when the dragon attempted once again to persecute the woman (Israel). However, God once again intervened by enabling her to fly like an eagle into a special hiding place in the wilderness (v. 14) where she was safely isolated from the "serpent" Satan.

In a desperate attempt to locate and destroy the woman, the serpent cast a destructive "flood" after the woman (v. 15). God intervened to protect her by causing the earth to absorb the flood (v. 16)—probably a picture of God's preservation of the righteous remnant (predicted by Paul in Rom. 11:26).

Unable to touch the woman, the dragon turns to vent his anger on the seed of the woman (v. 17). The "remnant of her seed" includes ethnic Jews who turn to Christ during the awful days of Tribulation. But a vast number of Gentiles will also be converted during the Tribulation (7:9-17), and many of them will suffer for Christ under the Antichrist's world regime, some to the point of martyrdom. They are those who "keep the commandments of God" and "have the testimony of Jesus Christ."

Application: Teaching and Preaching the Passage

Spiritual warfare has its own niche in the local Christian bookstore and is perhaps the preferred language of some when teaching, preaching, or conversing about Christian life. Unfortunately, this often gives the impression that there is a demon involved in every event. At the other extreme is a secular society that either scoffs at the reality of Satan's existence or capitalizes on it at the box office. Consequently, there is need for a balanced view on Christian warfare—a view that does not exaggerate inordinately the devil's power and presence on the one hand or take such a serious subject too lightly on the other.

Revelation removes all doubt about the reality of Satan's personal existence and about his destructive and deceptive nature. Satan is totally committed to destroying or persecuting as many souls as possible for the duration. As Hal Lindsey has indicated, "Satan is alive and well on planet earth." His presence in the world will be felt even more during the Tribulation just before the Second Coming.

Those who teach and preach the Word to others must be careful not to leave the impression that spiritual warfare ended with Christ's triumph on the cross. There is a sense in which the war has been won: Jesus finished the work God gave Him and achieved triumph (Col. 2:15) in His death, burial, and resurrection. The victory of Christ and the power of the Holy Spirit enable us to live and serve victoriously as Christians. Even so, Christians may experience tribulation, suffering, persecution, and ultimately death before entering Heaven. Victorious Christian living involves persevering faithfully through such things by the grace of God. We do a service to new converts when we prepare them to anticipate such hardships. (See 1 Pet. 4:12; 2 Tim. 3:12.)

Suggested Outline. The End of Accusatory Access, 12:7-12: (1) The war in Heaven that settled it, vv. 7-9; (2) The powers that denied further access, v. 10; (3) The legal basis that ended it, v. 11; (4) The result in Heaven and on earth, v. 12.

6. Two beasts (13:1-18)

The lengthy "parenthesis" between the seven trumpet judgments and the seven bowl judgments continues, focusing on two "beasts" whose identities are hotly disputed and especially important to our understanding of Revelation.

a. The beast out of the sea (vv. 1-10)

1 And I stood upon the sand of the sea, and saw a beast rise up out of the sea, having seven heads and ten horns, and upon his horns ten crowns, and upon his heads the name of blasphemy.
2 And the beast which I saw was like unto a leopard, and his feet were as *the feet* of a bear, and his mouth as the mouth of a lion: and the dragon gave him his power, and his seat, and great authority.
3 And I saw one of his heads as it were wounded to death; and his deadly wound was healed: and all the world wondered after the beast.
4 And they worshipped the dragon which gave power unto the beast: and they worshiped the beast, say-
ing, Who *is* like unto the beast? who is able to make war with him?
5 And there was given unto him a mouth speaking great things and blasphemies; and power was given unto him to continue forty *and* two months.
6 And he opened his mouth in blasphemy against God, to blaspheme his name, and his tabernacle, and them that dwell in heaven.
7 And it was given unto him to make war with the saints, and to overcome them: and power was given him over all kindreds, and tongues, and nations.
8 And all that dwell upon the earth shall worship him, whose names are not written in the book of life of the Lamb slain from the foundation of the world.
9 If any man have an ear, let him hear.
10 He that leadeth into captivity shall go into captivity: he that killeth with the sword must be killed with the sword. Here is the patience and the faith of the saints.

The first clause in v. 1 appears as v. 18 of the previous chapter in some versions, reflecting the fact that some manuscripts read "and he [the dragon] stood" instead of "and I stood." This would apparently mean that the dragon (Satan) stood there waiting for the first "beast" (the Antichrist) to arise out of the "sea" (Aune II:732), thus calling forth the one by whom he will persecute Tribulation believers. Here the majority reading, indicating that *John* saw this, makes better sense and is supported by the rest of vv. 1, 2. "And I saw" typically indicates a new vision or focus and reflects John's seashore vantage point.

Some equate the "sea" with evil, perhaps with pagan nations or evil mankind: "The ancient world commonly associated the sea with evil, and for the last great enemy of God's people to arise from the reservoir of chaos would be entirely appropriate" (Mounce 244). Beale (682) cites the arrival of a Roman governor, by ship, as possible background, which works well if the "beast" represents a Roman emperor. But the beast's origin, already indicated in 11:7, is clearly hellish and Satanic. Daniel saw "four beasts," symbolizing four great empires, arise out of the "sea" (Dan. 7:2, 3). Based on this, the "sea" probably refers to the beast's *worldly* origin from a nation or nations.

The beast is not named, but his caricatured appearance should not obscure his identity. Scriptures that help us identify this beast are Dan. 7:7-14 and Rev. 17:7-18 (see also "the beast" in 11:7; 14:9, 11; 15:2; 16:2, 10, 13; 19:19, 20; 20:4, 10). On the meaning of "beast" (vv. 1, 11) see 11:7: a "wild animal" is an appropriate symbol for *both* beasts (the Antichrist and the false prophet). The three—Satan, Antichrist, and the false prophet—are sometimes identified as an unholy trinity, in some respects a deliberate counterfeit of the real Trinity. The latter two figure prominently in the satanic agenda of the endtimes.

On "dragon" see comments on 12:3; the O.T. background and sea-monster image may correspond to the beast that arises out of the sea. At any rate, the dragon metaphor describes both Satan and the "beast" of 13:1, showing that Satan is the driving force behind the beast.

The beast has "seven heads" (cf. 12:3; 17:9), probably symbolizing some form of absolute earthly power. Thomas (II:155) says, "The seven heads stand for seven successive world monarchies: Egypt, Assyria, Babylon, Medo-Persia, Greece, Rome, and the regime represented by the ten simultaneous kingdoms—i.e. the ten horns." He reasons that "seven heads" indicate that they are *successive* since only one head may rule at a time. Swete (163), on the other hand, is an example of those who see the seven heads as "seven Emperors"; he identifies Nero as the beast that was wounded. (Other identifications are discussed below, following v. 10.) The first beast, then, may represent a man, a kingdom, or both.

He also has "ten horns," animal horns being an ancient and Scriptural symbol of power. "Ten" may also suggest *completeness*, perhaps in a more earthly sense, or "the measure of human responsibility" (Vine 622). The "ten horns" relate to the last of the four empires surveyed in Dan. 7, which most identify as the Roman Empire (Dan. 7:23, 24). In an eschatological setting it may take the form of a *revived* Roman Empire, a world confederacy of nations led by the Antichrist. However, "Babylon," rather than "Rome," is the name Revelation prefers to use for the world system. The ten horns of Dan. 7 are ten kings (Dan. 7:24); Antichrist (7:8) arises to subdue three of them and from this base gains supremacy over the rest.

Each horn wears a royal crown (Greek *diadema*). The "ten horns" therefore represent ten kings or kingdom-nations (17:9-13). Interpreters sometimes identify these as ten Seleucid rulers or some combination of Roman emperors. That there are "ten" conveys the worldwide scope and power of this end-time confederacy of nations ruled by the Antichrist. These arise during the seven-year Tribulation that culminates with the Second Coming. Beale (684) says, "The crowns symbolize the beast's false claims of sovereign, universal authority in opposition to the true 'King of kings and Lord of lords,' who also wears 'many diadems'"; see 19:12, 16.

"The name of blasphemy" is written on all seven heads (cf. 17:3); perhaps the same term or name is common to all. The name itself constitutes the blasphemy and is "indicative of radical hostility to God" (Hughes 145), possibly referring to his pretense of deity. If so, this title is a part of the beast's deceptive masquerade before the world, claiming to be God. The use of divine titles by Roman emperors—like lord, savior, Son of God—may shed light on the mind-set of the Antichrist.

Some manuscripts have "names" (plural) rather than "name," perhaps suggesting that each head has a different blasphemous title or verbal insult against God. In the end, it is inconsequential whether the beast wears one or many names or whether they are divine titles or defamatory insults. The beast is claiming to be God, either by wearing divine title(s) or by negatively slandering God.

The description of the first beast deliberately harks back to the great red dragon (12:3), using almost the same words. This virtual identity is close enough that what applies to one applies to the other. The beast of 13:1 is an extension and instrument of the dragon. Since the four aliases of the dragon (12:9) clearly marked him as Satan, the

beasts of chapter 13 are obviously satanic.

The primary difference between the "dragon" and the first "beast" is that where the dragon had seven crowns on his seven heads, the beast has ten crowns on its ten horns; perhaps this "accents the horns' importance" (Thomas II:154). The focus thus shifts: the seven heads represent seven world empires, and the horns are kings or rulers of the *seventh* empire (or a "revived" seventh empire). The fact that the crowns have now shifted to the horns is a way of indicating that *the last* of the seven empires is in view: specifically, an eschatological confederacy of ten nations led by Antichrist (cf. Dan. 7:7, 24; Rev. 17:10, 12).

As always, Scripture should interpret Scripture. "Same language" predictions in Dan. 7:1-28; 9:24-27 (and elsewhere) strongly suggest that this beast in chapter 13 is the eschatological world ruler in Daniel. Biblical passages, including the O.T. and N.T., often appear to refer to the same person or event, especially when eschatology is in view. When a significant amount of the *"same language"* is present, this is a strong argument that the references are in fact to the same person or event. In addition to Daniel, we must also reference 2 Th. 2:1-12, the predictions of Christ in the Olivet Discourse (Mt. 24:15), and related commentary in Rev. 17:3, 7-14: all these help interpret the symbolism of the beast in Rev. 13 and say important things about the nature of Antichrist.

Daniel saw *four* beasts—lion, bear, leopard, and a "dreadful and terrible" beast (cf. Rev. 13:2)—arise from the sea (Dan. 7:3), each representing an earthly king or kingdom (7:17; cf. Dan 2:31-44). The fourth had "ten horns" (7:7). A "little horn" arose from within the ten, uprooting three in the process (7:8). He is identified as a man with "a mouth speaking great things" (7:8). This world ruler, described as a "beast" in v. 11, is eventually slain and cast into a fiery Hell by God (7:11). His confederacy is also defeated (7:12) when the Son of Man comes to earth "with the clouds of heaven" and establishes His eternal kingdom (7:14; see Dan. 2:35, 44, 45).

Daniel also predicted (Dan. 9:26) that a world ruler ("prince") would destroy "the city and the sanctuary"—Jerusalem and its Temple—in what is commonly designated as "the seventieth week." Futurist interpreters envision this as the eschatological seven-year Tribulation that culminates with the Battle of Armageddon and the Second Coming. This prince will "confirm the covenant," or make a covenant with the nation of Israel, at the beginning of this final period; but in the middle of the week (after three-and-a-half years), he will break this covenant or treaty by causing the previously restored Temple ritual to cease. He will profane the Temple with some sort of abomination (9:27).

Some interpreters see an early fulfillment of this in the person of Antiochus Epiphanes IV (164 B.C.), who sacrificed swine in the Temple, thereby profaning it. Others suggest that the destruction of Jerusalem by Titus in A.D. 70 is a possible fulfillment; Titus conquered the city and profaned the Temple before destroying it completely. Indeed, some see these historical examples as legitimate foreshadowing but not ultimately fulfilling Daniel's predictions. The ultimate world ruler will be a man, the Antichrist, who will arise at the end of the age, not

someone who has arisen along the way, regardless how heinous.

A pivotal N.T. passage is 2 Th. 2:1-12, again using "same language" of an eschatological period. The context is clearly the Second Coming, designated by Paul as "the day of Christ" (2:2). One proof that Christ had not already come again is the necessity for "that man" (2:3) to appear first. This person will "oppose and exalt himself above God" (2:4; cf. Dan. 7:8) and "sit in the temple of God" as though God (2:4). Satan energizes this man with satanic power to work miracles and perform signs of deception in order to keep people from believing in Christ (2:9, 10). God permits this (2:11, 12; cf. the "divine passive" in Rev. 13:5, 7). Jesus Himself will return to intervene in history and destroy this evil man (2:8; cf. Dan. 7:11; Rev. 19:19-21).

Christ predicted in the Olivet Discourse that Daniel's "abomination of desolation" would be an eschatological event, happening in the end-times of earth's history (Mt. 24:15). Indeed, Daniel connected this "abomination" to the same period as Christ's Second Coming, thus effectively ruling out Antiochus Epiphanes IV, Domitian, Adolf Hitler, Mussolini, some Catholic pope, or anyone else to date as a possible fulfillment (it is possible that Antichrist is presently alive but still unrevealed). Christ spoke of a time future to His own and indicated that His Second Coming would bring about the end of the present world system (24:3, 14). He predicted unprecedented "great tribulation" (24:21) and rampant "deception" (24:24) as markers of the end. The "same language" principle connects vv. 29,30 of the Olivet Discourse with the concept of "the Day of the Lord" and its similar language of catastrophe in the O.T. prophets; see Jl. 2:10, 11; Zech. 14:1-21; Is. 2:10-21; 24:17-23; 2 Pet. 3:10-13; the sixth seal in Rev. 6:12-17; 16:18-20).

When the language of these passages is compared to the descriptions in Revelation, it is apparent that *the same person* is being described as living and defeated at the Second Coming. This clearly identifies him as "Antichrist" ("against Christ") and reflects his activity in 2 Th. 2:4; cf. 1 Jn. 2:18, 22; 4:3; 2 Jn. 7). He is more than a mere worldly or anti-christian spirit that opposes Christ and the church; these passages indicate that he is a real person whom Satan uses to wreak havoc on the eschatological earth.

John describes the beast in terms of the same four animals mentioned in Dan. 7 (v. 2), but with all four combined in one beast that must be symbolic of something that those four worldly kingdoms have in common. It is commonly agreed that the lion with eagle's wings represented the Babylonians, the bear with three ribs in its mouth the Medo-Persians, and the leopard with four wings (swiftness) and four heads (four successors of Alexander) the Greek Empire of Alexander the Great (Dan. 7:3-8). Revelation might have intentionally borrowed these to construct a composite creature representing the consummate world ruler (Antichrist) and his dominion over all worldly nations.

The "leopard" comparison may indicate the speed with which he carries out his purpose. Like Alexander the Great's swift conquest of the world around him, Antichrist's rise to power will be meteoric. The feet of a bear may reflect that Antichrist, like Antiochus Epiphanes IV, is sure-footed, powerful, fierce, or carnivorous. The lion's mouth may draw from the lion as a proud animal that is carnivorous, strong, loud, or even royal—perhaps suggesting either that Antichrist speaks with the voice of unchallenged authority or "devours" like a lion (cf. 1 Pet. 5:8), as with the Roman Empire. The three animal characteristics, combined, indicate that Antichrist's kingdom will manifest the strengths of many historical kingdoms in the end-times, surpassing any historical precedent in scope and in brutal domination.

Satan equips Antichrist for his earthly rule: "the dragon gave him his power, seat, and great authority." As "prince of this world" Satan promotes the beast to his political "seat" and the "great authority" that goes along with it. "Seat" (Greek *thronos*) is throne, as in 4:2, 4. Satanic power and authority are prerequisites for ruling the world, enabling Antichrist to control religious, economic, political, and social components during the Tribulation. However, God permits the transfer of power from the dragon to the beast for His own purposes.

One of the seven heads was "wounded to death" (v. 3; cf. Gen. 3:15). According to v. 14, a "sword" inflicted this wound, and interpreters differ as to whether the beast was actually killed or only wounded. Though "wounded" (Greek *sphazo*) typically means "to kill, slay, sacrifice" (Vine 342), "as" ("as it were wounded to death") may allow that the beast only "appeared fatally wounded" (Aune II:716). Since nothing states that he died, the miracle may have been healing (rather than resurrection) from an otherwise mortal wound (Barnes 321).

The world wonders at this healing or resurrection (v. 3). Either way, it was a miraculous, supernatural deliverance, effectively ruling out historical candidates like Julius Caesar, Caligula, Nero, or Domitian (cf. Charles I:349, 350). None of them recovered from mortal wounds. The resurrection myth of Nero (Aune II:738, 739), for example, that became legendary after his suicide, never materialized. Some interpreters attempt to offset this by suggesting that the Roman Empire, rather than a particular emperor, was "healed." Suggestions include the "healing" time of Vespasian after the disastrous reign of Nero (Moffat 430), or the "marriage" of the rapidly declining, secular Roman power to the papacy—"the Holy Roman Empire" of the Middle Ages (Barnes 330, 331). Unlike these historicists, futurist Walvoord (199) suggests that the healing refers to the *revival* of the long dead Roman Empire in the end-times. But all such historical identifications are premature since the Antichrist is an eschatological figure, not appearing until the Great Tribulation.

Some think that *God* inflicted the beast's wound by "the mortal blow of Christ's death and resurrection" (Beale 687, 688), for example. But the fact that the beast continued to live and function is not appropriate for a wound inflicted by God, nor does this idea fit the beast's healing (or resurrection)—though of course the beast continues to operate by divine permission.

Likewise, idealism's suggestion that the beast's resurrection applies to the recovery of any evil institution throughout the church age also misses the mark. "It is better to link the beast's resuscitation to the repeated rise and fall of oppressive states, world systems, or social structures that continue because the devil continues to inspire opposition to God's people, even though he has

been decisively defeated by Christ" (Beale 691). But "rise and fall" in this quotation is telling, opposite to the "fall and rise" in the beast's recovery; the analogy is therefore improper. It also seems incongruent to suggest on the one hand that the beast was "killed" (totally defeated) at the cross and yet have him soon "resurrected" to oppose Christ at the beginning of the church age.

Furthermore, only one of the seven "heads" was wounded (v. 3); the dragon, or the entire beast symbolizing Satan, is not in view. The beast as a whole continues to live while the seventh head suffers. Were this "wound" a "death-blow" from the death, burial, and resurrection of Christ, surely that would be adequately represented only by the death of the beast (cf. Gen. 3:15). This incongruity disappears if the beast, here, is seen as a future, real Antichrist rather than as a "transhistorical reality with many human manifestations in history" (A. Johnson 131).

That "all the world wondered after the beast" (v. 3) indicates the miracle's "dazzling effect" (Aune II:716). It is unlikely that the world would consider the recovery of a nation, either economically or politically, to be so miraculous that they would be prompted to worship Satan in response. The identity of the one who wounds the beast is not supplied, leaving us to speculate about a rival ruler or disloyal subordinate, but certainly an enemy who attempted to assassinate him. The result may be a diabolical attempt to counterfeit the death and resurrection of Christ, although the text does not explicitly indicate this.

After the beast was miraculously healed, he acquired the aura of indestructibility (v. 4). Interestingly, the unbelieving population of earth ("all the world") attributed his recovery to the *dragon*. They concluded (rightly) that the beast must get his power from the dragon, and (wrongly) that no one was *comparable* to the beast since he was apparently indestructible and all-powerful. As a result, the entire world worshiped them both.

"Worshiped" (Greek *proskuneo*, as in 4:10), means literally "to bow down, to kiss—someone's feet, garment hem, or the ground in front of" (ALGNT 334), thus "to make obeisance, do reverence to" (Vine 686). The text does not define this, but one may infer, from Paul's prediction that Antichrist will "sit in the Temple as God" (2 Th. 2:4), that some sort of Temple liturgy or expression or act of allegiance is required, perhaps bowing down to or kissing his image (13:15). In the ancient imperial cult the devotees were required to burn a pinch of incense to Caesar and confess him as Lord (DNTB 777, 1030).

Indeed, the people's expressions of admiration—"Who *is* like unto the beast?" "Who is able to make war with him?"—may be a mantra of "worship," confessing the beast's omnipotence or deity in a "parody" of the worship of God who delights to be worshiped as incomparable (Ex. 15:11; 20:3, 4; Ps. 71:19; Is. 40:18, 25; 44:8). Regardless, this is "the epitome of blasphemy" (Beale 694). Interpreters cite Ex. 15:11 as a model for this parody (if it is that); indeed, one of the central themes of heavenly worship in the doxologies of chapters 4 and 5 is the unique worthiness of God and the Lamb (4:11; 5:9, 12, 13).

In John's day, faithful Christians who refused to comply with the imperial cult in Asia Minor were perceived to be disloyal and therefore worthy of death. Faithful believers refused to confess Caesar as Lord or to offer sacrifices to an idol image of the emperor. Similar situations, with believers forced to choose between Antichrist and Jesus, will come into play again during the latter half of the Tribulation, when the pressures will be far more intense than anything yet experienced.

The dragon succeeds in redirecting to the beast the worship that should be offered to God alone, and the beast brazenly accepts it—as predicted in all the "same language" passages pointing to Antichrist. The two rhetorical questions expressing the masses' adulation imply that no one can expect to challenge the indestructible (divine) beast. But theirs is a false confidence: God alone is eternal, all-powerful, and worthy of worship (4:11; 5:4, 9, 10, 12), and His power is stronger than the dragon's—as demonstrated in Satan's expulsion from Heaven (12:10-12; cf. 11:15-18).

"And there was given to him" (v. 5) is another example of the "divine passive" to indicate divine origin, control, or authority; it appears four times here—twice each in vv. 5, 7—but *not* in active-verb clauses like "the dragon gave him his power" (v. 2) or "the dragon which gave power unto the beast" (v. 4). There are two tiers of authority at work, the divine *and* the nefarious. The devil's authority, including what he shares with his confederates, remains at all times under God's sovereign management. Even now, the devil has significant authority in the spiritual realm (Mt. 4:8, 9; 2 Cor. 4:4; Eph. 2:2; 6:12), but his work is providentially governed (Rom. 8:28; 1 Pet. 1:6, 7; 4:12; Jas. 1:2-4). God allows or uses evil and suffering to bring about greater glory to Himself and greater good for His people.

Thus God allowed the beast to demonstrate his hellish conceit and hate for God in "speaking great things and blasphemies" (vv. 5, 6). Some suggest that the "great things" define or constitute the "blasphemies" (Thomas II:161, citing Beckwith). While that is plausible, "great things" could be a separate category of self-serving propaganda indicating the Antichrist's conceited opinion of his own deity or his agenda for the world. Then "blasphemies" would be "verbal insults directed toward God" (Dan. 7:8; 2 Th. 2:4) and direct attacks against God's character (Dan. 7:25). (See Thomas II:162.) Narrowly, "blasphemy" (Greek *blasphemia*) is "defamatory speech spoken against God" (Vine 69), but it may include either defaming God or inflating oneself to be God. Antichrist is guilty on both counts.

Furthermore, to Antichrist "was given" (divine passive, again) authority to reign for "42 months" (v. 5), equivalent to the second three-and-a-half years, or last half, of the Tribulation (cf. 11:2; 12:6; Dan. 7:25; 12:7). Idealism regards the period as symbolic of the church age from the ascension to the Second Coming; but this is said to be a "short time" (12:12) against the backdrop of thousands of years of previous world history. Antichrist's behavior during this "short period" will be "frantic activity" (Thomas II:161); he knows that his time is limited. All this argues against the view that the beast began his activity shortly after Christ's death.

Verse 6 develops more precisely the beast's "blasphemy" by naming three specific objects of that blasphemy. The verbs "opened" and "to blaspheme" (Greek constative aorist) sum up the

practice of blasphemy as a whole for the entire period. The three targets of his blasphemy reveal the depth of the beast's hatred for God's name, God's tabernacle, and "them that dwell in heaven" at the time. Since most manuscripts do not have "and" before the third, some interpreters regard God's "tabernacle" as defined by "them that dwell in heaven." The final meaning is similar either way.

"Tabernacle" (Greek *skene*) means "a tent, booth, tabernacle" (Vine 614) and might refer either to the throne room in Heaven or a reconstructed "Temple" on earth during the Tribulation. But a *heavenly* "tabernacle" or "dwelling place of God" is more likely, so that all three objects of blasphemy are in Heaven. Here the meaning seems to be general: "the place where God dwells"— Heaven. Also, it would be awkward to represent Antichrist as profaning his own throne, which would result from identifying this as the rebuilt earthly Temple during the Tribulation (cf. 2 Th. 2:4).

"And it was given unto him" (v. 7) contains the third "divine passive" in this passage: though the dragon gave the beast power to make war, God gave the permission. All the evil activities within the Tribulation are managed by God according to His larger purpose to establish Christ's literal rule over the present earth, judge humanity, and usher in the eternal age. Consequently, the beast was divinely permitted not only to "make war with the saints" on earth during the Tribulation but also "to overcome" Tribulation believers (cf. Dan. 7:21; Rev. 11:7) during this relatively brief and intense period. It is important to note, however, that this overcoming is physical rather than spiritual, temporary and not eternal (cf. 7:9-17; 12:11), expressed in the martyrdom of many Tribulation saints who refuse to worship him or receive his mark (6:9-11; 7:9, 14; 13:15).

A fourth "divine passive" appears in "power was given him" (v. 7), further underscoring God's sovereign management of Tribulation events. God permits worldwide power, as seen in "all kindreds, tongues, and nations" of the earth—a triad used often in Revelation to indicate "the entire population of earth." "Kindreds" or "tribes" (Greek *phule*) are groups with well-defined, common characteristics. "Tongues" are language groups. "Nations" (Greek *ethnos*) are larger groupings of people bound together by common ancestry or geography. A number of manuscripts add a fourth grouping, "peoples." Regardless, the expression indicates the totality of the redeemed on earth, where Satan's activities have now been restricted since losing the heavenly war (12:7-9). "This cannot then refer to any situation in the past or present but must refer to the eschatological future when the rule of the beast will include the entire known world" (Aune II:746).

As before, "all that dwell upon the earth" (v. 8) indicates the unbelieving population of earth. The beast will use his powers of persuasion, the powers of his associate (the second beast or false prophet), and the power of life and death to coerce people to worship him. They will do so because they have been deceived, because they are in league with him (commercially or politically), or because they are afraid for their lives (cf. vv. 3, 4).

The clause "whose names are not written in the book of life" further characterizes the unbelieving population of earth from whom Antichrist recruits his worshipers (cf. 3:5; 13:8; 17:8; 20:12, 15; 21:27; Ex. 32:32, 33; Phil. 4:3). Believers' names *are* written in the Lamb's Book of Life; that a person's name is still there at the Great White Throne Judgment (20:12, 15) indicates victory in refusing to worship the beast and remaining faithful to Christ. Rowland comments, "Until the books are opened (20:12; cf. Dan. 12:1) and judgment takes place, the names contained in it are unknown....Thus the threat remains for all on earth, believer and unbeliever alike, that one's name might be removed" (Rowland 657)

Some link "from the foundation of the world" to "whose names are not written in the book of life," hinting at a predestinated group (parallel to 17:8). But it is more likely that the phrase links to "the Lamb slain" (Charles I:354). The fact that there are other N.T. references that speak of the foreordination of Jesus' sacrificial death before creation strongly supports this (Acts 2:23; Eph. 1:9-11; 1 Pet. 1:19, 20). (Further, this leaves the two prepositional phrases not separated in the sentence structure of the original.) Still, it is Biblical to affirm that, even before creation, God foreknew all who would eventually comprise the final number of "the elect" (1 Pet. 1:2). God's plan (decree, decision) of redemption through Christ was conceived before creation. Redemption is not an afterthought, but by design—not God's effort at crisis management because the entrance of sin into the world was unanticipated.

Earth-dwellers, whose names are not in the Lamb's Book, are contrasted to earth's *believing* population. There will be conversions to Christ during the Tribulation period from every people group, including believing Jews and Gentiles; see 7:9-17. Their names *have* been written in the Lamb's Book of Life. Even so, the possibility that names may be blotted out (3:5) means that security in a time of trial cannot be taken for granted; Thomas (II:164, 165) suggests that potential reasons for being blotted out include "disbelief and consequent disobedience."

John, whose passion for evangelism motivated him to write the Gospel of John (Jn. 20:31), inserts a universal invitation for all to "hear" what is being said. "If any man have an ear, let him hear" (v. 9) recalls "He that hath an ear, let him hear what the Spirit saith to the churches," given by Christ to each of the seven churches (2:7, 11, 17, 29; 3:6, 13, 22).

There are at least two ways of reading v. 10. As the text stands, "captivity" and "the sword" (v. 10) allude to the price some would pay for refusing to submit to the government or worship of the beast (cf. Jer. 15:2). "Captivity and the sword [i.e., death] are the fated consequences of those who practice the qualities of faith and endurance" (Aune II:750). Such was the choice some early Christians were compelled to make: whether to confess Christ or Caesar as Lord. Those who refused the demands of the imperial cult were in danger of being socially ostracized, losing personal property, or even losing life. Those first-century choices typify similar choices the final generation of Christians will be called on to make during the Tribulation. Worshiping the beast is mandatory, verified by a mark so that no one can hide his particular loyalty. Failure to comply leads to martyrdom (vv. 15-17); at best, any who escape will become fugitives. Correspondingly, the agents of

persecution will reap what they have sown. For each action there is a corresponding response from God: those who put believers into prison ("captivity") will themselves be put into a prison; those who kill with the sword will be killed in the same manner. This seems the more likely understanding of the verse.

The alternative reading takes v. 10 as an exhortation for Tribulation believers to expect and submit to captivity and execution. This view (in part based on different manuscript readings), views the verse as indicating that suffering and martyrdom are to be expected and must be endured by "patience and faith." (Note the NIV and NASB translations.) The last sentence—"Here is the patience and faith of the saints"—serves as an exhortation to submit to the inevitable. (Yet another perspective sees the couplet as a warning to believers against retaliation, but this requires too much reading between the lines.)

Correspondingly, the reference to "the patience and the faith of the saints" may mean that these virtues are *illustrated* by believers when they are killed or imprisoned (see NASB); "here is" fits well with this view. Or John may have cited these as an *exhortation* to encourage believers in light of the "inevitability" of the persecutions that were coming (D. Johnson 194); this meaning makes sense and is reflected in a number of translations (see the NIV). Both ideas may be intended, at least by implication: Tribulation believers must respond to threats about imprisonment and death in patience and faith.

"Patience" involves "the ability to bear a heavy load over an extended period of time." "Faith," John says elsewhere, is "the victory that overcometh the world" (1 Jn. 5:4, 5; cf. 1:9; 14:12). Beale (705) says, "Every use in the Apocalypse of 'faith' or 'faithful' of humans on earth speaks of enduring faith in the face of persecution."

b. The beast out of the earth (vv. 11-18)

The second "beast" which John saw is now introduced.

11 And I beheld another beast coming up out of the earth; and he had two horns like a lamb, and he spake as a dragon.
12 And he exerciseth all the power of the first beast before him, and causeth the earth and them which dwell therein to worship the first beast, whose deadly wound was healed.
13 And he doeth great wonders, so that he maketh fire come down from heaven on the earth in the sight of men,
14 And deceiveth them that dwell on the earth by *the means of* those miracles which he had power to do in the sight of the beast; saying to them that dwell on the earth, that they should make an image to the beast, which had the wound by a sword, and did live.
15 And he had power to give life unto the image of the beast, that the image of the beast should both speak, and cause that as many as would not worship the image of the beast should be killed.
16 And he causeth all, both small and great, rich and poor, free and bond, to receive a mark in their right hand, or in their foreheads:
17 And that no man might buy or sell, save he that had the mark, or the name of the beast, or the number of his name.
18 Here is wisdom. Let him that hath understanding count the number of the beast: for it is the number of a man; and his number is Six hundred threescore *and* six.

This "beast" (v. 11) is distinct from the first one—Antichrist—of v. 1. Whereas the first rose up from the sea, the second comes up ("arises," same verb as in v. 1) "out of the earth" and is subsequently called "the false prophet" (16:13; 19:20; 20:10). That this one arises out of the earth may imply "a degree of inferiority in power of the second beast to the first" (Thomas II:172), but that both are represented as *beasts* indicates the *evil nature* of both. Both "sea" and "earth" point to their literal humanity: they are real historical persons who will live during the Great Tribulation.

The second beast has often been called the third member of an "unholy trinity" with the dragon (Satan) and first beast (Antichrist). The nefarious personalities and activities of Satan, Antichrist, and the false prophet "parody" or "counterfeit" the three personalities of the triune Godhead. The second beast ("false prophet") glorifies the first (Antichrist) as the Holy Spirit glorifies Christ. The first beast (Antichrist) derives his authority from the dragon (Satan) as the Father gives authority to the Son.

"The relationship of the two beasts denotes an unholy alliance of the antichristian state with the apostate church, in such a way that the latter becomes subservient to the former" (Hughes 152). The satanic trio attempts to deceive the world with signs or miracles in order to usurp the true worship of God, perhaps *the* bedrock issue underlying the conflict between God and Satan. This conflict has existed throughout history; the final conflict between Christ and Satan at the end of the age will settle the issue once and for all.

The second beast's appearance is not as impressive or detailed as the first. He had "two horns like a lamb" (v. 11; cf. Dan. 8:3,20), perhaps intended to indicate a unique animal but certainly representing him as powerful in his own right. He performs great miracles, though he is subservient within the satanic economy. "As the first beast was characterized by political features, the beast from the land appears clothed in all the accoutrements of religion" (Boring 161). Mounce (255) suggests that all this conveys an "impression of gentle harmlessness," but the false prophet's coercive activities, authoritative speech, great miracles, and use of capital punishment to enforce policies are far from suggesting anything truly *veiled* or *harmless*.

When he speaks his voice sounds "as a dragon," not like a lamb. This is not necessarily a reference to great or frightening volume and certainly not the animalistic sound produced by a literal "dragon." The whole description makes clear that he is, in fact, a real man who speaks with great authority as the Antichrist's proxy and by the authority of "the dragon" himself, Satan. The comparison, then, may be that he speaks in a "deceitful or beguiling" way (Mounce 256) as Satan does.

That he "exerciseth all the power of the first beast before him" (v. 12) suggests that he taps the same satanic power that was given to the first beast by the great dragon (v. 2). "Power"

(Greek *exousia*) is right or authority. The second beast directs worship to the first, performing miracles on his behalf, whether "in his presence" ("before him") or perhaps even when Antichrist is not physically present.

Again, as throughout Revelation, "the earth and them which dwell therein" refers to the unbelieving population of earth. For the most part, those who end up worshiping the beast come from this group; but it is also possible that a number of professing believers will deny Christ and submit to the beast in order to save their lives (cf. v. 8a).

The appositional clause "whose deadly wound was healed" clarifies that the first beast of v. 3 (Antichrist) is the intended object of worship, with his miraculous recovery one of the things that prompts worship. Even so, Antichrist is a *man*, and the entire population of earth will be coerced to worship a man, with a pompous and evil personality at that, instead of God. This is one of the ways by which he seeks to take God's place (2 Th. 2:4).

The false prophet who assists him succeeds in recruiting worshipers of Antichrist for several reasons. One is his beguiling speech, patterned after the arch-deceiver, "the dragon" (Satan). Another is the charisma that accrues to him because of his ability to perform great miracles. But once his position and power are consolidated sufficiently through persuasive speech and miraculous powers, the government transitions to the use of coercion. The false prophet acquires the power of life or death over earth's population, threatening those who will not worship the beast; many Tribulation saints will probably be martyred for this reason. Enforcement of the Antichrist's agenda will be married to the world's economic system, implemented by a mark that enables only those who have it to carry on business and buy food.

The second beast's "great wonders" make him more believable to the masses (v. 13; cf. Mt. 24:24; 2 Th. 2:9, 10; cf. Dt. 13:1-3). "Wonders" (Greek *semeion*) means signs (as in 12:1, 3; 15:1), a miracle that goes beyond nature or any attempt to explain it scientifically; one reason it is effective as a "sign" is that it is superhuman. Jesus used miracles to authenticate His deity, to demonstrate that He had the authority to forgive sins (Mk. 2:10), and to prompt faith in Him (Jn. 20:30, 31; Mk. 4:41). As a result many rightly concluded that Jesus was God.

Though miracles typically point to the true God, Satan has some ability to imitate or perform them. He has incredible cunning and power. Knowing that miracles cause human beings to look to God, Satan performs them in an attempt to deceive people into worshiping him. Miracles "attract the uncommitted by making them wonder whether there might not be something in it after all" (Wilcox 127).

The false prophet calls fire down "from heaven on the earth in the sight of men" (v. 13; cf. 20:9), reminiscent of Elijah's miracle on Mt. Carmel (1 Kg. 18:36-39; 2 Kg. 1:10, 12). But where Elijah's "sign" glorified God and demonstrated that He alone is worthy to be served, the false prophet parodies Elijah's miracle with an ulterior motive. He means them as public demonstrations ("in the sight of men") that authenticate the authority of Antichrist. The deception (v. 14), whatever its nature, consists in convincing unbelievers of the lie that Antichrist is deity and is to be worshiped.

A significant part of the deception in the Tribulation, then, is *idolatry* in its most brazen and ultimate form, represented in the demand to make an idol-image of the first beast (Antichrist) and worship it. Satan seeks to destroy the righteous remnant of Israel and Gentile believers during the Tribulation period with this old falsehood. And, as with Daniel and the three Hebrew "children," failure to comply with the command to worship the Antichrist's image is a life or death issue (Dan. 3:1-30; cf. Mt. 24:15, 24).

Some interpreters reject the idea that Satan can perform miracles and suggest that the false prophet's miracles are feigned in some way, much like the illusions of an ordinary magician. "Ventriloquism" has been suggested as a way the false prophet enabled the image of the beast to speak. But, given the assuredly miraculous healing of Antichrist's mortal wound, there is no reason to discount the false prophet's miracles. Well-performed "magic" tricks hardly explain his ability to mesmerize the world into worshiping Antichrist. "These will be genuine miracles, supernatural accomplishments, not mere trickery or skill in pyrotechnics" (Thomas II:175).

Again, "them that dwell on the earth" (v. 14) means the unbelieving population. The deceit is successful and is attributed to the miraculous works of the false prophet. "Miracles" (v. 14) and "wonders" (v. 13) are the same word (in the original). The deception, then, is in pointing people to the worship of Antichrist (and Satan behind him) instead of God. Though one may assume that most Tribulation believers will not be caught up in this deception, many will. Jesus did not predict that "the elect" will *almost* be deceived (Mt. 24:24). The deception will be incredibly persuasive and intense; the love of many will grow cold and some may even become apostate. Only the faithful will be saved (Mt. 24:13).

Idealist Poythress (144-146) makes some helpful observations about the instruments of satanic deception and the spirit of Antichrist that we face even now—including the mass media, educational institutions, advertising, and all sorts of modern technology like computers and the television industry. Any of these may be commandeered by Satan to indoctrinate people with falsehood. "Technology, then, becomes the worker of miraculous signs" (145). He even suggests that television has taken the place of the image of the emperor in the first century. As true-to-life as these comments are, however, they fall short of matching the persons and powers of the eschatological Antichrist and his minister of worship. It would be difficult to envision someone being put to death because of refusal to watch television.

Antichrist and the false prophet will be real persons and should not be confused with mechanical instruments, media, or institutions. Poythress equates "being put to death" with the process of self-destruction that one brings on himself by being immersed in a godless or idolatrous culture; but Revelation attributes the killing to the agency of the beast: something done "to," not "by" the person deceived. True, something of the spirit of Antichrist is already at work, discernible in amoral, secular, anti-Christian programming and advertising. But speculation about contemporary media should not obscure the main point: "The

final form of apostasy is not simply the worship of some pagan deity but the worship of Satan himself who in his whole program seeks to be 'like God' [Is. 14:14]" (Walvoord 200). He does not lust for power so much as for worship.

"Which he had power to do" is, again, the "divine passive": literally, "which [signs] were given him to do." The deception is possible and effective only because God permits it. Paul offers helpful explanation in 2 Th. 2:9, 10, 11: "And for this cause God shall send them strong delusion, that they should believe a lie...who believed not the truth." God does not deceive them but allows the unholy trinity to do so as a part of His judgment for their unbelief.

"Saying...that they should make an image" has the effect of a coercive command (cf. Dan. 3:4): "He ordered them to set up an image" (NIV). Interpreters express interest in the precise form of the image intended here. The word (Greek *eikon*) can mean a "resemblance" or "likeness" (Vincent 529), which might take the form of an engraving on a coin, for example, or an actual "statue." Or a document might be marked with an official "imperial stamp" (Deissmann 341). But "an image to the beast" seems more likely to suggest a statue, perhaps in "a conspicuous place" (Aune II:761). In John's day, such statues were often found in public places and idol temples. Smaller versions might even be kept in the home (cf. Acts 19:24). Antichrist will doubtless employ technology or media, at least, to keep his image before the world.

The appositional clause "which had the wound by a sword, and did live" occurs again, this time adding that "a sword" was used. As observed earlier, the words may suggest a formal confession that earth-dwellers are compelled to recite in the Antichrist's worship. As discussed in connection with v. 3, some believe that "and did live" indicates a "resurrection"; but in that case "lived again" (Greek *anazao*) would seem more likely. "Did live" may as easily imply that the "beast" did not die from the wound, as expected (Aune (II:720). Antichrist was mortally wounded but miraculously continued to live. John states unequivocally in vv. 3, 12 that he was "healed."

The second beast also "had power" (again a "divine passive": literally, "it was given to him") to "give life unto the image of the beast" and enable it "to speak" (v. 15). This "wonder" is truly impressive if the image was a stone or metal statue, made to *appear* (at least) to be alive and to speak. It is not likely that the image actually lived in the same way that a flesh and blood being lives. "To give life" is literally "to give spirit (or, breath)," and the ability of speech may fully explain this; the image apparently does not develop any other anatomical life. Those who think the false prophet's "miracles" are bogus suggest that this is accomplished by "ventriloquism" (Ford 225) or some other "magic." Magicians or zealous devotees in the ancient world sometimes rigged an idol with the ability to speak (Aune II:764). At any rate, this complements the other miracles and further induces earth-dwellers to worship the beast. D. Johnson (195) compares the taunting observations of Ps. 115:5, 7 about idols ('They have mouths, but they cannot speak. They cannot make a sound with their throat.") and observes that this ability makes the image appear to be something other than a lifeless idol.

The second beast also enforces the idolatrous, worldwide state religion with *the power of life or death*. There is some question whether "the image of the beast" or "the false prophet" puts people to death, here, but the latter seems more likely (Thomas II:178). The commas setting off "that the image of the beast should both speak," suggest that the second beast is the subject or "cause that as many as should not worship the image of the beast should be killed." Regardless, the important point is the serious nature of the threat of death. The evil characters are confederate, working toward the same nefarious goal: the worship of the image, the worship of Antichrist, and the worship of the dragon (and so of Satan).

"As many as would not worship the image of the beast" specifies those (Tribulation martyrs) who are put to death (cf. 6:9). Mounce (258) says, "It is this decision that accounts for the apostasy that is to precede the return of Christ (2 Th. 2:1-3)." In the Roman Empire, many Christians faced such a threat: "At least by Trajan's day failure to worship the emperor was a capital offense" (Mounce 259). Failure to participate in civic festivals honoring the emperor as deity was equivalent to being unpatriotic and could lead to execution. In a similar way, in the Tribulation, Antichrist's demand to be worshiped will conflict with loyalty to Christ.

This does not mean that everyone who does not worship the beast is killed, though that is the standard policy. The remnant of converted Jewish believers is safely hidden away in the place prepared by God for her in the wilderness; these apparently escape the wrath of Antichrist and consequently the experience of martyrdom (12:6, 14-16).

Neither is it likely that every Tribulation believer will be "discovered" or "denounced" to Antichrist in spite of economic and spiritual coercion to worship the image. A great number of these will be alive at the Second Coming. But apparently a significant number will be discovered, who refuse to be unfaithful to Christ either by receiving the mark of the beast or by worshiping his image, and will be executed.

"And he causeth all" (v. 16) continues to refer to the second beast, who eventually facilitates Antichrist's control over the world's population by identifying those who comply with the "mark of the beast." Antichrist desires to be worshiped exclusively and exempts no one. Every cross section of humanity is listed for effect in antithetical couplets: "small and great," "rich and poor," and "free and bond": "a rhetorical way of stressing the totality of human society" (Mounce 259). One implication is that it will be very difficult to hide one's loyalty during the latter half of the Tribulation. There will be very little *fence-straddling*. The Antichrist's system of social identification and the potential consequence of martyrdom will effectively weed out insincere professions of faith.

What begins as a peace treaty with national Israel at the beginning of the period eventually turns into world domination by Antichrist. Israel buys into the promises of the Antichrist, only to be tragically betrayed in the middle of the period. The unbelieving nations of the world are also duped, at first, by the impressive satanic miracles and sweet-sounding promises. Unfortunately, Antichrist soon establishes a policy demanding exclusive worship. The Romans typically tolerated worship of other gods so long as allegiance was sworn to Caesar; Antichrist has no such tolerance and by coercion requires the worship of himself alone.

The "mark" is made on either the "right hand" or on the "forehead" (v. 16) and is thereby visible. Interpreters speculate about the precise form of this "mark" and whether it is a literal or legal marking. It may be a literal branding (tattoo?) of the flesh in some way, similar to the devotees of pagan gods in the ancient world. Keener (352) reports that "Ptolemy IV...of Egypt required Jewish people in his realm to be enrolled in a census and to be branded with an ivy leaf, the symbol of Dionysus [3 Macc. 2:28-29]." On "mark" (Greek *charagma*) Aune (II:721) says, "When applied to human or animal skin, it is always a *brand*." It has been popular to speculate about a mark or number such as a personal identification number (pin?) that may be assigned to a person or perhaps attached to their legal documents. Apparently a certificate was issued to "those who complied with the ritual of the imperial religion" (Charles I:365, citing Ramsay).

Some think the "mark" is only symbolic: "The *charagma* is not a literal impress seal, certificate, or similar mark of identification, but is John's way of symbolically describing authentic ownership and loyalty" (A. Johnson 136). Hendriksen (150) suggests that the forehead symbolizes "the mind, the thought-life, the philosophy of a person," and the right hand "his deed, action, trade, industry, etc." D. Johnson (196) suggests a reflection of the practice of ancient Israelites who tied quotations from the Law on their foreheads or hands "in order to signify that their thoughts and actions were in submission to the Word of the Lord (Deut. 6:8)." All such observations are appealing, but what will the beast's regime use to distinguish between those who may buy and sell and those who cannot? The bottom line seems to be that in the Tribulation, God marks those who belong to Him and the Antichrist does the same.

The mark must incorporate either "the name" or "the number" of the beast, or both (v. 17). In a way that perhaps parodies how God marks the 144,000 special servants (7:1-8; 9:4; 14:1), Antichrist counters with a mark of his own for those who belong to him. The significance of this cannot be underestimated: it becomes a standard of judgment used by God in assigning a person's eternal destiny (14:11; 15:2; 19:20; 20:4). Idealist Beale (716), who thinks the "mark" is transhistorical and on every unbeliever in every age, is forced to regard it as "invisible" and figurative of allegiance to "the beast." But the specific reference to one's "right hand" or "forehead" suggests visibility instead.

So does the need for clear identification in order to buy and sell on earth, and the "mark" is the basis for determining that during the Tribulation period (v. 17). The specter of such economic discrimination, poverty, and starvation are reminiscent of the kinds of external threats faced by the first-century church (chapters 2 and 3). But during the Tribulation everything is magnified (unprecedented historically) in degree and scope. The strictures are inevitable and worldwide, far exceeding the sporadic and occasional "discoveries" or persecutions in first-century Asia Minor.

The "name of the beast" and the "number of his name" apparently define the "mark" (Brighton 347). These serve to identify unbelieving earth-dwellers for legal participation in the world's economy. The mark identifies those who worship the beast and its lack exposes those who do not. Tribulation saints will be "discovered" to Antichrist if without this mark they attempt to use the normal channels of commerce. Faithfulness to Christ during the Tribulation dramatically narrows one's options. There will be great pressure to compromise in order to save one's life.

John equates "wisdom" and "understanding" with the ability to recognize or "count the number of the beast," which is "the number of a man" (v. 18). The number of man or of the beast is "666." The history of interpretation reveals that many have attempted to determine the identity of the beast (Antichrist) by comparing the numerical equivalents of letters in the Hebrew alphabet with the letters in someone's name—a method called "Gematria" (see Bauckham 384-389). These attempts often manipulate the mathematical equivalents of the letters in order to arrive at "666" for one's favorite candidate. Most such attempts are so blatantly arbitrary and inconsistent that the entire concept is highly questionable. One survey (Hughes 154) reports more than 100 names that have been identified as Antichrist by this method.

Yet Bauckham is convinced that this unquestionably means "Nero" since the numerical equivalents of the letters in his name equal 666—though there are legitimate questions about this. Caird insightfully points out that there is nothing in the text to indicate that John intends his readers to transliterate from Greek letters into the Hebrew alphabet; doing this probably indicates a presupposition that "Nero" is meant. An appropriate question is whether John is encouraging readers to attempt specific identification of Antichrist by citing this number. In the final analysis, an absolutely unquestionable identification of the Antichrist, by the alphabetical equivalents of the number 666, can never be certain. "This solution asks us to calculate a Hebrew transliteration of the Greek form of a Latin name, and that with a defective spelling" (Mounce 264).

The number 666 could be as simple as a symbol of the imperfection of man, since six is one short of seven, the number of perfection (and sometimes of deity) in Revelation (cf. Hendriksen 151). In that case, the only point is that Antichrist will be a real person, male in gender, and will use a mark to enforce the world's worship. Nothing necessarily indicates that the number is a "cryptic" reference to Nero (or another emperor) because John fears retaliation from secular authorities (cf. Gonzalez 85). Surely there will be better Scriptural indicators that the Tribulation has come than having to rely on a secret formula for identifying Antichrist. Popular attempts at identification in the past have failed: the Great Tribulation has not happened. When Antichrist is finally revealed, the inhabitants of the world will have no difficulty recognizing him or his regime.

Summary
(13:1-18)

John's visions in chapter 13 introduce us to two great beasts that are the evil associates of the great red dragon in chapter 12. They are the primary agents Satan uses, during the Great Tribulation, to carry out his agenda in the earth, to which he is then confined after being cast out of Heaven (12:7-9). This seven-year period culminates with the Second Coming of Christ, when Christ defeats Antichrist and establishes His millennial rule on earth. Conversely, Satan uses this eschatological period to persecute the "woman" (the nation of Israel) and her "seed" (Jewish and Gentile Tribulation believers). Most of this appears to take place in the latter half or last three-and-a-half years.

The first beast (vv. 1-10), Antichrist, rises up out of the sea, in description nearly identical to the great red dragon in 12:3. Both have "seven heads" and "ten horns." The dragon wears crowns on its heads. The beast of 13:1-10 wears them on his horns, indicating a shift in focus to one great world empire and the confederate nations or kings comprising it with Antichrist in control. Though there are many interesting views about the symbolism of the heads and horns, it seems best to rely on identifications made in Scripture. Daniel 7:4-8 presents four beasts, subsequently interpreted as four kings or kingdoms (7:17, 23). The "ten horns" (7:7) are identified as "ten kings" (7:24) that come from the fourth kingdom. The "little horn" (7:8) is identified as "another king" that subdues three of the ten kings (7:24). In a similar way, the symbolism of Rev. 13 becomes clearer in Rev. 17. There the beast symbolizing Antichrist appears again (17:8). The "seven heads" are identified as "seven mountains" (17:9) and the "ten horns" as "ten kings." (There is some question whether the "seven kings" of v. 10 relate to the mountains or the kings. Comment on this will be reserved for that section in the commentary.)

All the qualities of ancient world powers considered as enemies of God are epitomized in the first beast. The ancient kingdoms of Dan. 7 foreshadowed the final, eschatological world empire but are distinct from it. The world empire that emerges during the Tribulation is unprecedented in scope and degree when compared to anything before it. This is true of its leader, the Antichrist, and his associate, the second beast of chapter 13, the false prophet. Both are real historical persons. The personification of the lawless spirit of Antichrist in a future historical individual best satisfies the language of Scripture.

John indicates a number of the Antichrist's characteristics. He is blasphemous, with "the name of blasphemy" on his heads (v. 1). In terms of a composite monstrosity he embodies the characteristics of a "leopard," "bear," and "lion," and of the ancient kingdoms thus symbolized in Dan. 7—kingdoms that persecuted the people of God (v. 2). The dragon (Satan) has persecuted the seed of the woman since Gen. 3:15; he will continue this until the very end. These kingdoms and their rulers foreshadow the Antichrist's persecution of God's people in the Tribulation period.

The mortal wounding and miraculous healing of Antichrist catapults him into the spotlight of world attention in the end-times (v. 3). The unbelieving population of the world mistakenly concludes that the miracles of Antichrist indicate that he is God, and wonder turns into worship. In that worship they parody the O.T. question that emphasized how incomparable the true God is (v. 4). The agenda of the satanic trinity is to redirect worship from God to Satan by deception.

The Antichrist speaks great blasphemies against the name of God, His tabernacle, and those who dwell in Heaven (vv. 5, 6). Satan hates everything and everyone associated with God. Still, though Antichrist is inspired by Satan to do this, he is allowed to do so only by God who still retains sovereign control over all historical events including the Tribulation. Temporary authority is granted, for a 42-month period, to make war against the saints and "overcome" them (v. 7), apparently meaning that God will permit many faithful believers to be martyred. Further, some true believers may renounce Christ under the pressures of the period.

The worship of Antichrist is worldwide and exclusive (v. 8). All will be coerced, with no other option. Imprisonment and martyrdom are inevitable for those who profess faith in Christ. Two virtues will be required to endure such a hostile spiritual environment: patience and faith (v. 10).

The second beast (vv. 11-18) is closely associated with the first but distinct and subservient, subsequently given the title "false prophet" (16:13; 19:20). He arises out of the "land" instead of the sea, perhaps indicating an earthly connection (v. 11). His "two horns" symbolize that he has power, though not equivalent to that of the first beast with ten horns. His lamb-like appearance is deceptive: he has great power and speaks with authority reminiscent of the great red dragon (chapter 12). The false prophet has no independent interests but works entirely on behalf of the first beast (v. 12), to deceive the world into worshiping Antichrist. Toward this end he performs great miracles ("signs") that include causing fire to fall from the sky (v. 13) and "giving life" to Antichrist's image.

The false prophet influences the world to make an image to Antichrist (v. 14). The whole world witnessed the

REVELATION

miracles, and the power was attributed to Antichrist. They concluded that only God could do such things; an image would therefore be appropriate. But persuasion soon turns to coercion: the entire population of earth is eventually compelled to worship the image of the beast on pain of death (v. 15).

This mandatory worship is reinforced by means of a verifiable mark (v. 16), a visible one placed on every known person—either on the right hand or the forehead (or both). This may even extend to some sort of official documentation such as a pin number or official government stamp with Antichrist's seal. The ramifications of compliance extend to the marketplace, controlling whether a person can buy or sell (v. 17). The inability of faithful Tribulation believers to buy food, clothing, medicine, gas, or other basic necessities must lead either to their death or to a fugitive existence.

The number or mark of the beast is specific: "666" (v. 18). Rather than being a means of revealing Antichrist's identity (by gematria), this number is probably a literal part of the marking.

Application: Teaching and Preaching the Passage

Every student or teacher of Revelation should be familiar with the four major schools of its interpretation: preterism (past history), historicism (continuous history), futurism (future history), and idealism (para-history). These were briefly surveyed in the introduction to this commentary. Understanding these perspectives helps us both to evaluate the viewpoint of a particular interpreter on a given passage and to articulate our own viewpoint.

The first three of the schools just listed are all "historicist" in one way or another, thus willing to see in Revelation specific persons, places, and events of the past or future. By contrast, idealism looks for the abiding principle that applies to every generation of church history and is hesitant to limit the symbolism to any one fulfillment. Yet even many idealists allow for an eschatological application, as in a future, intense Tribulation period or personal Antichrist.

These four chronological perspectives typically govern commentators' interpretation of the visions of Revelation, though not necessarily slavishly or uniformly. Most preterists identify the first beast of chapter 13 with Rome or one of its emperors—like Nero or Domitian. Historicists tend to identify the beast as the Roman Catholic Church or papacy or some other infamous, historic personality like Hitler or Stalin. Futurists look to the end-time Tribulation for the revelation of Antichrist. Idealists tend to institutionalize "Antichrist" as an anti-Christian spirit manifested in all secular or pagan institutions and personalities of history between Christ's first advent and the Second Coming.

Teachers of Revelation must articulate a theology of Revelation that appreciates the value of all four perspectives but without compromising legitimate conviction. It is easy to understand why believers in the first few centuries of church history would be tempted to think of Nero or Domitian (or some other emperor) as Antichrist, since they led persecutions against believers. (Indeed, even for the advocates of other schools of interpretation the early church's relationship with the Roman Empire provides a helpful context for

347

discussing church-state issues.) Likewise, some of the leaders of the Protestant Reformation, in their struggle against the Roman Catholic Church, easily equated the papacy or pope with Antichrist. Similarly, some interpreters living during World War II, familiar with the horrors of the Jewish holocaust, could hardly help identifying Adolf Hitler as Antichrist.

In sympathy with the idealists we are able to recognize the *spirit* of antichrist in each of these scenarios while recognizing that none of them provided the actual fulfillment (see 1 Jn. 2:18). Since no generation knows the hour of Christ's return or when the Great Tribulation will begin, attempts at identifying him with some contemporary figure will no doubt prove premature. Christ warned us about making such predictions. The temptation to "sensationalize" our audience must be resisted. Speculation should be qualified as such. A simple exposition that does not go beyond what the text itself suggests is exciting enough!

The ways early believers related to the persecutions and idolatry of the Roman state reveal principles about how Christians of any generation should relate to secular authorities and live in countercultures. The commitment of many led to their martyrdom, an instructive example that should embarrass nominal Christian commitment in the twenty-first century. Conversely, the compromising attitude of some also serves as a negative example of how not to behave in the face of cultural pressure. Futurist interpreters should have an interest in the ancient Roman Empire since many see a *revived* Roman Empire in the end-times. The forces at work in ancient empires foreshadow the ultimate

expression of these in the Tribulation just before Christ returns.

Revelation is truly a handbook on Christian behavior under pressure. We must labor to rediscover how relevant it is to each generation, including our own. A more comprehensive description of various church scenarios and the problems they encounter cannot be found anywhere else in Scripture. (See chapters 2 and 3.)

The material in Revelation should not only be used to inform people about the future, it should be mined for principles for living in the present. The deceptive and destructive potential of the culture around us will continue to increase as the Tribulation draws closer. Even now, the *spirit* of antichrist is at work to redirect worship from God to the things of this world and ultimately to Satan himself. That spirit seeks to destroy genuine faith in Christ. Christians must develop an ability to discern between external appearances ("signs" that are often satanic deceptions) and truth or reality. We must develop "spirit eyes" that see things as God sees them and that weigh present behavior in light of eternity.

For example, even modern technology often breeds a false confidence that God is not needed. This is certainly reflected as American culture returns to paganism and fewer people attend church. God is left out inadvertently or by design. Indeed, God is often legislated out of sight. This pattern indicates a culture in the grip of idolatry, which may be defined as "getting from someone or something else what God alone desires to give," or as "giving to someone or something else what God alone deserves to receive." We must help fellow believers see that idolatry exists not only when there is an image to bow down to but when we find ourselves doing what has just been described in this practical definition.

Today's believers must recognize that the demands of genuine discipleship never change. Every believer must choose to be faithful to Christ whatever the cost. Believers are instructed in the N.T. to obey and pray for the secular authorities that govern them. But when the prevailing culture or government expects believers to violate Scriptural principle the choice is clear: we must obey God. In that moment we choose Christ instead of Caesar.

Suggested Outlines. The Appearance of Antichrist, 13:1-10: (1) Audition, v. 1; (2) Authority, v. 2; (3) Assassination, v. 3; (4) Acceptance, v. 4; (5) Accusations, vv. 5, 6; (6) Adversaries, vv. 7-10.

The False Prophet, 13:11-18: (1) Diverse deputy, v. 1; (2) Director of world worship, v. 12; (3) Deceptive deeds, vv. 13-15; (4) Designated disciples, vv. 16, 17; (5) Digits of false deity, v. 18.

7. The character of Christ's servants (14:1-20)

The third, lengthy parenthesis (which began at 12:1) continues, introducing another vision with "And I looked, and, lo" (v. 1). The focus changes back to the divine perspective, providing a chronological view of two "harvests" that take place at the end of the Tribulation. That the Lamb stands on Mt. Zion is in contrast to the previous scene on the seashore (13:1), thus picturing opposing forces at work.

Chapter 14 may be divided into three parts. The first relates to Heaven and earth, expanding on the special group introduced in chapter 7 by indicating

seven characteristics (vv. 1-5). The second records three angelic proclamations (vv. 6-13). The last (vv. 14-20) predicts two eschatological world harvests.

Caird (178) compares Ps. 2: "The psalm depicts a worldwide rebellion of the nations against God, and tells of God's plan to entrust the suppression of the revolt to his son, the anointed king... and it ends with an appeal to the rulers of the earth to do homage before they are overtaken by God's final day of reckoning." This gospel appeal is in v. 6.

a. The 144,000 (vv. 1-5)

**1 And I looked, and, lo, a Lamb stood on the mount Sion, and with him an hundred forty *and* four thousand, having his Father's name written in their foreheads.
2 And I heard a voice from heaven, as the voice of many waters, and as the voice of a great thunder: and I heard the voice of harpers harping with their harps:
3 And they sung as it were a new song before the throne, and before the four beasts, and the elders: and no man could learn that song but the hundred *and* forty *and* four thousand, which were redeemed from the earth.
4 These are they which were not defiled with women; for they are virgins. These are they which follow the Lamb whithersoever he goeth. These were redeemed from among men, *being* the firstfruits unto God and to the Lamb.
5 And in their mouth was found no guile: for they are without fault before the throne of God.**

"A Lamb" stood on Mt. Zion, surrounded by "144,000" servants of God (v. 1), recalling the Lamb of 5:6ff and the 144,000 of 7:3-8, though some interpreters do not precisely equate the two groups. Aune (II:804) thinks of "all Christians" in chapter 7, but only "the remnant of Christians who survive to the end" in chapter 14. Mounce (265) identifies these as "the entire body of the redeemed." Idealist Beale (733) sees them as "the totality of God's people throughout the ages."

The uniqueness of "144,000" argues for identifying this group as the same Jewish believers introduced in 7:4-8 (see comments there). Furthermore, both groups have the name of God written on each individual's forehead (7:3; 14:1). These are therefore a select group of *Jewish Christians* who serve Christ in the Tribulation. Though not necessarily tantamount to the righteous remnant of Israel predicted in Rom. 11:26, 27, they are saved in the same way and follow the same Christ, making it unproductive to differentiate between them.

Thomas suggests that vv. 1-5 are a "summary of the Millennium" (II:189). That would make this scene a proleptic view of their final state after the Tribulation. Mounce (263) calls it "glimpses of final blessedness" and "the bright morning of eternity," a glimpse given to encourage saints in the present or in the Tribulation to endure until then. More likely, these are pictured as having joined Christ at His Second Coming, positioned on Mt. Zion just before the great Battle of Armageddon (cf. Thomas II:191). Old Testament prophecies predict a rally around Mt. Zion in the Day of the Lord (Ps. 48:1, 2; Is. 11:9-12; 24:23; Jl. 2:32; Zech. 14:4, 5).

"A Lamb" is obviously "the Lamb" (as in most manuscripts), the slain Lamb of 5:6-14; 6:1; 13:8, *standing* "to suggest that he functions as a warrior prepared to destroy his enemies" (Aune II:803). Mt. Sion (Zion) probably stands for the entire city of Jerusalem, though some would idealize it to represent "every place on earth where God's Word is proclaimed and the Sacraments of Holy Baptism and the Lord's Supper are administered according to the Lord's institution" (Brighton 365). Mounce (265), on the other hand, sees it as "the heavenly Mt. Zion" based on Gal. 4:26. But this is clearly the city of Jerusalem on earth rather than "the heavenly Jerusalem" or God's people. "Without some special qualification, Scripture never uses Mt. Zion to denote a celestial abode of God or His people" (Thomas II:190).

Jerusalem, center of God's earthly activity in both testaments, will figure prominently in the end-times (Ps. 2:6; Is. 24:23; Jl. 2:32; Mic. 4:7; Zech. 14:4, 5). The picture here is perhaps a symbol of the Messiah's ultimate triumph and coming eternal enthronement over the world. The Lion of Judah, the Root of David, and the slain Lamb of the church all converge in Jesus Christ. The expectations of the nation of Israel and the N.T. church are fulfilled in His person and kingdom. These appellations will eternally be a part of Jesus' identity and do not disturb the unity or singular nature of God's family in eternity.

As noted, these 144,000 have God's name "written in their foreheads." Many manuscripts read "His name and His Father's name." Since their appearance together in the throne room (chapter 5), the Father and the Lamb continue to appear together throughout Revelation. Indeed, Jesus promised to write His own "new name" on the faithful believers of Philadelphia (3:12).

Such a mark signifies ownership and servitude; see comments on 7:3. The mark a person bears during the Tribulation has eternal consequences according to the proclamation of the third angel (14:9-11; cf. 19:20). Battle lines are forming for the last great conflict at Christ's return, and eternal destinies are being determined. God "seals" those who belong to Him, and the Antichrist does the same with his.

John "heard a voice from heaven" (v. 2), no doubt recognizing its source by the quality and volume of the voices and music. "Many waters" and "a great thunder" are analogies from the world of nature, indicating tremendous volume. "Voice" (Greek *phone*), used four times, can also mean "sound" and refers here to the sound made by a group. John distinguished the sound of a number of harpists, a "harp" (Greek *kithara*) being a "ten-stringed instrument" such as a lyre or harp (Vine 291, citing Josephus). These—perhaps the elders, saints, or angels—accompanied the heavenly singers; cf. 5:9, 10. Those ultimately victorious over the beast also have harps and sing "the song of Moses" in 15:2-4.

The 144,000 sing "a new song" in Heaven's throne room (v. 3). "Before the throne, and before the four living creatures, and the elders" is an unchanging snapshot of the permanent entourage of beings around God's throne. "Before the throne" indicates the presence of God in Heaven. None but the 144,000 could sing this song, appar-

ently excluding unredeemed persons, angels, and "the four beasts and the elders." The earth's inhabitants during the Tribulation period are hostile to God and those who follow Him. The judgments of God fall on them and earth's systems. Anyone saved or redeemed during this period escapes sharing in its doom. And since the 144,000 are positioned with the Lamb, standing on the earthly Mt. Zion, it is plausible that they are singing from this earthly position while gathered there with Christ, a fitting image indeed. Those who have faithfully followed the Lamb of God in life will finally stand with Him in His victory.

How can these be on earth and sing "before the throne" at the same time? The answer is that this is a *vision*, an expansive one that incorporates elements of Heaven and earth. It probably looks ahead chronologically, with the initial sight of the 144,000 on Mt. Zion (v. 1) expanded to include a future scene when they sing before God's throne in eternity (vv. 2-5). The vision, then, is a historical account of the 144,000 from their initial redemption and sealing in 7:1-8 to their eternal condition before the throne of God in eternity (14:5).

"Redeemed" in vv. 3, 4, (Greek *agorazo*) technically means *purchased* (Thayer 8), typically thought of as the purchase of believers through the payment of Christ's blood (1 Pet. 1:18, 19)—"redemption" indeed. Some interpreters think that the focus here is on their deliverance from Antichrist's persecution: "That they have been redeemed from the earth does not mean that they have been removed bodily from the earth [Jn. 17:15] but that they were separated from the evil ways of the world and the tyranny of its pernicious philosophies" (Mounce 266). But the word probably refers, simply, to their redemption out from among the population of earth (cf. v. 4).

The character of this select group is described (vv. 4, 5) in several particulars. (1) "Not defiled with women" means that they never had sexual intercourse with a woman and are cited positively for their celibacy. "Defile" (Greek *moluno*) means "causing something to be dirty: *soil, smear, stain*" (ALGNT 266) and may include spiritual defilement (3:4). If this is the meaning here, the defilement refers to spiritual adultery (idolatry), and "virginity" to spiritual faithfulness. Worshiping Antichrist would be equivalent to adultery (cf. Jer. 2:20; 3:1, 6, 8; 14:17; Is. 37:22).

But there is no indication that "not defiled with women" is to be taken spiritually; consequently, the literal sense may not be ruled out (Thomas II:196). But the literal interpretation, here, must not be taken to mean that lawful sexual intercourse is unholy. Jesus sanctioned marriage (Jn. 2:1, 2; Mt. 19:4-6), as did Paul (1 Cor. 7:1, 7, 8, 25-35) and the writer of Hebrews (13:4). The Tribulation provides a unique set of circumstances. (If the straightforward meaning is correct, the viewpoint that identifies the 144,000 as the church becomes problematic since not all believers are virgins.)

(2) They are *submissive* to the leadership of Christ: They "follow the Lamb whithersoever he goeth." They have been faithful to Him, even if called to martyrdom. This characterization is consistent with their past experience during the Tribulation as well as their present posture on Mt. Zion. Jesus is not only the eternal Lamb of God, He is the Good Shepherd of the sheep (Jn. 10:1-

18). As such, Christ invited His disciples to "follow" Him (Mt. 4:19; 16:24; cf. 1 Pet. 2:21; 5:4). The 144,000 willingly follow the Lamb—serve Christ faithfully—throughout the Tribulation.

(3) They are "redeemed from among men" as "the first fruits unto God and to the Lamb" (cf. 5:9; 7:1-8; Jer. 2:3). "Redeemed" is the same as in the previous verse. Identification as "first fruits" harks back to God's O.T. requirement of the best of things from His people: the "first fruits" of male children, animals, and produce were offered to the Lord (Ex. 13:1-16; 23:19; Lev. 23:9-14; 27:30; Num. 15:20; 18:12-17; Dt. 14:22, 23, 28; 26:1-10). Israel was "first fruits" of all nations (Jer. 2:3). In general: "The offering of 'first fruits' also foreshadowed that the rest would soon be gathered in accordance with the Owner's sovereign provision" (Beale 742). Even in the N.T. that principle is reflected in references to "new converts," "the Spirit," and "Christ's resurrection," each of which points to a greater end-times fulfillment or promises that there are many more to come (cf. Rom. 8:23; 1 Cor. 15:20; Jas. 1:18).

Then the "first fruits" principle is operative in the predicted end-times restoration of Israel on Mt. Zion (Ezek. 20:33-44). The 144,000 fill this role during the Tribulation, serving as an initial harvest that presages the larger and final group of Tribulation believers portrayed in vv. 14-16. "The connection between the first fruits of 14:4 and the reaping of the whole harvest in 14:14-16 would be obvious to any Jew" (Bauckham 291).

Aune (II:815) observes that the precise words, "first fruits," when applied to people, as here, "is a metaphor drawn from the first fruits of the field (barley, wheat, bread, grapes, etc.)." This insight corresponds to the two "harvest" visions of chapter 14: perhaps of grain (vv. 14-16) and grapes (vv. 17-20). The setting aside of the 144,000, therefore, points to a greater harvest to come (vv. 14-16). Objecting to a connection with a future harvest on the basis that the character of the 144,000 is somehow superior to the rest of the redeemed is not good theology. *All* the redeemed will be presented "blameless" before the throne on the basis of Christ's merits alone.

(4) The 144,000 are also commended that "in their mouth was found no guile" (v. 5; cf. Is. 53:9; Zeph. 3:11-20). Though some manuscripts have "lie" (Greek *pseudos*) instead of "guile" or "deceit" (Greek *dolos*), the meaning is the same. This may indicate their general truthfulness or maintaining their witness with integrity even in a threatening environment—or both. This characteristic is in sharp contrast to the ungodly culture around them. Liars are finally excluded from Heaven (21:8, 27; 22:15).

(5) They stand before God's throne "without fault" or "blameless" (cf. 1 Th. 3:13; 5:23; 2 Pet. 3:14). They have seen through the error of Israel's rejection of Christ and have refused to participate in the idolatrous worship of the Antichrist. Many of the elements of this blamelessness are found in 1 Pet. 1:21-25, where Peter exhorts believers to follow in Christ's steps. He committed no sin; no deceit was found in His mouth; He did not revile or threaten; He trusted God totally. These are reminiscent of the qualities attributed to the 144,000 in vv. 4, 5. They follow Christ, imitating His character even to martyrdom; but there is no hint that they are

blameless specifically because of their martyrdom (cf. Mounce 269).

"Before the throne of God," though not in all manuscripts, is clearly implied; it is equivalent to being in God's presence in Heaven. The end of such character and service as these 144,000 manifest is finally to be ushered into God's presence forever. Perhaps this group serves as successful evangelists, spreading the gospel and leading others to Christ during the Tribulation.

b. Three angelic proclamations (vv. 6-13)

6 And I saw another angel fly in the midst of heaven, having the everlasting gospel to preach unto them that dwell on the earth, and to every nation, and kindred, and tongue, and people,

7 Saying with a loud voice, Fear God, and give glory to him; for the hour of his judgment is come: and worship him that made heaven, and earth, and the sea, and the fountains of waters.

8 And there followed another angel, saying, Babylon is fallen, is fallen, that great city, because she made all nations drink of the wine of the wrath of her fornication.

9 And the third angel followed them, saying with a loud voice, If any man worship the beast and his image, and receive *his* mark in his forehead, or in his hand,

10 The same shall drink of the wine of the wrath of God, which is poured out without mixture into the cup of his indignation; and he shall be tormented with fire and brimstone in the presence of the

holy angels, and in the presence of the Lamb:

11 And the smoke of their torment ascendeth up for ever and ever: and they have no rest day nor night, who worship the beast and his image, and whosoever receiveth the mark of his name.

12 Here is the patience of the saints: here *are* they that keep the commandments of God, and the faith of Jesus.

13 And I heard a voice from heaven saying unto me, Write, Blessed *are* the dead which die in the Lord from henceforth: Yea, saith the Spirit, that they may rest from their labors; and their works do follow them.

"And I saw" introduces a series of visions in which an angel serves as a herald for future events (vv. 6-12). These separate the vision of the 144,000 from the vision of the two harvests in vv. 16-20 and are still within the larger parenthesis of 12:1—14:20.

The first angel was "flying through the midst of heaven" (v 6; cf. 8:13), which may indicate haste in light of rapidly disintegrating world conditions during the Tribulation. All the speculation about whether this is the same as an angel earlier in Revelation seems inconsequential: he is simply "another angel," similar to but different from the others. The "midst of heaven" (Greek *mesouraneima*) is "the highest point of the sun's circuit in the sky... *zenith, midair, directly overhead*" (ALGNT 259). The theater of action (as in 8:13) is the earth's sky, a vantage point from which the angel may be easily heard and seen.

This angel symbolically portrays *the preaching of the gospel* during the Tribulation. Some object that this is not what we know as the "gospel" of salvation by grace through faith in the finished work of Christ, either because of the lack of a "the" (in the Greek) with "everlasting gospel" or because of the content of v. 7. Aune (II:825), for example, thinks this "is a more general invitation given to the world in light of the pending judgment of God." But Beale (748) is more on track: "The meaning of the word here must be determined ultimately by the immediate context....The angel announces not a different gospel, but one that carries dire consequences if it is rejected." Even if v. 7 is this angel's *total* message—and that is not necessarily the case—the traditional sense of "gospel" is implied. Otherwise, the invitation to "Fear God, and give glory to him" would be meaningless without provision for a way of obeying it. The gospel is good news because it provides the way to escape the judgment of God. It would be incongruous to envision a message of judgment *alone* as "an everlasting gospel." The focus shifts to the blessings of the gospel once eternity has come.

People—Jews and Gentiles—will have opportunity to be saved throughout the Tribulation (cf. 7:4-10). For this to happen, the gospel must be preached (v. 6; cf. Rom. 1:16; 10:17; 1 Cor. 1:21) and the Holy Spirit must be at work. There is no Scriptural evidence that those who turn to Christ during the Tribulation experience salvation in a way different from anyone else. Salvation comes only through the blood of the Lamb and being born again by the Holy Spirit.

Again, "them that dwell on the earth" refers to unbelievers during the Tribulation, and "every nation, and kindred, and tongue, and people" emphasizes the *entire* unbelieving population and the universal scope of God's offer in the gospel. Indeed, it appears that the preaching of the gospel during the Tribulation is very successful, considering the numberless multitude of Tribulation converts from all nations in 7:9-17; cf. 11:13. God's mercy and grace are *available to everyone* until the Second Coming (Mt. 24:14; 2 Pet. 3:9).

The angel himself does not preach, but the vision represents that there will be those who proclaim the gospel during the Tribulation, the two witnesses (11:3-12) and perhaps the 144,000 Jewish servants included. Indeed, many Tribulation saints may proclaim the gospel, though in an environment of wonders, tribulations, and pending judgment. Warnings about the Second Coming, the millennial reign of Christ, the Great White Throne Judgment, and Heaven are likely included in the proclamation. Still, the angel himself was not silent, and this is where v. 7 comes in. The "loud" voice, typical for angels, points to the great importance of his warning, loud enough for the entire world to hear.

The angel issued a great gospel invitation and called people to worship, reflecting two potential responses. The tumultuous events of the Tribulation period are enough to cause the inhabitants of earth to live in fear, especially as the judgments of God against the unbelieving world intensify in succession with the seal, trumpet, and bowl events. They are calculated to bring glory to God by the destruction of God's ene-mies, the resurrection and rewarding of believers, and the establishment on earth of God's kingdom via the millennial reign of Christ.

This exhortation to fear, give glory to, and worship God is justified because "the hour of his judgment is come." God, who created "heaven, earth, the sea, and the fountains of waters"—the entire universe, in other words—has the power and right to judge His creation whenever and however He chooses. The Creator of all is the Judge of all.

All the sins and injustices of history have been reserved for this "hour," no longer merely prophesied, desired, or dreaded. "Is come" (Greek ingressive aorist) stresses the beginning of the event. The day of God's vengeance has begun (cf. 6:17; 11:18; 18:10), putting urgency in the angel's call; the judgment of God brings catastrophic and eternal consequences. The ever-narrowing window of *time* is rapidly closing; opportunities to repent are about to end.

We should probably assume that the circumstances of the first angel apply to the other two, including their flying and loud pronouncements. At any rate, the second angel followed the first with the emphatic announcement that the great city Babylon has fallen (v. 8; cf. Is. 21:9; Jer. 51:1-10). The verb "is fallen" apparently refers to an imminent event as though it has already occurred (Greek "prophetic" aorist; see Robertson 411). The doubling of the message—"is fallen, is fallen"—dramatically underscores the certainty (Aune II:829).

Ancient Babylon was the powerful capital of a world empire, "renowned for its luxury and moral corruption" and "the great enemy of the people of God...a symbol of the spirit of godlessness that in every age lures people away from the worship of the Creator" (Mounce 271). In effect, it came to represent the sum total of all earthly and satanic evil. But the way Revelation uses "Babylon" is disputed. Lenski (434) offers a helpful analysis of the schools of interpretation: "The preterists regard Babylon as pagan Rome alone; the historical interpreters as a reference to papal Rome; the futurists as a reference to the capital of the antichrist who is yet to come, either Rome or Jerusalem." Lenski himself, an idealist, identifies "Babylon" as *the entire antichristian empire throughout the whole of the New Testament Era.*"

Many interpreters think it is "a symbolic name for Rome," a way of textually disguising a reference to Rome for fear of antagonizing adherents of the imperial cult (Aune II:829, 830). Thomas (II:206, 207) cites the preterist viewpoint that "Jerusalem" rather than Rome is in view, but he favors identifying Babylon as a literal end-time capital city rebuilt on the Euphrates River. Idealist Beale (755) says, "Here in the Apocalypse Rome and all wicked world systems take on the symbolic name."

The background of any symbolism is probably found in the O.T. kingdom of Babylon. Nebuchadnezzar's desire to be worshiped, his idol image, and his use of coercion effectively foreshadowed Antichrist and his activities in the end-times. The end-time confederacy of nations in all likelihood will not even carry the name of Rome. Babylon is an appropriate symbol to designate an entity that is evil and overtly opposed to God. In Revelation, then, Babylon is a metaphor for the world's systems under the control of the Antichrist—religious, economic, political (see chapters 17, 18). Its manifestation will be "great" (v.

8), but the time of its judgment will come.

"Babylon" merits judgment because she makes the nations of the world *drunk* with the "wine of the wrath of her fornication" (cf. 17:2; 18:3). The getting drunk metaphorically represents coming under the persuasive influence of her "wine": that is, her deceptive doctrines, miracles, idolatry, and carnal behavior: "a symbol not only of sexual licentiousness but of every kind of excess which is the expression of unfaithfulness to God" (Hughes 162). The spirit of antichrist, as counterpart to the Holy Spirit who inspires believers to righteousness, inspires evil behavior in those who follow the Evil One, coercing them to conform to the idolatry of worshiping the Antichrist and his image. "Fornication" (Greek *porneia*) typically refers to sexual immorality in general, but it is used here as a metaphor for spiritual unfaithfulness—though literal fornication is often characteristic of those unfaithful to God. The nations of the world have committed spiritual adultery against God in their idolatrous relationship with Antichrist. "The wrath of her fornication" can be taken to mean either the wrath of God poured out because of her wickedness or, more subjectively, the wrath of those who have "committed fornication" with her and finally participate in her judgment.

The third angel immediately followed with another loud proclamation (vv. 9-11), announcing what those who are judged with "Babylon" have done (v. 9) and the nature of their judgment (vv. 10, 11). In short, they have worshiped the "beast" and received his mark, both verbs pointing to the actions as fact and habit (Greek present tense). For comments on the beast, his image, and his mark in the forehead or right hand, see chapter 13. The "if" clause is assumed true: there will be those who worship the beast and receive his mark during the Tribulation.

Two words for God's anger are used here: "wrath" (Greek *thumos*), an outburst of anger, and "indignation" (Greek *orge*), a deep-seated, abiding anger (Trench 131). The wicked behavior of Antichrist and the Christ-rejecting world angers God deeply enough both to pour out His wrath in destructive judgment and to consign those who offend Him to eternal torment.

"The same"—literally "he also" or "even he"—is emphatic: there will be no exceptions. Anyone who fulfills any of the conditions indicated in v. 9 will be judged severely and eternally. Even as beast-worshipers drank the wine of fornication (v. 8) they will "drink of the wine of the wrath of God" (v. 10). "Without mixture," typically meaning undiluted, indicates that the wine of God's wrath will be "full strength," without mitigation. The "cup of his indignation," continuing the wine metaphor, is probably the earth itself into which the wine of wrath is poured. Nor can this cup be refused.

The text provides its own interpretation of the judgment involved in "the wine of God's wrath": eternal torment with "fire and brimstone." "Brimstone" (Greek *theion*) is sulphur: "in the NT always associated with supernaturally kindled fire" (ALGNT 195). This is a literal fire, fueled by sulphur, extremely difficult to extinguish and burning with an intense heat (Mounce 273): a permanent "torment" in Hell (19:20; 20:10; 21:8; cf. 9:17, 18). That it is a *continual* torment from which there is no relief compounds the misery immeasur-

ably. "In the presence of the holy angels and the Lamb" apparently means that they will be witnesses when unbelievers are cast into Hell (cf. 20:15), further testifying to the divine sentence involved. The language makes clear that this is a casting into eternal Hell rather than judgment on earth during the Tribulation. There is some truth in saying that this is "primarily spiritual and psychological suffering" (Beale 760), certainly a part of the total experience, but physical pain from literal burning is a significant part.

The torment of v. 10 is "for ever and ever" (v. 11; cf. 9:2; 18:8-10, 18; Is. 34:8-10). Jesus taught that the fire of Hell torments its inhabitants (Lk. 16:23, 24). He also taught that the conditions endure eternally when he referred to "the fire that never shall be quenched," adding "where their worm dieth not" for emphasis (Mk. 9:42-48). "They have no rest day nor night"; the torment is unrelenting. Unbelievers are not annihilated in Hell but exist forever in a conscious state of awareness, in contrast with the eternal "rest" that believers will enjoy in Heaven (cf. v. 13). "The word *basanismos* ['torment'] in Rev. 14:10-11 is used nowhere in Revelation or biblical literature in the sense of annihilation of personal existence" (Beale 762).

The victims of this eternal torment are again identified as those "who worship the beast and his image" (cf. 13:15-18; 19:20; cf. 20:10). For "the mark of his name," equivalent to "the mark of the beast," see 13:17. Any advantages gained by accepting the mark of the beast are short lived. God will judge those so marked. "Whosoever" means that *all* those found wearing this mark after Armageddon are cast alive into "the lake of fire burning with brimstone" along with the beast and his associate (19:20; cf. 20:10, 14, 15; 21:8).

Verse 12 presents an entirely different group, in stark contrast. These are "the saints," different in nature, behavior, and future. The "patience of the saints" is the faithfulness of Tribulation saints that enables them to endure the persecutions, natural catastrophes, and temptations to compromise with the Antichrist (see comments on 13:10). They remain true to the commandments of God, though for many this leads to martyrdom. The "commandments of God," according to Beale (766), are "a holistic reference to the objective revelation of the old and new covenants." Commandment keeping is not incompatible with N.T. discipleship: see Mt. 5:17-20; 1 Jn. 2:2-5; 3:22-24; 5:2, 3.

That they "keep the faith of Jesus" apparently means that their faith in Jesus Christ endures to the end. Believers of all generations, particularly those during the Tribulation, find the inner strength necessary to endure the hardships and threats of the period because they believe that the future will be exactly as it is being portrayed in the revelations contained in this book.

After the three angelic proclamations, "a voice from heaven" commanded John to "write" (v. 13), specifically to memorialize those who "die in the Lord." This provides permanent commentary on how God feels about the deaths of His people. Many believers will die during the Tribulation, including a number of martyrs (some interpreters think this verse refers only to the latter), and some from natural causes. We have here God's own *eulogy* of those who die in a right relationship with Him—in principle applicable to faithful saints of every generation. Martyrs during the

Tribulation seem to be singled out in "from henceforth."

The deaths of *all* believers are "blessed" in the eyes of God, the word (Greek *makarios*) used for seven "beatitudes" in Revelation (1:3; 16:15; 19:9; 20:6; 22:7, 14). It means "blessed or happy" (ALGNT 252; Thayer 386)—perhaps even "divinely favored." It is flexible enough to include all the bliss of the personal benefits of salvation and the glory of God in Heaven, or to refer to spiritual well-being.

Furthermore, graduation into the Lord's presence means that the saints have entered into a state of perfect rest from the "labors" and "works" that were often fatiguing to body and soul. "Labor" (Greek *kopos*), originally a striking or beating, is "toil resulting in weariness, laborious toil, trouble" (Vine 349). "Work" (Greek *ergon*) is "work, employment, task" (Vine 683). The first may reflect the subjective aspect of the believer's works and the toll they take; then the second refers to the objective deed or accomplishment. That these "follow them" means that the effects of their works continue on earth long after they are gone and will follow them into Heaven at some point in the future.

c. Harvest time on earth (vv. 14-20)

14 And I looked, and behold a white cloud, and upon the cloud *one* sat like unto the Son of man, having on his head a golden crown, and in his hand a sharp sickle. 15 And another angel came out of the temple, crying with a loud voice to him that sat on the cloud, Thrust in thy sickle, and reap: for the time is come for thee to reap;

for the harvest of the earth is ripe.

16 And he that sat on the cloud thrust in his sickle on the earth; and the earth was reaped.

17 And another angel came out of the temple which is in heaven, he also having a sharp sickle.

18 And another angel came out from the altar, which had power over fire; and cried with a loud cry to him that had the sharp sickle, saying, Thrust in thy sharp sickle, and gather the clusters of the vine of the earth; for her grapes are fully ripe.

19 And the angel thrust in his sickle into the earth, and gathered the vine of the earth, and cast *it* into the great winepress of the wrath of God.

20 And the winepress was trodden without the city, and blood came out of the winepress, even unto the horse bridles, by the space of a thousand *and* six hundred furlongs.

Chapter 14 concludes the lengthy parenthesis (12:1—14:20) with two visions of Christ as a divine Harvester (vv. 14-20; cf. Mt. 13:24-30; 24:31; cf. Mt. 9:37; Jn. 4:34-38). The first harvest (vv. 14-16) may be positive, alluding to the gathering of Christ's elect at the Second Coming (Bauckham 292). The second (vv. 17-20) is clearly negative or judgmental, alluding to the Battle of Armageddon. Three angels introduce various components of these coming events.

"And I looked" reflects another change in subject matter, expanded to include Heaven and earth with the "Son of man" looming large to thrust a sickle from Heaven to earth. The first object for attention is "a white cloud": clouds are associated with the Second Coming (Dan. 7:13; Mt. 24:30; 26:64; cf. Acts 1:9-11). The cloud soon reveals someone sitting on it, one "like unto the Son of man"—a Scriptural designation for Christ. Some interpreters, noting the absence of "the" in the original, take it to mean a "human-like" figure, perhaps an angel, thinking that it would be incongruous for Christ to receive a command from an angel. But the identical wording is clearly applied to Christ in 1:13 and is determinative here. To identify this with anyone other than Christ is highly suspect. "Angels in Revelation... are always mere conveyors of messages representing the divine will" (Beale 772).

The Son of Man wears a "golden crown" (Greek *stephanos*), probably reflecting the *victorious* aspect of Christ's activity: "emblematic of His coming conquest over his enemies" (Thomas II:219). He also holds a "sharp sickle" (Greek *drepanon*), "a knifelike instrument with a curved blade used for reaping grain" (ALGNT 121). Since the 144,000 have already been designated as "firstfruits" (v. 4), a positive harvest term, this first "sickle" harvest may be for the remainder of the elect (Mt. 24:31; cf. Mt. 9:37, 38; Jn. 4:35-38).

But it is clear that the second harvest (vv. 17-20), of grapes, is negative—for wicked, unbelieving human beings. The metaphor takes on an ominous, negative tone. The second "sickle" is used to gather grapes that will be crushed in the winepress of God's judgment, the "wine" of human blood being the blood of unbelievers spilled in the great world battle near Jerusalem (19:17-21).

That the angel emerges from the *Temple* indicates that he is relaying the command from God, yet another reference to a heavenly "temple" (Greek *naos*), the place of God's presence. The Temple in Heaven and other components such as "the golden altar of incense" (6:9; 8:3, 4; see v. 18) are mentioned frequently (3:12; 7:15; 11:1, 19; 14:17; 15:5, 8; 16:1; cf. 21:22). These might be symbolic visual constructs that enable us to view abstract, heavenly realities. But for that matter they may indicate the existence of an actual temple in Heaven; after all, the Temple was patterned after heavenly realities (Heb. 8:5; 9:23, 24). Even so, in the final state of things in eternity there will *not* be a temple (21:22). If there is a Temple in Heaven now, it will disappear in the reconstitution of all things into their eternal state.

The angel's command to the Son of Man was to "thrust" and "reap" with the sharp sickle (v. 15), words often "used for the ingathering of men into the kingdom of God" (Caird 190); see Mt. 9:37f; Mk. 4:29; Lk. 10:2; Jn. 4:35-38. Harvest is indicated because the crop is "ripe" (Greek *xeraino*), literally meaning "to dry up, wither" (Vine 537). This convinces many interpreters that the metaphor here is a "wheat" harvest, since fruits and vegetables are not "dried up" when harvested. The condition pointed to occurs at the very end of the Tribulation period.

The one "sitting on the cloud" promptly obeyed the command and "thrust his sickle into the earth" (v. 16) and reaped. Both Jesus and angels are instrumental in both harvests of chapter 14, but Christ is more prominent in the first. Nonetheless, even for the "grape" harvest, alluding to the Battle of Armageddon, Jesus is the One who executes the terrible "harvest" of God (see Jl. 3:9-17; Is. 63:1-6).

After the first harvest vision, two other angels are dispatched, with the same divine authority, for the negative harvest of grapes (vv. 17-20; cf. Jl. 3:9-17; Is. 63:1-6; cf. Is. 5:1-7). The first of these exited the heavenly Temple, also with a "sharp sickle" (v. 17). "Another angel" (the third thus far) was dispatched from the "altar" area of the throne room (v. 18)—the golden altar of incense referenced previously in 6:9 (see comments there). The angel's "power over fire" (v. 18) may refer either to some duty of his in connection with the golden altar of incense or to a role as "custodian" of the fire used by God for judgment.

The angel repeats the commission given to Christ the divine Harvester by the first angel in v. 15, with an additional "and gather the clusters of the vine of the earth; for her grapes are fully ripe." The harvest is specified as clusters of grapes—apparently unbelievers "gathered" from "the earth." These too, are cut and gathered because they are "fully ripe." Indeed, the angel assisted the Harvester with his own sickle (v. 19), though as an instrument of God he does not act on his own. The clusters were cut and gathered and then cast into the "great winepress of the wrath of God." The picture is extremely somber: "a metaphor for eschatological judgment" (Aune II:846). "The image of 'treading a winepress' is without exception a metaphor for judgment in the OT" (Beale 774).

Caird (191) believes the grape harvest is also positive, but any viewpoint that sees both harvests in the same light creates a redundancy. In the end-times, the elect will be gathered (Mt. 24:31) and unbelievers will be judged; it seems best, then, to include both positive and negative harvest ideas here. The first and second "beasts," with their confederates and a great number of unbelievers, are the "grapes" being harvested and crushed by the wrath of God. The "winepress" is the Tribulation. The "wrath of God" is the outpouring of the seal, trumpet, and bowl judgments (19:15).

Ancient winepresses were pits with upper and lower levels connected by a conduit. The grapes were trodden with bare feet in the upper portion (winepress) and the juice would flow through the conduit into the lower receptacle (wine vat; ISBE IV:1072). That which flowed from "the winepress" of God's wrath represents the *literal blood* of unbelievers crushed in judgment. This blood is shed during the Battle of Armageddon (chapter 19), outside "the city" (v. 20) of Jerusalem. Jerusalem itself is spared, even as the judgment that fell on Jesus in His crucifixion was done outside the city proper. The Temple of Jerusalem has been "measured" for protection in 11:1, 2. An omnipotent Christ descends to deliver her from assault by the armies of Antichrist (19:11f.).

The amount of blood indicates the huge number of victims of judgment, in contrast to the amazing fact that Christ's armies do not experience a single casualty. The blood of unbelievers rose to the level of the horses' bridles over a distance of 1600 furlongs (v. 20)— about 180 miles. This is not hyperbole: we can envision the blood from such a battle pooling up into a river in the bottom of a narrow valley—in this case the valley of Jezreel (Esdraelon). The birds

of earth will eventually consume the flesh of unbelievers' dead bodies. These should be taken as literal predictions (see 19:17-19).

The victims of God's wrath are judged for their idolatrous worship of Antichrist, for evil behavior in general, and for their attack against Jerusalem. But they are judged ultimately because they have rejected the salvation of Jesus Christ as the risen Lamb and the rule of "the One sitting on the throne" as their Rightful King.

Summary
(14:1-20)

John's new vision began with Jesus the Lamb standing on Mt. Zion with the 144,000 Jewish servants first introduced in 7:1-8 (v. 1)—apparently a part of the righteous remnant of the nation of Israel that turns to Christ during the Tribulation. "Mount Zion" refers to a literal location within the earthly city of Jerusalem, perhaps to the "Temple Mount." That they have God's name written on their foreheads adds confirmation that they are the same group (7:3).

John heard them singing the new song of redemption before God's throne in Heaven (vv. 2, 3), picturing either their eternal bliss or their position with Christ on earth just before the Battle of Armageddon. They can sing this because they too have been redeemed by the blood of the Lamb.

Their special, spiritual character is described (vv. 4, 5). They are sexual virgins, implying that their time, energy, and affection is fully devoted to Christ alone. They follow Christ wherever He leads. They are firstfruits of an even greater harvest of Tribulation saints to come. They speak only the truth. They are blameless in God's presence. The vision of a victorious Christ and the 144,000 standing on Mt. Zion is in sharp contrast with the picture of the beast and his followers in chapter 13.

Three angelic proclamations precede two concluding harvest visions. The first angel, flying in the middle of the sky, indicates that the gospel is preached throughout the period (vv. 6, 7). It is the same everlasting gospel of Jesus Christ, but it also includes a warning about the coming judgment of God. The universal scope of the atonement comes into view in the epithet "every nation, and kindred, and tongue, and people." A gospel invitation is extended throughout the earth. A part of the gospel call is to fear God enough to give Him glory and worship that He alone deserves as Creator (v. 7). An important part of this particular proclamation is that the hour of judgment has come. It is therefore urgent to trust Christ immediately.

A second angel proclaimed the fall of the great city of Babylon (v. 8), reiterated to emphasize its certainty. "Babylon" could very well be a literal world capital in the end-times. But it is also fairly obvious that the name symbolizes the evil world systems and the transhistorical spirit of Antichrist. The reason for her judgment is that she coerced the world into committing spiritual fornication against God by various deceptions, false doctrine, and the involuntary worship of the Antichrist, portrayed in the analogy of drinking wine. The unbelieving inhabitants of the world "drink" and become intoxicated with the anti-Christian spirit and behaviors.

A third angel issued a stern warning about coming judgment (vv. 9-12). Those who worship the beast and his image, or who receive his mark in their forehead or hand, will be made to drink the wine of God's wrath at full strength (v. 10)—including literal "fire and sulphur." The physical and psychological torment will be unrelenting (eternal) and constant (day and night), factors that increase the miseries of Hell exponentially (v. 11). Tribulation believers who refuse the mark of the beast do so by patient endurance, obedience to God's commandments, and their faith in Jesus Christ (v. 12).

After the angelic proclamations John was commanded to memorialize the deaths of saints as a part of the record (v. 13). Though this focuses on Tribulation martyrs, the truth applies equally to the deaths of all saints. The inhabitants of Heaven are blessed with sweet rest from their labors on earth and with the satisfaction of knowing that their works will be rewarded and continue to bear fruit on earth after their deaths.

Chapter 14 concludes with the prediction of two great world harvests (vv. 14-20). The time is ripe for both. The first one (wheat) is apparently positive, referring to an ingathering of the elect according to Mt. 24:31 (vv. 14-16). The second (grapes) is clearly negative, referring to the eschatological slaughter of unbelieving followers of Antichrist, near Jerusalem, at the Battle of Armageddon in chapter 19 (vv. 17-20).

Application: Teaching and Preaching the Passage

The devotion of the 144,000 Jewish servants is remarkable. These are mere men who have a testimony of absolute devotion to Christ. They, as well as those Tribulation saints that are martyred during Antichrist's regime, illustrate well the essence of a conviction. A conviction is a principle that we adopt and determine to live by for the rest of our lives, whatever the cost. The example of these men constitutes a call to a high standard of discipleship for believers in every generation of church history.

Within the deafening crescendo of wrath and catastrophe at the end of the Tribulation, the compassionate voice of God continues in the preaching of the gospel for the sake of those who may yet turn to Christ in the last days. The first angelic proclamation is the eternal gospel of Jesus Christ, albeit with special focus on God's wrath and judgment (14:6, 7).

Equally illustrative of God's great love is the scope of the offer: "every nation, kindred, tongue, and people"—*the entire human race.* The good news of Jesus Christ is good news for everyone on earth and not just for a predetermined few. God is not willing that any should perish but that all should come to repentance, including those who are alive near the very end of history. The two witnesses, the 144,000, and a numberless multitude of Gentile converts (7:9) will spread the gospel in the world during the Tribulation.

This Scriptural perspective—the universal scope of the atonement and the potential for every single human being to be saved—should encourage us to share the gospel with as many as possible. This can be done sincerely and enthusiastically because we believe that anyone is a legitimate candidate for salvation. Furthermore, we believe that there is power in the preaching of the gospel, a power stronger than the spirit of antichrist (Rom. 1:16; 10:17; 1 Cor.

1:18, 21; 2 Cor. 10:4, 5; 1 Pet. 1:23-25).

Suggested Outlines. The 144,000—Servant Characteristics, 14:1-5: (1) Their Savior, v. 1; (2) Their Stance, v. 1; (3) Their Seal, v. 1; (4) Their Song, vv. 2, 3; (5) Their Sanctification, vv. 4, 5.

The Tribulation Period Gospel, 14:6, 7: (1) Duration is everlasting, v. 6; (2) Destination is earth, v. 6; (3) Defined as doxological, v. 7.

Harvest Time, 14:14-16: (1) The Harvester, v. 14; (2) The command to harvest, v. 15; (3) The condition for harvest, v. 15; (4) The gathering of the harvest, v. 16.

V. THE SEVEN BOWLS (15:1—16:21)

"Vial" (15:7, Greek *phiale*) is, more literally, a *bowl*; seven bowls contain the seven last judgments poured out on the world during the latter half of the Tribulation, which some call the "Great Tribulation." They are the most severe judgments to date and bring the Tribulation judgments of God to an end (15:1; cf. Lev. 26:21), being directed primarily against Antichrist and his followers—earth's unbelieving population.

Three groups of judgments began with the seal judgments (6:1), followed by the trumpet judgments (8:6), and concluding with the bowl judgments (15:1)—each group separated by a significant "parenthesis." The bowl judgments are best understood as distinct from the seals and trumpets, except for the seventh bowl: the sixth seal, seventh trumpet, and seventh bowl seem to reveal the same event (see 6:12-17; 14:14-20; 16:17-21): namely, the Day of the Lord (cf. Is. 2:19-21; 13:6-13;

30:2, 3; Jl. 1:15; 2:1, 28-32; 3:9-17; Zech. 14:1-21).

Revelation returns to the throne room to introduce each major new section (4:1-5:14; 8:1-5; 15:1-8), the point being that all the judgments come from God and are used to judge Antichrist and the unbelieving population of earth during the Tribulation. Even so, provision for evangelism may be one reason for three different phases of increasingly severe judgment. Many, perhaps most, of earth's unbelieving population will remain recalcitrant despite the judgments aimed to bring them to repentance (9:20, 21; 16:9-11). But the gospel will be preached successfully and a multitude of saints come out of the Great Tribulation (7:9, 14).

"Whenever in history the wicked fail to repent in answer to the initial and partial manifestation of God's anger in judgments, the final effusion of wrath follows" (Hendriksen 157). The seven bowls of wrath take us to that final effusion.

A. Preparation (15:1-8)

**1 And I saw another sign in heaven, great and marvellous, seven angels having the seven last plagues; for in them is filled up the wrath of God.
2 And I saw as it were a sea of glass mingled with fire: and them that had gotten the victory over the beast, and over his image, and over his mark, *and* over the number of his name, stand on the sea of glass, having the harps of God.
3 And they sing the song of Moses the servant of God, and the song of the Lamb, saying, Great and marvellous *are* thy works, Lord God Almighty; just and true *are* thy ways, thou King of saints.
4 Who shall not fear thee, O Lord, and glorify thy name? For *thou* only *art* holy: for all nations shall come and worship before thee; for thy judgments are made manifest.
5 And after that I looked, and, behold, the temple of the tabernacle of the testimony in heaven was opened:
6 And the seven angels came out of the temple, having the seven plagues, clothed in pure and white linen, and having their breasts girded with golden girdles.
7 And one of the four beasts gave unto the seven angels seven golden vials full of the wrath of God, who liveth for ever and ever.
8 And the temple was filled with smoke from the glory of God, and from his power; and no man was able to enter into the temple, till the seven plagues of the seven angels were fulfilled.**

"And I saw another sign in heaven" (v. 1) marks a major transition from the trumpet judgments (8:6—11:19) and third parenthesis (12:1—14:20) to the bowl judgments (15:1—16:21). Chapter 15 is an elaborate introduction to the seven bowl judgments. For "sign," see 12:1, 3.

"Great" and "marvelous" suggest that this vision is no less impressive than the preceding ones; John's senses remained sharp, and the revelations had not lost any of their wonder along the way. These seven angels (there is no "the" in the original) are apparently different from any previous group.

Special attention is drawn to the bowl judgments as "the seven last plagues" (cf. 22:18). "Plague" is the same as in 13:3: "a stripe, wound" (Vine 473), "used fifteen times in Revelation, always in an eschatological sense" (Thomas II:230). All three series have "plagued" the Christ-rejecting world during the Tribulation, with divine utility evident in the repeated use of the divine passive "it was given" (6:2, 4, 8; 7:2; 8:2; 9:1, 3, 5; 11:1, 2; 12:4; 13:5, 7; 16:8; 20:4) and in the angels' being commissioned from the throne room in Heaven (9:1; 10:1; 14:15, 17, 18; 15:1, 6; 16:1; 18:1; 20:1).

It seems clear that the three series indicate chronological progression rather than running parallel (parallelism) or recording the same events again (recapitulation). They have been generally sequential, increasing in intensity from "fourths" in the seals, to "thirds" in the trumpets, to "total judgment" in the bowls (Kistemaker 426). The end of the entire series is now in sight: "for in them is filled up the wrath of God." The passive "is filled up" indicates "that it is God who concludes history" (Aune II:870). Aune also emphasizes that this wrath "presupposes a universal divine law or standard, repeated violations of which are now thought to have caused a final eschatological manifestation of the wrath of God." The entire Tribulation is properly viewed as a time of God's wrath rather than Satan's, though the latter's rage is an important factor (12:12). Even so, there is no reason to exclude the seals or trumpets as expressions of God's wrath.

Tribulation judgments conclude with the Battle of Armageddon described in chapter 19. Indeed, God shortens the period for the sake of the elect (Mt. 24:22), otherwise there would be no one to survive and enter into Christ's millennial, earthly kingdom. (There will of course be other judgments following Satan's last uprising and the Great White Throne Judgment [20:11-15], both to occur at the end of the millennium).

"And I saw" (v. 2) introduces a change in focus, beginning with a spectacular "sea of glass mingled with fire"—as in 4:6 located before the heavenly throne of God and providing visual definition to the throne room. Its translucent quality creates a visual, prismatic enhancement of God's glory, majesty, holiness, and beauty: "designed to reflect the glory of God" (Walvoord 227). Heaven's throne room has now been used to introduce all three series of judgments (4:1-5:14; 8:1-5; 15:1-8).

"Mingled with fire" (not in 4:6) may refer only to a reflection of the fire or fiery colors associated with the throne of God (Hughes 170), used here for special visual effect (Mounce 284). But the imagery of fire is often associated with God's holiness and judgment; here, then, it may suggest "impending judgment" (Aune II:871). Other views are that it signals the blood of martyrs (Swete 194, 195) or the spiritual warfare of believers (Brighton 400). The fiery tone may hark back to the intense but victorious struggle of Tribulation saints over the beast, thus indicating God's response of judgment against the beast and his followers for persecuting His people.

Regardless, the glistening, fiery, crystal sea evokes a sense of holy awe and majesty associated with God's throne. Speculation beyond this is not suggested in the text. At the least, "This sea is the crystalline pavement proceeding from God's throne [4:6], the firmament that earlier prophets had seen as heaven's floor and earth's ceiling [Ex. 24:10; Ezek. 1:22]" (D. Johnson 216).

John saw a large group of people standing on the sea of glass (cf. 7:9-17). Idealist Hendriksen (159) identifies them as "the Church triumphant" from the entire church age. In this view, the implied warfare with Antichrist represents the spiritual warfare of believers of any period. Summers (184) sees them as believers of early church history, victorious over the Roman emperor cult. Futurists agree with Walvoord (227) that they are "the martyred dead destroyed by the beast of Revelation 13:1-10," who "remained faithful to death instead of yielding to the blasphemous demand of the beast" and whose "resurrection and reward are described in 20:4-6." In other words, those standing on the sea of glass in v. 2 are Tribulation saints; all the phenomena—the beast, his image, his mark, and his number—belong literally and exclusively to the eschatological, seven-year Tribulation.

The chief characteristic of this group is their total "victory" over (rather than being overcome by) "the beast, his image, his mark, and the number of his name" (cf. 13:17). Lenski (456) suggests that "over" (Greek *ek*) has the sense "out of"; their victory resulted in escape from their enemies' traps. They refused to compromise with Antichrist by receiving his mark or worshiping his image. Those who were "discovered" and martyred were no less victorious since martyrdom does not mean defeat. Those who escaped discovery existed as fugitives in the earth, unable to participate in its economy or society—an achievement as remarkable and commendable as martyrdom.

The blessed position enjoyed by this particular group—all Tribulation saints and not just martyrs—contrasts significantly with that of those on earth who follow Antichrist. Anyone who comes to Christ and endures faithfully to the end of the Tribulation is certainly "victorious." If the flow of the narrative is followed, this may specifically be a snapshot of those who have already been taken into Heaven before the bowl judgments begin, since that is how it appears to be arranged in the text (vv. 1-4, 5).

They (some or all) had the "harps of God," used for accompaniment in singing (cf. 5:8; 14:2). With the sea of glass for a choir loft, the victorious Tribulation saints sang "the song of Moses the servant of God" and "the song of the Lamb" (v. 3), apparently referring to the song in vv. 3, 4. Great victories have always been celebrated and memorialized in songs celebrating redemption (Ex. 15:1-21; Dt. 32; Ps. 90).

This theme, and the consequent glorifying of God, are central in the *songs* of Revelation (5:9; 14:3); the *doxologies* that extol God's attributes seem to be recitations instead of songs (4:8, 11; 5:12, 13; 7:12; 11:17; 19:2). The 24 elders, representing all the redeemed, sang the new song in 5:9; the 144,000 Jewish servants sang it in 14:3. Both groups are qualified because they experienced Christ's redemption. It is no less appropriate that these victors, having overcome Antichrist, sing their song celebrating their redemption out of the Tribulation.

The lyrics appear to be general truths about God drawn from many O.T. sources rather than directly quoting a specific passage (see Ex. 15; Dt. 32; Ps. 86:8-10; 92:4, 5; 139:14; Is. 66:23; Jer. 10:6, 7; Hos. 14:9). By singing this as "the song of Moses" and also "the song of the Lamb," the victors are glorifying God the Father as their Redeemer. The close connection between God and the Lamb in redemption was established in chapters 4 and 5 and continues throughout. The worship given to God in the O.T. is as justified for the Lamb as for the Father.

The song begins by extolling the works of the "Lord God Almighty" (cf. 1:8; 4:8; 11:17; 16:7, 14; 19:15; 21:22) as great and marvelous (cf. Ps. 92:5; 111:2). God's glory refers as much to His works as to His character. All God's attributes, His purposes throughout eternity, and His works of creation and redemption are expressions of "His glory." "Marvelous" (Greek *thaumastos*) means causing wonder or amazement. Like the Israelites amazed at God's parting of the Red Sea, or the people who were awestruck by Christ's miracles, those who witness the great judgment-works of God during the Tribulation will respond in wonder.

Three names for God are included. "Lord" (Greek *kurios*) means "strong, authoritative, having legal power, master" (ALGNT 240); it is the Greek word used to translate the O.T. personal name for God (Yahweh or Jehovah). "God" (Greek *theos*) is "the supreme divine being, the true, living, and personal God" (ALGNT 196). "Almighty" (Greek *pantokrator*) is a designation for God as the One holding all power and ruling all things, the omnipotent One.

The all-powerful God does not use His power without good reason, but with patience, love, and for a high purpose; His ways are "just and true" (cf. Ps. 111:7; Is. 44:6; 1 Tim. 1:17). "Just" (Greek *dikaios*) means "righteous, upright, just" (ALGNT 116); He always does what is right. "True" (Greek *alethinos*) means "real, ideal, genuine"

(Vine 645); applied to persons it means "characterized by integrity and trustworthiness, true, dependable" (ALGNT 43). "Ways" (Greek *hodos*), literally "any place along which one travels," is used here figuratively to mean "a way of life, type of conduct" (ALGNT 277). God's "ways" include not only *what* He does (works) but also the *way* He does things and the objective results.

From the eternal decrees of God before the creation of the universe to the creation of a new Heaven and earth, God's character, motives, plans, and acts are "just and true"—including even His severe judgments against unbelieving mankind in the end-times. In contrast to the righteous character of God and the Lamb is the nefarious character of Satan and Antichrist; theirs are the ways of deception and destruction. They deserve to be judged, and God is just to judge them. Indeed, humanity for the most part by the end-times is permanently recalcitrant, and God is just to confine all unbelievers in Hell forever.

Where the A.V. has "King of saints," a few manuscripts have "King of ages" and the majority have "King of nations" (matching "for all nations shall come and worship before thee" in v. 4). In fact, God is "King" of all of these!

The song continues with the rhetorical question, "Who shall not fear thee, O Lord, and glorify thy name?" (v. 4). "Fear" (Greek *phobeo*) means "reverential fear" (Vine 230), an essential component of worship. This fear or respect results from recognizing that no one else is as great, powerful, just, or true as God. "Glorify" (Greek *doxazo*) means "to magnify, extol, praise" (Vine 267). God's "name" here may be used as a metonymy for all that God is and for all that He does—His attributes as well as

His works of creation and redemption. All are components of His glory. The worship of God is the very thing Satan wants and so he seeks to redirect the worship of unbelieving humanity to Antichrist.

The response to the question provides three reasons the nations or inhabitants of the millennial earth will worship God alone (see 21:24-27), with the word "for" introducing each one. First, He alone is "holy" (Jer. 10:6, 7); no other person or pagan god is worthy of worship because no one else is holy. All people have sinned and are thereby disqualified. The gods of the nations are mere idols that cannot hear or speak (Is. 44:9-20).

Second is the Scriptural prediction that all nations will come and worship Him, a decree being directed to fulfillment by Almighty God (cf. Ps. 22:27; 66:4, 5; 86:8-10; Zech 14:16; Rev. 21:24, 26). The O.T. prophets foresaw an age in which all the nations of the world would turn to God (Is. 11:9, 10). The nations will not do this because they have been finally persuaded of God's love, greatness, or justice, but because there is no other option in the millennial reign of Christ. Though idealist interpreters see this as fulfilled in the multiethnic makeup of the church in the present age, or in eternity proper in the new Heaven and earth, premillennialists envision this happening during a literal reign of Christ on earth after His Second Coming. Only one is left standing to be worshiped after the Battle of Armageddon, God and the Lamb alone.

"Thy judgments are made manifest" provides a third reason that all must fear and glorify God alone, apparently referring to God's mighty acts of judgment on display during the Tribulation. "Manifest" (Greek *phaneroo*) means "to make clear, visible, manifest" or "to uncover, lay bare, reveal" (Vine 390). The seals, trumpets, and bowls are all *visible*, catastrophic judgments of God, demonstrating the superiority of God over Satan and Antichrist in ways reminiscent of the Exodus plagues and their effects. But they are more: they are "moral expressions of his just character" (Beale 795). Indeed some versions (NASB, NIV) translate "judgments" (Greek *dikaioma*) as "righteous acts," a meaning supported by the lexicons (Thayer 151). God's acts of judgment are right acts.

"After that I looked" (v. 5) indicates another change of focus, now directed to "the tabernacle of the testimony"—the Temple in Heaven from which the seven angels emerge with their "bowl" judgments. Nothing suggests that this refers to a rebuilt earthly temple or that it is symbolic of the church; only negligible time has passed since the beginning of the vision in v. 1. John designates the heavenly Temple as "the tabernacle of the testimony" (cf. Ex. 38:21; Num. 1:50; Heb. 8:5; Rev. 13:6). "Tabernacle" is a dwelling place, the place of God's presence, whether on earth or in Heaven. The "testimony" or "ark" was housed inside the most holy room of the O.T. Tabernacle, Solomon's Temple, and here in the Temple of Heaven.

"'The testimony' refers to what was written on the stones, which 'testified' against sin" (Thomas II:241, 242; cf. Ex. 32:15). The ark itself typically symbolized God's presence but also served as the object to which blood was applied on the Day of Atonement (Lev. 16:2, 13-16, 34). And since both O.T.

Tabernacle and Temple (and furnishings) were modeled after the heavenly pattern (Heb. 8:5), it is logical to assume that John saw their ideal counterparts in Heaven at this time. The heavenly golden altar of incense has already been described in 6:9, 8:3, and 9:13. Here, the Temple's doors were "opened" (perhaps by an angel or on their own) allowing John to see into the innermost room, the true Holy of Holies. Caird (200) points out that it is not the Tabernacle that is the focal point of the vision but the "testimony" or tablets of law within: "The time for mercy is over, and God's law must now take its course."

"The seven angels" with "the seven plagues" exited the Temple (v. 6). On "plagues" see the comments on v. 1; the negative nature of these angels' mission is obvious. That they were leaving the Temple indicates, again, that the judgments are divine in origin and utility. God will use the plagues to chastise the anti-Christian world, its evil rulers, and its unbelieving inhabitants.

The angels were "clothed in pure and white linen" robes, symbolizing their holiness (Lenski 460). "Pure" may be used literally or morally (cf. Mt. 5:8)—here obviously the latter. "White" (Greek *lampros*) is more literally "shining, brilliant, bright." The same two adjectives are used in 19:8 to describe the "fine linen" of the saints. "The linen worn by the angels represents righteousness in action as it does with the wife of the Lamb" (Thomas II:242).

Furthermore, the angels wore golden girdles (or "sashes") about the chest (cf. 1:13), "symbolic of royal and priestly functions" (Mounce 288; cf. Ex. 28:4; 39:29). The similarity to the description of the Son of Man (1:13) leads Beale

(804) to suggest that they "act as his representatives in carrying out judgment." At any rate, the clothing suggests, in a powerful way, that their mission is righteous and authoritative.

Each of the seven receives his respective "bowl" from "one of the four living creatures" (v. 7; 4:6-9). Aune (II:854) suggests that these "shallow, broad dishes" should be understood as cultic utensils, bowls used for offerings. Each is "golden" and "full of the wrath of God." In 5:8, the 24 elders were holding golden bowls filled with the prayers of all saints; the similarity may be coincidental. However, the timing of the judgments suggests that they are inaugurated at least partly in response to the prayers of the saints in 6:9-11. The utensils for priestly service and the furniture inside the earthly Temple were either made or covered in gold.

The judgments, then, come from God and are poured out on the kingdom of Antichrist and upon his followers. That they are "full"—full-strength, complete, final—is another indication of increasing intensity and progression in the three separate series of judgments. Even so, the seven bowl judgments as a whole are not the exact equivalent of the final judgment of 20:11-15. However, the seventh bowl (16:17) does in a sense encompass the final judgment process that begins with Armageddon and concludes at the Great White Throne Judgment.

That God lives forever increases the seriousness of being an object of His wrath. John thus reminded his readers that God is eternal in nature and in all His attributes. This magnifies the significance of the bowl judgments as expressions of the wrath of an Almighty and Eternal God. He may not be ignored or taken lightly and must be reckoned with forever. The wrath of man and the wrath of Satan last only for a season; God's wrath is forever. Neither Antichrist nor his image should be feared as much as the living God.

The preliminary introduction of the bowl judgments (to begin in 16:1) concludes with a manifestation of God's glory when the heavenly Temple is "filled with smoke"—the smoke of God's glory and power (v. 8). God's visible presence in the O.T. Tabernacle and Temple is often identified as the Shekinah glory. Though typically confined to the Holy of Holies above the mercy seat (Lev. 16:2), in John's vision the glory filled the entire heavenly Temple. Indeed, the smoke may also represent "the full and thorough operation of God's holy anger" (Hendriksen 160).

Access into the Temple of Heaven was thus suspended until "the seven plagues of the seven angels were fulfilled" (v. 8). No one was able to come near such intense divine presence—recalling the principles underlying the prohibitions in regard to God's presence on Mt. Sinai (Ex 12:16, 19). This may simply refer to anyone's ability to come into physical proximity with such an intense manifestation of God's infinite power. Or it may imply refraining from coming into contact with God's wrath (Kistemaker 433). Or: "Once the time of final judgment has come, none can stay the hand of God....The time for intercession is past" (Mounce 289). At any rate, the temporary inaccessibility draws attention to how serious the bowl judgments are, with all Heaven's attention directed to them, to continue until they are fulfilled: that is, at the end of the Tribulation (16:17-21; cf. 6:12-17; 11:15-19).

Summary
(15:1-8)

The fifteenth chapter is an introduction to the seven "bowl" judgments, the third and last major series of sevenfold judgments of the Tribulation. We are alerted to the great significance of the bowl series by John's vision of another "sign" that he described as "great and marvellous" (v. 1).

John saw seven angels with the seven last plagues. The word "plagues" (lit. "strike or wound") indicates that they are extremely negative or judgmental. They are administered in full strength and complete the cycle of Christ's conquest that began (6:1, 2) when the judgments were first inaugurated.

John's vantage point is the throne room of Heaven—another indication of the divine origin and utility of all 21 judgments (v. 2). The "sea of glass" before God's throne is prominent again, as in the original throne-room vision of 4:6. This crystal clear heavenly pavement magnifies in prismatic fashion the spectacular colors, sights, and glory associated with God's throne. The colors of fire are singled out. If any special symbolism is intended beyond the beauty, majesty, and glory of God that is always reflected in the crystal pavement, this may point to the remaining judgments to be poured out on the earth since fire is a symbol and instrument of judgment.

More important, John saw a large gathering of people standing on the glistening pavement before God's throne, in a stance of victory. Their victory is total; they have overcome the beast (Antichrist) in every way: his "image," "his mark," and "his number." In other words, they remained faithful to

Christ throughout the Tribulation. Furthermore, they were celebrating their victory in song, accompanied by harps.

The song of Moses and the song of the Lamb, which John heard them singing, is one song of redemption (5:9; 14:3). Some additional lyrics of this song have the form of a doxology (vv. 3, 4), praising God for His great and marvelous works and His just and true ways. The names of God recall two of His great attributes: "almighty" (all-powerful) and "King" over all things, whether saints, nations, or eternity.

A rhetorical question (v. 4) is a call to worship the one true God, who alone is holy. No one else is like Him in any of His attributes. Consequently—as predicted in the O.T.—all the nations of the earth will one day unanimously worship Him alone in the earth. The terrible judgments of the Tribulation have been working toward this end, ultimately to be fulfilled in the millennial reign of Christ on earth when all the nations of earth will submit to the rule of Christ.

That the angels exist from the heavenly Temple reiterates the divine origin of the seven bowl judgments (vv. 5-8). This Temple is "the tabernacle of the testimony," reflecting the two tablets of commandments given to Moses and stored inside the ancient Ark of the Covenant, housed in the innermost room of the Tabernacle and Temple. This may reflect a connection between the Law of God and the outpouring of His judgments against the earth at this time. These are not times of mercy as such; judgment is the dominant feature.

The bowl angels were dressed in heavenly regalia: white, shining, linen robes bound with gold sashes. These symbolize their own holiness and perhaps their priestly ministry in serving God by administering the plague judgments. As an official commission, one of the four living beings presented each with a golden bowl filled with the wrath of the Eternal God (v. 7). That they are full indicates the severity of the judgments.

The smoke of the Temple visibly manifested God's presence (Shekinah glory). The infinite and wrathful power being generated from within the Temple was so intense that no one was able to enter the Temple. The decision to judge is therefore final; the judgments will not be recalled or stopped until they are poured out in full.

Application: Teaching and Preaching the Passage

There are some positive things among the sobering predictions about how the Tribulation period of earth's history will come to an end. For one, the end is in sight. The wrath of God, and the bitter spiritual warfare that began as early as Gen. 3, will come to a catastrophic climax at Armageddon. The sovereign God maneuvers present history to an end before the re-creation of a new Heaven and earth where sin and Satan are banished forever.

One of the intentional comparisons in Revelation has been the contrast of futures between the righteous and the wicked, between those who follow Christ faithfully and the unbelieving who follow Satan and his personification, the Antichrist. This chapter is a proleptic view (a view of the future before it happens) of the heavenly celebration of those who decided to follow Christ instead of the beast and are victors.

Music has always been significant in expressing faith. It will be so in Heaven:

a song of redemption from the hearts of the redeemed, music based on personal experience. Those redeemed from Egyptian bondage sang about it on the other side of the Red Sea (the song of Moses). Those redeemed out of the Great Tribulation will sing about it on the shores of the crystal sea in Heaven (the song of the Lamb). Even now, Christian music should incorporate not only testimony about the wonder and blessing of personal redemption but also the worship of God's attributes. The heavenly music in Revelation reflects both.

The events of the Exodus——the plagues, the magicians' imitations, Pharaoh's recalcitrance, the Passover principles, and the display of God's power over the false gods of Egypt—help us understand the nature of redemption in Christ. They also reveal important things about the nature of God, man, and the devil. They should be studied and referenced today by all who teach and preach the Bible (1 Cor. 10:1-13).

Suggested Outline. The Songs of the Redeemed, 15:2-4: (1) The singers, v. 2; (2) The song of Moses, v. 3 (see Ex. 15); (3) The song of the Lamb, v. 3 (see 5:9; 14:3); (4) The song of doxology, v. 4.

B. First Bowl (16:1, 2)

**1 And I heard a great voice out of the temple saying to the seven angels, Go your ways, and pour out the vials of the wrath of God upon the earth.
2 And the first went, and poured out his vial upon the earth; and there fell a noisome and grievous sore upon the men which had the mark of the beast, and *upon* them which worshiped his image.**

"A great voice" ("great" means loud) commands the angels to pour out their bowl judgments on the earth (v. 1; see 16:17; cf. Is. 66:6; Ps. 79:6, 12). The unidentified voice resounded from within the heavenly Temple, pointing to the divine origin and use of the seven bowl judgments. The voice is probably God Himself (Mounce 292), given that the "temple" (Greek *naos*) is the innermost sacred place, the Holy of Holies associated with God's presence. The frequent use of "great" (11 times in this chapter alone) indicates how extraordinary the bowl judgments are.

The seven vials were filled with "the wrath of God." "Wrath" (Greek *thumos*) typically denotes a specific expression of wrath (Trench 131). The number seven shows that the designated area of judgment, "upon the earth," is *total*. The delivery is probably *sequential* rather than simultaneous. Logically these final catastrophic conditions of the seventh bowl come at the end of things.

The first angel poured out his bowl judgment on the earth without hesitation (v. 2). (Though sequential, the entire series appears to proceed rapidly.) The image of a "drink-offering" poured out at the brazen altar may correspond somewhat to the "pouring out" of the bowls (Aune II:883; cf. Ex. 30:9; Lev. 23:13, 18). "Just as the pouring out of sacrificial blood represented the cleansing of the tabernacle from defilement of sin, so the pouring out of the bowls cleanses the earth from the defilement of sin through judgment" (Beale 813). But why should cleansing the earth be necessary? It may be best to view the bowl judgments simply as the fulfillment of O.T. prophecies of an outpouring of God's wrath on the nations of the world, as in Ps. 79:6.

The effects of the first bowl recall the plague of "boils" in Ex. 9:8-11. This judgment afflicts unbelieving mankind with "a noisome and grievous sore," a "grotesque vividness" (D. Johnson 225): "loathsome and malignant" (NASB), "ugly and painful" (NIV). "Sore" (Greek *elkos*) is the same as "boil" in Ex. 9:9, 11 (Greek): "a suppurated, inflamed, running sore that refuses to be healed" (Lenski 464). Kistemaker (440) suggests that the judgment contaminates the food supply, which in turn causes the sores; but this would not explain how Tribulation saints escape the sores. The affliction is apparently more direct.

Some regard the bowl judgments as metaphorical rather than literal, others as manifested throughout church history (Brighton 409, 410), and others as manifestations of God's wrath "on the Roman Empire" (Summers 186) or "successive blows by which the Papacy will fall" (Barnes 356-360). But God is not beyond using literal boils as instruments of judgment (Lev. 26:21, 28; Dt. 28:27, 35). There is no good reason He may not use them to afflict unbelieving humanity during the Tribulation; nothing in the text suggests that any symbolism is intended here.

Though some scholars see equivalence between the first four trumpet judgments and the first four bowl judgments (Kistemaker 438, 439), the first trumpet and first bowl do not match up (A. Johnson 153). The first trumpet judgment was directed against one-third of the earth's vegetation; the first bowl is directed against the unbelieving population of earth who followed the Antichrist.

Those afflicted by the first bowl judgment are identified as the "men" (generic, including women and children) which had the mark of the beast and worshiped his image (cf. 7:3; 14:1). Those who do *not* have the mark—Tribulation believers—are spared.

C. Second Bowl (16:3)

3 And the second angel poured out his vial upon the sea; and it became as the blood of a dead *man*: and every living soul died in the sea.

The second bowl judgment is poured out on "the sea" or oceans of earth, killing all sea life (v. 3; cf. 8:8, 9; Ex. 7:19). All the saltwater sources become something *like* "the blood of a dead man," if not literal blood. The seas can no longer support life; every living thing in them dies.

"Soul" (Greek *pseuche*) has a wide range of nuances: "life, soul, *life-principle, physical life, breath, natural life, one's life on earth, mind, purpose, heart, desire*" (ALGNT 414). In each instance the precise meaning depends on the context. Here it serves as a way of referring to any being in whom is the breath of life.

The fourth horseman's killing affected only *a fourth* of the earth's population (6:8). The third trumpet brought death in the seas to a *third* (8:8, 9). Here, *every living soul* in the sea died, arguing against the recapitulation view that each series repeats the previous ones. The bowl judgments follow the earlier ones and are more severe.

Idealist Beale (815) calls this an "economic plague" that might occur at any point in the church age, interprets the "sea" as "a sea of nations," and views the sea being turned into blood as "the demise of the world's economic life-support system." But this would require the death of everyone on earth rather than life in the oceans. Thomas (II:250) is right to observe that the literal judgment effectively reverses God's creation of sea life in Gen. 1:21.

D. Third Bowl (16:4-7)

4 And the third angel poured out his vial upon the rivers and fountains of waters; and they became blood.
5 And I heard the angel of the waters say, Thou art righteous, O Lord, which art, and wast, and shalt be, because thou hast judged thus.
6 For they have shed the blood of saints and prophets, and thou hast given them blood to drink; for they are worthy.
7 And I heard another out of the altar say, Even so, Lord God Almighty, true and righteous *are* thy judgments.

The third bowl judgment fell on freshwater sources (v. 4; cf. 8:10, 11; Ex. 7:17-25), including rivers and "fountains of waters" (springs) above and beneath the earth's surface. Like the oceans, these are turned into "blood," further affecting anyone or anything dependent on these water supplies. The bowl judgments of the Tribulation are far worse than any in history (or earlier in Revelation): they are *total*, leaving humanity without freshwater sources for the remainder of the period.

Beale (816) interprets this as "famine" and "severe economic suffering." Lenski (468) suggests that the springs

and rivers are "natural good sense, knowledge, and wisdom, from which all men must constantly draw for all departments of life." According to the idealist hermeneutic, all the bowl judgments are instruments that God uses to afflict unbelieving people throughout the church age (Hendriksen 161).

At this point, John heard "the angel of the waters" confirm the justice of God's action (v. 5; cf. 9:14). This angel may be one who in some way assists in God's government of the created universe, perhaps with responsibility over earth's waters in some way. Or he may serve as a personified spokesman for the waters that have been affected in the second and third bowl judgments.

The angel praised God for His righteousness and His eternal existence. God's character, motives, and actions are eternally, absolutely righteous. ("O Lord" is omitted in most manuscripts, but it is clear that the angel is addressing God.) Righteousness is right behavior and character. The righteous God is completely justified in His motives in whatever He does, including His judgments.

"Which art, and wast, and shalt be" (cf. 1:4, 8; 4:8; 11:17) indicates God's eternal existence and points to His infinite wisdom. (Most manuscripts omit "and shall be" and have "holy one" instead. Both attributions are amply justified in Scripture.) Whatever the eternal God does to creation is within His rights as its sovereign Creator. Infinite wisdom will be needed to dismantle His creation and judge mankind properly at the end of the present order.

The angel's doxology affirms the righteousness of God's severe judgments, poured out upon the world with an end in view. The material elements (stars, continents, salt- and freshwater sources) are judged because these ultimately affect the Antichrist's regime and the unbelieving population of earth dependent on them. "Because thou hast judged thus" refers specifically to the bowl judgments. God's wrath is poured out for a reason: "For they have shed the blood of saints and prophets" (v. 6; cf. 17:6; 18:24; 19:2). "Shed" (Greek *ekcheo*) is the same as "pour out" in 16:1: the judgments are "poured out" because they have "poured out" the blood of saints. While the primary reference here may be to those martyred during the Tribulation (cf. 6:9-11; 7:9, 14), martyrs throughout O.T. and N.T. history are in principle included.

Furthermore, God *reciprocates* their duplicity in the bloodshed of martyrs by *giving them blood to drink in return*" with the earth's water sources turned into blood. Furthermore, this punishment is deserved ("they are worthy") because they are guilty of bloodshed. God's judgment against the guilty is based on law and works, not on the grace of Jesus Christ that they rejected. They must now reap what they have sown. The punishment fits the crime (cf. Is. 49:26).

Aune (II:889) raises the possibility that this reflects "internecine warfare" (cf. L. Morris 188), that unbelievers turn against one another to the point of bloodshed. But the judgment includes the whole earth, making that unlikely. The building toll of the three series of judgments is awesome: under the seal judgments (early in the Tribulation), one-quarter of earth's population; under the sixth trumpet judgment, a third of humanity by the demonic cavalry (9:18). The Battle of Armageddon, where the blood of the Antichrist's army rises to the level of a horse's bridle in the bottom of the valley, is yet to come. The angel's explanation is simply that even as the unbelieving have killed or shed the blood of God's people, so now their blood is being shed in catastrophic and unprecedented proportions. That those judged are "worthy" means that they *deserve* to have their own lives taken (Gen. 9:6). Their works of bloodshed have earned the judgment.

"The woe of the third bowl is part of God's answer to the saints' plea in ch. 6" (Beale 818). Martyred saints asked God when He would avenge their blood (6:10). The waiting is over. As the bowl judgments unfold, the vindication of the martyrs is in progress. But this is not mere *retaliation*; it is a *just* righting of great wrongs, including the martyrdom of saints, the rejection of the gospel of Jesus Christ, and lifestyles characterized by unbelief. Even so, the bowl judgments, though the most severe in the Tribulation period, are not comparable to being confined to Hell forever (cf. 20:15).

Gregg (352ff.) conveniently summarizes how the various schools of interpretation identify the bowl judgments. Preterists view them as attacks against the Roman Empire of the first century. Historicists tend to equate the bowls with attacks on the papacy around the time of the French revolution. Futurists interpret them literally as phenomena that will take place during the end-times Tribulation. Idealists usually look for repeated manifestations, in principle, throughout church history.

Verse 7 is probably an "antiphonal" response to vv. 5, 6 (Brighton 412). "Another" from "out of the altar" could be one of the martyrs or an angel, probably the same angel associated with the golden altar in 8:3-5, 9:13, and 14:18. Most manuscripts read "And I heard the altar (or, [one] from the altar) saying," but even in the first reading it is more likely that the voice came from the vicinity of the altar than that the altar is personified. The identity of the voice is not as significant as what is being said. "Altar" (Greek *thusiasterion*) is the word used previously to refer to the golden altar of incense in Heaven (6:9-11; 8:5; 9:13; 14:18). The voice here may represent the entire body of saints in Heaven. Regardless, the affirmation that God's judgments are "true and righteous" is emphatic.

"Even so" (Greek *nai*) is literally "Yes," perhaps synonymous with "Amen" (Aune II:888). The up-front positioning emphasizes the following doxology (cf. 1:7; 14:13; 22:20). The voice commended the "Lord God Almighty"; cf. 1:8; 4:8; 11:17; 15:3 (see comments there); 19:6; 21:22.

God is powerful enough to do anything He desires and has demonstrated this sovereign power throughout history. But it is *power under control*: He uses His power righteously, for holy objectives that are "true and righteous" (cf. 15:3; 19:2). These adjectives reflect two important components of a right judgment: they are executed on the basis of true facts (evidence) and carried out in a just or right way, always commensurate with what is deserved.

"Judgments" (Greek *krisis*) indicates "the action of a judge" (ALGNT 238), "*a separation, selection, judgment/ opinion/decision given concerning anything*" (Thayer 361). Here it refers to a determination already made, perhaps to the objective instrument or action of judgment. The bowls are good examples

of God's final decisions and the subsequent actions taken.

E. Fourth Bowl (16:8, 9)

8 And the fourth angel poured out his vial upon the sun; and power was given unto him to scorch men with fire.
9 And men were scorched with great heat, and blasphemed the name of God, which hath power over these plagues: and they repented not to give him glory.

The fourth bowl judgment affected the "sun" (vv. 8, 9; cf. 8:12). "Was given" (another *divine passive*) indicates that God Himself authorized the judgment and its effects. The purpose was simple, terrible, and dedicated: to inflict great physical suffering on the unbelieving population of the earth (cf. 7:16; Is. 49:10). Still, the next verse suggests that retribution was not God's *only* purpose.

God created the sun as a giant ball of *fire* to give light and warmth to the earth (Gen. 1:14-19). Initially, the sun's temperature was perfectly regulated by God for optimum life-giving benefit. But this was very likely altered in some way when God cursed the creation because of original sin, and perhaps again at Noah's flood; the human lifespan decreased dramatically after that catastrophe. Still, the sun has continued to serve the earth and mankind beneficently and consistently. But with the outpouring of the fourth bowl judgment God's management of the sun is dramatically altered once again.

This judgment produced a "scorching" effect on mankind. "Scorch men with fire" is probably a reference to "the sun" itself: that is, to its rays. Even now, overexposure to the sun leads to sunburn and other damage; the pain from a burn is intense. The scorching or burning of the flesh that occurs as a result of the fourth bowl judgment is far worse: "great heat" implies severe torment. Though this is not said to cause death, some may in fact die as a result. But God's purpose is torment, not execution; and it is but a foretaste of the suffering that Hell will provide forever.

Perhaps the sun's temperature increases significantly, or the atmosphere is altered so that its protective properties are diminished—another instance of a pattern that emerges toward the end of the Tribulation when the order of nature begins to unravel. This happens in increasingly catastrophic ways as the Day of the Lord proper approaches (see 6:12-17; 16:17-21). God uses the very things that formerly sustained human life on earth—including land, water, and sunlight—as instruments of His judgments.

Those scorched responded in two negative ways. First, they "blasphemed the name of God" (v. 9; cf. vv. 11, 21; 13:1, 5, 6; 17:3). Blasphemy is "*harmful, abusive speech* against someone's reputation; *slander, reviling, evil speaking*" (ALGNT 91). Blaspheming the name of God is speaking against Him. Men will know on some level that the bowl judgments come from God. Their "blasphemy" suggests that they impugn or curse God in some way: perhaps personally or maligning His motives or questioning His justice.

Second, "they repented not to give him glory." "Repent" (Greek *metanoeo*) means "to change one's mind, be converted" (ALGNT 260). Not only did the chastisement fail to prompt repentance, they also failed to give God glory. That they blasphemed His name means they recognized that the plagues were from Him; they may even have recognized that their evil behavior was the reason. Whatever they recognized, their rebellious attitude deepened.

The fact that "repentance" is introduced in this context near the end of the Tribulation is noteworthy, suggesting that repentance may have been God's desired outcome. That this judgment did not result in death allows that repentance was at least theoretically possible. All God's acts of judgment before the *final* judgment are limited and allow for this. Not that God *expects* mass conversions at this time, but He acts on principle, extending an offer of mercy until the very end. Perhaps a number were converted ("gave glory to God") after the earthquake of 11:13. The response here is the opposite.

Idealist Beale (821, 822) suggests that the scorching is symbolic: "This woe includes suffering involving deprivation of forms of earthly security, likely with an economic focus." But equating heat so scorching that it causes men to blaspheme God, with economic deprivation seems incongruous. Nothing in the text encourages this reticence about physical suffering. When the world's economy or material deprivation is intended, Revelation indicates that (18:3, 11, 12-19).

F. Fifth Bowl (16:10, 11)

10 And the fifth angel poured out his vial upon the seat of the beast; and his kingdom was full of darkness; and they gnawed their tongues for pain.

11 And blasphemed the God of heaven because of their pains and their sores, and repented not of their deeds.

"There are few visions in Revelation more awe-inspiring than that of the fifth Bowl" (Wilcox 147), poured out on "the seat of the beast" (v. 10; cf. 2:13; 13:2); the kingdom and followers of Antichrist are subjected to chaos and panic. "Seat" is the same as "throne" (4:2, 4), used here of the central location of Antichrist's government on earth (wherever that is). Thus God dramatically illustrates His sovereignty over Antichrist, reminiscent of His challenge to Egypt's Pharaoh: "Since the worshipers of the beast and its image refuse to repent, even though struck by these various plagues, God now strikes the object of their worship and allegiance" (Brighton 414).

Darkness often represents judgment (Ex. 10:21-29; Is. 13:10; Jl. 2:31; 3:15; Amos 8:9; Mt. 24:29; 25:30; Acts 2:20; Jude 6, 13), in both Testaments the antithesis of God as Light (Is. 9:2; Jn. 3:19; Rom. 2:19; 13:12; Eph. 5:8, 11; 6:12; Col. 1:13; 1 Pet. 2:9; 1 Jn. 1:5, 6). The entire confederacy of Antichrist is enveloped in such "darkness" (v. 10), perhaps corresponding to similar cosmic phenomena with the sixth seal judgment (6:12) and the fourth trumpet judgment (8:12). To suggest that this is *spiritual* darkness creates an unnecessary redundancy since that kind of darkness already characterizes the beast's kingdom and way of life.

The darkness causes people to "gnaw their tongues for pain"—difficult to interpret only if "darkness" is viewed as the cause, since darkness is normally painless in itself. "Pain" (Greek *ponos*) can mean distress or physical pain (ALGNT 322). Distress, both physical and psychological, is brought on by many potential sources of pain during the Tribulation. Indeed, v. 11 indicates that the cause of the pain includes the previous bowl judgments and not just the darkness alone.

Certainly, the darkness may cause people to dwell on their torments, magnifying the painful effects, and it may enhance the fear caused by the rapidly disintegrating world conditions, thus contributing to chaos and panic. But there is no need to make this darkness symbolic of psychological torment, as in the view of idealist Beale (824). That the victims "gnawed their tongues" indicates *physical* pain. Since spiritual darkness characterized the kingdom of the beast from its beginning in 13:1, and since a miracle of literal darkness is frequently associated with end-time prophecies in a number of *same language* passages (O.T. and N.T.), the plague of darkness should be interpreted literally.

The response to the fifth bowl judgment, as to the fourth, was: they "blasphemed the God of heaven...and repented not" (v. 11). Their "pains and sores" came from the first four bowl judgments that directly affected unbelieving humanity, including the "boils" of the first and the "blisters" of the fourth. Physical suffering has psychological impact; the cumulative effect prompted a visceral response of blasphemy against God. Totally devoid of a spirit of "repentance" that acknowledges guilt, turns to God for relief, and results in changed behavior, they continued their evil "deeds." Their allegiance to Antichrist was unaffected, perhaps even reinforced.

G. Sixth Bowl (16:12-16)

12 And the sixth angel poured out his vial upon the great river Euphrates; and the water thereof was dried up, that the way of the kings of the east might be prepared.
13 And I saw three unclean spirits like frogs *come* out of the mouth of the dragon, and out of the mouth of the beast, and out of the mouth of the false prophet.
14 For they are the spirits of devils, working miracles, *which* go forth unto the kings of the earth and of the whole world, to gather them to the battle of that great day of God Almighty.
15 Behold, I come as a thief. Blessed *is* he that watcheth, and keepeth his garments, lest he walk naked, and they see his shame.
16 And he gathered them together into a place called in the Hebrew tongue Armageddon.

The sixth bowl judgment is poured out on "the great river Euphrates" (v. 12); the sixth trumpet judgment also involved the Euphrates (9:13-21). An army from the East—perhaps a two-hundred-million-member cavalry (9:16)—must cross the Euphrates in order to invade Israel. The earlier loosing of the four angels bound there (9:14, 15) may be preparatory and complementary to the action here. Even so, the two judgments are distinct and each description is unique. Here, the purpose for drying up the Euphrates is to facilitate crossing by the eastern kings; a highway is thus prepared for those who will participate in the Battle of Armageddon (v. 16): "The invading armies are gathered by the lies of the dragon, the beast, and the false prophet" (D. Johnson 231). God is not doing them any favors by drying up the Euphrates. He is virtually leading them to their slaughter.

"And I saw" introduces a small parenthesis (vv. 13-15) between the sixth and seventh bowl judgments. "Three unclean spirits like frogs" came from the mouths of the so-called *satanic trinity*—the dragon, the beast, and the false prophet (the first time the second beast of chapter 13 is called "the false prophet": cf. 19:20; 20:10). Given that the N.T. commonly refers to demons as "unclean spirits," these are demonic spirits of anti-Christian "propaganda" (Thomas II:264), employed by the satanic trinity to deceive the world into invading Israel (v. 14). The comparison to "frogs" may simply reflect that they looked as if they *leaped* from their mouths. The demon spirits receive their authority, message, and miracle-working power from "the dragon" (Satan).

These "spirits" are able to work miracles (v. 14); "sign" (Greek *semeion*) is the same as in 13:13; 19:20 (see there), often used to mean a miracle that is "contrary to the usual course of nature and intended as a pointer or means of confirmation" (ALGNT 348). As suggested earlier, Antichrist successfully diverts the worship of God to himself through the use of "signs" (13:13); these demons employ the same deceptive technique.

They are sent to "the kings of the earth," further qualified as "the whole world" or "the whole *inhabited* earth." The "kings of the east" and their armies would be numbered among these (v. 12). This *dual* reference to the worldwide scope of their mission points to eschatological fulfillment. This is not a gathering of nation against nation; the scenario does not compare with any historical precedent to date. It is a gathering of the entire antichristian world against God, with the end-time confederacy of nations forming the bulk of the movement.

The demon spirits "go forth" to recruit anti-Christian forces for the Battle of Armageddon, using miraculous signs as successful persuaders (cf. 13:13, 14). Whether these are personified as persons in order to carry out their mission or are simply symbols of *spirits* working invisibly behind the scenes in a variety of ways is not clear. Regardless, the miracles are visible.

Aune (II:894, 895) compares the "lying spirit" that deceived King Ahab (1 Kg. 22:19-23). Likewise, these succeed in leading the anti-Christian forces to their eventual destruction at Armageddon. "The nations are deceived into thinking that they are gathering to exterminate the saints, but they are gathered together ultimately by God only in order to meet their own judgment at the hands of Jesus" (Beale 835).

The battle itself is "the battle of that great day of God Almighty" (v. 14), referring to "the well-known eschatological battle" (Aune II:858, 896). This makes it distinct from repeated battles throughout church history (as idealism suggests) or from some fulfillment within past history (as historicism suggests) and indicates that it is a solitary end-time event yet to be fulfilled.

"Great day" is apparently synonymous with the "Day of the Lord," prominent in both testaments (Ps. 2:1-10; Jl. 2:1-11; 3:2; Zech. 14:1-9, 12-14). There are at least three major components to the "Day of the Lord" proper, in its most narrow sense the culmination of God's wrath at the end of the Tribulation. (1) Catastrophic changes in the material universe precede or occur in connection with this day, including the heavenly luminaries and the physical topography of the earth itself: sun, moon, stars, comets or asteroids, displaced mountains and islands, earthquakes, and polluted water sources. (2) The Second Coming of Christ follows. (3) The decisive world battle itself, "the Battle of Armageddon," occurs (19:19-21; see v. 16).

Scripture unwaveringly connects the Day of the Lord with the Second Coming of Christ; this is determinative for eschatology. Jesus gave the definitive standard for the associated catastrophes in the Olivet Discourse (Mt. 24:29, 30; cf. Rev. 6:12-17). Paul spoke of a battle that would destroy the Antichrist on the "day of Christ"—equivalent to "his coming" (2 Th. 2:2, 8, 9). Peter followed suit; see 2 Pet. 3:10, 12. These N.T. verses connect the catastrophes associated with the Day of the Lord in the O.T. with the coming of Christ. Jesus' own words here—"Behold, I come as a thief" (v. 15; cf. 22:7, 12, 20)—add to this synthesis of three major Scriptural components of eschatology: the Day of the Lord, the Second Coming of Christ, and the Battle of Armageddon with its attendant catastrophes. All these are integral parts of what the Scriptures identify as "the Day of the Lord."

The Second Coming of Christ and the Battle of Armageddon are so closely associated in chapter 19 that the abrupt interjection, here, of "Behold, I come as a thief" is appropriate. Even as the anti-Christian forces gather at Armageddon, the one who they will fight against, "the exalted Christ" (Aune II:896), prepares His entry.

"Blessed is he" (v. 15) is the third of seven beatitudes in Revelation (1:3; 14:13; 16:15; 19:9; 20:6; 22:7). The conditions of this blessing are watching and keeping one's "garments," spiritual requirements to be ready for the Day of the Lord or the Second Coming (cf. Mt. 24:42, 46; 25:13, 31f.). The two complementary disciplines indicate a right relationship with God. A person may be unprepared in two ways: he may fail to watch or have "soiled" garments at Christ's return. Christ will look for evidence of fresh faith and a present, righteous lifestyle. Faith and faithfulness (righteous behavior) constitute readiness.

The armies of the world, under the leadership of Antichrist, are finally gathered at "Armageddon" (v. 16), "a Hebrew place name meaning *Mount* or *Hill of Megiddo* and generally identified as the fortress overlooking a pass through the Carmel Range into Galilee" (ALGNT 74). Megiddo was a Biblical city, though a specific *mountain* named Megiddo is not known. "Whatever the derivation of the name, it is clear that John means by Armageddon the place of the final struggle between the powers of evil and the Kingdom of God" (Ladd, *Commentary* 216). Surely Armageddon refers to a geographical location in northern Israel near the end of the age, whatever its precise location.

H. Seventh Bowl (16:17-21)

The *same language principle* in Scripture should be observed for the sake of hermeneutical consistency: identical or similar words, synonyms, concepts, persons, places, and events throughout Scripture are more than likely references to the same things. Recognizing this facilitates interpretation, identifications, and a systematic understanding of the predictions contained in both Testaments. The repetition of essentially the same language reaches a point at which the evidence for a particular interpretation or identification becomes overwhelming.

This principle applies when comparing the sixth seal, the seventh trumpet, and the seventh bowl: each is a unique member within its own group of seven, with each "telescoping" to the grand climax of the Tribulation. The language and subject matter of these three are so similar that they obviously refer to the same events and time.

**17 And the seventh angel poured out his vial into the air; and there came a great voice out of the temple of heaven, from the throne, saying, It is done.
18 And there were voices, and thunders, and lightnings; and there was a great earthquake, such as was not since men were upon the earth, so mighty an earthquake, *and* so great.
19 And the great city was divided into three parts, and the cities of the nations fell: and great Babylon came in remembrance before God, to give unto her the cup of the wine of the fierceness of his wrath.
20 And every island fled away, and the mountains were not found.
21 And there fell upon men a great hail out of heaven, *every stone about the weight of a talent:* and men blasphemed God because of the plague of the hail; for the**

plague thereof was exceeding great.

The seventh angel poured out his bowl "into the air" (the atmosphere), setting in motion two historically unprecedented catastrophes (v. 17), each accompanied by related catastrophes affecting both the earth and its unbelieving population (v. 20).

First, another "great voice" came from the heavenly Temple, for the first time associated with "the throne" (cf. 14:15). This may suggest the voice of God Himself and imply that the throne is inside the heavenly Temple. (Previously unidentified voices *may* have been God's; regardless, the source of all such voices points to their divine origin. The revelation is no less divine or authoritative when an angel speaks for God.)

"It is done" corresponds to what the mighty angel said after the sixth trumpet judgment in 10:6, "that there should be time no longer" and to the language of finality in the seventh trumpet (11:15-19). Likewise, the seventh bowl judgment finishes the "wrath of God" (15:1). "It is not surprising that there are a number of similarities between the last trumpet and the final bowl: they both bring history to a close" (Mounce 302).

"A great earthquake" (v. 18) occurs, and the description shows just how "great." First, the typical heavenly phenomena associated with the throne room of Heaven—"voices, thunders, and lightnings"—herald the announcement (cf. 4:5; 11:19). Earthquakes are sometimes theophanic: one accompanied God's presence on Mt. Sinai, for example; cf. the crucifixion and resurrection of Christ. But they may also be instruments of judgment (11:13). Thus, though the "earthquake" may symboli-

cally underscore the significance of what is about to happen from Heaven's point of view, this one could just as well be literal, closely linked to events in the earth's atmosphere and the great hailstorm of v. 21 (thus explaining why this vial was poured into the "air"). Regardless, the effect is no less devastating to the earth, and its magnitude is emphasized by the twice-used "great," the addition of "mighty," and the comparison "such as was not since men were upon the earth." Thomas (II:274) says, "The seventh bowl sweeps away time and history, and so must be more than just an [ordinary] earthquake and hail."

This end-times earthquake will be the "mightiest" or "greatest" earthquake in the history of the world (cf. Hag. 2:6; Zech. 14:4; Heb. 12:26, 27). Presumably, this will involve greater devastation than by any of the more notable ones of earth's history. Earthquakes have the potential to destroy civilizations and to rearrange earth's topography. This may account for the displacement of earth's islands and mountains in v. 20.

The epicenter of this particular earthquake is "the great city" (v. 19). In 11:8, 13 an earlier earthquake affected the city of Jerusalem, identified as "where also our Lord was crucified." In that case, the city alone—and only one-tenth of it—was affected. But this earthquake is not that one, for two reasons. First, a different city is indicated: namely, "Babylon" (v. 19). Second, the scope is different: this earthquake causes all the cities of the nations to fall.

The fact that "great" modifies the "city" of Babylon in 17:5, 18; 18:2, 10, 16, 18, 21 suggests that "the great city" of 16:19 is the same. "Babylon," an ancient city whose name came to be used as a symbol of the enemies of God's people, is also used this way in Revelation, representing the evil world system as a whole; it may also exist literally as the seat of the Antichrist's government during the Tribulation. Identification with a revived ancient empire or city of Babylon is not necessarily in view (cf. 14:8; 17:5; 18:10, 21; cf. 11:8); but idealist Beale (843) is not inconsistent in saying, "Indeed, 'the great city' itself is 'Babylon the Great,' which is the evil world system."

As noted, the seismic waves of this earthquake destroy cities worldwide, so that it "must therefore be understood as affecting the entire inhabited world" (Aune II:901). This judgment is against the anti-Christian world capital in the end-time Tribulation period and the cities allied with her in other nations throughout the world. "Divided into three parts" indicates that the earthquake split "Babylon" into three parts and may suggest God's judgment of three components—religious, economic, and political—of the world system (see chapters 17, 18). "Came in remembrance before God" is equivalent to saying that God decided that the time for judgment was right. "The fall of Babylon is the central teaching of the seventh bowl" (Thomas II:275).

Reference to "the wine of God's wrath" (in 14:8, 10, 18-20) resumes in v. 19 (cf. 17:2; 18:3). God's motivation to judge Babylon is in order to reciprocate her for "the wine" she has offered to the "kings, nations, and merchants" of the world, intoxicating them with her philosophy of materialism and idolatry. The cup of wine that God gives her to drink is "the fierceness of his wrath," a phrase using both common N.T. words

for wrath and therefore emphasizing that the wrath is full strength or undiluted.

Verse 20 affirms the catastrophic degree, the worldwide scope, and the eschatological nature of this earthquake. Every island "fled away" or disappeared. The mountains "were not found": they disappeared or were destroyed as a result of the earthquake. (Note the *same language* in 6:12-17 and Mt. 24:29, as well as in O.T. descriptions of the Day of the Lord.)

The seventh bowl judgment ends with a supernatural hailstorm (v. 21; cf. Jos. 10:11; Ezek. 38:18-22). The hail is truly "great": individual stones weigh a talent, roughly a hundred pounds. John describes the effects as "exceeding great." This adds significantly to the death totals and material devastation. Regrettably, yet predictably, unbelievers remain recalcitrant in spite of this final provocation to repentance. They "blaspheme God" because of the hail.

Summary
(16:1-21)

After the introduction to the seven last plagues (chapter 15), John heard an unidentified voice—perhaps God Himself—command seven angels to pour out their bowls of wrath on the earth (16:1).

The first produced sores or boils on those who had the mark of Antichrist and worshiped his image—implying that those who do not have that mark are spared (v. 2). These believe in Christ and remain faithful to Him throughout the Tribulation.

The second was poured out on all the saltwater sources on earth (v. 3), turning them into something like the blood of a dead person that can no longer sustain life. Every living thing in them dies. The third judgment affected the freshwater sources of earth in the same way (v. 4).

These judgments prompted an angelic doxology affirming God's righteousness and justice (vv. 5-7). The judgments are poured out because people deserve them, having shed the blood of martyred saints.

The fourth bowl judgment was poured out on the sun (vv. 8, 9), resulting in an increase in the amount of heat that consequently scorched the unbelieving population. The significant blistering or scorching caused the victims to blaspheme the name of God instead of repenting and giving God glory.

The fifth bowl brought darkness, directly challenging the Antichrist in affecting the headquarters of his kingdom (vv. 10, 11). This darkness compounds the already significant suffering caused by the previous judgments, exacerbating the social panic and escalating chaos. The cumulative effect of the judgments caused victims to gnaw their tongues in pain.

The sixth bowl judgment was poured out on the Euphrates River (v. 12). God miraculously dries up this great river's bed to allow the kings of the East to cross on their way to the Battle of Armageddon. Three demonic, miracle-working spirits recruit from all over the world (vv. 13, 14), speaking successfully on behalf of the satanic trinity; but they are divinely manipulated for the eventual destruction of the anti-Christian forces at Armageddon.

The Second Coming will occur in conjunction with the Battle of Armageddon (19:11-21). John restates Christ's promise about the thief-like, unpredictable nature of His return (vv.

15, 16), adding an exhortation to be faithful in watching and readiness.

The seventh bowl judgment was poured out into earth's atmosphere (v. 17). An unnamed voice—probably God Himself—pronounced the judgments finished with this one, which affects the earth in unprecedented, catastrophic ways. First, the greatest earthquake in history divided the city of "Babylon" into three parts and destroyed the cities of the nations confederated with her (vv. 18, 19). The earth's topography was dramatically affected, destroying every island and mountain of earth (v. 20).

The second catastrophic effect was a supernatural hailstorm (v. 21), producing hailstones that weighed about 100 pounds each. The unbelieving population of earth remained recalcitrant and blasphemous to the end, in spite of the awesome displays of God's power.

Application: Teaching and Preaching the Passage

The present world system and material universe are coming to an end. Everyone ought to be informed about this, about the catastrophic ways by which this end occurs, and that there is an eternal existence beyond the present life. The end comes at the Second Coming of Christ and the Battle of Armageddon. This knowledge provides powerful motivation to change human behavior (2 Pet. 3:10-14). Revelation provides details that should be referenced as we teach and preach about the Second Coming.

The last generation of humanity will not surrender willingly to Christ as the rightful King. Christ will come and take control by the use of omnipotent force. The world is not bound to get better, but worse (2 Tim. 3:1). This perspective should temper any idealism that seeks to reconstruct or reform present society in the world at large. Though many will be saved in the future, and it is important to reach as many as possible, the church will not ever successfully convert the world by its preaching and good works.

This raises questions about the role of believers in America or other nations. Should believers try to band together in sufficient numbers in order to reconstruct what is now post-Christian America? It does not appear that such efforts will ever succeed, and some movements toward that end in the last quarter of the twentieth century have fallen by the wayside. Perhaps more concern and effort should be devoted to carrying out the Great Commission and living out personal holiness. Significant change comes about by changing the hearts of men one at a time (Mt. 5:13-16). Society will not endure forever, but the souls of individuals will. Though civil concern and service are significant, the transitory nature of human institutions should be kept in view.

Suggested Outline. Prelude to Armageddon, 16:12-16, (1) Divine preparation, v. 12; (2) Demonic assistance, vv. 13, 14; (3) Duties of devoted, v. 15; (4) Destination determined, v. 16.

VI. THE CONQUEST BY CHRIST (17:1—20:15)

Most of chapters 4-20 refer to the seven-year Tribulation at the end of the present age. World conquest by Antichrist is not the primary emphasis, which is Christ's conquest of the present world. Christ defeats Satan, Antichrist and his followers, and the world's systems (reli-gious, economic, and political) before establishing His own millennial kingdom (Dan. 2:35, 44, 45). Nor is this a post-millennial or reconstructionist accomplishment: Christ's victory is by force, instituting a millennial reign on earth, achieved through three series of judgments (seals, trumpets, and bowls) and the Battle of Armageddon. The identity of the first horseman in the first seal (6:2) is Christ as the One who rides forth to conquer.

Chapters 17, 18 visually depict the end of the present world system: "Whether referred to as an appendix or as an extended footnote, it is an expansion and explanation of the seventh bowl judgment" (Thomas II:279). God has used the seals, trumpets, and bowls to bring the world to this point, judging unbelievers, dismantling the world system, and altering the material earth in dramatic ways. Clearly, the wrath of God is essentially finished with the seven bowl judgments (15:1; 16:17). After the seventh bowl, the calendar of world events moves rapidly toward a climax at Armageddon and the Second Coming of Christ.

A. The Great Prostitute (17:1-18)

1. The vision (17:1-6)

1 And there came one of the seven angels which had the seven vials, and talked with me, saying unto me, Come hither; I will shew unto thee the judgment of the great whore that sitteth upon many waters:
2 With whom the kings of the earth have committed fornication, and the inhabitants of the earth have

been made drunk with the wine of her fornication.

3 So he carried me away in the spirit into the wilderness: and I saw a woman sit upon a scarlet coloured beast, full of names of blasphemy, having seven heads and ten horns.

4 And the woman was arrayed in purple and scarlet colour, and decked with gold and precious stones and pearls, having a golden cup in her hand full of abominations and filthiness of her fornication.

5 And upon her forehead *was* a name written, MYSTERY, BABYLON THE GREAT, THE MOTHER OF HARLOTS AND ABOMINATIONS OF THE EARTH.

6 And I saw the woman drunken with the blood of the saints, and with the blood of the martyrs of Jesus: and when I saw her, I wondered with great admiration.

One of the seven "bowl" angels reappears to introduce new revelation (v. 1) and subsequently interpret the vision (vv. 7-18). John is summoned to view "the judgment of the great whore." "Whore" (Greek *pornos*) involves illicit sexual activity but metaphorically can indicate unfaithfulness to God: "In prophetic language prostitution or adultery equals idolatry" (Ford 277). Indeed, the analogy of a prostitute is used frequently in the O.T. to portray Israel's idolatry and unfaithfulness to God (Is. 1:21; Jer. 2:20-31; 13:27; Ezek. 16:15; Hos. 2:5; 4:10-12).

Revelation adapts this analogy to portray idolatrous, sinful behavior by the world system during the Tribulation. More than an apostate religious institution is meant, though such an institution may satanically drive the whole. But all the nations of the world and their institutions are included, as is God's purpose to be worshiped and served exclusively. Satanic seduction has led the world to spiritual harlotry against God. One reason "prostitution," rather than "adultery," is charged, is found in the defining characteristic of prostitution as done for money. This "prostitute" has become wealthy from plying her trade with the clientele of kings, merchants, nations, and the inhabitants of earth.

That she is "sitting upon many waters" (cf. Is. 17:12, 13; Jer. 15:13) is figurative, suggesting a position of authority or ruling: an "indication of enthronement" (Aune III:930). Some take "upon" (Greek *epi*) to mean *by* or *beside* and suggest that this implies Babylon or Rome, both situated by rivers. But "upon" or "on" is more likely, and "many waters" does not refer to *one* river but symbolizes the worldwide influence referenced in v. 2 and later interpreted as "peoples, and multitudes, and nations, and tongues" in v. 15.

"The description is not a matter of geography but theology and Scripture: Rome is Babylon, enthroned upon her multinational commercial empire that spans the seas" (Boring 180). "Babylon" apparently came to mean "Rome" in Jewish tradition after the destruction of Jerusalem. But this does not settle the identity of "Babylon" here: whether ancient Babylon or Rome is meant, interpreters may regard either as literal or symbolic. There are various views.

Mounce (306) identifies the great prostitute as "Rome, that citadel of pagan opposition to the cause of Christ." Many think "Babylon" is Rome, and chapters 17, 18 describe the downfall of the Roman Empire as a severe threat to the early church—a *historicist* view. But such a look back into church history is woefully out of place by now in Revelation. These revelations come at the very *end* of the present order. It seems inappropriate for the great prostitute to be judged *before* her 2,000-year history of sins against the church!

Thomas (II:283) says that this prostitute "represents all false religion of all time, including those who apostatize from the revealed religion of Christianity." Walvoord identifies her as "false religion" or "the apostate church" (243, 244). Though the reformers identified her with the Roman Church, the tendency now is to identify her more broadly as a world religion, including all branches of the Christian church and non-Christian religions.

Ryrie ("Apostasy" 51), citing Alexander Hislop's work *The Two Babylons*, is convinced that the Roman Church practices Babylonian religion in the form of "mother-child worship." He therefore identifies this "Babylon" as "the final form of apostate Christendom," with Rome as its "pillar church."

Some futurists think that ancient Babylon will be rebuilt by Iraq and become prominent in the world by the end of the age and oppress Israel (Allen 407). Some suggest that it will become the physical capital of Antichrist's world empire.

Ford (285) identifies the great prostitute as "Jerusalem" (based on Ezek. 16) and her gaudy appearance as "a parody of the high priest" (288). Although the historical unfaithfulness of Jerusalem is an established fact, this identification should be rejected because the Second Coming is about the city of Jerusalem's *deliverance*, not her judgment.

The prostitute's *judgment* is the central subject of chapters 17 and 18. Though "judgment" (Greek *krima*) at root means the judicial verdict, it can also refer to "the result of the action" of judgment (Vine 337). The arraignment of Babylon before God is the burden of chapter 17. The *grand jury* in God's court has determined there is sufficient evidence to indict. The revelations made in chapters 17 and 18 flow out of this guilty verdict already rendered (16:5-7). "St. John has heard the sentence pronounced, and is now to see it carried into effect" (Swete 213).

"The kings of the earth" are among the whore's clientele (v. 2; cf. 18:3, 9; Is. 23:17; Jer. 51:7). As noted above, their "fornication" with her is a metaphor for spiritual unfaithfulness to God. But in what sense were the kings or nations of earth "married" to God? Idealist Hughes (182) thinks of this as "the general unfaithfulness to God represented in mankind's pride and sinfulness." But as true as this picture is, it fails to face up to the eschatological manifestations involved here, portraying the "prostitute's" *final* judgment and how it affects the real world. The world's acceptance and worship of the Antichrist and his image during the Tribulation will be the most brazen and universal form of idolatry ever, far surpassing the client relationships of ancient nations with the Roman Empire. God judges equally the prostitute *and* her clientele.

The analogy seems to suggest that the "whore" had been initially "married" or related to God in order to be charged with unfaithfulness. Then a prior relationship to God may indeed be implied: the once faithful woman became unfaithful to God by her complicity in the agenda and idolatries of Antichrist. She corrupted the world by influencing the kings, nations, and inhabitants of the earth to do the same: the unbelieving population is part of her tangled web.

This corrupting of unbelieving humanity ("the inhabitants of the earth") compounded the prostitute's wickedness. "Made drunk with the wine of her fornication" describes her evil influence on others. "The inhabitants of the earth" means, again, *the unbelieving population* of earth (3:10; 6:10; 11:10; 13:8, 12, 14; 14:6; 17:8). Like their leaders (kings of the earth), the rank and file of earth have also committed spiritual "fornication" against God with the "whore."

In the end-times, unbelievers will become drunk with "the wine of her fornication," manifested primarily in spiritual or religious unfaithfulness but perhaps also involving sexually immoral behavior (Beale 849). The "intoxication" indicates that unbelievers are overcome by the whore's evil influences: anti-Christian spirit, worship of Antichrist, atheistic materialism, etc. (cf. Eph. 2:2, 3; 5:18). They will be judged with her because they willingly followed her; that many are coerced into compliance makes no difference.

After the introduction of "the great whore," John was transported "in the spirit into the wilderness" (v. 3). Though he remained physically on Patmos he was transported by the Spirit in his spirit to the vantage point from which he observed the vision (cf. 1:10; 4:2). "Wilderness" (Greek *eremos*) means "an uninhabited place or desert" (Vine 676). This "wilderness" seems to be distinct from the one in 12:6, 14, here perhaps for effect as a backdrop against which to display ironically the "beauty" of the prostitute. It is at least symbolic of the

sinful, barren, or even hostile spiritual conditions of the world (cf. Is. 21:9).

The woman was "sitting" (as in v. 1) on "a scarlet-coloured beast." If Aune (III:930) is correct that "sitting" indicates "enthronement" all four times it is used in chapter 17, then some type of rule or control is indicated. Indeed, a rider on an animal is typically considered to be in control. But this may be more a picture of mutual cooperation between the two: "Her position atop the beast is quite fitting to picture the influence of the religious power over the secular leader" (Thomas II:285). Walvoord (244) views this as representing "the alliance of the apostate church with the political powers of the world."

"Beast," or "wild animal," is the word used for both beasts in chapter 13, appropriate for beings (or systems) with a destructive nature. That this beast is scarlet (or crimson) may be "primarily descriptive," highlighting its "terrifying appearance" (Mounce 310). But the color may symbolize the bloody or destructive nature of the beast since the blood of the martyrs is in view in v. 6. Thomas (II:286) cites scarlet as "the color of sin" (Is. 1:18). Although red is often associated with prostitution and is worn by the great prostitute (v. 4), the color is assigned to the beast as well.

Two additional characteristics of the beast appear. One, it is "full of names of blasphemy": perhaps specific blasphemies were written all over it. To blaspheme is to impugn God's name or His works in some evil way. More likely, this refers to wearing the names of deity rather than slanders against God, with perhaps an allusion to "the blasphemous claims to deity made by Roman emperors" (Mounce 310). This view is supported by the Apostle Paul's characterization of the Antichrist in 2 Th. 2:4: he will position himself in God's Temple and masquerade as God.

Two, it has "seven heads and ten horns," using the *same language* of 12:3 and 13:1 for the dragon and the first beast; see comments there (and on vv. 7-18 below). "Seven" typically indicates completion or perfection, "heads" usually represent kings or rulers, "horns" symbolize power, and "ten" implies fullness. This "scarlet beast," then, as well as the prostitute riding it, are closely identified with both the dragon (Satan) and the beast (Antichrist). Indeed, Mounce (310) identifies the scarlet beast as the beast of 13:1. Thomas (II:286) identifies the seven heads as "seven consecutive world empires throughout history" and the ten heads as "ten kingdoms contemporaneous with the final false Christ" (cf. Dan. 7:7, 19-27).

Verse 4 returns to the woman's appearance, typical of an ostentatious prostitute. She was dressed in "purple and scarlet" (cf. 18:16), bright colors designed to draw attention and reflect opulence. Her fine jewelry—"gold, precious stones, and pearls"—serve the same purposes. Swete (216) suggests that John would have remembered "the finery of the temple prostitutes of Asia." Nothing suggests that this implies a priestly or religious role even though the colors and stones are similar to those worn by Israel's high priest (cf. Ford 288). But if religious garb were in view it would likely be connected with an apostate church rather than Israel. Unfortunately, a prostitute acquires material wealth at the expense of her clientele, true on a grander scale here since the prostitute's clientele has included the kings of nations and their unbelieving population. From this standpoint,

her attire suggests that she has amassed incredible wealth (cf. 18:17), specifically through her participation in the end-time world economy.

A golden cup in her hand (cf. Jer. 51:7) was "full" with the wine of "her fornication," "abominations and filthiness" being the mixed ingredients that she "drinks" and offers to others. "Abominations" (Greek *bdelugma*) means "what is extremely hated or abhorred, *abomination, destestable thing*," including "anything connected with idolatry" (ALGNT 89). The concept is prominent in the O.T. in regard to such things as unclean foods, forbidden sexual activity, and idols. Drinking from her golden cup may thus be equated with acquiescence to the idolatrous worship of Antichrist during the Tribulation. This idolatry and its associated materialism make up the "fornication" that she, the kings and nations, the merchants of earth, and the unbelieving population have committed together. "Filthiness" (Greek *akathartos*) indicates "what is ritually not acceptable...*defiled, unclean*" or "morally, of vices *indecent*" (ALGNT 39). As some interpreters suggest, this may further explain the abominations: "*even* the filthiness of her fornication."

A name was written on her forehead (v. 5). The lengthy name may be analyzed in three parts: "Mystery," "Babylon The Great," and "The Mother Of Harlots and Abominations Of The Earth." "Mystery" (Greek *musterion*) apparently indicates something unknown unless revealed by God, and there are different views (among editors of the text, translators, and interpreters) whether this is part of the prostitute's name or John's introduction to the name: "It is probable that the term *musterion*, mystery, is not part of what is written on the woman's forehead in v. 5 but a way of indicating that the phrase 'Babylon the great, the mother of whores' itself is a mystery in need of interpretation" (Aune III:936). Regardless, the "mystery" about Babylon is being revealed here.

The mystery being revealed is that "Babylon," the great prostitute, is the one responsible for spreading corrupting "abominations" throughout the world during the Tribulation. To the degree that she manifests a transhistorical satanic spirit, she has carried on this corrupting activity throughout previous history as well. The "mystery" of Babylon may involve surprise in discovering that *she* is the one responsible for so much corruption. "Babylon is called a 'mystery' because to the world at large her true identity as the *false* church and great *enemy* of God's saints on earth will not be fully disclosed until the end, when it will be revealed by her judgment by God" (Brighton 444).

As "mother" she may be viewed as the source or origin of all such behaviors: idolatry, sexual immorality, the murder of saints, etc. If taken literally and futuristically, Babylon is a city, perhaps the seat of the anti-Christian world government during the Tribulation, with the idolatrous cult of Antichrist originating and enforced from there. That she is "tattooed" on the forehead, as a whore, may indicate that she is the worst kind (Aune III:936).

"And I saw" (v. 6) indicates a shift in focus to the whore's drunken condition. "Drunken" (Greek present participle) probably suggests a habitual condition. But what has made her drunk is even more disturbing: the blood of martyred saints. The martyrdom of the saints should be considered as heinous an

abomination as any other wicked behavior of hers. The vision strongly suggests that she, together with Antichrist's regime, is *guilty* in this regard, even if she does not bear sole responsibility.

It seems clear that "and" has the sense of "even" here, and that "the martyrs of Jesus" further defines "the saints," thus indicating one group rather than two. This is helpful because it explains the nature of their death and how the great prostitute became "drunk": making martyrs of saints because of their "witness" for Jesus. The "martyrs of Jesus" probably means that they bore witness, even to death, to Jesus (Greek objective genitive) and not simply that they belonged to Jesus (possessive genitive). The analogy of drunkenness may also imply that the great prostitute truly *enjoyed* her role in martyring believers (cf. 11:10).

"Great admiration" has the sense of amazement or wonder: a natural reaction on John's part to the vision of the great prostitute—not in sympathy but in a revulsion approaching horror. Literally, the words are, "I wondered with great wonder"—obviously emphatic. Here is perhaps an attractive woman (though ostentatious and drunk), but she is riding a monstrous animal and has gorged herself on the blood of the saints. The impressive visual spectacle would be followed immediately by questions as to what it all meant. The interpreting angel supplied the meaning of the visual experience for the awestruck apostle.

2. The interpretation (17:7-18)

7 And the angel said unto me, Wherefore didst thou marvel? I will tell thee the mystery of the woman, and of the beast that carrieth her,

which hath the seven heads and ten horns.

8 The beast that thou sawest was, and is not; and shall ascend out of the bottomless pit, and go into perdition: and they that dwell on the earth shall wonder, whose names were not written in the book of life from the foundation of the world, when they behold the beast that was, and is not, and yet is.

9 And here *is* the mind which hath wisdom. The seven heads are seven mountains, on which the woman sitteth.

10 And there are seven kings: five are fallen, and one is, *and* the other is not yet come; and when he cometh, he must continue a short space.

11 And the beast that was, and is not, even he is the eighth, and is of the seven, and goeth into perdition.

12 And the ten horns which thou sawest are ten kings, which have received no kingdom as yet: but receive power as kings one hour with the beast.

13 These have one mind, and shall give their power and strength unto the beast.

14 These shall make war with the Lamb, and the Lamb shall overcome them: for he is Lord of lords, and King of kings: and they that are with him *are* called, and chosen, and faithful.

15 And he saith unto me, The waters which thou sawest, where the whore sitteth, are peoples, and multitudes, and nations, and tongues.

16 And the ten horns which thou sawest upon the beast, these shall hate the whore, and shall make her desolate and naked, and shall eat her flesh, and burn her with fire.

17 For God hath put in their hearts to fulfill his will, and to agree, and give their kingdom unto the beast, until the words of God shall be fulfilled.

18 And the woman which thou sawest is that great city, which reigneth over the kings of the earth.

The angel's explanation began with the rhetorical question (v. 7), "Wherefore didst thou marvel?" John needed help for two reasons. First, only the author of the vision could know its precise meaning, and that was God. Second, the meaning itself was introduced as a "mystery" (vv. 5, 7). Like Joseph and Daniel, John must have supernatural revelation to understand his vision. God is able to reveal future events because He has a sovereign plan and foreknowledge of the future, as well as the power to execute His plan (Eph. 1:11; Rom. 8:28).

Since God desired to reveal rather than obscure the future, He provided an interpretation of John's mysterious vision. The angel promised to interpret the two major components in the original vision: the "prostitute" and the "beast" on which she was seated: the beast first (vv. 8-14) and then the prostitute riding it (vv. 15-18).

"The beast that thou sawest" (v. 8) means the scarlet beast (17:3), closely associated with Satan (12:3) and Antichrist (13:1) by the seven heads and ten horns. The angel's explanation offers four points as a concise overview of Antichrist's life history: "was," "is not," "shall ascend out of the bottomless pit," and "[shall] go into perdition." The first three stages as a whole—repeated at the end of v. 8 as "was," "is not," and "yet is"—are germane to the beast's success in galvanizing the world's support (cf. 13:3). Some interpreters think this parodies Christ's death, burial, and resurrection (Beale 864) or perhaps the description of God's eternal nature in 1:4, 8 and 4:8 (Aune III:939). But the comparison may be coincidental rather than intentional.

Some see the "Nero resurrection myth" of the late first century as a background (Moffat 449, 450): after Nero's death, urban legend had it that Nero would rise from the dead. But that this is reflected here may be rejected if for no other reason than that it never happened. Nor has anyone else in two thousand years of church history fulfilled the "yet is" of these predictions (see comments on 13:1-8). Those who think "the beast" represents the Roman Empire see the historic downfall of the empire in the mortal wounding of the beast. Idealist interpreters tend to equate the "is not" stage with Christ's defeat of the beast on the cross at the beginning of the age (A. Johnson 161), meaning that Antichrist presently "is not."

For futurist interpreters, the time period is eschatological and applies to one specific individual person, the Antichrist, in the seven-year Tribulation. This satanically inspired man will establish a world empire and rule the world through a confederacy of kings and nations. He successfully coerces the unbelieving population to worship himself instead of God.

The first stage of the life history of the scarlet beast (Antichrist) is reflected by "was," referring to his existence before receiving the mortal wound. Daniel 9:27 predicted that he would make a covenant of peace with Israel at the beginning of an eschatological seven-year period. At some point, he receives a mortal wound and dies or nearly dies from it. The phrase "and is not," indicating the second stage, refers either to his death or to his incapacitation from the mortal wound. An unspecified period of nonexistence follows. The clause "and shall ascend out of the bottomless pit" is the third stage and implies two things: his "resurrection" from the second stage and his satanic origin (cf. 9:1, 2, 11; 11:7; 13:1; 20:1, 3).

"And go into perdition" marks the final stage of the beast's history, telescoping forward to 19:20 when he is cast into Hell. "Perdition" (Greek *apoleia*) means "utter or complete destruction" (Vine 164) and is a synonym for Hell—a much-deserved outcome for Antichrist. The period of his life between the third stage (healed) and fourth stage (cast into Hell) is equivalent to his appearance and subsequent activity that begins in 13:1. Thankfully, the beast's nefarious glory is short-lived. The beast, the false prophet, and all who have marveled after him will eventually be sent to perdition (Hell) by the conquering Christ.

Idealist interpreters view all this, instead, as the recurring pattern of a transhistorical satanic spirit throughout church history: "It is characteristic of the beast to appear and disappear and then appear again in a sequence of would-be world conquests which are essentially antagonistic to God and his sovereignty" (Hughes 184).

"They that dwell on the earth" refers again to unbelievers; they witness the beast's resurrection or healing and are "amazed" (Greek *thaumazo*, as in v. 6). This amazement is a major part of the psychology that leads to their worship of Antichrist; his recovery is deemed miraculous. Apparently invincible, he overcomes the saints (13:7). All this seems to support his claim to deity (cf. 13:3, 4; 2 Th. 2:4).

Those who worship the beast are identified as "whose names were not written in the book of life from the foundation of the world" (cf. 3:5; 13:8; 20:12, 15), showing that they *are not* written in the Lamb's "book of life." In 13:8, "from the foundation of the world" connects to the Lamb's being slain; here it goes with "written" or "the book of life." But this need not imply unconditional predestination: "John is not teaching a form of determinism...but emphasizing the great distinction that exists between the followers of the Lamb and those who give their allegiance to the beast" (Mounce 314). It is possible that the words speak to the preexistence of "the book of life," not that names are eternally written in it. Even if the latter, the phrase may indicate God's *foreknowledge* rather than "predestination" as often defined.

The angel proceeded to interpret "the seven heads" (v. 9): "Here is the mind which hath wisdom" serves as an invitation to heed the angel's interpretation (cf. 13:18). Wisdom is the ability to interpret the meaning of the vision, and perhaps in this case to understand the interpretation provided by the angel. It further implies "a warning to interpret with care" (Mounce 315).

The seven heads are equated with "the seven mountains on which the woman sits." The "mountains" may be literal, symbolic, or both. The seven hills

of Rome match so well that identification as Rome has become dogma for many interpreters. Mounce (315), for example, thinks that the seven mountains would leave "little doubt in the mind of a first-century reader about what was intended by the reference"— Rome. But it is the great prostitute that is identified as a "city" in this particular vision (17:18); if the beast on which she rides is also a city, that is awkward at best. In line with the Roman identification, some suggest that the seven mountains, apparently identified as "kings" in v. 10, represent seven Roman emperors in succession, usually ending with Nero or Domitian.

Other interpreters see the seven hills not as Roman emperors or Rome but as successive world "kingdoms" or "empires," with the Roman Empire usually designated as the sixth. "In apocalyptic tradition there is a tendency to associate the heads of many-headed creatures seen in dreams or visions with rulers" (Aune III:945; Dan. 7:6). Since "mountain" may symbolize a kingdom (Dan. 2:35), and since "kings" and their "kingdoms" are virtually synonymous, the reference could be to seven kingdoms (cf. Is. 2:2; Jer. 51:25). Those often mentioned are Egypt, Assyria, Babylon, Persia, Greece, Rome, and eschatological Babylon or Rome (cf. Dan. 7:17-27; see Thomas II:296; Seiss 393; Ladd, *Commentary* 227). Rome was certainly the ruling empire at the time John was writing. The seventh kingdom is future to John and eschatological according to futurists (Walvoord 254).

Additionally, since the number "seven" is the number of perfection or completion, the reference could be symbolic of something like the worldwide domination of Rome—if Rome is in view at all. Hughes (185) rejects all views that focus on Rome or any specific kingdom and opts for a *symbolical* one: "Seven being the number of divine authority, it may be taken here to indicate the desire of the empire-builders of this fallen world to dethrone God and to exercise authority that is universal and absolute." Kistemaker (470) agrees that the symbolism "comprises all rulers and their times."

"Seven kings" (v. 10) may refer either to the rulers of seven successive world empires or to seven kings from one empire. Regardless, the Roman Empire is prominent as either the sixth of seven world kingdoms or as one kingdom represented by seven of its emperors. The way one reads "And there are seven kings" can make a subtle difference: this reading may imply an *additional* fact and allow for the dual interpretation suggesting that the city of Rome *and* her emperors are both in view. But if it is read as "And they are seven kings" (as in the NASB), this suggests *equivalence*, meaning that the seven mountains *are* in fact the seven kings.

That "five are fallen" indicates that five kings have preceded and are out of power, with a sixth one in power at the time of John's writing. "Yet to come" indicates that the seventh king or kingdom ("the other") will reign at some future point. The reigns of ten confederate kings associated with this seventh king are also future at the time of John's writing (v. 12). The reign of the seventh king is significantly limited in duration: "he must continue a short space." Thomas (II:298) identifies the seventh kingdom as "the future kingdom of the beast," adding that the time of the seven

heads "spans essentially the entire history of Gentile world empires."

Such views—that "the seven kings" are seven Roman emperors or seven world kingdoms—are handicapped by the lack of a standard starting point and are often subject to arbitrary manipulations that produce the desired result. Some begin with Augustus, for example, ignoring Julius Caesar, considered the first Roman emperor by ancient historians. And three of the lesser-known emperors (Galba, Otho, Vitellius) are often omitted in the formulas, a "questionable procedure" (Aune III:947). The text is not explicit enough to enable us to say which particular historical kings or kingdoms are in view here. What is more certain is their historicity in general and whether they reigned before or after the time of John. In other words, there may be latitude in identifying the seven kings or kingdoms, but there is no doubt that five were before him and one after him.

On balance, it seems preferable to view the seven kings as *literal* rather than symbolic. John's breakdown into five, one, and one does not match the use of seven as a mere symbol of perfection or completion. In Revelation seven not only represents completion but usually refers to specific things like seven "stars" as pastors, candlesticks as churches, seals, trumpets, or bowls for judgments, etc. Thus the seven mountains for kings indicate literal kings or kingdoms who reign for a time. Furthermore, kings rather than kingdoms are apparently meant; their personal nature is suggested by the fact that the seventh king goes into perdition or Hell. The kingdom in power when John wrote was the Roman Empire, its emperor Domitian. The seventh one, future and final, will be eschatological and governed by Antichrist, even though the transhistorical spirit of Antichrist was present in John's day (1 Jn. 2:18) and exerts itself against Christ throughout history until Jesus comes.

When v. 11 repeats the formula, "was, is not, is, and goeth into perdition," the scarlet beast, alias Antichrist and his dominion, is obviously meant (cf. v. 8, twice; 13:3, 14). "And is of the seven" reveals that the beast is actually *one of the seven* previously identified historical kings (vv. 3, 10) who somehow emerges to become the "eighth" (Dan. 7:8, 20, 24), dominant over the rest. "His reign following his ascent from the abyss will be far more dynamic and dominant than before" (Thomas II:299). Thus the final world kingdom is reminiscent of those that precede it in history but is distinct from them chronologically and comparatively. The final world ruler will become the most satanically endowed monarch ever; the worldwide scope of his government will be unprecedented—only to have the additional distinction of being destroyed by Christ in Person.

The future of all this is clearly indicated by the clause "*and* the other is not yet come" (v. 10). Furthermore, the fact that Antichrist is numbered as "the eighth" (v. 11) clearly indicates a point in time after the sixth and seventh members. The sixth king, reigning at the time Revelation was composed, was Domitian; the seventh king had not yet appeared. Nerva followed Domitian rescinding John's banishment but is not a likely candidate as the Antichrist.

The "ten horns" are ten eschatological kings that form a future world confederacy ruled by Antichrist (v. 12), not to be confused with the seven heads of the beast (12:3; 13:1; 17:3)—whether those are interpreted as kings or kingdoms. Their reigns are "contemporaneous" rather than "successive" (Aune III:950). Like the future ruling king predicted in the phrase "yet to come," these kings are neither before nor contemporaneous with John but have kingdoms in the future.

That these kings have kingdoms and reign simultaneously with Antichrist has a precedent in the ancient Roman Empire that allowed for "client" kings—like king Herod in Palestine—who exercised relative autonomy but remained subservient to Rome. As Mounce (319) observes, "The ten kings are not the ten emperors of Rome because, unlike the Roman emperor, these have received no kingdom as yet." Still, various interpretations are given. Charles (II:71, 72) cites "governors of senatorial provinces," thus adding to the list of preterist viewpoints. Swete (222) mentions "subordinate potentates of Asia Minor." Idealist Beale identifies the ten figuratively as "a transtemporal force opposing the Eternal Lamb," "earthly agents through whom the spiritual forces of Satan and the beast work, both throughout the age and the end of the age" (878, 879). Hendriksen (171) says, "The ten kings are really all the mighty ones of this earth in every realm: art, education, commerce, industry, government, in so far as they serve the central authority."

Beckwith (cited by Mounce 319) identifies these as "purely eschatological figures representing the totality of the powers of all nations on the earth which are to be made subservient to Antichrist." Walvoord (255) suggests they are a "world" or end-time form of the Roman Empire, revived. A. Johnson (165) feels that their number itself is not literally "ten" but rather "the multiplicity of sovereignties" in the world.

"One hour" represents a short period of time, the three-and-a-half-year duration of their confederate power, the latter half of the seven-year Tribulation (cf. Dan. 7:20-28). "Receive power as kings one hour" suggests God's sovereign control governing end-time persons and events (Aune III: 951, 952; see 17:17).

The fate of the ten kings is tied to Antichrist's since they are in league with him (v. 13). "These have one mind" (or one accord) indicates unanimity of purpose and philosophy, a worldly, materialistic disposition that complements Antichrist's idolatrous agenda. Whether by coercion, because of a shared pagan worldview, or for pragmatic reasons, they "give" their support to the beast and unite in their opposition to Christ the Lamb.

"Power" (Greek *dunamis*) means ability and may refer to the pledge of their material and military resources. "Strength" (Greek *exousia*) means "*authority, right, power*" or "the power of decision making" (ALGNT 157). Here it may refer to a transfer of governmental or decision-making powers to Antichrist's government, perhaps indicating that they are willing enforcers of his policies. Antichrist uses these resources and governing powers to enforce his worship and policies in the world.

That "these"—the ten kings—"shall make war with the Lamb" (v. 14) reflects the basic spiritual conflict between Christ and the counterfeit kingdom of the Antichrist, perhaps pointing to the decisive Battle of Armageddon (19:11-21). This worldly conglomerate of kings, nations, and unbelieving inhabitants, fol-

lowing Antichrist during the Tribulation, will wage war against the Lamb and the followers of the Lamb (12:17; 13:7; 17:6). The diabolical goal of the conflict is world domination, and Christ and His followers stand in the way (Dan. 7:21-25). "The only way in which earthly kings can wage war on the Lamb is through his followers" (Caird 220). The conflict leading to Armageddon may very well involve continuing persecutions against Tribulation believers, perhaps specifically the 144,000 of 7:1-8 and 14:1.

"Make war" can, of course, be applied to *spiritual* warfare (Eph. 6:10-18; 2 Cor. 10:4, 5; 1 Pet. 5:8), an ever-present reality throughout history; Brighton (452, 453) gives this idealist perspective. But the ultimate expression of this conflict is more likely in view here: the underlying spiritual conflict of the ages will culminate in a literal, eschatological battle. The thing inspiring spiritual conflict is no doubt the satanic spirit, but this spirit manifests itself in the literal shedding of the saints' blood. This has happened throughout history and will also produce a significant number of martyrs during the Tribulation. Even this, however, is secondary to the ultimate event in view: Armageddon and the Second Coming. The final event of this war is the gathering of "these" against Jerusalem for the great battle described in 19:11-21 (cf. 16:14-16; Ezek. 38, 39; cf. 20:8, 9). Since the blood of many believers has been shed during the period, it is not surprising that the blood of unbelievers will also be spilled.

Several things are worth noting about the absolute victory of the Lamb predicted in "the Lamb shall overcome them" (v. 14). One is that this confident expectation of victory is based on the deity of the Lamb, "Lord of lords and King of kings" (cf. Dt. 10:17; Dan. 2:47; 1 Tim. 6:15; Dan. 4:37). As God, the Lamb's powers and resources are infinite; He has no equal. Christ wins the battle in the same way that He created the universe, overcame temptation in the wilderness, or performed great miracles while on earth: by verbal command. His choice of weapons is His spoken Word (19:15, 21). The same power that can speak a universe into existence can also dismantle one or defeat the enemies of Christ.

This is more than mere *spiritual* victory, it is victory in and over the eschatological world, involving the annihilation of the Antichrist's confederacy in literal bloodshed. It may include causing them to turn their own weapons against one another (cf. Zech. 14:13).

"They that are with him" might be taken to mean all believers, but this seems more specific and might be understood in more than one way. One possibility is those believers who are already with Christ in Heaven whether by natural death or martyrdom. These will accompany Christ at His Second Coming (1 Th. 4:14; Rev. 19:14). A second possibility is an indeterminate but significant number of believers (Jew and Gentile) still alive in the Tribulation period awaiting Christ's return. Yet a third is the 144,000 select servants of Israel (14:1) standing with Christ on Mt. Zion. The adjectives "called," "chosen," and "faithful" can apply to all these groups equally well. But since the immediate context points to Armageddon, the reference is probably either to the 144,000 standing with Christ on Mt. Zion or to those who accompany Christ and are mentioned in 19:14.

"Called" (Greek *kletos*) designates "one who has accepted a calling or an invitation to become a guest or member of a select group" (ALGNT 232). Both Paul and Peter often applied the term to themselves and to believers in general (Rom. 1:1, 6, 7; 2 Pet. 1:3). "Chosen" (Greek *eklektos*) may imply being "choice, select, excellent" (ALGNT 138) and is another way of designating believers. The 144,000 of Israel were sealed, implying their selection, from each tribe of Israel. "Faithful" (Greek *pistos*), from the verb "to trust or believe," can mean either "believing" or "faithful"; here it may imply those who have both placed their trust in Christ and remained faithful in spite of great tribulations.

Verses 15-18 refocus on the great prostitute, interpreting "the *waters* where the whore sitteth." The "many waters" (v. 1) are "peoples, and multitudes, and nations, and tongues" (v. 15). For these words, see comments on 7:9. The formula indicates the entire world or human race, demonstrating that the great prostitute's seduction is worldwide, affecting all areas and classes of people.

The angel predicted that the ten kings represented as "ten horns" (v. 12) would turn against the whore (v. 16). The initial cooperation between them disintegrates, at some point during the Tribulation, into "hate"; the reason is not supplied. The degree of their hate is significant, prompting them to "make her desolate and naked," to "eat her flesh," and to "burn her with fire" (cf. Ezek. 38:21; Hag. 2:22; Zech. 14:13). This portrays the merciless destruction of whatever institution "Babylon" symbolizes. Aune (III:956) suggests that "make her desolate" means "to depopulate her." "Make her naked" apparently means to strip her of her clothing and jewels, prominent in the original vision (v. 4) as symbols of her seductions and great wealth (cf. Ezek. 23:10, 29). "Eat her flesh" suggests "wild beasts tearing at the body of their prey", portraying "the fierceness with which the prostitute is attacked by her assailants" (Mounce 320; cf. 2 Kg. 9:30-37). "Burn her with fire" could very well suggest the destruction of material assets; it may reflect the O.T. precedent of burning a priest's daughter who turned to harlotry (Lev. 21:9; cf. 20:14). "The political side of the ungodly world system will turn against the heart of the social-economic-religious side and destroy it" (Beale 883).

"God hath put in their hearts" (v. 17) reminds us of God's sovereign design and control of the events in this period, but does the clause indicate His causation or mere permission? Beale (887) says, "Only inspiration from God could cause them to commit such a short-sighted and foolish act." God providentially commandeers the activities of these ten kings to become His agents of judgment against the great whore. Such sovereign utility of kings and their worldly empires to achieve God's purposes is a prominent O.T. theme, where He periodically used ungodly nations to chastise the nation of Israel. His manipulation of the diabolical events and characters of the Tribulation period to achieve His ultimate design should be viewed likewise: namely, to "fulfill his will."

This divine prompting included moving the hearts of the confederate kings to "give their kingdoms to the beast," recalling v. 13 and manifesting the depth of their commitment to the Antichrist and his agenda. Ironically,

their activities are utilized by God against them. "Until the words of God shall be fulfilled" refers to the certainty of these events. Furthermore, these things have been predicted in Scripture and point specifically to the end of the Tribulation. Unlike their tenuous relationship with the great prostitute, the ten-king confederacy remains loyal to "the beast" (Antichrist) throughout the period.

The vision of chapter 17 ends as it began, with "the woman" identified in v. 1 as "the great whore" (v. 18). This part of the interpretation seems to have been saved until last for effect. The great prostitute is actually a city of earth identified as "that great city" (v. 18), "Babylon the Great" (v. 5), a city that "reigneth over the kings of the earth."

In light of Antichrist's more fundamental and worldwide rule, in what sense does "Babylon" reign? How can both rule over the kings of the earth at the same time? The answer may be the existence of a religious ruler and a political ruler. The religious would be necessarily be subservient to the political, and therefore expendable, since the political is obviously controlled by Antichrist.

The greatest mystery regarding the whore, then, is not about her activity but her precise historical identity: is she a literal woman, a city, or a religious institution? Or (as idealists insist) does she merely symbolize a transhistorical anti-Christian spirit that manifests itself repeatedly in history? Many futurist interpreters suggest that this is a world capital city during the Tribulation, or a revived Roman Empire, or old Babylon rebuilt on the Euphrates. Often Rome and Babylon are equated as the same entity, making "Babylon" a cryptic reference to Rome. Some identify her as both a city, like Babylon, and "the whole anti-Christian religious system of the future" at the same time (Thomas II:306, 307). Many take her to be Rome (Aune III:936, 959). A. Johnson (159) identifies Babylon the prostitute *symbolically*: "the archetypal head of all entrenched worldly resistance to God." Beale (885) defines her as "both the pagan world and the apostate church that cooperates with the world," including unbelieving Israel. Brighton (436) identifies her as "false Christianity and the apostate church." Lenski (492) identifies her as "*the antichristian empire*." Walvoord (245) implies that she is "the Roman Catholic and Greek Orthodox churches" or "papal Rome." Thomas (II:304) labels her as "false religion" or "the world-city Babylon." Ford (285) opts for a less popular view by identifying her as "Jerusalem."

The destruction of the great prostitute by the ten-nation confederacy will occur in the Tribulation just before the Second Coming. This rules out a first-century fulfillment with the destruction of Jerusalem in A.D. 70 (*preterism*). Neither does the eventual destruction of the Roman Empire at the hands of Germanic hordes in the fifth and sixth centuries fit the bill, as in Barnes' *historicism*. *Idealism's* basic hesitance to identify a specific historical manifestation diminishes the significance of the crescendo of universal catastrophe that envelops literal history just before Christ's return.

Summary
(17:1-18)

The vision of the great prostitute adds perspective to the Tribulation events that culminate with the Second Coming of Christ. One of the seven bowl angels invited John to see "the great whore sitting on many waters," symbolizing her universal or worldwide influence. The clients of the great prostitute were also revealed: the "kings of the earth" and "the inhabitants of the earth" (v. 2). The degree of the prostitute's influence over her clients is illustrated with the "wine" analogy: they have been made drunk with "the wine of her fornication."

Within his spirit John was taken into the wilderness to see the vision (v. 3): the great prostitute seated on a beast. It was scarlet, apparently symbolizing its destructive, bloody, satanic nature. It had blasphemous names written on it, and seven heads and ten horns, characteristics clearly connecting it with previous visions (12:3; 13:1). In appearance (vv. 4-6) she was dressed in purple and scarlet clothing, representing her royal associations and immoral behavior. Her gaudy jewelry of gold, precious stones, and pearls reflected the lucrative rewards of her profession. The golden cup in her hand was filled with a mixture consisting of the abominations of her wicked behavior and the blood of martyred saints. She had a title written on her forehead: "MYSTERY, BABYLON THE GREAT, THE MOTHER OF HARLOTS AND ABOMINATIONS OF THE EARTH."

The angel interpreted the vision for John (vv. 7-18). While John marveled, the angel explained, beginning with an identification of the beast, the same one that he had previously seen (13:1-10). The beast's history (v. 8) includes that he had existed previously but did not then exist (at the time John received the vision). But he would live again in the future, after arising out of the bottomless pit. And then he will be destroyed, cast into perdition (Hell). Before that end, those *not* written in the Lamb's Book of Life will witness his miraculous "resurrection" and worship him as a result.

The beast's seven heads perform double duty: they represent "the seven mountains" the great prostitute is seated upon (v. 9) as well as "seven kings" (v. 10). Five of these were no longer in power when John wrote. Domitian is the most likely identification for "the one who is": that is, the one then reigning. The seventh had not yet appeared on the scene.

The "seven mountains" may refer to ancient Rome, located on seven hills, or to seven great world kingdoms like Egypt, Assyria, Babylon, Persia, Greece, Rome, and eschatological Rome ("Babylon"). Either way, Rome figures prominently. The "seven kings" are probably either seven emperors of Rome or the kings of the seven world kingdoms. The beast, identified both as "of the seven" and as an "eighth" king, did not exist when John wrote. In the future he will reign for a short period of time before going into perdition (v. 11). He is the Antichrist who arises in the end-times of world history to become world ruler during the Tribulation.

The "ten horns" are kings in their own right (vv. 12-14), who also did not exist at the time Revelation was written. Their kingdoms will exist in the same future period as the seventh/eighth king of v. 10. They form a confederacy and give their allegiance to Antichrist, galvanizing his control over the earth. They eventually join together in war against their common enemy, Jesus the Lamb and His faithful followers. The ultimate event of this war is the Battle of Armageddon where the beast and his followers are totally destroyed (v. 14).

The angel then interpreted the symbolism of the great prostitute herself (vv. 15-18). First, the "waters" on which she was seated represent the entire unbelieving population of the earth: "peoples, multitudes, nations, and tongues." Second, the "ten horns"—kings or kingdoms of the Antichrist's coalition—in a surprise move turn against the great prostitute and destroy her (v. 16). God Himself turned the hearts of the kings against her and moved them to destroy her. He did this to achieve His greater purposes, thus revealing the parallel and superior track of God's activity in these times (v. 17).

The final interpretation is that the great prostitute is in reality "that great city" (v. 18), further described as a great city that reigns over the kings of the earth. This city may be some type of world capital during the Tribulation.

Application: Teaching and Preaching the Passage

Idealism errs in its hesitancy to find literal, end-time references in Revelation. However, just as there are distinct perspectives within dispensationalism, some recent idealists (like Beale and Brighton) have modified classic idealism by allowing for literal, historical fulfillment in certain instances. They remain idealistic in believing that Revelation generally portrays spiritual realities present throughout church history from the cross to the Second Coming. But they allow for a greatly intensified, literal tribulation just preceding Christ's return; they also seem to speak of a literal "Antichrist" during that tribulation.

Preterism errs in confining everything in Revelation to a first-century context surrounding the destruction of Jerusalem in A.D. 70. Historicism likewise errs when it suggests that these visions portray the fall of the ancient Roman Empire. Such views severely limit the significance of the end-times emphasis in Revelation. Revelation does not repeat truths already given in the gospels and epistles. It does not portray (or predict) events within past church history that pale in comparison to the unprecedented and catastrophic Great Tribulation. God gave us a clear picture of the beginnings; surely He would not leave us ignorant about the catastrophic events that will befall the final generation.

The proper way to interpret Revelation is not by being predisposed toward either literalism or symbolism; it often requires both. We should recognize abiding principles of spiritual truth and their manifestations in real persons, places, and events when so indicated. Transhistorical spiritual truths (idealism) must interface with history literally at some point; preterism, historicism, and futurism are *historical* viewpoints. It is true that great mistakes have been made in regard to predicting the time of Christ's return, identifying Antichrist with certain historic figures, or otherwise assigning historical fulfillment prematurely. Such predictions have often proven wrong, damaging the credibility of true preaching.

For example, many feel that the great prostitute is some form of apostate church or religion; but great care must be exercised in identifying her as any particular religious institution in the world today. For the Reformers and others it is the papacy. Though such a connection is plausible, she could just as easily be some form of apostate Protestant church, a hybrid of both apostate Catholics and Protestants, or something not presently recognizable at all.

A significant aspect of the Tribulation is the great number of Jewish and Gentile believers martyred for their faith (6:9; 13:15; Mt. 24:9). Tribulation believers have experienced typical N.T. salvation; nothing indicates any other way to be saved during the Tribulation. They are washed in the blood of Christ and regenerated by the Holy Spirit (see 7:9-14). Their faithfulness to the Lamb is demonstrated either by martyrdom or by enduring to the end of the period in the face of Antichrist's persecutions and rapidly disintegrating world conditions.

The consensus of interpreters, whatever their view of the rapture, is that Tribulation saints will escape *the wrath of God* (1 Th. 5:9). The wrath of God is poured out on *unbelievers* throughout the Tribulation. Escape for *believers* will be either by "rapture" before the Tribulation begins (pretribulationism) or by preservation from God's wrath during the period (posttribulationism)—if not some of both (a midtribulation, prewrath rapture). Of course *Antichrist* will manifest wrath on believers; God never promised to shield believers from persecutions but to provide the resources necessary to endure them.

Suggested Outline. The Great Prostitute, 17:1-6: (1) Her district—many waters, v. 1; (2) Her clientele, v. 2; (3) Her companion, v. 3; (4) Her clothing, v. 4; (5) Her cup, v. 4; (6) Her cryptic title, v. 5; (7) Her casualties, v. 6.

B. Babylon the Great (18:1-24)

Chapter 17 introduced the great prostitute and her symbiotic relationship with Antichrist and his ten-king coalition and identified her as "Babylon," "that great city, which reigneth over the kings of the earth" (17:18). The introduction to the mystery of Babylon the Great included her destruction (17:16); now chapter 18 gives detail and indicates how that destruction affects the world, causing its economy—*economic Babylon*—and social institutions to collapse. The destruction of *political* Babylon occurs at the Second Coming and the Battle of Armageddon (chapter 19).

The revelations focus, now, on the absolute destruction of the world's economies (land and maritime) and society itself, a "collapse of civilization" (L. Morris 208) unprecedented in history since Noah's flood. "All that makes the city emblematic of human culture and achievement—music, craftsmanship, food preparation, domestic life, and commerce—will cease" (D. Johnson 254). This completes God's judgments against the present anti-Christian world system, one that may well include a literal capital city. But idealist Kistemaker is right: "Babylon is not confined to the city on the banks of the Euphrates or to Rome as the capital of the Roman empire...Babylon is the capital of the entire world, the center of the universal kingdom of darkness" (484, 485).

1. Affirmation of her collapse (18:1-3)

1 And after these things I saw another angel come down from heaven, having great power; and the earth was lightened with his glory.
2 And he cried mightily with a strong voice, saying, Babylon the great is fallen, is fallen, and is become the habitation of devils, and the hold of every foul spirit, and a cage of every unclean and hateful bird.
3 For all nations have drunk of the wine of the wrath of her fornication, and the kings of the earth have committed fornication with her, and the merchants of the earth are waxed rich through the abundance of her delicacies.

"After these things I saw" indicates chronological progress and a shift in focus. The new revelations describe the worldwide results of great Babylon's destruction (v. 1). "Another angel" descended from Heaven (cf. 10:1; 20:1), apparently a new angel entirely, with "another" distinguishing him from Christ Himself—who will be clearly indicated in 19:11-21. The portrayal of angels endowed with such great size, power, and glorious appearance is frequent in Revelation, and "come down" indicates the heavenly origin of the angel (cf. 10:1).

That "the earth was lightened with his glory" is especially impressive, suggesting that the angel lights up the entire earth (cf. Ezek. 43:2). The angel possesses this radiance in the same way that Moses' face was illuminated after having been in God's presence (Ex. 34:29, 30). The great light may have revealed the condition of the earth after the judgments of God had fallen: "In the light of his heavenly glory the ruin of Babylon on earth is fully revealed" (Lenski 515).

In a characteristically strong or loud voice, the angel "cried mightily" to announce: "Babylon the great is fallen, is fallen" (v. 2; cf. Is. 13:17-22; 21:9; 47:1-15; Jer. 50:39, 40; 51:8; Rev. 14:8). "Fallen" is repeated to underscore the certainty or finality of God's judgment.

"The prophecy and fulfillment of Babylon's past fall [in the O.T.] is viewed as a historical pattern pointing forward to the fall of a much larger Babylon" (Beale 893). The reference is primarily to the judgment of eschatological Babylon as a whole in all its components, encompassing the destruction of all her major systems——economic, social, religious, and political. "Is fallen" (Greek aorist, usually past time) apparently emphasizes "that the great purpose of God in triumphing over evil is a *fait accompli*" (Mounce 325).

"Babylon" symbolizes "the great satanic system of evil that has corrupted the earth's history" (A. Johnson 169) but may well identify a literal world capital in the end-times. Rome on the Tiber, Babylon on the Euphrates, and Jerusalem are most often suggested as candidates. It is only logical that the world ruler, Antichrist, will have an official seat of government somewhere on the earth during the Tribulation, probably one of these three.

The second part of the angel's proclamation underscores the sordid, satanic nature of Babylon itself: judged by God, her ruins become "the habitation of devils, and the hold of every foul spirit" (v. 2). "Devils" (Greek *daimonion*) is, literally, "demons." "Foul" (Greek *akathartos*) means "unclean" (Vine 649), used often in the gospels of "unclean spirits" (Mt. 10:1; Mk. 1:23, 26, 27; cf. also 16:13). Assuming that "and" has the

sense "even" here (as often), the demons and unclean spirits are the same.

"Hold" (Greek *phulake*) means "to guard or watch" and, by metonymy, a prison or guardhouse or even a place of refuge or safe-dwelling—the sense it apparently has here. "It is not a place of detention but a place where they dwell undisturbed" (Mounce 326). "The evil spirits...build their eyries in the broken towers which rise from the ashes of the city" (Swete 227). Even so, from God's perspective, this could certainly be a form of confinement in the destroyed city; Lenski (515) thinks of it as banishment, and Thomas (II:317) as involuntary.

That she becomes "the cage of every unclean and hateful bird" is parallel, with "cage" the same word as "hold." Again, then, though an element of confinement may well be involved, this refers to their haunt, den, or refuge. The phrase pictures demonic spirits, like scavenger birds, hovering to feed on the rotting corpse of Babylon (cf. 19:17, 18). "Hateful" has the sense "hated," reminding us that scavengers were considered "unclean" in the Mosaic Law (Dt. 14:12-19; Is. 34:11-15). Wild animals inhabit forsaken cities when people desert them; since the destruction of a literal world capital city is probably in view, the reference to scavenger birds may also be taken literally

The presence of lurking, unseen demons and visible scavenger birds adds to Babylon's residual aura of evil. The picture testifies to total destruction, much like the ruins of a city destroyed in war. The despised scavengers take up residence to harvest what remains. Furthermore, "In the repetition of the word *unclean* there is no doubt a contrast intended with the holy city, into which nothing unclean may enter [21:27]" (Caird 223).

Verse 3 provides three reasons for *eschatological* Babylon's demise. The first revives the "wine analogy" (14:8), indicating how the world has been intoxicated by—come under the control of—the great prostitute's "wine" of (spiritual) fornication (v. 3). "Have drunk" (Greek perfect) points to a settled state resulting from a process. All classes of society remain in an intoxicated spiritual condition, their behavior controlled or influenced by "the wine" of illegitimate intercourse with her. "The cause of Babylon's judgment lies in her idolatrous seduction of nations and rulers" (Beale 895).

Perhaps "the wrath of her fornication" means the *passion* (NASB) associated with this illegitimate intercourse. The word (Greek *thumos*) often means "a strong passion of soul or mind" (ALGNT 200), and the context refers to the intoxicating influence, not to wrathful judgment. Understanding the word in this way provides additional insight into the alluring and overcoming nature of the great prostitute's "fornication." In effect, the world has participated in her fornication because it has been unable to resist her allure: "maddening wine" (NIV).

Many believers in first-century Asia Minor experienced various trials because of pressure to take part in the pagan festivals or imperial cult. Those trials of faith foreshadow similar but much more aggravated conditions during the Tribulation. Those who refuse the mark of the beast will be unable to participate in the economy (13:17). Those who refuse to worship the beast will be put to death (13:15). No doubt many will

choose survival over faithfulness to Christ.

The great prostitute's fornication is spiritual: "Fornication is a biblical word for idolatry...the worship of the beast instead of worship of the Lamb" (Ladd, *Commentary* 236). Furthermore, "The city has promoted herself by instilling an unquestioning faith in her supposedly inexhaustible resources, thereby discouraging any sense of a deeper need for God" (Thomas II:319). Instead of directing the inhabitants of the earth to depend upon God for their resources, Babylon has pointed mankind to mammon instead, corrupting others in various ways. The intoxicating effects of her "wine" include materialism, idol (demon) worship, violence, sorcery, sexual immorality, stealing, lying, and blasphemy—characteristic sinful behaviors during the Tribulation (9:20, 21; 16:9, 11; 21:8).

Brighton (466) goes further: "This describes how all the pagan nations and political and economic rulers and powers shared in her deceptive piety." He then identifies the great prostitute as *corrupted Christianity* during the Tribulation; unfortunately, the dogmatic identification of Babylon as a corrupt church must be tempered, since that is never stated in the text.

Three classes of society are implicated as clientele of the great prostitute. First, the unbelieving population of the earth is implied in "all nations," consistent with "the inhabitants of the earth" (17:2). Second are "the kings of the earth" (cf. 17:2), earthly monarchs who bear additional responsibility for leading those under their rule to take part. This is often identified as "political Babylon." Third, "the merchants of the earth" are singled out for having especially benefited from their relationship to the great prostitute. They have become materially "rich" through hawking "the abundance of her delicacies."

"Delicacies" (Greek *strenos*) denotes "*luxury, sensuality,* a way of life characterized by headstrong pride" (ALGNT 358). Material luxuries are excesses that go far beyond basic needs like food, clothing, and shelter. Such abundance tends to breed a sense of independence from God and pride. "The idea of the term is that of insolent luxury, self-indulgence with accompanying arrogance and vicious exercise of strength... the impudence of wealth" (Thomas II:319). The inordinate desire for material things is a form of idolatry in itself (see Col. 3:5). These merchants of the earth have been unfaithful to God in the idolatry of materialism, becoming rich through their cooperation with Babylon. "Abundance" (Greek *dunamis*) is, literally, "power" or "ability": the power of her luxury. Wealth breeds power.

The symbiotic, mutually beneficial way in which this comes about is obvious: patrons of the world's merchants are drunk with the same spirit of materialism. The merchants profit from their materialistic clientele and the rulers prosper from the increase of wealth. The world *economy*, often identified by interpreters as "commercial Babylon," is thereby implicated in the sin of the great prostitute. She is worthy of judgment because she facilitates a spirit of self-sufficiency, materialistic idolatry, and a failure to worship God through an excessive desire for luxury.

God's judgment against Babylon is thereby total, a threefold judgment against the world religion (great whore), the world economy (merchants), and the world government (kings). These are inextricably related to one another: judgment against one affects all three.

Walvoord (259) reasons that the religion of the great whore cannot coexist with the demand of the Antichrist to be worshiped. He therefore concludes that the destruction of the woman referred to in 17:16 is specifically religious and refers to *Antichrist's* destruction of the world church, early in the Tribulation, in order to obtain unmixed allegiance for himself. Then economic and political "Babylon" continue a while longer, only to be destroyed as depicted in chapter 18. But if in fact the prostitute's religion and the worship of Antichrist are basically identical, no such distinction is needed. As A. Johnson (169) advises, "It is important not to separate this chapter from the portrayal of the prostitute in chapter 17, for there is no warrant for making the prostitute in chapter 17 different from the city in chapter 18." Indeed, John does not so differentiate, as 17:18 shows: Babylon the Great is the same entity in both chapters.

2. Crimes of Babylon (18:4-8)

**4 And I heard another voice from heaven, saying, Come out of her my people, that ye be not partakers of her sins, and that ye receive not of her plagues.
5 For her sins have reached unto heaven, and God hath remembered her iniquities.
6 Reward her even as she rewarded you, and double unto her double according to her works: in the cup which she hath filled fill to her double.
7 How much she hath glorified herself, and lived deliciously, so much torment and sorrow give her: for**

she saith in her heart, I sit a queen, and am no widow, and shall see no sorrow.

8 Therefore shall her plagues come in one day, death, and mourning, and famine: and she shall be utterly burned with fire: for strong *is* the Lord God who judgeth her.

Because God's judgment against the world ("Babylon") is certain, a special appeal is given to believers alive on earth at the time by "another voice," perhaps another angel but more likely God Himself: note "my people." "Nowhere else in Revelation does an angel use the possessive pronoun in the first person" (Brighton 466). If the voice is God's, He speaks about God in v. 5, but that may seem awkward only to the reader.

God's people are warned to disassociate themselves from the world's system (v. 4), because it is doomed for destruction. The only way to avoid a common fate, implied in "partakers of her sins," is to "Come out of her": out of doomed "Babylon" and all it represents (cf. Gen. 19:12, 17; Num. 16:25-27; Jer. 51:45; 1 Jn. 2:15-17). Those who participate in Babylon's sins will suffer judgment with her.

There are two reasons, then, to "come out." One is that God's people are holy; compare 2 Cor. 6:14-18. "Separation is the order of the day: sometimes physical, always ideological" (Mounce 327). The second is "that ye receive not of her plagues." There should be no question about the "plagues": the same word has been used for the seven bowl judgments (15:1) and would fit any remaining plagues suggested in 18:8.

"My people" indicates the presence of at least some of God's people *within* the Tribulation period, already pointed to in John's vision of a vast multitude of believers who came out of the Great Tribulation (7:9, 14). A great number of Jewish and Gentile believers will be present during this time, regardless of one's view of the rapture. But those who come to Christ will face unprecedented catastrophes and persecutions. The appeal to "come out," then, "is addressed to professing Christians who were being seduced by Satan through the wiles of the queen prostitute to abandon their loyalty to Jesus...If this occurred, Christ would be forced by their own decision to blot out their names from the book of life and include them in the plagues designed for Babylon when she is judged" (A. Johnson 171).

Aune (III:991) has, therefore, a misplaced chronological perspective when he suggests that "the summons to flee from the city is used symbolically...[and] refers to the necessity of Christians disentangling themselves...from the corrupt and seductive influences of Roman rule in Asia." In principle, this would apply, but the exhortation here more accurately applies to believers during the end-times Tribulation.

The explanation of God's judgment of Babylon resumes after the exhortation: "For her sins have reached unto heaven" (v. 5; cf. Gen. 18:21, 22; Jer. 51:9). "Sins" (Greek *hamartia*) is a general word, defined as "a missing of the mark" (Vine 576). Babylon has committed many, accumulating to a point that prompts God to respond decisively. Instead of "reached" (Greek *akoloutheo*) most manuscripts have "piled up" (Greek *kallao*). Either conveys the image of sins being joined together all the way to Heaven so that God is reminded of them. The tremendous accumulation of Babylon's sins merits God's judgments. His response is just and timely.

God is eternally patient and merciful. But after long-suffering, a time for judgment arrives; compare Gen. 15:16; 2 Chr. 36:16-21. That "God hath remembered her iniquities" suggests that there is a point in the eschatological future when God will judge Babylon decisively. "Remembering" equates with God's decision to act in judgment.

The commands "reward," "double," and "fill" (v. 6) are directed to a group. "Reward" (Greek *apodidomi*) means "to give back" (Vine 533), even "pay a debt" (Walvoord 261), signifying payback or retribution. "Double" (Greek *diploo*) means *"pay back twice as much"* (ALGNT 118). "Fill" (Greek *kerannumi*) means *"cause to be at full strength, prepare, pour out, cause to be fully experienced"* (ALGNT 228). Babylon will be judged in a measure that fully satisfies the demands of holy justice, receiving no less than she deserves.

To whom are these commands addressed? Most manuscripts read, "Give back to her as also she gave back," omitting "to you." In that case, the agents addressed are not necessarily "my people" of v. 4, thus leaving them unidentified—perhaps specially commissioned angels (as throughout Revelation). With "to you" included, God's people may be the agents. The best view, however, is that the agents of judgment are the ten kings of the Antichrist's confederacy (Beale 900); this is grounded in 17:16, 17, where the same degree of devastation is portrayed as here. The explanation that God moved the hearts

of the ten kings to destroy Babylon (17:17) is convincing.

The *measure* that God uses in administering judgments against Babylon reflects the principle of sowing and reaping (13:10) but is based on specific reciprocation for offenses against God's people. The *double* measure (three times in v. 6) not only underscores the certainty and completeness of the judgments but also reveals how God feels when His people have been mistreated or martyred. The pagan empires of world history —Egypt, Assyria, Babylon, Persia, Greece, and Rome—have never been kind to God's people. The final empire, Antichrist's kingdom during the Tribulation, will be hostile to believers to an unprecedented degree. Many, refusing to worship him and wear his mark, will be martyred, as first glimpsed in 6:10. When God's wrath is finally and fully poured out on the earth, the pendulum quickly swings the other way. The Antichrist, false prophet, world rulers, and unbelieving inhabitants of earth will experience the wrath of God to the fullest degree.

"According to her works" serves as the primary basis of Babylon's judgment, as of all unbelievers (20:12, 13). No doubt the word includes all sinful attitudes and behaviors, arising as they do from a wicked heart. Babylon's wicked works are the external expressions of her wicked spiritual disposition. The sins that are listed reveal her character, thereby demonstrating the justice of God's judgments. The "cup" recalls the golden cup filled with her abominations, fornication, and martyrs' blood (17:4; cf. 14:10).

God will turn Babylon's false glory and luxurious living into "torment and sorrow" (v. 7). The proud and self-sufficient attitude of Babylon, and of those influenced by her, reflects the satanic inspiration behind her. God hates pride (Prov. 16:5,18). All glory belongs to Him, as emphasized throughout Revelation (1:6; 4:9, 11; 5:12, 13; 15:3, 4; 16:9; 19:2). Pride is self-glori-fication, related to the self-sufficiency that causes one to trust in something other than God.

Babylon's pride is reflected in "I sit a queen, and am no widow, and shall see no sorrow" (cf. Is. 47:8; Rev. 3:17). We call this *hubris:* "an arrogant self-asser-tiveness that insults and abuses others" (Mounce 328). The great prostitute "Babylon" apparently recognizes her subordinate relationship ("marriage") to the beast (Antichrist) as her king by claiming the title "queen." She is con-vinced that this lucrative, luxurious, pro-tective relationship will continue: "[I] shall see no sorrow." Aune (III:996) thinks that this reflects Roman pride as "the eternal city." But it recalls the proud attitude of ancient Babylon as well, and perhaps of any pagan mon-arch (Is. 13:19; 47:7, 8; Jer. 51:41).

The word "widow" implies depriva-tion and vulnerability. Babylon's proud assertion amounts to another statement of the hubris of self-sufficiency. Indeed, all has gone well for her until now, under the protection of the powerful beast upon which she rides. Her boasts are intertwined, since sorrow is caused by loss; she expects neither. One of the objectives of God's judgment was a direct attack against this satanic, self-confident hubris.

She has caused the people of God "torment and sorrow." "Torment" (Greek *basanismos*) has already appeared in 9:5 and 14:11: "*testing by torture, torture, torment*" (ALGNT

88). "Sorrow" (Greek *penthos*) is "*grief, lamentation, mourning*" (ALGNT 305). In a great reversal, God will cause her to experience the pains she has inflicted on others, foreshadowing the eternal tor-ment and sorrow of Hell (Lk. 16:19-31; Rev. 20:10).

The correlatives "how much" and "so much" also indicate the standard of judgment. Babylon the prostitute has enjoyed opulent, luxurious living and sinful behavior; God will measure out judgment on her to a similarly excessive or "luxurious" degree. Such judgments do not violate the *lex talionis,* they fol-low it. She sinned excessively, God judges her excessively—and righteously (15:3, 4; 16:7; 19:2).

God will again use "plagues" as instruments of Babylon's destruction: "death, mourning, famine" (v. 8). "Fire" will be included (8:3-5, 7, 8, 10; 9:18; 11:5; 16:9) and is a permanent compo-nent of eternal judgment in Hell (19:20; 20:14, 15). The picture of Babylon's judgment (vv. 2, 8) is the classical depic-tion of the destruction of a city and its populace; "utterly burned with fire" is the finishing touch of a destroyer (cf. 17:16, 17). The use of death, mourn-ing, famine, and fire may be *an ironic parody* of what many of God's saints have suffered in church history from Nero to the Reformation and beyond. God will cause Babylon to feel the "tor-ment and sorrow" that she has caused His people to feel. He will give her blood to drink since she enjoyed shed-ding the blood of saints so much. He will take away from her all the material wealth, power, and security that she has idolized and denied to His people.

Babylon's false sense of perpetuity and security is likewise contrasted with the abrupt way in which she is destroyed.

God will destroy her "glory" and "delicious living," ironically, in a relatively short period of time: "in one day." The process began with the seal judgments, continued and intensified in the trumpet judgments, and becomes total with the bowl judgments. All occur within the seven-year Tribulation that culminates with the Second Coming and the Battle of Armageddon. Babylon's final collapse begins in earnest with the bowl judgments in chapter 16; chapters 17 and 18 provide additional perspective on this process of events.

"One day" may therefore refer at most to the entire Tribulation or to the climactic collapse toward the end. Regardless, it is "a symbol for suddenness" (Thomas II:326). This language of *suddenness* is consistent with O.T. and N.T. "Day of the Lord" predictions and particularly the sudden nature of the Second Coming portrayed in the N.T. as a "thief" (Is. 2:10-21, etc.; Mt. 24:29-44; 1 Th. 5:1-3; 2 Th. 1:8-10; 2 Pet. 3:10).

"Strong is the Lord God who judgeth her" refers to sheer strength. When the sovereign God determines to judge Babylon, her false security will be woefully exposed; nothing she or anyone else may do can stop Him. Her judgment will be sudden, severe, thorough, and final. In direct contrast to her former, conceited expectations, she will no longer function or exist.

3. The laments of the world (18:9-20)

9 And the kings of the earth, who have committed fornication and lived deliciously with her, shall bewail her, and lament for her, when they shall see the smoke of her burning.

10 Standing afar off for the fear of her torment, saying, Alas, alas that great city Babylon, that mighty city! for in one hour is thy judgment come.

11 And the merchants of the earth shall weep and mourn over her; for no man buyeth their merchandise any more:

12 The merchandise of gold, and silver, and precious stones, and of pearls, and fine linen, and purple, and silk, and scarlet, and all thyine wood, and all manner vessels of ivory, and all manner vessels of most precious wood, and of brass, and iron, and marble,

13 And cinnamon, and odours, and ointments, and frankincense, and wine, and oil, and fine flour, and wheat, and beasts, and sheep, and horses, and chariots, and slaves, and souls of men.

14 And the fruits that thy soul lusted after are departed from thee, and all things which were dainty and goodly are departed from thee, and thou shalt find them no more at all.

15 The merchants of these things, which were made rich by her, shall stand afar off for the fear of her torment, weeping and wailing.

16 And saying, Alas, alas that great city, that was clothed in fine linen, and purple, and scarlet, and decked with gold, and precious stones, and pearls!

17 For in one hour so great riches is come to nought. And every shipmaster, and all the company in ships, and sailors, and as many as trade by sea, stood afar off,

18 And cried when they saw the smoke of her burning, saying, What *city is* like unto this great city!
19 And they cast dust on their heads, and cried, weeping and wailing, saying, Alas, alas that great city, wherein were made rich all that had ships in the sea by reason of her costliness! for in one hour is she made desolate.
20 Rejoice over her, *thou* heaven, and *ye* holy apostles and prophets; for God hath avenged you on her.

The great angel chronicled the responses of three affected groups: "the kings of the earth" (vv. 9, 10), "the merchants of the earth" (vv. 11-17a), and those who "trade by sea" (vv. 17b-19); compare Ezek. 26-28. In light of the fact that the unique confederacy of ten kings—Antichrist's close inner circle—is the actual agent of judgment employed by God to destroy Babylon (17:16, 17), they are probably not included here as mourners.

"The kings of the earth" have "committed fornication" and "lived deliciously" with her (v. 3; 17:2): these are the sins of idolatry and rampant materialism. God's judgment is based on the established pattern of their behavior, as reflected in this resumé. Their sin is a matter of historical record. As noted previously, "fornication" can metaphorically mean *idolatry*. On "lived deliciously" see v. 7.

These wicked rulers will "bewail" and "lament" Babylon's judgment because the primary means of their wealth and pleasure has been destroyed, visible to them in "the smoke of her burning." This apparently indicates the destruction of a literal world capital or seat of government and commerce (cf. Gen.

19:28). "Bewail" (Greek *klaio*) refers to the external expression of grief such as the shedding of tears and perhaps audible groaning. "Lament" (Greek *kopto*) means to "*beat one's breast* as a strong expression of grief or remorse" (ALGNT 235). Altogether, this constitutes "a cry of sorrow over the loss of a lover; but it is also a cry of fear, for the husband now realizes that his mistress was struck down because of her sins and their illicit affair" (Brighton 471).

"Standing afar off" (v. 10) indicates that these kings are at some distance from the immediate fallout of God's judgment directed against Babylon, a distance maintained because of "the fear of her torment." "They are helpless to do anything to help the city and are probably afraid that the same thing will happen to them" (Thomas II:328).

Ancient Babylon prided herself as self-sufficient and impregnable, but God judged her through the Medes and Persians. Just so, His judgments against eschatological "Babylon" in the end-times, through the ten-king confederacy of the Antichrist, prove that such hubris (v. 7) is always foolish. The outpouring of God's wrath understandably produces fear that takes hold of everyone, king and commoner alike.

The castastrophic devastation is shocking, as is the identity of the agents of destruction: the ten confederate kings. Equally shocking is the *suddenness* of her destruction. The "great city Babylon, that mighty city," crashed in just "one hour"—a short period of time indicating her sudden collapse. "Alas, alas" is the verbal expression of their "bewailing and lamenting" (v. 9) and is the identical response of the merchants (v. 16) and marine traders (v. 19) over Babylon's destruction. "Alas" (Greek *ouai*) is the same as "woe" (8:13; 9:12; 11:14), "expressing extreme displeasure and calling for retributive pain on someone or something" (ALGNT 287). The despair is immediate, overwhelming, and unrelenting.

From this point the sense of doom escalates as events crescendo toward Armageddon, bringing a growing awareness that all is lost forever! This is a disaster of epic proportions for those who have everything dear to them tied up in the world. They are forced to watch the world capital city, the symbol and center of the world systems, destroyed before their very eyes.

"The merchants of the earth" are likewise affected by Babylon's destruction (v. 11), grieving over the collapse of the world's material economy. "Merchant" (Greek *emporos*) refers to *"one who travels about for trading"* (ALGNT 147). They "weep and mourn" because their materialistic way of life, their prestigious positions and possessions in life, are being destroyed along with Babylon (cf. v. 9). "Mourn" (Greek *penthos*) means "to grieve with a grief which so takes possession of the whole being that it cannot be hid" (Trench 239). The shedding of tears by these merchants is an expression of their great, ignoble grief.

That "no man buyeth their merchandise anymore" (v. 11) explains their grief and indicates that buying and selling are now forever disrupted. "Buy" (Greek *agorazo*) means to trade or do business, buying or selling, and has the flavor of the public marketplace. "Merchandise" (Greek *gomos*) is "load, freight, or cargo" (ALGNT 101). In ancient times, a great deal of the world's merchandise was transported via the earth's seas. A maritime economy continues in modern times, evidenced by huge tankers, ocean liners, cargo ships, and seaports. This will continue to be the case during the Tribulation.

A lengthy list illustrates the wide variety of this period's merchandise (vv. 12, 13), thus suggesting "extensiveness and abundance by means of an exhaustive summary" (Aune III:981). The 28 items may be grouped in broad categories: (1) precious metals or stones; (2) cloth; (3) furniture or housewares; (4) spices and perfumes; (5) foodstuffs; (6) domesticated animals; (7) means of transportation; and (8) slaves: "an exotic catalog of precious cargo goods" (ISBE IV:349). Bauckham (350, 351) indicates that the list is "accurate in representing the imports of the city of Rome in the first century A.D." and that it is "the longest extant list of Roman imports to be found in the literature of the early empire." (He comments on all 28 items.) Beale (909) suggests that the ones selected "represented the kind of luxury products in which Rome overindulged in an extravagantly sinful and idolatrous manner."

Precious metals and jewels include "gold, silver, precious stones, and pearls" (compare the prostitute's attire in 17:4). Ancient Rome's gold and silver came from Spain and was plentiful, an obvious sign of significant wealth. Most "precious stones" were from India (Bauckham 353) and were used for jewelry by both men and women. "Pearls," highly valued in the ancient world, were harvested from the Red Sea, the Persian Gulf, and India.

Clothing materials, curtains, or rugs are made of "fine linen, purple, silk, scarlet," thus "varieties of expensive fabric" (Aune III:998). Indeed, the expense of a luxury item was often associated with how difficult it was to obtain. "Fine linen" was made from expensive and delicate flax from Egypt, Spain, or Asia Minor (Thomas II:332). The "purple" dye required large quantities of tiny shellfish and was therefore "more expensive than any of the materials which it was used to dye and accounts for the exorbitant price of purple cloth" (Bauckham 354). It was, consequently, a symbol of high status. Scarlet dye (Greek *kokkinou*) was also produced in Asia Minor (Bauckham 356). Silk was imported from faraway China. Expensive clothing, like the precious metals of gold and silver, indicated significant wealth in ancient society. Such abundance will still identify the rich and famous at the end of history.

"Thyine (scented) wood" might be used as an ornament for wearing or for fine furniture. It apparently is "citron wood" (perhaps a type of cypress), prized for its aroma and fine veining, often used for costly tabletops (ISBE IV:349). "All manner vessels of most precious wood" broadens to include all sorts of expensive woods.

The limitless supply of household "vessels" of "ivory, precious wood, brass, iron, and marble" further illustrates the manufacturing capability of the nations of the world that produce an almost incomprehensible superabundance of material things. "Vessels" (Greek *skeuos*) include "any kind of instrument, tool, weapon, equipment, container, or property" (Aune III:969). Elephant herds of Africa were endangered because of ancient Rome's voracious appetite for ivory (Bauckham 357, 358). Imported iron was used for making weapons and statues. Marble was not only for public buildings and ostentatious houses but also for dishes and containers.

Other household or personal luxuries are "cinnamon, odours, ointments, and frankincense" (v. 13). Cinnamon, both an odor and a spice, came from eastern Asia (Thomas II:333). Some manuscripts have "spice" (Greek *amomon*) in the list between "cinnamon" and "odours," used as "an aromatic balsam for the hair" (Thomas II:334). "Odours" (Greek *thumiama*) is "fragrant stuff for burning, incense" (Vine 322), often used for "perfuming the rooms and funerals of the rich" (Bauckham 360). "Ointments" and "frankincense" may be read as examples of the incenses or perfumes, or as additional items. Either way, "ointments" (Greek *muron*) refers to "myrrh-oil" (Vine 444), an imported, sweet-smelling substance that could also be used in medicines (Aune III:1001).

Foodstuffs include "wine, oil, fine flour, and wheat" (v. 13). "Africa and Egypt supplied most of Rome's 'wheat' via the imperial grain fleet" (Keener 429). "Fine flour" was the "finest wheatened flour" (Vine 243), imported from Alexandria (Thomas II:335), in contrast to the cheaper grades on which the poor subsisted. The ability of the modern world to manufacture durable goods depends on the ability of the farming industry to grow, store, and distribute large amounts of food. These blessings will begin to diminish with the seal judgments, eventually coming to an abrupt end with Babylon's destruction.

Domesticated animals—"beasts, sheep, and horses"—are probably produced in abundance in the end-times. There were horse and chariot races in the ancient world, and the thrill of racing will likely continue to exist in the final, eschatological generation.

"Chariots" may reflect civilian transportation as opposed to the stereotypical military image: "These were the four-wheeled, horse-drawn, private chariots used by the rich for travel in Rome and to their country estates" (Bauckham 360). There is no reason to doubt that technology, industry, and wealth ensure that there will be no shortage in meeting the needs of the eschatological world for transportation or warfare.

"Slaves" (Greek *soma*), literally "bodies," by metonymy refers to slaves (ALGNT 372). Slavery was extremely common in the ancient world, varied in degree, and may not always have carried the stereotypical, American civil-war-era meaning. The list points to those rich enough to have slaves, viewed as commodities to be bought and used. Furthermore (or perhaps "and" means "even"), the merchants are guilty of trafficking in the "souls of men." This carries a negative connotation, referring to the corruption of men's souls. It refers to the damage done to the slave's soul.

The material objects, being mainly expensive items, are objects of the world's "lust" (Greek *epithumia*), "*strong impulse* or *desire*" (ALGNT 164). Here it is used negatively as a desire for evil things, the "strong desire" of the merchants (and much of the world's population at this time) for the items mentioned in the preceding catalogue. The rich typically crave excessive amounts of such luxuries and are willing to pay extravagant prices.

The products are now characterized as "fruits" and "dainty" and "goodly" things (v. 14). "Fruits" (Greek *opora*) originally means the season (late summer or early autumn) of ripening fruit, then by metonymy "the *ripe fruit* itself"

(ALGNT 284). Here the word may be a metaphor to describe how "delicious" the acquisition and enjoyment of these material things has been to them: they are "the good things of life" (Aune III:969). "Dainty" and "goodly" expand on the luxurious living. "Dainty" (Greek *liparos*) means "*fat, oily*" but is used "figuratively in the NT, of a sleek, easy way of life *luxurious, costly*" (ALGNT 247). "Goodly" (Greek *lampras*) means "*shining, bright, radiant, clear, sparkling, elegant, splendor, lavish*" (ALGNT 243). The material goods valued by these end-times merchants are *expensive, luxurious,* and *beautiful.*

That these "are departed from thee," and "thou shalt find them no more at all" reveal that all this luxurious wealth and visible beauty is lost forever in the judgment of Babylon, causing the great grief displayed by the merchants of the earth. God's judgment of great Babylon destroys the system that has promoted the idolatry of crass materialism. Abundance of material wealth typically creates self-sufficiency and independence from God in any age, person, or nation. John's vision describes and predicts the drastic intervention of a wrathful God within eschatological history. He has decided to dismantle eternally what tends to destroy faith in Him: the idolatry of mammon. These objects of material lust and the means of procuring them have disappeared. The loss is final; nothing remains to be found.

These material "things" made the merchants "rich" (v. 15). Like the kings of the earth (vv. 9, 10), and for the same reasons, the merchants will also "stand afar off for the fear of [Babylon's] torment." This reflects an attempt to remain at a safe distance and perhaps the intuitive fear that they are likewise guilty and deserving of destruction. That they will "weep and wail" at her destruction is repeated; see comments on v. 11. God's destruction of the world's economy is a final commentary on the temporal quality of earthly treasures and the absence of eternal treasures.

Likewise, the merchants' lament— "Alas, alas that great city" (v. 16)—echoes the lament of the kings of the earth (see comments on v. 10), different only in perspective: "Each group sees her fall in terms of its own interests. Whereas the kings focused on the destruction of her great 'power,' the merchants focus on the destruction of her wealth" (Mounce 335). The initial description of "that great city" in terms of the prostitute's attire (see 17:4) is repeated here, with the addition of "linen" (v. 16). The bright clothing—"linen, purple, and scarlet"—is symbolic of success in plying her trade with the kings and merchants of earth and reflects items included in the 28 luxuries (v. 12). Likewise, the jewelry (v. 16); see v. 12. All these are abruptly and finally destroyed.

Her great material wealth—"so great riches"—and her position in the world are suddenly changed, again in "one hour" (v. 17; see vv. 10, 19). God's judgment of Babylon is *swift* and *thorough.* "Is come to nought" (Greek *eremoo*) means to "*become desolate…of a prosperous city, be depopulated, be destroyed, be ruined*" (ALGNT 172). The verb views the action holistically (Greek aorist passive), implying a sudden and decisive historical action against her by God.

Her destruction has devastating implications for her associates in the world's maritime economy (vv. 17-19): "every shipmaster, all the company in ships, sailors, and as many as trade by the sea." "Shipmaster" (Greek *kubernetes*) is "the steersman or pilot" of the ship (Vine 396), equivalent to the captain. "The company" apparently refers to those who travel by ship: passengers— or perhaps the traveling merchants (Aune III:1005), though they were mentioned earlier in vv. 11, 15. Those who "trade by sea" are the common workers in a maritime economy: divers, fishermen, dockworkers, shipbuilders, and others; "trade" is the usual word for "work, labor" (Greek *ergazomai*). "Every," "all," and "as many as" underscore the totality of God's judgment in this arena.

These too (like the kings and merchants) witnessed "the smoke of her burning" (v. 18; cf. vv. 8, 9; Gen. 19:28), leading to the emotional exclamation, "What *city is* like unto this great city!" The destruction of such a great city did not seem possible; Babylon's wealth and power seemed secure and permanent. What must have been equally shocking was the sobering realization that their own fate was connected with hers: Babylon's ruin was their ruin.

"Alas, alas that great city" repeats for the third time the world's mantra of despair bemoaning the destruction of beloved Babylon (v. 19). That they "cast dust on their heads" and (literally) "were crying out" reflects deep emotion. The "weeping and wailing" are the same as in the kings' and merchants' mourning (vv. 9, 11, 15). "Costliness" (Greek *timiotes*) means "valued at great price, precious" (Vine 131) and "figuratively, as honor and value" (ALGNT 380). Babylon was not only wealthy, she was honored for it; the great wealth of Babylon helped make everyone else wealthy. But the chain of wealth is completely severed by the destruction of the capital city. The world's economy collapses suddenly, totally, and permanently. Again, "for in one hour is she made desolate" indicates amazement and grief at the suddenness of Babylon's destructive judgment (vv. 8, 10, 17).

In stark contrast to the world's grief and shock is the exhortation to joy of those designated as "*thou* Heaven, the holy apostles, and prophets" (v. 20). "Rejoice" (Greek imperative of *euphraino*) means "*be merry, enjoy oneself, rejoice, celebrate, be jubilant*" (ALGNT 181; cf. 12:12; cf. 11:10). The sudden turn of events is reason for great rejoicing by the entire host of Heaven, apparently included in the exhortation: "It is the church glorified, not believers on earth, who are invited to rejoice" (Mounce 336). These three groups are singled out since they have often suffered the brunt of the world's persecution. Many of them were martyred at the hands of "Babylon."

This is not an exhortation to rejoice about God's judgment of unbelievers; that should be viewed soberly and compassionately. "The focus is not on delight in Babylon's suffering but on the successful outcome of God's execution of justice, which demonstrates the integrity of Christians' faith and of God's just character" (Beale 916). Ladd (*Commentary* 242) calls it "a cry of rejoicing that God at the end will show himself to be God in the face of all satanic foes." Perhaps the rejoicing is more over the destruction of the system and the satanic trio than over the unbelievers who are victims of their deceit.

Most manuscripts, instead of "holy apostles and prophets," read "holy ones, and apostles, and prophets." Either way, all saints are no doubt included, as inhabitants of heaven. The "apostles"

are probably Jesus' original ones (with perhaps a few additions like Paul), memorialized in the twelve foundations of the New Jerusalem (21:14). Indeed, most of them were martyrs at the hands of one segment or another of the world's system. "Prophets" may include those of the O.T. and the N.T. dispensations, many of whom suffered persecution at the hands of evil kings and pagan world empires. Thomas (II:342) disagrees: "The prophets singled out are not representatives of the old covenant, but are those who have been persecuted for Jesus' sake."

"God hath avenged you on her" refers to God's *action* (not just His judicial verdict) in pouring out devastating judgments against the world's systems as represented in the capital city of Babylon. The judgment affects all components of the worldly system: religious, economic, social, and governmental. God has judged Babylon because she judged God's people, a judgment that is not only punitive but vindicates all who have been faithful to God in all of history, with special focus on those martyred or persecuted during the Tribulation (2:10, 13; 6:9-11; 13:7, 15-18; cf. Mt. 5:10-12; 24:9, 10). It also answers the question "When?" originally asked in 6:10.

4. Comparison of her fall (18:21-24)

21 And a mighty angel took up a stone like a great millstone, and cast *it* into the sea, saying, Thus with violence shall that great city Babylon be thrown down, and shall be found no more at all. 22 And the voice of harpers, and musicians, and of pipers, and trum-

peters, shall be heard no more at
all in thee; and no craftsman, of
whatsoever craft *he be*, shall be
found any more in thee; and the
sound of a millstone shall be heard
no more at all in thee;
23 And the light of a candle shall
shine no more at all in thee; and
the voice of the bridegroom and of
the bride shall be heard no more at
all in thee: for thy merchants were
the great men of the earth; for by
thy sorceries were all nations
deceived.
24 And in her was found the blood
of prophets, and of saints, and of
all that were slain upon the earth.

At this point John saw another
"mighty" angel portrayed as larger than
life (v. 21; cf. 10:1; 18:1), apparently
commensurate in size with the earth and
its oceans. This angel picked up "a
stone like a great millstone" and promptly threw it into one of the earth's oceans.
"Mighty" (Greek *ischuros*) suggests the
raw strength (ALGNT 206) necessary to
do this. A great splash and subsequent
sinking are implied, the action illustrating the destruction of the "great city
Babylon" by God.

Millstones were large and heavy, used
for grinding grain into flour. Two things
are evoked by this image: its ability to
crush and its great weight. Once thrown
into the ocean it would cause violet
upheaval and sink rapidly. The vision
thus symbolizes the total, sudden, and
permanent destruction of eschatological
Babylon (cf. Jer. 51:59-64; Ex. 15:4, 5;
Mt. 18:6), as indicated by the interpreting angel (v. 21). The passive verb "be
thrown down" points to an external
agent of destruction, previously identified as God (vv. 5, 8, 20). "Found no

more at all" indicates that the action
results in total destruction, symbolized
by the sinking of the millstone out of
sight. The final resting place of Babylon
will no longer be visible; some form of
"never again" is used six times in this
context (Kistemaker 501).

Verses 22, 23 provide examples of
things typical in a great city, things that
cease to exist there when Babylon is
destroyed (cf. Jer. 25:10). "Harpers,"
"musicians," "pipers," and "trumpeters"
are musicians. "Voice" (Greek *phone*),
used broadly, means "sound." "Harpers"
are those who play stringed instruments
like the ten-stringed lyre or harp (Greek
kithara). A "musician" is a person
skilled in music, perhaps a "singer"
(Aune III:1008) or "minstrel" (Robertson
444). The "piper" plays "a musical wind
instrument shaped like a tube *flute,
pipe*" (Greek *aulos*: ALGNT 81). "Flutes
were used both at festivals and at funerals...Trumpets served for games and in
the theater" (Mounce 338). Music has
always been an integral component of a
society for entertainment, celebration,
and worship; once God judges "Babylon,"
it will no longer exist there.

"No craftsman, of whatsoever craft
he be" is, literally, "every craftsman of
every craft." Such crafts include "metal-
working, brick-making, glassmaking,
carpentry, perfume-making, tent-mak-
ing, spinning, weaving, tanning, dyeing,
pottery-making, carving, sculpture, and
stonemasonry" (Aune III:1009). Again,
that none of these "shall be found anymore" expresses the universal scope
and total degree of the destruction.

"The sound of a millstone" may represent the production of food. Whether
a large millstone at the local mill or a
handmill used in homes, the message is
the same. This sound, too, is "heard no

more at all," perhaps implying famine toward the end of the Tribulation; cf. the "third seal" judgment (6:5-8).

All these disruptions signify the collapse of world society. What began incrementally and intensified now becomes total. The visual landscape changes rapidly and the silencing of normal sounds—which may indicate the absence of people—underscores the total and sudden nature of God's judgments. The use of the double negative (Greek *ou me*) with all three examples— music, craftsmen, and millstones— makes the finality of their judgment emphatic.

The extinguishing of "candlelight" (the smallest light source) in Babylon implies, by metonymy, that *all* of Babylon's lights are extinguished (v. 23). A city cannot function without light; its lights at night indicate its habitation and that all is well. On the other hand, darkness in Scripture is a symbol of evil and God's judgment—appropriate here in the picture of God's judgment of Babylon. In a modern world this might well refer to the destruction or disruption of utilities that provide electricity.

Yet another thing absent from the society of judged Babylon is "the voice of bridegroom and bride"—"a metaphor that represents the vitality of a thriving city" (Aune III:1009). This may well include the cessation of "joy" along with the institution of marriage itself. At a deeper level, this may allude to the cessation of idolatry previously represented as the great whore's "marriage" to the world system. Indeed, the interpretation suggests as much when it cites the "merchants or great men of earth" and "all nations"—members of this unholy union. The materialistic society of Babylon had made her merchants into "the great men of the earth," who owed their prestige, prosperity, and position in the earth to her. So God's judgment is directed against the hubris of self-sufficiency and pride in men whose god has become the abundance of their material possessions and other wicked behaviors.

Verses 23, 24 indicate two reasons Babylon has merited such total and final judgment. First, she has successfully seduced or deceived the nations of the world into being unfaithful to God. This has been done by Babylon's "sorceries" (cf. 9:21; 21:8), a word (Greek *pharmakia*) indicating "the use of medicine, drugs, spells" (Vine 587). The explanation is spiritual in nature: her power is satanic, stronger than those she deceives. The only ones who successfully resist the "magic spell" of her influence are believers, indwelled by a stronger and wiser power, the Spirit of God (1 Jn. 4:4, 5).

Second, Babylon is guilty of bloodshed. Though God will judge all sins, violent bloodshed is one of the most heinous in His sight (Gen. 4:10; 6:11-13; 9:5, 6). That man is made in the image of God and the finality of the act of murder are reasons for this. "In her was found the blood" reveals the guilt of Babylon for all who have ever been martyred for their faith (cf. Jer. 51:49).

Three classes of those killed are identified, with the first two in the category of martyrs. Whether "prophets and saints" refer to O.T. or N.T. eras is unclear, perhaps in both dispensations. "All that were slain upon the earth" is the third category, general enough to include saint and sinner alike in one grand category and thus placing the guilt of *all* the murders of world history on Babylon's account (cf. Jer. 52:49).

(Alternatively, this last phrase might simply amplify the first two categories and refer to all the prophets and saints who have been martyred.)

Summary
(18:1-24)

Chapter 17 introduced the great prostitute Babylon, riding upon a scarlet-colored beast, subsequently identified as "that great city" (v. 18). Chapter 18 then chronicles the destruction of this world capital in the end-time Tribulation. The world economy collapses as a result and is greatly mourned by Babylon's economic allies.

Another great angel who descended from Heaven to earth announces this (v. 1), pointing to the divine origin and authorization of the proclamation. The angel's radiant heavenly glory, within the context of the vision itself, may also have illuminated the devastation of the city of Babylon.

The great angel loudly proclaimed the fall of Babylon the great (v. 2), repeating *fallen* to emphasize the certainty of her destruction. As a result of God's judgment (through the agency of the ten-nation confederacy of the Antichrist that turns against her, 17:16, 17), the once great and proud city is reduced to a ghost town inhabited only by demons and scavenger birds.

Such total judgment by God is justified for several reasons, the first being that Babylon has corrupted the kings and merchants of earth with the wine of her fornication (v. 3). This is the wine of idolatry or materialism.

Before being given other reasons, John heard another voice coming from Heaven (v. 4). In a way that recalls the warning given to Lot's family before the

destruction of Sodom and Gomorrah, the angelic voice exhorted God's people to "come out" of the city of Babylon for the sake of holiness and to escape the plagues God had determined to send against her.

A second reason for the severity and timing of God's judgments against Babylon (v. 5) is that her sins had piled up as high as Heaven. Her sins had accumulated enough that God determined to act in final judgment against her.

The standard of punishment is the principle of "an eye for an eye and a tooth for a tooth" (*lex talionis*); her punishment must be commensurate with her crimes (v. 6). Having rejected Christ, Babylon was judged according to her works. The cup of her works was full of the abominations of the earth and the blood of martyrs (17:5, 6). Her judgment was just, consistent with the principle of sowing and reaping.

She was guilty of pride arising from her excessive materialism and luxury (v. 7). She was conceited because of her relationship with the beast and her earthly clientele of kings and merchants. She was self-confident about what she believed to be her permanent and happy future.

However, her destruction will be sudden and complete, carried out by the strong, Almighty God (v. 8). The sight of her destruction caused her economic allies to lament her. The kings, merchants, and mariners all stood at a safe distance in fear and grief since their fate is bound up in hers. They all saw the smoke of her burning. They all marveled that her destruction was so sudden and complete.

A list of 28 luxury items illustrates the world's materialistic emphasis (vv. 12,

13): precious metals, jewelry, fine fabrics, fine wood, home furnishings, spices, perfumes, fine food, domesticated animals, luxury transportation, and slaves. Commerce in these comes to an abrupt end; they cannot be found (v. 14). The merchants wept and mourned over Babylon's great loss (vv. 15, 16). They too marveled at the suddenness of her destruction (v. 17).

The maritime economy is also completely destroyed, affecting all connected with trade by seas and rivers (v. 17). These collectively marvel over the sudden destruction of the icon of earthly security (vv. 18, 19).

By contrast, the destruction of Babylon is reason for all the host of Heaven to rejoice (v. 20), including apostles and prophets as well as all saints and martyrs in Heaven. God's judgment of Babylon is in part recompense against those who have martyred His people.

The vision concludes with the appearance of another mighty angel (v. 21), portrayed in cosmic dimensions. The angel picked up a huge millstone and threw it into one of the earth's oceans. The violent splash and sudden sinking to the ocean's bottom illustrated the fall of mighty Babylon into eternal oblivion.

The vision portrays the total collapse of earth's society (vv. 22-24), selecting several components of society that dramatically highlight the scope and finality of God's judgment. All music ceases, affecting both singers and those who play musical instruments. Manufacturing shuts down. Food production ceases. Cities and houses become uninhabited. There are no marriages or other joyous celebrations. The great men of the earth suffer the loss of their wealth.

What has justified such catastrophic judgment of God against Babylon? For one thing, the nations of earth have been victimized by the deceitfulness of Babylon's religion and riches. Furthermore, Babylon is accountable for shedding the blood of those who have been martyred throughout history and during the Tribulation. God will judge the great prostitute and her clientele for the idolatry of materialism and for martyring a great number of saints.

Application: Teaching and Preaching the Passage

Many interpreters see an analogy, for the destruction of Babylon the Great, in the ancient Roman Empire of John's day: "For John, the judgment brought against the city of Rome was at the same time the eschatological judgment that would bring history to its close.... The forces exemplified by Rome will in fact be those very forces which will play the major role at the end of time" (Mounce 340). This means that John's prophecies were *not* fulfilled in the conditions and destruction of the ancient Roman Empire, but will be fulfilled in the Tribulation period of earth's history that culminates with the Second Coming.

"Possession of wealth is not the reason for God's judgment of Babylon... The cause lies, rather, in 'the arrogant use of it' and trust in the security that it brings, which is tantamount to idolatry" (Beale 924). Jesus warned disciples about the deceitfulness of riches in the parable of the sower (Mt. 13:22), about the difficulty of entering Heaven as a wealthy person when testing the rich young ruler (Mt. 19:23, 24), and about not being rich toward God (Lk. 12:15-

21). The exhortations by Christ to lay up treasures in Heaven (Mt. 6:19, 20, 24, 33) and by Paul to be heavenly minded (Col. 3:1-6) provide the proper perspective. Abundance of material things tends to create a false sense of self-sufficiency and security, turning our focus away from God and from our need for Him. The value system condemned and symbolized by end-times Babylon is rampant materialism. It is this kind of culture that prompted the exhortation to "Come out of her, my people" (v. 4). Christians in every generation of church history are called to do the same whenever the culture of the society around them reflects the greed, idolatry, and humanistic pride portrayed by the great prostitute, Babylon the Great.

We must teach our children how to be rich toward God and how to be successful in life from God's point of view.

Suggested Outlines. Cry Out In A Mighty Voice! 18:1-4: (1) Prediction of Babylon's fall, vv. 1, 2; (2) Participants who fall with her (nations, kings, merchants, seafarers of earth), v. 3; (3) Plea to come out, v. 4.

The World's Lamentation, 18:10, 16, 19: (1) Babylon's judgment is fearsome; (2) Babylon's judgment is sudden; (3) Babylon's judgment is total.

C. Celebration in Heaven (19:1-10)

These heavenly doxologies stand in contrast to the worldly laments of chapter 18. The pendulum of history swings back in favor of God's people with force and finality. In the remainder of Revelation, visions will reveal details about the Second Coming of Christ, Antichrist's defeat at Armageddon, the binding of Satan and millennial reign of Christ, the final conflict leading to the Great White Throne Judgment, and the new heavens and earth. The celebratory worship of 19:1-10 serves as an introduction to these climactic events.

1 And after these things I heard a great voice of much people in heaven, saying, Alleluia; Salvation, and glory, and honour, and power, unto the Lord our God:
2 For true and righteous *are* his judgments: for he hath judged the great whore, which did corrupt the earth with her fornication, and hath avenged the blood of his servants at her hand.
3 And again they said, Alleluia. And her smoke rose up for ever and ever.
4 And the four and twenty elders and the four beasts fell down and worshiped God that sat on the throne, saying, Amen; Alleluia.
5 And a voice came out of the throne, saying, Praise our God, all ye his servants, and ye that fear him, both small and great.
6 And I heard as it were the voice of a great multitude, and as the voice of many waters, and as the voice of mighty thunderings, saying, Alleluia: for the Lord God omnipotent reigneth.
7 Let us be glad and rejoice, and give honour to him: for the marriage of the Lamb is come, and his wife hath made herself ready.
8 And to her was granted that she should be arrayed in fine linen, clean and white: for the fine linen is the righteousness of saints.
9 And he saith unto me, Write, Blessed *are* they which are called unto the marriage supper of the

Lamb. And he saith unto me, These are the true sayings of God.
10 And I fell at his feet to worship him. And he said unto me, See *thou do it* not: I am thy fellowservant, and of thy brethren that have the testimony of Jesus: worship God: for the testimony of Jesus is the spirit of prophecy.

"After these things" (v. 1) marks transition to another subject and indicates chronological progression. This locates these doxologies just before the Second Coming and Battle of Armageddon (19:11-21), at the very end of the Tribulation (Walvoord 268). The focus also shifts from earth back to the throne room of Heaven, where we hear jubilant response to God's judgment of the great whore (vv. 1-7). The doxologies of "much people" (vv. 1-3), "the 24 elders" (v. 4), "the four living beings" (v. 4), "a voice" (v. 5), and "a great multitude" (vv. 6, 7) apparently come in response to the invitation in 18:20. They are offered to God because He alone is responsible for judging Babylon and gloriously vindicating His people.

The "great" voice of this group is loud, perhaps a "roar" (NIV). Interpreters are divided between identifying them as "saints" or "angels"; "people" (Greek *ochlos*) means "throng...multitude" (ALGNT 290), whether of one or the other. But it is usually applied to human beings, and the experiential terminology of "salvation" suggests that this first doxology is given by the redeemed. Other groups and their doxologies are subsequently identified. The final doxology (vv. 6, 7) may come from the whole host of Heaven: living creatures, elders, angels, and the redeemed.

The people in Heaven at this time are O.T. and N.T. saints who have died and come into God's presence: "the church triumphant" of 7:9 (Mounce 341). "The focus in 19:1-3, 5b-8 is on the entire assembly of saints as they praise God at the consummation of history, though angels could be included" (Beale 926). This group would include, of course, the full complement of martyrs portrayed in 6:9-11 but should not be limited to them. Those in 6:9 were instructed to patiently await their ultimate vindication, not to occur until the full number of martyrs in Heaven was completed.

The first word of praise is "Alleluia," used four times here (vv. 1, 3, 4, 6) and nowhere else in the N.T. It is a Hebrew word, often transliterated "hallelujah," meaning "praise Yahweh/Jehovah," used to introduce and conclude various Psalms.

"Salvation" (Greek *soteria*) can refer to physical or spiritual *deliverance* (ALGNT 373)—here the latter since even martyrs, who were not delivered from physical death, are among those who offer this praise to God. It is the salvation of Lk. 19:10 and Rom. 1:16, the redemption made possible by the risen Lamb that is highly extolled throughout Revelation (5:9; 7:9-17).

"Glory" (Greek *doxa*) is also ascribed to God: "radiance, brightness, splendor; a manifestation of God's excellent power, glory, majesty" (ALGNT 119). It is reflected by everything God is (attributes) and does (works) and ultimately belongs to Him alone. The first "alleluia" is offered for the glory manifested in God's incomparable attributes, the second for what He has done in judging Babylon the Great.

"Honor" (Greek *time*) reflects a valuing of something as "costly, precious"

(ALGNT 380), "*honor* which belongs or is shown to someone" (Thayer 624). When honor is given to God it carries this meaning. (Though "honor" is not in most manuscripts, all the doxological terms used here have appeared in earlier doxologies to God in Revelation [4:11; 5:12, 13; 7:12; 15:3,4; 16:5-7].)

"Power" (Greek *dunamis*) is defined as "*power, might, strength*," or "*ability, capability*" (ALGNT 121). Great power is necessary to manage end-time events and persons in a sovereign way: to produce the catastrophic judgments poured out on the earth, to defeat Satan and his minions completely, and to create and eternally sustain the new Heaven and earth. In this doxology its linking with "salvation" implies that it is necessary to achieve the salvation of all believers (Rom. 1:16).

"The Lord our God" is the one who deserves this tribute; He alone has the power to save His people, defeat His and their enemies, and judge the great prostitute, Babylon the Great. "The purpose of this first hymn appears to be the attribution of power, victory, etc. to God rather than to human strength" (Ford 316). At this point in the Revelation, God's feats have become realities: He has redeemed His people through the risen Lamb, judged Babylon for idolatry and persecution of God's people, and avenged those who followed Him to martyrdom.

"True" and "righteous" describe God's judgments, particularly those rendered during the Tribulation (v. 2; cf. 15:3; 16:5, 7). The view is proleptic, portraying future judgments as having already happened. "Judged" (Greek *krino*) has a broad range of meanings including "*divide out* or *separate off; think of as better, prefer; evaluate,*

think, judge; resolve, determine, decide; find fault with, condemn; administer justice; punish; rule, govern" (ALGNT 238). Here it includes the whole process of arraignment, evaluation, verdict, and punishment. God's "judgments" are based on specific truth or fact. The prostitute Babylon was guilty of seeding ("corrupt") the earth with spiritual "fornication" (idolatry, materialism) and was guilty of great bloodshed (martyrdom of saints).

That God's judgments are "righteous" means that the judgments are right in themselves and administered rightly. They are commensurate with the crimes Babylon has committed, consistent with the principle of sowing and reaping. She has lived and behaved excessively or luxuriously, and her judgments are imposed with matching excess. God judges her guilty and executes the prescribed punishment.

Furthermore, this satisfies the martyrs' question "how long?" (6:9-11; cf. 16:6; 17:6; 18:20, 24; cf. 8:3-5). "Hath avenged the blood of his servants at her hand" indicates that the heavenly throng (v. 1) views the judgment of Babylon (chapters 17, 18) as God's vengeance on their behalf. "Avenged" (Greek *ekdikeo*) means "to vindicate a person's right" (Vine 46).

Perhaps while still viewing "the smoke" of Babylon's destruction the heavenly throng offered a second "Alleluia" (v. 3). The first "alleluia" was offered in praise of certain attributes of God. The second is connected to the fact that the smoke of Babylon's judgment rises "*for ever and ever*" (cf. 14:11) praising His actual work in judging Babylon.

Verse 4 cites the affirming response of the 24 elders and four living beings to the doxology of the heavenly throng. These elders and living beings (see 4:1-11) also prostrated themselves and offered an "Amen" and an "Alleluia."

From the vicinity of the throne a solitary "voice" commanded "all" God's servants to praise Him (v. 5). This voice probably belonged to someone other than God or Christ since it refers to "our God," apparently putting the speaker on the same level as "servants" and "God-fearers." While it would not be inconsistent for Christ to view Himself as a servant, that does not seem to be the case here; He makes a dramatic appearance later in the chapter. The voice might belong to one of the living creatures, but more than likely it was the voice of yet another angel—as often in Revelation. At any rate, the connection with the throne of God implies divine origin and authority.

"Ye his servants," "ye that fear him," and "both small and great" (v. 5) identify those exhorted to praise the Lord, broad enough to call for a doxology from the vast host of Heaven and even from Tribulation saints still alive on the earth. "Servants" (Greek *doulos*) may be translated "slaves," thus indicating both service and ownership (cf. 11:18). Indeed, the "and" may mean "even," referring to the same group: God's servants *are* those who fear Him (Aune III:1016). "Fear" as experienced by God's people (not by the wicked) refers to a healthy respect for God's power and holiness (1 Jn. 4:18). "Small and great" includes everyone in between—all believers. The redeemed of all ages share in the vindication, conquest, and rewards of God in the end-times.

"And I heard" indicates a change in subject matter and calls attention to "a great [heavenly] multitude" in v. 6,

apparently the same group as in v. 1. The doxological tone continues. The doxologies given in vv. 1-5, and also in v. 6, may be viewed as pointing backward in praise for what God has already done and forward in terms of the continuing results. The shift into a future perspective is more discernible in v. 7, pointing to the upcoming marriage supper of the Lamb.

The immense size of this group is underscored by John's use of two different analogies. First he compares the multitude's "voice" (or "sound") to that of "many waters"—perhaps like "many people talking at the same time" (Kistemaker 513) or the roar of a rushing river or waterfall or ocean breakers; cf. 1:15, which uses the same expression of the risen Christ's voice. Then he compares the sound to "mighty thunderings" that typically evoke awe in those who hear (cf. 6:1; 10:3, 4). The combined voices of angels and all the redeemed would indeed produce such an awe-inspiring sound.

The great multitude begins its doxology with "Alleluia" (see above on v. 1), but the motivation is different. Whereas the doxologies of vv. 1-5 commemorate God's destruction of Babylon, the doxologies of vv. 6-10 extol the coming establishment of God's reign over the earth in its place. Though "the Lord God omnipotent reigneth" can accurately affirm the *timeless* nature of God's rule in history, Revelation indicates here that Christ is about to establish His millennial kingdom by great force, having judged and conquered the world and all His enemies during the Tribulation. "Reigneth" should then be understood as the inauguration of that reign (Greek ingressive aorist). At this point in time God imposes His rule over the world in an unprecedented way. The act of judgment against Babylon, and against Antichrist's kingdom (about to be described in the Battle of Armageddon), opens the door for the reign of God to be established on earth.

The triple name—Lord God omnipotent (almighty)—leaves no doubt as to who is taking sovereign control on earth. Babylon has been overthrown; Antichrist is about to be overthrown; Satan will be bound. No emperors or potentates, whatever their claim to deity, will prevail. This conquest—happening during the Tribulation—is symbolized by the rider on the white horse (6:1, 2). Daniel predicted that the Kingdom of God would one day overcome all the kingdoms of earth (Dan. 2:34, 35, 44). Jesus instructed the disciples to *pray for God's kingdom to come*, and for His will to be done "in earth as it is in heaven" (Mt. 6:10). All that is about to come to pass and Revelation shows us how and when.

"Let us rejoice and be glad" (v. 7), by which the heavenly multitude rhetorically exhorts itself, introduces a personal reason for such jubilant praise to the Lord. They are about to be "married" to the Lord Jesus Christ, using an analogy frequent in both testaments to describe the relationship between God and His people (Jer. 31:32; Hos. 2:19-23; Eph. 5:25-33; 2 Cor. 11:2). The long-anticipated marriage of the Lamb of God to His glorious bride has arrived. Although the church and each believer have already been placed in union with Christ, the relationship between Christ and His bride is formally and eternally ratified on this occasion.

In Jewish marriage tradition a period of betrothal was followed by a waiting period and payment of dowry before the actual wedding day. On the day of the wedding the bridegroom would go to the bride's home in order to bring her back to his house for the marriage feast and consummation. The occasion was joyously celebrated for a week or more by family, attendants, and friends (DNTB 685, 686). Christ's coming for His bride, the church, follows a similar pattern. The church age is the rough equivalent of the waiting and preparation period. The redeemed in Heaven feel the joy and anticipation of a bride in those moments just preceding the coming of Christ the groom. Nor can the marriage feast itself take place until that time. This implies that the rapture of the church occurs at some point before the marriage supper begins (Walvoord 271).

The multitude also exhorts itself to give honor (Greek *doxa*, "glory") to God. God deserves glory for arranging the marriage between His Son and the bride. Loving and generous parents should not be forgotten on a wedding day. Were it not for the infinite resources of God the Father there would not be any such wedding.

The announcement that "the marriage of the Lamb is come" puts the time of the Lamb's marriage, at the earliest, near the end of the Tribulation. This allows *all the saved* to be present, including those martyred during the Tribulation. But there are different perspectives here. Mounce (347) thinks that the announcement is "proleptic," looking ahead to the blessedness that follows the millennium. Thomas (II:367) thinks that the "initial phase" of the wedding is imminent, at this point in the account, but that "the celebration of that union with a grand wedding feast ensues on earth for the span of the millennial and eternal kingdoms."

On the opposite end of the interpretive spectrum is a focus on the fact that believers are already married to Christ by virtue of their union with Him. The marriage supper itself may simply formalize and celebrate what has already taken place in the truest sense of the word. In this case there is no need for prolonging the process. Indeed, the idea that it is necessary to spread the marriage supper out over the entire millennial reign of Christ seems awkward; better to place the actual supper between the end of the Tribulation and the start of the millennium.

The Lamb's bride is the church, redeemed by the blood of Christ— perhaps including Jewish believers, as one with Gentiles, on the same N.T. basis. Eventually, all the redeemed of both dispensations are incorporated together into the one family of God. But the emphasis here seems to be on the N.T. church.

"Hath made herself ready" may suggest human responsibility. Neither the sovereignty of God nor the principle of justification by faith alone mitigates human responsibility in personally appropriating redemption. "The church is given the garment to wear, but it must still put it on" (Wall 222); and it must be left on. Without this N.T. "readiness" a given individual could be left out or left behind (Mt. 25:1-13). There are certain things that God expects of every believer that may not be done after the Lord's coming. One makes himself ready to participate in the marriage supper by washing his clothing in the blood of the Lamb (7:14), by refusing to worship the beast or receive his mark (v. 20; 14:6-13; 15:2), by practicing daily watchful-

ness for the Second Coming (Mt. 24:36-44), and by faithful service (Mt. 25:1-46).

But the specific preparation of the bride in the present context is described in v. 8, beginning with how she has dressed herself. Her "wedding gown" (Is. 1:18; 61:10) is in direct contrast to the attire of the great prostitute, Babylon (17:3, 4). It is made from "fine linen, clean and white." Linen was the cloth of choice for priestly service in the O.T. White implies holiness, purity, or even victory: all these ideas apply appropriately to the redeemed church. The linen became clean and white by being washed in the blood of the Lamb (7:14). This no doubt reflects having been justified with the righteousness of Christ; but it also symbolizes righteous behavior as well.

There are two threads in the fabric of the "fine linen" given to believers. One is imputed righteousness, appropriated by faith in Jesus Christ (Rom. 3:21, 22; 4:13, 22; 5:1; Gal. 3:6, 11; Eph. 2:8-10). This is the major thread, bestowed solely on the basis of the grace of God by faith in Christ. The divine passive "was granted" indicates that the wedding gown is God's design and provision.

The other thread in this linen gown is the *practical* righteousness of the saints. "Righteousness" (Greek *dikaioma*) may be defined as "righteous deed, act of justice" (ALGNT 117). The wedding gown that merits entrance into the wedding, then, is woven with the threads of both faith (imputed righteousness of Christ) and faithfulness (righteous behavior). "This does not deny the Pauline doctrine of justification based on the righteous obedience of Christ [Rom 5:18-19], but suggests that a transformed life is the proper response to the call of the heavenly bridegroom" (Mounce 348). The privilege of participating in the marriage supper of the Lamb may be viewed as a reward of faithfulness in a way that does not compromise the principle of justification by faith alone (see Rom. 6:18-23).

The "marriage supper of the Lamb" is a major milestone in salvation history (cf. Mt. 26:29; Lk. 22:18) and a time of great celebration in Heaven. It stands in sharp contrast to the feast that God prepares for the scavenger birds of the earth after the Battle of Armageddon (vv. 17, 18). "Blessed *are* they which are called" (v. 9) refers to those qualified to participate. "Called" (Greek *kaleo*) means "invited": "a formal summons to friends and relatives to join the festive occasion" (Aune III:1034). The "called" are identical to the redeemed, identified earlier as "people" (v. 1), "servants" (vv. 2, 5), "God-fearers" (v. 5), "saints" (v. 8), and as "his wife" (vv. 7, 8). In this sense the "call" is distinct from God's universal "gospel call" to all men to be saved—a call that may be rejected (1 Tim. 2:4-6; 2 Pet. 3:9; 1 Jn. 2:2). Many whom God calls, in that sense, do not heed His call.

The analogy of a marriage and wedding feast is not always used, in Scripture, in precisely the same way, especially in the freedom and flexibility of parables. In Mt. 22:11-14 *the wedding guests* (rather than the bride, as here) are those who have the proper attire. In Mt. 25:1-13 *the wedding entourage* accompanying the bride are those qualified to participate. But there is no need to identify either of these as distinct from the bride or "wife" of Christ in Rev. 19. All the positive comparisons refer to the redeemed, to those who have faithfully followed Christ to the end.

The saints are "blessed"—vindicated and rewarded by the privilege of attending this supper. The enemies of Christ have been excluded and are being judged. The prediction of this feast, given in the O.T. (Is. 25:6-9), has been long anticipated: the *same language* principle suggests that the predicted O.T. event and the marriage supper in chapter 19 are one and the same (cf. Mt. 26:29).

The throne-room focus ends with the angel's pronouncement, "These are the true sayings [Greek *logoi*, literally "words"] of God" (v. 10). This provides a closing commentary on what has been revealed in vv. 1-9 and assures readers that these things are indeed true and trustworthy. God Himself has spoken them. "These" should not be limited to the beatitude in v. 9: everything spoken in Revelation thus far is equally true.

John was apparently so moved that he bowed in worship at the feet of the angel whose "voice" he had heard (cf. 22:8). The angel promptly forbade him (cf. Acts 10:26): the "voice" he had been hearing (vv. 5,9) belonged to a "fellow servant" of John and all believers ("thy brethren"). On "servants," see v. 5; the term implies both servitude and ownership. Christians relate to Christ in both ways, without negative connotations.

"That have the testimony of Jesus" again raises the question whether it means testimony given for or about Jesus (Greek objective genitive) or Jesus' own testimony (Greek subjective genitive). Probably it is another way of referring to someone who knows Christ, that is, to the redeemed. Admittedly, those who know Christ share their testimony about Him with others. If it is correct that this is an angel, then he can rightly say that he is a "fellow servant" with believers, and no doubt he too gives testimony of Jesus; but he cannot bear witness, with them, to having been redeemed.

The angel exhorted John to "worship God" instead, quickly deflecting John's honest but improper response. God and the Lamb alone are worthy of worship. Some suggest that John thought this one to be Jesus, or that it was "impulsive reverence" (Swete 248). Another suggestion, which does not seem likely, is that this is "staged" in order to serve as a polemic against angel worship; but this application, though appropriate, comes after the fact.

The spokesman concludes by equating the "testimony of Jesus" (cf. 1:2, 9; 12:17; 20:4) with the "spirit of prophecy" in some way. The precise relationship between the two may be understood in a number of ways and includes the meaning of "spirit." The Holy Spirit as "the spirit of prophecy" is the author who moved men to compose Scripture (2 Pet. 1:20, 21). But He also indwells every believer and gives promptings to share the Word or witness for Christ. The Holy Spirit is necessarily present in the preaching and teaching of the Word (1 Cor. 2:4, 10-16).

More specifically, Jesus is the *object* of the Spirit's ministry or of prophesying: "True prophecy witnesses to Jesus" (Aune III:1039). The Holy Spirit, indwelling every believer, seeks to reproduce the character and mind of Christ within the believer and prompts every believer to bear witness to Christ. This often becomes the basis of persecution in an environment of people hostile to the gospel. John was not banished to Patmos because he was silent about his faith in Christ (1:2).

D. Battle of Armageddon (19:11-21)

This book is a "revelation of Jesus Christ" (1:1) in two senses: He gives the revelations and they are about Him. The visions in chapters 1-3 indicate that Jesus is eternally alive and that He is God. In chapters 4, 5 He is the slain Lamb, redeeming mankind. In chapters 6-19 He is revealed as riding forth to conquer, judge, and establish His kingdom: a Warrior-Messiah. The passage before us reveals His final conquest over the nations of the world at the Battle of Armageddon.

In order to do this, Christ must make His long-awaited Second Coming to the earth: a coming that is prophetic, literal, militaristic, and triumphant. This event, often designated as the *parousia* (Vine 111), is predicted in the O.T. (Dan. 7:13; Zech. 12:10; 14:3, 4) and in the N.T. (Mt. 10:23; 16:27; 24:3, 27, 37, 39; 26:64; Acts 1:11; 1 Cor. 15:53; 1 Th. 1:10; 4:16; 2 Pet. 1:16; etc). It was predicted at the very beginning of Revelation (1:7, 8), thus casting its shadow over the entire book. That moment has arrived in the Revelation record. It is one of the most significant milestones of world history in all of Scripture.

11 And I saw heaven opened, and behold a white horse; and he that sat upon him *was* called Faithful and True, and in righteousness he doth judge and make war.
12 His eyes *were* as a flame of fire, and on his head *were* many crowns; and he had a name written, that no man knew, but he himself.

427

13 And he *was* clothed with a vesture dipped in blood: and his name is called The Word of God.

14 And the armies *which were* in heaven followed him upon white horses, clothed in fine linen, white and clean.

15 And out of his mouth goeth a sharp sword, that with it he should smite the nations: and he shall rule them with a rod or iron: and he treadeth the winepress of the fierceness and wrath of Almighty God.

16 And he hath on *his* vesture and on his thigh a name written, KING OF KINGS, AND LORD OF LORDS.

17 And I saw an angel standing in the sun; and he cried with a loud voice, saying to all the fowls that fly in the midst of heaven, Come and gather yourselves together unto the supper of the great God;

18 That ye may eat the flesh of kings, and the flesh of captains, and the flesh of mighty men, and the flesh of horses, and of them that sit on them, and the flesh of all *men, both* free and bond, both small and great.

19 And I saw the beast, and the kings of the earth, and their armies, gathered together to make war against him that sat on the horse, and against his army.

20 And the beast was taken, and with him the false prophet that wrought miracles before him, with which he deceived them that had received the mark of the beast, and them that worshiped his image. These both were cast alive into a lake of fire burning with brimstone.

21 And the remnant were slain with the sword of him that sat upon the horse, which *sword* proceeded out of his mouth: and all the fowls were filled with their flesh.

"And I saw heaven opened" (v. 11) marks another transition. John looked once more into Heaven (cf. 4:1; 11:19; 15:5), this time with the curtain of the future drawn aside to reveal a great army in waiting. He saw, first, "a white horse"—the second time a white horse has introduced a vision (6:1, 2)—"whose rider is to wage a holy war and bring to close the present age" (Mounce 351). The vision dramatically portrays the Second Coming, depicting Christ as the *divine-warrior*, "employing military imagery strongly reminiscent of Divine Warrior passages in the OT" (Longman 298).

Again, "white" is the preferred color of Heaven, generally symbolic of holiness, victory, and reward: in this case the holy character and triumphant conquest of Jesus Christ. The risen, glorified Christ rides forth to reclaim what rightfully belongs to Him as Creator and Redeemer. The picture thus forms an *inclusio* (like bookends) with the first seal in 6:1, 2. I have taken the position that the rider of the white horse in 6:1, 2 is Christ, not Antichrist; this rightly places emphasis on what God is doing in the end-times rather than on Satan's secondary agenda.

The white horse's rider has the name "Faithful and True" (cf. 21:5; 22:6): His title and His character (cf. "the faithful and true witness," 3:14)—obviously Jesus Christ. He was faithful in every way, especially in executing the mission of redemption. A faithful person can be depended on to do what he says, and Jesus can be trusted absolutely. And if the connection with 3:14 is noted, that He is "faithful and true" may subtly recall Christ's "martyrdom": that is, His faithfulness to bear witness to the truth of God before the Roman authorities, even unto death. As the very incarnation of absolute truth, He lived and spoke the truth with great authority (Mt. 7:28, 29).

His standard for "judging" and "making war" is "righteousness": *right behavior* (cf. 16:5-7; 19:2; Ps. 72:1-4; Ps. 96:10-13). "Judge" (Greek *krino*), as used here, includes the idea of exercising judgment in ruling or governing, and making war is part of that work of judgment or justice: what Beale (951) calls "legal war." The conquering Christ's motives and objectives are legitimate ("righteous") because He is totally submitted to God's will. The cause of this particular war is based on the truth about God and about Antichrist and his followers. They have martyred many Christians (13:15; 16:5-7) and have coerced the world into worshiping the beast. They are guilty and unrepentant and deserve to face the wrath of God in full force. The proud, idolatrous hubris of the Christ-rejecting, eschatological world warrants God's judgment. Christ's own name and followers also await final vindication. This is, indeed, a just and holy war.

The rider's eyes looked like "flames of fire" (v. 12; cf. 1:14; 2:18), this penetrating gaze suggesting that he is omniscient. He was wearing "many crowns," perhaps "fillets or bands of cloth encircling the brow" as compared to a traditional crown (Trench 78-80; cf. 6:2; 12:3; 13:1). But these are the crowns of royalty (Greek *diadema*), not just vic-tors' or celebrants' crowns. The "many crowns" suggest that the rider is omnipotent.

Further, the rider had a name known only to Him (cf. 2:17; 19:16), recalling Christ's promise to the faithful at Pergamum (2:17). This name may have been written on His forehead or on the crowns, or even on a banner draped around His body (cf. v. 16) and may indicate the absolute sovereignty of Christ: "In the OT to know a name means to have control over the one named" (Beale 955). If this nuance is intended, it indicates the inability of Antichrist or his armies to defeat Christ since they know and control nothing about their opponent. While some think that the ignorance of the name is only for unbelievers, the words "but he himself" seem to exclude *everyone*. It is therefore probably not any of the names by which we know God or Christ: "The most common interpretation is that it is a secret name whose meaning is veiled from all created beings" (Mounce 353).

The rider also wore a floor-length (cf. 1:13) "vesture" or robe that had been "dipped in blood" (v. 13; cf. Is. 63:1-6), a graphic symbol of the wrath and destruction of God as Judge. "Vesture" (Greek *himation*) is the outer garment or *stole*. Here the blood-stained garment does not represent Christ's blood, or the blood of martyrs, but the blood of unbelieving members of Antichrist's army to be slain in the winepress of God's wrath at Armageddon. "Dipped" works well with the image of someone walking around in a winepress treading on grapes; the juice would invariably splatter on one's garments. This connects the rider to the great "harvest" of judgment in 14:17-20. The fact that the garments are *already* stained with blood simply symbolizes the coming conflict.

The rider has another name, this one well-known: "The Word of God" (cf. 1:2, 9; 20:4); compare Jn. 1:1, 14, where Jesus is both Creator of the Universe and the Word of God incarnate. This title indicates how the imminent battle will be fought: the spoken Word is the rider's weapon of choice to "smite the nations" (v. 15). Sovereign, creative power resides in the Word of God, whether to speak the universe into existence, to regenerate and sanctify an individual, to perform a miracle, or to defeat His enemies (1 Pet. 1:23-25; Rom. 1:16; 10:17).

Following the rider as leader were the "armies in heaven," also riding "white horses" (v. 14). "Clothed in fine linen, white and clean" is a description of their battle dress; see the comments on v. 8. That they appear to be *unarmed* seems startling, but their relationship to Christ explains their lack of need for weapons. This battle dress is apparently no different from the attire normally worn by the redeemed in Heaven (3:4, 5, 18; 4:4; 6:11; 7:9, 13, 14) or from typical angelic garb (15:6). As in v. 8, then, the clothing symbolizes both the imputed righteousness of Christ and righteous behavior; and this connection may suggest that the riders are saints rather than angels—though angels are similarly clothed and are in fact closely associated with the Second Coming (Mt. 16:27; Mk. 8:38; 2 Th. 1:7). Kistemaker (522) and Walvoord (277) include both saints and angels in this "cavalry" (cf. Dt. 33:2). But 17:14 identifies those "with him" as "called, and chosen, and faithful," meaning saints. No doubt both saints and angels are present with Christ at the Second Coming, but whether both ride in this retinue is not clear and relatively unimportant.

The most unusual feature of the rider was the sword protruding from His mouth (v. 15; cf. 2:12, 16; Is. 11:4; 49:2). Compare the glorified Christ in 1:16. The "sword" (Greek *hromphaia*, not *machaira*) is the larger kind (Vine 613), powerful and sharp, best understood here as a symbolic representation of the spoken Word of God, supernaturally "sharp" and highly effective (Heb. 4:12). But the spoken Word is not simply used to *pronounce* judicial condemnation; it *executes* the judgment. The Lord must personally subdue the earth by force before establishing His millennial rule (Ps. 2:9).

This personal, "hands-on" activity is emphasized by the repetition of the otherwise unnecessary pronoun "he" (Greek *autos*) twice in the last half of v. 15. "Smite" (Greek *patasso*) means "giving a blow with the hand, fist, or weapon" (Vine 581), definitely warlike in tone. Christ deals with the nations of the earth and their armies, gathered against Jerusalem and His faithful remnant, in a destructive and final way: "Messiah's words have death-dealing power against His foes" (Thomas II:389). "It would violate the nature of apocalyptic language to spiritualize this passage to the point where it is taken to designate God's judicial acts in ordinary historical events" (Ladd, *Commentary* 252).

"He shall rule them with a rod of iron" (cf. 2:26, 27; 12:5; Ps. 2:8, 9) indicates universal dominion. "Rule" (Greek *poimaino*) literally means to tend a flock (as a shepherd does): "*tend, feed, pasture*" (ALGNT 320). The tense points to a *future* role as shepherd over the nations. The expression thus looks beyond Armageddon to a world led or ruled by Christ after Armageddon, helping us distinguish this future rule from Christ's present government of the church. This future government is an absolute, worldwide rule of Christ over those who know Him as well as those who have no other choice but to accept His rule. It is true that Christ ascended to the Father's right hand shortly after His resurrection (Acts 1:9-11). It is also true that He presently reigns over His church and in the hearts of believers on earth. But He has not yet demonstrated any rule over "the nations" of the earth. Unprecedented world dominion (Ps. 2:6-12) will be established as a result of Christ's conquest at Armageddon; then He will rule or shepherd the nations during a literal, millennial reign on earth.

"He treadeth the winepress of the fierceness and wrath of Almighty God" focuses again on the Battle of Armageddon (cf. 14:17-20; Is. 63:1-6), by which that reign will be established. The doublet—fierceness (anger) and wrath—intensifies the depth of God's anger. The fierce wrath of an offended God requires satisfaction. Christ bore God's wrath for the redeemed (1 Th. 5:9), but His wrath will be poured out in full force on Antichrist and his followers at Armageddon. The Christ who created and redeemed humanity will one day judge those who have rejected and opposed Him, ultimately confining them to eternal Hell.

"KING OF KINGS, AND LORD OF LORDS" (v. 16) was the rider's title (cf. 1 Tim. 6:15; Phil. 2:9-11), written on His garment in the area of His thigh. As often, "and" means "even": "even on his thigh" (Aune III:1044). Swete (255) suggests that the thigh area of a person sitting on a horse is the most visible place. At any rate, the rider's sover-

eignty is in view: He possesses all the power, authority, and justification necessary to "make war." There is no other king or lord comparable to Him. Ruling over the earth, with its kings and lords, rightfully belongs to Him as Creator, Redeemer, and Conqueror.

"And I saw" (v. 17) represents another change of focus, to an event that takes place immediately after the Second Coming. As in 10:1-5; 11:1, etc., "standing in the sun" suggests cosmic dimensions: the angel superimposed against the sky with the sun for a background and calling out with a "great" (loud) voice. The reason may be that his invitation to the supper is directed to the birds of earth that move about the sky. These fowls, scavengers especially, are exhorted to assemble for a feast. "Unto the supper of the great God" suggests that the event is a banquet prepared for them by God (cf. Ezek. 39:4, 7, 12, 17-21; Mt. 6:26)—whether "great" modifies God or the supper (as in most manuscripts). That the Battle of Armageddon turns into a great banquet for the birds and beasts of the earth points to a terrible loss of human life.

In keeping with the ironic analogy of a banquet, v. 18 lists several items on the "menu." In sharp contrast to the marriage supper of the Lamb for the redeemed (v. 9), the followers of Antichrist *become the menu* for another banquet provided by God for scavengers. The grotesque menu is human flesh: "corpses," "carcasses," or "carrion" (Aune III:1044). Seven categories suggest the completeness of the slaughter: kings, captains, mighty men, horses and "them that sit on them" (horsemen), "all men," "bond and free," "small and great"—in other words, earth's unbelievers, many of them in Antichrist's armies. "To remain unburied for the pleasure of the predators was considered by the ancients to be an ignominious fate" (Mounce 358). The *same language* principle strongly suggests that these events are identical to those prophesied in Ezek. 39 (Kistemaker 525). Ezekiel adds that other "beasts" are invited and that the dead bodies will lie exposed for up to seven months. The degree of slaughter portrayed at Armageddon and the amount of time suggest that the scavengers will have plenty of flesh and time to gorge themselves.

Some think that "the only survivors of this awful confrontation will be those loyal to Christ who have not died or suffered martyrdom" (Thomas II:395). But the context seems to imply that only those who are members of the Antichrist's armies are slaughtered. "The remnant" ("the rest," v. 21) are the assembled forces of v. 19; others on the earth are not slaughtered. It would be highly unlikely and totally unnecessary, from a military perspective, to gather all the earth's unbelieving population near Jerusalem to put down what would appear to be an easy target.

"And I saw" (v. 19), as usual, marks another change of focus within the vision that began in v. 11. The gathering referred to probably coincides with the heavenly activity that began with the arrival of Christ. Even as John witnessed the muster of the armies of Heaven, he also saw the muster of the Antichrist's forces on earth. God Himself had providentially maneuvered the arrival of the kings of the East by drying up the Euphrates River with the sixth bowl judgment (16:12; cf. vv. 13, 14). These kings would join the evil confederacy of "the beast," "the kings of the earth,"

and "their armies" that were gathering near Jerusalem at "Armgeddon"; see the comments on 16:16. Though the name Armageddon does not occur here, that passage makes clear that it is meant: "a Biblical city in whose vicinity many famous battles were fought (Jg. 5:19; 2 Kg. 23:29f.). In Jl. 3:2, 12 it is called 'the valley of Jehoshaphat' and is roughly equivalent to 'the valley of Jezreel' or 'the plain of Esdraelon'" (ISBE II:1059, 1060).

The purpose of the world confederacy, whose armies gather in this valley, is "to make war" (cf. 17:14). An army needs a staging area and this large valley serves the purpose well. Their opponents are Christ ("him that sat on the horse") and "his army," following Him at the Second Coming to link up with a remnant of God's people in or around Jerusalem (v. 14). Christ has ridden forth from Heaven with His armies to engage the armies of the world in battle (cf. Is. 13:4; Ezek. 38, 39; Jl. 3:2, 9-17; Zech. 12:3, 8-10; 14:1-9). Perhaps the Second Coming is partly intervention on behalf of Jerusalem or the righteous remnant congregated there, perceived as a threat by Antichrist and his confederacy and prompting a move against Jerusalem. (Thomas II:396 suggests various scenarios.)

John records relatively few details about this battle except the outcome: Christ is victorious! The true Sovereign of the earth takes rightful control and establishes His millennial kingdom. Several O.T. texts, noted above, provide details; Zech. 14:1-15 is especially helpful. The nations not only gather against Jerusalem, they attack it and inflict significant damage (Zech. 14:2). This prompts the Lord Himself to intervene, accompanied by "all the holy ones with

Him" (Zech. 14:5), probably a direct reference to the Second Coming (Zech. 14:3-5). Sunlight and moonlight dramatically diminish in a rearrangement of the solar day (Zech. 14:6, 7; Jl. 3:15; cf. Rev. 6:12-14; 8:12; Mt. 24:29). There is a great eschatological earthquake (Zech. 14:4, 5; Is. 2:19, 21; Ezek. 38:19, 20; Jl. 3:16; cf. Rev. 16:18-20). The Lord literally causes the flesh of Antichrist's soldiers to dissolve (Zech. 14:12) and throws the armies into such chaos and panic that they turn against one another (Zech. 14:13; Ezek.38:21). Even the animals are affected (Zech. 14:15). The result is the annihilation of these nefarious armies, the rescue and restoration of Jerusalem's supremacy over the nations, and the establishment of the worldwide rule of God (Zech. 14:16-21).

John skips right to the result of the battle: the disastrous destruction of the "beast" (Antichrist) and his followers and the unambiguous victory of Christ expressed in "the beast was taken" (v. 20). In order to cut off the "head" of the confederacy against Him, Christ captures the beast and the false prophet (second beast) and promptly casts them into Hell. A brief summary of the second beast's activity is rehearsed (cf. 13:11-17): he used miracles to "deceive" the earth's unbelieving inhabitants into receiving the mark of the beast and worshiping his image. This history serves to legitimize the harsh but deserved judgment.

Both beasts, Antichrist and the false prophet, are alive (literally "living") when cast—probably by an angel (20:1-3; 12:7-9)—into Hell (cf. Dan. 7:7-11). "Brimstone" (Greek *theion*) is literally "sulphur" (Vine 80); burning sulphur is known for its ability to produce intense heat. When this occurs, those who follow them will no doubt fall into immediate chaos and demoralization.

Idealist Beale (969) suggests that these are not two literal individuals "but...all who function in the corporate role of beast and false prophet at the end of history." But "the beast" and "the false prophet" are definite ("the" is with both), pointing to their identity and suggesting that they are in fact individual persons.

Christ next turns His wrath on Antichrist's followers, identified as the rest ("remnant") of the beast's army (v. 21). "Slain with the sword" conveys the result: a horrific amount of literal bloodshed (14:20)—much of which may be caused by their turning against one another in battle (14:20; Zech. 14:13). As noted, the primary "weapon" against them is the "sword" protruding from Christ's mouth—the Word of God spoken (v. 15). That He "sat upon the horse" with a sword that "proceeded out his mouth" links this specifically to the rest of the vision that began in v. 11.

The army following Christ (v. 14) does not appear to be actively involved. Christ produces the desired effect by commanding the desired outcome: "a decree of death" (Beale 971). This is literal slaughter, not to be allegorized as the ultimate spiritual destruction of Hell or of "converting the nations throughout the course of history" (Chilton, cited in Beale 971). The vision of graphic slaughter does not serve well to portray the blessedness of evangelism or personal redemption. The account depicts devastating judgment without any redemptive flavor.

The carnage is catastrophic: the entire army arrayed against Christ is annihilated, so many that the victims' blood is as high as "horse bridles" for a distance of approximately 200 miles (see commentary on 14:20). The "fowls" (scavenger birds) of earth gather to gorge themselves on the bodies of men and horses (vv. 17, 18), leaving much after they are filled (v. 21).

Summary
(19:1-21)

In chapter 19 the focus returns to Heaven to survey the response of Heaven's host to the news of Babylon's destruction. The triumphant praise contrasts sharply with the laments of the world's inhabitants.

The first doxology is given by a great multitude who praise God for His salvation, glory, honor, and power (v. 1). God was absolutely justified in judging the great prostitute; it was a judgment based on true facts or guilt, carried out in a just way. She corrupted the earth with her "fornication" and martyred many saints. Her judgment therefore was the answer to the martyrs' question in 6:10, 11 and may rightly be considered as God's vengeance against her and vindication of His own faithful servants (v. 2).

The smoke of Babylon's burning is an ominous reminder that her judgment is complete and final, likewise a reason to praise the Lord and cause for another doxological tribute (v. 3). This is followed by a tribute of praise from the 24 elders and by a command originating from God's throne for all of God's servants to join in (v. 4, 5).

Another multitude continues the doxological theme (v. 6), perhaps similar to the group mentioned in v. 1 and comprised of saints—and angels as well, if the entire host of Heaven is meant. Angels, though not direct beneficiaries

of redemption, have always been interested in and assisted the heirs of salvation. These offer collective praise that God has exerted His rule over the earth. The defeat of all Christ's enemies makes way for the establishment of Christ's kingdom on earth.

There is also great celebration that the time for the marriage supper of the Lamb has come. His bride or wife, the church, has prepared herself by putting on the proper wedding garment, provided by God (v. 7): fine, clean, and white linen that represents the twofold righteousness of the saints. It consists of the imputed righteousness of Christ (justification) and the righteous behavior and good works of believers (faithfulness). These, being bidden to the marriage supper, are thereby blessed (v. 9).

John, perhaps enraptured in spirit or misjudging the angel's identity, bowed spontaneously in worship (v. 10). But the angel prevented him, commanding him to worship God instead. He reminded John that he was but a fellow servant himself, in that respect like those who had the testimony of Jesus which is the goal of prophecy.

In one of the most significant revelations of all, John saw Heaven opened to reveal the Second Coming of Christ (v. 11). Jesus sits on a white horse, ready to ride forth, wearing the title "Faithful and True." The purpose of His mission is for judgment and to make war. He will execute this mission righteously.

Jesus' other features receive notice (vv. 12, 13). His eyes flicker like flames of fire, recalling 1:14 and 2:18 and indicating intensity, knowledge, or judgment. He wears many diadems, signifying His absolute power or rule over all. He has a mysterious name that no one can decipher. He wears a blood-soaked garment, like a harvester treading grapes in a winepress, pointing to the harvest of blood at Armageddon in 14:20 (v. 13). His name is also "The Word of God" (cf. John 1:1-14), another revelation of the deity of the rider on the white horse.

Following the rider were the armies of Heaven (v. 14), dressed in fine, clean, white linen recalling the attire of the bride of Christ (the redeemed) in v. 8. Since angels wear similar clothing, and some Scriptures indicate that angels accompany Christ at His Second Coming, the riders could therefore be either the redeemed or angels, or both.

The conquering Christ also had a sharp sword, symbolizing the Word of God and its power, protruding from His mouth (v. 15). The spoken Word is Christ's weapon of choice to smite the nations and win the Battle of Armageddon. Assurance is given that Christ will rule the conquered nations of the world with a rod of iron, suggesting that He will establish His universal rule over the earth in what is commonly called the millennial reign of Christ.

The name "KING OF KINGS AND LORD OF LORDS" was written on the thigh area of the rider's garment (v. 16). This title reinforces the divine identity of the rider leaving no doubt about who He is or His ability to wage a victorious war.

An additional vision introduces the Battle of Armageddon and its results (vv. 17, 18). An angel in cosmic dimensions, standing tall as the sun, issued an invitation to the scavenger birds of the earth to come to a banquet. God Himself has prepared this grotesque banquet of the flesh of kings, captains or military men, strong men, horses and their riders, and the ranks of the armies from all classes of society.

John also provides an account of the results of the battle (vv. 19-21). The participants include the beast (Antichrist), the kings of the earth, and their armies (v. 19). In addition to the slaughter of these forces, Antichrist himself and the false prophet—who did much of his work—are captured by Christ and are thrown *alive* into a fiery Hell (v. 20). The army regulars, now leaderless, are slain by the Word of Christ and left exposed for the scavenger birds and animals to devour (v. 21).

Application: Teaching and Preaching the Passage

By the *same language principle*, the descriptions given in the O.T. by Zechariah and others often refer to the same persons, places, and events in Revelation. Whatever adjustments this requires one to make to his eschatology is secondary to the importance of recognizing the unity and consistency of the Scriptures. The eschatological prophecies of the O.T. are going to agree with John's eschatology. We should marvel as we discover those connections being made right before our inquiring eyes!

The question of the rapture of the church intersects this material at some point, even though it is not explicitly mentioned in the text of Revelation. The best text on the rapture is 1 Th. 4:13-18 (cf. 2 Th. 2:1; 1 Cor. 15:23). And though some pretribulationists "see" the rapture between Rev. 3:22 and 4:1 it is not a part of John's revelations at that point. My approach has been to treat only what is said in the text and not to harmonize it with some system along the way. The reader must decide what this means for a given presupposition brought to the text.

Suggested Outlines. Five Reasons to Praise the Lord, 19:1-3: (1) His salvation, v. 1; (2) His glory, v. 1; (3) His honor, v. 1; (4) His power, v. 1; (5) His judgments, vv. 2, 3.

The Marriage Supper of the Lamb, 19:6-9: (1) Arranged by God the Father, v. 6; (2) Parties—The Lamb as the groom, the Church His wife, v. 7; (3) The wedding gown, v. 8; (4) The blessed guests, v. 9.

The Mother of All Battles, 19:11-21: (1) The heavenly Conqueror and His cavalry, vv. 11-14; (2) The Weapon of choice—the Word of God, v. 15; (3) The cleanup of the carnage, vv. 17, 18; (4) The capture and casting of the beast and false prophet, vv. 19, 20; (5) The completed conquest, v. 21.

E. The Millennial Reign (20:1-10)

Though Antichrist and his forces are annihilated at Armageddon, the conquest of Christ is not complete until His rule is established on the earth and His archenemy, Satan, is put away forever. The Great White Throne Judgment follows Christ's millennial reign on earth, in turn followed by the creation of a new Heaven and earth for eternity. For a helpful overview, see 1 Cor. 15:24-28.

For Scripture references to the millennial reign of Christ, see the list included in the "Excursus" after the commentary on v. 6. There are a number of reasons for such a millennial reign; Newport (296, 297) categorizes them: (1) to provide "an open manifestation of Christ's kingdom" where it has previously been "invisible or spiritual"; (2) to prove "the truthfulness of the Word" in its O.T. and N.T. prophecies

of such a kingdom; (3) to display "personal and political righteousness"; (4) to confirm man's basic sinful nature in the final rebellion; and (5) to provide a time of unprecedented justice and peace under the rule of Christ.

The passage before us, including the millennium it refers to, is one of the most passionately debated matters in all of Scripture. Idealist or amillennial interpretation suggests that the millennial conditions predicted in Scripture are fulfilled either in the church during present history (or in Heaven), or in the new Heaven and earth in eternity. Premillennialism finds here a literal, one-thousand-year reign of Christ on earth inaugurated as a result of the Second Coming and the Battle of Armageddon. That way, Revelation portrays events that are chronologically "sequential"; amillennialism typically suggests that Christ is *presently* reigning—in the church on earth or with saints in Heaven (Gregg 464), which places His reign *before* the Second Coming. Idealist interpreters regard 19:1-10 as chronologically "recapitulating" the events leading up to the final battle and judgment of Armageddon in 19:11-21. (For some, Armageddon is not a literal battle at all but a symbolic portrayal of the Great White Throne Judgment; see Beale, Brighton, Hendriksen, Lenski, Kistemaker.)

Neither amillennialism nor postmillennialism advocate a future, one-thousand-year reign of Christ on earth. For additional information, see the survey of millennial views in the Introduction to this commentary and a brief but thorough survey in ISBE III:356-361. There is an abundance of recent and well-articulated scholarship on various eschatological issues, much of which has been codified in books. I have tried to reference these in the exposition. An exhaustive presentation of any viewpoint is beyond the purview of this commentary.

1. The binding of Satan (20:1-3)

1 And I saw an angel come down from heaven, having the key of the bottomless pit and a great chain in his hand.
2 And he laid hold on the dragon, that old serpent, which is the Devil, and Satan, and bound him a thousand years.
3 And cast him into the bottomless pit, and shut him up, and set a seal upon him, that he should deceive the nations no more, till the thousand years should be fulfilled: and after that he must be loosed a little season.

Christ will not forfeit His right, as Creator and Redeemer, to rule over the nations of the present world. With all earthly resistance successfully defeated and removed at Armageddon, He moves to "bind" the one who inspires all rebellion against His rule, Satan himself. This amounts to a total restriction of his activity: Christ's millennial reign would not be truly blissful if Satan remained in the world to continue corrupting the nations of earth.

"And I saw" (v. 1) represents a major change of focus from that of chapter 19 and introduces a new vision entirely. With nothing in the text to suggest otherwise, the reader should assume that the events of chapter 20 transpire chronologically *after* those in chapter 19.

John's vision begins with sight of yet another "angel," apparently one not mentioned previously. This angel could be the one already given a key to the abyss in 9:1, 2 (cf. Mounce 360), or the archangel Michael who previously fought and defeated Satan in 12:7-9. Regardless, the mission—overpowering Satan—requires God-given authority and strength, and all the holy angels derive such from God.

That the angel came down from Heaven indicates (1) the holy nature of the angel, (2) the divine origin and authorization of his mission, and (3) the fact that the devil roams the earth exclusively after being cast out of Heaven (12:7-17). The fact that the abyss had to be opened indicates that he was not already inside but on the earth: the present earth is the sphere of Satan's activity and presence (cf. 1 Pet. 5:8; Eph. 2:2; 6:11).

"The key to the bottomless pit" and "a great chain in his hand" are essential to the angel's mission. The "key" is symbolic of Christ's authority or control over the bottomless pit; compare "the keys of hell and of death" in 1:18. The deeper significance of possessing keys is given in 3:7: "he that openeth, and no man shutteth; and shutteth, and no man openeth." The risen Christ governs access, in or out (v. 7), to Hell. He has already cast Antichrist and the false prophet into Hell, where they remain forever (19:20).

The abyss or "bottomless pit" in Revelation is associated with the origin of evil things: the hellish smoke and demonic locusts of 9:1-3 and the beast (Antichrist) of 11:7. Lewis (ISBE: I:22) says that "*abyssos* in the N.T. means the 'abode of the demons". It is "a vast subterranean cavern that served as a place of confinement for disobedient spirits awaiting judgment" (Mounce 360). It does not equate precisely to "Hell," being apparently an intermediate holding place used by God to house the nefarious minions that He allows to afflict unbelieving humanity during the Tribulation. Other fallen angels are likely held here as well. Throughout the millennium it imprisons the chief spiritual criminal of all time (cf. Jude 6).

The "great chain in his hand" is symbolic and dramatic, emphasizing the angel's mission to confine Satan in the "bottomless pit." "Great" points to the chain's sufficiency for its intended purpose. The binding is more than house arrest: it restricts Satan's freedom and typical behavior, as the following verses will show. The "chain" may of course be conceived as either metaphorical (Brighton 548) or literal, with neither viewpoint necessarily serving the cause of a particular view of the millennium— though our sense of the completeness of the restraint fits well with a literal chain. Regardless, the concept of binding is the important thing.

The angel locks Satan away from the earth during this period in the abyss. He is shut up, sealed, restrained: confined without the privilege of going in and out. The restriction therefore appears to be *total* and does not fit well with the idea of presently restricted activity in the world or restriction in the lives of those who respond positively to the gospel.

"And he laid hold on the dragon" (v. 2) indicates the angel's success. "Laid hold" (Greek *krateo*) means "*to take hold of* [forcibly], *seize, grasp; to take into custody, arrest*" (ALGNT 236). It implies a show of force. The devil's fury intensified when he was cast out of Heaven (12:7-17); no doubt he remains

extremely angry until the bitter end— though nothing is said about any resistance he might offer.

Seven verbs delineate the angel's mission: "come down," "laid hold," "bound," "cast," "shut up," "set a seal," and "loosed" (vv. 1-3). These actions manifest the angel's divinely given authority and suggest absolute confinement in the abyss. (The loosing occurs at the end of the confinement but probably involves the same angel.) The subject to be confined in this way is identified by the same four aliases used earlier (12:9; cf. 12:3, 7, 13, 17; 13:2, 4; Gen. 3:1, 2): "dragon, serpent, Devil, and Satan," leaving no question about identity. The other two members of the satanic trinity have already been cast into Hell (19:20); there is clear distinction between the three personages.

"Bound" is the word used for the four angels "bound" in the Euphrates River in the sixth trumpet judgment (9:14; cf. Mt. 12:29). A cognate word appears in 2 Pet. 2:4 in reference to evil angels bound in chains awaiting future judgment (cf. Jude 6). The binding effect in each of these examples is total, roughly comparable to what it means to be put in prison. Even if "binding" were merely restrictive, they are also confined within the abyss and are therefore not free to do anything on the earth.

Verse 3 relates this binding to "the nations" of the world. The scope is therefore too great to be limited to an individual's conversion experience, even though similar principles are involved. Neither should this be confused with the outcome of the heavenly war of 12:7-12 since there Satan is cast to the earth to carry on his deception and wrath against God's people.

Brighton (549) expresses the essence of the symbolical or spiritual approach of the amillennial or idealist viewpoint on the nature of this "binding": "According to the four gospels, then, the devil was bound, conquered, judged, and cast out as a result of Jesus' saving ministry, culminating in his death on the cross and his resurrection." For the idealist, then, the inauguration of this "binding" by Christ's redemptive work continues whenever the gospel is preached, or Satan's activities are curtailed by the presence of the church in the world, or an individual Christian is victorious in spiritual warfare. This view means that throughout this age "Satan cannot hold the nations in darkness, blinded to the gospel." (D. Johnson 282). Kistemaker (532) says that "the decision to bind Satan was first made in chapter 12 and not in chapter 20." For many preterist interpreters this "binding" is specifically about the triumph of the early Christians over the imperial cult of Asia Minor in John's time (Summers 202).

Against all such views is 2 Cor. 4:3, 4, which affirms that "the god of this world hath blinded the minds of them which believe not, lest the light of the glorious gospel of Christ, who is the image of God, should shine unto them." Add to this all the "isms" of religious deception and atheistic, humanistic philosophies that are rampant in our world, or such forms of increasing unbelief as are manifested in the "postmodern" or "post-Christian" spirit. Not only is Satan deceiving many, he is deceiving even some believers! It cannot be said that the nations are not being deceived during the present age. And Kistemaker is surely mistaken: after the events of chapter 12 Satan is able to redouble his efforts in persecuting God's people.

Furthermore, the "sealing" is problematic for such idealist or preterist interpretations. Unlike the positive sealing of believers in 7:3, Satan is "sealed" inside the abyss. Futurists are satisfied that "the intention of the passage is not to represent Satan as merely restricted but as rendered completely inactive during the thousand-year millennial period following the second advent" (Mounce 361; see Lk. 22:3; Acts 5:3; 2 Cor. 4:3, 4; Eph. 2:2; 1 Th. 2:18; 2 Tim. 2:26; 1 Pet. 5:8). Satanic activity is highly discernible in our world, and believers must be on guard. If, indeed, the N.T. warns against apostasy and true believers turn away from Christ, then Satan is most certainly not bound and may succeed in destroying the faith of some who were genuinely saved.

The period of the binding is "one thousand years" (vv. 2, 3), obviously the same as the thousand years of the reign described below (vv. 4-7). (The word "thousand" is *chilia*, whence "chiliast" for anyone who believes in a one-thousand-year future reign of Christ on earth following the Second Coming.) Premillennialists take this to refer to a *one-thousand-year period* to begin with Christ's return to earth. Non-premillennialists, instead, interpret it to mean an indeterminate, lengthy period of time symbolic of the entire church age. Amillennialists, for example, advocate that Christ's "reign" began at His ascension (Acts 1) and continues until His Second Coming. In that case, the final resurrection and judgment follow the Second Coming immediately, and the eternal state begins at that point. Such views think of the number 1,000 as a symbol of completeness (Brighton 551, 552).

It is simply too difficult to reconcile any "binding" of Satan in the present age with Biblical teaching. He walks about freely like a ravenous lion (1 Pet. 5:8). Peter rebuked Ananias for listening to him (Acts 5:3). Paul does not equivocate about Satanic freedom and power (Eph. 2:2; 2 Cor. 4:4). Indeed, Satan in the present age is "deceiving the nations" (v. 3), the very thing he must discontinue during his binding. The death, burial, and resurrection of Christ did indeed provide total spiritual victory over Satan, but they did not immediately restrict his activities. The "already-not yet" understanding of Christ's kingdom applies in a similar way to Christ's defeat and conquest of Satan on the cross (Col. 2:14, 15). He has been defeated but remains to be cast into the abyss for Christ's millennial reign and finally into Hell forever (20:10).

Meanwhile, for unbelievers Christ's victory is provisional until appropriated personally by faith. The Holy Spirit is powerful enough to successfully draw people to Christ (Jn. 12:32). For believers, the indwelling Spirit is powerful enough to overcome Satan's power, deceptions, and activities. Satan has no power to prevent someone's conversion when the gospel is preached, if that person desires to be saved. He cannot successfully oppose the work of sanctification in those who walk in the Spirit, nor can he prevail against the faithful church. Only in such ways is the power of Satan "bound" in the present age; only his success is limited, not his efforts. This limitation does not at all satisfy the expressions used for the 1,000 years: he is "bound," "cast into the pit," "shut up" there, "sealed," and prevented from

deceiving the nations any longer until the end of the 1,000 years. "Shut up" (Greek kleio; NIV "locked") means "to shut, lock, or bar" (ALGNT 231). "Sealed" (Greek phragizo) has the same root as the seven "seals" around the scroll (5:1). It indicates a condition that is fixed until broken or loosed, true of all prisons: going in or out is denied when something is sealed shut (Brighton 551). "The elaborate measures taken to insure his custody are most easily understood as implying the complete cessation of his influence on earth" (Mounce 362). And, obviously, the abyss where Satan is confined should not be confused with the earth in any way. The angel in 9:1, 2 had to open the shaft to the abyss before the demonic locust-creatures could come out and plague the earth.

"That he should deceive the nations no more" (v. 3) explains the purpose of the confinement. "Deceive" (Greek planao) means "lead astray, cause to wander; mislead, deceive, cause to be mistaken" (ALGNT 314). After his initial rebellion in Heaven, Satan turned deception into an art, perhaps the defining characteristic of his method. He is, above everything, a liar and the father of lies (Jn. 8:44). He uses deceit to lead souls astray and usurp God's glory to himself, beginning with the original sin of Adam and Eve (Gen. 3:1-15). In the Olivet Discourse, Jesus warned that rampant deceit would be a sign of the end-times (Mt. 24:5, 24; cf. 2 Th. 2:3-10; 2 Tim. 3:13, 14). Most people do not willingly choose to worship Satan but must be deceived into doing so (2 Cor. 11:14). Deception figures prominently in the Tribulation period, including Antichrist's betrayal of Israel (Dan. 9:27), the false prophet's successful effort to persuade the world to worship the Antichrist, and the three evil frog-spirits' effective recruitment of the kings of the earth for the Battle of Armageddon (13:13-15).

The world's population is not annihilated at the Battle of Armageddon; the "nations" survive to inhabit the millennial earth. Those who perish are the beast, and the kings of the earth, and their armies (19:19, 21). Perhaps millions of unbelieving people do not participate in the battle in Palestine and survive Armageddon. "The smashing of the nations therefore cannot mean disappearance from the face of the earth, but rather the breaking of that political power which, with the undergirding of idolatrous religion and materialist seduction, has organized them in resistance to the sovereignty of God" (Caird 252).

The last part of v. 3 ("till the thousand years should be fulfilled: and after that he must be loosed") looks ahead to the end of Satan's confinement that precipitates the final rebellion; see below on vv. 7-10. Satan will be freed to resume his typical, deceptive, unrestricted activity for a short period of time: "a desperate but unsuccessful attempt to regain power" (Thomas II:403). That he "must" (Greek dei, "it is necessary") indicates nothing other than God's sovereign control of events. "Apparently a thousand years of confinement does not alter Satan's plans, nor does a thousand years of freedom from the influence of wickedness change people's basic tendency to rebel against their creator" (Mounce 363).

One reason for the release, then, may be to show that the nature of unbelieving men and devils never changes. Further, the rebellion confirms the existence of true "free will" in the millennial period. Those living on the millennial earth have a legitimate option of choosing to serve the Lord or not. Presumably, there will be children born in the millennium who must decide for themselves whether they will follow Christ. After all, a choice with no other option is not really "a choice." There were two trees available to Adam and Eve in Eden, and it is plausible that the same dichotomy of choice exists during the millennium. "It may be that the Christian nations which have long acquiesced in the faith without conviction will need to be sifted before the end....A short exposure to the stress of Satan's *energeia planeis* [activity of deception] may suffice to separate the wheat from the chaff" (Swete 261).

2. The millennial reign of Christ (20:4-6)

**4 And I saw thrones, and they sat upon them, and judgment was given unto them: and I *saw* the souls of them that were beheaded for the witness of Jesus, and for the word of God, and which had not worshiped the beast, neither his image, neither had received *his* mark upon their foreheads, or in their hands; and they lived and reigned with Christ a thousand years.
5 But the rest of the dead lived not again until the thousand years were finished. This *is* the first resurrection.
6 Blessed and holy *is* he that hath part in the first resurrection: on such the second death hath no power, but they shall be priests of God and of Christ, and shall reign with him a thousand years.**

"And I saw thrones" (v. 4) introduces the next vision, revealing the new world government (Christian) that displaces the evil one defeated at Armageddon. The "thrones" are on the millennial earth rather than in Heaven (cf. Mt. 25:31), though idealists disagree. The binding of Satan (vv. 1-3) is necessary so that nothing may interfere with Christ's rule over the nations.

John first saw "thrones" and those who occupied them, number and identity not given (cf. "thrones" in 4:4). "Thrones" speak of royalty and ruling or perhaps judgment. Christ will be King but will delegate the functions of priesthood and government to faithful followers. These offices are awarded to believers in fulfillment of promises made to the original disciples (Mt. 19:28) and to overcoming believers (Rev. 2:26, 27; 3:21). It is also plausible that these are the 24 thrones of the permanent representatives of O.T. and N.T. saints (4:4). For that matter, all believers are promised the privilege of reigning with Christ (2:26; 3:21; cf. 1:6; 5:10; Dan. 7:9, 22, 27; 1 Cor. 6:2) and may be included, though the 24, as representative, seems more manageable. Or martyred saints only may be in view, but they receive their recognition later in v. 4. Least likely is the view that they are angels.

Most likely, then, the thrones are the 24 introduced in 4:4 and represent all the redeemed. In that case, "the souls of them that were beheaded for the witness of Jesus" are not the same as those on the thrones. (Many versions place a period or colon after "judgment was given to them" to make this distinction.) These Tribulation martyrs, then, are perhaps singled out for special mention because they suffered most for Christ

during that period. Those occupying the thrones include, representatively, all the redeemed, and the "souls...beheaded" identify the more exclusive group, Tribulation martyrs.

"Was given" is another example of *the divine passive*, pointing to God as source and authorization for their new office as judges, though the nature of their judging is not revealed (cf. Dan. 7:9-22). At any rate, the judgment or rule exercised *by* the saints must be distinguished from the judgment rendered favorably *on behalf of* the saints by the court of Heaven. And whatever this judging includes, it is rendered under the authority of Christ as millennial King. As Caird (252, 253) notes, this is not the last judgment or a determination of others' destinies. It is surely what Paul predicted in 1 Cor. 6:2: "Do you not know that the saints shall judge the world?"—a governing, political, judicial, and religious (note "priests" in v. 6) position of service to Christ the King.

The rest of v. 4, except for the final clause (below), describes this group of martyrs. They paid the ultimate price in faithfulness to Christ during the Tribulation. (The difficulty was laid out in 13:7-18.) "Beheaded" reflects a classic method of execution (cf. 6:9-11)—typically, under the Romans, by use of a double-bladed axe or sword. This group recalls "the souls of martyred saints" introduced in 6:9, 10 (see comments on "souls" there), but at that point their number was incomplete.

A number of things led to their martyrdom. First, they were beheaded because of their profession and witness for Christ (taking "Jesus" as "objective genitive" in Greek) and for preaching "the word of God." "Witness" (Greek *martus*) is actually the source of our

English "martyr," indicating the close association between a witness for Christ and a martyr: the one often meant the other. Further, they "had not worshiped the beast or his image" and thus avoided the compromise of idolatry. They had refused the beast's (Antichrist's) "mark" on the forehead or hand (13:16-18). They were therefore not able to buy or sell during the final half of the Tribulation.

As a result, along with the rest of believers, they are rewarded in a way that recalls the compensation sections of Christ's messages to the seven churches: they live and reign with Christ during the 1,000 years of His earthly rule. Since both groups of the redeemed are in view in v. 4 and have been resurrected by this point, "and they lived and reigned with Christ a thousand years" should not be limited to the martyrs only. (Again, many versions punctuate to make this clear.) The same promise of reigning with Christ is made to believers in general (2:26, 27) and Laodicea (3:21); compare 1:6; 5:10. All believers will be resurrected to participate in the millennial reign of Christ.

The verbs "lived" and "reigned" (Greek aorists) can be read in subtly different ways. Some regard them as focusing on the beginning of the actions (Aune III:1073): they "came to life" and "took their seats to reign." But the focus may as easily be on the whole period (constantive aorists): the 1,000 years tends to support this nuance. Regardless, both resurrection and reigning are special rewards for faithfulness to Christ.

The change of status requires the bodily resurrection designated in "This is the first resurrection" (v. 5). "Resurrection" (Greek *anastasis*) means "coming back to life after having died"

(ALGNT 52). The resurrection of all deceased saints occurs with the rapture of the church (1 Cor. 15:23, 51-57; 1 Th. 4:13-18; cf. Dan. 12:2). Consequently, the rapture must be included as part of "the first resurrection," translating living saints and transforming those already dead. But in order to include those martyred (or remaining alive) during the Tribulation, this "first resurrection" must also incorporate a second stage for them, at the end of that period.

There are numerous views about this "first resurrection." All premillennialists, though they have differing views about the rapture, place it *before* the millennial reign of Christ. Amillennialists and idealists often equate the "first resurrection" with *the new birth experience of believers* during the church age (a symbolic "millennial reign"), though some think of it as "the translation of soul from earth to Heaven" (Hendriksen 192) or Christ's resurrection (Hughes 214) or the "spiritual" reign of Tribulation martyrs with Christ between their martyrdom and the Second Coming (Poythress 182).

According to such views there is but one bodily resurrection, of saints and sinners, which occurs at the Second Coming. For premillennialists, however, it is clear that the "first" resurrection implies a "second": namely, at the end of the 1,000 years (v. 5) when all the *unbelieving* dead are resurrected to appear before God at the Great White Throne Judgment (vv. 11-15 below). Obviously, that would also include any who might have died during the millennium; it may also include O.T. saints—unless they were included in the rapture of the church (Dan. 12:2).

"Lived not again" (v. 5) therefore implies another bodily resurrection for those not in the "first" resurrection. (Most manuscripts do not include "again," but its sense is clearly justified.) Here again, "lived" (the same as in v. 4) can mean "came to life" or view the entire period as a whole. Premillennialists interpret both instances of "lived" (vv. 4, 5) consistently, as bodily resurrections. Idealists must interpret the first and second differently. This seems highly incongruous; there is not even a hint, in the text, that two different meanings are attached to the same word in the same context. Furthermore, "resurrection" (Greek *anastasis*), in 41 uses in the N.T., refers to physical resurrection in all but one or two instances (Lk. 2:34; Jn. 11:25). And since some of those in the first resurrection were "beheaded," it is all the more clear that resurrection from physical death is meant.

"Blessed and holy" are predicated of those who experience the first resurrection (v. 6), further confirming its exclusive nature. Not one unbeliever will experience the first resurrection, only those who have trusted Christ by faith and remained faithful to Him—a vast number after all! The first resurrection, then, applies only to deceased *believers*. The two terms also reflect the joy of the redeemed and their sanctified spiritual condition before God. "Blessed" (Greek *makarios*) means "characterized by transcendent happiness or religious joy...*happy*" (ALGNT 252)—the fifth of seven "beatitudes" in Revelation. "Holy" (Greek *hagios*) means "brought near or into God's presence...set apart for God's purpose," then "*dedicated, sacred... holy, pure, consecrated to God*" (ALGNT 32). The very fact that believers are resurrected indicates their holy

relationship with God. They have been made God's in Christ and are set apart to serve Him alone (see 14:1-5).

Furthermore, those in the first resurrection are no longer subject to "the second death," equated in Scripture with eternal confinement in Hell (v. 14; cf. 2:11; 21:8). To the contrary, believers have eternal life through faith in Christ. Again, the fact that there is a "second" death means that there is a "first" one: the spiritual death that passed from Adam to the entire human race as a result of original sin (Gen. 2:17; 3:3,19; Rom. 5:12-21; Eph. 2:5). The ultimate punishment for sin is death (Rom. 6:22, 23), separation from the life-giving Spirit of God, and the ultimate death is eternal death (21:8). Thus all men have experienced the "first" death, which may be remedied by faith in Christ. The second death—also fundamentally spiritual in nature—is permanent and cannot be remedied.

First resurrection participants will also be blessed to serve as "priests of God and of Christ" during the millennium (cf. Ex. 19:6; 1 Pet. 2:5, 9; Rev. 1:6; 5:10), apparently suggesting an active priestly mission on behalf of the nations of the earth during that period. This may relate to the potential for leading some who are born during the millennium to receive and worship Christ, and perhaps for assisting the nations of the earth in worshiping the Lord. There will be a large number of unbelievers on earth at that time; Satan recruits a huge army from their number at the end.

There is also a *ruling, judging, political* function: they "shall reign with him" (cf. Dan. 7:14, 22, 27; Mt. 5:5; 19:28; Lk. 22:30; Rev. 2:26, 27; 3:21; 4:4; 11:16) throughout the 1,000 years (cf. v. 4). In assisting and serving King Jesus,

His people rule over the millions of people dwelling upon the earth who survive Armageddon.

Excursus: The Nature of the Millennial Period

See Ps. 2:8, 9; 110:1-7; Is. 2:1-4; 9:6, 7; 11:6-10; 35:1-10; 65:17-25; Ezek. 37:21-28; 39:21, 25, 27; Dan. 7:14, 18, 22, 27; Hos. 3:5; Am. 9:13-15; Zech. 9:10; 14:9; Mic. 4:1-4; Mt. 5:5; 19:28; 25:31-46; Rom. 11:1-36; 1 Cor. 6:2, 3; 15:23-28; Rev. 2:26; 3:21; 12:5; 19:15; 20:1-10.

"This interim kingdom is transitional in that it is depicted as a synthesis or compromise between this age and the age to come, combining characteristics of both worlds or ages" (Aune III:1105).

The passages listed above, with others, predict a literal, eschatological time when God's kingdom is established on earth. It is true that the reference to "1,000 years" does not come into view until Rev. 20. But the concept of a messianic, Davidic reign of righteousness over the nations of the entire earth is frequent. This includes the role of a restored Israel and the existence of blissful conditions, different from the present order and from eternity proper. (See Clowney 214-218 for a concise survey of this O.T. hope.) Those who believe that this millennial period is the present church age (that the church has displaced Israel) or refers to eternity proper (as in Rev. 21, 22) discount unnecessarily the predictions and covenant promises that God has included in the Scriptural record.

My view is that God made eschatological promises to Israel, specifically, and that He will keep them as surely as His promises to the church. He can fulfill both sets, and that without diluting the gospel or compromising the true oneness of saved Jews and Gentiles as members of the same body throughout remaining time and eternity. Classic dispensationalism's dualism of two eternally distinct groups of people and programs, coexisting throughout eternity, appears too radical. It seems far more Scriptural that there is but one final family of God. From Adam to Abraham to Christ, it has been God's eternal design to call forth a people and to tabernacle among them forever. This unity is ultimately brought about through the new covenant of Christ's blood and will be fulfilled in the eternal age in Heaven. Jews and Gentiles are now and forever saved in the same way.

The earthly, millennial reign of Christ should not be viewed as retrogression to an antiquated Levitical system or as a pointless interlude between ages. It is about unfinished business from God's point of view: the fulfillment of His original design for Israel and the nations of the present earth and the vindication of the church on earth. Jesus said that He had not come to destroy the law or the prophets but to fulfill them (Mt. 5:17, 18). He also instructed us to pray "Thy kingdom come. Thy will be done in earth, as it is in heaven" (Mt. 6:10).

The O.T. portrait of Christ as a suffering servant who bears the sins of the world (Is. 53) exists simultaneously with the portrait of Him as the Warrior-Messiah who will conquer and rule the nations of the earth (Ps. 2; cf. Ps. 110). He will bear the government on His shoulders and rule as a Davidic king forever (Is. 9:6, 7); "forever" points to millennial improvements carried over into the eternal age. Daniel predicted a worldwide kingdom that would conquer all pagan kingdoms and allow all the peoples, nations, and people of every language to serve Him, with the saints sharing therein (Dan. 2:44; 7:13, 14, 18).

This motif carries over into the N.T. Jesus predicted that He and His disciples would sit upon thrones to rule Israel (Mt. 19:28; 25:31-34). Paul alluded to the reign of Christ (1 Cor. 15:23-28). This theme is especially prominent in Revelation (2:26; 3:21; 12:5; 19:15; 20:1-10) since it deals with the fulfillment of such predictions. There is no sense in which Christ may be seen as presently ruling over the nations of the earth in the ways indicated in such prophetic Scriptures. His messianic rule is universal, exclusive, and uncontested.

Other defining characteristics of the millennial period which distinguish it from the present world order, or the eternal state, are: (1) the institution of the Messiah (Christ) as King over Israel (Ezek. 34:23-31; 37:21-28; 39:21, 25, 27; Hos. 3:5; Zech. 12:10); (2) the restoration of the nation of Israel and exaltation of Jerusalem as the world's chief city and center of worship (Is. 2:2,3; 56:6-8; Ezek. 40-48; Am. 9:8-15; Mic. 4:1; Zech. 14:10; Acts 15:15-18); (3) worldwide knowledge and worship of the Lord (Is. 11:9b,10; Mic. 4:2; Zech. 14:16-21); (4) worldwide peace that leads to the destruction of weapons of war (Is. 2:4; 11:9a; 65:25b; Mic. 4:3, 4; Zech. 9:10; 14:11); (5) counter-intuitive changes in nature (Is. 11:6-8; 35:1-9; 65:20, 25; Am. 9:13); (6) greatly lengthened life spans (Is. 65:20); (7) unmolested joy for God's people (35:10; 65:18); and (8) interaction in society between those with resurrected bodies (saints) and those with natural bodies

(unbelievers and believers, including children born during the time). By contrast, some characteristics of the millennial period illustrate continuity with the present order, including (1) building houses and planting gardens (Is. 65:21, 22; Am. 9:14; and (2) the birth of children (Is. 65:23).

The present world system will not voluntarily submit to the rule of Christ. Nor will the church conquer or reconstruct society (as in postmillennialism). Christ must use catastrophic force to wrench control of the earth from Satan and the pagan nations that control it, as revealed in the seal, trumpet, and bowl judgments culminating in the Battle of Armageddon. Satan is then apprehended and bound in the abyss for the duration of Christ's millennial rule.

Life on the millennial earth will therefore be free from satanic deception. It will be characterized by vastly different and improved conditions, though not absolutely perfect ones: death still occurs, as well as unbelief among those who join Satan's last revolt. Christ's reign is thus a real one: the possibility of inward resistance remains. But sincere worship of Christ will be the norm. The meek will have inherited the earth (Ps. 37:11; Mt. 5:5), leaving the Lord and His saints in control of the government.

The curse of nature is mitigated: wild animals and children lie down together without danger. Life spans are extended. Deserts blossom and the earth's ability to yield increases dramatically. The glory of Israel and Jerusalem is restored as the peoples of the earth make pilgrimages to her in order to worship the Lord (and are punished if they do not). The prediction that *every* knee will bow and *every* tongue confess that Jesus is Lord applies especially well (Phil. 2:9-11). It is not hard to envision such changes when Jesus Himself presides over nature and humanity.

Resurrected believers (and perhaps O.T. saints) will live in resurrection bodies. Those who survive Armageddon and the righteous remnant of Israel will live to repopulate the earth. Both they and children born to them will have bodies that have not been resurrected and do not exhibit resurrection qualities. (Jesus was able to continue interacting with the disciples after His resurrection: Mt. 28:9, 10, 17; Lk. 24:15, 39, 42, 43; Jn. 20:26-28.)

Physical existence for unbelievers will be similar to life at present except for enhanced life spans and things necessary to that. On the spiritual side, life will be minus Satan's troubling presence, but those in the natural body will have a sinful nature, making death and unbelief still possible. Apparently children born to unbelieving parents or Israelites will have the privilege of choosing or rejecting Christ, and significant numbers may turn to Him and practice sincere worship. True believers in natural bodies will no doubt be translated into glorified bodies at some point, perhaps toward the end of the period. Those who survived Armageddon will probably not have another opportunity to trust Christ, providing the pool of humanity from which Satan recruits his final rebellion at the end of the period.

Many things about the period are mysterious and must remain enigmatic to us. Indeed, as with most of the Bible, we take this teaching by faith, not rejecting it because it is hard to understand. All believers should anticipate the millennial reign of Christ as a time of vindication, reward, learning, worship, joy, and further service for Christ.

3. The final rebellion (20:7-10)

7 And when the thousand years are expired, Satan shall be loosed out of his prison,
8 And shall go out to deceive the nations which are in the four quarters of the earth, Gog and Magog, to gather them together to battle: the number of whom *is* as the sand of the sea.
9 And they went up on the breadth of the earth, and compassed the camp of the saints about, and the beloved city: and fire came down from God out of heaven, and devoured them.
10 And the devil that deceived them was cast into the lake of fire and brimstone, where the beast and the false prophet *are*, and shall be tormented day and night for ever and ever.

The millennial period, being transitional, eventually "expires" (v. 7; cf. vv. 3, 5). This verb (Greek *teleo*) means *"bring to an end, conclude, complete...be over, end, be finished"* (ALGNT 377). The period itself should not be confused with the final state that follows the Great White Throne Judgment.

The bottomless pit (abyss) in which Satan was bound is now depicted as his "prison" (cf. v. 3), the same word translated as the "hold" of demonic spirits in 18:2. Satan's confinement during the millennium was imprisonment, his freedom and activities (including deceiving the nations) totally restricted and his presence removed from the earth. At the end of the period, however, he "shall be loosed": another *divine passive* indicating God's sovereign activity. When the blissful millennial conditions predicted in the O.T. are considered (see above), conditions on the earth return nearly to the original Edenic conditions. In this sense, Christ is finally able to fulfill God's original design forfeited by the first Adam. However, as noted, there will be many unbelievers on earth during the millennium, and when Satan is released he recruits from them for his final rebellion.

After being freed, Satan will resume activities in a final attempt "to deceive the nations" (v. 8). "The four quarters of the earth" indicates the worldwide scope of this effort, as does "the breadth of the earth" (v. 9). Though short-lived, the rebellion is significant: Satan recruits an army of unbelievers for one final assault against Christ's millennial headquarters in Jerusalem.

As names, "Gog and Magog" are probably either specific nations that figure prominently in this episode or symbolically designate all the ungodly in the world at this time. A final end-time battle prophesied in Ezek. 38, 39 also refers to "Gog and Magog" (Ezek. 38:2, 3), but it also includes representative nations from around the world (Ezek. 38:5, 6). The battle portrayed here in 20:8, then, may not be the one portrayed in Ezekiel. Both are significant wars but there are differences of degree and in certain particulars (cf. Walvoord 303; Ryrie, *Revelation* 133).

The commonness of "Gog and Magog" to Ezek. 38 and Rev. 20 does not necessarily identify them as the same, since the terms were widely used as symbols. "In the OT and early Jewish tradition, Gog and Magog are understood in a bewildering variety of ways" (Aune III:1094), referring, for example, to individuals or nations (Gen. 10:2; 1 Chr. 1:5-7). Jewish literature, at times, used the terms for Ethiopia, the Scythians, Edom, Assyria, and the Gentiles in general (Beale 1024,1025) or "the rebellious nations of Ps. 2" (Caird 256, citing the Talmud). Here, then, Gog and Magog may be symbolic, indicating all the rebellious nations and people at the end of the millennium. As a figure, then, "Gog and Magog" may roughly parallel the cryptic use of "Babylon," earlier, for a worldwide anti-Christian kingdom or spirit rather than the one ancient city. "The most that one can discern from these names is that they are emblems for the enemies of Messiah during the end-times" (Thomas II:423).

Why does God allow another rebellion? For one thing, it validates the righteousness and strength of Christ's millennial reign to the nations of the world (see Ezek. 36:21-24; 38:23; 39:7, 21, 22) by demonstrating His commitment to suppress all unrighteousness or rebellion against God. In this God also demonstrates His ability to keep Satan forever in prison and preserve millennial-type conditions in Heaven forever. For another, it validates the continuing existence of free will during the millennium. True worship of Christ is verified when there is a real alternative to do otherwise. Finally, it confirms the sinful nature and recalcitrance of the unregenerate even in a near perfect environment, at the same time revealing that Satan is eternally incorrigible.

The differences between the Battle of Armageddon and this battle after the millennium are significant. Armageddon is directly associated with the Second

Coming; this battle comes at the end of the 1,000 years. Following Armageddon, Satan was not cast into Hell permanently, as were Antichrist and the false prophet (19:20); after this battle he joins them in the Lake of Fire (v. 10). Those at Armageddon were destroyed primarily with the sword from Christ's mouth, their bodies consumed by scavengers; these are "devoured" by fire, with nothing left for scavengers.

The names "Rosh, Meshech, and Tubal," often linked to Gog and Magog (Ez. 38:2, 3) are somewhat enigmatic, and investigation goes beyond the scope of this commentary. Beale (1025) has a helpful discussion supporting one conclusion that seems important: namely, that the three names are *not* related to Russia, Moscow, or Tobolsk and cannot be identified with any specific, twentieth-century country. I would add that it is certainly possible that the primary fulfillment of Ez. 38, 39 is the Battle of Armageddon, and that the battle here at the end of the millennium is a secondary fulfillment that reflects similar characteristics.

Revelation provides little detail about the final rebellion and battle mentioned here. It is clear that Satan's confinement did nothing to change his character or goals, and that a significant part of the unbelieving population of the earth remained gullible. It is also clear that the sovereign God manages everything according to His greater purposes. God knew what Satan would do and released him anyway.

He will succeed in deceiving people from nations all over the earth (apparently identified as "Gog and Magog")—people who have conformed externally to Christ's strong rule but inwardly remained recalcitrant, gullible to Satan's

final deception. "To gather them together for battle" is his purpose: a huge army assembles, as numerous as "the sand of the sea" (cf. Josh. 11:4; Jg. 7:12; 1 Sam. 13:5; cf. Gen. 22:17; 2 Sam. 17:11). This success is amazing, considering the absolute rule of Christ and blessed earthly conditions during the millennial period. But those born during the millennium continue to exercise freedom of the will. Even during the millennium, the choice to worship and serve Christ is voluntary, a fact that the final rebellion authenticates. As in Eden (Gen. 2:9, 15-17), the righteous environment of the millennium does not preclude the responsibility to choose Christ. In the end, many will listen to Satan instead.

The army gathers in Palestine to "go up" and "compass" (surround) the city of Jerusalem and the saints' camp (v. 9). This "reflects the central strategy of ancient warfare, to surround a city and besiege it until it surrendered" (Aune III:1097). "The breadth of the earth" is interpreted variously as the distance from which the armies traveled, or "from everywhere," or even "the backbone of central Palestine" on the way to Jerusalem (Thomas II:425). "The beloved city" reaffirms the identification of Jerusalem as the center of Christ's millennial rule. The "New Jerusalem" will not descend until 21:1, 2 (see Jer. 3:17; Is. 24:23; Ezek. 43:7; Zech. 14:9-21).

The N.T. sense of "camp" (Greek *parembole*) carries a military denotation. It could denote a "distribution of troops" such as in battle formation or "castle or barracks" (ALGNT 300). If "the camp of the saints" *equals* the city of Jerusalem, "and" means "even" again. But it may as likely mean a military encampment created in anticipation of an attack (Aune III:1097); the march of a huge army toward Jerusalem could hardly be concealed. At the same time, a Warrior-Messiah would hardly need such a camp. But the distinction seems inconsequential: both camp and city are made up of the Lord's people and surrounded.

Idealistic interpreters view "the camp of the saints and the beloved city" as symbolic of "the church throughout the earth" (Beale 1022) and equate this battle with the Battle of Armageddon in 16:12-16 and 19:19 (Beale 1023). "These verses describe the last battle in which the dragon desperately attempts once and for all to destroy the church and her mission of witness to Christ" (Brighton 571)—equating this battle with the tribulation of Mk. 13:19 (Mt. 24:22).

The attack of the millennial rebels is interrupted decisively: "fire came down from God out of heaven"—in some ways recalling the destruction of Sennacherib's army (Is. 37:36). In this case, those who have marched against Jerusalem are "devoured" (Greek *katesthio*), meaning *"eat up, consume, devour"* (ALGNT 224). Here it suggests virtual annihilation by fire; the rebels are consumed bodily (cf. Ezek. 38:22; 39:6).

Satan—"the devil that deceived them" (v. 10)—disturbs the righteous, millennial environment in one final act of deception and rebellion. This time, his judgment is total and eternal: he is "cast into the lake of fire and brimstone"—the scriptural equivalent of Hell—where he will remain in torment forever. He thus joins "the beast and the false prophet" who had been cast there after Armageddon (19:20). The entire evil confederacy comprised by the satanic pseudo-trinity, all fallen angels or demons, and all who have followed them (unbelievers) are now "tormented day and night for ever and ever" (cf. vv. 14, 15; 21:8; Mk. 9:43, 44, 46, 48). "Day and night" emphasizes the constant nature of the torment; "for ever and ever" is obviously broader, indicating that the torment is permanent or eternal. Together, these indicate that there will be no intermittent period of relief in the suffering forever. There is no basis, here, for the doctrine of annihilation of the wicked.

F. The Great White Throne (20:11-15)

11 And I saw a great white throne, and him that sat on it, from whose face the earth and the heaven fled away; and there was found no place for them.
12 And I saw the dead, small and great, stand before God; and the books were opened: and another book was opened, which is *the book* of life: and the dead were judged out of those things which were written in the books, according to their works.
13 And the sea gave up the dead which were in it; and death and hell delivered up the dead which were in them: and they were judged every man according to their works.
14 And death and hell were cast into the lake of fire. This is the second death.
15 And whosoever was not found written in the book of life was cast into the lake of fire.

Again, "and I saw" (v. 11) marks movement to a new subject: "With this vision we close forever the chapter on sin and stand ready to enter the eternal state of glory" (Mounce 374). The vision takes us back to the throne room of God but is distinct from the other throne-room visions in several ways. Literally, we read "a throne, a white one, a great one," emphasizing the throne's awesome appearance and size. Again, white represents God's holiness, purity, righteousness, victory, or justice. The judgments about to be rendered are authoritative, true, and righteous (see 15:3; 16:7; 19:2). The revelations about the end of time finish where they began, at the throne of God.

The focus narrows to the theme of judgment. "Him that sat on it" is God the Father and His "face" refers to His immediate presence (Lenski 602); cf. "before God" in v. 12. As on several occasions (4:1, 3, 9; 5:1, 7, 13; 6:16; 7:10, 15; 19:4; 21:5), this is apparently a way of identifying God without using His name, perhaps because of John's high reverence for the name of God (as was common in Jewish practice).

The Lamb of God is not the judge, here. Though God has given the right of judgment to the Son (Jn. 5:22-29; Mt. 25:31-46; Rom. 14:10; 2 Cor. 5:10), the millennial rule of Christ on earth has been completed at this point. The throne of Christ in Mt. 25:31, apparently for His millennial reign, is *on the earth* and is *not* this "great white throne," which follows the millennial reign *after the dissolution of the present universe* so that there is nothing of the present earth left for Christ to rule (Walvoord 305). Christ has finished His judging and ruling; His enemies have been put down forever. This therefore falls within the transfer of authority, predicted by Paul, when Jesus gives control of the Kingdom back to God the Father (1 Cor. 15:24-26, 28). Even so, the Father and the Son are one; both occupy the throne throughout eternity (22:3), thus preserving Christ's eternal rule.

The Great White Throne Judgment, then, is but the final one in a series of eschatological judgments. While the idea of one general resurrection and judgment has some appeal, it oversimplifies the Biblical picture. The judgment of believers at "the judgment seat of Christ" (2 Cor. 5:10), for example, seems clearly distinct (in purpose and chronology) from the Great White Throne Judgment. "It is difficult to believe that those who have lived and reigned with Christ for 1,000 years should be regarded as on trial at the close" (Glasson 529).

That "the earth and the heaven fled away" indicates the unprecedented nature of the "great white throne" vision when compared with other judgment scenes located either in Heaven or on earth. "Fled" (Greek aorist of *pheugo*) may suggest "a sudden and violent termination of the physical universe" (Thomas II:429, citing Kiddle). The similar dissolution language of 2 Pet. 3:10-12 suggests that Peter was describing the same event. Fire, supernaturally intensified, is instrumental in either: (1) the annihilation of every material and temporal thing that presently exists (time, space, and matter) or (2) the refurbishment and renovation of the cosmos to begin anew with infinitely purified remains. Either would be in preparation for the new Heaven and earth to come (Ps. 102:26; Is. 51:6; Mt. 5:18; 1 Jn. 2:17). Irenaeus thought that the "substance" of the earth will not be annihilated, but that its "external form" will be radically changed. But it is equally plausible that God may create a new universe entirely (cf. Walvoord 305; Heb. 1:10-12; Rev. 6:14).

The judgment of vv. 11-15, then, is not only *final* for unbelieving humanity, it is also the final purge of sin's curse from the created universe (cf. Rom. 8:19-22). The location of this judgment scene is unique. "There was found no place for them" indicates that the present earth and heavens no longer exist, and the new ones have not yet come into place (21:1). Then it appears that God has specially created a unique courtroom for this one-time event. Regardless, the focus is totally on God upon His throne and on what is happening.

"And I saw" (v. 12) shifts the focus to another object within the larger vision: the gathering of a vast number of *unholy* persons standing before God—unusual since God does not normally allow the unholy in His presence. These are "the dead, small and great" (cf. 11:18; 13:16; 19:5,18), their death being physical rather than spiritual—although they are dead in that sense as well. As previously, "small" and "great" includes the extremes and *everyone* in between, emphasizing that all the unredeemed, including those who died during the millennium, are present. (Although not specifically mentioned, any millennium unbelievers who remained alive at the end would also be included. One may also assume that millennium converts—from children born in the period—will be translated at some point during the transition into eternity proper.)

Idealist and amillennial interpreters envision one general resurrection and judgment for everyone at the time of the Great White Throne Judgment. They cite the use of the Lamb's Book of Life here (v. 15), to support their view that believers are included with unbelievers in this group standing before God, as well as Dan. 12:1-3 and Mt. 25:31-46. But "the Book of Life comes into the discussion only to show that the names of these dead are not written there" (Thomas II:431). "As in 13:8 and 17:8 the 'book of life' is introduced to bring attention to those excluded from it" (Beale 1033). For argument's sake, it would not make any difference in the outcome if believers were present in this judgment scene. They would pass safely because their names are in fact written in the Lamb's Book of Life. But (to borrow a word from Aune) it is "striking" that the elements associated with the judgment of believers at *the judgment seat of Christ*, as well as the Lamb Himself, are conspicuously absent from this scene (see 2 Cor. 5:10,11).

That these dead are "standing" before the throne implies their *resurrection*— the one predicted in v. 5 for "the rest of the dead" after the millennium. Since believers have been raptured, resurrected, or translated by this time, this resurrection (joining bodies and souls) must refer to all *unbelieving* humanity. Every unbeliever who has ever lived is raised to be present at what may now be legitimately designated as *the* final judgment (Dan. 7:9,10).

Though the redeemed may witness this they are certainly not objects of this judgment, which relates exclusively to the works of unbelievers and confirms their eternal condemnation. Exemption from the Great White Throne Judgment is by whether one's name has been recorded in the Lamb's Book of Life, consulted to confirm that the names of the unbelieving are not there.

God uses two different books as standards in the judgment of unbelieving humanity. There is no way to tell whether these "books" are in scroll or book form, but the difference is not important; what matters is the content. The reference to plural "books" is understandable in view of the vast amount of information they contain: enough to record the behavior (works) of each unbelieving person in human history, both their relatively good acts and their evil ones. "God keeps his accurate record of each individual's life and deeds....The 'books' are a visual representation of God's indelible and unerring mind and remembrance" (Brighton 583; cf. Mal. 3:16). "The sentence of the Judge is not arbitrary; it rests upon written evidence" (Swete 272).

The other book is "the book of life" (cf. 3:5; Phil. 4:3), apparently the same as "the Lamb's book of life" in 21:27 and not necessarily the same as the "book" of God in the O.T. (Ex. 32:32, 33; Ps. 56:8; 139:16). Other N.T. references to such a book are largely synonymous with this Lamb's Book of Life, mentioned six times in Revelation (3:5; 13:8; 17:8; 20:12, 15; 21:27). This book has the names of those who have placed (and kept) saving faith in Christ. The works of believers are not up for review at this particular judgment, having already been dealt with at "the judgment seat of Christ." The Book is used here simply to verify that the names of unbelievers are absent, so that the basis of their judgment defaults to being "according to their works" recorded in "the books." (It seems better to view all these "books" as literal records rather than merely "metaphorical for God's unfailing memory" [Beale 1037].)

Even then, the final standard for determining the eternal destiny of persons is whether their names are in "the book of life" (v. 15). But just as believers' works are considered at the judgment seat of Christ, so will unbelievers' works be considered at the Great White Throne Judgment. For that matter, their works recorded in the books will match the absence of their names from the Book of Life. An unbeliever's "works" are also evidence of unbelief (cf. Mt. 7:16-23; Jn. 15:2; Acts 26:20; Eph. 2:10; 2 Pet. 1:5-11; Jas. 2:14-26). Mounce (376) is therefore correct to point out that the books recording unbelievers' works complement the Lamb's Book of Life.

The universality of this judgment is further indicated in the breakdown (v. 13) into "the sea," "death," and "hell," amplifying v. 12. The judgment extends to those who lost their lives in the oceans of the earth, or who were "buried at sea": even the dead with no visible remains are raised bodily. "Death and hell" in essence repeat "the dead, small and great." "Every man" adds emphasis: there are no exceptions. "According to their works" repeats from v. 12, again probably for emphasis; see the comments above.

There are two kinds of death, of course: physical and spiritual. The phrase "death and hell," then, may imply something like "the fact and its consequences" (Swete 273). "Hell" (Greek *hades*), in the time of the N.T., apparently referred to the place of all the dead in the underworld or to an intermediate holding place for the dead. Thus many scholars have reservations about translating the word as Hell (see Walvoord 307). But it seems clear that Jesus Himself sometimes used the word in a way that corresponds to *Hell* as we use the word (Lk. 16:23; Mt. 16:18; cf. Mt. 11:23; Lk. 10:15). There is no reason for taking the word any differently here.

If it seems awkward that "hell" (*Hades*) is cast into "hell" (the lake of fire), as in v. 14, we need only view the first as metonymy, with "the container substituted for the contained." In other words, it is the *inhabitants* of *Hades* that are meant. Furthermore, this may be a symbolic way of affirming that death and Hell will never threaten the redeemed again, while by contrast unbelievers experience death—as a state of eternal spiritual punishment or separation from God—throughout eternity. The suffering of Hell then is physical, spiritual, emotional, and eternal.

"Whosoever" (v. 15) is often used positively of the opportunity for salvation (22:17); here, however, it is negative, referring to those who have ultimately rejected Christ, further implying that there are no exceptions among unbelievers. "When taken seriously, this final note evaporates all theories of universalism" (A. Johnson 194). "Not found written in of the book of life" implies a search, and the absence of one's name constitutes the most serious indictment brought against anyone who stands at the Great White Throne Judgment. Without exception those whose names are not found will be "cast into the lake of fire." *The lake of fire* (19:20; 20:10, 14, 15; 21:8) is unique to Revelation in the N.T. but is used synonymously with the terms "second death" and "hell" and is another way of referring to Hell.

We should note, in passing, that the absence of a person's name from the Book of Life may occur in either of two ways: having never been written there or having been erased after being there (3:5). We should also note that this Great White Throne Judgment makes clear that people are not cast into Hell *only* for having rejected Christ but *also* for their wicked works. Furthermore, we must note that this is the *final* judgment, with its verdict standing for eternity; beyond this there is no hope of reexamination.

A list of the verbal actions in vv. 11-15 is impressive and implies that God is ultimately behind each one: (1) the dissolution of the old universe, v. 11; (2) the resurrection of all the unbelieving dead, v. 12; (3) the opening of the books, v. 12; (4) the judgment rendered, vv. 12, 13; (5) the gathering of the dead from the sea, death, and hell, v. 13; (6) the casting of death and hell into the lake of fire, v. 14; and (7) the casting of all the unbelieving dead into the lake of fire, v. 15. God's sovereign control over all things is thereby reaffirmed in the dissolution of creation and consignment of unbelievers to eternal Hell.

Summary
(20:1-15)

Another angel descended from Heaven with a key to the bottomless pit and a great chain in his hand (v. 1), indicating the angel's heavenly origin and authority and God's sovereign control over Satan and over access to the abyss. The angel apprehended Satan, further identified by various aliases: "the dragon, that old serpent which is the Devil, and Satan" (v. 2; cf. 12:9). With the chain he bound Satan for a literal, one-thousand-year period—the millennial reign of Christ on earth—thus totally restricting his activities on the earth for the period.

Then the angel cast him or confined him in the bottomless pit (the abyss), a holding place for demons and fallen angels (v. 3). The terms indicate total restriction from deceiving the nations: "cast," "shut up," and "sealed"—though he will be loosed at the end of the millennium for a short period.

A new vision introduced those who would reign with Christ during the millennium (v. 4): these, representing all the redeemed (not just martyrs), were sitting on thrones for the purpose of judging and included those who had been beheaded for Christ. The latter had been martyred for two reasons: witnessing for Christ and preaching the Word of God. They also refused to receive the mark of the beast and worship his image. They are resurrected to live and reign with Christ during His millennial reign over the earth.

The unbelieving dead are resurrected at the *end* of that millennial reign (v. 5). The "first resurrection" looks back to v. 4: a resurrection of believers only, a physical or bodily resurrection occurring at the "rapture" of the church (whenever that occurs).

The first resurrection participants are "blessed and holy" (v. 6) and not subject to the "second death," another way of describing eternal confinement in Hell. They are compensated with the privilege of serving Christ as priests and reigning with Him for the duration of the millennium.

At the end of the millennium God releases Satan from his confining imprisonment in the bottomless pit (v. 7). Freed, Satan disturbs the prevailing righteous conditions by resuming his activity of deceiving the nations. This serves to legitimate the rule and worship of Christ by offering subjects a real option, there-

by confirming the unchanging sinful nature of Satan and of the human heart—even against the backdrop of a nearly perfect environment. It ushers in the end of the present cosmic order (cf. 2 Pet. 3:10-13).

Satan's final deception succeeds in recruiting a significant number of rebels against Christ's millennial reign (v. 8). These are recruited from the entire earth, indicated by the designations "four quarters" and the title "Gog and Magog"—terms symbolizing all those nations that rebel against God in the end-times. This results in the gathering of a huge army of rebels, "the number of whom is as the sand of the sea."

Once mobilized, the nefarious army marches toward Jerusalem, by then known as "the camp of the saints" and surrounds it (v. 9). At this point, in a way reminiscent of God's defense of Jerusalem in Hezekiah's day, God intervenes miraculously to deliver the city and His people, sending fire down from Heaven to "devour" the enemy.

As a result, God casts Satan permanently into Hell, described as "the lake of fire and brimstone" (v. 10), to share the same fate as the beast and the false prophet who were cast there after the Battle of Armageddon. The counterfeit trinity is thereby to be tormented constantly and eternally for all that they have done in deceiving the world, corrupting their victims, and usurping the worship of God to themselves.

John's attention is drawn to a "great white throne" (vv. 11-15), seeing first God the Father who sits there (v. 11). Equally significant the old universe passes away into oblivion before his very eyes. A courtroom setting is convened for the purpose of judging the works of mankind and determining the ultimate destinies of every human being from Adam to the last one born during the millennium.

Those who had been resurrected appear before the throne: "small and great" includes "everyone" (v. 12). Two kinds of books are opened and serve as the basis of God's just judgments, determining each person's ultimate reward. The books of "works" are examined in order to judge all the unbelieving dead.

There are no exceptions as to who will appear before God at this time: even those who were buried at sea or who had already been in Hell were called forth (v. 13). All are judged on the basis of their works or behavior in life.

The impersonal enemies of mankind that spoiled the old created universe are also judged, eliminated from any influence in the new heavens and earth (v. 14). These are "death" and "hell" (*Hades*)," confined to the boundaries of eternal Hell, which is identified as "the lake of fire" and "the second death."

God uses "the book of life" (elsewhere "the Lamb's book of life," as in 21:27), to determine every individual's eternal destiny. The names of all who have experienced salvation in Christ and remained faithful to Him (3:5) are found there. Every person whose name is *not found* there is thereby ultimately cast into the lake of fire (v. 15). The merits of the righteous works of Jesus Christ have been imputed to all believers whereas those who have ultimately rejected Christ are judged on the basis of their own efforts, invariably proven to be sinful and to fall short of God's standard of acceptance in Heaven.

Application: Teaching and Preaching the Passage

We must recapture a sense of soberness in regard to the themes and events predicted in Revelation. The messages to the churches in chapters 2 and 3 challenge believers to be faithful to Christ in the present age, in part because present faithfulness impacts our future destiny and reward. Eschatology is a great sanctifying, motivating message (2 Pet. 3:11). Teachers and preachers who would motivate others spiritually and help them prepare for what is ahead should study and utilize it in their teaching, preaching, and witnessing. Glasson (537) quotes Johanan ben Zaccai, who lived in the late first century A.D. and "wept bitterly on his death-bed," to say:

They are about to bring me before the King of kings, the Lord, the Holy and Blessed one, who liveth and abideth forever. And if he is wroth with me, his wrath is eternal; and if he bind, his bonds are eternal... and beside all this there are before me two paths, one to Paradise and the other to Gehenna, and I know not in which they are about to lead me. How can I do ought but weep?

In reality, the unbelieving world is not prepared for the Second Coming of Christ or for judgment at the Great White Throne. For that matter, many professing believers may also be woefully unprepared for end-time events and judgments, in particular the Judgment Seat of Christ (2 Cor. 5:9-11). The unpredictable, castastrophic, and final nature of these things should sober us and cause us to be greatly concerned for

others. The fact that they may be imminent magnifies the importance of recognizing the signs of the times around us
and of doing all we can while there is a
window of opportunity. Jesus said, "I
must work the works of him that sent
me while it is day: the night cometh,
when no man can work" (Jn. 9:4). We
need not panic but neither should we
bury our heads in the sand. The events
of the Great Tribulation may not begin
for another thousand years, or the
machinery may already be in place.
Regardless, we must determine to be
faithful every day for "as death finds us
eternity will leave us."

Every believer should study Revelation
personally and determine what he or
she believes about it. Our epistemology
(knowing the basis of our beliefs) must
be founded not simply on what some
tradition has taught us but be subject to
the Word itself. Consequently, one
should not fear examining what one
believes about eschatology in the light of
Scripture.

Suggested Outlines. The Binding of
Satan, 20:1-3: (1) Authorization, v. 1;
(2) Apprehension, v. 2; (3) Restricted
Activity, v. 3.

The Great White Throne Judgment,
20:11-15: (1) The seating of the Judge,
v. 11; (2) The arraignment of the defen-
dants, v. 12; (3) The presentation of the
case or evidence, vv. 12, 13; (4) The
verdict and sentence, vv. 14, 15.

VII. THE ETERNAL AGE (21:1—22:5)

The rest of Revelation describes the
final disposition of things as they will
exist in eternity. The millennial reign of
Christ on earth has ended, Satan has
been finally defeated and cast into Hell,
the old creation has passed away, the
Great White Throne Judgment has taken
place, and every unbeliever and vestige
of sin and death have been cast into
Hell. The newly created Heaven and
earth are similar to the former ones, in
some ways, but there are significant
material and spiritual differences. The
stage is thus set for the eternal state,
with Heaven and its glories, new heavens and earth, and eternal union of God
with His people who forever worship,
fellowship with, and serve Him.

This new vision, then, not only serves
to inform us about the glorious future
that awaits all of God's family but also as
a present comfort, as a motivation to
continue serving faithfully, and even as
an evangelistic tool used to invite others
to come to Christ (21:6).

A. The New Heaven and Earth (21:1-8)

**1 And I saw a new heaven and a
new earth: for the first heaven and
the first earth were passed away;
and there was no more sea.
2 And I John saw the holy city,
new Jerusalem, coming down from
God out of heaven, prepared as a
bride adorned for her husband.
3 And I heard a great voice out of
heaven saying, Behold, the tabernacle of God is with men, and he
will dwell with them, and they shall
be his people, and God himself
shall be with them, and be their
God.
4 And God shall wipe away all
tears from their eyes; and there
shall be no more death, neither
sorrow, nor crying, neither shall
there by any more pain: for the
former things are passed away.**

5 And he that sat upon the throne said, Behold, I make all things new. And he said unto me, Write: for these words are true and faithful.

6 And he said unto me, It is done. I am Alpha and Omega, the beginning and the end. I will give unto him that is athirst of the fountain of the water of life freely.

7 He that overcometh shall inherit all things; and I will be his God, and he shall be my son.

8 But the fearful, and unbelieving, and the abominable, and murderers, and whoremongers, and sorcerers, and idolaters, and all liars, shall have their part in the lake which burneth with fire and brimstone: which is the second death.

"And I saw a new heaven and a new earth" (v. 1), as often, introduces a new vision and with it a significant historical change. This is the end and beginning again to which all redemptive history has been inexorably striving since the day humanity died in the Garden. All that has been designed in the eternal counsels of God before the world was created and prophesied subsequently in Scripture is finally realized. The "not yet" of eschatology is fulfilled. Faith becomes sight. God will shepherd and dwell in unmediated, loving fellowship with His people forever. "It is remarkable that John's picture of the final age to come focuses not on a platonic ideal heaven or distant paradise but on the reality of a new earth and heaven" (A. Johnson 196). Heaven is more than an ideal, it is a real place.

There is emphasis here on "new" (Greek *kainos*), used four times (cf. 2:7; 3:12; 5:9; 14:3): the word implies "what was not there before," thus "*new, recently made, not yet used, fresh* [Mt. 9:17]" (ALGNT 212), but its primary focus is on new as a matter of quality: "the new as set over against that which has seen service, the outworn, the effete or marred through age....commonly better than the old" (Trench 220). (Both those who see the new Heaven and earth as an entirely new creation and those who see it as renovation of the old order appeal to this word for their position.)

That "the first heaven and first earth were passed away" appears to suggest that the new order is more than a limited destruction and subsequent reconstruction of old, purged elements. This clause, with 20:11 (the old heaven and earth "fled away" and "there was no place found for them"), argues for an entirely new order, making it "difficult to avoid the conclusion that the author has in view the complete destruction of the physical universe" (Aune III:1117). Add to this the language of 2 Pet. 3:10-13: "pass away," "melt," "burned up," and "dissolved"; this further supports the annihilation of the present heavens and earth and their replacement by an entirely new creation. (See also Is. 51:6; 65:17-19; 66:22; Zeph. 1:18; 3:8; Mt. 5:18; 19:28; Rom. 8:19-22; Heb. 12:27; Rev. 6:14; 16:18-20.)

"No more sea" indicates that at least this much of the old earth ceases to exist in eternity. Thomas (II:440) thinks this is "decisive" for "an entirely new creation." Even Ladd (*Commentary* 276), who allows for "renovation," thinks that this suggests a new *order*. "On the present earth approximately 70 percent of the earth is covered by the sea....The whole [new] world will consist of inhabitable land surfaces on the new earth" (H. Morris 437).

This is but the first of a number of things in the present age that will be absent from the eternal one, and startling at that: the oceans of the earth have been such an integral part of our present system that it seems hard to conceive of an earth without them.

Some view the missing seas as symbolic of sin or evil nations (and some of them allow for a literal "sea" in the new earth!). Along these lines, various interpreters suggest all sorts of evil associations for the missing seas: they reflect "the ancient Israelite tradition of the opposition of Yahweh and the sea" (Aune III:1119); or "the mythological dragon Tehom/Tiamat, an ancient nemesis of God" (Moffat 479); or "a principle of disorder, violence, or unrest that marks the old creation" (Thomas II:440); or "the primeval ocean, symbol of chaos; its disappearance is assurance of God's total victory" (Harrington, cited by Brighton 593).

But if the seas symbolize such "evil," this would seem to require the literal absence of seas in the new earth, lest they remind those in Heaven of that evil. There is nothing in the text, implicit or explicit, that suggests anything other than the absence of a literal sea, or "oceans," from the new earth. At the same time, that absence may also dramatically represent the absence of such evils as have been mentioned. In the final analysis, the sea seems to be excluded in the new Heaven and earth because of its historical association with evil and also because the new source of water and food is the freshwater river that flows from the throne of God (22:1). Furthermore, oceans divide continents and nations, and there will be no division among God's people in the eternal state.

The vision passes quickly to the descent of "the holy city, new Jerusalem" from God to the new earth (v. 2; cf. 3:12). "The holy city" is commonly used in Scripture to designate the earthly city of Jerusalem (v. 10; 22:19; 3:12; 11:2; Is. 48:2; 52:1; Mt. 4:5; 27:53; cf. Gal. 4:26; Heb. 13:14), so designated because of the salvation history associated with it in both Old and New Testament eras. Jerusalem alone is God's beloved city, selected by Him above all other earthly locations, "graven...upon the palms of [His] hands" [Is. 49:16]. The New Jerusalem is even more so, described as "holy" because it is His dwelling-place and He allows nothing unholy there (cf. 21:8; 22:15).

"New" probably carries the same sense as in "new heaven and new earth" above: an entirely new creation not to be confused with the city on the former earth and surpassing it in every way. The eternal New Jerusalem is in many ways the antitype or ideal of all that was good about the old one. God's love for the historical city of Jerusalem is well documented: it was the place God chose as His special dwelling place; His presence was manifested in the Temple there; it was the seat of government for Israel's monarchy; it was central for Christ's redemptive work; it will figure prominently in the Tribulation, Second Coming, and Israel's restoration; it will be the capital city from which Christ governs during the millennium. God's love for this "place" carries over into eternity, being transferred to the New Jerusalem.

Considering the tremendous size of the city, in the form of a gigantic cube (vv. 16,17), the quality of the "building materials," the beautiful, prismatic effect of God's glory shining through and illuminating all the colors, this is perhaps the most impressive vision the apostle has received. No doubt he felt a sense of awe, excitement, and privilege, viewing the redeemed as finally gathered into the presence of God to share in His glory and live with Him forever.

Many interpreters take the "New Jerusalem" as figurative, a symbol of the church in its perfected and eternal state, including premillennialist Mounce (382). Idealist Beale (1064-1066) agrees, adding that in 3:12 there is a hint that in chapter 21 "the concepts of city and temple would be collapsed into the one concept of the presence of Christ and God with his people" (1070). Along similar lines, many emphasize that the "place" is essentially a metaphor for "transformed human existence" (Wall 243); or "spiritual states" rather than "physical realities" (L. Morris 236); or "the community of men who have fellowship with God" (Hendriksen 201).

But the fact that the names of the tribes of Israel are inscribed in the city on an equal basis with the N.T. apostles suggests that more than the N.T. church is in view. It is "plain that saints of all ages are involved and that what we have here is not the church per se but a city or dwelling place having the freshness and beauty of a bride adorned for marriage to her husband." (Walvoord 313). He emphasizes that the marriage analogy for the union between God and His people is used in both testaments. As true as this is (see 19:7-9; Mt. 22:3-12; 25:1-13; Eph. 5:22-32), the primary point here is that the descending city is "prepared as" a bride rather than *being* the bride—whether the church or Israel. In other words, the city is "decked out,"

and the description later in the chapter confirms this.

Granted, this may be an instance ("synecdoche") where two objects—city and people—are so closely related to one another that a reference to one is a reference to both: "The bride is both the people of God and the seat of their abode, the new Jerusalem" (Thomas II:442). Still, we must maintain the important distinction between the object (the New Jerusalem as a real, celestial city) and what the object symbolizes (God dwelling in the midst of all His saints).

Viewing the New Jerusalem as a literal city is also attractive because it is apparently the "place" that Jesus has been preparing for His bride (the church) according to Jn. 14:1-3. Its heavenly origin, in distinction from the earthly Jerusalem, is reflected in the clause "coming down from God out of heaven." When John saw the city, it was already "prepared" and "adorned" (Greek perfect tense), thus in a finished state distinct from previous earthly states of the earthly Jerusalem. Of this New Jerusalem God Himself is Architect and Builder (Heb. 11:10), though Jesus also must be credited (Jn. 14:1-3). A. Johnson (197) notes that this eternal city finally fulfills the O.T. expectation of a "renewed Jerusalem, rebuilt and transformed into a glorious habitation of God and his people," and that millennial Jerusalem is therefore transitional between the old Jerusalem and its final form. (He offers some helpful discussion how the imagery of this chapter reflects Is. 60, 65, and Ez. 40-48.)

Indeed, trying to make sense of all the strands of Biblical prophecy is daunting. Whether a given passage is literal or figurative, whether it is fulfilled in the near or distant future, whether it applies to Israel or the church, or whether it refers to a millennial or eternal period— these are but some of the large issues with which one must wrestle. What is clear is that God's great love of Jerusalem and the nation of Israel manifested in the O.T. era led the prophets to believe that the city and her people would be eternally restored. The fact that the names of their tribes are inscribed on the gates of the New Jerusalem shows that He never goes back on a promise. While much of O.T. expectation was fulfilled in Christ's millennial reign, some "forever" aspects of those promises may correspond better with fulfillment in eternity proper.

In this literal, heavenly city, New Jerusalem, God's O.T. bride (Israel; Is. 52:1; 61:10) and the bride of Christ (the church; Rev. 19:7-9), who comprise the entire body of "saints," will live forever with God (Is. 61:10; 62:5; Rev. 19:7-9). Both the patriarchs of the tribes of Israel (gates) and the N.T. apostles (foundations) are literally inscribed in her, symbolizing their place in the city: that is, their eternal inclusion in the one family of God (see Is. 52:1-15). The New Jerusalem thus reflects the plurality, variety, holiness, beauty, and unity of God's family or "bride" in eternity. What began with one man, Abraham, and was envisioned in the Abrahamic covenant, that progressed through the nation Israel, and that eventually found its most perfect expression and fulfillment in the church of the N.T., is fully realized in Heaven. (See Gen. 12:1-3; Dt. 29:10-29; Rev. 5:9; 7:9; see Ezek. 37:24-28; Lev. 26:11, 12.)

"Prepared as a bride adorned for her husband" suggests that the city is strikingly beautiful, its "coming down" remi-niscent of a grand bridal procession (cf. 19:7, 8). Her beauty and adornment are strikingly described in vv. 10-21 and may well stand in conscious contrast to the adornment of the whore, Babylon, in 17:1-6 (Aune III:1122). The analogy is similar to the bride analogy in 19:7-9 where the church and her righteous garments are clearly in view. But here the bride analogy more precisely refers to the features of the heavenly city itself as implying her physical appearance.

In the final analysis, the lengthy and detailed description of the city in vv. 10-21 and the associated features in vv. 22-27 weigh heavily in favor of identifying "the holy city, new Jerusalem" as a literal, celestial city where God and His people (O.T. and N.T. varieties as one family of God) dwell together forever in the new Heaven and earth.

"And I heard a great voice out of heaven saying" (v. 3) introduces an auditory revelation that supplies divine interpretation of the vision of the New Jerusalem's descent from Heaven. (Some manuscripts have "out of the throne"; either way, the heavenly origin and divine authority of the voice are clear.) The unidentified voice was likely that of an angel. God is the speaker in vv. 5-8, but there He is identified.

God's long-desired intention of dwelling in the midst of His people forever, to enjoy their worship and fellowship, has become eternal reality (Ex. 29:45; Lev. 26:11, 12; Dt. 23:14; Jer. 31:33; Ezek. 37:23-28; 43:7; Zech. 2:10, 11; Jn. 1:14; 2 Cor. 6:16; Rev. 7:15). This realized relationship is officially inaugurated with the descent of the New Jerusalem, referred to here as "the tabernacle of God" and thus the eternal residence of God Himself. Though "tabernacle" (Greek *skene*) often means a tent or temporary habitation (Vine 614; ALGNT 350), its sense here is "dwelling place"—and, as an eternal one, a fixed and permanent location. This word, complemented by the accompanying verb "dwell" (Greek *skenoo*, the same root as "tabernacle"), suggests that God will inhabit that dwelling place with His people. When we remember that the old universe cannot contain God's essence, we are amazed by and appreciate the heavenly voice's explanation: the Almighty, Omnipresent God actually dwells with "His people."

On a starlit night upon a Judean hillside a shepherd once marveled that such a great and holy Creator would involve Himself with mankind (Ps. 8). God first thought of mankind in His own eternal counsels, created him in His own image, exalted him within creation, redeemed him after the fall by ultimately incarnating Himself as a man who died and arose for his justification and was exalted to an eternal glory that surpasses conditions in the Garden of Eden. God will gladly dwell with His people in eternity because He is their Creator and Redeemer, their all-loving God.

In some manuscripts (apparently including the text used by the A.V. translators), "people" (Greek *laos*) is plural, perhaps suggesting the pluralistic makeup of God's family in eternity; in others it is singular, in that case perhaps conveying more of an emphasis on the oneness of God's family even though made up of a great variety of peoples. Both truths apply; either way, "his people" expresses the privileged relationship between God and all the saints in Heaven, including all the redeemed of history, memorialized in the twelve gates and twelve foundations of the city (vv. 12, 14) and represented by the 24

elders (4:4, 10). Jews and Gentiles have entered into the one family of God through Christ (Eph. 2:14-22) and include "all nations, kindreds, people, tongues" (Rev. 5:9; 7:9; cf. Gen. 12:3; Acts 3:25; Is. 49:12; 60:1-22; Mt. 8:11). "Thus 21:3 declares all the nations to be God's covenant peoples" (Bauckham 311).

The nation of Israel was never conceived to be an end in itself but a priestly instrument of God used to reflect His glory, execute His purpose, and bless all the nations of the earth (see Gal. 3:7-9). The N.T. body of Christ, comprised of believing Jews and Gentiles, is a continuation of what God began in Abraham and continues to have a priestly function in the world (1 Pet. 2:9,10). Hence, the multiethnic makeup of God's eternal, heavenly family sheds light retrospectively on what was being said in the Abrahamic covenant. (This "progressive dispensational" concept of continuity between covenants stands in some contrast to "classic dispensationalism's" emphasis on rigid distinctions between Biblical covenants or dispensations.)

The glorious concept of the saints' unmediated access to God in eternity is repeated for emphasis in the clause "God himself shall be with them, and be their God" (see Lev. 26:11,12; Dt. 23:14; Jer. 31: Ezek. 37:23-28; Jn. 1:14; 2 Cor. 6:16; Rev. 7:15). (Some manuscripts do not include "and be their God," but the truth of this is obvious even if not stated.) The fact that God dwells with His people necessarily implies that He is their God. What is paramount is the practical significance of this relationship with God: dwelling in the midst of His people, with His infinite love, an omnipotent, omni-resourceful heavenly Father will minister to the needs of His children forever (see Mt. 7:9-11; Rom. 8:32).

One of the ways God will ensure the perpetual joy of His children is to banish from Heaven everything that can hinder joy. First, "God shall wipe away all tears from their eyes" (v. 4; cf. 7:17; Is. 25:6-9). Any tears that might issue from life in the former earth are permanently wiped away, and no other tears can arise since all the things that can cause human tears are banished forever. Apparently, one's memory continues to function, but otherwise painful memories are touched in some way (resolved) to prevent grief or tears. "Behold, I create new heavens and a new earth; and the former things shall not be remembered or come to mind" (Is. 65:17, NASB; cf. Is. 66:22).

Four causes of tears are banished from Heaven: "death," "sorrow," "crying," and "pain" (v. 4). "Death" was cast into the lake of fire at the Great White Throne Judgment (20:14) and is not experienced in the new order—whether physical or spiritual death. This cause for grief was swallowed up in victory in each believer's resurrection and permanent transformation (1 Cor. 15:26, 51-58).

"Sorrow" (Greek *penthos*) is "an outward expression of sorrow: *grief, lamentation, mourning*" (ALGNT 305)—the kind of mourning or grief that is visible to others, painful both to experience and to observe (see Is. 35:10; cf. 51:11; 65:17-19). "Crying" (Greek *krauge*) is any kind of outcry, clamor, or shouting, whether of one or many, and here apparently is used (as often) with the sense of the loud sound accompanying grievous weeping: "*crying, wailing*" (ALGNT 237). "Pain" (Greek *ponos*) first means "hard, exhaustive work...

toil, labor, great exertion," and then, as here, the "distress caused by hard, difficult circumstances"—"*pain, affliction, anguish*" (ALGNT 322).

None of these—unavoidable parts of experience in the present age—will exist in the new Heaven and earth; they are among "the former things" (literally, "the first things") that (literally) "passed away" (Greek aorist), indicating in this context a once-for-all, completed action.

"He that sat upon the throne" (v. 5) applies more precisely to God the Father in the context of Revelation and of eternity proper; Jesus is typically portrayed with the Father but distinguished from Him (4:2, 9, 10; 5:7, 13; 6:16; 7:10, 15; 12:5; 14:5; 19:4; 20:11; 22:1, 3). God the Father, then, is the speaker in vv. 5-8, saying first "Behold, I make all things new" (cf. Rom. 6:4; 2 Cor. 5:17), and then "I am Alpha and Omega"—though both of these expressions can be equally applied to Christ in the Scriptures. "Make" (Greek *poieo*) is used here with the sense of "create" (Vine 386, 387; ALGNT 319). Here it indicates the creation (*ex nihilo*) of something entirely "new," and the statement is a futuristic present in the vision: at the time God spoke to John, He was looking ahead to the new order He would create after the old passes away.

After the first three chapters of Revelation, direct speech from God is rare in Revelation. What is heard from the vicinity of God's throne is typically by an angel, an elder, or an unidentified voice. "Now for the first time in the prophetic message proper God speaks directly....It is quite fitting that...it should be his creative word by which he will make his original creation new" (Brighton 600). This fourth use of "new" underscores again that the things that characterized the old dispensation according to v. 4 are absent in the new Heaven and earth. They have passed away with the old universe and God has created a new order in which they do not exist.

The repetition of John's commission to "write" emphasizes that "these words are true and faithful." "True" (Greek *alethinos*) applies to "words that conform to facts," thus *"true, correct, dependable,"* or to "what conforms to reality" and is thus *"genuine, real, true"* (ALGNT 43). "Faithful" (Greek *pistos*) can be used passively—"trusted, reliable or active"—or actively—"believing, trusting, relying" (Vine 223); here, as applied to words, the first applies. God's words conform to the facts and are true and trustworthy, including His words about the new Heaven and earth. What the vision says is "true and faithful," based on the word of a sovereign God who always brings to pass what He promises. God cannot lie. The holy character of God and the truthfulness of God's Word legitimate one's trust in God and what He has spoken about the future.

"It is done" (v. 6) may refer directly to the revelations given in vv. 1-5 and plausibly to all the revelations thus far—perhaps even to all that God has done in history since the Genesis creation, particularly the work of redemption that finally culminates in the new creation. In light of the story of redemption and where it leads, everyone has ample incentive to respond to the gospel. The glorious prospect of eternal life with God in the new Heaven and earth, along with the fact that the present system and its devotees face utter destruction at the Second Coming, offers people who read and hear Revelation compelling incentive to repent and believe while they may.

But "it is done" could as easily apply to the inauguration of the eternal age. On "Alpha and Omega" see the comments on 1:8; the expression includes everything in between and applies, here, to the old creation. Recognizing God and Christ as "the Alpha and Omega" of history draws attention to every point of history; they are not only present at the beginning and end. "The point of the title is that the God who transcends time guides the entire course of history because he stands as sovereign over its beginning and end" (Beale 1055).

It is a natural reflex for Bible students to think of Christ when the gospel invitation is extended the way it is in v. 6. These are the very words used by Christ in Jn. 4:10-13 and Rev. 22:17, and given the equality of Father and Son this is not surprising. Yet, God the Father continues to be the speaker.

The narration about the eternal age pauses with the insertion of a gracious, gospel invitation into John's exposition (v. 6b): "I will give unto him that is athirst of the fountain of the water of life freely" (cf. Mt. 5:6; Jn. 4:4-15; 6:35; 7:37; Rev. 7:17; 22:1, 2). Essentially the same invitation is repeated in 22:17. "Fountain" (Greek *pege*) is a spring or living well, "a source of water; to be distinguished from [a place for] storing surface water" (ALGNT 312). This may well draw attention to both the source (God) and the supply of water (Christ). Drinking from this water assuages thirst (brings salvation): the very same invitation that Jesus shared with the woman at the well (Jn. 4).

The form of the invitation implies the conditional, universal, and gracious nature of salvation. The analogy of "thirst" is helpful: thirst arises out of a drought in the soul of man brought on by the effects of sin, and it can become an active desire to seek Christ to satisfy this thirst of the soul. In the same way that physical thirst prompts someone to seek water, spiritual thirst prompts one to seek satisfaction in Christ. Sadly, though the souls of all are in this sinful state of drought, and some may even be woefully aware of their misery and its cause, not everyone has the desire to quench that thirst with the water of life in Jesus Christ. Here, then, "athirst" implies both the condition and the desire, thus signifying clearly the conditional element in salvation.

"I will give to him...freely" indicates the "grace element." God freely gives salvation on the merits of Jesus' death, burial, and resurrection; it is never merited or aided by human effort though it must be appropriated by faith. Salvation has been provided for all mankind (1 Jn. 2:2), so that anyone may be saved (universal provision and offer); but it is not automatically applied to anyone. Only those who put faith in Christ are saved (see Is. 49:10; 55:1, 2; 1 Pet. 1:18-20). Even so, that faith is not meritorious; it is the opposite of works, looking away from oneself to Christ, and so it is entirely gracious. The "water of life" (salvation) may be had simply and freely for receiving it as a gift of God in Christ.

Once again, then (reflecting the letters to the seven churches), the readers are exhorted to "overcome"—as a *condition* for "inheriting all things" (v. 7). The verb means "intransitively *be victorious, win, prevail*; transitively *overcome, defeat, conquer*" (ALGNT 271). Jesus' concept of "overcoming" is well amplified in His messages to the seven churches. Overcoming is possible only through the Spirit's regeneration and the indwelling that begins at conversion. Though faith brings a person all the way into the household of the saved, there is much more to follow, and "overcoming" sums it up.

Then if someone does not "overcome" in the sense meant here and in the messages to the churches (chapters 2, 3), he will not inherit the joys of eternal life. The obstacles to faith reflected in the seven letters included: "loss of first love" (2:4), "persecution and poverty" (2:9), "idolatry and false doctrine" (2:13-15), "immorality" (2:20), "lack of watchfulness" (3:3), "fruitlessness" (3:8), and "lukewarmness" (3:15-17). Such problems persist throughout church history, and the warning extends to every generation of believers. Christ's expectation of victorious Christian living and service for believers is not antithetical to the principle of justification by faith alone. It is complementary in that genuine faith produces such living. Saving faith can be verified and not simply guessed at (Jas. 2:14-26). True faith in Christ overcomes the world (1 Jn. 5:4, 5).

Three promises are made to those who overcome. The first taps the N.T. idea of the believer's inheritance: "He that overcometh shall inherit all things" (see Acts 20:32; Eph. 1:11; Col. 1:12; 3:24; Heb. 9:15; 1 Pet. 1:4; cf. Eph. 5:5). "All things" is the specific content of the inheritance, a general reference to everything associated with eternal life, all of it infinitely good and everlasting. In the seven letters Christ promised to reward "overcomers" in a variety of ways: (1) eat from the tree of life (2:7); (2) not be hurt by the second death (2:7); (3) receive the hidden manna, a white stone with a new name (2:17); (4)

have power over the nations (2:26); (5) wear white raiment (3:5); (6) become a pillar in God's temple (3:12); and (7) sit with Christ on His throne (3:21). Other "things" to be inherited include: (8) eternal worship of and fellowship with God Himself; (9) the joy of fellowship and encouragement shared with others in God's family; (10) the glories of the New Jerusalem and of the new Heaven and earth; (11) an environment free from sin, problems, or an enemy; (12) the banishment of things that cause tears and sorrow; (13) infinite resources, provisions, and a permanent dwelling place; and (14) glorified bodies with supernatural qualities.

Second, God promises the overcomer that He will "be his God"; and third (correlatively), each overcomer will become God's "son" (cf. v. 3). "This is probably a metaphor based on ancient adoption law, providing an appropriate basis for the right of inheritance mentioned in v 7a" (Aune III:1129). Adoption is indeed an appropriate metaphor for a believer's relationship to God presently (Rom 8:15, 23; Gal. 4:5; Eph. 1:5). Thus God bestows heavenly inheritances on believers because they are His children. But the primary emphasis here is that "overcoming" is also a condition of inheritance. The benefits of adoption that accrue immediately as a result of "adoption" are mainly spiritual in nature for the present. The believer, already adopted through Christ, is given the Holy Spirit as an "earnest" on the fuller inheritance to be received in Heaven (Rom. 8:15; 2 Cor. 1:22). But the believer's ultimate inheritance is received in eternity proper in the form of a dwelling place in the New Jerusalem, life in a new Heaven and earth, and unmediated access to and fellowship with God (see 22:4).

The promise verbs are future: "shall inherit," "will be," and "shall be"—focusing attention on the *not-yet* reality of the believer's final inheritance and unmediated relationship with God in Heaven. The Christian's present relationship with God continues to be mediated; it is not direct or *face-to-face* as it will be. During the present dispensation, then, the focus is on overcoming, and v. 7 appears to emphasize the believer's responsibility in this regard, aimed at finalizing the adopted relationship forever. The converse of overcoming is being overcome and the converse of receiving an inheritance is being disinherited (cf. 1 Cor. 6:9-11).

"But" (v. 8) begins a list of eight types of unbelievers whose eternal future stands in tragic contrast to that of believers. These do *not* inherit good; they are excluded from the blissful conditions of the new Heaven and earth on the basis of their sinful behaviors recorded in the books of works (20:12, 13). Their names were not found written in the Lamb's Book of Life (20:15). Their behaviors—the list is a sampling, not exhaustive—characterize unbelief and arise from the sinful nature ("the flesh" see Mt. 15:11, 19; Gal. 5:19-21; 1 Cor. 6:9, 10).

"And shall have their part in the lake which burneth with fire and brimstone" indicates the future ironic "inheritance" of unbelievers, in contrast to the inheritance of believers. Every person characterized by these sinful behaviors will inherit an eternal future that is opposite to the one described in Heaven. Eternity in Hell is as infinitely bad as living in Heaven is infinitely good.

(1) "Fearful" (Greek *deilos*) means "*timid, fearful, cowardly*; substantivally, of persons showing fear in a shameful way" (ALGNT 105). "'Cowardice' was a designation in the Greek world for general moral degradation" (Aune III:1131). Interestingly, many interpreters view these as former believers who have denied their faith: they "succumb to the pressures of persecution and do not remain loyal when called on to admit that they are followers of Christ" (Beale 1059). Mounce (386) suggests, "In fact, all eight classes of people mentioned in the verse may refer to professing believers who have apostatized [although after the second or third class they apply to pagans as well]." But since apostates are not specifically identified, the references should be taken as universally applied to anyone who does not exercise or persevere in faith. Though fear often hinders people, it is not an acceptable excuse from God's point of view (see Mt. 8:26; 10:28; Prov. 29:25; cf. Prov. 1:7; 2 Tim. 1:7).

(2) "Unbelieving" (Greek *apistois*) can mean "*not believable, incredible*," or "*lacking in faith, unbelieving, not trusting*," or even "*unfaithful, untrustworthy*" (ALGNT 65). The middle meaning predominates here: the sin of unbelief in Christ (cf. Jn. 3:16, 18). This term is appropriate for those who have never trusted Christ but may include those who professed faith but relapsed into unbelief (apostasy).

(3) "Abominable" (Greek *bdelugma*) generally refers to "what is extremely hated or abhorred...*destestable thing*; as anything connected with idolatry," including the worship of Antichrist (ALGNT 89). Some (like Aune III:1131) think it refers to sexual sins like homosexuality or sodomy, as in Lev. 18. But many sins are cited as abominations in the O.T., including idolatry (Dt. 7:25), and many think that is the primary implication here. But since "idolatry" is singled out later in the list, the reference here is likely more general. Among the things called abominable were certain foods (Lev. 11; Is. 66:17) and the "ways" of the nations defeated by the Israelites, including sorcery (Dt. 18:9-12). Solomon listed "seven things the Lord hates" (Prov. 6:16-19); ultimately, anything that God finds detestable might be included.

(4) "Murderers" (Greek *phoneus*) are those guilty of the unjustified taking of human life: "*murderer, slayer, killer*" (ALGNT 401). Murder is especially reprehensible to God because man is made in the image of God, and this sin was a key reason in His decision to send the flood (Gen. 6:11b; 9:5, 6).

(5) "Whoremongers" (Greek *pornos*) ranges from meaning "a man who has sexual intercourse with a prostitute" to any "*sexually immoral person*" (as here), typically "distinguished from [*adulterer*] in 1 Cor. 6.9 and [*sodomite or homosexual*] in 1T 1:10" (ALGNT 324). "The 'sexually immoral' are mentioned because the practice had become the major vice of paganism" (Mounce 387). Equally, those who are unfaithful to God by worshiping or serving pagan gods or who have made material possessions their god are guilty of committing spiritual whoredom against God.

(6) "Sorcerers" (Greek *pharmakos*) means "one who prepares and used drugs for magical purposes or ritual witchcraft," thus: "*sorcerer, poisoner, magician*" (ALGNT 397). Thomas (II:452) suggests that the false prophet may have used sorcery to deceive (see 9:21; 13:13, 14; 22:15).

(7) "Idolaters" (Greek *eidololatria*) are those who worship idols or false gods. Beginning with the golden calf incident (especially reprehensible because a major component of Israel's deliverance and God's judgment upon Egypt occurred against the backdrop of Egypt's pantheon of false gods), this sin eventually infiltrated, corrupted, and destroyed the nation of Israel. Furthermore, the idolatrous environment of the Roman world posed a real threat to the purity, health, and even existence of the seven churches, particularly Pergamum (2:12-17) and Thyatira (2:18-29). The most significant expression of idolatry in history occurs during the Tribulation in regard to the Antichrist's image.

(8) "Liars" (Greek *pheudeis*) means "*lying, false, deceitful*, opposite to Greek *aletheis* [*truthful*]; substantivally, *one who tells lies, liar*" (ALGNT 413). The unbelieving Jews in the synagogue at Philadelphia claimed to be a "synagogue of Jews" but were in reality a synagogue of Satan (3:9). John associated lying with unbelief (1 Jn. 1:6, 8, 10; 2:4, 22; 4:20; 5:10). Jesus identified Satan as the father of all murders and lies (Jn. 8:44). In contrast, Heaven's citizens emulate Christ, the faithful and true witness.

"Their part" will be an eternal, tormented existence in "the lake which burneth with fire and brimstone," also identified as "the second death" (cf. 2:11; 20:6,14). The "lake" in Hell is not filled with water but with fire and brimstone. The "burning" is continual or unending (Greek present participle). "Brimstone" (Greek *theion*) is "*sulfur*" (ALGNT 195), known as extremely difficult to put out when ignited. Indeed, the fire and brimstone of Hell will never burn out (Is. 66:24; Mk. 9:43, 44; Lk. 16:23, 24, 28). On "second death," as implying a "first," see the comments on 20:14 and consult the definitive Scripture on the subject, Rom. 5:12-21.

It is difficult to imagine eternal existence in Hell. The prospects behoove one to avoid going there at all costs (Mt. 18:8, 9) and to continue preaching the gospel to others.

B. The New Jerusalem (21:9—22:5)

The continuing vision of the New Jerusalem contrasts the eternal heavenly city with the worldly city of Babylon in chapters 17 and 18. Both cities are presented as "women," each beautifully adorned. Both have a citizenry and worldwide influence. But the character of the women, the character of their citizens, the character of their rulers, their values, their relationship to God, and their ultimate eternal destinies are diametrically opposite. The fact that a bowl angel introduces both visions invites such a comparison (17:1; 21:9). The city's identification in v. 10 is linked with v. 2 and thus is a more detailed look beyond the initial introduction given earlier in the chapter.

1. As the Lamb's wife (21:9-27)

**9 And there came unto me one of the seven angels which had the seven vials full of the seven last plagues, and talked with me, saying, Come hither, I swill shew thee the bride, the Lamb's wife.
10 And he carried me away in the spirit to a great and high mountain, and shewed me that great**

city, the holy Jerusalem, descending out of heaven from God,

11 Having the glory of God: and her light was like unto a stone most precious, even like a jasper stone, clear as crystal;

12 And had a wall great and high, *and* had twelve gates, and at the gates twelve angels, and names written thereon, which are *the names* of the twelve tribes of the children of Israel:

13 On the east three gates; on the north three gates; on the south three gates; and on the west three gates.

14 And the wall of the city had twelve foundations, and in them the names of the twelve apostles of the Lamb.

15 And he that talked with me had a golden reed to measure the city, and the gates thereof, and the wall thereof.

16 And the city lieth foursquare, and the length is as large as the breadth: and he measured the city with the reed, twelve thousand furlongs. The length and the breadth and the height of it are equal.

17 And he measured the wall thereof, an hundred *and* forty *and* four cubits, *according to* the measure of a man, that is, of the angel.

18 And the building of the wall of it was *of* jasper: and the city was pure gold, like unto clear glass.

19 And the foundations of the wall of the city *were* garnished with all manner of precious stones. The first foundation was jasper; the second, sapphire; the third, a chalcedony; the fourth, an emerald;

20 The fifth, sardonyx; the sixth, sardius; the seventh, chrysolite; the eighth, beryl; the ninth, a topaz; the tenth, a chrysoprasus; the eleventh, a jacinth; the twelfth, an amethyst.

21 And the twelve gates were twelve pearls; every several gate was of one pearl: and the street of the city was pure gold, as it were transparent glass.

22 And I saw no temple therein: for the Lord God Almighty and the Lamb are the temple of it.

23 And the city had no need of the sun, neither of the moon, to shine in it: for the glory of God did lighten it, and the Lamb *is* the light thereof.

24 And the nations of them which are saved shall walk in the light of it: and the kings of the earth do bring their glory and honour into it.

25 And the gates of it shall not be shut at all by day: for there shall be no night there.

26 And they shall bring the glory and honour of the nations into it.

27 And there shall in no wise enter into it any thing that defileth, neither *whatsoever* worketh abomination, or *maketh* a lie: but they which are written in the Lamb's book of life.

One of the seven "bowl angels" escorted John on a "guided tour" in order to take a closer look at "the bride, the Lamb's wife" (v. 9; cf. 17:1): New Jerusalem. "Showed" (Greek *deiknumi*) means "drawing attention to something, *point out, show, cause to see*" (ALGNT 105). After taking the apostle, in spirit, to the selected mountain site, the angel may have initially let the spectacle speak for itself. But "talked with me" (here and v. 15) suggests that there was a running dialogue between the angel and John. Given the probability of John's ignorance and amazement, the angel may have offered both moral support and information.

The angel continued to participate in the vision when he measured the city's physical dimensions (vv. 15-17), when he showed John the "river of life" flowing from God's throne (22:1), and in various affirmations, rebuffs, and commands (22:6, 8, 9, 10). If there is an example in Scripture when Jesus takes the form of "the angel of the Lord," chapter 22 would certainly be it. At times the transition between the angel and Jesus in the narration is so smooth that a distinction is not that apparent.

Of special interest is the identification of the New Jerusalem as both the bride or wife of the Lamb (v. 9) and "that great city" (v. 10; cf. 19:7-9). The text thus provides its own interpretation of the symbolism. The flexibility of the term "bride" to refer to the church elsewhere in Scripture and to the heavenly city here is not problematic. See the comments earlier on v. 2 relative to this, and also relative to the important question whether "the New Jerusalem" refers to the church or to a real, heavenly city.

"Bride" (Greek *numphe*) means "a young woman engaged or newly married" and is metaphorically used "of the church as the bride of Christ" (ALGNT 273). "Wife" (Greek *gune*) means a "*woman*, as distinct from a male" or "a married woman...[or] bride or fiancée legally considered as *wife*" (ALGNT 102). The "saints" (the church) are identified as the Lamb's wife in 19:8; and

Israel is regarded as a wife in Is. 54:5; Hos. 2:19. Building on this in v. 10 the Lamb's wife is identified as "that great city, the holy Jerusalem, descending out of heaven from God."

The elaborate and detailed description in vv. 11-27 suggests that more than a mere symbolic reference to the glorious church (saints) is intended. Certainly symbolism is involved here: in fact, a chief feature. But a symbolic viewpoint that leaves God's family without a corporeal or tangible dwelling place, located on and distinct from the new earth, is unsatisfactory. Such an exclusively symbolic viewpoint is hard put to account for the symbolism of *all* the particulars without a governing standard or consensus. In contrast, a literal viewpoint that interprets this passage as describing a real, heavenly dwelling place for the redeemed with highly symbolic features is not so challenged. This approach recognizes the truth in both perspectives and is the most consistent model of interpretation.

The correct interpretation, then, begins with the particulars of the New Jerusalem. These include the foundations, walls, gates, precious stones, gold, colors, lights, mathematical dimensions, configuration, and inhabitants—including God the Father, Jesus the Lamb, all the saints, and angels. In this respect, the heavenly city literally exists as a dwelling place for God and His people on the newly created earth. Though the church is designated elsewhere as the bride of Christ, it is also true that Jesus promised that bride a specific location with "many dwelling places." "The bride-figure cannot be limited to the individuals who will live in the city....It must also include the literal city with her physical inhabitants" (Thomas II:460).

The "great and high mountain" is apparently the one that will serve as a location for the New Jerusalem in the new Heaven and earth (v. 10). This was the vantage point from which John observed the New Jerusalem descending. But it was "more than a vantage point....It is Mount Zion itself [14:1], on which the city stands, or rather 'lands' in its descent from the sky" (Michaels 241).

The O.T. predicted a restored, eschatological Jerusalem that would rest on a high mountain above all others (Is. 2:2-5; Ezek. 17:22, 23; 20:40; 40:2; Mic. 4:1-3). Jerusalem's eschatological, millennial prominence carries over into the eternal age when the New Jerusalem, "the holy city" (vv. 1, 2), descends from Heaven to the new earth. The mountain is both "great" and "high," beyond comparison with any mountain in our present experience. The huge dimensions of the New Jerusalem (vv. 16, 17) require an immense foundation.

"The holy Jerusalem, descending out of heaven from God" links this city to the one initially introduced in v. 2: they are one and the same. Consequently, there is no justification for suggesting that 21:9 22:5 reverts back to 20:4-6 as a description of the millennium—as some interpreters do (Charles, Preston, and Hanson, cited in Beale 1062; Lee and Beasley-Murray, cited in Thomas II:457). This is an unnecessary and inappropriate attempt to avoid attributing "millennial" features to eternity proper ("nations," "kings," and "unbelievers"—21:24; 22:2,15) and introduces too many contextual inconsistencies. To place 21:9ff. in the millennium puts the absence of night, the absence of sun and moon, and the absence of a Temple into

the millennial period that obviously has all these (Thomas II:458).

"Descending" (Greek present participle) means that John actually observed (in the vision) the descent of the city from God, through the new heavens (the sky) down to the new earth, as that descent was in progress. "Out of heaven from God" makes clear that this is a new version of Jerusalem that differentiates it from any former earthly or millennial one.

"The glory of God" (v. 11) recalls the Shekinah or visible manifestation of God's glory that inhabited the O.T. Temple (Ex. 40:34, 35; 2 Chr. 5:14; 7:1-3). "Shekinah...personalizes this visible manifestation of God's presence with His people....and as a result was used at times as a periphrasis for the divine name of Yahweh, for it represented the holy, ineffable God dwelling with his people" (Brighton 598). As indicated earlier, God's glory is the sum total of His nature and activity. The feature of His glory specifically in view here is how it is expressed in the New Jerusalem. This manifestation flows from God's nature as Light and is expressed as "light" (cf. 1 Jn. 1:5; 1 Tim. 6:16).

"Light" (Greek *phoster*) in v. 11 first means a "light-giving body, luminary, star," then "a state of brightness, radiance, shining, brilliance" (ALGNT 404): "a heavenly body which generated its own light, like a star" (Brighton 610). The New Jerusalem generates its own light from the glory of God and the Lamb that resides there. The transparent city, like a gigantic prism, radiates that light throughout, obviating the need for sun or moon or any other source of light. The light of God's glory illumines the city (the new, eternal dwelling of

God) and the new earth; the nations and kings walk in that light. That the saints live eternally in God's light in Heaven is remarkable, considering Paul's observation that the light of God's presence is "unapproachable" (1 Tim. 6:16). God enables the saints to approach Him without being blinded or consumed; the former barrier becomes a blessing as the saints, kings, and nations of the new earth "walk"—live—in it (21:23-25; the light in v. 11 corresponds to the light in v. 23, where the risen Lamb is Heaven's light source).

John compared the New Jerusalem's light to a "precious" jasper stone (cf. 4:3), referring to the intrinsic quality of the light itself as distinct from or as assisted by the other colorful properties of the building materials in the heavenly city. "Precious" (Greek *timios*) means "*valuable, costly…*of great worth…very expensive" (ALGNT 380). "Jasper" (Greek *iaspus*) is a precious stone "found in various colors and ordinarily opaque" (ALGNT 201). Thus it is clear like crystal which "underlines its purity and value" (Aune III:1154): "probably the white Levantine variety which is precious" (Ford 335). Mounce (390) suggests that this may even be a reference to a diamond.

John also observed "a wall great and high" (v. 12), such as is "used as a strong fortification" (ALGNT 376). John used "great" (Greek *megas*) 80 times in Revelation to express features larger than life in the visions. To appreciate the wall's height one must refer to the physical dimensions of the city given in v. 16, though it does not have to be as tall as the city itself. One measurement of the wall was "144 cubits" (v. 17), but this is clearly not its circumference around the city (1,400-1,500 miles) and

so may refer to its height or thickness. Ancient cities were noted for having thick, high walls. Assuming a "cubit" of 18 inches, then, the wall may have been approximately 216 feet in height. Indeed, given the cubic nature of the city itself, it may have been 216 feet in height and thickness. (And some suggest that the angel is of superhuman size, and therefore that an angelic "cubit"— the distance between elbow and tip of forefinger—would be much greater than "human" cubits. This, of course, we cannot know; see further on v. 17, below.) Furthermore, it was constructed of "jasper" (v. 18); see the comments on v. 11. The transparent quality of jasper would be capable of transmitting and even magnifying the great reflections of color and light radiating throughout the New Jerusalem (cf. v. 23; 22:5.) Nothing is hidden behind the walls (or anywhere else) in Heaven. There is nothing to hide.

Though a real wall, there is no need for a wall in Heaven. But "need" is a category we do not know now how to apply; caution should be exercised before rejecting the literalness of something simply because *we* do not understand its purpose. The wall is apparently both literal and symbolic, although the "meaning" is not given in the text. Paradoxically, the symbolism may be the primary reason for having a wall. Idealist Beale (who typically rejects literalness) says, "The 'great and high wall' represents the inviolable nature of fellowship with God, as implied by 21:27 and 22:14-15" (1068). Or Brighton (611) takes the wall to represent the fact that "God's people will forever be under God's gracious protection so that never again will they suffer attack or be afflicted." But as sensible as this is, nothing in the text directs us to make such a connection; there is simply no way for us to be sure what lesson the wall might teach us. What we do know is that John saw a tall (or wide) jasper wall surrounding the city, punctuated by 12 gates of pearl and supported by 12 foundations decorated with precious stones. Symbolic or not, it is a beautiful, permanent, well-defined place, lit by the glory of God.

With the city's "twelve gates" (v. 12), compare the 12 gates of O.T. Jerusalem (Neh. 2:13, 14; 3:1, 3, 6, 13, 15, 26, 28, 29, 31; 12:37, 39) and the 12 gates of Ezekiel's millennial Temple (Ezek. 48:30-34). These literal gates punctuate the perimeter of the wall around the heavenly city. The number 12 may symbolize "abundant entrance" (Brighton 611; Hendriksen 204); or, "Completeness is implied in the number twelve and its multiples [21:12-14, 16-17, 21] and fullness in the cubical dimension of the city [21:16]" (A. Johnson 195). There were three gates per wall in the square city, facing east, north, south, and west (v. 13). Apparently the compass points carry over into eternity since the New Jerusalem is situated on a new Heaven and *earth*.

These gates obviously function, practically, for entering and exiting the city to and from the rest of the new Heaven and earth. The gates were constructed from "twelve pearls," apparently requiring one large pearl per gate (v. 21). Just as ancient cities took pride in the architecture of their gates (Aune III:1154) so the great gates of the celestial city are triumphant, majestic memorials to God's kingdom and the eternal victory of the New Jerusalem and her saintly citizens.

John also saw "at the gates twelve angels" posted as sentries (v. 12; cf. 1 Chr. 23:5; Is. 62:6). Angels have been posted as guards before (Gen. 3:24; cf. 1 Kg. 6:32). The passive posture of these angels standing watch at the always-open gates may draw attention to the permanently authorized access of the saints who enter and exit the heavenly city freely.

These gates have symbolical significance, with "the names of the twelve tribes of the children of Israel" inscribed on them, one tribe per gate. This implies "the realization of one of the central concerns of Jewish eschatology, namely, the restoration of the twelve tribes of Israel, which is repeatedly mentioned in post-exilic OT and early Jewish literature" (Aune III:1155). Thomas (II:463) thinks of this as being "in fulfillment of their distinctive role in history throughout the centuries of their existence." The inscription suggests that God has neither divorced nor displaced Israel in eternity. They, along with saints from every nation on earth, comprise God's one family in Heaven (Eph. 2:11-22). Which names are on which gates is not specified; compare the list of tribes in 7:5-8 and see the comments there. Whatever else is intended, it is clear that the nation of Israel is by this memorialized eternally. God used Israel to showcase His glory and laws in the world and to give the world its Redeemer (Rom. 9:4, 5), and His special love for His "chosen people" never diminishes.

The same may be said for "the twelve apostles of the Lamb," whose names are likewise inscribed eternally in the city's "twelve foundations" (v. 14)—we assume with Matthias's name instead of Judas's. The nation of Israel was never conceived to be an end in itself to exist independently of the church in eternity; Jesus Christ brought about the reconciliation of all things as one in Himself

(Eph. 1:10; 2:11-22; 3:1-11). The wall of separation between Jew and Gentile came down long ago at Calvary, resulting in equal fellowship for all peoples as members of one family of God. Though historical identities are not forgotten in eternity (1 Cor. 13:12), the inscription of the names of Israel's patriarchs and Christ's apostles is not the symbolism of separateness but of unity. They are portrayed as integral parts in the same city.

A. Johnson (200) explains, "Foundations of ancient cities usually consisted of extensions of the rows of huge stones that made up the wall, down to the bedrock." He reports that the foundations of the second Temple have been excavated, with unbelievably huge stones going down "fourteen to nineteen layers below the present ground level." That the names of the apostles are inscribed on the foundations may recall Eph. 2:20, which refers to "the foundation of the apostles and prophets, Jesus Christ himself being the chief cornerstone." Thus the foundations of the heavenly city confirm the place of the N. T. church in God's family and in Heaven.

The foundation seen by John might be a twelve-layered foundation all around or twelve connected sections reaching all the way around. Those who would take this as entirely figurative might say that this pictures how the New Jerusalem and its citizens are founded on the Word of God. In reality, this is a literal foundation inscribed with names that have symbolical significance. Buildings and walls have had names or other inscriptions on them from time immemorial, so that it is no stretch to imagine that the New Jerusalem is similar. (An extensive description of the various types of precious stones embedded in the foundations is given in vv. 19, 20.)

The fact that the 12 tribes of Israel and Christ's 12 apostles are memorialized in the New Jerusalem suggests the fundamental unity of God's family in eternity (cf. Walvoord 322). This recalls the throne-room vision of 4:4, 10 where 24 thrones, representing both O.T. and N.T. saints, flank God's throne. Thus, there are distinctions within the basic oneness of God's eternal family that do not compromise that oneness in the least.

"He that talked with me" (v. 15) is the bowl angel of v. 9, John's "tour guide" as it were. This angel took a "golden reed" for a measuring tool in order to measure the city (New Jerusalem; cf. Ezek. 40-42; Rev. 11:1, 2). Reeds in antiquity were suitable measuring instruments about four to ten feet long (ISBE III:295), more rigid than rope, and typically used for measuring shorter distances. These measurements are acted out for dramatic effect in order to draw attention to the truly incredible dimensions, the reality of the New Jerusalem, and its perfection: "a seal on the perfection of the city" (Ford 341).

The New Jerusalem is configured as *a gigantic square cube* ("foursquare"): "a symbol of perfection" (Kistemaker 568). The O.T. precedent is perhaps the Holy of Holies in Solomon's Temple, configured as a square (1 Kg. 6:19-22). That "the length is as large as the breadth" means that their measurements are equal, as is its height (v. 16). The length of each side (though some think this is the distance around all four sides), and its height, apparently, was 12,000 furlongs (a furlong being about 600 feet) or approximately 1,400-1,500 miles. H. Morris (450-452) calculates that this would provide some 75 acres per person in a city with 20 billion residents!

All this adds up to an incredibly large city, 1,400-1,500 miles in every dimension, including its height. It would be an understatement to say that this will provide for ample stacking of "stories" to house the huge number of saints who will likely dwell there (cf. Jn. 14:1-3). The rooms (or apartments or condominiums) will accommodate uncountable numbers. Indeed, the dimensions are so incredibly large that some seem to take the language figuratively simply to make the picture more believable.

The same faith that one exercises in the resurrection of Christ, or any other miracle of the Bible, is required to accept the size of the New Jerusalem: we need only accept God's Word. Nothing in the text suggests that any modifications downward are justified; Aune refers to such attempted modifications as "highly speculative emendations, however, and there is no convincing reason to reject the author's intention to depict a city of gigantic dimensions." The figures are too definite to intend something different from what they are, though idealist Beale (1073) observes that the equality of sides and height "reinforces the figurative idea of the completeness of God's people found earlier in the mention of the twelve tribes and twelve apostles." A square configuration certainly suggests perfect order or symmetry, but this is no reason to take the dimensions as anything other than specific and literal.

"The measure of man, that is, of the angel" (v. 17) may indicate that the angel used his own arm for measuring the wall (cf. 11:1). If so, there is a question whether these are man-sized "cubits"

(about 18 inches) or oversized, "angelic cubits." In that case, we have no basis for assigning dimensions to the wall, though a wall of 216 feet high seems dwarfed by a city of 1,400 miles in height! Considering this, it actually makes more sense if a cosmic-sized angel (and "cubit") is involved.

As already noted, the "wall" surrounding the city is constructed out of "jasper" (v. 18); see the comments on v. 12. The city itself is constructed from pure, transparent gold, "like unto clear glass." This characteristic would contribute to an increased prismatic effect, dispersing the colors and the great light generated from God's glory. The sheer size, unimaginable beauty, and unprecedented architectural design and engineering will be appropriate, visible expressions of God's infinite glory. Heavenly gold is of such quality that it is transparent, showing that there are no impurities and far exceeding the quality of any gold in our present experience.

The foundations of the wall are decorated with "all manner of precious stones" or gemstones (vv. 19, 20; cf. Is. 54:11, 12; cf. Ex. 28:15-21; 39:8-14). Some see the High Priest's breastplate as a precedent; if so, these may symbolize the priestly character of the redeemed (Glasson, cited by A. Johnson 202). "The prerogatives that once belonged exclusively to the High Priest are now reflected in the entire city" (Poythress 191). But the analogy breaks down since only eight of the stones used in the High Priest's breastplate are used in the New Jerusalem's foundations (Thomas II:470); D. Johnson (314) sees the "remaining four as equivalents." The priestly analogy is certainly better than the idea that the stones are selected from the pagan zodiac (Farrer, cited by

Ford 343) or as a rebuff to it (Charles II:167) or drawn from the king of Tyre's wardrobe. Regardless, the selections have certainly come from the mind of the Architect and Builder of the heavenly city, God Himself.

Each of the 12 parts of the foundation is decorated by one gemstone, described in consecutive order, as follows.

(1) For "jasper" see comments on v. 11. Ford (335) says, "Jasper is a variety of quartz found in various colors, commonly red, brown, green, and yellow, more rarely blue and black, and seldom white....The jasper here is probably the white Levantine variety which is precious."

(2) "Sapphire" is "a precious stone, blue-colored gem" (ALGNT 345).

(3) "Chalcedony" is "a valuable stone that can be highly polished, like the modern agate, onyx, carnelian, chrysoprase" (ALGNT 406).

(4) "Emerald" is "a transparent bright green precious stone" (ALGNT 352).

(5) "Sardonyx" is "a precious agate stone marked by layers of colors of the red *sardius* and white onyx" (ALGNT 346).

(6) "Sardius" is "a variety of translucent quartz regarded as a precious stone," also called "*sard, carnelian,* regarded as equivalent to a ruby" (ALGNT 346).

(7) "Chrysolite" is "a gold-colored gem, known today as *topaz*" (ALGNT 411).

(8) "Beryl" is "a valuable stone or gem of sea-green color" (ALGNT 90).

(9) "Topaz" is "a greenish-yellow precious stone, perhaps the modern chrysolite" (ALGNT 382).

(10) "Chrysoprasus" is "a translucent gem, a variety of quartz of golden green color" (ALGNT 411).

(11) "Jacinth" is "a precious stone either dark blue or dark red" (ALGNT 387).

(12) "Amethyst" is "a gem of deep purple or violet, so-called from its supposed power to ward off drunkenness" (ALGNT 46).

Each of the twelve gates was of one "pearl" (v. 21), from early times until now counted as a valuable gem. "Among the ancients, pearls were ranked highest among precious stones, because their beauty derives entirely from nature, improvement by human workmanship being an impossibility" (Thomas II:473). This suggests that the gate is not the modern stereotypical "iron" or "wooden" variety that swings on hinges. It is more accurately conceived as *an entrance or opening only*, one that remains open throughout eternity (v. 25).

The "street of the city" may refer to the "main street" by which a great city is known to others, as well as, collectively, to any other streets that may exist. Like the city proper, the streets are of "pure gold," again described as like "transparent glass" (v. 21). See comments on v. 18. The huge pearls and the volume of pure gold used as construction materials suggest infinite quality, infinite resources, and eternal permanence.

"And I saw no temple therein" (v. 22) marks a change in focus within the vision and another instance (like no sea or oceans, v. 1) of what is *not* in the new Heaven and earth. "Temple" (Greek *naos*) was the Holy of Holies, the innermost room where the Ark of the Covenant was housed and God's visible presence was manifested in Shekinah glory. The absence of a Temple in the eternal age clearly distinguishes it from the past, present, Tribulational, and millennial periods of earth's history (cf. 3:12; 7:15; 11:1, 2, 19; 14:15, 17; 15:5, 6, 8; 16:1, 17; Acts 15:16; Am. 9:11; Ezek. 40-48), thus representing the significant changes that will take place in the final constitution of things. Earlier references to a heavenly temple in Revelation are not simply metaphors for God's presence but point to the existence of a corporeal temple and altars (7:15; 14:15, 17; 15:5, 6, 8; 16:1, 17). To suggest that these are only metaphors for God's presence, applied consistently, would also suggest the absurdity that God is no longer present in Heaven since John saw no temple there.

Rather than a corporeal Temple, "the Lord God Almighty and the Lamb are the temple of it." God and the Lamb ultimately replace all previous historical symbols or instruments of salvation history because their purpose has been fully realized. The need for mediation is obviated by the new relationship between God and His people. The citizens of Heaven live in God's immediate or direct presence forever. They do not need the former Temple that portrayed a graduated approach into the presence of God; instead they enjoy the constant and permanent presence of Jesus the slain and risen Lamb. This will be pure fellowship, unhindered by sin, face to face with God Himself (22:4). God will dwell in the midst of His people forever; the goal of redemption is thus finally realized.

Also remarkable in the New Jerusalem is the absence of "the sun" and "the moon" (v. 23). "The glory of God" and "the light of the Lamb" replace the for-

mer earthly light sources as a matter of honor and logistics. (See the comments on v. 11.) "Lighten" (Greek *photizo*) can be used intransitively to mean "*shine, give light*" or transitively, "*give light to, light up, illuminate*" (ALGNT 405). This infinite light, radiating from within and throughout the New Jerusalem, would dwarf the light of any other source. Lesser lights like the sun or moon would be useless and undetectable (cf. H. Morris 457).

The New Jerusalem's divine light will provide enlightenment and guidance for "the nations" and "the kings of the earth" (vv. 24, 26). (Nearly all manuscripts do not include "of them which are saved," but of course only the saved are here.) Indeed, all the saints of Heaven will walk by means of the light of God in the New Jerusalem. But a question arises: some think that the reference to the presence of "nations and kings" is inappropriate for the eternal state, leading them to realign this text somewhere else in the chronology of Revelation, as during the millennium for example. But this fails for more than one reason. There is no Temple here, and there is one during the millennium. Furthermore, the same New Jerusalem is in view, here, as in vv. 2, 10. And there is neither sun nor moon here, whereas the millennium is still governed by those heavenly bodies in regular nights and days.

Such exegetical manipulations are entirely unnecessary. All that the presence of "nations and kings" indicates is that eternal life in Heaven is not restricted to the boundaries of the New Jerusalem itself. There will also be a new earth, and society in the eternal state will evolve into new nations and new "kings of the earth" who presumably rule those nations, under God. The existence of "kings" may imply some degree of governmental structure, with responsibilities assigned as rewards for faithful Christian service in present history (see Mt. 6:19, 20; 25:14-30). These nations and kings "bring their glory and honor into" the New Jerusalem. "John sees a vision of social life, bustling with activity....Life in the age to come will certainly involve continuing activities and relationships that will contribute to the glory of the Holy City throughout eternity" (A. Johnson 202). There will be no unredeemed inhabiting the new Heaven and earth or having access to the New Jerusalem.

The character of the New Jerusalem and its saintly citizenry is diametrically opposite to the character of Babylon, and the great prostitute's worldly clientele. The nations, merchants of Babylon and the kings of the nations were made rich, idolatrous, and immoral by their association with Babylon (18:3). They grieved inconsolably over her destruction because they owed their wealth to her. In contrast, the kings and nations of the new Heaven and earth have a totally different outlook. Instead of living to accumulate riches and build their own selfish empires as their wicked predecessors had done, the citizenry of Heaven live to bring their honor and glory into the New Jerusalem (v. 24). Beale interprets this "glory" figuratively: "The only thing that the redeemed can carry with them from the old world to offer to God is not literal riches but the reputation of their good works [so 14:13; 19:8], which they can continue to perform by praising God." But "glory and honor" could also be something tangible, brought to the Lord as an expression of genuine worship and praise or thanks-

giving. "Actually the phrase 'glory and honor' probably has a double meaning and includes wealthy gifts as well as fame and adoration" (Aune III:1173).

The entire new Heaven and earth is bathed in the light of the New Jerusalem (vv. 24, 25; cf. Is. 60:1-22). Everyone in Heaven will worship, serve, and live ("walk") in the knowledge of the Lord and His Word. "The glory of God as the light of the New Jerusalem is not just a beacon that attracts the nations to it...It is the light by which they live" (Bauckham 315). That "there shall be no night there" indicates that the light of God and the Lamb never cease shining. The New Jerusalem's light source is an omnipresent, eternal God who never slumbers or sleeps. The present phenomenon of nighttime, where the rotation of earth blocks the sun's light to half the earth's population, is impossible in Heaven. Nor is there reason to shut or lock any of the gates: there is neither sin, sinful people, nor darkness. Heaven is one eternal day that begins somewhere between the events of 20:11-15 and 21:1. The gates into the Holy City are always open; indeed, they are apparently *openings*.

Verse 27 gives special commentary about the holy environment and the exclusive citizenship of Heaven. John is *not* suggesting that any of the things named are possible in Heaven; they have been done away with by the final consignment of unbelievers to Hell and the annihilation of the old order entirely. Instead, he is underscoring once more (as in v. 8) that access to God cannot be taken for granted but is a carefully regulated privilege. Denying the presence of these things emphasizes their absence, and warns against them. It also underscores the exclusive makeup and holy character of those who live in Heaven, in sharp contrast with those who are no longer present. Furthermore, Heaven will remain this way forever.

Excluded, then, are three influences (as examples rather than an exhaustive list): "any thing that defileth," "whatsoever worketh abomination," and "liars." Nothing sinful can ever contaminate the holy environment of Heaven. (Like the Garden of Eden, the millennial period was predominantly good but not without the presence of evil.)

As noted, this may be an attempt to influence the readers of Revelation to change their present behavior in order to enter Heaven someday. Any readers or hearers still manifesting such behavior may expect to be rejected. The final phrase, "but they which are written in the Lamb's book of life," confirms this evangelistic intent and harks back to 20:15 (see comments there). Only those whose names are written there may expect to enjoy eternal life in the new Heaven and earth.

There is an implicit connection in v. 27 between one's belief and his behavior. In Scripture the two are married to one another. Those whose names are in "the Lamb's book of life" will not be guilty of the behaviors that disqualify them from the New Jerusalem. Conversely, those who are guilty of such sinful behaviors may be prompted to consider turning to Christ in repentance.

2. As Eden restored (22:1-5)

These verses continue the vision that began in 21:9, with perhaps a narrowing of focus as the bowl angel continued with John's guided tour of the New Jerusalem. John was privileged to see the "river of life" flowing from God's throne (v. 1) and a "tree of life" growing beside it by the main street of the city (v. 2). As Mounce (398) observes, though these verses continue the description of the city, "they also portray the eternal state as Eden restored, thus 'book-ending' the Christian Bible. In Genesis we were introduced to the tree of life planted in the middle of the garden (Gen. 2:9)....Now in Revelation we see redeemed humanity back in the garden, able to eat the bountiful fruit of the tree of life (22:1-2)."

1 And he shewed me a pure river of water of life, clear as crystal, proceeding out of the throne of God and of the Lamb.

2 In the midst of the street of it, and on either side of the river, was there the tree of life, which bare twelve *manner* of fruits, *and* yielded her fruit every month: and the leaves of the tree *were* for the healing of the nations.

3 And there shall be no more curse: but the throne of God and of the Lamb shall be in it; and his servants shall serve him:

4 And they shall see his face; and his name shall be in their foreheads.

5 And there shall be no night there; and they need no candle, neither light of the sun; for the Lord God giveth them light: and they shall reign for ever and ever.

"He" (v. 1) is the bowl angel of 21:9, continuing to reveal to John the glories of the new Heaven and earth and New Jerusalem. The immediate focus is on "a pure river of water of life" flowing from God's throne (cf. 7:17; Ps. 46:4; Ezek.

47:1-12; Zech. 14:8; Jl. 3:18; Gen. 2:10). Rivers historically have been associated with great cities, notable for their ability to sustain life and bring prosperity. Rivers thus doubly symbolize life, for the commerce they generate and because water is the most basic nutrient to sustain physical life.

But real water is only the *agent* of life on God's behalf. God ultimately controls and has invested water with its life-sustaining properties. Thus the literal river flowing out from God's throne is also symbolic of this (see Ps. 1:3); that it flows from God's throne confirms that He is the source of life and of all literal water in eternity. Even idealist Brighton (625) recognizes the literal and symbolic nature of this river, saying first that it "refers to the spiritual power of God and of the Lamb that will sustain forever the communal life of God's people with him in the new Heaven and earth"; and then that it "indicates that all physical life will also be richly supplied by pure natural water as in the first Eden." (This river should not be confused with a similar one, depicted in Ezek 47:1-12 and Zech. 14:8, that exists during the millennium. The old earth has passed into oblivion by 22:1.)

That the throne belongs to the Lamb not only points to the deity of Christ but also attributes to Him an eternal role as King and Shepherd, fulfilling prophecies that suggest He will rule and shepherd His people forever (7:17; 3:21; 11:15; cf. Lk. 1:33). God and the Lamb have appeared at the throne together since 5:6 (7:9, 10, 17; 14:4, 10; 15:3; 21:22, 23: 22:1, 3).

"Pure" (Greek *katharos*), as applied to the river (literally and figuratively), means "*clean, pure*; literally, as free from dirt" (ALGNT 209). It is free from

all pollutants, which also represents the holy nature of the heavenly environment. Though many manuscripts do not include "pure," essentially the same meaning is indicated by "clear as crystal," which affirms a visible purity (cf. 21:11, 18, 21.). (On this expression, see 21:11.) The river is pure because its Source is "the throne of God and of the Lamb," both infinitely pure or holy (Jas. 3:11,12). The sparkling quality of the river of life suggests that its waters may reflect the radiant light of God's glory that illuminates the New Jerusalem.

Clear, refreshing, sparkling, flowing water is unavoidably inviting. The river of life has a singular beauty that is commensurate with the other beautiful things in Heaven. "Proceeding" (Greek *ekporeuomai*) means "*go from or out of a place, depart from, emerge, come forth*" (ALGNT 139). In other words, the river is *active*, flowing constantly from the throne, apparently symbolizing the ongoing nature of eternal life. There is no apparent reason to equate the flowing river to the Holy Spirit or as the eternal procession of the Spirit from the Father (see Lenski 649).

Editors and interpreters of the text differ on punctuation here. Some place a period after v. 1, others a comma. If the latter, the sentence continues and the river flows from the throne into the midst of the street (NIV: "down the middle of the street"). However, most editions of the text separate the two sentences with a period and it seems best to recognize it. Even so, the river apparently flows through "the midst of the street of it" (v. 2; see 21:21; Is. 35:6-9), thus marking the river's course. "It" is the New Jerusalem, the heavenly city. Indeed, the "street" (Greek *plateias*) may be more like a "city-square" or "plaza": ancient cities were often laid out square with a plaza or open area in the center. John portrays the river of life flowing through it and on through the wall of the city out into the new earth beyond. Such an open, central plaza would provide a location for God's throne, suitable for worship services. Regardless, this emphasizes "the river's centrality to the city as a whole and its visibility to all residents" (Michaels 246). (Compare the street or plaza of Babylon where the two witnesses' bodies were displayed for ridicule, 11:8, 9.)

In addition to the river of life was the "tree of life" (singular) growing in the middle of the "street"—or plaza—in the New Jerusalem (2:7; 22:14). "Tree" (Greek *xulon*) is not the usual word for a living tree but usually denotes "wood"; it is typically used for an object made of wood, and it is often used for the cross of Christ (Acts 5:30; 10:39; cf. Gal. 3:13). This is unusual (and apparently deliberate) enough that it may subtly blend the ideas of the cross of Christ and the tree of life (Hendriksen 206; Thompson 185). Even so, here it refers to the ultimate tree of life in Heaven.

The tree of life first appeared in the Garden of Eden along with the tree of the knowledge of good and evil (Gen. 2:9), the two trees representing true freedom of choice. By contrast, the tree of the knowledge of good and evil (the potential to sin) does not exist in Heaven; the existence of only the tree of life memorializes the wisdom of those who have chosen life over death by choosing Christ. It represents their final choice and their final condition in God's sight. They are awarded eternal life and will live forever with God and Christ in eternity. (One implication from Gen. 3:22 is that had Adam and Eve chosen, instead,

to eat from the tree of life, they would have received eternal life at that point.)

All life has its beginning in God. If the river of life flowing from the throne suggests that God is the source of life, the tree alongside the river and street signifies that God "sustains" life throughout eternity. Again, it is appropriate for literal things (river and tree) to have rich symbolism. The eternal life of God's people is no less real if God employs glorified but literal objects to sustain it. Like the river, the tree and the life sustained by them are *pure*; pure life is eternal life, since nothing can compromise it.

Does this mean a single tree on "either side of the river"? Some think so; Walvoord (330), for example, conceives a tree "large enough to span the river." More likely, "tree" is a "collective" term referring to more than one tree; a number of interpreters take this approach and conceive "numerous trees found along both banks of the river" (Aune III:1177). Literally, the words read: "from here and from here (or, there)," surely meaning on each side; and there is no "the" with "tree of life." This seems to support the idea of a beautiful tree-lined avenue on both sides of the river of life. It is possible, of course, that a solitary "tree of life" parents others along the riverbanks.

In 2:7 Jesus placed the "tree of life" in the "paradise" of God; here the tree of life is in Heaven (as the eternal state); obviously, then, "paradise" is synonymous with "Heaven" as we typically use the term. (See the commentary on 2 Cor. 12:2-4.) Based on the background of "paradise" as a Persian loan-word for an enclosed garden or park (TDNT II:760, 761), Brighton conceives of Heaven as a restored Garden of Eden, "a garden which was rich and luxurious in its vegetation and contained every delightful pleasure of life in communion with God" (627). He adds: "It may be that the *entire orb of the physical earth* in its restored condition will be a virtual Garden of Eden" (631). Michaels (247) suggests that the new garden is inside "the heart of the city," but it is possible that if the river flows out of the city into the new earth it will produce Edenic conditions wherever it flows. In light of 21:1, the river of life may be the only water source in the new Heaven and earth, conceivably forming additional rivers, streams and lakes. "The theology of the incarnation itself suggests that, as a result of Christ's redemptive activity and his own bodily resurrection, those in Christ in the resurrection will be restored to God's original design for humanity's bodily state, and so also will the present earth be restored to its original, divinely intended state as the home for God's resurrected people" (Brighton 632). The story of Revelation is in many ways the story of paradise restored.

The tree (or trees) of life will bear "twelve manner of fruits," perhaps different kinds of fruit on the same tree (Ladd, *Commentary* 288) or the same fruit twelve different times (L. Morris 249). The italicized *"manner of"* has been added by the translators; the words, literally (according to Marshall's interlinear 775) are: "producing fruits twelve according to month each rendering the fruit of it," thus possibly suggesting a monthly yield—whether one or two or many trees. Regardless, the expression of "time" must be regarded as figurative of *frequency*, since time is not measurable in Heaven as now. Clearly, the new earth is infinitely more fertile and produces better fruit than the present earth.

Further, the twelve different kinds of fruit suggest significant variety. Ripe, perfect fruit is always *in season* in the New Jerusalem.

The evergreen leaves of the tree of life provide "healing for the nations," likewise to be regarded as symbolic of eternal provision for well-being since no disease, imperfection, or death exists in the eternal state. All these were banished (21:4). God, however, delights to shepherd and provide for all the needs of His children. A significant component of a good shepherd's care for his sheep included anointing their wounds with oil (Ps. 23). Jesus cared for the physical needs of people and healed many. "Healing" (Greek *therapeia*) "primarily denotes 'care, attention'; then, 'medical service, healing' (Vine 295). Thus in this context the word need not be limited to medical help; it may as easily indicate "care" or "provision" for all sorts of needs. In the final analysis, "The healing leaves indicate the complete absence of physical and spiritual want" (Mounce 400). "In other words, the leaves of the tree promote the enjoyment of life in the new Jerusalem, and are not for correcting ills which do not exist" (Walvoord 330).

On "the nations," compare 21:24 and see comments there. What began as one nation of God in the O.T. (Israel) has expanded to include representatives from every nation, fulfilling God's promises in the Abrahamic covenant (Gen. 12:1-3). "Heaven" includes a multinational family that makes regular pilgrimages to the New Jerusalem to bring God all their glory and honor (21:24, 26). Christ's redemption has restored that original design. Importantly, the family of God remains as one forever but not in a way that erases historical distinctions. We shall know even as we are known.

Verse 3 affirms yet another difference between the new Heaven and earth and the present order of things: "There shall be no more curse." "Curse" (Greek *katathema*) is not the pronouncement but the thing cursed: anything "delivered over to divine wrath" and thus "*accursed thing*" (ALGNT 217). Here this apparently means that which God Himself has devoted to destruction, specifically the curse of sin, which is death—spiritual, physical, and eternal. The death, burial, and resurrection of Christ conquered these forever, so that the curse and its consequences are cast into the lake of fire after the Great White Throne Judgment (20:14). Nothing in Heaven is under any curse; everything is consecrated to God. Furthermore, since the devil and all his followers (human and angelic) are banished to Hell forever, no such curse can occur again: as noted, the tree of knowledge of good and evil is not present. Again, then, the theme of paradise restored is implied: "The theme of returning to Eden continues with the reversal of the curse [v. 3], which answers Genesis 3:14-19" (Poythress 193).

Instead of any accursed thing is "the throne of God and the Lamb" eternally present, guaranteeing a permanently holy environment and holy worship, conduct, and service. One may rightly anticipate significant service activity on the part of God's family throughout eternity, given the doubly emphatic ""his servants shall serve him." According to 7:15-17, such "service" is constant: "day and night." Jesus the Lamb, as Eternal Shepherd, feeds them and leads them to drink from living fountains of water—the river of life flowing from God's throne.

Furthermore, His people "shall see his face" (v. 4), in significant contrast to the Biblical tradition that no one sees God and lives (Ex. 33:20-23; cf. Jn. 1:18; 6:46; 1 Jn. 4:12; 1 Tim. 6:16). This is itself a commentary on the confirmed holiness of the redeemed in eternity. Even great Bible heroes like Isaiah and Daniel were terrified in God's *mediated* presence, but the reasons for such fear are absent in Heaven. Perfect love casts out fear and such love is perfected between God and man in Heaven. Each believer's redeemed, resurrected, and glorified body exists in Heaven in an absolutely holy condition, enabling a close personal relationship with an absolutely holy God—and all by the grace of God through Jesus the Lamb.

That God's "name shall be in their foreheads" has precedents in Revelation and is a reward given in fulfillment of Christ's promise to faithful followers (2:17; 3:12; 7:3; 14:1; 13:16). Swete (301) suggests that such a "branding" represents "entire consecration to the service of God"; it may also suggest "ownership," "protection," or "authority." Other interpreters suggest similar meanings for the name on the foreheads: "they reflect the divine glory in their persons" (Thomas II:487); "the priestly nature of God's new people" (based on the O.T. High Priest who wore God's name on his forehead, Ex. 28:36-38) and "a figurative way of speaking of God's presence with his people" (Beale 1114).

On "there shall be no night there" (v. 5), see the comments on 21:23 (cf. Is. 60:19, 20). Heaven will be one eternal day illuminated by the light of God's glory and the Lamb. No lesser sources of light, whether the sun as strongest or "candles" at the opposite end of the spectrum, are needed because of the incomparable brightness of the Lord God who gives light (cf. "the light of his countenance," Num. 6:25, 26). God's glory is diffused by the New Jerusalem throughout the new Heaven and earth; if any other buildings are constructed, they only need openings to let the light of God's glory shine through.

"They" (three times in vv. 4, 5) are God's "servants" (v. 3). That they will "reign for ever and ever" serves to remind that all the conditions being described in the vision that began in 21:1 are permanent, in contrast to the limited millennial reign in 20:4-6. The blessed relationship with God and all the glorious conditions of the new order will never come to an end (cf. Dan. 7:18, 27). The reign of God's servants in the new Heaven and earth recalls the dominion over created things in the Garden of Eden originally given to Adam and mankind—again fulfilling God's original design.

Summary
(21:1-22:5)

The visions in chapter 20 revealed the millennial reign of Christ, the dissolution of the old universe, the Great White Throne Judgment, and the assignment of personal ultimate destinies to either Heaven or Hell. After that, John saw the new Heaven and earth come into being (v. 1), a world so new and different that there are no oceans there. John then observed the holy city, the New Jerusalem, beautifully adorned like a bride on her wedding day, descending from Heaven to the new earth (v. 2).

A great angelic voice from Heaven interpreted the significance of what John had just seen (v. 3). God will per-

sonally and permanently dwell with His people in the New Jerusalem, thus fulfilling His original design in creating mankind. History is the story of God's redemption of His people through Christ and that goal has finally been realized at this point in the revelations.

In the final, eternal disposition of things—that is, in this eternal, blessed relationship—God will nurture His people, meeting every need. He will wipe away their tears and banish everything that plagued mankind in the old order: death, sorrow, crying, and pain (v. 4). God promised to make all things new, and all His words are true and faithful. They come from the sovereign God who sits on the throne over all (v. 5).

Thus "It is done" marks the end of the story of redemption (v. 6). This statement reaches back to the decrees of God before creation and covers everything done in history up to the beginning of the eternal state. As Alpha and Omega, God has conceived, created, controlled, consummated, and recreated the universe. He is the beginning, the end, and everything in between. In this light, a gospel invitation is in order, inviting all to receive the water of life and become part of God's family. This invitation to the "thirsty" includes anyone willing to come and drink and so to receive a salvation and eternity that are gracious and free for acceptance by faith. Such faith is equal to "overcoming" and is rewarded by inheritance of all that Heaven is, including unmediated fellowship with God as His child (v. 7).

Those who will not enter Heaven are listed, illustrating the character of those who do not know God. They include the fearful, unbelieving, abominable, murderers, whoremongers, sorcerers, idolaters, and liars. Individuals manifesting such behaviors are judged on this basis (works) and cast into a fiery Hell forever (v. 8).

A more detailed description of the New Jerusalem follows (vv. 9-27). The angel took John to the mountain that would serve as the pedestal for the heavenly city (v. 10). John recorded what he saw, including the actual dimensions and building materials used to construct the heavenly city.

The most conspicuous thing about the New Jerusalem was the incredible light of God's glory illuminating it (v. 11). The light was compared to a clear (opaque) "jasper" stone of exceptional quality, "clear as crystal." The light shone through, significant enough that it served as the only light source of the new Heaven and earth illuminating the entire new earth.

The city had a great wall surrounding it (v. 12), measured 144 cubits in either height or width (v. 17), or both. The wall had 12 gates, three per side (v. 13), each made of one great pearl (v. 21). Each gate was inscribed with the name of one of the tribes of Israel, memorializing Israel's distinctive role in salvation history and continuing place in God's family (vv. 12, 21). An angel was posted, a symbolic sentry, at each gate (v. 12).

The city also had 12 foundations, perhaps layered underneath the wall, decorated with precious stones: jasper, sapphire, chalcedony, emerald, sardonyx, sardius, chrysolite, beryl, topaz, chrysoprasus, jacinth, and amethyst. These foundations were named after the twelve apostles of the Lamb (v. 14), perhaps symbolizing the founding of the church on the preaching of the gospel and the Word of God. Regardless, this portrayed the distinctive role of the church in salvation history and the eternal place of the N.T. church in the family of God.

The measurements of the city, taken by the angel, were staggering (v. 15). It was configured as a giant, square cube (v. 16), with length, breadth, and height equal: 12,000 furlongs—roughly 1,400-1,500 miles—for each side and its height. This translates into literal adequacy for multiplied millions of dwelling places. The building material of choice for the city proper and its streets was an infinitely pure gold, clear as crystal and exceeding any gold in our experience (vv. 18, 21).

There was no Temple in the new Heaven and earth (v. 22): the unmediated, personal presence of the Lord God Almighty and the Lamb obviate the necessity for a temple. Further, since the glory of God and the Lamb illumine her, the city has no need of other luminaries like sun and moon (v. 23). The new light source is fully adequate, enabling the saved nations and kings of the new earth to live in its light (v. 24). The redeemed kings who rule these nations bring all their glory and honor into the New Jerusalem where it rightfully belongs (vv. 24, 26).

The gates of the city are never closed at night: there is no nighttime in Heaven's eternal day (v. 25). Nor is there any potential for unauthorized access; anything that would bring "defilement" or any person who practices "abominations" or "lies" has been eternally removed (v. 26). Only those whose names are in the Lamb's Book of Life may enter (v. 27).

The angel-guide of 21:9 continued showing the New Jerusalem and the new Heaven and earth (22:1-5), especially with its Eden-like features. A river symbolizing eternal life flowed from the throne of God and the Lamb (v. 1) through the middle of the city's street or plaza. A tree (also symbolizing eternal life) grew on each side of the river; indeed, perhaps twelve of them grew from it and lined the river on both sides. These trees constantly bore fruit in twelve varieties or seasons. The fruit and leaves of these trees symbolized God's eternal provision for His people inhabiting the new earth as "nations" (v. 2).

There was no curse (death, disease, hunger) in the new order (v. 3), its central focus being the throne of God and the Lamb as the source and sustainment of eternal life (v. 3). Heaven is not only a place of worship, it is a place of activity since God's servants will actively serve Him.

God's servants will also see God face-to-face (v. 4): they will have unmediated access into His very presence with a real holiness of their own. They will wear God's name in their foreheads, indicating that they have the character of God, that they belong eternally to Him, and that He protects and provides for them.

In the eternal state, the solar day no longer exists; God and the Lamb serve as the only sources of light for the new Heaven and earth (v. 5). His servants will reign with Him and the Lamb forever, fulfilling Bible prophecies predicting the eternal reign of Christ and those who follow Him.

Application: Teaching and Preaching the Passage

One of the key differences between premillennial-futurist interpretation and amillennial-idealist interpretation is about how O.T. promises or predictions in regard to the nation of Israel and Jerusalem are actually fulfilled. Premillennialism advocates that such promises are fulfilled in a millennial reign of Christ over the present earth after the Second Coming of Christ and before eternity proper begins. Amillennialism advocates a spiritual reign of Christ that began with His first advent and that continues until the Second Coming, followed immediately by a general judgment and the inauguration of eternity proper. Thus, idealism views as happening in Heaven and the eternal age a lot of what futurism views as happening in the literal millennial period of earth's history. The two viewpoints see God's promises fulfilled in different ways and in different times. What futurists see fulfilled in a literal millennial period is blended into the eternal age by the idealist.

Many idealists regard the "New Jerusalem" in Rev. 21 as symbolic rather than a literal city with physical dimensions stated. The "city" represents the redeemed as they exist in the presence of God in eternity. It seems more likely, however, that even though elements of the description represent important truths, the details are meant to be taken literally. If the saints will inhabit corporeal, glorified bodies, then it is appropriate to view the description as applying to a corporeal, glorified place. Christ, in His glorified body, could both eat and pass through a closed door. The eternal state of things may well have elements beyond human understanding, but we may not push something aside simply because we do not fully understand it. There are many mysteries (the Holy Trinity, for example) that will only be understood when our minds are made perfect. To argue against literal objects in Heaven on the basis that they are supposedly not "needed" misses the point. God does not need a throne to sit on but He has one.

Conversely, it also follows that we need not ignore the symbolism in order to uphold the reality of the features of the New Jerusalem. The literal, created universe declares the glory of God (Ps. 19:1-6), and so is both corporeal and symbolic. Just so, it is reasonable to think that there will be literal objects in Heaven that also have symbolic meaning. A. Johnson (197) asks, appropriately, "How different is this concept of heaven from that of Hinduism, for example?...Here heaven is depicted as a city, with life, activity, interest, and people, as opposed to the Hindu ideal of heaven as a sea into which human life returns like a raindrop to the ocean."

We must be careful to distinguish when such symbolic interpretation is being supplied to the text or taken from it: we may be absolutely confident only when the Scripture supplies its own interpretation—as when the great prostitute "Babylon" is subsequently interpreted (chapters 17 and 18) as "a great city"; cf. 12:3 and 12:9, or 19:8. The provision of such detailed dimensions of the New Jerusalem points to the existence of a literal city rather than viewing it as *only* a symbol of God's presence with His people. The concept of a future, literal, heavenly city and the cohabitation of God with His people are not antithetical.

Along these lines, the literal walls, with gates that are never shut, serve as permanent symbols of the gracious access into Heaven made possible by Christ. Such thick, high walls would normally keep people out, but the fact that they are permanently open reflects God's grace. Otherwise, access would not be possible.

Faith must sometimes be exercised in regard to the incredible realities portrayed that we do not yet fully understand. We must simply take God at His Word rather than rationalizing them away.

In a different vein, evangelicals who believe that the present world is going to be destroyed have sometimes been accused of neglecting their responsibilities to the present environment or of abandoning the political process and any hope of revival in the present. This certainly prompts legitimate questions about our present responsibilities as believers toward the environment or the political process, or about what God might do through us in the here-and-now. How much attention or labor should we devote to earthly causes lest we become "too heavenly minded to be of any earthly good"?

If believers and churches are sometimes apathetic about present concerns—whether about conservation, social causes, political activity, or the hope of revival—the blame may not be placed on conservative Biblical eschatology. To suggest that the literal schools of eschatological interpretation advocate such is to misrepresent them and to impugn the Scriptures. We who believe in a real, future judgment cannot escape into irresponsible futurism. What we do now will be the basis for our judgment then.

The Bible is not silent about stewardship of creation, civic responsibility, and an optimistic view of life in the present. We must examine our Bibles afresh to find direction in such matters. Ours is not an eschatology of doom; the knowledge that time is running out should stimulate us to redeem the time responsibly. Consciousness of the Second Coming and the Day of the Lord motivates us to change our behavior for the good in the present time (2 Pet. 3:10-13).

Suggested Outlines. The Newness of Eternal Life, 21:1-7: (1) A new Heaven and new earth, v. 1; (2) A new Jerusalem, v. 2; (3) A new relationship with God, v. 3; (4) A new existence without former problems, v. 4; (5) A new assurance, v. 5; (6) A new invitation to accept the gospel, v. 6; (7) A new inheritance, v. 7.

Some Things That Will Not Be In Heaven, 21:1, 4, 8, 22, 23, 25, 27: (1) No sea or oceans, v. 1; (2) Nothing that causes tears: death, sorrow, crying, or pain, v. 4; (3) None who are mentioned in Hell's rollcall, v. 8; (4) No temple, v. 22; (5) No sun or moon, v. 23; (6) No night, v. 25; (7) No defilement, v. 27.

EPILOGUE (22:6-21)

"Rev. 22:10-20 constitutes an 'epilogue' in that it exhibits striking thematic similarities with the 'prologue' in 1:1-8" (Aune III:1236). At this point the revelations have basically come to an end and the work concludes with a mixture of remarks from the bowl angel, John, the Holy Spirit, and even "the bride." These voices challenge all humanity to live in the light of the book's sobering truths, to prepare for the awesome future events predicted, and to change behavior if necessary.

A. Assurances (22:6-17)

6 And he said unto me, These sayings *are* faithful and true: and the Lord God of the holy prophets sent his angel to shew unto his servants the things which must shortly be done.

7 Behold, I come quickly: blessed *is* he that keepeth the sayings of the prophecy of this book.

8 And I John saw these things, and heard *them.* And when I had heard and seen, I fell down to worship before the feet of the angel which shewed me these things.

9 Then saith he unto me, See *thou do it* not: for I am thy fellowservant, and of thy brethren the prophets, and of them which keep the sayings of this book: worship God.

10 And he saith unto me, Seal not the sayings of the prophecy of this book: for the time is at hand.

11 He that is unjust, let him be unjust still: and he which is filthy, let him be filthy still: and he that is righteous, let him be righteous still: and he that is holy, let him be holy still.

12 And, behold, I come quickly; and my reward *is* with me, to give every man according as his work shall be.

13 I am Alpha and Omega, the beginning and the end, the first and the last.

14 Blessed *are* they that do his commandments, that they may have a right to the tree of life, and may enter in through the gates into the city.

15 For without *are* dogs, and sorcerers, and whoremongers, and murderers, and idolaters, and whosoever loveth and maketh a lie.

16 I Jesus have sent mine angel to testify unto you these things in the churches. I am the root and the

**offspring of David, *and* the bright
and morning star.
17 And the Spirit and the bride
say, Come. And let him that heareth
say, Come. And let him that is
athirst come. And whosoever will,
let him take the water of life freely.**

The bowl angel (21:9) begins the
concluding remarks by affirming the
trustworthiness of the revelations:
"These sayings are faithful and true" (v.
6); compare 21:5 (the reversed order is
not significant). The revelations are
trustworthy because God gave them and
because Christ's own faithfulness and
truthfulness were demonstrated in His
own life, death, burial, and resurrection.
Christ gave the world all the words of
God that had been given to Him and
remained faithful under pressure unto
death—the ideal martyr.

The revelations may also be trusted
because of their divine inspiration. They
have come from "the Lord God of the
holy prophets" (cf. 1:1-5, 11, 19; 5:1;
10:1, 2, 8-11; 2 Pet. 1:20, 21; 2 Tim.
3:16; Eph. 2:20). The angel's own role
is included: he was commissioned by
God as an agent in the process of transmission, consisting of God, Jesus Christ,
the angel, John, the pastors of the
seven churches, and their congregations
(1:1). "Of the holy prophets" apparently
includes both O.T. and N.T. prophets,
thus affirming that the God of Revelation
is the God of both and maintaining continuity in the story of redemption. "All
true prophecy originates with God and
comes through people moved by the
Holy Spirit [2 Pet. 1:21]" (Mounce
404). (Most manuscripts read "the Lord
God of the spirits of the [holy] prophets," which does not change the overall

meaning.) As Swete (303) notes, the
spirits "are the natural faculties of the
prophets, raised and quickened by the
Holy Spirit, but still under the prophets'
control, and standing in a creaturely
relation to God" (1 Cor. 14:32).

The original commission in 1:1 is
repeated here: "to show unto his servants the things which must be shortly
done"; see the comments there. The
"things which must shortly be done" (cf.
1:19) are the events revealed thus far,
especially from 6:1—22:5. (On "shortly" see below on v. 7.) The things "near"
in God's plan for the future are: (1) the
Tribulation (seal, trumpet, and bowl
judgments); (2) the Second Coming of
Christ; (3) the Battle of Armageddon; (4)
the millennial reign of Christ; (5) the
annihilation of the old universe; (6) the
Great White Throne Judgment; and (7)
the transition into the eternal age, including the creation of a new Heaven and
earth and descent of the New Jerusalem.
This is the context for 2 Pet. 3:10-14.

The revelations were for the benefit
of God's "servants" (cf. 1:1; 19:10;
22:9). As noted, the word refers to
bondservants and implies ownership
and service for life: "one that is in a
permanent relation of servitude to
another, his will altogether swallowed up
in the will of the other" (Trench 30).
Many interpreters suggest that a major
motif of Revelation is the encouragement of God's people to persevere in
faith and service in the midst of tribulations. The revelations about the victorious outcome of faith and the catastrophic end of unbelief provide this encouragement to remain faithful in the present and thus to be prepared to meet
Christ in the eschatological future. Future
judgment is based on present behavior,

proving the value of the study of eschatology.

The idea here is that the revealed events will take place very soon or that the time is near (cf. 1:3; 3:11; 22:10, 12, 20), not (as some suggest) that once they start happening they will take place swiftly. The time of Christ's coming is unpredictable; consequently, a spirit of expectancy and watchfulness for the Lord's return is a Biblical mandate for every believer in every generation. Both Jesus and the apostles promoted such an attitude, even in the first century of church history. This theme continues into the next verse with a specific reference to the Second Coming in v. 7.

Christ's first-person prediction of His coming in v. 7 may be a direct quote from Him by the angel-guide, or perhaps an insertion by John himself (Lenski 659); regardless, Jesus was the original speaker. This concluding remark, predicting the future from John's original vantage point (and from ours), reflects the revelation of the Second Coming in 19:11-21, which takes place at the end of the Tribulation. This is the central theme of the revelations (see 1:7; 3:3, 11; 16:15; 22:12, 20). "Quickly" (Greek *tachu*) is the same word as "shortly" in v. 6 (see comments there): it can qualify an action as done *"quickly, swiftly, rapidly"* or a time as being *"without delay, right away, at once, soon"* (ALGNT 376). The latter is surely the meaning here.

Given that 1,900 years of history have elapsed since John recorded these words, what did Jesus mean by "soon"? Preterists suggest that Jesus did in fact come *in judgment* in A.D. 70 when Jerusalem and the Temple were destroyed by the Romans. But Christ's prediction cannot reasonably be taken to mean anything other than His bodily return at the end of the present age; nothing in the text warrants any other view. The tension that exists between Jesus' use of "soon" and a delay of 1,900 or more years is resolved by viewing the word against *God's* sense of timing. That is, a thousand years are as one day and vice versa to God (2 Pet. 3:8); in light of God's eternal existence, the whole history of the cosmos is brief! As already noted, one of the reasons for this pronouncement is that every generation of believers must know that His Coming is soon and maintain a sense of urgency and expectation. He could in fact come within the span of any generation. In that sense, "I come quickly" is timeless.

"Blessed is he that keepeth the sayings of the prophecy of this book" likewise picks back up from 1:3; see the comments there. This emphasizes being doers of the Word, being "overcomers" in an anti-Christian culture, and weighing present behavior against the realities of the future—including the prospect of personal judgment and the possibility of the "second death" as measured against the joy of eternal life. "Keepeth" (Greek present participle) suggests the habitual observance of God's Word.

The "sayings of the prophecy of this book" are, first, its entire contents: the letters to the churches, the visions, doxologies of worship, proclamations by angelic messengers, gospel invitations, etc. But at this point there is special reference to the immediately preceding revelation of eternity proper (21:1—22:5). "Sayings" (Greek *logos*) may also be translated as "words"; the Word of God generally and Revelation specifically are in view. Furthermore, the blessing pronounced includes the blessing of receiving a revelation of God's Word and will (Wall 262). A significant part of the blessing may be *the "inspiration" that comes from God* to us within our souls as we read, hear, and obey.

John has received the revelations in two (sensory) ways: he *heard* and *saw* (v. 8). Many of the revelations had an *audible* component: the voices of elders and angels offering doxologies, commands, interpretations, proclamations, and encouragements; the peal of thunder and lightning; beautiful vocal and instrumental music; perhaps even the voices of God or Christ. Even more prominent was the *visual* component: "I saw" appears almost 40 times. It may well be that this emphasis "reflects the widespread ancient view that the only reliable access to knowledge of past and present events is through the two senses of hearing and sight" (Aune III:1185; cf. 1 Jn. 1:1-3; Jn. 20:24-31).

As in 19:10, John's initial response was to fall before the angelic agent of the revelations in worship. Having been rebuked there, we wonder why John would make that mistake again—if it should be viewed as a mistake. John's humble and grateful attitude was correct but misdirected. He might not have been thinking of the angel *per se*; no doubt he was very much aware that the revelations were from God Himself, and he certainly knew the difference between God and an angel and that only God is worthy of worship. Perhaps John associated the angel so closely with God that the prostration seemed appropriate and was actually directed to God. The angel's rebuff, each time, may have been more didactic than anything else, serving to emphasize that God alone is to be worshiped and secondarily as a polemic against angel worship.

Therefore the angel rightly interrupted John: "See thou do it not" (v. 9). The message, however divine, is not just cause for deifying the messenger. The angel was but "a fellow servant" of John, of John's brothers "the holy prophets" (as in v. 6), and of "them that keep the sayings of this book." The last phrase is significant as a description of believers, identifying true Christians as those in the habit of obeying God's Word (see comments on v. 7). Belief and behavior are not divorced in the N.T.

The angel also commanded, "Seal not the sayings of the prophecy of this book" (v. 10). "Seal" (Greek *sphragizo*) is used often in Revelation (5:1; 7:1; 9:4; 14:1; 20:3), meaning either "*seal up, secure by putting a seal on*" or "*providing a sign of identification or ownership (mark with a seal)*" (ALGNT 371). The former is apparently the meaning here, but with John instructed *not* thus to "seal" up what he had recorded: "for the time is at hand" (cf. 1:1-3; 19; Dan. 8:26; 12:4, 9). In other words, the Second Coming of Christ is near. The unveiling of this message assists and challenges humanity to prepare for the denouement of world history. "At hand" is to be explained in the very same way as "quickly"; see comments on v. 7. The potentiality and unpredictability of Christ's return serves each believer as a constant motivation for readiness. The reminder "for the time is at hand" is for the express benefit of each generation of church history: "The tension of imminence is endemic to that span of redemptive history lying between the cross and the parousia" (Mounce 406).

The imperatives in v. 11 have the form of commands or exhortations that carry the sense of a final pronouncement. Each confirms what the individual has already personally decided, thus affirming how a person has lived (and perhaps died) and reflecting final choices for good or bad. "The time arrives when change is impossible because character has already been determined by a lifetime of habitual action....The arrival of the end forecloses any possibility of alteration" (Mounce 406). God deals with us on the basis of how we are today, a principle that can work to our advantage or disadvantage (cf. Ezek. 33:12-16). He deals with each of us on the basis of our *final* decision, whenever it is made (even at the last minute if sincere, as in Lk. 23:39-43). At least theoretically, repentance is always an option as long as a person remains alive.

The first two character qualities named, "unjust" and "filthy," are negative and refer exclusively to unbelievers. "Unjust" (Greek *adikos*) is defined as "generally *characterized by violation of divine law*; as doing what is contrary to right, *unrighteous, wrong*" (ALGNT 35). This may have reference to external behavior or works, while "filthy" (Greek *hruparos*) may focus on inner condition or sinful nature and means "*dirty, filthy, foul...morally impure, degenerate, completely bad*" (ALGNT 343).

"Righteous" and "holy" are positive and refer to believers, also probably indicating behavior and character respectively. "Righteous" (Greek *dikaios*) is a moral and ethical term, meaning "*righteous, upright, just...law-abiding, honest, good*" though it often indicates being "rightly related to God, *righteous, just*; *put right*" (ALGNT 116). This may refer to the external behavior or works of a believer. "Holy" (Greek *hagios*) is "the quality of persons or things that can

be brought near or into God's presence," thus "*holy...dedicated, sacred... consecrated to God*" (ALGNT 32). This may refer to the inner spiritual condition, the regenerated nature of the believer.

The first part of v. 12—"Behold, I come quickly"—repeats from v. 7 for emphasis, in both instances a direct quotation, either by the angel, or John, of Christ Himself (see comments there, and on v. 20). The Second Coming effectively freezes in place the spiritual condition of all mankind—yet another reason Jesus strongly emphasized the importance of being ready and watching for His return (Mt. 24:36-44; 25:13).

The Second Coming is also the cutoff point for "reward" (Greek *misthos*), which means "*pay, wages...reward, compensation*" and sometimes in a strictly negative sense "*punishment, reward*" (ALGNT 264). Christ comes to reward either positively or negatively according to one's works. When He returns, He will bring His "reward" with Him in order to "give" or reward "every man according as his work shall be" (see Ec. 12:13, 14; Jer. 17:10; Mt. 6:19, 20; 16:27; 25:14-30; Rom. 2:6-10, 16; 1 Cor. 3:8-15; 2 Cor. 5:10; Rev. 2:23).

The N.T. portrays an even balance between the importance of grace and good works. "Grace" (Greek *charis*) appears 156 times, "works" (Greek *ergon*) 176 times. The principle of justification by faith alone is not antithetical to a proper concept of the place of "works" in a believer's life. Even the believer's works will be scrutinized by God, at the Judgment Seat of Christ, and rewarded accordingly, as will the works of unbelievers at the Great White Throne Judgment. The most basic "reward" that Christ brings to believers is eternal life—certainly reward enough. But Scripture also suggests that other rewards will be bestowed, based on faithful service. The reward of unbelievers' works is *ironic* because being sent to Hell is not really "reward" at all.

"I am Alpha and Omega" (v. 13), spoken by Christ Himself, expresses His timeless and sovereign nature, with "the beginning and the end" and "the first and the last" essentially restating the same truth (see comments on 1:8). In these expressions Christ is both Creator and Consummator of all things, and everything in between—Sustainer and Redeemer.

"Blessed are they that do his commandments" (v. 14) signals the importance of believing behavior. The Bible never separates faith and walk, nor does justification by faith alone mitigate personal responsibility in doing good works (Mt. 5:17-20; Acts 26:20; Eph. 2:8-10; Tit. 2:7,14; 3:1, 8). The right to eat from "the tree of life" and to enter "through the gates of the city" are equivalent to inheriting eternal life and are properly viewed as the consequence or reward of good works that reflect the existence of true faith (Rom. 6:19, 21, 22; Acts 26:20; Jas. 2:14-26). (A few manuscripts have "that wash their robes" instead of "that do his commandments." Though the two readings express different aspects of truth, both indicate "believers" equally well and are not contradictory.)

Having a "right to the tree of life" and to "enter in through the gates into the city" recalls that Adam and Eve were denied access to the Garden of Eden after the fall (Gen. 3:22-24). Again, then, the analogy of paradise lost and regained is invited. Adam and Eve were expelled because of their sinful condition. In contrast, all the redeemed will have unhindered access to the tree of life and may freely enter and exit the New Jerusalem at will.

Verse 15 gives a sevenfold list of those excluded from Heaven: dogs, sorcerers, whoremongers, murderers, idolaters, those who love a lie, and those who make a lie. The deliberate use of seven suggests that *all* unbelievers, with these being representative, are excluded from the joys of eternal life. The list is similar to 21:8; see the comments there on sorcerers, whoremongers, murderers, idolaters, and liars (equivalent to loving and making lies).

"Dogs" (Greek *kuon*) is obviously figurative: "a term of reproach for persons regarded as unholy and impure" (ALGNT 240). No doubt some of a dog's habits make the figure appropriate: Jesus represented "dogs" as unworthy of holy things (Mt. 7:6); Paul used "dogs" for Judaizers who corrupted the doctrine of justification (Phil. 3:2; cf. 2 Pet. 2:22). Charles (II:178) indicates that the word, in ancient times, "was used to denounce the moral impurities of heathen worship"; in Dt. 23:18 it means male prostitutes.

"I Jesus" (v. 16) takes readers back to the divine origin of the revelations in 1:1, 2 (see comments there). Jesus is both the revealer ("I Jesus have sent") and the revealed ("these things"). Again, His use of an angel as an intermediary in transmitting the revelations is indicated. "To you" is plural, apparently referring to John and all believers (the churches) in the chain of transmission, matching the plural used in the messages to the churches in chapters 2 and 3 and elsewhere. John was commissioned directly by the risen Christ (1:11-20) to record and deliver the revelations to local pastors of the seven churches in Asia Minor ("the churches"). From this base in Asia Minor the revelations would eventually be disseminated throughout the ancient world and Revelation would be canonized as the last book of the Bible.

"I am the root and the offspring of David, *and* the bright and morning star" (v. 16) consciously emphasizes Christ's historical identity as the prophesied Messiah of Israel (Is. 11:10; Num. 24:17; Rev. 2:28). The historical connection with Israel must be important because it continues to be repeated and, as we have seen, is permanently etched into the gates of the New Jerusalem (21:12; see 5:5). As the "root" of David, Jesus is more *ancestor* than *descendant* of David though the latter is obviously applicable as well (Thomas II:510). "The bright and morning star" is *prominent* and *permanent* in the sky; as applied to Christ it is "the brightest in the whole galaxy, the Light which lightens every man by its coming into the world [Jn. 1:9]; the Star of Dawn, whose coming precedes the Day of God....He does not fall or set" (Swete 310). It not only rules the morning as the brightest star (planet), its position in the sky never changes. Just so is Christ's character: He is the Messiah of Israel, exalted at the throne of God as the Lamb of God forever, His position and prominence settled in Heaven. The testimony of Christ is absolutely trustworthy because of who He is.

At the conclusion of the revelations, an invitation is expressed four times to "Come" (v. 17). The fourth of these does not use the word "come" but it is implied in the clause "let him take" (v. 17). Three different speakers extended the invitation, the fourth unidentified. There are at least three ways of looking at the invitation to "come." (1) It is plausible that the command is directed to Christ, imploring Him to return (see Thomas II:511). (2) It is equally plausible that this is an invitation directed to unbelievers to receive the gospel. (3) It is possible that both ideas are contained in the verse. In support of the first option is the fact that the Second Coming is clearly in view in v. 20 where John speaks directly to Christ in the words "Amen. Even so, come, Lord Jesus." Jesus had just said, "Surely I come quickly" (v. 20), referring to the Second Coming. In support of the second alternative is the fact that the last two clauses in v. 17 are clearly evangelistic.

"The Spirit" who invites Christ or people to come is the Holy Spirit; He has something to say to unbelievers even as He spoke to the church in all seven messages in chapters 2, 3 (2:7, 11, 17, 29; 3:6, 13, 22). "The bride" could either be the church or the New Jerusalem (comprised of O.T. and N.T. saints dwelling there), since the analogy of bride is applied to both (19:7-9; 21:2, 9, 10). "Him that heareth" (v. 17) is general, referring to anyone. To have "hearers" join in extending the call to come seems a bit awkward. This is because it appears at first to have the hearer either giving or repeating his own invitation. The difficulty may be resolved if the reference is to the remaining host of Heaven to join in giving out the gospel call. Or better, as Mounce (409) explains, "Those who hear and accept repeat the invitation to others who thirst for the water of life."

It seems more natural to envision the church as the bride who is speaking in this instance since N.T. believers have experienced Christ's redemption, have already come to Christ, and are anticipating the future marriage supper. But the all-inclusive nature and tone of the gospel is also very apparent in v. 17 so that all the saints (O.T. and N.T. varieties) may be a part of this collective voice. Regardless, one cannot help noticing an evangelistic emphasis throughout Revelation. This was true even in the midst of the terrible judgments since a special note is appended about their failure to repent. This suggests that the revelations about the future should be used as a tool to evangelize unbelievers. It also serves to inform saints about present responsibilities weighed against the same future predictions. The mention of the Spirit and the church might also reflect their respective roles in the proclamation of the gospel. The Holy Spirit of course works toward that end and the church has a vital role: "It is the testimony of the church empowered by the Holy Spirit that constitutes the great evangelizing force of this age" (Mounce 409).

The basic *precondition* of those who may potentially respond to the invitation is given in the clause "And let him that is athirst come" (v. 17; see comments on 21:6). "Hunger and thirst are frequent metaphors and are often used in the OT, early Judaism, and early Christianity for the need for spiritual satisfaction and fulfillment that can only be provided by God" (Aune III:1229; cf. Mt. 5:6; Jn. 4:1-42).

"Whosoever will" (v. 17) reveals the universal scope of the gospel (Jn. 3:15,16; Rom. 10:13; 2 Pet. 3:9; 1 Jn. 2:1, 2.), consistent with the universal nature of the invitations ("he that hath an ear, let him hear") to the seven churches in chapters 2 and 3. The gos-

pel of Christ is indiscriminately offered to every "kindred, tongue, people, and nation" (5:9; 7:9), including Jews and Gentiles (Eph. 2:11-22).

The invitation to "come" becomes specific: "Let him take the water of life freely." "Water of life" is a metaphor synonymous with salvation provided by Christ (Jn. 4:10, 14; Is. 55:1; Rev. 21:6; 22:1). It is similar to the "river of water of life" that symbolizes eternal life and flows eternally from the throne of God in 22:1.

B. Warnings (22:18, 19)

18 For I testify unto every man that heareth the words of the prophecy of this book, If any man shall add unto these things, God shall add unto him the plagues that are written in this book:
19 And if any man shall take away from the words of the book of this prophecy, God shall take away his part out of the book of life, and out of the holy city, and *from* **the things which are written in this book.**

"For I testify" (v. 18) introduces a sobering warning attached to the end of Revelation (cf. Dt. 4:2). Regardless who spoke the words, Christ or His angel, the words are from Christ Himself, making the warning emphatic and authoritative. Like the invitation, the warning is for "every man that heareth," which emphasizes that those who interact with the Book of Revelation in any way are thereby placed under responsibility for how they respond.

John strengthens his warning with the principle of reciprocation. "If any man shall add" addresses the first of two great errors: reading *more* into the revelations than God intended. "These things" means all John's revelations ("written in this book"); but the warning can apply equally to all of God's Word. Adding to Scripture distorts its meaning and damages people spiritually. Those who do this will be severely judged by God. God will reciprocate by *adding* "the plagues that are written in this book" to those who *add* to Scriptures—an emphatic play on words and another way of saying that God will send such a person to Hell.

John likewise warned about *subtracting* from Scripture: "If any man shall take away from the words of the book of this prophecy" (v. 19) involves the same principle of reciprocation. This warning, too, applies to "any man" who distorts the revelations by taking something away from God's Word, reading *less* into the Scriptures than God intended. For such a person, as for those who add to His Word, God will "take away his part out of the book of life." (Most manuscripts read "the tree of life," but the result is the same since both are metaphors for eternal life.) Further, God will take away his part "out of the holy city." And, third, "the things which are written in this book" will be taken away from the guilty person, referring to the great blessings of eternal life (all the glories of Heaven) described previously. A part of the agony of Hell is missing out on the joys of eternal life; adding to or subtracting from the Bible is that serious.

These warnings also serve as a strong reason for including Revelation in the canon of Scripture: "The warning is a 'stereotyped and vehement form of claiming a canonicity equal to that of the O.T." (Mounce 410, citing Moffat).

Modern interpreters must also handle the Book of Revelation with care, and what applies to it specifically applies to the entire Bible.

C. Conclusion (22:20, 21)

**20 He which testifieth these things saith, Surely I come quickly. Amen. Even so, come, Lord Jesus.
21 The grace of our Lord Jesus Christ *be* with you all. Amen.**

Revelation closes as it began, with a word from Jesus Christ about the great and central theme: His Second Coming (1:7). The combination of such epistolary elements with an overwhelmingly dominant apocalyptic format makes Revelation a unique literary product. "He which testifieth these things" (v. 20) reminds us again that the revelations came from Him as "the true and faithful witness"; they may therefore be trusted.

Two other points are noteworthy in Christ's promise, "Surely I come quickly." One is that "surely" makes the Second Coming *certain*. The other is that "quickly" (or "soon"; *see* on v. 7) makes the Second Coming *near*" (cf. 3:11; 22:7, 12, 20). Christ's promise to return soon is a challenge for *every* believer in *every* generation, implying that Christ's return is unpredictable and could occur at any time. Preparation for the Second Coming is maintained by being ready and watching in the present.

John's concluding response to this truth is "Amen. Even so, come, Lord Jesus"; this suggests that the thought of Christ's return was extremely refreshing to the aging, banished apostle. He was ready for Christ to come and prayed for it in a literal, *eschatological* sense. Caird's idealist interpretation falls short: "It is a prayer that Christ will come again to win in his faithful servant the victory which is both Calvary and Armageddon (288). This sees the prayer as a request for victorious Christian experience only, and every believer can appreciate the need for that without avoiding the obvious reference to the Second Coming. Indeed, with John, we are also challenged to express in prayer our longing for that momentous event.

The Second Coming will right all wrongs in the present world and eventually usher God's people into the bliss of eternal life and direct fellowship with God in Heaven. "The context of this concluding prayer...is indeed a situation of extreme need and stress" (Aune III:1234); such a prayer, therefore, is appropriate for saints in trial in every generation. Compare *maranatha* in 1 Cor. 16:22: "O Lord, come!"—"an Aramaic formula used in early Christian liturgy" (ALGNT 253).

John's final thought was of "grace" (v. 21), appealed to in a benediction more or less common among early Christians. John knew that it would certainly take the grace of God and of Christ to be overcomers in the anti-Christian world, to face the catastrophic future predicted in the revelations, and to be ready for the unpredictable return of Christ. The concluding "Amen" seals the fact that nothing is left to add or subtract: Revelation offers the final Word.

Summary
(22:6-21)

The angel assured John that the revelations he had received were faithful and true and that they were primarily revelations about the future (v. 6).

The scene abruptly retrogressed from eternity to John's own time when the angel quoted Christ's prediction of His own Second Coming. Christ promised that He would come soon and pronounced the sixth beatitude of blessing in Revelation on the person who obeys the words or commands given in the book (v. 7).

When the angel finished, John bowed in worship before him but was stopped immediately. The bowl angel further identified himself as a fellow servant of John, of the prophets, and of all believers, and commanded John to worship God alone (vv. 8, 9).

The angel also instructed John not to seal the revelations he had been given because the end-time events predicted in them were near (v. 10). Present behavior and character determine personal readiness for the end of earth's history (v. 11).

A number of vital concluding remarks from Christ are added (vv. 12-21). First is the fact that Jesus has promised to come soon and man's destiny will be frozen at that moment. When He comes He will reward every human being according to his or her works (v. 12).

Jesus repeated His claim of being the Sovereign God from creation to consummation in the titles "Alpha and Omega," "the beginning and the end," and "the first and the last" (v. 13).

The seventh beatitude of blessing in Revelation is, "Blessed are they that do his commandments." Those who keep God's commandments inherit eternal life and have unhindered access into Heaven (v. 14).

In contrast are those who do not inherit eternal life and are denied access into the New Jerusalem: these are "dogs," "sorcerers," "whoremongers," "murderers," "idolaters," and "liars" (v. 15).

The revelations originated with Jesus, were mediated through an angel to John, and were to be passed on to the churches. Jesus further reassured John—as the Messiah, "the root and offspring of David"—that things would be permanently as He revealed them, since He was also "the bright and morning star" that is preeminent and unchanging in the sky (v. 16).

John included either a prayer for Christ's coming or a gospel invitation as the revelations drew to a close. The Holy Spirit, the church, and the newly converted all repeat this invitation to "come." The universal scope of salvation is reflected, with all those who are spiritually thirsty ("whosover will") invited to come; furthermore, it is free (v. 17).

The revelations conclude with a stern warning about the errors of adding to or taking away from the Word of God. God will add the plagues of revelation to those who add to it; He will take eternal life away from those who take away from it (vv. 18, 19).

Jesus repeated His promise to come again soon for the third time (v. 20). John responded with a confirming "Amen" and prayer for Christ to come, then closed with a benediction of the grace of God (v. 21).

Application: Teaching and Preaching the Passage

Such topics as the timing of the rapture and the nature of the millennial reign of Christ have received a lot of the attention in eschatological teaching and preaching. A defining pillar of pretribulational dispensationalism is the imminent or "any-moment" rapture of the church. This cherished doctrine is viewed as something that leaves "the teeth" in eschatological preaching and tempers present behavior. It is appropriate to use eschatological themes in this way—as Peter did in 2 Pet. 3:10-14, and as Jesus did on several occasions, exhorting His disciples to be ready and watching for His return. The imminence of the rapture is a powerful motivator to trust Christ immediately or, for believers, to maintain personal readiness.

But there is a more immediate and primary concern for all of us, as important as the rapture and Second Coming are: the prospect of personal, physical death. This is just as unpredictable—an immediate, constant possibility. It is certain. No one has promise of tomorrow.

A student once asked his teacher what would be the best day to repent. The teacher responded: "the last day of your life." The perceptive student recognized that it was impossible for anyone to know when that would be and called this to the teacher's attention. The wise teacher concluded with the obvious: "Then the best day to repent is today!"

The rapture may or may not happen in our lifetime. But what concerns every person presently is the day of his or her death. This is certain within each one's generation and could come personally at "any moment." When death occurs a person's spiritual condition is fixed for eternity; he goes immediately into the presence of the Lord or into Hell. Then we must recognize the jeopardy of each moment. Our focus must be on personal, daily preparedness—even more for this reason than for the rapture.

C. S. Lewis in *The Last Battle* (173) speaks indirectly to the significance of the last chapters of Revelation:

The things that began to happen after that were so great and beautiful that I cannot write them. And for us this is the end of all the stories, and we can most truly say that they all lived happily ever after. But for them it was only the beginning of the real story. All their life in this world and all their adventures in Narnia had only been the cover and the title page: now at last they were beginning Chapter One of the Great Story which no one on earth has read: which goes on for ever: in which every chapter is better than the one before.

Suggested Outline. The Fountain of Eternal Youth—The Water of Life, 22:1-2,17: (1) A pure, bright, clear river, v. 1; (2) A divine river, v. 1; (3) A flowing river, v. 1; (4) A tree-lined river, v. 2; (5) A thirst-quenching river, v. 17; (6) A free river, v. 17.

REVELATION

BIBLIOGRAPHY: WORKS CITED IN THIS COMMENTARY

Books (cited by author's last name)

Allen, J., *What the Bible Teaches - Revelation* (Ritchie, 1997)

Archer, Gleason L. Jr., and others, *Three Views on the Rapture* (Zondervan, 1996)

Aune, David E., *Revelation* (three vols., WBC, Nelson, 1998)

Bahnsen, Greg, *Theonomy in Christian Ethics* (The Craig Press, 1979)

Barnes, Albert, *Notes on the New Testament: Revelation* (Baker, 1958)

Bauckham, Richard, *The Climax of Prophecy* (T. & T. Clark, 1993)

Beale, G. K., *The Book of Revelation* (Eerdmans/Paternoster, 1999)

Beasley-Murray, G. R., *Revelation* (NBC, IVP 1994)

Benware, Paul N., *Understanding End Times Prophecy* (Moody, 1995)

Blaising, Craig A., and Bock, Darrell L., *Progressive Dispensationalism* (Victor, 1993)

Bock, Darrell L., ed., and others, *Three Views on the Millennium and Beyond* (Zondervan, 1999)

Boettner, Loraine, and others, *The Meaning of the Millennium: Four Views* (IVP, 1977)

Boring, M. Eugene, *Revelation* (John Knox, 1989

Borland, James A., "The Meaning and Identification of God's Eschatological Trumpets" *Looking into the Future*, Ed. David Baker (Baker Academic, 2001)

Brighton, Louis A., *Revelation* (Concordia, 1999)

Caird, George B., *The Revelation of Saint John* (BNTC, Hendrickson, 1966)

Charles, R. H., *Revelation* (ICC two vols., T. & T. Clark, 1989)

Clouse, Robert G., ed., and others, *The Meaning of the Millennium: Four Views* (IVP, 1977)

Clouse, Robert G., and others, *The New Millennium Manual* (Baker, 1999)

Collins, Adela Yarbro, *The Apocalypse Revelation* (NJBC, Prentice Hall, 1990)

Couch, Mal, *Dictionary of Premillennial Theology* (Kregel, 1996)

Deissmann, Adolf, *Light from the Ancient East* (Hendrickson, 1927)

Edersheim, Alfred, *The Temple: Its Ministry and Services* (Hendrickson, 1994)

Ellul, Jacques, *Apocalypse: The Book of Revelation,* trans. George W. Schreiner (Seabury Press, 1977)

Erickson, Millard J., *A Basic Guide to Eschatology* (Baker, 1998)

Ford, J. Massyngberde, *Revelation* (AB, Doubleday, 1975)

Gentry, Kenneth L. Jr., and others, *Three Views on the Millennium and Beyond* (Zondervan, 1999)

Gentry, Kenneth L. Jr., and others, *Four Views on the Book of Revelation* (Zondervan, 1998)

Gonzalez, Catherine C., and Gonzalez, Justo L., *Revelation* (WBC, John Knox, 1997)

Gregg, Steve, *Revelation: Four Views a Parallel Commentary* (Nelson, 1997)

Gundry, Robert, *First the Antichrist* (Baker, 1997)

REVELATION

Guthrie, Donald, *New Testament Introduction* (IVP, 1976)

Hamstra, Sam Jr., and others, *Four Views on the Book of Revelation* (Zondervan, 1998)

Harris, R. Laird, *The Inspiration and Canonicity of the Bible* (Zondervan, 1969)

Hemer, Colin J., *The Letters to the Seven Churches of Asia in their Local Setting* (Eerdmans, 1989)

Hendriksen, William, *More Than Conquerors* (Baker, 1940)

Hoekema, Anthony A. and others, *The Meaning of the Millennium: Four Views* (IVP, 1977)

Hughes, Philip E., *The Book of Revelation* (IVP/Eerdmans, 1990)

Johnson, Alan F., *Revelation* (EBC, Zondervan, 1996)

Johnson, Dennis E., *Triumph of the Lamb* (Presbyterian & Reformed, 2001)

Josephus, Flavius, *The Works of Josephus*, trans. W. Whiston (Hendrickson, 1987)

Keener, Craig S., *Revelation* (NIVAC, Zondervan, 2000)

Kistemaker, Simon J., *Revelation* (NTC, Baker, 2001)

Ladd, George E., *A Commentary on the Revelation of John* (Eerdmans, 1972)

Ladd, George E., and others, *The Meaning of the Millennium: Four Views* (IVP, 1977)

Ladd, George E., *The Presence of the Future*, (Eerdmans, 1974)

LaHaye, Tim F., *Left Behind Series*, (Tyndale, 1995)

LaHaye, Tim F., *Revelation Unveiled* (Zondervan, 1999)

Lenski, R. C. H., *The Interpretation of St. John's Revelation* (Augsburg, 1966)

Lewis, C. S., *The Last Battle* (MacMillan, 1988)

Lindsey, Hal, and Carlson, Carol C., *Satan is Alive and Well on Planet Earth*, (Zondervan, 1972)

Mare, W. Harold, *Mastering New Testament Greek* (Baker, 1977)

Marshall, Alfred, *The Interlinear KJV-NIV Parallel New Testament in Greek and English* (Zondervan, 1975)

Metzger, Bruce M., *The Text of the New Testament* (Oxford, 1968)

Michaels, J. Ramsey, *Revelation* (IVPNTC, IVP, 1997)

Moffat, James, *Revelation* (EGT, Eerdmans, 1976)

Morris, Henry M., *The Revelation Record* (Tyndale, 1999)

Morris, Leon, *Revelation* (TNTC, IVP/Eerdmans, 1987)

Mounce, Robert H., *Revelation* (NICNT, Eerdmans, 1998)

Newcombe, Jerry, *Coming Again* (Chariot Victor Publishing 1999)

Newport, John P., *The Lion and the Lamb* (Broadman & Holman, 1986)

Pate, C. Marvin, ed., and others, *Four Views on the Book of Revelation* (Zondervan, 1998)

Poythress, Vern S., *The Returning King* (Presbyterian & Reformed, 2000)

Ramsay, W. M., *The Letters to the Seven Churches* (Hendrickson, 1994)

Reiter, Richard R., and others, *Three Views on the Rapture* (Zondervan, 1996)

Robertson, Archibald T., *Word Pictures in the New Testament,* vol. 6 (Broadman, 1960)

Rosenthal, Marvin J., *The Pre-Wrath Rapture of the Church* (Nelson, 1990)

Rowland, Christopher C., *Revelation* (NIB, Abingdon, 1998)

Russell, J. Stewart, *The Parousia* (Baker 1999)

Ryrie, Charles C., *Dispensationalism* (Moody, 1995)

Ryrie, Charles C., *Revelation* (EBC, Moody, 1996)

Sanders, Cecil, *The Future: An Amillennial Perspective* (Randall House, 1990)

Saucy, Robert L., *The Case for Progressive Dispensationalism* (Zondervan, 1993)

Schurer, Emil, *A History of the Jewish People in the Time of Jesus Christ* , vol. 5 (Hendrickson, 1998)

Seiss, J. A., *The Apocalypse: Lectures on the Book of Revelation* (Zondervan, 1975)

Summers, Ray, *Worthy is the Lamb* (Broadman, 1951)

Swete, Henry B., *Commentary on Revelation* (Kregel, 1977)

Thomas, Robert L., *An Exegetical Commentary of Revelation* (two vols., Moody, 1992/1995)

Thompson, Leonard L., *Revelation* (ANTC, Abingdon, 1998)

Trench, Richard C., *Synonyms of the New Testament* (Eerdmans, 1976)

Van Kampen, Robert, *The Sign* (Crossway, 1992)

Vincent, Marvin R., *Word Studies in the New Testament*, vol. 2 (Eerdmans, 1946)

Wall, Robert W., *Revelation* (NIBC, Hendrickson, 1991)

Walvoord, John F. *The Revelation of Jesus Christ* (Moody, 1966)

Wilcox, Michael, *The Message of Revelation* (BST, IVP, 1975)

Worth, Roland H. Jr., *The Seven Cities of the Apocalypse and Greco-Asian Culture* (Paulist Press, 1999)

Zahn, Theodor, *Introduction to the New Testament*. vol. 3 (Kregel, 1953)

Reference Works (cited by the abbreviations indicated)

ALGNT: *Analytical Lexicon of the Greek New Testament*, ed. Barbara and Timothy Friberg and Nerva F. Miller (Baker, 2000)

ANF: *The Ante Nicene Fathers*, ed. Alexander Roberts and James Donaldson (ten vols.: Eerdmans, 1951)

DBI: *Dictionary of Biblical Imagery*, ed. Leland Ryken, James C. Wilhoit, Tremper Longman III (IVP, 1998)

DNTB: *Dictionary of New Testament Background*, ed. Craig A. Evans and Stanley Porter (IVP, 2000)

DNTT: *The New International Dictionary of New Testament Theology*, ed. Colin Brown (three vols.: Zondervan, 1975)

ISBE: *The International Standard Bible Encyclopedia*, ed. Geoffrey W. Bromiley (four vols.: Eerdmans, 1979)

NPNF: *A Select Library of the Nicene and Post Nicene Fathers*, ed. Philip Schaff (14 vols.: Hendrickson, 1994)

TDNT: *Theological Dictionary of the New Testament*, ed. Gerhard Kittle (10 vols., tr. Geoffrey W. Bromiley: Eerdmans, 1967)

REVELATION

Thayer: *Thayer's Greek-English Lexicon of the New Testament*, ed. Joseph H. Thayer (Hendrickson, 1999)

TWOT: Harris, R. Laird, and others, *Theological Wordbook of the Old Testament*, vol. 2 (Moody Press, 1980)

Vine: *Vine's Complete Expository Dictionary of Old and New Testament Words*, ed. W. E. Vine (Nelson, 1996)

Articles (cited by author's name)

Clowney, Edmund P., "The New Israel," in *A Guide to Biblical Prophecy*, ed. Carl E. Armerding and W. Ward Gasque (Wipf and Stock, 2001), 207-220.

DeSilva, David A., "The Social Setting of the Revelation to John: Conflict Within, Fears Without" (*Westminster Theological Journal* 54:2 [1992] 273-302)

Glasson, T. F., "The Last Judgment" (*New Testament Studies* 28:4 [1982] 528-539)

Hill, David, "Prophecy and Prophets in the Revelation of St. John" (*New Testament Studies* 18:4 [1972] 401-418)

Hodges, Zane C., "The First Horseman of the Apocalypse" (*Bibliotheca Sacra* 119 [1962] 324-334)

Longman, Tremper III, "The Divine Warrior: The New Testament Use of an Old Testament Motif" (*Westminster Theological Journal* 44:2 [1982] 290-307)

McComiskey, Thomas E., "Alteration of OT Imagery in the Book of Revelation: Its Hermeneutical and Theological Significance" (*Journal of the Evangelical Theological Society* 36:3 [1993] 307-316)

Picirilli, Robert E., "Hell in the New Testament" (*Integrity* 2 [2003] 55-83)

Ryrie, Charles C., "Apostasy in the Church" (*Bibliotheca Sacra* 121:481 [1964] 44-53)

Townsend, Jeffrey L., "The Rapture in Revelation 3:10" (*Bibliotheca Sacra* 134:534 [1980] 252-266)

Wong, Daniel K., "The First Horseman of Revelation 6" (*Bibliotheca Sacra* 153·610 [1996] 212-226)

CPSIA information can be obtained at www.ICGtesting.com
Printed in the USA
LVOW091808091211

258526LV00006B/1/P